Also in the Variorum Collected Studies Series:

PETER LINEHAN
Spanish Church and Society, 1150–1300

JEAN GAUTIER DALCHE
Economie et société dans les pays de la Couronne de Castille

ARCHIBALD R. LEWIS
Medieval Society in Southern France and Catalonia

JOSEPH O'CALLAGHAN
The Spanish Military Order of Calatrava and its Affiliates

C. J. BISHKO
Studies in Medieval Spanish Frontier History

C. J. BISHKO
Spanish and Portuguese Monastic History, 600–1300

PHILIP GRIERSON
Dark Age Numismatics

PETER HUNTER BLAIR
Anglo-Saxon Northumbria

R. A. MARKUS
From Augustine to Gregory the Great
History and Christianity in Late Antiquity

W. H. C. FREND
Religion Popular and Unpopular in the Early Christian Centuries

W. H. C. FREND
Town and Country in the Early Christian Centuries

JOHN MATTHEWS
Political Life and Culture in Late Roman Society

ALAN CAMERON
Literature and Society in the Early Byzantine World

T. D. BARNES
Early Christianity and the Roman Empire

HENRY CHADWICK
History and Thought of the Early Church

Visigothic Spain, Byzantium and the Irish

J.N. Hillgarth

Visigothic Spain, Byzantium and the Irish

VARIORUM REPRINTS
London 1985

British Library CIP data

Hillgarth, Joscelyn N.
Visigothic Spain, Byzantium and the Irish. —
(Collected studies series; CS216)
1. Spain — Civilization — To 711
I. Title
946′.01 DP96

ISBN 0–86078–164–X

Published in Great Britain by Variorum Reprints
20 Pembridge Mews London W11 3EQ

Printed in Great Britain by Butler & Tanner Ltd
Frome, Somerset

VARIORUM REPRINT CS216

CONTENTS

This volume contains a total of 336 pages.

PREFACE

The articles selected for this volume, originally published from 1958 to 1984, reflect a continuing interest in early medieval intellectual and religious history. The first article to appear (IV, to which V is an addendum) came out of my doctoral thesis at Cambridge on Julian of Toledo (*ca.* 640–690). With what must have seemed to my Cambridge mentors deliberate perversity, I had chosen what used to be considered the darkest of all "Dark" Ages, the seventh century, Spain under the Visigoths, and, in that century and country, the works of a practically unknown author. The choice reflected, as I now see, my lifelong fascination with Spain and with the history of ideas. It also reflected the years when my work began. Living — as we have all lived since the Second World War — in a time of radical transition, it was natural that I should have been drawn to explore the centuries which saw the crucial changes from Antiquity to the Middle Ages.

As work on Julian of Toledo advanced it became clear that, if he was almost unknown to modern scholars, he had been extremely well known to the Middle Ages. His works are documented in virtually all medieval libraries — at least before the thirteenth century — and they are preserved in over two hundred manuscripts. Since they are very largely a mosaic of quotations from earlier patristic authors, research into them necessarily constituted a practical training not only in paleography but in source-criticism. It involved one in tracing how learning was transmitted, how books travel and how they are used, often in very different contexts from that in which they originated. It became evident that one could not understand Visigothic Spain without studying its relation to other countries. In reaction to the older view that Spain under the Visigoths was a largely isolated world, I have tried to show its links, on the one hand with Byzantium, and on the other with Ireland.

The place of Spain in the late antique Mediterranean world, of which Byzantium was the intellectual and political centre, is reflected in the political and religious ideas which dominate both the struggles of the sixth century and the historical writings — in the broadest sense — of the seventh (see articles II and III). Seventh-century Spain saw one of the most striking revivals of the classical tradition in the Latin West. The leading writer of the age, Isidore of Seville, was the author of perhaps the most influential book (apart from the Bible) of the whole Middle Ages, the *Etymologiae* or *Origines*. The "two faces" of Isidore, a product of Late Antiquity but a master of the Middle Ages, make him a man whose thought spans the transition between these ages. The longest article reproduced here (IX) represents an attempt (begun in 1960) to assess recent research into Isidore and his age and to determine the problems that most urgently demand attention. The study of Isidore's works and of their influence illustrates very clearly the way Visigothic Spain passed on to the rest of Europe what it had received from classical Antiquity and contemporary Byzantium. In this transmission — as I argue in papers VI to VIII — the first and perhaps the most vital link was with Ireland.

Transmission is not a term which should be understood in a mechanical sense. What was handed on were not merely books but ideas which, being alive, change and are changed in the historical worlds they successively penetrate. As with relations between Byzantium and Spain, so with those between Spain and Ireland one should be concerned not simply with "Quellenforschung" but with investigating how what is transmitted is transformed, how, to take two examples, Isidore and Julian, working with late antique materials, construct — out of the mosaic of quotations I referred to — new models in history, theology, and political philosophy, or how, working with Isidore's grammatical synthesis, the Irish proceed beyond it.

The first article in this volume, in that it attempts to ascertain something of the beliefs and practices of the inhabitants of Spain as a whole, and not the ideas and influence of a small group of leading thinkers, differs somewhat from the rest. My use of the word "popular" is not intended, however, to suggest a divorce between the history of ideas and that of religion. The religion of Visigothic Spain was largely that presented to, if not always assimilated by, its people by Isidore and his successors. In my book, *The Conversion of Western Europe 350–750* (1969) — to appear in expanded form from the University of Pennsylvania Press in 1985 as *Christianity and Paganism*, and in a study of *Modes of Evangelisation of Western Europe in the Seventh Century* — contributed to the third symposium on Ireland and Europe (Dublin, 1984) — I have continued the type of investigation represented by this article, while broadening its scope beyond Spain.

My debt to one institution is particularly apparent in the focus of the articles collected here. It is not only that a number of these papers — or earlier versions of them — were written at the Warburg Institute in London. No one who has belonged to the Warburg, as I was fortunate enough to do for several years, can fail to be drawn, by contact with its scholars and by the use of its extraordinary library, into trying to see how one discipline can assist another, how — to choose two instances from the articles assembled here — archaeology, literary and artistic history can work together to illuminate the connections between Spain and Ireland in the seventh century, or how coins can be brought to the aid of chronicles when one is studying the exiguous sources for sixth-century Spain.

My debts to individual scholars are stated in the notes to the articles. I am much indebted to the editors and publishers of the different papers listed in the Table of Contents for permission to reproduce them here, and to Variorum Reprints for undertaking this volume. Given the emphasis of the book it seems right to dedicate it jointly to my Spanish and Irish friends.

J. N. HILLGARTH

Toronto,
October 1984

PUBLISHER'S NOTE

The articles in this volume, as in all others in the Collected Studies Series, have not been given a new, continuous pagination. In order to avoid confusion, and to facilitate their use where these same studies have been referred to elsewhere, the original pagination has been maintained wherever possible.

Each article has been given a Roman number in order of appearance, as listed in the Contents. This number is repeated on each page and quoted in the index entries.

I

Popular Religion in Visigothic Spain

IF one holds the view that 'history deals with activity not process, that it deals with men who can express their thoughts, deliberations and imaginings in speech, literature, action and artifacts', and not with 'feelings and drives to which men are subject', which have *not* found expression in recorded forms,[1] then one has obvious difficulties when approaching a subject such as Popular Religion in Visigothic Spain. Most of the inhabitants of Spain under the Visigoths were not able to express their 'feelings and drives' in forms which have reached us. Most of our knowledge of their views on religion—as in other matters—derives from what was done, or attempted to be done, *to* them by their rulers, secular and spiritual. Professor Southern observed some years ago: 'The first thing to emphasize about the religion of the laity [in 600–1000] is the extent of our ignorance.' How can one try to lessen this ignorance as to the immanent aspect of religion—to adopt Professor Meslin's distinction—for as to 'the apprehension of the sacred' this is more difficult, often impossible, to assess.[2]

It has been said that we can hardly hope to recapture the inward aspect of ancient religion, 'a state of mind, a complex of beliefs and feelings' about supernatural forces. As Professor Dodds has remarked: 'How shall we recover the beliefs and feelings of persons long dead, the vast majority of whom have left us no report of what they thought and felt?' But he goes on to suggest that one can study the outward, ritual aspect of religion, more important to the Greeks than theology or even

[1] Elie Kedourie, 'New histories for old', *Times Literary Supplement*, 7 Mar. 1975, reviewing, *inter alia*, Jacques Barzun, *Clio and the Doctors*, with whose views in this matter Kedourie (and I) agree.

[2] R. W. Southern, 'The Church of the Dark Ages, 600–1000', *The Layman in Christian History*, ed. S. C. Neill and H.-R. Weber (Philadelphia, 1963), p. 88. M. Meslin, *Pour une science des religions* (Paris, 1973), p. 8.

than myth.[1] In the same way one can to some extent recapture the collective saving rituals and the models presented to the people of Spain as a substitute for their pre-Christian beliefs—the rituals of prayer, thanksgiving, sacrifice, the classic stories, symbols, and formulas, and the new model of life represented by the professional holy man of Christianity, the monk.

'Popular Religion' is a term which can be interpreted in different ways—as religious folklore, as the religion *of* a people, considered as more or less divergent from 'official' religion, or as the religion presented *to* them, which may one day, but not at once, become their own. It is this last sense that one is obliged to use here. The author of the one work known to me on popular religion in Visigothic Spain (mainly confined to Septimania) begins by saying he intends to exclude 'ce que pensent et sentent les clercs et les moines'. It seems to me impossible to separate the lay world in this way from that of the clergy and monks, and, if one could do so, one would end by knowing hardly anything of the subject. In fact Canon Delaruelle refers to hymns, sermons, and liturgical offices, all, of course, written by clerics.[2] Presumably most of the inscriptions we have (at least after 500 A.D.) were also composed by them. Did laymen choose the design of the sarcophagi they would rest in? Toledo IV (633) tells us that the faithful built churches but did they design them? In 500 or 600 there appear to have been few laymen with the gifts of a Prudentius in the Visigothic kingdom.

What sources can one use in an attempt to reconstruct popular religion in Visigothic Spain? The difference between the sources for Visigothic Spain and Merovingian France is well known. For Spain we have a wonderful series of laws,

[1] E. R. Dodds, *The Ancient Concept of Progress and other Essays on Greek Literature and Belief* (Oxford, 1973), pp. 141, 144.

[2] E. Delaruelle, 'La vie religieuse populaire en Septimanie pendant l'époque wisigothique', *Anales toledanos* iii (= *Estudios sobre la España visigoda*) (Toledo, 1971), 3 (see pp. 23–9). J. Le Goff, in *Annales ESC* xxii. 2 (1967), 781–91, also sharply separates the clerical and lay worlds; clerical culture is seen here as far more homogeneous that it was in fact. (But see p. 51 n. 3 below.) See also E. Patlagean, on Byzantine hagiography, *Annales ESC* xxiii. 1 (1968), 106–26. Different views of 'popular religion' by P. Boglioni, in *Les Religions populaires* (Quebec, 1972), pp. 53–7, and by J-C. Poulin, ibid., pp. 67–9 (the latter view is closer to my own). Natalie Z. Davis, in *The Pursuit of Holiness in Late Medieval and Renaissance Religion*, ed. C. Trinkaus and H. A. Oberman (Leiden, 1974), p. 309, points out that many religious presuppositions were shared by learned clergy and laity in a much later period than that dealt with here.

almost always datable, and of Church Councils, but very few Lives of Saints. For France we have a great many Lives of Saints but very few laws. The question here is how close do royal or ecclesiastical laws get one to reality. Speaking of a later period in Spanish history Peter Linehan has observed, 'though the survival of synodal and conciliar statutes may provide information about the prelates who issued the legislation, it is no guide to the condition of the people at whom that legislation was directed.' He continues, 'the existence of piety at any level . . . cannot be deduced from an analysis of . . . conciliar or synodal legislation.'[1] One may ask what can be deduced from this material; perhaps a series of problems and the fact that the bishops were aware of them. But one has to turn mainly, for our subject, to other sources. New analyses of the art of the period have been made. Its inscriptions—unfortunately relatively few in number—can be studied. We now have in print virtually all the Spanish sermons of the age. The so-called 'Mozarabic' Liturgy has attracted new attention, as have a number of the Spanish Fathers.[2] No one has as yet discovered more Lives of Spanish Saints. There is a need to apply to those we have methods of analysis which have proved fruitful with Gregory's *Dialogues* and with Eastern Lives.[3]

Some preliminary remarks as to the social and political framework within which the religion of our age existed.

Any student of the Iberian Peninsula, in any age, must be struck by the violent contrasts between its different regions. These contrasts were fully as great in Roman and Visigothic Spain as they were in the Middle Ages. To use the terms 'Roman' or 'Visigothic' Spain is, in a sense, to beg the issue, to assume that one is dealing with one entity. As Marcel Bénabou has said, speaking of North Africa, Romanization in the sense of a Roman *way of life* could only follow when the earlier stages

[1] P. Linehan, *The Spanish Church and the Papacy in the Thirteenth Century* (Cambridge, 1971), pp. 99 f. See also Fontaine (on the Synod of Elvira), *L'Art préroman* i. 33.

[2] For the art see Fontaine, *L'Art préroman*, and the works cited in the Bibliography. For the inscriptions, Vives, *Inscripciones*, and, for sermons, Grégoire (see the Bibliographical Note, below). Information can be gleaned from unpromising sources, e.g. Julian of Toledo, *Prognosticum futuri saeculi* (see below, nn. on p. 30).

[3] See R. Gillet, in *Dictionnaire de spiritualité, ascétique et mystique*, vi. 2 (Paris, 1967), 879.

of conquest and colonization had been completed.[1] In the north and north-west of Spain conquest was more or less complete by the time of Augustus (except for Vasconia, which was never conquered) but colonization was feeble indeed, in comparison to the south or south-east.

Even in the countryside of Baetica we find native names surviving into the Empire. In the north Latinization was far more gradual.[2] A recent study has noted the 'absence of real urbanization' in Galicia. In the third century A.D. the native element was still strongly represented there both in personal names and in those of gods. Persons with completely Roman names continued to erect inscriptions to Celtic gods. The Roman element in the population was relatively slight, compared to Baetica.[3] In Galicia what interested Rome were the gold mines, which merely needed slaves to work them and troops to keep the peace. There were a few cities but large-scale colonization was not necessary.[4] In Castile Clunia declined sharply in the late third century and other cities were not of great importance.[5] If one turns from Galicia or Castile to Cantabria (later Asturias) one finds a tribal, matriarchal society surviving from pre-Roman times into the Visigothic period, as it probably survived in the whole of the Meseta, the north and north-west.[6]

[1] M. Bénabou, 'La résistance africaine à la romanisation d'Auguste à Dioclétien', paper presented to the Sixth International Congress of Classical Studies (Madrid, 1974).

[2] A. García y Bellido, 'La latinización de Hispania', *AEA* xl (1967), 3–29, at 13, 16 n. 29. J. Mª. Blázquez, 'Problemas en torno a las raíces de España', *Hispania*, xxix (1969), 245–86, insists on a more absolute Romanization of most of Spain (outside the north) than does García y Bellido. But he admits (p. 270) that excavations in cities in the interior reveal native names, native gods, and some native decoration. The fact that Roman *villae*, 'with excellent mosaics', are found in regions apart from main roads is hardly proof that 'not only the upper classes but the rural people were well Romanised in the third century' (ibid). See n. 4 below, and the excellent summary by P. de Palol, 'Etapas de la romanización', *I Symposium de Prehistoria de la Peninsula Ibérica* (Pamplona, 1960), pp. 303–17.

[3] P. Le Roux and A. Tranoy, 'Rome et les indigènes dans le Nord-Ouest de la Péninsule ibérique. Problèmes d'épigraphie et d'histoire', *Mélanges de la Casa de Velásquez*, ix (1973), 177–231, esp. 215, 229.

[4] J. Mª. Blázquez, 'Las invasiones nórdicas en la Hispania romana de los siglos IV–V', paper presented to the Sixth International Congress of Classical Studies (Madrid, 1974), also his earlier paper in *Actas del III Congreso Español de Estudios Clásicos*, ii (Madrid, 1968), 137–42, and idem, in *Actas del Coloquio Internacional sobre el Bimilenario de Lugo* (Lugo, 1977), pp. 67–81.

[5] P. de Palol, *Castilla la vieja entre el Imperio Romano y el Reino visigodo* (Valladolid, 1970), pp. 36–40; idem, *Guía de Clunia*, 3rd edn. (Valladolid, 1974).

[6] A. Barbero, M. Vigil, 'La organización social de los cántabros y sus trans-

The task of the Christian Church in the peninsula has to be seen against these sharp contrasts between Romanized Baetica and the largely un-Romanized north. The opposition of city and countryside which existed throughout the Roman Empire was here particularly acute. The fact that there were Christians even in León and Astorga in the 250s did not facilitate the conversion of the non-Roman countryside around these small islands of a foreign culture. There were prosperous *villae* to be found in late Roman Castile, in contrast to declining Clunia.[1] But the contacts of the *domini* of these *villae*, whether Christian or not, with the peasants on their estates were not likely to be easy when, in the far more Romanized eastern Spain of the late fourth century, it was unusual for an estate owner to be able to communicate with her *rustici*.[2] The contrasting types of later Iberian monasticism, and of piety in general, are largely explicable as a reaction to the different societies (urban or rural) with which the Spanish Church was confronted.[3]

If 'Roman' Spain was disunited socially and culturally there are also signs that by 400 the Imperial Government's political control over the north was slipping.[4] The invasion of Sueves, Vandals, and, shortly after, of Visigoths brought about a general disintegration. From 409 to the end of the sixth century there was no one central power in the peninsula, nor did the Visigoths ever achieve effective control over Cantabria, let alone Vasconia.[5] The Visigothic settlements, which only began

formaciones en relación con los orígenes de la Reconquista', *Hispania Antiqua*, i (Madrid 1971), 197–232 (quoted from the republication, in Barbero and Vigil, *Sobre los orígenes sociales de la Reconquista* (Barcelona, 1974), pp. 141–95). See J. González Echegaray, *Los Cántabros* (Madrid, 1966), esp. pp. 225–47, also David, *Études*, pp. 81 f. Greater detail in F. Jordá Cerdá, in *Actas del Coloquio . . . Lugo*, pp. 29–40.

1 Palol, *Castilla*, pp. 41–6. For Galicia see idem, in *Actas*, pp. 157–73.

2 Eutropius (possibly of Aquitaine but writing to an apparently Hispano-Roman lady), *De similitudine carnis peccati*, in *PL*, Suppl. i. 555; see J. Madoz, *Estudios eclesiásticos*, xvi (1942), 27–54; P. Courcelle, *RÉA* lvi (1954), 387–90.

3 See below, and J. Orlandis, in *AEM* viii (1972–3), 17–33, who points to the difference between the hermit Valerius in the Bierzo and the rich bishops of Mérida, who could build a hospital and establish a credit loan organization.

4 Apart from the controversial question of a *limes* in northern Spain (for which see Barbero and Vigil, cited in the next note, and the criticism of Palol, *Castilla*, pp. 17 ff.) there is the inscription of 399, commented on below (see p. 11 n. 3).

5 A. Barbero, M. Vigil, in *BRAH* clvi. 2 (1965), 271–339 (quoted from *Sobre los orígenes*, pp. 13–102). The criticism of this article by C. Sánchez-Albornoz, *CHE* xlvii–xlviii (1968), 341–52, does not affect its main theses. The maps at the end

on a large scale in the 490s, were apparently concentrated in a little populated area, the central Meseta, though small Gothic garrisons and noble families entered the Roman cities of the south.[1]

The regional and social disunity of Spain under the Romans becomes even more evident under the Visigoths. Ramon d'Abadal remarked some years ago that the idea of uniting the Goths and Hispano-Romans in one country (alluded to, or, perhaps more correctly, *wished for*, by the Fourth Council of Toledo) is not found in the Visigothic Code, or in the oath taken by a Gothic king's subjects after his elevation to the throne: instead we find phrases such as 'infra fines patriae Gothorum', or (in the oath) 'pro patriae gentisque Gothorum statu'. In general, Abadal concludes, the Goths continued to reserve for themselves 'the structure of real power'.[2]

The Church reacted to this situation and tried to use it. Most visibly by anointing, but also in other ways, it sought to confer a sacred character on the Visigothic kings (just as it visibly removed this character, when it tonsured Wamba, and apparently Ervig). But long before anointing became normal the king had been recognized (the fact is clear at Toledo III, with the first Catholic Visigothic king, other than Hermenegild) as a Byzantine monarch, the successor of Constantine. Toledo III had decreed that while the Goths should rule, the Hispano-Roman bishops should correct and control abuses of government. But it was the Visigothic king who selected the bishops.[3]

(pp. 101 f.) show particularly clearly the absence of Visigothic power from the north, compared to the Roman posts. For mints see *Sobre*, pp. 115–18.

[1] P. de Palol, 'The Christian Monuments of Roman and Visigothic Spain', *Classical Folia*, xxiii (1969), 42 and Map VI. See also J. Orlandis, 'El reino visigodo. Siglos VI y VII', *Historia económica y social de España*, i (Madrid, 1973), 464–71. W. Hübener, *MM* x (1970), 187–211, throws doubt on the 'Visigothic' nature of the necropoli of the Meseta. For the legal evidence see A. García Gallo, 'Notas sobre el reparto de tierras entre visigodos y romanos', *Hispania*, i. 4 (1940–1), 40–63.

[2] R. d'Abadal, 'La Monarquia en el Regne de Toledo', *Homenaje a Jaume Vicens Vives*, i (Barcelona, 1965), 191–200 (quoted from Abadal, *Dels Visigots als Catalans*, i (Barcelona, 1969), 57–67, at 57 f.). See IV Toledo, 2, probably due to Isidore (p. 22 n. 3 below).

[3] Abadal, *Dels Visigots*, i. 61 f., 65, and 'Els concilis de Toledo', ibid. 69–93 (originally published in *Homenaje a J. Vincke*, i (Madrid, 1962–3), 21–45). See III Toledo, 18 (*PL* lxxxiv. 355; Vives, *Concilios*, p. 131). See also my article, 'Historiography in Visigothic Spain', *La Storiografia Altomedievale* (*Settimane di studio*, xvii. 1: Spoleto, 1970), pp. 280–4. The sacred character of the king is brought out by Julian of Toledo, *Historia Wambae*, on which see Claude, *Adel*, pp. 157–61.

If, in the seventh-century West, 'kings move into an ecclesiastical atmosphere', in Spain the Church was centred on the Crown as no other Western Christian society. The theocratic nature of the Visigothic monarchy and its drive towards ideological unity explains a great deal about seventh-century Spain, not least its policy towards religion.[1] The appearance of a cross in the king's hand on Wamba's and Ervig's coins, or, even more strikingly, of a Cross on Ervig's head, symbolized to these rulers' subjects the union of spiritual and secular authority.[2]

The Spanish churchmen of the late sixth and seventh centuries, with which we are especially concerned, used Latin as their normal language. They were surrounded by the 'monuments of the ancients', artistic as well as literary. But they were aware, as Braulio says of Isidore, that they were separated from those 'antiqui' by centuries of 'boorish rusticity'. They had to contend not only with rusticity in their flocks but with that of their inferior clergy. And they were the servants, though privileged, of a 'religiosus princeps', a state of affairs which had disadvantages as well as advantages.[3]

After the official conversion of the Visigoths in 589 the Spanish Church appears to have made little effort to evangelize the Arian Visigoths, now officially Catholic. We know virtually nothing about the religion of the Visigoths, as such, either as Arians or Catholics.[4] Only occasionally do Arians earn an

[1] J. M. Wallace-Hadrill, *Early Germanic Kingship in England and on the Continent* (Oxford, 1971), p. 47 (for Isidore's ideas see pp. 53 ff. and also Mullins, *The Spiritual Life*, pp. 173–6). See King, *Law*, esp. chapter 5; Thompson, *Goths*, p. 282: 'It was the kings, not the bishops, who governed Spain, and with it the Spanish Church.' See W. A. Chaney, *The Cult of Kingship in Anglo-Saxon England* (Berkeley, 1970), e.g. pp. 55 f.

[2] G. C. Miles, *The Coinage of the Visigoths of Spain, Leovigild to Achila II* (New York, 1952), pp. 375 f., 382, 386 (cited by Claude, *Adel*, pp. 168 f. but Claude does not refer to Wamba's use of the first type). These two types were also employed by Egica; for Egica and Witiza see Miles, p. 65. See also F. Mateu y Llopis, in Vives, *Inscripciones*, pp. 148–50. For 'In Dei Nomine' (normal from Wamba onwards) and 'In Christi Nomine' (only used by Ervig) see Miles, pp. 67 f. Compare the gold coin of Justinian II (692–5); cf. E. Kitzinger, *Byzantine Art in the Making* (Cambridge, Mass., 1977), p. 121 (fig. 218).

[3] Braulio, *Renotatio Isidori*, ed. P. Galindo–C. H. Lynch, *San Braulio, obispo de Zaragoza* (Madrid, 1950), p. 359 (*PL* lxxxi. 7A), trans. C. W. Barlow, *Iberian Fathers*, ii (Washington, D.C., 1969), 142. See below, p. 46 n. 1.

[4] So already Delaruelle (above, p. 4 n.2), pp. 5, 9 f. Schäferdiek, *Kirche*, is not concerned with Arian religion but with the interrelationship of conflicting creeds

incidental mention in a probably Spanish sermon. At Pentecost the congregation is told: 'There are some blasphemers who say: The Holy Spirit is not God'; he is 'a creature'. They are primed to reply: 'Where is it written in the canonical books . . . that the Holy Spirit is a creature?'[1]

The heretical groups which appear in Spain in the fourth century seem to have disappeared by the sixth. In 619 the Second Council of Seville was confronted with a Syrian bishop whom Isidore and the other Fathers considered heretical. But this was exceptional. Some decades later King Recceswinth was to declare that 'all other heresies' had disappeared from Spain other than Judaism.[2] Even Priscillianism was merely a literary reminiscence, though in the 530s it had still been honoured around Palencia and in the late sixth century in Galicia.[3]

---

and of politics. Conciliar decrees provide for the conversion of Arian churches, the reordination of Arian clergy, and the re-use (after proof by fire) of Arian relics (III Toledo, 9, II Saragossa, 1–3, *PL* lxxxiv. 353, 317 f.; Vives, *Concilios*, pp. 127, 154). For disputes between Catholics and Arians *before* 589 see J. Fontaine, 'Conversion et culture chez les Wisigoths d'Espagne', *La conversione al cristianesimo nell' Europa dell' alto medioevo* (*Settimane di studio*, xiv) (Spoleto, 1967), pp. 87–147. (On the paganism of many Visigoths see p. 130.) See also J. Orlandis, 'Problemas canónicos en torno a la conversión de los visigodos al catolicismo', *AHDE* xxxii (1962), 301–21.

[1] R. Grégoire, *Les Homéliaires du moyen-âge* (Rome, 1966), p. 208, 51–4: 'Solent enim blasfemantes fari: Spiritus sanctus deus non est . . . Creatura est, quibus dicendum est: Ubi scribtum est in canonicis libris nouis siue ueteribus quia creatura sit spiritus sanctus?' Caesarius of Arles, *De Trinitate*, Praef., ed. Morin, *Opera*, ii. 165, refers to Arians who pose subtle questions on the Trinity to 'simple Catholics'.

[2] For the fourth century see C. Baraut, 'Espagne', *Dictionnaire de spiritualité, ascétique, et mystique*, iv. 2 (Paris, 1961), 1095. II Seville, 12, in *PL* lxxxiv. 598; Vives, *Concilios*, p. 171. *LV* xii. 2. 3 (ed. Zeumer, 413. 17–19). See McKenna, *Paganism*, pp. 65–73. Spanish Judaism has been omitted from this paper because there is almost no evidence on its internal life under the Visigoths. See, however, J. Juster, in *Études d'histoire juridique offertes à P-F. Girard* ii (Paris, 1913), 299–310, 315–19.

[3] Montanus, *Epistulae* (*PL* lxxxiv. 338–42; Vives, *Concilios*, p. 49); I Braga, II Braga, 10 (ed. C. W. Barlow, *Martini episcopi Bracarensis Opera omnia*, pp. 107–9, 113, 122; *PL* lxxxiv. 563 f., 573; Vives, *Concilios*, pp. 67–9, 84 f.). The comparison between Priscillianism and Donatism, as two 'protest' movements, made by A. Barbero, *CHE* xxxvii–xxxviii (1963), 5–41, is not convincing. Even on Donatism the 'social protest' view has received severe criticism. See P. Brown, *Religion and Society in the Age of St. Augustine* (London, 1972), pp. 335–8 (a review of E. Tengström, *Donatisten und Katholiken*). See below, p. 15 n. 1.

The Pagani

But Recceswinth was to prove hasty in dismissing other opposition to his 'State Church' than Judaism. There remained—there was to remain for centuries—the problem of the *pagani*. This continuing problem was not, of course, peculiar to Spain. Paganism is found in Italy, Sicily, and Sardinia in 600, in Gaul in 625. In the Byzantine Empire, with its far older Christian traditions and more efficient government, missionaries to provinces of Asia Minor which had heard the preaching of the Apostles discovered 80,000 candidates for baptism in the mid-sixth century; in great cities of the East the ancient rites were being secretly celebrated in 578.[1] Nevertheless, in Spain the regional and social disunity and, later, the political confusion of the fifth and sixth centuries assisted the survival of the worship of the gods.

As one would expect, there is more evidence for pagan cults in the north than elsewhere. In the north the native gods had survived Romanization. Whereas in the south and east only one native deity's name is known, in the regions north of the Guadiana some 400 are documented.[2] Not all of these deities certainly survived into the fourth century. But in 399 an altar was publicly dedicated to the native god Erudinus on the peak of Dobra, in the modern province of Santander.[3] This dedication came some years after Theodosius' laws against paganism. It shows that neither the Imperial Government nor the Christian Church possessed great influence in Cantabria at this period.[4] Far later than this, in the Visigothic period, ritual sacrifice appears to have been practised near Santander.[5]

[1] A. H. M. Jones, *The Later Roman Empire 284–602* ii (Oxford, 1964), 939 f.

[2] García y Bellido, op. cit., p. 24.

[3] J. Mª. Blázquez Martínez, *Religiones primitivas de Hispania*, i. 211 ff. See M. Vigil, *BRAH* clii (1963), 225–33.

[4] One may compare the altar to Erudinus to the repair of a temple in Roman Britain under Theodosius, carried out 'in full view of the town of Dorchester'. See W. H. C. Frend, 'The Winning of the Countryside', *Journal of Ecclesiastical History*, xviii (1967), 1–14, at p. 10.

[5] J. González Echegaray, *Orígenes del cristianismo en Cantabria* (Santander, 1969), p. 10 (for a pagan inscription of 444 see p. 9). J. M. de Navascués, *Classical Folia*, xxviii (1974), 141–80, argues there are two Christian funerary inscriptions from Asturias of late *saec*. IV. He admits this is a feeble proportion of the inscriptions from the area.

The ancient gods did not survive in Cantabria alone. In 385 Pope Siricius was concerned at the relapse of many Christians into paganism in the far more Romanized diocese of Tarragona.[1] Many *rustici*, who 'thought it death not to see their idols', angered the priest Eutropius in eastern Spain about 400.[2] In Barcelona itself Bishop Pacian was obliged to combat paganism.[3]

To understand the situation in Spain on the eve of the collapse of Roman power one has to look not only at the continuing paganism but at the Christian Church. Iberian Christianity first appears in the light of day in the 250s, when we hear of churches in León-Astorga, Mérida, probably Saragossa, and Tarragona.[4] The scanty evidence available suggests that the new faith had been diffused by Roman soldiers and merchants, probably coming from Africa.[5] In this respect it can be compared to the Eastern mystery cults, which were carried by the same type of worshipper, and also failed, as did early Christianity, to make a deep impression on the native population of the central Meseta or the north-west.[6]

At the time of the Council of Elvira (313) Christianity was clearly far more important in Baetica than it was elsewhere. Throughout the fourth century Baetica, the Mediterranean coast, and the Balearic Isles continued to predominate. Palol's map of early Christian funerary inscriptions, with 158 places listed, reveals a virtual absence of evidence before the sixth

[1] Siricius, *PL* lxxxiv. 632.

[2] Eutropius (cited above, p. 7 n. 2).

[3] Pacian, *Paraenesis*, ed. L. Rubio Fernández, *San Paciano, Obras* (Barcelona, 1958), pp. 136, 144. For other evidence of paganism in fourth-century Spain see McKenna, *Paganism*, pp. 42–9, and the collection of evidence by J. Arce Martínez, *Principe de Viana*, xxxi–xxxii (1970–1), 245–55.

[4] M. C. Díaz y Díaz, 'En torno a los orígenes del Christianismo español', in *Las Raíces de España*, ed. J. M. Gomez-Tabanera (Madrid, 1967), pp. 423–43, is rightly sceptical as to apostolic foundations in Spain (cf. Baraut, 'Espagne' (cit.), p. 1089).

[5] The derivation from Africa, already indicated by Díaz, ibid., p. 436, is developed by J. Mª. Blázquez Martínez, *AEA* xl (1967), 30–50. See now the synthesis of D. Iturgaíz, 'Entronque hispano-africano en la arquitectura paleocristiana', *Burgense*, xiii. 2 (1972), 509–43.

[6] See McKenna, *Paganism*, p. 23. A. García y Bellido, *Les Religions orientales dans l'Espagne romaine* (Leiden, 1967), pp. 23, 44, notes the special reasons behind the presence of the cults of Mithra and Cybele in these regions (soldiers and slaves, respectively); of the fifty-eight monuments to Isis recorded by García (pp. 109–23, 166) only ten are from the north-west and centre (see the map on p. 107).

century from the whole Meseta, northern Portugal, Galicia, or León.[1] There is also very little evidence for the Rioja or for Aragon, outside Saragossa. Only six of the fifty places where Palol indicates early Christian monuments are to be found in the centre or the north-west.[2] This picture appears to agree with the recent conclusions of studies on Cantabria—where there is no evidence for Christianity before about 450—and on Vasconia, where the Church was virtually confined during the Visigothic period to a bishopric in Pamplona.[3]

What can one say of the inner state of fourth-century peninsular Christianity? From the Council of Elvira one gains the impression of a Church whose members are hardly emerging from paganism. The canon forbidding Christian matrons lending their best dresses to adorn pagan processions is perhaps as revealing as the decree forbidding Christians to sacrifice at the city temples.[4] Other canons appear to be aimed at the kind of picnics in cemeteries (but banquet would be a better word) provided for in the necropolis at Tarragona, deplored by Ambrose and Augustine.[5] Other surviving monuments

[1] Palol, 'Christian Monuments', pp. 36 f. and Map I. There is one tomb at Toledo of *saec.* V and one at Orense (Vives, *Inscripciones*, Nos. 67, 186). For Christianity in the Rioja see the Alfaro mosaic, Vives, 258, and for Aragon, 374.

[2] See Palol's Map III and his List, pp. 67–71. Nos. 18 (Puebla Nueva, Toledo); 27 (a Roman villa in the province of Toledo); 42 (Sta Eulalia de Bóveda, Lugo); 46 (Conimbriga); 49 (Marialba, near León); 50 (near Braga). For the places where Christian sarcophagi have been found see Palol, Map IV and List, pp. 72–4. Toledo and its surroundings, Galicia and León and the province of Burgos are represented here (Nos. 15–19, 21–8). There is no evidence of Christianity in the necropoli of *saec.* IV–V along the Duero (see p. 41 and Map II), which may be those of *limitanei*. M. Chamoso Lamas, *AEM* ii (1965), 433–49, discusses a series of necropoli in Galicia but it is very hard to date most of them. See also, for monuments in the whole north-west, H. Schlunk, in *Legio VII Gemina* (León, 1970), pp. 477–509; for 'Gallaecia', idem, in *Actas . . . Lugo*, pp. 193–236.

[3] González Echegaray, *Orígenes*, pp. 11 f. J. Mª. Lacarra, *Estudios de historia navarra* (Pamplona, 1971), pp. 1–31, esp. pp. 3–8. For a criticism of recent attempts to maintain as historical the legends of early Christianity in the north-west see B. de Gaiffier, *Analecta Bollandiana*, xci (1973), 140. On Galicia see M. C. Díaz y Díaz, in *La romanización de Galicia* (La Coruña, 1976), pp. 105–20, and idem, in *Actas . . . Lugo*, pp. 237–50, where the role of Priscillianism is stressed; on this see also H. Chadwick, *Priscillian of Avila* (Oxford, 1976), esp. chap. IV.

[4] Elvira, 57, 59 (*PL* lxxxiv, 308; Vives, *Concilios*, pp. 11 f.). On Elvira see McKenna, *Paganism*, pp. 28–38.

[5] Elvira, 34–5 (*PL* lxxxiv. 305; Vives, *Concilios*, pp. 7 f.). See A. Schneider, in *Spanische Forschungen der Görresgesellschaft*, i. 5 (1935), 79 f.; and, for Cartagena, P. de Palol, in *Actas del VIII Congreso Internacional de Arqueología Cristiana* i (Barcelona, 1972), 454–8.

suggest a Church of the affluent—as does the Elvira canon concerning the masters whose slaves are too attached to the domestic idols to allow them to be removed.[1] The worldly side of the Spanish Church in the later fourth century is revealed not only by the scandals of the Priscillianist affair but by the virtually hereditary succession to the see of Saragossa of Prudentius' friends, 'sacerdotum domus Valeriorum'. Prudentius' insistence on preserving the statues of the gods—though their worship was now prohibited—as 'the works of great artists', may perhaps be connected to the mixture of Christian and pagan themes in the *villae* of the fourth century, in Spain as elsewhere. A great distance, in any case, separated such cultivated landed proprietors from the 'stupid paganism' of the Basque countryside not far from Prudentius' Calahorra.[2]

The gradual breakdown of the Empire complicated the problems of the Church. Laws against pagans existed—even if not always enforced, or enforceable—in the Theodosian Code. These laws were omitted from the *Breviarium* of Alaric II, though Alaric kept the laws against magicians.[3] In the 530s Bishop Montanus of Toledo was praising Toribius of Palencia for his (apparently exceptional) zeal against idolatry.[4] The absence of documented dedications of churches and depositions of relics before the mid-sixth century has been noted.[5] No doubt a number of pagan sanctuaries were being turned into churches, as in Gaul. This appears to have happened, at some

[1] Elvira, 41 (*PL* lxxxiv. 306; Vives, *Concilios*, p. 9). On the artistic evidence see H. Schlunk, *MM* vii (1966), 210–31; P. de Palol, *Arqueología cristiana de la España romana* (Madrid, 1967), pp. 116–45; idem, in *Actas de la I^a. Reunión Nacional de Arqueología Paleocristiana* (Vitoria, 1967), pp. 18 f., and in *Actas del VIII Congreso*, i. 169–172. Fontaine, *L'Art préroman* i. 52–5, 86 f., 99 f.

[2] Prudentius, *Peristephanon*, i. 94 f., iv. 79 f.; *Contra Symmachum*, 502 f. (*CC* cxxvi. 255, 289, 203). On the double culture, classical and Christian, of Prudentius, Ausonius, Paulinus of Nola, see the recent studies of J. Fontaine, esp. 'Valeurs antiques et valeurs chrétiennes dans la spiritualité des grands propriétaires terriens à la fin du IVe siècle occidental', *Epektasis, Mélanges patristiques offerts au Cardinal Jean Daniélou* (Paris, 1972), pp. 571–95; 'Société et culture chrétiennes sur l'aire circumpyrénéenne au siècle de Théodose', *Bulletin de littérature ecclésiastique* (1974), pp. 241–82, esp. pp. 259 ff.

[3] As is noted by Thompson, *Goths*, p. 54.

[4] Montanus, *PL* lxxxiv. 340; Vives, *Concilios*, p. 50. Toribius even tried to convert 'terreni domini', presumably the Visigoths.

[5] See P. de Palol, in *Rivista di archeologia cristiana*, xliii (1967), 192. For Marialba see Fontaine, *L'Art préroman* i. 95–97; Th. Hauschild, and A. Viñayo, in *Legio VII Gemina* (León, 1970), pp. 513–21, 551–68 (the date of dedication is probably *saec.* IV or V).

uncertain date, to the sanctuary of the Celtic god Endovellicus, 50 km from Evora. As a guide to the future life he was suitably replaced by the Archangel St. Michael. The process of conversion of the *pagani* was slow, however. A number of Catholics were attracted to Arianism. The Council of Lérida of 546 speaks of Catholics presenting their children to be baptized 'in heresy', and of a class of rebaptized. Priscillianism also survived.[1]

Paganism was still alive. Pagans are mentioned in Romanized Mérida at the beginning of the episcopate of Masona (*c.* 570). They appear in the canons of Braga II (572), in the Suevic kingdom (the Sueves had only just been converted to Catholicism), of Toledo III, and of Narbonne in 589. II Braga stresses the need to instruct the *ignari* and to warn against idolatry. The canons freely translated by St. Martin of Braga from the Greek also contain decrees against divination, astrology, etc. The provincial Council of Narbonne was concerned with divination and 'observing' Jove's day by not working. But it was the Third Council of Toledo, at which sixty-two bishops celebrated the conversion of the Visigoths, which declared that 'the sacrilege of idolatry is implanted throughout almost all Spain and Gaul.' The measures ordered were revealing; judges and bishops together were to coerce idolaters (by all measures short of death). Landowners who did not 'extirpate this evil from their estates' would be excommunicated.[2]

The Visigothic Code does not contain laws against idolatry, though (like earlier Arian legislation) it is concerned with magic and divination.[3] For almost a century Church Councils were

[1] Blázquez Martínez, *Religiones*, i. 147–164. For Sta Eulalia de Bóveda (Lugo) see Fontaine, *L'Art préroman* i. 92–5 (a nymphaeum transformed into a church, but when?). Lérida, cc. 13, 14 (*PL* lxxxiv. 324; Vives, *Concilios*, pp. 58 f.). With the survival of Priscillianism, once coercion had ceased, one can compare that of Donatism. See R. A. Markus, in *Studies in Church History*, i (London, 1964), 118–26, who suggests almost 'complete fusion' existed between Catholics and Donatists by 600.

[2] *VPE* v. 11. 7, ed. Garvin, 192. II Braga, 1, *Canones* 71–5, in Barlow, pp. 119, 140 f.; *PL* lxxxiv. 571, 584; Vives, *Concilios*, pp. 81, 103 f. (On these *canones* see G. Martínez Díez, *Bracara Augusta*, xxi (1967), p. 18 of the offprint.) Narbonne, 14, 15 (*PL* 612 f.; Vives, pp. 149 f.) III Toledo, 16 (*PL* 354; Vives, p. 130). Ibid., 1 (*PL* 351; Vives, p. 125) says that by 'haeresis vel gentilitatis necessitate' (pressure?) church discipline has been cast into confusion.

[3] *LV* vi. 2. 1–5 (Zeumer, pp. 257–60). See King, *Law*, pp. 147 ff.; McKenna, *Paganism*, pp. 120–5. See Brown, *Religion and Society*, p. 126 n. 5, who considers that Martroye 'underestimates the use to which [Roman laws against magic] were put to victimize paganism in general'. On this see now D. Grodzynski, in *Divination et rationalité* (Paris, 1974), pp. 267–94.

also concerned with magic rather than idolatry.[1] But in 681 and 693 two Councils of Toledo again denounced 'formal' idolatry. In 681 those guilty were considered to be mainly slaves but in 693 'nobiles personae' appear to be involved, at least as protectors of idolatry.[2]

We learn far more about the nature of pagan cults from a short sermon of Martin of Braga than we do from the conciliar decrees. The *De castigatione rusticorum* (of *c.* 574) has been repeatedly analysed by historians of pre-Christian religion and of folklore. Martin's personal knowledge of the rites he was attacking seems undeniable. He is concerned with divination but more so with a complex of propitiatory rites, directed towards the gods governing certain days, the home, cross-roads, the sea, rivers, fountains, woods, and the crops. The Council of Toledo of 681 was still concerned with the sacred stones, fountains, trees, referred to by Martin. When the temples were abandoned—perhaps because they afforded too obvious targets for Christian zealotry—the older cults survived.[3]

They survived largely because they were so closely ingrained into the lives of the people. They afforded not only protection against a world of invisible dangers but an opportunity to rejoice when the back-breaking labours of the fields were over. To many of the inhabitants of Spain the Church must have appeared principally in the role of the enemy of their few pleasures, mainly concerned to put down their dances on festivals and the celebrations on the Kalends of January, which were intended to ensure the prosperity of the New Year. The Church was always afraid, as a sermon in use in Spain puts it, of the faithful turning 'from singing Psalms to bacchanal

[1] See IV Toledo, 29; Mérida, 15; see V Toledo, 4 (*PL* lxxxiv. 375, 622, 391; Vives, *Concilios*, pp. 203, 336, 228). See McKenna, *Paganism*, pp. 119 f., 125 f.

[2] XII, Toledo 1; XVI, 2 (*PL* lxxxiv. 478 f., 537; Vives, *Concilios*, pp. 398 f., 499 f.). See McKenna, pp. 128–33. The second canon was in response to Egica's *Tomus* (*PL* 529C; Vives, p. 486). It added to the *Tomus* the provision that offerings to idols should not only be transferred to neighbouring churches, but exhibited there, 'coram ipsis qui hoc voto sacrilego dedicanda crediderant'.

[3] Martin of Braga, *De castigatione rusticorum*, ed. Barlow, pp. 183–203; see McKenna, *Paganism*, pp. 84–107. For the treatise as a sermon see below. Compare Isidore, *Orig.* viii. 10, ed. Lindsay; 'Ibi enim in locis agrestibus et pagis gentiles lucos idolaque statuerunt.' Some supplementary information on the cult of the astral gods, the sun and moon, can be culled from Isidore, *De natura rerum*, and Sisebut's *Epistula*, sent in reply, ed. J. Fontaine (Bordeaux, 1960); see pp. 4 f., 331, 18–22. M. Meslin, in *Hommages à M. Renard*, ii (1969), while pointing to Martin's

chants'.[1] Toledo III remarks: 'The irreligious custom is to be totally extirpated by which the vulgar on Saints' days, instead of attending divine office, give themselves up to filthy dances and songs, not only harming themselves but disturbing the church services.'[2] To the Church such dances savoured of heathenism. And indeed ritual dances in honour of the gods are recorded in Spain by Strabo and are represented in art.[3] The Council's prohibition was not effective. In the late seventh century the ascetic Valerius of Bierzo witnessed a priest 'hopping on shaky feet, singing wicked ditties, the frightful songs of a sinful dance, the devil's ruinous obscenity'.[4]

The war on the celebrations on the Kalends of January also continued in Visigothic Spain but it seems that here the Church finally recognized 'the error of the Gentiles' was ineradicable. The institution of the Feast of the Circumcision may have been originally a Spanish attempt to replace the pagan festival; the *fast* appears to have been moved to 2 January.[5]

There must have been many sixth and seventh-century men who took the same view which had exasperated St. Augustine: 'To be sure I visit the idols. I consult magicians and soothsayers, but I do not forsake the Church of God. I am a Catholic.'[6] In the 1830s an English visitor to the Caucasus remarked of a nominally Islamic country (one converted, however, only a few generations before): 'The religious groves are still objects of a veneration far more real and sincere than the mosques, and the festivals still solemnized in them draw much greater

debts to earlier authors, remarks (p. 523) that his treatise reflects 'l'existence d'un paganisme rural, à-théologique, fondé sur l'adoration de sacralités naturelles'.

[1] Grégoire, *Homéliaires*, p. 198. 54 f.: 'In fide Christianitatis meretricat, cum de psallendi officio ad baccanalibus concurrit cantibus.' See the sermon, perhaps from Spain, ed. J. Leclercq, *Revue bénédictine*, lix (1949), 200 f., also M. Meslin, *La Fête des Kalendes de janvier dans l'empire romain* (Brussels, 1970).

[2] III Toledo, 23 (*PL* lxxxiv. 356; Vives, *Concilios*, p. 133). See McKenna, *Paganism*, p. 116.

[3] Blázquez Martínez, i. 36 f.

[4] Valerius, *Ordo querimoniae*, 6, ed. C. M. Aherne, *Valerio of Bierzo* (Washington, D.C., 1949), p. 93. 57–9.

[5] M. Férotin, *Le Liber Ordinum*, p. 450 n. 1; the sermon already cited in Grégoire, p. 198. 41 f. IV Toledo, 11 (*PL* lxxxiv. 370; Vives, *Concilios*, p. 195) was still attempting to keep the Kalends as a fast. See King, *Law*, p. 146 n. 6, and, in general, Meslin, *La Fête*, pp. 114–29.

[6] Augustine, *Enarratio in Ps. 88*, ii. 14 (*CC* xxxix. 1244), trans. by Frend (above, p. 11 n. 4), p. 8.

multitudes.'[1] Perhaps Martin of Braga might have recognized his own problem here.

The Church's Reaction

The rich and varied range of literary culture in seventh-century Spain has often been admired. The level would appear to rise from the time of Isidore to that of Eugenius II and Julian of Toledo. This is the culture of a few great bishops and abbots and an occasional lay noble.[2] Could this high culture be communicated in some form to the residually pagan populace, to 'rustics' whom the clergy in general probably viewed as semi-savages? That Braulio should tell Pope Honorius that the Spanish bishops kept constant watch over the flock of the Lord and should speak of the 'continuous and lengthy treatment [of converts from Judaism] by preaching', might not mean very much.[3] The portrait of Julian of Toledo by Felix, with its contraposition of 'theorica, i.e. contemplativa quies' (the monastic life) and 'proximorum salus'—the latter the aim adopted by Julian, might be no more than an official episcopal ideal. Even so, official ideals can be significant, and the whole eulogy, with its stress on counsel, almsgiving, relief of the *miseri*, of the oppressed, and (a discreet reference to Julian and 'la haute politique'?) of a bishop 'strenuous in directing affairs, equable in judgement . . . singular in vindicating justice, outstanding in the defense of all the churches', is worth quoting. The main note is one of vigilance and charity, of a man

[1] J. A. Longworth, *A Year among the Circassians* (London, 1840), i. 198.

[2] See, recently, M. C. Díaz y Díaz, 'Aspectos de la cultura literaria en la España visigótica', *Anales toledanos*, iii (1971), 33–58 (on the basis of the surviving manuscripts), and idem, in *La Patrología toledano-visigoda* (Madrid, 1970), pp. 45–63 (on the bishops of Toledo; on p. 53 he refers to the educated laymen). See also P. Riché, 'L'enseignement et la culture des laïcs dans l'Occident pré-carolingien', *La scuola nell' alto medioevo* (*Settimane di studio*, xix. 1: Spoleto, 1972), pp. 231–53.

[3] Braulio, *epist*. xxi (on behalf of VI Toledo), ed. Riesco, p. 110. 54 f., 45 f., trans. Barlow, *Iberian Fathers*, ii. 53. For the low view of the *rustici* in Gaul see J. Le Goff, in *Agricoltura e mondo rurale in occidente nell' alto medioevo* (*Settimane*, xiii. 2: Spoleto, 1966), esp. pp. 738 f. For Spain see *VPE* iii. 11 (Garvin, p. 158); *Vita Fructuosi*, 11 (Nock, p. 107; Díaz, p. 98); Valerius, *Replicatio sermonum*, 14 (Aherne, p. 145. 16).

'praestabilem hominibus'.[1] There is evidence that the defensive reaction of Braulio and the portrait of Julian represent a constant attempt on the part of the leaders of the Spanish Church to respond to the needs of their people. One may note the frequent insistence on 'brevity',[2] and how, in one letter, Braulio displays reluctance to embark on a non-crucial question. As a bishop he felt, with St. Paul, 'the time is short' and he and other priests should devote their efforts to 'love which edifies'.[3]

III Toledo recognized in 589 that under Arian rule ecclesiastical discipline had broken down.[4] The first necessity was to re-establish the character of the clergy. A great many conciliar decrees were concerned with this. IV Toledo, in particular, taking up earlier decrees and practice, insisted that bishops and priests should know the Scriptures and the Church canons, and that the young clergy should be brought up together under proper masters.[5] How limited the education the clergy received in episcopal schools was, as compared to that available in the monastic schools where almost all the leading bishops of Spain were trained, is a matter of dispute into which I need not now enter.[6] What is clear is the interest in the education of the clergy which appears in many of Isidore's works and later in the

[1] Felix, *Vita Iuliani*, 2–3, 5 (*PL* xcvi. 445 ff.). Cf. Isidorus, *Differentiae*, ii. 24, 130 (*PL* lxxxiii. 90C). The contrast with Ildefonsus' exaltation of the monastic character of his predecessors at Toledo in his *De viris illustribus*, esp. v–vii, ed. Codoñer (Salamanca, 1972), pp. 122–6, is striking. On this work of Ildefonsus see J. Fontaine, in *Anales toledanos*, iii (1971), 59–96, and Codoñer, pp. 32–46. Both these authors accentuate the 'pastoral' concern of the work; see Codoñer (p. 45) for the emphasis on *praedicatio*. See below, p. 24 n. 1.

[2] For the theme of *brevitas* see my article, 'Las Fuentes de San Julián de Toledo', *Anales Toledanos*, iii. 105 f.

[3] Braulio, *epist.* xii (Riesco, p. 86. 29 f.). See also Taio, *Sententiae*, ii, 36 (*PL* lxxx. 829–31), using a catena from Gregory the Great. The influence of Gregory's *Regula pastoralis* in Spain is brought out by J. Fernández Alonso, *La cura pastoral*, pp. 125–9. See his whole chap. III, 'Santidad y vida del clero'. Isidore on 'The Ideal of Perfection' is discussed by Mullins, *The Spiritual Life*, pp. 151–68 (on the clergy).

[4] III Toledo, 1; see 13 (*PL* lxxxiv. 351, 354; Vives, *Concilios*, pp. 125, 129).

[5] Notably IV Toledo, 19, 24–5 (*PL* lxxxiv. 372, 374; Vives, *Concilios*, pp. 198 ff., 201 f.).

[6] See Fernández Alonso, *Cura pastoral*, pp. 71–118, and M. Hernández in *La Patrología toledano-visigoda* (Madrid, 1970), pp. 65–98, but esp. Riché, *Éducation*, pp. 331–6, 339–45, and J. Fontaine, 'Fins et moyens de l'enseignement ecclésiastique dans l'Espagne wisigothique', *La scuola* (*Settimane di studio*, xix: Spoleto, 1966), pp. 145–202; see also the discussion of Riché and Fontaine, ibid. 217–22.

Ars grammatica which condenses the teaching of Julian of Toledo.[1]

The attempt of Augustine and Caesarius 'to reach the attention of the humblest masses', by the deliberate use of simplified style and presentation is again found in Spain.[2] Martin of Braga claimed to write 'rustico sermone' in his sermon for the rustics: that this was not a meaningless statement appears from the 'deliberate use of vulgarisms which would make his words more appealing'.[3] Braulio, in his *Life of Aemilian*, remarks he was writing 'in the plain and clear style (plano apertoque sermone) that is becoming to such things', i.e. Lives of Saints.[4] He makes it clear that he is employing 'sermo simplex', and writing in a different style from that suitable for 'disciplinae saecularium studium'.[5] The author of the *Vitas Patrum Emeritensium* declares: 'we will narrate simply and truly, for the simple, things that are true'. The use of non-classical vocabulary and syntax appears in this and other Spanish seventh-century hagiographical works.[6] Even when writing for monks, and in civilized Baetica, Isidore found it necessary to use 'sermo plebeia vel rustica'.[7]

However simplified the message it had somehow to be conveyed to its audience. For this step two things were needed, church organization outside the cities, and a measure of literacy on the part of the clergy and of some laity. We know that a relatively efficient parochial system existed in Galicia by the

[1] See now Mª. A. H. Maestre Yenes (ed.), *Ars Iuliani Toletani Episcopi, una gramática latina de la España visigoda* (Toledo, 1973).

[2] For Augustine etc. see Brown, *Religion and Society*, pp. 287–94 (the quotation is from Augustine, *Retract.* i. 20), also R. MacMullen, *Journal of Theological Studies*, N.S. xvii (1966), 108–12.

[3] Barlow, *Martini . . . Opera*, pp. 161 ff. (as against earlier editors). See *De castigatione*, i. 8–9 (p. 183: 'cibum rusticis rustico sermone condire').

[4] Braulio, *Vita S. Emiliani*, 2, ed. L. Vázquez de Parga (Madrid, 1943), p. 4. 21 f.; ed. Cazzaniga, p. 23. 1 (trans. Barlow, *Iberian Fathers*, ii. 114).

[5] Braulio, 5 (p. 11. 14 f., p. 12. 3–4; Cazzaniga, p. 25. 14, 21). See the study of variants etc. by Cazzaniga, pp. 14–19; idem, *Acme*, vii (1954), 533–49.

[6] *VPE* iv. 1 (Garvin, p. 160): 'ea quae omnibus modis vera sunt simplicibus simpliciter veraciterque narramus.' See the very detailed study in Garvin's edition, pp. 36–132. The article of M. Rabanal Alvarez, 'La lengua hablada en tiempos de San Isidoro', *Archivos Leoneses*, xxiv (1970), 187–201, tells us little that is relevant here.

[7] Isidore, *Regula*, Praef. (*PL* lxxxiii. 868). See J. Fontaine, *Vigiliae Christianae*, xiv (1960), 93 ff. In his *De viris*, 10 (Codoñer, p. 130), Ildefonsus praises one bishop for use of 'communis eloquium'. See Fontaine, *Anales toledanos*, iii. 68 f.

late sixth century.[1] Throughout Spain, by 633, many rural churches had been built by local landowners, not always for the best of motives, and their endowment was a matter of importance.[2] The question of literacy is more complex. Perhaps some scepticism with regard to the significance of apparent signatures on one at least of the recently discovered *pizarras* might be warranted, in the light of the case of Bishop Marcianus of Écija in the 620s. A document was produced against him signed by two women, with Roman names, though 'viles personae'. Unfortunately it later appeared that neither could read what they had signed.[3] However, in view of the importance of the Visigothic Code and of Braulio's and other correspondence, it seems that the nobility, Roman or Gothic, officials, notaries, etc., could read more complicated Latin than that of sermons and Lives of Saints.[4] The sermon already quoted in which the faithful are told to memorize answers to (presumably Arian) 'blasphemies' presupposes a degree of sophistication in the probably urban congregation.[5]

Did royal or noble women, one may ask, provide the kind of bridge between the intellectuals and the ordinary people which Professor Momigliano has seen them as holding in fifth-century Byzantium?[6] The 'taste for theological controversy' does appear, in a rather crude form, in the Arian Queen Goiswintha, confronted with a recalcitrant step-daughter-in-law and later with a turncoat step-son, but not, to my knowledge, later.[7]

[1] In the dioceses of Braga, Porto, and Tuy, more than in the rest. See David, *Études*, pp. 1–82.

[2] A. H. M. Jones, in *Christianity in Britain, 300–700* (Leicester, 1968), pp. 9–15 (but one cannot use the exceptional state of affairs in II Seville, 7, to prove the existence of *chorepiscopi* in Spain). See P. Séjourné, *Le Dernier Père de l'Église, St. Isidore de Séville* (Paris, 1929), pp. 233–7, and, in general, Fernández Alonso, *Cura pastoral*, pp. 202–13.

[3] For the *pizarras* etc. see Díaz in *La Patrología*, p. 53; the case of Marcianus is analysed by Thompson, *Goths*, pp. 287 ff. See the text in F. Dahn, *Die Könige der Germanen*, vi[2] (Leipzig, 1885), 617: 'quia se litteras ignorabant, rusticitate se deceptas dicebant.'

[4] For written proceedings, see King, *Law*, pp. 94 ff. See Braulio, *epist.* xvi (Riesco, p. 96). In the 'Discussione' on Riché's paper (p. 18 n. 2 above), pp. 340 f., both Riché and Bertolini agreed on the far higher level of Spanish law, as against that of the Lombards or Franks. [5] See p. 10 n. 1, above.

[6] A. Momigliano, in *Popular Belief and Practice* (*Studies in Church History*, viii) (Cambridge, 1972), pp. 12 f.

[7] See Gregory of Tours, *Historia Francorum*, v.38, ix. 1, and John of Biclar, *Chronicon*, *s.a.* 579, 589 (*MGH AA* xi. 215, 218). See my article in *AST* xxxiv (1961), 26 n. 12.

'The cult of relics' no doubt attracted noble women, as it did everyone else at this period.[1] But probably intellectuals in Visigothic Spain, even the authors of the highly complicated credal formulas of Toledo, were not as far distant, in their mental presuppositions, from the people as was the case in Byzantium.

Both the scanty evidence one has from this age and the comparison with much later medieval centuries suggests that the ordinary country clergy did not preach. For peasants a sermon, even one read aloud from a homiliary, must have been a far less central part of their religion than the liturgy of the year. In some ways, despite the abundance of material, it is more difficult to reconstruct the seventh-century Spanish liturgy than it is that of (say) the thirteenth century. This was a time when the liturgy was being organized, the cult of non-martyrs was beginning, Christian art was growing and developing.[2] The insistence on uniformity in the liturgy of IV Toledo ('unus ordo orandi atque psallendi . . . unus modus in missarum sollemnitatibus, unus in vespertinis matutinisque officiis') was all the more important because of the existing variety (even the form of the *Gloria Patri* was not the same throughout Spain).[3] IV Toledo laid down a complete programme of liturgical composition—'let hymns, masses, prayers . . . be composed'.[4] The response was a long series of hymns, *passiones*, and masses, offices, and 'occasional prayers', constituting a very large proportion of what is preserved in the books of the 'Mozarabic' Liturgy.[5]

[1] Vives, *Inscripciones*, appears to contain only one example of a church built by a noblewoman, the presumably Celto-Iberian Anduires, together with her husband (No. 505, undated). The Gothic Count Gudiliuva constructed three churches in 594–610 (Vives, No. 303).

[2] These characteristics of the age are noted by Delaruelle (cited p. 4 n. 2,) pp. 5 f. (on reading sermons, ibid., pp. 26 f.).

[3] IV Toledo, 2. See Mérida, 2; XVII Toledo, 2, 6 (*PL* lxxxiv. 365, 616, 556, 558; Vives, *Concilios*, pp. 188, 327, 528 f., 532). J. Mª. Pinell, in *DHEE* ii (Madrid, 1972), 1304 ff., sees an attempt to suppress the Roman liturgy in Galicia in IV Toledo. He summarizes well the complex history of the Spanish liturgy. For the 'Gloria Patri' see IV Toledo, 15 (*PL* 371; Vives, p. 197).

[4] IV Toledo, 13 (*PL* lxxxiv. 371 B; Vives, *Concilios*, p. 197). 'Componuntur ergo hymni . . . missae sive preces vel orationes . . .'

[5] See my article, cited above (p. 8 n. 3), pp. 304 f., nn. 179, 180, and M. C. Díaz, in *Estudios sobre la liturgia mozárabe* (Toledo, 1965), p. 58. It is only occasionally that one can date a Mass immediately after 589, e.g. the 'Missa S. Engratie' (Férotin, *Liber mozarabicus sacramentorum*, pp. 272 ff.).

The Spanish bishops of the seventh century created a liturgy of great splendour, a splendour difficult to envisage today without the large churches built for it. The theological complexity of the liturgy is as notable as its 'grandiose style' and rhetorical qualities. Despite the relatively high level of spoken Latin in Visigothic Spain the liturgy was well removed from, though influenced by, popular speech.[1]

The drama of the liturgy's action comes through the play of synonyms. The Holy Week liturgy was particularly dramatic.[2] But drama appears elsewhere also, for instance in the hymn, 'De nubentibus'; after a prelude on Adam and Eve, joyfulness breaks out suddenly, with a whole orchestra of instruments striking up, the lyre, flute, lute, cymbals, dulcimer depicted in lively Latin.[3]

A recent account speaks of the 'active part' of the faithful in the liturgy.[4] This would appear anachronistic in view of the structure of the surviving Visigothic churches (or plans made from excavations). The care taken to separate the presanctuary from the nave by partitions and the sanctuary from the presanctuary by curtains indicate that mystery and transcendence rather than participation were what was aimed at.[5]

Although the liturgy did not stress, or necessarily involve, preaching, the leaders of the Spanish Church were aware of the

[1] J. A. de Aldama, 'Valoración teológica de la literatura litúrgica hispana', *La Patrología toledano-visigoda*, pp. 137–57. Díaz, loc. cit., pp. 78–82, 65, and, more generally, Fernández Alonso, chap. VI.

[2] Delaruelle, pp. 24 ff. An elaborate study of the Paschal vigil by J. R. Bernal, in *Hispania Sacra*, xvii (1964), 283–347.

[3] Díaz, *Index*, 364. Blume, *Analecta*, xxvii. 283 f. The 'Ordo ad benedicendum eos qui noviter nubent', in Férotin, *Liber ordinum*, pp. 436–40, is less dramatic—or joyful. It ends by an admonition to the newly wedded couple 'pro sancta communione a pollutione in ea nocte se custodiant.' See Isidore, *DEO* ii. 18. 5 (*PL* lxxxiii. 805): 'Nuptiae enim peccatum non sunt, sed per sollicitudinem mundi qui nubunt legem Dei servire vix possunt', and i. 18. 9–10 (ibid. 756 f.). In general, see L. Bopp, in *Spanische Forschungen der Görresgesellschaft*, i. 20 (1962), 123–38.

[4] Baraut (cited p. 10 n. 2), p. 1108.

[5] A. Rodríguez G. de Ceballos, in *Miscelánea Comillas*, xliii (1965), 295–327. See also F. Iñiguez Almech, *Cuadernos de trabajos de la Escuela Española de Historia y Arqueología en Roma*, vii (1955), 7–180, e.g. 75 f.; and esp. H. Schlunk, *MM* xii (1971), 205–40. This is not to deny the elements of 'dialogue' in the Mass, for which see Fernández Alonso, pp. 318–23. M. C. Díaz y Díaz (Chapter 2 below, pp. 61–76) holds that the liturgical texts were mainly addressed to the clergy and monks. I Braga, 13 (Barlow, p. 113, *PL* lxxxiv. 567; Vives, *Concilios*, pp. 73 f.) prohibits laymen from entering the sanctuary to receive communion. IV Toledo, 18 (*PL* 372; Vives, p. 198) is more explicit still: 'sacerdos et levita ante altare communicent, in choro clerus, extra chorum populus.'

importance of sermons, normally given by a bishop. In 549 the Council of Valencia insisted that the 'catechumens and penitents', as well as the faithful, should hear the Gospel and the bishop's sermon, 'because', the canon adds, 'we know with certainty that some have been drawn to the faith by the preaching of pontiffs'.[1]

The clearest presentation of Christianity in Spain is Martin of Braga's *De castigatione rusticorum.* The work contains a capsule history of salvation, focused on the Creation and Incarnation. The main point appears to be, however, that demons—whose existence Martin fully admits and stresses—need not be frightening, because they have fallen and man is called on to ascend above them.[2] Demons have tricked man in the past but the Incarnation has freed man from them. (The Resurrection is brought home by emphasizing that Christ ate after it. His *body* was risen.) We have more powerful 'incantations' than the Devil's, in the shape of the Creed, the Sign of the Cross, and the Lord's Prayer. Finally, if you have sinned, you can repent. 'Do not doubt the mercy of God.'[3]

Many of the sermons prescribed to be read in Visigothic Spain are contained in the Homiliary of Toledo.[4] Over half of the 118 items contained in the Homiliary (and addenda to it) were taken from Caesarius of Arles (48) or Augustine (13), with other patristic sources, such as Maximus of Turin or Gregory the Great, drawn on to a much lesser extent. The number of possibly 'original' (anonymous) Spanish sermons in the collection is small. This indicates that Spanish congregations were perhaps more likely to hear a sermon—or an extract from a sermon—from Caesarius of Arles than from their own bishop. The emphasis on practical morality typical of Caesarius is therefore particularly important. This note also appears in probably Spanish sermons in the collection.[5] The general tone

[1] Valencia, 1 (*PL* lxxxiv. 325; Vives, *Concilios*, p. 61). See Fernández Alonso, chap. VII, 'La predicación', pp. 395–414.

[2] Martin (cited p. 16 n. 3), 4 (Barlow, p. 185).

[3] Ibid. 13, 16, 17 (pp. 193. 17 f., 199. 20–30, 200. 5).

[4] Grégoire, *Les Homéliaires*, pp. 161–85 (analysis); pp. 197–230 (unpublished sermons). He notes other publications.

[5] e.g. Grégoire, pp. 197–8 (on the Feast of the Circumcision): 'Circumcise your *hearts*'. On Caesarius see H. G. J. Beck, *The Pastoral Care of Souls in South-East France during the Sixth Century* (Rome, 1950), pp. 276–83.

is one of fairly simple allegorizing, in the sense of drawing moral precepts from the Scriptures.[1]

Yet, as with the liturgy in general, so in the sermons one finds a dramatic appeal to the theatrical sense of late Roman man. In the sermon on the resurrection of Lazarus the preacher exhorts the congregation, 'Clamate et plorate! Plorate sicut Maria et Marta!'[2]

Six sermons on the plague were included in the collection.[3] Three of them were intended for use on successive days. The avoidance of repetition and the ability to hold attention are masterful. On the first day the sermon begins: 'Behold a mournful message hath dismayed us'. The wrath of the Just Judge is upon us. On the second day the preacher is to instil hope into his chastened hearers ('Ipse autem dominus . . . nos anuntiato flagello eripiat'). On the third day he is to bring them to resignation to God's Will.[4]

The Religion of the Laity: Rituals

The Church endeavoured to incorporate the uneducated mass of the population into its ranks by initiating it into a ritual cycle which covered the whole life of man from baptism to death. The laity's opportunities of salvation (and their corresponding obligations) stemmed from their character as baptized members of the Church. By 600 the old preparation for adult baptism, lasting at least two years, had disappeared.[5] Braga II, in 572, still envisages the instruction of adults but it sees this as mainly accomplished in the twenty days before Easter.[6] In mid-seventh-century Spain, although catechumens were supposed to have been present for years at the liturgy, up to and

[1] e.g. Grégoire, p. 201. 17–19.

[2] Ibid., p. 203. 99–101.

[3] Ibid., pp. 172 f.

[4] Ibid., p. 214. 2–3, p. 219. 77 f. In the third sermon we have quotations (not indicated by Grégoire) from Augustine, *De ciu. Dei*, i. 11 (quoted in Julian of Toledo, *Prognosticum*, i. 12, my edition, *CC* cxv. 27. 17–19 = Grégoire, p. 220. 11 f.) and from Cyprian, *De mortalitate* (also in Julian, i. 15, pp. 31. 63–32. 68 = Grégoire, p. 220. 42–7). See also Julian, p. 32. 77–82 = G., p. 221. 71–7. This may perhaps indicate a common source, unless Julian is the author of the sermon. On the Toledan Homiliary see also Delaruelle, pp. 28 f.

[5] Elvira, 42; baptism could be postponed to the hour of death in certain cases (see 4, 11, 68, 73). *PL* lxxxiv. 306, 302 f., 309; Vives, *Concilios*, pp. 9, 2 f., 13 f.

[6] Braga, II, 1 (Barlow, p. 119; *PL* lxxxiv. 571; Vives, *Concilios*, p. 81).

including the sermon, formal preparation for baptism began two weeks before Easter. This preparation included fasting, exorcism, and anointing.[1] Although, by 572, and more clearly in the seventh century, infant baptism was the norm, in about 660 Ildefonsus of Toledo still considers the case of some adult coming 'reluctantly', from paganism to Christianity. In such cases the bishop would instruct the convert individually.[2]

One of the main features of the whole preparation for baptism was the memorization of the Apostles' Creed. The Spanish liturgy prescribed sessions explaining the Creed during the twenty days before baptism.[3] On Palm Sunday we have the solemn *traditio* of the Creed to the *competentes*, with the following words: 'Before you sleep, before you go out, fortify yourselves with your Symbolum . . . Let your memory be your codex.' In reply the *competentes*, first making the sign of the Cross, would recite the Creed.[4] On Holy Thursday there was the *redditio symboli*, another formal recitation to the bishop.[5]

These actions, whether performed by adult converts or—as in most cases after 600—by godparents on behalf of infants,[6] were of great significance. The Creed, Isidore, followed by Ildefonsus, proclaimed, contained in itself 'enough for salvation'.[7] For Ildefonsus it was 'vera fidei regula', 'a compact' (foedus).[8] The importance of the Creed for Spanish religion at this period can hardly be exaggerated. The recitation of the Nicene Creed every Sunday was prescribed (an innovation in the West) by III Toledo, as a guarantee against Arianism. Later Councils of Toledo were continually occupied in refining their

[1] Fernández Alonso, pp. 273–96. For Ildefonsus, *De cognitione baptismi*, see L. Robles, in *La Patrología toledano-visigoda*, pp. 263–335, esp. pp. 274–303 (also in *Saitabi*, xx (1970), 73–146). The identification of sources here is used, with some additions, in the reprint of the Migne edition (*PL* xcvi. 111–72), in *Santos Padres Españoles*, i, ed. J. Campos Ruiz (Madrid, 1971), with a Spanish translation.

[2] Ildefonsus, 17 (*PL* xcvi. 118; ed. Campos, p. 253); see Robles, pp. 277 f. (citing also different policies towards the Jews).

[3] Robles, p. 283, citing the *Liber commicus*.

[4] *Liber ordinum*, ed. Férotin, p. 184.

[5] *Capitula Martini*, 49 (Barlow, 136; *PL* lxxxiv. 581D; Vives, *Concilios*, p. 99). Ildefonsus, 34 (*PL* xcvi. 127; Campos, p. 274).

[6] See Isidore, *DEO* ii., 21. 3 (*PL* lxxxiii. 815).

[7] Isidore, ii. 23. 3–5 (*PL* lxxxiii. 816 f.), copied by Ildefonsus, 33 (*PL* xcvi. 126 f.; Campos, p. 274); 'sufficientem scientiam salutarem'.

[8] Ildefonsus, 31, 33 (*PL* xcvi. 125D, 126C; Campos, pp. 271, 273). These passages do not appear to be directly taken from Isidore.

view of it.[1] On a more popular level the Apostles' Creed was a binding compact entered into at baptism. Martin of Braga reminded his peasants: 'Consider the nature of the pact you made with God in baptism.' After reciting the promises made, the abjuration of the Devil and the Apostles' Creed (in the form of questions and answers), Martin concludes: 'See what a bond and confession God holds against you!' By pagan practices the *rustici* had 'broken the pact which you made with God.'[2] Isidore and Ildefonsus also insist on 'two pacts', the renunciation of the Devil and the statement of belief.[3] All this reinforces the view that in this age the Creed 'is not the expression of mysteries but a canonical collection, every word of which has juridical force.'[4] The Credal inscription from the royal foundation of St. Leocadia at Toledo, and another Toledan fragment, 'he who *believes* in Him shall not be judged' (John 3:18), express a whole legalist ethos which also extended to bishops and other clergy, who, before they were ordained, had first to guarantee 'sub cautione', that they would live 'honourably and piously' and not break canonical rules.[5]

The Church's expectations from the laity were realistically minimal. Martin of Braga put it as a question of merit and reward. Those 'who lived faithfully and well will enter into the kingdom of God . . . and will be in eternal *rest*. . . . There will be no toil or pain there, no sadness, no hunger or thirst, no heat or cold' (in fact it would be the precise reverse of the normal existence of his audience). How *do* you 'live faithfully and well'? Apart from avoiding idolatry, murder, adultery, fornication, theft, and perjury, you should feed the poor, take in the weary, often visit church or the saints' shrines, and honour the Lord's Day by doing no 'servile work'.[6] The last point was also emphasized by the Council of Narbonne in 589. The Visigothic

[1] III Toledo, 2 (*PL* lxxxiv. 351; Vives, *Concilios*, p. 125). See J. Madoz, *El simbolo del Concilio XVI de Toledo* (Madrid, 1946) (with earlier bibliography on the creeds of different councils).

[2] Martin, *De castigatione*, 15, 16 (Barlow, pp. 196. 2–3, 197. 1, 198. 17).

[3] Isidore, ii. 25. 5 (*PL* lxxxiii. 821C), Ildefonsus, 111 (*PL* xcvi. 158; Campos, p. 343).

[4] Delaruelle, p. 27 n. 72.

[5] Vives, *Inscripciones*, Nos. 552, 554, and especially M. Jorge Aragoneses, *Archivo español de Arte*, xxx (1957), 295–323, and H. Schlunk, *MM* xi (1970), 175–86. See XI Toledo, 10 (*PL* lxxxiv. 462; Vives, *Concilios*, p. 363).

[6] Martin, 14 (p. 194. 4–8); 17 (p. 200. 6–9, p. 201. 17 f.); 18 (p. 202. 10–15).

Code was to enforce Sunday rest on Jews, under pain of a hundred lashes.[1]

The Church possessed a number of rituals to cover crucial moments in life, the offering of a child to a clerical school, the rite for adolescence (the 'first beard'), for marriage.[2] But, if one sinned gravely after baptism what remedy was there? Frequent communion was urged by Isidore and Ildefonsus in terms which make one suspect that it was unusual, and the insistence on due preparation may have tended to diminish the number of communicants.[3] One could undergo penance and become a penitent, but, as has been recently demonstrated, in Spain—as elsewhere before the Irish innovations—penance could only be received once in one's life. Its reception meant a lifelong isolation from society (as well as, for a time at least, from receiving the Eucharist). The (not infrequent) penitent who returned to the lay life was seized on by his bishop and forced back into monasteries or subjected to indefinite excommunication. The result was that it was very rare for anyone to receive penance before their death-bed.[4]

Death closed the ritual cycle in which men had been embarked at baptism. When a man died he might hope to merit the rest from toil promised by Martin of Braga to those who had lived well.[5] He might be comforted by some story such as the boy Augustus, 'innocent, simple and untaught in letters', told of his reception (in a dream) by Christ, surrounded by 'a high multitude of saints', of a banquet in a meadow, and of Christ's promise: 'Know that I shall be your protector. Never shall

[1] Narbonne, 4 (*PL* lxxxiv. 611; Vives, *Concilios*, p. 147). *LV* xii. 3. 6 (Zeumer, p. 434). See Fernández Alonso, pp. 345–8. For almsgiving see e.g. the Homiliary (Grégoire, pp. 199 f.): in Lent he who cannot fast should give alms (and eat by himself).

[2] *Liber ordinum*, pp. 37–9, 43–6 (and see, above, p. 23 n. 3). Fernández Alonso, pp. 311 ff. For exorcisms etc. see below, nn. on pp. 53 f.

[3] Fernández Alonso, pp. 333–5; see esp. Isidore, *DEO* i. 18, 9–10 (*PL* lxxxiii. 756 f.), and the text from the *Liber ordinum*, cited above (p. 23 n. 3), also formulae in the Masses: 'Accedentes ad mensam terribilis omnipotentis Dei', or, 'ad terribilem thronum altaris . . . properantes' (Férotin, *Liber mozarabicus sacramentorum*, 13, 266), Beck, (cited p. 24 n. 5), pp. 150–3, comes to similar conclusions for the region he studies.

[4] G. Martínez Díez, in *La Patrología toledano-visigoda*, pp. 121–34 (or in *Miscelánea Comillas*, xlix (1968), 5–19), has demonstrated the lack of foundation of the earlier work of S. González Rivas, *La penitencia en la primitiva iglesia española* (Salamanca, [1950]) on which Fernández Alonso, chap. X, partly relied.

[5] See above, p. 27 n. 6.

anything be lacking to you. I shall always feed you, I shall always clothe you, I shall protect you at all times and I shall never abandon you.'[1]

But even this promise of absolute security was accompanied by the appearance before Christ's 'tribunal' of men 'screaming and howling and wailing', 'wicked servants', whom Christ orders to be taken out as 'not worthy of seeing my face'. In his accounts of visions enjoyed by men he had known Valerius of Bierzo normally balances his account of heaven, seen either as a beautiful garden or a high mountain, or in terms of the Apocalypse, with one of Hell, which is much more enthusiastically described, with the Devil bound in iron chains and on his head an iron bird in the form of a raven, inferior devils, of different sizes and skills, and 'archers', who shot at the visitor, their arrows feeling like drops of ice-cold water. In another work Valerius remarks that the volcano of Sicily 'spreads flame over that land, lest those who do not believe what they have heard [in Scripture] of the fires of Hell may at least fear what they see.'[2]

Perhaps one of the most vivid expressions of the struggle expected after death over man's soul is that found in an anonymous Spanish sermon which attained popularity. First we have a description of a battle over a soul between 'a black Ethiopian' and another enemy, in gleaming garments. The soul is led off to Hell and promised future torments as the demon choir sings Psalm 51: 'Why dost thou glory in malice, why art thou powerful in iniquity?' 'But Michael did not release the soul until he assigned him before the tribunal of the Trinity.' Then we have a corresponding (though tamer) description of a just soul led off to Heaven, angels, on this occasion, singing Psalm 64: 'Blessed is he whom Thou hast chosen and assumed, Lord, into Thy tabernacles.'[3]

[1] *VPE* i. 1. 11, 15 (ed. Garvin, pp. 138. 2; 140. 49; 142. 68–70). I use Fr. Garvin's translation.

[2] Ibid. 18 (pp. 142. 79–143. 82). See Martin, *De castigatione*, 14 (Barlow, pp. 194. 12–195. 21); for the visions see Valerius' three short works (Díaz, *Index*, 286–8), *PL* lxxxvii. 431–6. The summary of these works by C. M. Aherne, *Valerio of Bierzo*, pp. 57–61, while useful, confuses two of the visions. For Etna as an *exemplum* see Valerius, *De vana saeculi sapientia*, 11, and in 12–13, the contrast between Hell and Heaven.

[3] Grégoire, pp. 224 f., esp. pp. 224. 11, 225. 29–32, 53 f. See p. 177 (No. 80).

A man's dying would have been to the sound of the Psalms' recitation (and also to the sound of his relations asking him to remember them). After his death God would have been asked to send His angels to meet his soul, to repel the 'princes of darkness'. 'Although he sinned, he did not deny the Father, Son and Holy Spirit, but *believed* . . .' As the body was borne before the church doors a great lament would be made. It would be accompanied to the tomb by chants and antiphons, while the priest prayed: 'Bring, O Lord, his soul out of prison', and other prayers evoked Christ's descent into Hell and triumph over death.[1]

Julian of Toledo's *Prognosticum futuri saeculi*, though mainly concerned with theological problems and drawn from earlier authors, contains some information which appears contemporary. 'Since', he says, 'the Devil labours at the end of our life to entangle us in his snares, if we are protected at that going out by the prayers of our brethren and by sedulous psalm-singing, he is always driven off . . . For we have read that some, in the hour of their passing, have often been freed from the Devil lying in wait [by these means].'[2]

Julian also remarks that the survival of the soul is proved by the fact that what the survivors ask the dying man to perform for them has often been granted without delay.[3] Meanwhile the dead person can be assisted by burying him beside or in the shrines of martyrs.[4] His relations would be exhorted to pray 'daily before God for his repose'. The most effective method to secure his salvation was to offer Mass for him.[5] Only those whose sins are 'indissoluble' cannot be helped by this.[6]

[1] *Liber ordinum*, pp. 107–26, esp. pp. 108 f., 110. 11–14, 22–4, 117. 18, 122. 35 f. One should also consult the very interesting 'Officium mortuorum' in *PL* lxxxvi. 976–89, which is now considered almost entirely genuine and untouched by the editor of 1500. For the Biblical texts used in the office for the dead see J. Llopis Sarrió, *Hispania Sacra*, xvii (1964), 349–91; see also (more briefly) J. Pinell, *Concilium*, xxxii (1968), 25–35. See Fernández Alonso, chap. XI, pp. 577–87 (on extreme unction, viaticum, the funerary liturgy). For the relations' request see Julian, *Prognosticum* ii. 26 (*CC* cxv. 63. 20–2).

[2] *Prognosticum* i. 18 (p. 36. 16–23). See A. C. Rush, 'An Echo of Christian Antiquity in St. Gregory the Great: Death a Struggle with the Devil', *Traditio*, iii (1945), 369–80.

[3] *Prognosticum* ii. 26 (pp. 63. 28–64. 31).

[4] Ibid. i. 21 (p. 38. 4–7).

[5] Braulio, *epist.* xx (Riesco, p. 106. 13–15, 24 f.); see *epist.* xlii (p. 160. 135–8).

[6] Julian, i. 21 (38. 8–10): 'insolubiles culpae, quae eos non sinant, etiam oblatis Deo sacrificiis, adiuuari post mortem.' See the *Capitula Martini*, 68 (Barlow, p. 140; *PL* lxxxiv. 583; Vives, *Concilios*, p. 102), where priests are rebuked for celebrating Mass on tombs, rather than in the martyrs' church.

Presentation of Doctrine to the Laity

The influence of rural milieux on the evolution of Christian theology has been suggested for an earlier period.[1] For the simpler Christian, what was always most important was that Christ should be fully God in order to save from sin and guarantee victory over demonic powers. To sixth- and seventh-century Spain, just emerging from Arian rulers, Christ was certainly fully God. One prayer describes him as 'Christ Jesus, our terrible God and our King'.[2] Hymns approximate Him to God the Father.[3] He appears even in the letters of a careful theologian as 'Christus Omnipotens', and in Braulio's *Vita Aemiliani* as 'Christ who *alone* doest marvels', who possesses 'great power'. In inscriptions 'famulus Christi', instead of 'famulus Dei', becomes more frequent after 450 and in some regions totally replaces the older usage.[4]

God is mainly seen as Judge and King. The whole Trinity has, as we saw, its Tribunal.[5] God's residence is a palace with gates.[6] God the Father is 'iudex terribilis'.[7] The plague is 'furor irae Dei'.[8] Christ is a King. In one sermon we are told that just as the faithful courtier would reject all riches and power on earth if their acceptance meant separation from the 'face'of the king, so the faithful Christian should prefer death to eternal life on earth with consequent separation from 'Christ our King'.[9]

[1] Frend (cited p. 11 n. 4), p. 9, for Monophysitism see idem, in *Popular Belief* (cited p. 21 n. 6), pp. 26–9.

[2] For the effect of the Arian controversy on the development of Western Christology see J. A. Jungmann, *Zeitschrift für Katholische Theologie*, lxix (1947), 36–99, esp. (for Spain) pp. 53–6, 61–6. 'Christe Iesu, terribilis Deus noster et Rex noster' (*Liber orationum psalmographus*, ed. J. Pinell, p. 158, No. 508). See No. 359 (p. 106): 'Deus summe et terribilis, et rex magne super omnem terram'.

[3] 'In sacratione basilicae' (Díaz, *Index*, 349, Blume, p. 263, v. 1); also in Blume, p. 270 v. 12, Christ is addressed as 'Tu regum pater omnium'.

[4] Braulio, *epist.* xx (Riesco, p. 106. 14); *Vita Aemiliani*, 4 (p. 9. 12, 10, 6; Cazzaniga, p. 24. 12, 23), Vives, *Inscripciones*, Nos. 9, 37.

[5] See p. 29 n. 3 above, also n. 2, and Valerius, *De vana saeculi sapientia*, 12 (*PL* lxxxvii. 428D): 'terribile tribunal'.

[6] *Liber ordinum*, p. 110. 13.

[7] *Sermo in vigilia pasche* (from the Toledan Homiliary), ed. Díaz, *Anecdota Wisigothica* i (Salamanca, 1958), 70. 29. See Valerius, *Ordo querimoniae* i. 10 (Aherne, p. 69. 11–12, p. 107. 11–12).

[8] *Sermo de clade*, Grégoire, p. 214. 21.

[9] Sermo, *die tertio, de clade*, Grégoire, pp. 220 f. See also *VPE* v. 6. 22 (Garvin, p. 216. 102 f.), where Masona is made to compare Leovigild to God, the true King: 'ecce regem quem timere oportet' (since He can terrify men by thunder), and a Mass 'de Sabbato pasche' (Férotin, *Liber mozarabicus*, p. 291. 13 ff.): 'Cohors militorum terrenorum celestis Regis terribili regressu perculsa diffugit.'

The hymn 'Christe, rex, mundi creator' sees Christ as an emperor triumphing over the power of death.[1]

References to the Passion are less frequent in sermons and hymns, than to Easter and the Resurrection of Christ. Braulio speaks, in a private letter, of 'memoria Passionis' stirring up 'tristitia animae', but he ends with the joy of Christ's Resurrection.[2] The Toledan Homiliary contains perhaps two sermons on Good Friday, one on Holy Thursday, one on the Vigil of Easter, but *nine* on Easter, or Easter week.[3]

A number of seventh-century Spanish bishops wrote on Biblical themes.[4] None of their commentaries was intended for a wide audience. Although conclusions here are highly tentative it seems safe to see greater interest in the Old than the New Testament, especially in works intended for a popular audience. The proportion in which the two Testaments are drawn on in Braulio's different works is interesting. In the *Letters*, apart from 44 (which discusses Old Testament exegetical problems) there are 119 quotations from or references to the New Testament, compared with only thirty-six to the Old. When writing to Pope Honorius an appeal to the New Testament, in general, clinches the argument.[5] On the other hand, Braulio's (quite short) *Life of Aemilian* contains twenty quotations from or references to the Old Testament, as opposed to only fourteen to the New. The proportions are reversed. We

[1] Díaz, *Index*, 345, Blume, p. 286 (the hymn may be earlier than *saec.* VII). See also the hymns 'De defuncto' (Díaz, *Index*, 354, Blume, p. 286, where we have 'rex Deus'), and 'In restauratione basilicae' (Díaz, *Index*, 356, Blume, p. 264), where we hear of 'rex superne'. In Taio, *Sententiae*, v. 30 (*PL* lxxx. 985–7), and in Julian of Toledo, *Prognosticum*, iii. 4–9 (*CC* cxv. 83–8) we have, drawn from different sources, a similar picture of 'Omnipotens Deus Filius', acting as terrifying judge at the end of time.

[2] Braulio, *epist.* xiv (Riesco, p. 92. 20 f.). See also the way that Julian of Toledo, Praef., begins by sorrow at the Passion (*CC* cxv. 11. 16 f.) but goes on to draw up the plan for a book which is concerned with the future life, and especially with the resurrection of the body. This is a doctrine which also preoccupied Braulio, *epist.* xlii (Riesco, pp. 156 f.) and Taio, *Sententiae*, v. 29 (*PL* lxxx. 983–5). See also such inscriptions as Vives, *Inscripciones*, No. 151 (based on Job 19: 25–6), also Nos. 193, 220–2.

[3] Grégoire, pp. 166–8.

[4] See a list by U. Domínguez del Val, in *La Patrología*, pp. 25 f. In contrast, Díaz, in *Estudios sobre la liturgia mozárabe*, p. 59, has noted its theological, rather than Biblical, character.

[5] The Biblical references ín Braulio's work were collected for me on the basis of Barlow's translation from Latin (based on Madoz) by my former student Mr. James Copple. For Honorius see *epist.* xxi (Riesco, p. 114. 128).

will come later to the influence of the Old Testament on the presentation of saints in Spain. It is worth noting here that when writing to King Chindaswinth Braulio's usual preferences in his letters change. References to Joshua, David, and Solomon appear.[1] One is reminded of the Spanish hymn, 'In profectione exercitus', which refers to Moses crushing Pharaoh, to the defeat of Amalec, and to David, as models for the defeat of 'gentes barbaricas' (!) by the Visigothic king of a New Israel.[2]

A parallel study of the use of Biblical *exempla* in art and in literature would be useful. Both Old and New Testament cycles appear in the Roman sarcophagi imported into Spain in the fourth century—the Old Testament 'types' of Christ, Abraham, Daniel, Suzanna, the Three Hebrews in the Fiery Furnace, and New Testament miracles of Christ and representations of the Apostles.[3] In the sarcophagi produced *in* Spain there are representations of the Sacrifice of Isaac, of Moses and Abraham, of David killing Goliath, and of Daniel, but also of the Good Shepherd and the resurrection of Lazarus, and the very unusual

[1] *Epist.* xxxvii (Riesco, p. 148. 28 f.). See also *epist.* xxxi, p. 132. 4 (five O.T. quotations or references, one N.T.).

[2] Díaz, *Index*, 358, Blume, pp. 269–71. See the hymn, 'In ordinatione regis' (Blume, p. 269), with its reference to anointing, and the *Ordo quando rex cum exercitu ad prelium egreditur* (*Liber ordinum*, pp. 149–53). In the sermons on the plague the proportion of quotations from the O.T. appear larger than usual (twenty-six quotations or references are noted by Grégoire, pp. 214–23, compared to only seven from the N.T.). In the prayers for blessing of the baptistery Rebecca, Agar, Rachel are referred to (*Liber ordinum*, pp. 162 f.). See also the comparison of the Martyrs to the Maccabees in 'Officium in diem S. Felicis' (Férotin, *Liber mozarabicus*, pp. 584–8), and the O.T. references in the 'Ordo de primitiis' (ibid., pp. 647 f.). The canticles used in the liturgy comprised 40 from the O.T. and only three from the New. See J. Pinell, 'Los cánticos del oficio en el antiguo rito hispánico. *El Liber canticorum* de la tradición B', *Hispania Sacra*, xxvii (1974). Biblical references in the *Passiones* earlier than 711 are not noted by the editor, A. Fábrega Grau, *Pasionario hispánico*, 2 vols. (Madrid, 1955). There are some to the Psalms in the *Passio* of St. Felix of Gerona (ii. 325) and in that of St. Eulalia of Mérida (pp. 74 f.), and one to Abraham in the former *Passio* (p. 321). The *VPE* appear to contain twenty-six references to the O.T. against only eight to the N.T. (Garvin, p. 553), Martin of Braga's works (excluding I and II Braga), forty-two to the O.T., thirty-two to the N.T. (Barlow, pp. 312 f.). The *Vita S. Fructuosi* apparently contains only two Biblical quotations, and Ildefonsus, *De viris*, none. A rapid examination of the literature written for monks and nuns (Martin of Braga and Paschasius' translations from the Greek, the *Rules* of Leander, Isidore, Fructuosus, and the *Regula communis*) shows that the N.T. predominates, most notably in Paschasius, edited J. Geraldes Freire, i (Coimbra, 1971), where we have thirty-four references as compared to twenty-three from the O.T., and in the *Regula communis* (thirty, as compared to thirteen).

[3] Fontaine, *L'Art préroman* i. 102.

scene of the Passion of St. Perpetua.[1] One may end by concluding that Daniel, who appears throughout Christian art from the fourth to the seventh century (San Pedro de la Nave) and even on belt-buckles enjoyed greater popularity than any other Old or New Testament figure, perhaps because he was thought of as providing magical protection against monsters, visible or invisible.[2] After 400 there may be fewer representations based on the New Testament and there is a definite increase in non-representational pieces.[3]

Models for the Laity

The Church presented the laity not only with rituals and a simplified version of Christian doctrine but also with holy men, whom they might or might not be able to take as models for themselves, but through whom they could reach the divine.[4] It has been shown that in the Byzantine East the saints made a distant God (and even Christ, as in Spain, often seemed distant) approachable. In Byzantium a professional expert was needed who could 'make the connection' between the laity and God, who could provide the answers which the later system of private

[1] Fontaine, *L'Art préroman* i. 103 f. For other scenes apparently derived from the Apocryphal Gospels or early traditions see H. Schlunk, *Actas del VIII Congreso Internacional de Arqueología Cristiana* i (Barcelona, 1972), 200–8.

[2] So Delaruelle, pp. 30 f.

[3] Ibid., pp. 12 ff. The scenes of N.T. miracles on the pillar of the church of San Salvador in Toledo (the curing of the blind man, the resurrection of Lazarus, the encounter of Jesus and the Samaritan woman, etc.), of *saec.* VII, reveal a continuity with the sarcophagi. See Fontaine, *L'Art préroman*, p. 142 and pls. 44–5, also H. Schlunk, in *MM* x (1970), 161–75, who notes the exceptional N.T. emphasis and possible non-Spanish connections. This pillar and the churches of Quintanilla de las Viñas and San Pedro de la Nave contain the only representations of human figures apart from fragments in the Visigothic period. The scene of the Magi on a circular gold brooch found at Turuñuelo is an example of imported art (*saec.* VI, Syrian); see Fontaine, p. 240, and M. J. Pérez Martin, *Una tumba hispano-visigoda excepcional hallada en el Turuñuelo. Medellín (Badajoz)* (Madrid, 1961). See now Fontaine, 'Iconographie et spiritualité dans la sculpture chrétienne d'Espagne du IVe au VIIe siècle', *Revue d'histoire de la spiritualité*, l (1974), 285–313. See below, p. 52 n. 2. For realism as an impediment to devotion at this time see Kitzinger (cited p. 9 n. 2), p. 107.

[4] Braulio, *Vita Emiliani*, 6 (p. 12. 16–23; Cazzaniga, p. 26. 6–11), remarks that in some special ways Aemilian was *not* to be imitated. See also Isidore, *Sententiae* iii. 18, 1 (*PL* lxxxiii. 693C): 'Alia sunt praecepta quae dantur fidelibus communem vitam in saeculo agentibus atque alia saeculo huic renuntiantibus.'

penance would one day provide through skilled confessors.[1] In the sub-Byzantine Spain of the sixth and seventh centuries we can also find saints acting as channels of communication between God and men—as in Gaul one can point to Martin of Tours or the later Fathers of the Jura: one does not have to cite the 'embarras de richesses' of saints in Ireland or in Bede's Britain.

There appears to be an important difference which divides Spanish hagiographical texts into two. On the one hand there are the texts emanating from urbanized, Romanized Spain. These comprise the *passiones* which were written during the Roman and Visigothic periods and the *Vitas* of Mérida. On the other hand there are the seventh-century northern texts, by Braulio of Saragossa, Ildefonsus of Toledo, Valerius of Bierzo, and the anonymous *Life of Fructuosus*. These two groups differ in several essential respects.[2]

In Visigothic Spain general *official* cultus was almost restricted to Spanish (and some non-Spanish) martyrs, to the Virgin Mary, the Apostles, and a few other Biblical saints. The martyrs were of great importance for popular devotion. Each city had its martyrs, and hymns and *passiones* were written to celebrate them, and were read aloud in the liturgy. The feelings of the citizens for their patron are well expressed in the sixth-century sermon of Justus of Urgel on St. Vincent, 'nobis vernula quadam et gentili pietate coniunctus, eo quod sit noster ex genere, noster ex fide, noster in stola, noster in gloria, noster in officio, noster in tumulo, noster in patrocinio'.[3] In the Spanish liturgy, unlike the Roman, many prayers were directed to the saints or the Virgin, and not only to God the Father or to Christ. There are similar examples among masses. The saints are invoked for every type of problem, spiritual and physical

[1] P. Brown, 'The Rise and Function of the Holy Man in Late Antiquity', *Journal of Roman Studies*, lxi (1971), 97 f.

[2] A general parallel could, perhaps, be drawn with the contrast between Caesarius of Arles in southern France and Gregory of Tours in northern France. See Beck (cited p. 24 n. 5), pp. 307–10.

[3] C. García Rodríguez, *El culto de los santos en la España romana y visigoda* (Madrid, 1966); Fernández Alonso, pp. 370 ff.; J. Vives, *AST* xiv (1941), 31–58. See also B. de Gaiffier, *Analecta Bollandiana*, lxxii (1954), 157 f. Justus of Urgel, *Sermo*, in J. Villanueva, *Viage literario a las iglesias de España* x (Valencia, 1821), 219 (Díaz, *Index*, 10). See García, pp. 271–8; for the cult of martyrs in Roman Spain see Fontaine, 'Société' (cited p. 14 n. 2), pp. 264 f.

(especially against the plague, famine, war), and against the terrors of the Last Judgement.[1] Buildings were placed under the protection of a saint. 'Possess this house which is yours, Martyr Eulalia', an inscription in Mérida reads, 'that knowing this the enemy may go away in confusion.' The same principle was applied on a large scale when King Wamba placed the fortifications of Toledo under the protection of martyrs 'whose presence shines out here'. An earlier Toledan inscription speaks of Christians as 'servi sancti Vincenti martyris'.[2]

Despite the similarity of sources and style connecting it with the Northern literature, the *Vitas* of Mérida should be placed, I suggest, with the *passiones*, the celebration of martyrs of the official church of Romanized Spain. A careful reading of the *Vitas* tends to show that their real heroes are not the bishops of that city, still less a dimly remembered figure such as Abbot Nanctus, but the patron saints of the basilicas, to whom the author urges his readers to show reverence.[3] There are continual references to the churches of Mérida and to their inhabitation by the saints.[4] Even Bishop Masona, in his contention with King Leovigild, is overshadowed by the greatest saint of Mérida, the martyr Eulalia, who appears in visions to cheer Masona or to 'beat up' Leovigild—as well she may, since the battle concerns her basilica and her tunic.[5] At the end the author acknowledges that he has written because of 'his love of Christ and affection for the most holy Eulalia' (the reference to Eulalia is inserted in the middle of a phrase borrowed from Sulpicius Severus and is thus doubly personal).[6]

St. Martin of Tours was not the only *non*-martyr to be venerated in Spain.[7] Most of the new saints were monks, either from the East, like Martin of Braga, or from Africa, like Donatus, or

[1] García, pp. 374 f. L. Brou, *Hispania Sacra*, iii (1950), 371–81.

[2] Vives, *Inscripciones*, Nos. 348, 361, 67. See also the dedication of San Juan de Baños by King Recceswinth in 661 (No. 314). Even in the north a man could shut himself up as a recluse at the martyrs' shrine in León: Valerius, *De Bonello monacho* (*PL* lxxxvii. 435). A complete distinction between types of holy patron is clearly impossible.

[3] *VPE* iv. 10. 3–7 (Garvin, pp. 186 f.).

[4] *VPE* iv. 7–9 (Garvin, pp. 178–86). In these chapters the churches of St. Faustus, St. Lucretia, St. Eulalia, St. Mary, and St. John are referred to.

[5] *VPE* v. 8. 1–4 (Garvin, pp. 222 f.).

[6] *VPE*, epilogus 2 (Garvin, p. 258. 10–12). See Sulpicius Severus, *Vita S. Martini*, 27, 7, ed. J. Fontaine, i (Paris, 1967), 316.

[7] García Rodríguez, pp. 97, 342–6.

native growths, such as Aemilian. In the seventh century there is a new development (new for Spain, Martin of Tours had provided the model three centuries earlier), the monastic bishop, of whom Fructuosus of Braga is the outstanding but far from the only example.[1]

The growth of the monastic life in Spain cannot and need not be discussed here. All that is necessary is to point to the rich variety of the written sources available for Spanish delectation and imitation.[2] To the Pachomian writings, which appear in Jerome's version in the Visigothic collection of rules, Martin of Braga and his disciple Paschasius added translations of sections of the Egyptian *Vitae Patrum.*[3] Augustine's writings on the monastic life were soon known in Spain. Augustine's pleasure that so many of the poor were entering monasteries and his view of monks as servants of the Church no doubt affected Spain.[4] While an urban, or, more strictly, suburban, monasticism developed around Seville, Toledo, and Saragossa, a more rigorous native tradition, far from Leander's 'ascétisme du luxe', emerged in the north.[5] Instead of the example of the Apostles, stressed by Isidore, in the north we have that of the Desert Fathers, and instead of the great monasteries such as

[1] For Donatus see Ildefonsus, *De viris*, 3, ed. Codoñer, pp. 120 f.: 'monumentum eius honorabiliter colere perhibentur incolae regionis.' For Toledan monastic bishops in Ildefonsus, and for St. Martin of Tours as a model, see J. Fontaine, *Anales toledanos*, iii (1971), 73–5. C. J. Bishko, *Bracara Augusta*, xxi (1967), 63 f., suggests that Fructuosus led an attempt to 'convert the hierarchy from a secular to a regular basis'. With this one may perhaps connect a change in the view of how the peninsula was converted, with a new emphasis on monks as apostles. See M. C. Díaz, 'Los orígenes del cristianismo en la Peninsula vistos por algunos textos del siglo VII', *Cuadernos de estudios gallegos*, xxviii (1973), 277–84.

[2] See, in general, C. Baraut (above, p. 10 n. 2), 1099 f.

[3] Martin, *Sententiae patrum Aegyptiorum*, ed. Barlow, *Martini Opera*, 11–51; idem, *Iberian Fathers*, i. 17–34, 113–71. For Paschasius see the works of José Geraldes Freire, analysed by B. de Gaiffier, *Analecta Bollandiana*, xcii (1974), 357–64.

[4] See R. Arbesmann, in *The Heritage of the Early Church* (Orientalia Christiana Analecta, 195) (Rome, 1973), pp. 245–59. The work of monks, insisted on by Augustine, is praised by Isidore, *Regula*, v (*PL* lxxxiii. 873), and by Fructuosus, *Regula*, vi (*PL* lxxxvii. 1102). See also the anonymous work cited in the following note, pp. 83, 98–200.

[5] The need to justify urban monasticism appears in the anonymous sixth-century sermon, *De monachis perfectis*, ed. Díaz, *Anecdota* i. 71–87. In the article cited on next page, n. 2, p. 20 n. 55, Díaz supposes the work may have come from Catalonia or Septimania. For Leander see his *De institutione virginum*, esp. 27 (ed. Vega, pp. 121 f.; *Santos Padres Españoles* ii. 68 f.). See J. Madoz, in *Miscellanea G. Mercati* i (Città del Vaticano, 1946), 26 ff. of the offprint.

Agali near Toledo, to which leading courtiers retired (to re-emerge later as bishops) in Galicia we have a monastic population consisting largely of slaves, who could even become abbots. The entry of whole families into the religious life, dependence on a pastoral economy, the harshness of the discipline observed, and the constant menace of armed attack are other features which distinguish the Galician monasteries, 'contractual, egalitarian, unstable and potentially short-lived', from those in the south.[1]

As we have seen, it was the north of Spain which had been least influenced by Rome and, before 500, by Christianity. As in Asia Minor and Syria so also in Spain it was hermits or wandering monks, such as Aemilian, Fructuosus, and Valerius, who acted as the spearheads of Christianity in the countryside, who expelled demons and destroyed pagan shrines.[2] In the last third of the sixth century the hermit Aemilian began to evangelize Cantabria—largely without, or against, the wishes of the bishop of Tarazona (who appears, with his clergy, to descend, as literary types, from the worldly clergy of Gaul who had been opposed to Martin of Tours).[3] Other hermits who penetrated further into Cantabria are only known through finds of liturgical objects, which indicate that they deliberately settled in the caves which had formed centres for pagan cults.[4]

[1] See Isidore, *Regula*, iii (870), and other texts cited by M. C. Díaz y Díaz, in *Théologie de la vie monastique* (Paris, 1961), pp. 377–82. See also A. Linage Conde, in *Bracara Augusta*, xxi (1967), 123–63, and J. Orlandis, 'Notas sobre sociología monástica de la España visigoda', *Yermo*, vi (1968), 1–16. (This and other relevant articles are collected in Orlandis, *Estudios sobre instituciones monásticas medievales* (Pamplona, 1971; see esp. chapters IV, VI). For Agali and the bishops of Toledo see Fontaine (cited p. 37 n. 1), and, for the examples of the Desert Fathers, Díaz (next note), p. 12 n. 23. I also use the *Consensoria monachorum* (Díaz, *Index*, 317), on which see C. J. Bishko, *American Journal of Philology*, lxix (1948), 377–95 (the quotation from p. 393). In *Bracara Augusta*, xxi (1967), 328–45, R. Grégoire has some more theoretical considerations on the Galician Rules. The article of G. Penco, 'La composizione sociale delle comunità monastiche nei primi secoli', *Studia Monastica*, iv (1962), 257–81, is useful for the background.

[2] For Eastern parallels see Frend (cited p. 11 n. 4), pp. 1–14. For Spain, M. C. Díaz, in *Revista Portuguesa de História*, vi (1964), 25 pp. (trans. in *Classical Folia*, xxiii (1969)). Even Valerius, despite all his trials, enjoyed considerable prestige. See his *Ordo querimoniae*, 2, *Replicatio*, 9 (Aherne, pp. 73, 137).

[3] Braulio, *Vita S. Emiliani*, 13 (p. 19; Cazzaniga, p. 30); the comparison of Aemilian to Anthony and Martin in 12 (p. 18. 23; Cazzaniga, p. 29. 20). See Fernández Alonso, *Cura pastoral*, pp. 485 f.

[4] González Echegaray (cited p. 11 n. 5), pp. 14 ff. Lacarra (cited p. 13 n. 3) notes that there are traces of hermits in the Visigothic period in the present province of Alava. For an oratory in caves at Valdecanales (Jaén) see R. Vañó Silvestre, *et al.*, *MM* x (1970), 213–29.

Braulio describes Aemilian's struggle with the Devil: the site mentioned suggests that he was confronted with the local god Dercetius.[1] A century later Valerius of Bierzo refers to pagan worship on a mountain near Astorga. He may have led the local Christians in the destruction of the shrine there.[2]

Spanish writers were always aware of the standards against which their heroes had to be measured. These standards were largely provided by the *Life of Anthony* by Athanasius, the monastic biographies of Jerome, Sulpicius Severus' *Life of Martin of Tours*, later Latin lives, Cassian's *Collationes*, and a few other texts. This is the literature possessed or asked for by Fructuosus and even by Valerius in his solitary cell. Valerius also possessed the *Itinerarium* of Egeria, which he used to show that 'feminea fragilitas' (in such a remarkable pilgrim to the East) could surpass the strength of holy men. In his *De vana saeculi sapientia* Valerius speaks of the 'Oriental Theban Fathers, flying to deserts and vast solitudes, living in small and narrow huts, and in caves . . .'[3] The *Dialogues* of Gregory the Great were a later but important addition to this literature, which provided models to imitate and, if possible, to excel. In the north of Spain it did not seem too difficult to surpass past models.[4]

In his letter to Fructuosus Braulio explicitly compares the Galicia of the new monasteries to the Egyptian desert described by Jerome.[5] In his *Life of Aemilian* he dwells on the forests and hills of the Sierra de la Demanda, the cold, solitude, rains, and

[1] Braulio, 11 (p. 16; Cazzaniga, 28. 4 f.). See Blázquez Martínez, *Religiones* i. 88; McKenna, *Paganism*, p. 6.

[2] So McKenna, *Paganism*, p. 131, but Valerius, *Replicatio*, 1 (Aherne, p. 115), merely seems to say that the destruction was something he knew about.

[3] Fructuosus, in Braulio, *epist.* xliii (Riesco, pp. 164 f.). For Valerius see Díaz, *Hispania Sacra*, iv (1951), 3–25; idem, in *Anales toledanos* iii. 56 f. I cite Valerius, *Epistola beatissimae Egeriae laude* and *De vana saeculi sapientia* (Díaz, *Index*, 285, 290). See the latter work, 10 (*PL* lxxxvii. 427C) 'Orientales Thebaei Patres, ad deserta vastasque solitudines confugientes, parvisque et angustis tuguriis inhaerentes, atque per antra et diversis terrae cavernis permanentes.'

[4] Valerius, *De celesti revelatione* (*PL* lxxxvii. 435): Fructuosus lives 'ad instar orientalium monachorum . . . ut antiquis Thebaeis Patribus se facile coaequaret' (cf. the same phrase in the *Vita Fructuosi*, i (Nock, p. 89. 18–19; Díaz, p. 80. 11 f., and pp. 19 f.—Valerius depends on the *Vita*). For the sources of the *VPE* see Garvin, pp. 30–3, for those of the *Vita Fructuosi*, Díaz, pp. 24–31; for Ildefonsus, *De viris*, Fontaine (cited p. 37 n. 1), pp. 59–96.

[5] Braulio, *epist.* xliv (Riesco, pp. 168 f.). See *Vita Fructuosi*, i (Nock, p. 89, Díaz, p. 80. 11 f.).

wind with which the hermit had to contend.[1] He sees Aemilian as similar to Saints Anthony and Martin (of Tours), surpassing the 'ancient philosophers of the world' by Divine Grace (a theme of the *Vita Antonii*), and actually spending twice as long as Anthony in one desert place (forty years, as compared to twenty). At the same time Aemilian is 'a second Martin', and outdoes the first by offering the whole of his cloak, not half, to a beggar.[2]

Behind the great saints of the Egyptian Desert of fourth-century Gaul there loomed the figures of Old Testament prophets. Aemilian, in particular, is a prophet. In his case, in that of Fructuosus, and for three of the bishops described by Ildefonsus, mockery of the saint brings down the same punishment as attended those who mocked the prophets of Israel.[3] Aemilian is compared in his beginnings to Samuel, in his spiritual struggles to Jacob, in his end to a second Elisha, who, like Elisha, can raise the dead.[4] The prophecy of destruction to the 'senate' of Cantabria, satisfactorily fulfilled, brings Aemilian's career to a triumphant close.[5]

Braulio was a greater artist than the author of the *Life of Fructuosus*. But in the latter document—and also in the *De viris* of Ildefonsus and in Valerius—one can find not only the same models but some of the same themes—reluctance to be trapped into the service of the Church and tied down to a parish or a bishopric, a quest for solitude and love of wandering, a definite depreciation of education (Isidore is compared very unfavourably to Fructuosus).[6] Fructuosus' letter to Recceswinth also

[1] *Vita*, 11 (pp. 15–17; Cazzaniga, p. 28).

[2] *Vita*, 12 (p. 18. 19 f.; Cazzaniga, p. 29. 17 f.); 11 (p. 16. 5 f.; C., pp. 287 f.); see 27, 'alter Martinus' (p. 28. 9; C., p. 35. 3).

[3] Braulio, *Vita*, 31 f. (pp. 32 ff.; Cazzaniga, pp. 37 f.) *Vita Fructuosi*, e.g. xi (Nock, pp. 107 f.; Díaz, pp. 98 f.). Ildefonsus, *De viris*, Praef., ed. Codoñer, pp. 112 f. See Fontaine, *Anales toledanos* iii. 81. One should also see *VPE* v. 13. 14 (Garvin, p. 252), in this connection.

[4] Braulio, 9, 11, 38 (pp. 15, 37; Cazzaniga, pp. 27, 28, 40). See also the Mass (by Eugenius II of Toledo?), which compares Aemilian to Moses, Elijah, Elisha, and Daniel (Férotin, *Liber mozarabicus*, p. 606).

[5] Braulio, 33 (p. 34; Cazzaniga, p. 38).

[6] *Vita Fructuosi*, e.g. vi, vii, xvii f., i (Nock, pp. 95 f., pp. 123 f., 87; Díaz, pp. 88 f., 110 f., 80). Ildefonsus, *De viris*, stresses the reluctance of his heroes to become bishops; see especially 13, Codoñer, p. 132, on the 'sagax fuga' of Eugenius II, but also Asturius' abandonment of his see (1, p. 118), Helladius (6, p. 126), and Eugenius I (12, p. 132). Education—and especially writing—is less esteemed than pastoral work, and monks are the best Christians (and the best bishops). See e.g.

has a tone quite different from the deferential communications of Isidore, or even Braulio, with Visigothic kings. The threat of God's Judgement on the king and his bishops, with which Fructuosus closes, is worthy of an Old Testament prophet.[1] Like Athanasius on Anthony, Braulio found it necessary to stress Aemilian's obedience to the Church.[2] But the main point the biographers of Aemilian and Fructuosus were concerned to make was that God was intervening in history *now*—on the frontier of *romanitas*—new miracles—'non prisca, sed moderna; non vetera, sed novella', as the *Vita Fructuosi* put it—were happening at the hands of charismatic, apostolic men.[3]

Throughout Spain—throughout the whole of contemporary Christendom—this was an age of miracles, attractive to the 'business-like' attitude of most men to religion. Miracles were wrought by prayer and good works, but most of all by a holy man such as Aemilian who could be persuaded 'to display the power of our God'.[4] The *Vitas* of Mérida are largely concerned with God's power over nature, with visions and prophesies. There are no exorcisms. In contrast, the *Vita Fructuosi* and the *Life of Aemilian* display the numinous power of the holy man.[5] This comes out most incontrovertibly in the struggle with demons.

It was difficult to escape from demons in seventh-century Spain. They appear in the Visigothic Code, inspiring the

6, p. 126. 23 f., and Fontaine, loc. cit., pp. 85–8, who comments on Ildefonsus' critical attitude towards Isidore (not too dissimilar to that of the *Vita Fructuosi*). One may also contrast the metrical inscriptions referring to bishops (Vives, *Inscripciones*, esp. Nos. 272, 279), which refer to their writings, with those for abbots (Nos. 280–1, 283–4). For Valerius see his *Ordo querimoniae*, 5, 7 (Aherne, pp. 81 f., 99 f.).

[1] Fructuosus, *Epistola ad Reccesvindum regem*, ed. W. Gundlach, *MGH*, *Epist.* iii. merov. i (Berlin, 1892), 688 (trans. from a later edition by Barlow, *Iberian Fathers* ii. 210–12).

[2] Braulio, *Vita*, 9 (p. 15. 4–6; Cazzaniga, p. 27. 17 f.).

[3] Braulio, *Vita*, 4 (p. 8; Cazzaniga, p. 24. 4): 'rei nouitas'; (9. 13; Cazzaniga, p. 24. 12): 'per eum carismata operatus'. *Vita Fructuosi*, i (Nock, pp. 87. 5 f.; Díaz, p. 80. 1 f.), 'nova . . . claritas'; xii (Nock, p. 109; Díaz, p. 100). See also the Mass (cited p. 40 n. 4), comparing 'nova cum veteribus . . . nunc insignia operari per christicolas sanctos' (Férotin, *Liber mozarabicus*, p. 606. 22–6).

[4] Braulio, *Vita*, 24 (p. 25. 11 f.; Cazzaniga, p. 33. 12 f.): 'ad ostendendam Dei nostri virtutem'.

[5] There is only one general reference to healings (at the tombs of the bishops), *VPE* v. 15. 2 (Garvin, p. 256). Compare the *Vita Fructuosi*, xvii (Nock, p. 123; Díaz, p. 112), when Fructuosus, like Peter or Paul in Acts, cannot be kept in prison.

soothsayers, in Isidore's *Origines* (all magical arts are due to them), at a bishop's consecration—where he is warned whom he will have to contend with—in hymns, in prayers, during the day as at midnight, in sermons, *passiones*, and in Lives of Saints, for, as Professor Momigliano has observed, this is an age when historiography is invaded 'en masse' by devils. An extreme case is constituted by the writings of Valerius of Bierzo, where the Devil is ubiquitous. When he is not trying to shake Valerius' cell to its foundations, inflicting him with a plague of fleas, or trying to delude him by appearing as an angel of light, he is inspiring the considerable range of Valerius' enemies, which included the local priesthood and 'pseudo-monks', the nobleman Ricimir and Bishop Isidore of Astorga. It is only in the literature written for monks and nuns that little attention is paid to demons.[1] The legislator, the grammarian, the bishop, the preacher, the martyr, the confessor, were all expected to deal with them. The bishops were expected not only to be 'hospitable, loving the brethren', but also 'shining in signs, by power expelling the demons'.[2] A hymn on St. Felix of Gerona states that here (at the martyr's tomb) 'oppressed by God's power, demons are destroyed, beaten, conquered and burnt. They fade away as smoke and ashes.' The hymn chronicles the miracles of St. Felix, granting 'sight to the blind, speech to the dumb, hearing to the deaf'. The author—probably the local bishop—says that the 'faithful people will ask what it needs *here*.'[3]

[1] *LV* vi. 2. 4 (Zeumer, p. 259). Isidore, *Orig*. viii. ix. 31. Díaz, *Index*, 362 (Blume, p. 102). For the psalm collects' preoccupation with demons and other foes of the Church see J. Pinell, in *Repertorio de historia de las ciencias eclesiásticas en España* ii (Salamanca, 1971), 44 ff. See also the sixth-century blessing quoted ibid., p. 54 (from J. P. Gilson, *The Mozarabic Psalter* (London, 1905), p. 365). A. Momigliano, in *The Conflict between Paganism and Christianity* (Oxford, 1963), p. 93, but esp. Valerius, *Ordo querimoniae*, *passim*, 2, 5, 6, 7, 8 (Aherne, pp. 75, 81, 89. 29 f., 99. 41–4, 101). (See n. on pp. 166 f. on Valerius' epithets for the Devil.) Martin of Braga's spiritual teaching (in the *Sententiae Patrum Aegyptiorum*) is close to Cassian's. Martin's disciple, Paschasius, has more stories about demons, but he concentrates on man's own faults (see esp. c. 19, ed. J. Geraldes Freire, i. 178–81).

[2] Blume, pp. 267 f. (Díaz, *Index*, 338): 'In ordinatione episcopi'.

[3] Díaz, *Index*, 351; Blume, p. 177. See Julian of Toledo, *Historia Wambae*, 26 (*MGH SRM* v. 522, 9 f.), the offering of a crown to St. Felix by Reccared. There are similar hymns to Saints Justus and Pastor (Alcalá), Díaz, *Index*, 357, Blume, p. 211 v. 12; to St. Leocadia (Toledo), Díaz, *Index*, 363, Blume, p. 213 v. 8, etc. See also the Sermon on St. Lawrence in Grégoire, p. 212.

Outside Roman cities, where there were martyrs' shrines, one had to turn either to a holy man such as Aemilian (half of whose recorded miracles are exorcisms)[1] or, failing a saint, to relics. In the fourth century Prudentius already makes St. Fructuosus beg the Christians of Tarragona to return the small relics they had taken from his body.[2] Relics multiplied, but not fast enough to meet the demand. Braulio had to tell one priestly correspondent that his predecessors at Saragossa had lost so many relics, either by theft or against their wills and by the coercion of the piety of many that he had only seventy left and they were in use.[3] In another letter, on some possible relics of the Blood of Christ, Braulio adopted the general principle 'not to go against the authority of the multitude'. In 652, and perhaps in 627, before and slightly later than the date of Braulio's letter, relics of the Blood of Christ are in fact recorded in the dedication of two churches, one in Mérida, the other in Guadix. The later dedication, of 652, also lists relics of the 'bread', 'the Cross', the 'tomb' and the 'clothing' of Christ, as well as of the Seven Sleepers of Ephesus and other Eastern saints. Relics from the East were evidently reaching Baetica and Lusitania in the seventh century.[4]

Success or Failure?

A major theme of the Spanish writers of the age is a weariness at this life—'a river of mortality', 'the condition of mortals', as Braulio calls it, and a corresponding desire for the

[1] Six exorcisms (19–24) and four other struggles with demons (11, 14, 25, pp. 16, 6–10, 20 f.; 26; Cazzaniga, p. 28. 8–11, pp. 30 f., 33 f.). The most elaborate description of the exorcism of a poltergeist is in c. 24. See also the Hymn, probably by Braulio, to Aemilian, Díaz, *Index*, 158, Blume, p. 126, vv. 12 f., and the Mass (cited, p. 40 n. 4), which describes him as 'agonista fortissimus, qui Satane durissimos in congressione conflictus et invisibiliter edomuit et visibiliter effugavit' (Férotin, *Liber mozarabicus*, pp. 605 f.).

[2] Prudentius, *Peristephanon* vi. 130–41 (*CC* cxxvi. 319).

[3] Braulio, *epist*. ix (Riesco, p. 78. 28 f.): 'aut furtim aut etiam invito ipsi coacti multorum caritate'.

[4] Ibid, xlii (p. 160. 131 f.): 'neque auctoritati contraire multitudinis'. See Vives, *Inscripciones*, Nos. 304–31, 548–51; Nos. 307b and 548 refer to 'cruore Domini', as does Braulio, and 307b also to 'pane Domini, cruce Domini, sepulcro Domini, veste Domini'. For relics in a later age see the remarks of Southern (cited p. 3 n. 2), pp. 89 f.

next.[1] Braulio's words, 'I see the fatherland of the pious is not here', and the contrast he draws between 'regio mortalium' and 'terra vivorum', his view of life as a pilgrimage, while no doubt expressing the feelings of many Spanish churchmen,[2] is less striking than Julian of Toledo's transformation of Virgil in the Preface to the *Prognosticum*. For Virgil's 'sunt lacrimae rerum, et mentem mortalia tangunt' (*Aeneid* i. 462) Julian writes that he does not intend to teach anything unknown until now, 'sed potius, ut sub uno collecta hic futurorum ratio mentes mortalium et vehementius tangeret'.[3] The transference from man touched by human sorrows to man touched by consideration of the Last Things, in itself expresses a vast change in culture, in the values of an age.[4]

Was this change felt by more than a few scholars? To what extent, in other words, was the Church successful in conveying its values to the people, in creating a popular version of Christianity which would win the adhesion of the Iberian population and especially of the great majority of that population, the (mainly non-free) *rustici*? While no complete answer to this question is possible, some suggestions may be made.

For the ruling élite there were no doubts in the matter. At the end of the seventh century, when, to modern historians, the shadows appear already, in Visigothic Spain, to obscure the stage, King Egica could claim that Spain was known throughout the world for the fullness of its faith (plenitudo fidei).[5] But a Council held in 693, a year before this boast was made, had to decree that conciliar decisions should be communicated within six months to the abbots, clergy, and people of each city.[6] Communications between the leaders of the Church and their subjects were clearly in need of attention.

[1] Braulio, *epist.* xxix, xxx (Riesco, p. 128. 20, p. 130. 17): 'fluvius mortalitatis', 'mortalium condicio'. See the concept of 'fluctus saeculi' in the *Liber orationum psalmographus*, ed. J. Pinell, pp. 148 ff.

[2] Braulio, x (p. 80.19 f.). See Fructuosus, *apud* Braulio, *epist.* xliii (p. 164.17).

[3] Julian, *Prognosticum*, Praef. (p. 14. 107–9).

[4] Compare Braulio's apparent transformation of Virgil, *Aen.* xi. 508, 'O decus Italiae virgo', to praise of Fructuosus as a model of asceticism 'O decus Hispaniae sacrum' (*epist.* xliv, 170.60), or Isidore, *De viris*, 27, ed. Codoñer, p. 149. 27 f.: 'Felix tamen et nimium felix . . .', applied to Gregory the Great, with *Georg.* ii. 490 (probably intended for Lucretius), and *Aen.* iv. 657 (see Fontaine, cited above (p. 19 n. 6), p. 153 n. 13).

[5] XVII Toledo, Tomus (*PL* lxxxiv. 553A; Vives, *Concilios*, p. 524).

[6] XVI Toledo, 7 (*PL* lxxxiv. 541; Vives, *Concilios*, p. 504).

The few churches which survive from Visigothic times are found in the rural north. Their existence does not prove a 'conversion' of the population; at most it may indicate an attempt by the local proprietor to enforce outward conformity on his *coloni* and slaves.[1] These churches represent the chapels built by patrons throughout the west, on their estates. In 655 founders of such churches received the right to select their clergy.[2]

The Clergy

The non-Roman element, which became predominant in the lay aristocracy in the seventh century, also triumphed in the church. The number of Visigoths in the Spanish episcopate increased from about 20 per cent in 633 to 40 or 45 per cent in the 690s.[3] There were doubtless excellent Visigothic bishops (Fructuosus, Ildefonsus) as well as others whose talents seem more suited for armed rebellion than for pastoral care.[4] What is worth noting here is that the areas of Gothic and Suevic settlement in the Meseta and the north-west continued normally to have bishops of Gothic origin.[5] Is it possible that the deficiencies in religious education which appear in the peculiar creed found on one of the *pizarras* are connected with this Germanic type of ecclesiastical hierarchy?[6]

Perhaps even more important, in its effect on the Church, than the Germanization of its leadership was the fact that Spanish bishops were selected by the King. The Spanish Clovis, Recared, was no wiser than his prototype as regards clerical

[1] At times such churches merely represented a commercial speculation, which brought in half the offering of the faithful. See II Braga, 6, ed. Barlow, pp. 120 f. (*PL* lxxxiv. 572; Vives, *Concilios*, p. 83).

[2] See R. Bidagor, *La 'iglesia propia' en España* (*Analecta Gregoriana* iv: Rome, 1933), pp. 58–76, and G. Martínez Díez, 'El patrimonio eclesiástico en la España visigoda', *Miscelánea Comillas*, xxxii (1959), 70–81.

[3] J. Orlandis, 'Los hispano-romanos en la aristocracia visigótica del siglo VII', *Revista Portuguesa de História*, xiii (1970), 189–96; idem. 'El elemento germánico en la iglesia española del siglo VII', *AEM* iii (1966), 27–64. See also Thompson, *Goths*, pp. 289–96.

[4] e.g. Sisebut of Toledo (see XVI Toledo, *PL* lxxxiv. 546 f.; Vives, *Concilios*, pp. 513 f.). Other cases could be cited.

[5] Orlandis, (cited p. 8 n. 1), pp. 469–71.

[6] Díaz, in *Studi medievali*, 3 ser. i (1960), 52–71; idem, in *La Patrología*, p. 53 n. 34. I find it hard to believe that the growth in the number of Gothic bishops is unimportant or unrelated to other changes.

appointments,[1] and Recared's successors appear to have been no wiser than he. In 633 IV Toledo lamented a series of appointments as bishops of criminals, men born as heretics, or outright simoniacs.[2] Later Councils continued to denounce simony, though in 675 the penalty was reduced to two years' suspension from office.[3]

As for the rural clergy below the rank of priest, one of the few provincial councils from the seventh century tells us that they could be recruited from slaves, who, although ordained, remained slaves of the Church.[4] The clergy in general displayed, according to the councils, a lack both of chastity and of training. In 653 some ordained priests did not even know the psalms, canticles, hymns, or how to baptize.[5] Their superiors were not much better off. They had to be told to preach, to enforce chastity on their subordinates, and to practice it themselves.[6] Perhaps as serious was their inveterate greed which made some bishops confiscate the endowments of churches in their dioceses, so that it was impossible to maintain either the local clergy or the buildings. In 693 this abuse ('consuetudo inordinata sacerdotum') was still as rampant as it had been in the sixth century.[7]

Monks

I have already alluded to the growing importance of monasticism in Spain. Towards the end of the seventh century the

[1] For Clovis see Remigius, in *Epistulae Austrasiacae*, 3 (*CC* cxvii. 409 f.); for Recared, Thompson, *Goths*, p. 110, citing II Seville, 6 f., 3.

[2] IV Toledo, 19 (*PL* lxxxiv. 372 f.; Vives, *Concilios*, pp. 198 f.). See Thompson, *Goths*, pp. 296 f.

[3] See VIII Toledo, 3; XI Toledo, 9 (*PL* lxxxiv. 422, 462; Vives, *Concilios*, pp. 277, 362).

[4] Mérida (666), 18 (*PL* lxxxiv. 623; Vives, *Concilios*, p. 338).

[5] VIII Toledo, 8 (*PL* lxxxiv. 424; Vives, *Concilios*, p. 281). For a sixth-century parallel see Licinian of Carthagena, *epist.* i, 5, ed. J. Madoz (Madrid, 1948), pp. 90 f. Fernández Alonso, *Cura pastoral*, p. 168, points to the institution of oblates as a cause for trouble over celibacy.

[6] For preaching see XI Toledo, 2; for lack of chastity ibid. 5. (*PL* lxxxiv. 458, 459 f.; Vives, *Concilios*, pp. 355, 358–60). See also King, *Law*, pp. 152 ff., Thompson, *Goths*, pp. 301, 304. Braga, III (675), 2 (*PL* lxxxiv. 588; Vives, *Concilios*, p. 374) reveals a curiously low level in the Galician bishops who used sacred vessels for their own meals.

[7] XVI Toledo, 5 (*PL* lxxxiv. 539; Vives, *Concilios*, p. 502). See Thompson, *Goths*, pp. 47–50, 298–301; King, *Law*, pp. 154–6, and, more generally, Fernández Alonso, pp. 174 f. See *LV* iv. 5. 6 (Zeumer, pp. 202 f.).

sources (as in Anglo-Saxon England a little later) suggest a deterioration here too, notably the creation of 'monasteries' as a tax-dodging device. Tension between monks and secular clerics also appears to increase.[1]

Magic and Superstition

'The twilight world of magic and superstition was never far away.'[2] To this quotation from a recent study of Visigothic Spain one can add the comment by Professor Dodds, inspired by an earlier age, that 'simple people are commonly unaware of any distinction in principle between religion and magic and . . . their religion very often *grows out of* their magic.'[3] The most one can say of general Christian influence in this respect is that it 'mobilized a current drift, in the Late Antique world, towards explanations of misfortune through suprahuman agencies.'[4] Christian sorcerers appear in Spain as early as Elvira.[5] Clerical diviners are mentioned in the Council of Agde (which concerned Spain) in 506, and in Martin of Braga's canons; clerics were consulting magicians in 633.[6] Bishops were accused of magic and appear to have practised it. The remarkable canon of XVII Toledo, which declares that 'many bishops' celebrated mass of the dead for the living, is well known.[7]

One may, in passing, note the way in which Spanish Lives of Saints show their heroes breaking the most important prescriptions of Spanish Councils. Bishops Paul and Fidelis of Mérida both clearly infringed church law, Paul by using as his private property large estates given him for his church to procure the

[1] Valerius of Bierzo, *De genere monachorum*, in Díaz, *Anecdota* i. 56 f.; idem, *Ordo querimoniae*, 3, 6, 9 f. (ed. Aherne, pp. 77, 93, 103–7). *Regula communis*, 1–2 (*PL* lxxxvii. 1111 f.). Cf. Bede, *Epistola ad Ecgbertum episcopum*, 10–13 ed. Plummer, *Baedae Opera* i. 413–17. See Díaz, 'El eremetismo en la España visigótica', *Revista Portuguesa de História*, vi (1964), 230 ff.

[2] King, *Law*, p. 148.

[3] Dodds (cited p. 4 n. 1), p. 148 (the italics are mine).

[4] Brown, *Religion and Society*, p. 131.

[5] Elvira, 6 (*PL* lxxxiv. 302; Vives, *Concilios*, p. 3).

[6] Agde, 42, in *CC* cxlviii. 211. Martin, *Canones*, 59 (Barlow, p. 138; *PL* lxxxiv. 582; Vives, *Concilios*, p. 101). IV Toledo, 29 (*PL* 375; Vives, p. 203). See *Lex vis.* vi. 2. 1, 4, 5 (Zeumer, pp. 257, 259 f.).

[7] XVII Toledo, 5 (*PL* lxxxiv. 557; Vives, *Concilios*, p. 531); see the Tomus (*PL* 554 A; Vives, p. 525).

succession of his nephew Fidelis, whom he had uncanonically consecrated, and Fidelis by concurring in this purchase of office. The author of the *Vitas* of Mérida, writing decades later, justifies Paul's arrangement, which he knew was irregular, by saying it was made 'because of a revelation of the Holy Spirit', and refers to both bishops as saints.[1] The author of the *Vita Fructuosi* describes his hero, when angered with his brother-in-law's taking money from his family's estates (and so from the Church), as 'stripping the altars and covering them with sack-cloth': he then sent a warning letter, while he himself turned to fasts and prayer. The result, as the biographer saw it, was his brother-in-law's sudden death without children, and damnation. If the first case is one of simony the second is surely one of magic, and indeed XIII Toledo, canon 7, seems directed against just such a practice.[2] Lives of Saints and church laws thus spoke with conflicting voices.

Coercion

Faced with a crowd of abuses within their own ranks and with a society essentially divided into great landowners and oppressed *rustici*, the leaders of the Spanish Church, if they wished to further the spread of religion, had to choose between an alliance with one class or the other. Perhaps the option was never a real one. In any case, by 589, the decision had long been made; it was merely ratified by the conversion of Recared. Christianity in Spain, as elsewhere in the Roman or post-Roman world, was to spread through alliance with the crown and the dominant few. The most that a man such as Isidore could do was threaten the nobles who excluded the poor from their lands, the tyrannical judges, and all the 'pauperum oppressores' with Hell in the next world. He could not prevent them ruling the present *saeculum*.[3]

The chaos left by two centuries of absence of central power had to be repaired. 'Il faut faire vite', Professor Fontaine has

[1] *VPE* iv. 4. 4 f. (p. 172. 24 f.): 'revelante sibi Spiritu sancto'. See Garvin, pp. 385–7; Thompson, *Goths*, pp. 43 ff.

[2] *Vita Fructuosi*, iii (Nock, 93; Díaz, p. 84). See XIII Toledo, 7 (*PL* lxxxiv. 494; Vives, *Concilios*, p. 423).

[3] Isidore, *Sententiae* ii. xli. 9, iii. lvii. 1–2 (*PL* lxxxiii. 647A, 728B). For earlier developments see A. Balil, 'La España del Bajo Imperio', *Actas del III Congreso Español de estudios clásicos* i (Madrid, 1968), 204.

remarked of Isidore,[1] and the saying would apply to councils and laws. The quickest way to convert men—in practice pagans, who, as we saw, still posed a very serious problem in 589—was to revert to Roman models and use coercion.[2] Martin of Braga—who wrote in the Suevic kingdom but under a Catholic ruler—was exceptional in not threatening pagans with physical punishments.[3] Gregory the Great and the Spanish Fathers were less patient.[4] Isidore declared: 'where the bishop cannot prevail by preaching the [secular] power should act by fear.'[5] In 686 Julian of Toledo admitted that there may still be 'increduli', but they cannot escape 'the dominion of Christ —since they are hard pressed by rulers in whose hearts Christ already dwells.'[6] That this remark was enunciated as a general principle does not obscure its relevance to XII Toledo, presided over by Julian five years earlier, which had applied coercion to pagans—as it was also applied to Jews in Spain.[7]

The Religion of the Age

A choice of religion, as Isidore and Julian implied, and as the Visigothic Code and Church Councils insisted, did not exist in

[1] Fontaine, *Isidore de Séville*, ii. 884.

[2] For coercion against pagans in Roman Africa and for its application through the local bishops see Brown, *Religion*, pp. 305, 321 f.

[3] In his *De castigatione rusticorum*. Nor do such threats appear in II Braga, over which Martin presided, or in the *Canones* he translated from the Greek.

[4] For Gregory, see F. H. Dudden, *Gregory the Great* ii (London, 1905), 147–51.

[5] Isidore, *Sententiae*, iii. li. 4 (*PL* lxxxiii. 723B): 'quod non praevalet sacerdos efficere per doctrinae sermonem, potestas hoc imperet per disciplinae terrorem.'

[6] Julian, *De comprobatione sextae aetatis* i. 14 (*CC* cxv. 161. 18–22): 'etsi in quibusdam locis increduli adhuc populi habeantur, dominatum tamen Christi in hoc penitus non effugiunt, cum a talibus principibus premuntur in quorum cordibus iam per fidem Christus ipse habitare dinoscitur.' I have not found any source for this passage.

[7] XII Toledo, 11 (*PL* lxxxiv. 478; Vives, *Concilios*, p. 398). While the theme of the Jews in Visigothic Spain has been omitted from this paper it is not possible not to refer to the problem created by repeated forced conversions of Jews under Sisebut, Chintila, and Ervig. In the last case the King foresaw that most of the 'converts' would continue to observe Jewish practices. The clergy were given the task of preventing this and of supervising the lives of large numbers of nominal Christians, still considered 'perfidi', 'infideles', 'Antichristi ministri'. This must have taken a large part of the clergy's time and have prevented them attending to genuinely pastoral tasks. And the bishops were also charged not only with supervising morals in general but with cases of treason, assisting local judges, and even finding stray animals. Thus the clergy were handed tasks far too heavy for their shoulders. See King, *Law*, pp. 133–9, 157.

Spain. The Christianity of the age was one of conformity—even the *pagani* were 'Occasional Conformists'—as occasional as possible. The Church, in Augustine's phrase, was Noah's Ark, with all sorts of beasts inside. In the seventh century only monks and nuns and some religious (*conversi*), living in the world but distinguished by tonsure or habit—were 'converted', in the sense one can use for many ordinary Christians in the early Church.[1] Even the converted now *grew up into* Christianity rather than assuming it by a deliberate decision. Peasants were hardly expected to aspire to sanctity. No *rusticus* was to be canonized until the thirteenth century.[2]

One is tempted to see in the attitude not only of most of the laity but of the lesser clergy and of a not inconsiderable number of the bishops a quasi-total *non-participation* in the religion all these men officially professed. This may, however, be an unduly gloomy view, induced by reading too many conciliar texts. I will end by suggesting some ways in which the Church may have not only provided channels for ordinary men's existing religious feelings but also opened new windows on their lives.

In the 'two Spains', which I have suggested existed, the Church offered different alternatives to men. In the Romanized cities of southern Spain—as of southern Gaul—it provided new institutions which they could take pride in, monasteries, churches, hospitals, in place of theatres and aqueducts. The bishop of Mérida—the seventh-century Spanish city we know best, but not, probably, a unique case—was the most important man in Mérida. When he went 'in procession to the church [at Easter] many attendants walked before him as before a king, clothed in silk robes, a thing that no one at that time could do or presumed to do . . . giving him the homage that was his due.' In Mérida the bishop had eclipsed the local landowner, Roman or Goth, as source of wealth and patronage, of employment and excitement. In the countryside, a thaumaturge such as

[1] See *Liber ordinum*, 'Ordo conversorum conversarumque', pp. 82–5, and the remarks of Díaz (cited p. 38 n. 2), pp. 22 ff., who considers the rite *saec.* VI. See Isidore, *Sententiae*, ii. vii–xi (*PL* lxxxiii. 606–13), and Mullins, *The Spiritual Life*, pp. 169–72.

[2] F. Graus, *Volk, Herrscher und Heiliger im Reich der Merowinger* (Prague, 1965), esp. pp. 88–120. It is in *saec.* VI–VII that 'laicus' begins to assume the meaning of worldly or secular in Latin Europe. See J. Hervada, *Tres estudios sobre el uso del termino laico* (Pamplona, 1973), pp. 133–6, 139.

Aemilian had eclipsed the local augur, the medicine man of the tribe.[1]

In its liturgy, with its ceremonies and processions, the Church offered a new framework for man's life. To an extent it replaced the amphitheatre, as the main form of urban entertainment.[2] It also attempted to enter and operate within the mentality of the peasantry. Given the fact that clerics and laymen largely shared the same mentality, this attempt was so inevitable as to involve little deliberation. That neither clergy nor laity distinguished between natural and supernatural, material and spiritual, is illustrated by the prevalence of supposedly miraculous events in daily life, by the cult of relics and exorcism.[3]

The basic problem of the Church in dealing with paganism lay in persuading the pagans that only one God existed and that He was enough for them. The problem was—in the end—largely solved by allowing reverence to be paid to a host of saints and holy men. The *Vitas* of Mérida describe how 'every time that rain failed . . . the people of the city would gather together and with [the bishop] make the rounds of churches of the saints, imploring the Lord in prayer.' Thus, when rain came, it could be attributed at the same time to God, the Martyrs of Mérida, and the bishop.[4] Other processions are recorded in the *Vitas*, 'all the people clapping their hands and singing hymns . . . Rejoicing *after the manner of the ancients* with great uproar in the streets, they shouted the praise of the Lord.'[5] In 541 another procession went round the walls of Saragossa, carrying the tunic of St. Vincent, the citizens, fasting, in sackcloth, their wives in black, their hair let down and covered with ashes. The besieging Frankish army, seeing this, believed magic was being worked against them; when they heard that St. Vincent was being invoked they withdrew.[6]

[1] See Brown, *Religion*, p. 296; *VPE* v. 3. 12 (Garvin, p. 196—his translation). For the hospital etc. see v. 3. 3–9 (pp. 192 f.), and, in general, R. Collins, 'Mérida and Toledo', Chapter 7 below, pp. 189–219. For southern Gaul see Beck (cited p. 24 n. 5), pp. 328–35.

[2] See e.g. A. Grabar, *Christian Iconography* (Princeton, 1968), p. 16.

[3] The presence of 'certaines structures mentales communes aux deux cultures' is admitted by Le Goff (cited p. 4 n. 2), p. 785, despite his—in my view—far too sharp distinction between two mental worlds, clerical and lay.

[4] *VPE* v. 14. 2 (Garvin, p. 254).

[5] *VPE* v. 11. 2, 12. 6–7 (pp. 236, 246).

[6] Gregory of Tours, *Historia Francorum*, iii. 29.

Processions appear to have constituted one of the main expressions of the communal religion of the city. Even on private occasions they were important. If the Church ordered the cessation of the 'funebre carmen', with women beating their breasts, at burials, it substituted for this the chant of the Psalms (but the bishops recognized that it was probably impossible to prevent laymen continuing to act as they had always done).[1]

The Spanish Church never attacked popular religious beliefs, as such, unless these beliefs were unmistakably involved with pagan practices. It allowed, for instance, votive offerings, crowns, crosses, veils, to shrines of saints (instead of to temples of gods). José Vives has spoken of the attempt 'to impress the seal of Christianity on all kinds of buildings and on objects of personal, family and social use'. One finds Christian inscriptions not only on patens, votive crowns and crosses but ('viva' or 'spes in Deo', with a Christian symbol) on rings, brooches (Christian amulets), tiles, and bricks. 'Xps Hic', with A†W, appears on the bronze hinge of a door, 'Pax, ic Christus', in calligraphy as rustic as its orthography, on a tile. Christian inscriptions and symbols appear on harness. Byzantine (at times Persian) models inspire much of the sculptural decoration of Spanish churches. A simpler imagery is more significant for our purpose. A number of pre-Roman symbols, stars, wheels, vines, trees, reappear in seventh-century art. The solar wheel, used on pre-Roman funerary stones, reappears in the decoration of San Pedro de la Nave in the seventh century. The indigenous solar religion, as at Quintanilla de las Viñas, seems to be taken up into a religion which celebrated Christ as the Sun of Justice.[2] Rather than saying, as does a recent author, that the Church 'replaces pagan realism by a universe of symbolism and signs', I would prefer to say that the Church, in

[1] III Toledo, 22 (*PL* lxxxiv. 356; Vives, *Concilios*, p. 133).

[2] García Rodríguez, pp. 371 f. See *Liber ordinum*, pp. 163 ff. Vives, *Inscripciones*, p. 303 (see Nos. 373–418, 514–22, 559–85, esp. nos. 404, 576.) Palol, *Arqueología cristiana*, pp. 352–66; idem, *Arte hispánico de época visigoda* (Barcelona, 1968), pp. 44, 64 f., 120, etc. The gold brooch referred to above (p. 34 n. 3) is also a type of amulet; it bears an inscription asking the Virgin Mary to help the wearer. See, in general, Fontaine, 'Iconographie' (cited p. 34 n. 3), pp. 304 ff., 312, and J. Puig i Cadafalch, *L'Art wisigothique et ses survivances* (Paris, 1961), pp. 53–65. For Byzantine influences see H. Schlunk, *MM* v (1964), 234–54.

Spain as elsewhere, incorporated an earlier, 'primitive' approach to religion in its own art. For the classical art of Rome, 'at once importation and artifice, there are substituted mystical symbols, formulas of exorcism.'[1]

One can sum up the main features of the religion presented to the people as a saving formula of faith, the Creed, seen as a binding pact between God and men; a short statement on the Creation and Incarnation, in mythical form, found in its simplest terms in Martin of Braga; new rituals, songs, symbolism, and new heroes for old. The replacement of old rituals by new is explicitly stated by Martin of Braga, who speaks of new 'incantations' (the Creed and the Our Father), as opposed to 'diabolical incantations and chants'.[2] On the correct observance of ritual depend the coherence of early societies and their view of man's fate after death. In Visigothic Spain the faithful were told that if they failed to observe the correct ritual before death—presumably by undergoing penance—they could be saved *after* it by Masses. 'Unless the Catholic Church believed this,' Isidore says in a revealing passage, 'it would not give alms or offer Masses for the dead.'[3] To this magical view of the efficacy of Mass later Spanish writers apparently had objections.[4]

During life the Church provided rituals for every occasion. Salt was exorcised, for instance, so that 'wherever it is sprinkled it may expel all the cunning of the devil.'[5] It replaced the pagan purification ceremonies, alluded to by Martin of Braga.[6] There were blessings for new seed, pruning instruments, the first fruits of harvests, for a new threshing floor, a new well, for the sick (to be anointed with a special *unguentum*,

[1] For the first quotation see Le Goff (cited p. 18 n. 3), p. 730, for the second Puig i Cadalfalch, p. 77 (but one need not accept his derivation of 'symbols and formulas' from 'très anciennes conceptions asiatiques et du mystère des steppes'. On Puig's views see Fontaine, *L'Art préroman* i. 133).

[2] Martin, *De castigatione*, 16, ed. Barlow, p. 199. 23–6.

[3] Isidore, *De officiis* i. 18, 11 (*PL* lxxxiii. 757A): 'nisi crederet fidelibus defunctis dimitti peccata, non pro eorum spiritibus vel eleemosynam faceret, vel sacrificium Deo offeret.'

[4] Ildefonsus, *De cognitione baptismi*, 93–4 (*PL* xcvi. 145), and Julian of Toledo, *Prognosticum* i. 22 (*CC* cxv. 40) copy Augustine, *Enchiridion*, 119. Isidore (12–13) also copies this text but leaves unmodified his earlier statement.

[5] *Liber ordinum*, p. 16. 7 f. See Braulio, *Vita Emiliani*, 24 (p. 25. 18; Cazzaniga, p. 33. 17).

[6] Martin, *Canones*, 71 (Barlow, p. 140; *PL* lxxxiv. 584; Vives, *Concilios*, 103).

blessed on the day of the Doctor Saints Cosmas and Damian), for travellers . . . [1] That these blessings proved effective appears in stories told by Valerius of Bierzo. A veil was blessed and hung in a field to protect growing crops. When a thief was stupid enough to dig up some of the vegetables he was at once struck by a serpent, 'whereas through the grace of the Lord no one else was found who had been wounded by a serpent in these mountains.' In another incident blessed oil immediately cured a paralysed arm.[2]

There were also elaborate exorcisms and Masses for those possessed by the devil.[3] Devils also appear in other exorcisms —from the nuptial bed to a fisherman's nets.[4] In one exorcism oil was blessed to repel 'the attack of demons, the incursions of unclean spirits, and legions and shades, and assaults or entries of demons, and also the arts of magicians, Chaldeans, augurs, and the incantations of diviners, and poisons, and those things which are done by the unclean spirit and abominable power, or by the diabolical army.'[5] It was advisable to sprinkle blessed salt in the foundations of a church, in those of houses, while standing still, when greeting others, when walking, and on manure heaps.[6] It was particularly advisable to sprinkle salt on graves, where 'it will give great security, expelling from that place all the arts of demons.' Wherever it was scattered the Devil and 'his aerial lewdnesses' ('aeria nequitia') would find their travels suddenly interrupted.[7]

The elaborate nature of these exorcisms, many of which are peculiar to Spain, are surely the best proof one could require that the Spanish Church entered sufficiently into the minds of the people to understand the terrors that beset them. For these terrors it provided remedies. That it did not attempt to deny the mysterious divinities of the countryside but transformed them into demons or countered them with saints; that it may have sometimes erred in permitting magical beliefs (as with Isidore on Masses for the dead); that it did not totally eradicate

[1] *Liber ordinum*, pp. 166–8, 172, 69 ff., 93 f.

[2] Valerius, *Replicatio sermonum*, 11–12 (Aherne, p. 141). I use Sr Aherne's translation.

[3] *Liber ordinum*, pp. 73–80, 364–71 (Masses).

[4] Ibid., pp. 433, 174. Note the play of words on the Devil's nets.

[5] Ibid., p. 11. 1–7. See p. 13. 15 f., 'all kinds of monsters'.

[6] Ibid., p. 17. 5–8.

[7] Ibid., p. 16. 15–17, 26–9.

the superstitions it denounced, can hardly be held against it. If priests were still dancing at weddings and women still tearing their hair at funerals in fifteenth-century Spain, if some of the rites attacked by Martin of Braga were still in force in nineteenth- or twentieth-century Galicia and Asturias, in Greece too rituals of the Early Minoan age can still be found today.[1]

Bibliographical Note

I. Sources

1. *Written sources.*

M. C. Díaz y Díaz, *Index scriptorum latinorum medii aevi hispanorum* (Madrid, 1960) (cited by number, not page), is comprehensive for publications until about 1958. See also L. A. García Moreno, *Prosopografía del reino visigodo de Toledo* (Acta Salmanticensia, Filosofía y Letras, 67) (Salamanca, 1974) (from 569 onwards). For the Church Councils, apart from González's edition, reproduced in *PL* lxxxiv, I use J. Vives, *Concilios visigóticos e hispano-romanos* (Barcelona–Madrid, 1963). For inscriptions see Vives's revised and expanded edition of his *Inscripciones cristianos de la España romana y visigoda* (Barcelona, 1969).

The most important individual written sources for our purpose (apart from liturgy and sermons, for which see below) are, in chronological order:

Martin of Braga (d. 579), *De correctione* [recte *castigatione*] *rusticorum*, ed. Claude W. Barlow, *Martini episcopi Bracarensis opera omnia* (Papers and monographs of the American Academy in Rome, 12) (New Haven, 1950), pp. 159–82. See the corrections by A. F. Kurfess, *Aevum*, xxix (1955), 181–6, and the

[1] C. Cabal, *Las costumbres asturianas* (Madrid, 1931), is of limited use here. See L. Chaves, *Bracara Augusta*, viii (1957), 243–77. See Dodds (cited p. 4 n. 1), pp. 144 f., 152. Meslin (cited p. 16 n. 3), appears to blame the Church for its attitude to the nature-cults—'une autre explication tout autant mythique' (p. 515). One wonders what other approach was then possible. A more sympathetic attitude in Lynn White, 'The Life of the Silent Majority', in *Life and Thought in the Middle Ages*, ed. Robert S. Hoyt (Minneapolis, 1967), pp. 98 f. Tacit complicity with pagan survivals is noted for a much later period in France by M. Vovelle, in *Le Monde alpin et rhodanien, Revue régionale d'ethnologie*, v (1977), 7–32, at 27. In this valuable article Vovelle sees the vital change in popular religion in the fourteenth–sixteenth centuries, when there is perceptible the first real attempt to Christianize the rural world, largely with the fear of damnation, and to combat the existing mélange of Christian and pagan customs.

valuable observations of M. Meslin, in *Hommages à Marcel Renard*, ii (Brussels, 1969), 512–24. The work is translated by Barlow, together with Martin's other writings, in *Iberian Fathers*, i (The Fathers of the Church) (Washington, D.C., 1969), and by me, in *The Conversion of Western Europe 350–750* (Englewood Cliffs, N.J., 1969), pp. 55–63.

Braulio of Saragossa's (d. 651) letters, *Epistolario de San Braulio*, are edited by L. Riesco Terrero (Seville, 1975). The older edition, by J. Madoz (Madrid, 1941), has valuable notes. The letters are translated (from Madoz's edition) by Barlow, *Iberian Fathers*, ii. 15—112. Braulio's *Vita S. Emiliani* was edited by L. Vázquez de Parga (Madrid, 1943), and again by I. Cazzaniga, in *Bolletino del Comitato per la preparazione della Edizione Nazionale dei Classici greci e latini*, N.S. iii (Rome, 1954), 7–44. It is translated in Barlow, pp. 113–39. On Braulio see C. H. Lynch, *Saint Braulio, Bishop of Saragossa (631–651), His Life and Writings* (The Catholic University of America, Studies in Mediaeval History, N.S. 2) (Washington, D.C., 1938), translated into Spanish, with some additions and the use of recent editions, by P. Galindo, *San Braulio . . .* (Madrid, 1950).

Ildefonsus of Toledo (d. 667), *De viris illustribus*, ed. (with a translation) C. Codoñer Merino (Acta Salmanticensia, Filosofía y Letras, 65) (Salamanca, 1972). The work of Sr A. Braegelmann, *The Life and Writings of St. Ildefonsus of Toledo* (The Catholic University . . . 4) (Washington, D.C., 1942), is still useful. See also *San Ildefonso de Toledo* (*Santos Padres Españoles*, i) (Madrid, 1971), which includes his other works, with a Spanish translation.

The anonymous seventh-century work, *Vitas Sanctorum Patrum Emeritensium*, is edited and translated with a very extensive commentary, by Joseph N. Garvin (The Catholic University of America, Studies in Mediaeval and Renaissance Latin Language and Literature, 19) (Washington, D.C., 1946).

The anonymous *Vita Sancti Fructuosi* (*c*. 680) was edited with a translation, by Sr F. C. Nock (The Catholic University . . . Studies in Mediaeval History, N.S., 7) (Washington, D.C., 1946). The new critical edition by M. C. Díaz y Díaz, *La vida de San Fructuoso de Braga* (Braga, 1974) (with a Spanish translation) provides a definitive text; Sr Nock's volume remains useful for its introduction and notes.

Valerius of Bierzo (dates uncertain) was partially edited and discussed by Sr C. M. Aherne, *Valerio of Bierzo, an ascetic of the late Visigothic Period* (The Catholic University . . . 11) (Washington, D.C., 1949), and again by M. C. Díaz y Díaz, *Anecdota wisigothica*, i (Acta Salmanticensia . . . 12. 2) (Salamanca, 1958), 49–61, 89–116.

The main monastic Rules coming from Spain are by Leander of Seville (see Díaz, *Index*, 72), Isidore of Seville (Díaz, 115), Fructuosus of Braga (Díaz, 218) and the anonymous *Regula monastica communis* (No. 314). They are all included, edited by J. Campos, with use of the manuscripts, in *Santos Padres Españoles*, ii (Madrid, 1971) (with Spanish translation) and are translated into English, together with other documents, by Barlow, *Iberian Fathers* (Leander), i. 183–228, and (Fructuosus and the *Regula communis*), ii. 155–220. Díaz, *Anecdota*, i. 9–35, 71–87, discusses and publishes other writings on the monastic life. See Díaz, 'La vie monastique d'après les écrivains wisigothiques', *Théologie de la vie monastique* (Théologie, 49) (Paris, 1961), pp. 371–83.

Liturgy. Bibliographies. L. Brou and J. Mª. Pinell, in *Estudios sobre la liturgia mozárabe* (Toledo, 1965), pp. 1–31 (1936–64). See also, ibid., Pinell, pp. 109–64, and J. Mª. Mora Ontalva, pp. 165–87. A. Roche Navarro, in *Archivos Leoneses*, l (1971), 323–69. J. Mª. Pinell, 'Liturgia Hispánica', *Diccionario de historia eclesiástica de España*, ii (Madrid, 1972), 1318–20. J. Mª. de Mora Ontalva, *Hispania Sacra*, xxvi (1973), 209–37.

The sources most used here are, in chronological order of publication:

M. Férotin, *Le Liber Ordinum en usage dans l'Eglise wisigothique et mozarabe d'Espagne du Vᵉ au XIᵉ siècle* (Monumenta ecclesiae liturgica, iv) (Paris, 1904) (cited as *Liber ordinum*). Idem, *Le Liber Mozarabicus Sacramentorum et les manuscrits mozarabes* (ibid. vi) (Paris, 1912) (cited as *Liber mozarabicus*).

A. Fábrega Grau, *Pasionario hispánico*, 2 vols. (Monumenta Hispaniae Sacra, ser. Litúrgica, vi) (Madrid–Barcelona, 1955) (cited as Fábrega, *Pasionario*).

Hagiography. C. García Rodríguez, *El culto de los Santos en la España romana y visigoda* (Monografías de historia eclesiástica, i) (Madrid, 1966). See also the articles of B. de Gaiffier, *Analecta Bollandiana*, lxvi (1948), 299–318; lxxvii (1959), 188–217; lxxx

(1962), 382–422; lxxxiv (1966), 457–99; lxxxvii (1969), 469–98; xci (1973), 133–62; xcii (1974), 387–408.

Sermons. R. Grégoire, *Les Homéliaires du moyen-âge* (Rerum ecclesiasticarum documenta, ser. major, Fontes, vi) (Rome, 1966).

2. *Art and archaeology*

The most valuable general syntheses, in chronological order:

E. Campos Cazorla, 'El arte hispano-visigodo', *Historia de España*, ed. R. Menéndez Pidal, iii (Madrid, 1940), 435–608. J. Ferrandis, 'Artes decorativas visigodas', ibid. 611–66 (in the 2nd edn. (Madrid, 1963), there are supplements by M. López Serrano, pp. 727–830). P. Batlle Huguet, 'Arte paleocristiano', *Ars Hispaniae*, ii (Madrid, 1947), 183–225. H. Schlunk, 'Arte visigodo', ibid. 227–323. P. de Palol, 'Demografía y arqueología híspanicas de los siglos IV al VII, ensayo de cartografía', *Boletín del Seminario de estudios de Arte y Arqueología* [Valladolid] xxxii (1966), 5–66 (English trans. cited above, p. 8 n. 1). Idem, *Arqueología cristiana de la España romana, siglos IV–VI* (Madrid–Valladolid, 1967). Idem, 'Arqueología cristiana hispánica de tiempos romanos y visigodos', *Rivista di archeologia cristiana*, xliii (1967), 177–232 (also published in *Diccionario de historia eclesiástica de España*, i. 96–113, with more bibliographical references. Other publications by Palol are cited here). J. Fontaine, *L'Art préroman hispanique*, i (La Pierre-qui-vire, 1973).

M. Sotomayor Muro, *Datos históricos sobre los sarcófagos romano-cristianos de España* (Granada, 1973), is a catalogue of the sarcophagi imported into the peninsula from outside. Many articles by H. Schlunk on sarcophagi, both those imported and those produced in Spain, are published in *Madrider Mitteilungen* and elsewhere. See especially 'Nuevas interpretaciones de sarcófagos paleocristianos españoles', *Actas de la* 1ª. *Reunión Nacional de Arqueología Paleocristiana* (1966) (Vitoria, 1967), pp. 101–16 (and see below). This volume, also published as *Boletín de la Institución 'Sancho el Sabio'*, x, contains a number of other relevant studies, as do the *Actas del VIII Congreso Internacional de Arqueología Cristiana* (*Barcelona, 1969*), 2 vols. (Barcelona, 1972) (see especially the general articles of Palol and Schlunk). Reviews of recent research by J. Fontaine, *REL* xlvi (1968), 90–7; *Bulletin hispanique*, lxxiv (1972), 261–74; *REAug* xxii

(1976), 402–35. A work comparable to E. Salin, *La Civilisation mérovingienne*, 4 vols. (Paris, 1949–59), is much needed for Spain.

II. Modern Studies

1. *The general background*

Bibliography. On Roman Spain see the very full 'Bibliographía' in *Hispania Antiqua*, ii (1972) and iii (1973). For late Roman Spain see J. Mª. Blázquez, *Estructura económica y social de Hispania durante la anarquía militar y el Bajo Imperio* (Madrid, 1964). For the Visigothic period the studies collected in *Historia de España* iii (1940), only slightly updated in the 2nd edn., continue to be useful but more valuable are E. A. Thompson, *The Goths in Spain* (Oxford, 1969), and P. D. King, *Law and Society in the Visigothic Kingdom* (Cambridge, 1972) (the latter work has an extensive bibliography). The recent studies of A. Barbero and M. Vigil, and others by Blázquez, Le Roux and Tranoy, and Palol, to cite a few names, have shed much light on the social background. See above, nn. on p. 6, and p. 7 n. 5. W. Hübener, 'Zur Chronologie der westgotenzeitlichen Grabfunde in Spanien', *MM* x (1970), 187–211, questions some of the main conclusions of the earlier studies of Zeiss, Reinhart, and Palol as to the distribution of the Visigothic settlements, but a new picture has yet to emerge which could be substituted for the older syntheses.

2. *Religion*

Earlier studies have been replaced, for native Spanish cults, by J. Mª. Blázquez Martínez, *Religiones primitivas de Hispania*, i (Rome, 1962), with a supplementary study in *Homenaje a A. Tovar* (Madrid, 1972), pp. 81–90, and, for Eastern religions, by A. García y Bellido, *Les Religions orientales dans l'Espagne romaine* (Leiden, 1967). The older synthesis of S. McKenna, *Paganism and Pagan Survivals in Spain up to the Fall of the Visigothic Kingdom* (The Catholic University of America, Studies in Mediaeval History, N.S. 1) (Washington, D.C., 1938), remains valuable for the Visigothic period. V. Martínez, 'El paganismo en la España visigoda', *Burgense* xiii. 2 (1972), 489–508, is more recent but the author does not know McKenna's work.

J. Fernández Alonso, *La cura pastoral en la España romanovisigoda* (Rome, 1955), while needing correction in detail, remains a valuable synthesis, which can usefully be compared at many points to the work of H. G. J. Beck, *The Pastoral Care of Souls in South-East France during the Sixth Century* (Analecta Gregoriana, 51) (Rome, 1950). One can also consult B. Jiménez Duque, *La espiritualidad romano-visigoda y muzárabe* (Madrid, 1977). There is no earlier general discussion, known to me, of the precise subject of this paper, such as we have, for Gaul, in the still valuable work of A. Marignan, *Etudes sur la civilisation française*, ii, *Le Culte des saints sous les Mérovingiens* (Paris, 1899).

Pontifical Institute of Mediaeval Studies, Toronto

Reproduced from Visigothic Spain: New Approaches, *ed. Edward James, (Oxford, 1980), pp. 3–60, by permission of Oxford University Press*

II

COINS AND CHRONICLES: PROPAGANDA IN SIXTH-CENTURY SPAIN AND THE BYZANTINE BACKGROUND

I. The Literary Sources for Leovigild and Hermenegild

The reigns of Leovigild (569–586) and his son, Recared (586–601), constitute the main turning point in the history of Spain under the Visigoths. Instead of succumbing, as the Vandals in Africa and the Ostrogoths in Italy had done, to the Byzantine advance, the Visigoths, under Leovigild and Recared, succeeded in achieving the political and, later, the religious unity of Spain. The sharp division between an Arian barbarian ruling class and the Catholic Hispano-Roman mass of the population was brought to an end. This was not achieved without a major crisis, which began with the conversion *ca.* 580 of Leovigild's elder son, Hermenegild, to Catholicism. This event precipitated a civil war in Spain between Hermenegild and Leovigild, which ended in Hermenegild's defeat and eventually in his murder in 585. It is very remarkable that this crisis did not prevent the official entrance of the Visigoths, led by Hermenegild's brother, Recared, into the Catholic Church in 589.

The questions associated with the conversion, revolt and death of Hermenegild have been repeatedly discussed since the sixteenth century and have been raised again in recent years but we do not seem much nearer an agreement. In this paper I shall look again at the evidence supplied both by the literary and the numismatic sources.[1] But before entering on questions of detail it may

[1] This article is, in part, based on "La Conversión de los Visigodos: notas críticas," *Analecta sacra Tarraconensia*, xxxiv (1961), 21–46. The first part of "La Conversión" consisted of some (unnecessarily polemical) comments on an important article by Professor E. A. Thompson, "The Conversion of the Visigoths to Catholicism," *Nottingham Mediaeval Studies*, iv (1960), 4–35; most of these comments are not reproduced here. In this paper I have tried to place the Hermenegild episode in its historical context. I have born in mind a remark of Marc Bloch's, *Journal des Savants* (1926), 419f., when he was speaking of this period, "that the sources of one region are ordinarily so poor that they need to be constantly compared in the light of documents from neighbouring countries." My own estimate of the situation, and in particular of Hermenegild, has altered. I should not now conclude, "sans phrase," that "the conflict between Hermenegild and his father was essentially a religious war."

In this article I use the following abbreviations: *MGH, AA* = *Monumenta Germaniae historica, Auctores antiquissimi*; *SRM* = *ibid.*, *Scriptores rerum Merovingicarum*; *PL* = *Patrologia latina*, ed. J-P. Migne; Campos = Julio Campos, *Juan de Biclaro, obispo de Gerona. Su Vida y su obra* (Madrid, 1960). I cite the *Chronicon* of John of Biclar by the editions of Mommsen (*MGH, AA*, xi) and of Campos; Isidore, *Chronicon* and *Historia*

be well to recall briefly the political situation and what one may call the intellectual climate of the late sixth-century Mediterranean world. To understand either of these things we have to begin with Byzantium. If we begin, as many historians still do, with the *a posteriori* view that the restoration of the empire in the West by Justinian was "an anachronistic enterprise, necessarily ephemeral,"[2] we deprive ourselves (even if this estimate – as is highly debatable – should be correct) of the possibility of understanding the minds of Justinian's contemporaries. *In the sixth century* it was the barbarian kingdoms that seemed ephemeral and different *in nature* from the ageless imperial rule.[3]

The first half of the sixth century had seen the collapse of the Vandal and Ostrogothic kingdoms before the Byzantine troops. It is true that the reign of Justinian's successor, Justin II (565–578), was marked by new wars on every front but the situation cannot have seemed, and was not, in fact, hopeless. The empire remained economically and financially powerful.[4] Justinian's reign, too, had seen the apparent failure of his plans for the West but the failure had been redeemed. The Emperor Maurice (582–602) was to succeed in stabilizing the situation in Italy and Africa, on the Danube and in the East. Maurice had plans to send one of his sons to rule in Rome and another in Carthage.[5] It is clear that Justinian's successors had no intention of abandoning his revindication of the empire's rights in the West. The imperial navy continued to dominate the Mediterranean and it was to Constantinople that all cultivated

Gothorum by Mommsen (*ibid.*); Isidore, *De viris illustribus*, by the new edition by Carmen Codoñer Merino (Salamanca, 1964), and by *PL*, lxxxiii; Gregory of Tours, *Historia Francorum*, according to *MGH*, *SRM*, i², ed. B. Krusch and W. Levison (Hannover, 1951); Gregory the Great, *Dialogi*, according to the edition of U. Moricca = *Fonti per la storia d'Italia*, lvii (Rome, 1924), and his *Registrum* according to *MGH*, *Epistulae*, ed. P. Ewald and L. M. Hartmann (Berlin, 1891–99). Since 1961 an article by Professor Karl Friedrich Stroheker, "Das spanische Westgotenreich und Byzanz", *Bonner Jahrbücher*, clxiii (1963), 252–274, has appeared, to which I am much indebted. I should also like to thank Professor R. L. Wolff for his kindness in reading this article and for his valuable suggestions and criticisms.

[2] Ramón Menéndez Pidal, *Historia de España*, *iii* (Madrid, 1940), xxiii, "empresa anacrónica, efímera por fuerza." One could quote many other similar judgements.

[3] See, for example, the famous letter of Gregory the Great to Phocas (of 603), *Registrum*, xiii, 34, also *ibid.*, xi, 4.

[4] See the classic work of Ernst Stein, *Studien zur Geschichte des byzantinischen Reiches vornehmlich unter den Kaisern Justinus II u. Tiberius Constantinus* (Stuttgart, 1919), also P. Goubert, *Byzance avant l'Islam*, i (Paris, 1951), 51–3, 55–9; A. H. M. Jones, *The Later Roman Empire, 284–602*, i (Oxford-Norman, Oklahoma, 1964), 298–302, 315; A. R. Lewis, *Naval Power and Trade in the Mediterranean A.D. 500–1100* (Princeton, 1951), 38–49.

[5] See Goubert, i, 183, 271 f.; G. Ostrogorsky, *Geschichte der byzantinischen Staates*² (Munich, 1952), 67 and n. 2. John of Biclar, *s. a.* 587, 3 (Mommsen, 218; Campos, 95) records Byzantine successes in Italy.

men in Italy, Africa and Spain still turned as the principal Christian power in the world, as the natural defender of the Faith "against barbarian foes."[6]

While Rome after the Gothic War, in the words of Pope Gregory the Great, "lay buried in its own ruins," Constantinople, the "new Rome" of the African poet Corippus, remained "the royal city" by definition, even to a Visigothic writer such as John of Biclar. It doubtless struck him very much in the same way that it had impressed Jordanes, who, writing in 551, describes its effect on an earlier Gothic visitor, writing of "the coming and going of the ships, the splendid walls and the people of diverse nations gathered like a flood of waters streaming from different regions into one basin." To the world of the sixth century the ruler of Constantinople was "truly a god on earth (*Deus sine dubio terrenus*)."[7] It was to Constantinople that Gregory the Great was sent as ambassador by Pope Pelagius II (579–590), mainly to obtain imperial aid against the Lombards, and it was thither that Bishop Leander of Seville travelled, probably in 580, to seek for help for the Catholic Hermenegild against his father Leovigild.[8]

When one studies the literary sources for the civil war between Hermenegild and Leovigild one would do well to begin by establishing the position of the authors concerned with regard to Byzantium. Our main authors are four in number, two writing in Spain, John of Biclar and Isidore of Seville, one in Gaul, Gregory of Tours, and, lastly, Pope Gregory the Great.

The position of Gregory the Great with regard to Byzantium was complex. Rome and with it the papacy had been reincorporated into the Empire in the time of Justinian. Gregory always saw the laws of this world in the light of the Last Judgment, which seemed to him imminent. At times imperial edicts appeared to infringe the individual's right to find salvation (most especially in monasticism); at other times the emperor acted uncanonically in other ways. Then Gregory would (privately) make his views known to the emperor. But he saw the empire much as Augustine had done. For him the Church and the Christian State were inseparable joint organs of the City of God. The empire was still, as Fischer says, "the ideal expression of Christian universalism" and in fact the frontiers of the empire and of the Christian world still largely coincided – in the West the only Christians definitely outside the imperial borders were the Frankish kingdoms, most of Spain and the far distant Irish; in the East only the heretical Christians of Persia. For Gregory it was in the empire that "we see God is worshipped." May it expand, he prayed, "so that the name of Christ

[6] See Lewis, *op. cit.*, 26–32 and the inscription cited below, n. 81.

[7] Gregory, *Dialogi*, ii, 15; Corippus, *In laudem Iustini*, i, 344, ed. J. Partsch, *MGH, AA*, iii, 2, 126, *et alibi*; John of Biclar, e.g. *s. a.* 573, 4 (Mommsen, 213; Campos, 83); Jordanes, *De origine actibusque Getarum*, xxviii, 143, ed. Mommsen, *MGH, AA*, v, 95 (trans. C. C. Mierow, *The Gothic History of Jordanes*, Princeton, 1915).

[8] See, e.g., T. Hodgkin, *Italy and her Invaders*, v (Oxford, 1895), 240f., and, for Leander, below, n. 67.

may be known on all sides, by preaching the Faith to subject peoples." Gregory's wish to further the harmony of Church and empire led him to remark, "what the emperor does, if it is canonical, we follow it, if it is not canonical we bear with it, as far as can be done without sin."[9]

Gregory's predecessor, Pelagius II, tried to bring the Franks into Italy, as the emperor's allies against the Lombards. The popes were principally anxious to secure the safety of Rome but at times they can only have appeared as imperial agents. This was how the emperor saw them.[10] It seems very possible that the long delay of Recared in communicating to Pope Gregory the official notice of his conversion and that of the Visigoths was due to the king's suspicion of the close relations between the papacy and the empire.[11] Later on Recared had recourse to the pope as the natural intermediary when he wished to secure a text of the peace treaty between his predecessor Athanagild and the Emperor Justinian.[12] In the *Dialogi* Gregory was not interested in recording the political actions of Hermenegild. He had other reasons, as I shall show, for introducing this Visigothic prince into his work. But Gregory's whole view of Hermenegild shows that he considered that his rebellion against Leovigild was legitimate, since it was directed against an unjust and heretical father, and also, very possibly, since it was supported by the authority of Byzantium.[13]

[9] The texts cited are *Registrum*, i, 73 and xi, 29. For the liturgical form of prayer for the emperor, that he may triumph over all barbarian nations, see also *Reg.* vii, 5 and 7, etc. Erich Caspar, *Geschichte des Papsttums*, ii (Tübingen, 1933), 467f., notes how different were the tone and the actions of Gregory from those of St Ambrose or of Pope Gelasius I. When protesting against the edict prohibiting soldiers or those holding civil office from becoming monks Gregory took care to stress that he was writing, "neque ut episcopus neque ut servus iure rei publicae, sed iure *privato*" (*Reg.* iii, 61). The letter concludes with the statement that Gregory has published the edict. Thus, by at once publishing the law and privately protesting against it, he has shown his obedience to the emperor and his duty to God. See also *Reg.* iii, 64 and E. F. Fischer, "Gregor der Große und Byzanz," *Zeitschrift der Savigny-Stiftung für Rechtsgeschichte*, Kanon. Abt., xxxvi (1950), 15–144, especially 18–20, 57–68, 129–144.

[10] Cf. the inscription placed by Pelagius II in the altar of St Peter's (J. B. de Rossi, *Inscriptiones christianae urbis Romae septimo saeculo antiquiores*, ii [Rome, 1888], 145f.); Hodgkin, *loc. cit.* For the position of the papacy under Justinian and his successors cf. Caspar, *op. cit.*, chaps. VI and VII and L. Duchesne, *L'Église au VIe siècle* (Paris, 1925), 262–69. See n. 12 below.

[11] Cf., in the same sense, J. M[a]. de Lacarra, "La Iglesia visigoda en el s. VII y sus relaciones con Roma," *Le Chiese nei regni dell'Europa occidentale e i loro rapporti con Roma sino all'800 = Settimane di studio*, vii. 1 (Spoleto, 1960), 367f. and the "Discussione," 406f.

[12] See Gregory, *Registrum*, ix, 229. Gregory excused himself from intervening, on the grounds that the imperial archives had been destroyed. He did act as mediator between the Franks and Byzantium (see *Reg.* viii, 4 and esp. xiii, 7 and 9) and between the empire and the Lombards. He even notified the emperor of the conversion of the Anglo-Saxons of Kent (xi, 35).

[13] See n. 44 below and, above, n. 3.

The main contemporary Spanish source for Hermenegild is the *Chronicle* of John of Biclar, of those active in Spain in the crucial years alone in having left a record that survives. Isidore of Seville largely depends on John, though he was himself a contemporary of the civil war of the 580s (he was probably born *ca.* 560), and his elder brother, Leander, was deeply involved, being active in the conversion both of Hermenegild and of Recared to Catholicism.

John's attitude to Byzantium is of interest. He was born in Lusitania in South-West Spain, where classical culture was more strongly rooted than in the North. He spent seventeen years as a young man (559–576) at Constantinople. He was a Visigoth by birth, although brought up as a Catholic. It is difficult to assess his attitude to the empire before the official conversion of the Visigoths in 589 since his *Chronicle* was written after this event. His sympathies would naturally have been divided. Constantinople, as has been said, was for him "the royal city," Spain was "the province of the Goths."[14] (It had been granted to them by the empire in the fifth century and had been held by them, at least nominally, for over a century, though part of it was in imperial hands since 552.) It is only gradually that events in Spain begin to assume in John's *Chronicle* an importance comparable to happenings in the empire.

The *Chronicle* begins in 567, very significantly, with one of the first important acts of Justinian's successor, Justin II, one that concerned religion. Justinian had roused strong opposition in the Latin West by his attempts to pacify the Monophysite opponents of the Council of Chalcedon in Egypt and Syria. Justinian's (Fifth Ecumenical) Council of Constantinople (553) had condemned several authors approved by Chalcedon and this condemnation had created a schism in North Italy; another schism had only been prevented in North Africa by the exile of leading ecclesiastics.[15] These events were well known in Spain, where the Church, in Visigothic times, never accepted the Fifth Council as Ecumenical.[16] But Justin II, John of Biclar tells us, "destroyed all that had been done against the synod of Chalcedon."[17] Justin II's action

[14] John. *s. a.* 569, 4 (Mommsen, 212; Campos, 80). Similarly, he speaks (*s. a.* 587, 3) of "provincia Italiae."

[15] See Duchesne, *op. cit.*, 188–255; E. Amann, "Trois-Chapitres," *Dictionnaire de théologie catholique*, xv (Paris, 1950), 1868–1924.

[16] J. Madoz, *Revista española de teología*, xii (1952), 189–204; Lacarra, *art. cit.*, 382 f. For the restricted sense of "ecumenical" in the sixth century see R. Devreesse, "Le cinquième concile et l'oecuménicité byzantine," *Miscellanea G. Mercati*, iii (Città del Vaticano, 1946), 1–15.

[17] John, *s. a.* 567, 2 (Mommsen, 211; Campos, 78): "ea, quae contra synodum Chalcedonensem fuerant commentata, destruxit." Justin II, by his first *Henoticon*, also annulled Justinian's last theological aberration. At the same time he repeated the condemnation of the Three Chapters of 553. Cf. Duchesne, 270–3; Campos, 103–5. John's statement was repeated by Isidore, *Chronicon*, 401; cf. his *De viris*, xviii–xix, xxv (ed. Codoñer, 144, 147; *PL* lxxxiii, 1099, 1101). I am unable to agree with Srta. Codoñer (pp. 71 f.) that Isidore's attitude is neutral.

was important because it at once reestablished Byzantium, in the eyes of the Catholic West, as the champion of the orthodox Faith. John proceeds to show us this champion intervening, even at the price of war with Persia, to protect the Armenian and Iberian Christians against persecution for their religion.[18] Two years later, in 569, the emperor appears as the apostle of barbarian nations, for John records that the "Garamantes [a tribe of the Fezzan] sent envoys to ask for peace with the Roman State and for the Christian Faith... They received both [things] at once."[19] The conversion of pagans, for John as for Gregory the Great, was part of the duty of the emperor, while it was also a means of expanding his political influence.[20]

In the early years of John of Biclar's *Chronicle* his attention is concentrated on the empire. It is only after 577 that it shifts to Spain. This change in emphasis is certainly due in part to John's return to Spain *ca.* 576,[21] but it is also due to the reorganisation of the Visigothic kingdom by Leovigild and his victories over all his enemies, including the local Byzantine forces. Under Leovigild there appeared to be emerging a new centre of power in the Mediterranean, which could stand against Byzantium. It was natural that John of Biclar should welcome the rise of a great king of his own race.[22] While chronicling Leovigild's victories John does not appear, however, as definitely hostile to the empire. In contrast, John's younger contemporary, Isidore of Seville, delights in recording the defeats of the "Roman troops" and their final ejection from Spain.[23]

The attitude of Gregory of Tours to Byzantium is less definite than that of Gregory the Great or John of Biclar. There was no question of direct opposition between the empire and the Frankish kingdoms. Contact between Constantinople and Gaul was sporadic and was mainly due to the empire's attempts to induce the Franks to intervene in Italy against the Lombards. On the other hand Gregory of Tours was well informed of events in Spain. The Merovingian and Visigothic royal houses were allied by several (generally unfortunate) marriages and embassies frequently travelled between the two countries.[24]

[18] John, *s. a.* 567, 3 (Mommsen, 211; Campos, 78).

[19] Idem, *ibid.*, 569, 1 (Mommsen, 212; Campos, 79).

[20] Cf. Duchesne, *op. cit.*, 650–2, and the text of Gregory the Great quoted above (*Reg.* i. 73).

[21] For John's seventeen years in Constantinople cf. Isidore, *De viris*, xxxi (Codoñer, 151; *PL*, lxxxiii, 1105). E. Florez, *España Sagrada*, vi[3] (Madrid, 1859), 362f., dates his return in 575; Mommsen, 207f., in 576.

[22] John only reckons years in Gothic kings, as well as emperors, from Leovigild (from 569 or 570). See n. 76 below.

[23] Throughout his *Chronicon* John devotes considerable attention to the East, on which he is generally well informed. Byzantium, to him, is always a great Christian power. Cp. Isidore, e.g. *Historia Gothorum*, xlvii, liv, lxii.

[24] Cf. N. H. Baynes, *Byzantine Studies and other Essays* (London, 1955), 312–5, also the valuable article by W. Goffart, "Byzantine Policy in the West under Tiberius II and

We thus have four points of view with regard to Byzantium in the existing literary sources for Hermenegild's life – that of Gregory the Great, who naturally saw events from within the empire, though he was principally interested in the struggle between Arians and Catholics; that of John of Biclar, familiar with Constantinople but whose admiration was aroused by Leovigild's victories; the nationalist (better, perhaps, isolationist) view of Isidore of Seville, deeply hostile to Byzantium; and, lastly, the neutral Gregory of Tours, whose neutrality was, however, relative, since his detestation of Arianism was no less pronounced than that of the other three writers in question.

If the would-be universal empire dominated the Mediterranean it was largely because of its intimate connection with the would-be universal Catholic Church. All men of the sixth century were bound to be concerned with the question of religious unity, without which no state could seem secure. Procopius writes of Justinian in the *Secret History*, "Anxious to unite all men in the same opinion about Christ, he destroyed dissidents indiscriminately, and that under the pretext of piety; for he did not think that the slaying of men was murder unless they happened to share his own religious opinions." Procopius was indeed willing, in the *Secret History*, to use any smear against Justinian but it is interesting that it should have occurred to him to use this charge.[25] The conduct satirised would have seemed normal and praiseworthy to most men, provided it was exercised on behalf of their own beliefs. In his work on Justinian's *Buildings*, written some years after the unpublished *Secret History*, Procopius numbers among Justinian's major achievements, on a level with his conquests, his legal codifications, his fortifications, etc., his imposition of theological unity on the empire's inhabitants.[26] The Arian rulers of the barbarian kingdoms were, in general, more tolerant than the rulers of Byzantium, but their tolerance, one may suspect, was mainly due to the weakness of their position. There were persecuting Arian kings, as certain as any Catholic ruler that they had the truth on their side. The Vandal King Hunneric (477–484) saw the Arians as the "true worshippers of the Divine Majesty," and the Visigothic King Leovigild held that *his* was the Catholic Faith. Both sought to impose their views on their subjects.[27]

Maurice: the Pretenders Hermenegild and Gundovald (579–585)," *Traditio*, xiii (1957), 73–118. Gregory's account of Justin II (*Hist. Franc.*, iv, 40) is inaccurate.

[25] *Anecdota*, 13. 7, trans. J. B. Bury, *History of the Later Roman Empire*, ii (New York, 1958), 428. I owe the characterisation of the *Secret History* as a smear to Professor R. L. Wolff.

[26] *Aedificia*, I. 9, trans. H. B. Dewing (Loeb Classical Library), 4 f. Cf. Ch. Diehl, *Justinien et la civilisation byzantine du VIe siècle*, ii (New York, 1960), "L'oeuvre religieuse," 315–366.

[27] Hunneric's edict is cited by Victor of Vita, *Hist.*, iii, 3–14, ed. M. Petschenig (Vienna, 1881), 72–8. On Hunneric and the Catholic Church cf. C. Courtois, *Les Vandales et l'Afrique* (Paris, 1955), 293–9. For Leovigild cf. below, n. 121. For other Visigothic Kings see Thompson, *art. cit.* (n. 1), 9 f.

Both Gregory the Great and John of Biclar were always conscious of the Catholic-Arian issue and it played a great part in the minds of Isidore of Seville and Gregory of Tours.[28] The introduction of Hermenegild into the *Dialogi*, a work officially concerned with the miracles of Italian saints, was due, as Gregory the Great himself says, to a desire "to display the [divine] condemnation of the Arian heresy."[29] In this section of the *Dialogi* we have a series of miracles revealing the power of the True Faith against Arian Lombards in Italy, Arian Visigoths in Spain and Arian Vandals in Africa.[30] The fact that Gregory's account of Hermenegild's death for the Catholic Faith appears in this apologetic context does not mean that it is worthless. Gregory must have possessed, through his close friendship with Leander of Seville, an accurate knowledge of Hermenegild's conversion and rebaptism by that bishop and of the events that followed, at least up to Leander's mission to Constantinople.[31] Before writing the *Dialogi* (*ca.* 594) Gregory had ample time to receive further information from Leander after the latter's return to Spain; at least one letter of Leander to Gregory is mentioned in the latter's reply of 591 but is unfortunately lost.[32] It is curious, however, that Gregory does not refer to Hermenegild in any of his letters to Spain; this silence is especially notable in *Registrum*, V, 53a, where the pope refers to Leander's mission to Constantinople; it is in striking contrast to the enthusiasm for Hermenegild in the *Dialogi*. Gregory knew, of course, that his letters to Leander would circulate widely in Spain, as in fact they did. And in Spain, as we shall see, Hermenegild was not a name of happy remembrance.[33]

[28] For Isidore cf. *Hist. Vand.*, 78–79, 81; *Hist. Suev.*, 90; *Hist. Goth.*, 50 (*et alibi*); also *De viris*, i (defection of Osius), xxii (conversion of the Sueves), xxviii (conversion of the Goths), xxx–xxxi (anti-Arian champions), ed. Codoñer, 133f., 145, 149, 151f.; *PL*, lxxxiii, 1087, 1100, 1103, 1105. Common phrases are "arriana impietas," "arriana insania," "arriana pravitas." For Gregory of Tours cf. his long debates with Visigothic envoys, *Hist. Franc.*, V, 43; VI, 40.

[29] Gregory, *Dial.*, III, 30 (Moricca, 204): "Quamvis sola quae in Italia gesta sunt narrare decreveram, visne tamen ut, pro ostendenda eiusdem arrianae hereseos damnatione, transeamus verbo ad Hispanias, atque inde per Africam ad Italiam redeamus?".

[30] *Ibid.*, 29–32. The miracle Gregory recounts of Africa (III, 32, prisoners without tongues continue to speak) is a garbled version of a often repeated story. Cf. C. Courtois, *Victor de Vita et son oeuvre* (Algiers, 1954), 82 n. 108. For Gregory's view of Theodoric's fate as a persecuting Arian king cf. *Dial.*, IV, 31.

[31] See John Chapman, *St. Benedict and the Sixth Century* (London, 1929), 5 n. 1. Fr. Görres, always a severe critic, admits the authenticity of Gregory's information as to Hermenegild's conversion, though not as to his martyrdom; cf. *Zeitschrift für die historische Theologie*, xliii (1873), 11–13. See n. 67 below.

[32] Cf. *Registrum*, i, 41. In the *Dialogi* (iii, 31) Gregory states his sources for Hermenegild's martyrdom, "sicut multorum, qui ab Hispaniarum partibus veniunt, relatione cognovimus" (Moricca, 204).

[33] Sisebut's use of *Reg.* i, 41 was pointed out by Görres, *Zeitschrift für wissenschaftliche Theologie*, xlii (1899), 311. The *Dialogi* appear only to have reached Spain after Isidore's

John of Biclar felt as strongly as Pope Gregory the importance of the Arian problem. The longest section of John's *Chronicle* and its triumphant conclusion consists of the account of the Third Council of Toledo in 589, which celebrated the conversion of the Visigoths from Arianism to Catholicism. At this Council King Recared, in John's words, "renewed in our times the example of Constantine the Great at Nicaea and of the Most Christian Emperor Marcian at Chalcedon."[34] The Arian heresy first condemned at Nicaea was at last, after 280 (really 264) years "cut off at the roots."[35] John here forgot the Arian Lombards, as Gregory the Great, despite the congratulations he addressed to Recared, was unlikely to do.[36] But it was certainly a great day and a great triumph for Catholicism in the West, balanced, as John (inaccurately) believed, in the East by the contemporary conversion of the "Emperor of the Persians."[37]

The power and prestige of Byzantium and its brilliant exploitation of the anti-Arian issue dominate the sixth-century Mediterranean world and some of the more obscure points of the Leovigild-Hermenegild conflict may become clearer if we bear this fact in mind.[37a]

There exists, as is well known, a flat contradiction between the early Spanish and non-Spanish literary sources for the 580s, as regards the rebellion of Hermenegild. The Spanish sources, John of Biclar and Isidore, completely ignore the existence of any religious motives for the civil war. They ignore the conversion of Hermenegild to Catholicism, which is attested by Gregory of Tours and Gregory the Great. John of Biclar, after recounting Hermenegild's marriage in 579 to Ingundis, the daughter of the Frankish King Sigebert, states that Leovigild gave his son "a part of the province [apparently Baetica] to rule." (Hermenegild and his brother Recared had been made "consortes

time. Apart from the *Vitas SS. PP. Emeritensium* (below, n. 78), generally dated in the 630s, the *Dial.* are only used by later Visigothic authors, of whom the earliest is Taio, *Sententiae* (*ca.* 652). Cf. I. M. Gomez, Dictionnaire d'histoire et de géographie ecclésiastiques, xv (Paris, 1961) 410f., for possible use by Braulio.

[34] John, *s. a.* 590, 1 (Mommsen, 219; Campos, 98): "renovans temporibus nostris antiquum principem Constantinum Magnum sanctam synodum Nicaenam sua illustrasse praesentia, nec non et Marcianum Christianissimum imperatorem ..." Cf. *Concilium Toletanum* iii, *PL*, lxxxiv, 345C, the acclamations of the assembled bishops, "Ipse (the king) novarum plebium in Ecclesia catholica conquisitor: Ipse mereatur veraciter apostolicum meritum qui apostolicum implevit officium." For John's view of Arianism cf. Campos, 169.

[35] "Radicitus amputata" (*ibid.*).

[36] *Reg.*, ix, 228.

[37] John, *ibid.* 2. Cf. Campos, 149. There was some foundation for John's optimism about the Persian emperor, who (while in exile) was actually receiving instruction from the Bishop of Melitene in Armenia. Cf. Gegory, *Registrum*, iii, 62, written in 593, when it was clear that the effort would fail. (I owe this reference to Professor Wolff.)

[37a] Otto G. von Simson, *Sacred Fortress, Byzantine Art and Statecraft in Ravenna* (Chicago, 1948) has shown how Justinian used the mosaics of Ravenna to advance his plans for the reintegration of Italy into the Orthodox empire. One can justly speak of a successful blend of "political realism and religious fantasy" (p. 9).

regni" in 573; that is, they had been associated in the royal power.[38]) "Then," continues John, "while Leovigild was reigning peacefully, a domestic quarrel disturbed the land. For the same year [579] his son Hermenegild, by the impulse (*,actione*) of Queen Goiswintha assumed a tyrannical power in Seville ... and made other cities and fortresses rebel against his father. This was a cause of greater destruction for the province of Spain, both for Goths and Romans, than the invasion of foreign enemies."[39]

Under 580 John records an Arian synod in Toledo, which attempted to bring about conversions from Catholicism. He does not connect this event with Hermenegild.[40] Under 582–584 John describes the civil war, Leovigild's successful siege of Seville, his capture of Hermenegild at Cordoba and his exile to Valencia. His murder in Tarragona is recorded under 585. There is still no word of religion.[41] Isidore of Seville, writing *ca.* 624, has two brief references to Hermenegild. In his *Chronicle* he states, "The Goths, divided into two factions by Hermenegild, the son of King Leovigild, were destroyed in mutual slaughter."[42] In the *Historia Gothorum* Hermenegild appears as just one more tyrant, one more opponent of the attempts of Leovigild to achieve the unity of the country. Isidore writes, "Leovigild determined to enlarge the kingdom by war and to increase its power." (He gained many victories, conquering various rebels and defeating the Byzantines.) "Then he besieged and overcame his son Hermenegild, who had set up as a tyrant."[43]

In contrast to this attitude, Gregory the Great, while ignoring Hermenegild's political actions, tells us that Hermenegild died because he refused to receive communion from an Arian bishop. He had previously been "deprived of his kingdom" and thrown into prison by his father because he refused to return to

[38] John. *s. a.* 573, 5 (Mommsen, 213; Campos, 83).

[39] *Ibid.*, 579 (Mommsen, 215; Campos, 89): "Liuuigildus rex ... provinciae partem ad regnandum tribuit ... Liuuigildo ergo quieta pace regnante adversariorum securitatem domestica rixa conturbat. Nam eodem anno filius eius Hermenegildus factione Gosuinthae reginae tyrannidem assumens in Hispali civitate rebellione facta recluditur et alias civitates atque castella secum contra patrem rebellare facit. Quae causa provincia Hispaniae tam Gothis quam Romanis maioris exitii quam adversariorum infestatio fuit." For Goiswintha see "La Conversión" (n. 1 above), 26 n. 12.

[40] See below, n. 121.

[41] John (Mommsen, 216f.; Campos, 91–3). See n. 44 below.

[42] Isid., *Chron.*, 405: "Gothi, per Ermenegildum Leuvigildi filium bifarie divisi mutua caede vastantur."

[43] Idem, *Hist. Goth.*, xlix: "Leuvigildus adepto Hispaniae et Galliae principatum, ampliare regnum bello et augere opes statuit ... (A resumé of John's information) Hermenegildum deinde filium imperiis suis tyrannizantem obsessum exsuperavit." A third Spanish source, the Acts of the Third Council of Toledo (589) contains no clear reference to the events of the preceding decade; though Recared's address and Leander of Seville's homily both contain (*PL*, lxxxiv, 343B, 361A) veiled references to the persecution of the Catholic Church by Leovigild, he is not mentioned by name.

Arianism. His murder was ordered by his father.[44] Gregory of Tours is the only contemporary authority who explicitly states that the cause of the war between Hermenegild and Leovigild was Hermenegild's conversion to Catholicism, an event which closely followed his taking up the government of Baetica.[45] "When Leovigild," Gregory remarks, "heard of [Hermenegild's rebaptism as a Catholic] he began to seek occasion to bring his son to ruin. But Hermenegild learnt his intent and went over to the emperor's side, entering into friendly relations with his prefect," i.e. the governor of the Byzantine province in Southern Spain. Then Leovigild invited his son to a conference. "But his son answered: 'I go not, since thou art mine enemy because I am a Catholic'." In other words Hermenegild would have claimed that he was in danger because of his religious beliefs and was obliged to defend himself.[46]

It is, of course, questionable how far this plea can be received. Religious and political motives were inextricably intertwined in the civil war between Leovigild and Hermenegild and one may agree with Don Manuel Torres that "history will never be able to establish up to what point political motives may have influenced the conversion of the future martyr."[47] The point is, however, that the Spanish sources deliberately ignore a *part* of the truth, the religious side of the quarrel.[48] Why do they do this?

The key to this problem surely lies in the radical change that must have taken place with the conversion of King Recared. It is essential not to forget

[44] *Dial.*, iii, 31 (Moricca, 205): "iratus pater eum privavit regno, ... in arcta illum custodia concludens." Gregory of Tours (*Hist. Franc.*, viii, 28, ix, 16) also states that Leovigild was responsible for his son's death. For a possible corroboration of Gregory the Great's account by a MS. of Isid., *Hist. Goth.*, cf. "La Conversión" (n. 1 above), 29 n. 17.

[45] I have shown in "La Conversión," 29 n. 18, that the *Historia Ps.-Isidoriana* (*MGH, AA*, XI, 385) is totally unreliable. It cannot usefully be adduced as evidence for Leovigild's or Hermenegild's motives or indeed for this period at all.

[46] *Hist. Franc.*, v, 38: "Tandem commotus [Hermenegildus] ad eius (his wife's) praedicationem, conversus est ad legem catholicam, ac dum crismaretur, Iohannis est vocitatus. Quod cum Leuvichildus audisset, coepit causas quaerere, qualiter eum perderet. Ille vero haec intellegens, ad partem se imperatoris iungit, legans cum praefectum eius amicitias... Et ille [Hermenegildus]: 'Non ibo, quia infensus es mihi, pro eo quod sim catholicus'." One might attribute Gregory of Tours' harsh censure of Hermenegild on another occasion to inconsistency (*Hist. Franc.*, vi, 43), but it seems that it was not Hermenegild's resistance to his father that Gregory blamed (cf. v, 38), but plans he is supposed to have formed against his father's life. Gregory is blaming Hermenegild's plan to ambush Leovigild at Osset, near Seville. For further evidence that Hermenegild claimed to be acting in self-defence see n. 108 below.

[47] M. Torres, in *Historia de España*, iii (n. 2 above), 103: "la Historia no logrará nunca aclarir hasta qué punto los motivos políticos pudieron influir en la conversión del luego mártir."

[48] Gregory of Tours' account is reinforced, to some extent, by the coin-legends I discuss below. These coins show, at least, that both sides found religious slogans useful as propaganda.

that almost all our sources for the attitude of the Spanish clergy during the revolt of Hermenegild are later than this event of 587. Before 587 the Catholics of Spain were in the same position as the Gallo-Romans before Vouillé, the African provincials under the Vandals and the Italians under Odoacer and, to a lesser extent, under the Ostrogoths. All these Roman provincials were ruled over for varying periods by barbarians who were also Arian heretics. Their natural friends were, in the first place, the emperor in Constantinople, and, later, the barbarian princes who had become Catholics, the Franks under Clovis and, in Spain, the Sueves in Galicia.[49]

The Byzantines knew perfectly how to make use of the latent antipathy between the Roman provincials and their Arian rulers. In particular, the Byzantines made use of the leaders of the Catholic population, the landed proprietors and the Church. In Africa under the Vandals the Church, in close alliance with the landed proprietors dispossessed by Geiseric, was in a permanent state of opposition: it can be said virtually to have solicited persecution by the Arians, a persecution which was far more serious and continuous than elsewhere.[50] This persecution of Catholics provided a powerful justification for the Byzantine "Reconquest" of Africa in 533, an intervention which the African Catholics had long demanded. The Reconquest began with the revolt of a wealthy Roman landowner in Tripolitana, who called in Byzantine troops. Justinian, hesitating as to whether or not to intervene, was promised divine aid by a bishop who recounted a well-timed vision.[51] Later, Justinian tried to invoke the motive of orthodoxy to persuade the Catholic Franks to join him against the Ostrogoths.[52] But the surest allies of the Byzantines in Italy were the Church and the senatorial nobility; the latter controlled and could arm hordes of peasants during the greatest crisis of the Ostrogothic war.[53]

Seen against the background of contemporary events in Africa and Italy the conflict between Hermenegild and his father and the respective attitudes of Spanish and non-Spanish authors become more intelligible. One should also recall the recent and incomplete character of the Visigothic occupation of

[49] For Hermenegild and the Franks and Sueves cf. below, n. 64.

[50] Cf. Courtois, *Les Vandales* (n. 27 above), 286–310; idem, *Victor de Vita* (n. 30), *passim*. For an author like Victor of Vita the cause of African Catholicism was inseparable from that of Roman civilisation. Arians = barbarians. Cf. Victor, *Hist*, iii, 62 f. (Petschenig, 102 f.).

[51] Procopius, *Bellum Vand.*, I, x, 19, 22. See now W. E. Kaegi, "Arianism and the Byzantine Army in Africa", *Traditio*, xxi (1965), 32–53, esp. 32–45.

[52] Idem, *Bellum Goth.*, I, v, 9: "It is proper that you should join with us in waging this war, which is rendered yours as well as ours not only by the Orthodox Faith, which rejects the opinions of the Arians," but also by a common enmity against the Goths (H. B. Dewing, Loeb).

[53] Cf. S. Mazzarino, in *Il Passaggio dall'antichità al medioevo in Occidente* = *Settimane di Studio*, ix (Spoleto, 1962), 415 f.

Spain. By the time of the Byzantine intervention in Spain in 552 the Visigoths had been settled for some generations in the Meseta of Castille and had succeeded in conquering South-Eastern Spain but the province of Baetica (Andalusia) and probably part of Lusitania remained independent. There is, at least, no evidence in our scanty sources of Gothic occupation and it is significant that the papacy, in 521, should have appointed a separate Vicar of the Apostolic See, the Metropolitan of Seville, "for Baetica and the province of Lusitania," whereas Caesarius of Arles had been Vicar "in the provinces of Gaul and Spain" from 514. The South of Spain was apparently controlled by the local aristocracy, in collaboration with the episcopate.[54] It was the attempt of the Visigoths, first possibly under Theudisclus (548–49) and later under Agila (549–54), to conquer the South which provoked an appeal to Byzantium, then triumphant over the Vandals and engaged in a long-drawn out struggle with the Ostrogoths in Italy.

This appeal was made by a Gothic noble, Athanagild, who was probably in alliance with the Hispano-Roman provincials, provoked by King Agila's anti-Catholic and expansionist policy.[55] The Byzantines were always delighted to make use of rebellious barbarians. Their official reasons for intervening in Africa and Italy had not only been religious: they had also claimed to intervene on one side of a dynastic dispute. Later one finds the same attempt to use native Lombard pretenders to divide and weaken resistance.[56]

The choice of a general to lead the expeditionary force to Spain in 552 is significant. The Patrian Liberius was a man of great age and experience, a member of the Italian Senatorial nobility who had served under Theodoric as Prefect of the Gauls and had some previous knowledge of Spain. Justinian's choice of Liberius implies that the emperor understood that the expedition to Spain must rely largely on the help of "collaborators."[57] In fact the Byzantines succeeded in defeating King Agila. Athanagild succeeded to the Visigothic throne but he was unable to expel the Byzantines, who secured their hold on the

[54] *PL*, lxxxiv, 827f. Cf. Duchesne, *op. cit.*, 553–55; R. d'Abadal y de Vinyals, *Del Reino de Tolosa al Reino de Toledo* (Madrid, 1960), 57f. The commission of 521 may be compared to an earlier commission (not limited to specific provinces) given to Bishop Zeno of Merida (*fl.* 468–483). Zeno was associated, however, with the Visigothic King Euric; cf. J. Vives, in *Römische Quartalschrift*, xlvi (1938), 57–61; *PL*, lviii, 35.

[55] Theudisclus was murdered at Seville, but probably in the main for non-political reasons, though he had prepared "necem multorum." Agila "adversus Cordubensem urbem praelium movens," profaned the tomb of St Acisclus. He was heavily defeated by the local population. Isid., *Hist. Goth.*, xlivf. Cf. Gregory of Tours, *Hist. Franc.*, iv, 5; Abadal, 64f.

[56] Courtois, *Les Vandales*, 268f.; Bury, *op. cit.*, ii, 160f.; Goffart, *art. cit.*, 97f. One reason why Byzantium decided to send an expeditionary force to Spain may have been to prevent further attacks on Byzantine North Africa, such as that made by King Theudis in the 540s (Isid., *Hist. Goth.*, xlii).

[57] For Liberius cf. Stroheker, *art. cit.* (n. 1), 254.

Mediterranean coast from Cartagena to Gibraltar and inland to Cordoba and Seville.[58] Athanagild (554–567) and his greater successor, Leovigild (569–586), were able to take some cities from the Byzantines but they still preserved their Mediterranean ports at the time of Hermenegild's conversion in 579. Seville, the capital of the province Leovigild gave Hermenegild to rule, had only recently come under Visigothic control and the Visigothic conquest of the South from the Byzantines had been bitterly resisted by the Hispano-Roman population.[59] When Hermenegild became a Catholic it was natural for him to look for support to the Church and the provincial aristocracy, which, until recently, had been independent. His appeal to Byzantium for aid followed a pattern set by Athanagild and, outside, Spain, by other barbarian princes.[60] The Byzantines were delighted to respond to the appeal. Burdened with wars elsewhere – in North Africa, Italy, on the Danube and against the Persians – they had been unable to prevent Leovigild's advance. Their only chance in Spain was to use another pretender, and what better pretender than the king's son, a Catholic, himself associated in the throne and already in control of the traditionally independent South?[61] At the same time Hermenegild appealed to the Sueves in Galicia (converted to Catholicism *ca.* 560 and traditional enemies of the Visigoths) and probably also to the Frankish relations of his wife, Ingundis.[62]

But the Emperor Tiberius (578–582) was not able to send effective aid and his successor, Maurice, withdrew from this new commitment. It has been suggested that his withdrawal was wise.[63] It meant, however, the loss of the best chance open to the empire in Spain. Leovigild was able to buy off the Byzantines and the Frankish and Suevic attempts to intervene were late and ineffective.[64] That Hermenegild, with little outside aid, contrived to resist

[58] Isid., *Hist. Goth.*, xlvif. The most elaborate study of Byzantine Spain is by P. Goubert, *Études Byzantines*, ii (1944), 5–78; iii (1945), 127–143; iv (1946), 71–133. Cf. Stroheker, 255–57, 272–4 (he shows that the empire probably never possessed Algarve). The map in Menéndez Pidal, *Historia de España*, iii (after p. 96) needs some correction.

[59] This can, I think, be deduced from the following passages of John of Biclar. For 572 he records (Mommsen, 213; Campos, 82): "Liuuigildus rex Cordubam civitatem *diu Gothis rebellem* nocte occupat et caesis hostibus propriam facit multasque urbes et castella *interfecta rusticorum multitudine* in Gothorum dominium revocat," and, for 577 (Mommsen, 215; Campos, 87): "... non multo post *rustici rebellantes* a Gothis opprimuntur et post haec integra a Gothis possidetur Orospeda." See also *s.a.* 573, 5, 575, 2. Resistance is naturally described as rebellion. Cp. the resistance of the Spanish provincials to the Goths in the late fifth and early sixth centuries (cf. Abadal, *op. cit.*, 43–7) and to Agila (n. 55 above).

[60] See above and n. 56.

[61] See n. 38 above. Isid., *Chron.*, 402f., evidently saw the relation between the attacks on the empire in Italy and its weakness in Spain.

[62] See Torres, in Menéndez Pidal, *op. cit.*, 105f. For an embassy from the Sueves to Burgundy in 580 cf. Gregory, v. 41.

[63] So Goffart, 74.

[64] Torres, *ibid.*; Thompson, *art. cit.* (n. 1), 14f.

until 584 shows that he possessed considerable support in the local population, as well as from a party of the Visigothic nobility, always ready to turn against a strong king such as Leovigild.[65] During these years Leovigild was attempting to convert Catholics to Arianism, although apparently more by means of bribes than by force.[66] One of the leading Spanish bishops, Leander of Seville, who had received Hermenegild into the Church, was in Constantinople, hoping to gain further support from the emperor for his convert.[67] Up to this time the situtation was reasonably clear. Hermenegild, converted to Catholicism and the heir to the throne, was engaged in a struggle with his father, the Arian ruler of Spain. In this struggle he could not fail to enjoy the support of the Church and the Hispano-Roman aristocracy, at least in the South. There the Church, like the papacy in Italy, moved within the orbit of Byzantium, for Catholics living under Arian kings the only legitimate source of political authority.[68]

The conversion in 587 of Hermenegild's brother, Recared, completely changed the situation. While Gregory the Great, who became pope in 590, continued to remember Hermenegild as a deserving Catholic prince and was to describe his death as a martyrdom for the Faith, in Spain the aspect of truth had altered. The Spanish historians who deliberately suppressed any mention of Hermenegild's Catholicism, John, Abbot of Biclar and later Bishop of Gerona, and Isidore, Metropolitan of Seville, were statesmen, preoccupied, inevitably, with the unity of Spain, so recently achieved by the efforts of Leovigild and Recared. This unity was too precious and too incomplete to be endangered by inconvenient memories. That it had been achieved at all was astonishing. The unstable Visigothic kingdom of the first half of the sixth century, menaced by religious dissension, attacked from outside by Franks, Byzantines and Sueves, whose internal history consisted principally in the assassinations of its kings,[69] with no permanent institutions strong

65 According to Gregory of Tours (*Hist. Franc.*, vi, 43) Hermenegild was followed by "many thousands." John of Biclar, *s. a.* 579 and 583, confirms the seriousness of the struggle, as does Isidore (n. 42 above). 66 See nn. 73, 121 below.

67 Isidore, *De viris*, xxviii (Codoñer, 149f.; *PL*, lxxxiii, 1103B) records his elder brother Leander's "exile," without saying why or where he was exiled. That he was in Constantinople is stated by Gregory the Great, *Reg.*, v, 53a, where his "legatio pro causis fidei Wisigotharum" is mentioned. Cf. also a letter of Licinian of Cartagena (whose see was in Byzantine Spain) to Gregory, *ca.* 595, recording Leander's return from his mission ("remeans de urbe regia"), some years before (ed. J. Madoz, *Liciniano de Cartagena y sus cartas* [Madrid, 1946], 92; *MGH, Epist.*, i, 60). On the interpretation of Leander's mission cf. Goffart, *art. cit.* (n. 24), 89f. and n. 71.

68 See n. 10 above. For the importance of Byzantine recognition of Clovis cf. recently J. M. Wallace-Hadrill, *The Long-Haired Kings and other studies in Frankish History* (London, 1962), 175–77, 184f. There were, of course, a number of Hispano-Romans in the service of Leovigild (cf. Thompson, 12).

69 Gregory of Tours, *Hist. Franc.*, iii, 30, remarks on the "custom" of the Goths of

enough to weld the different races together, survived, alone of the old type of German state, principally because Leovigild and Recared knew how to learn from their enemies and how to make use of Byzantine institutions and ideas. Leovigild, in his association of his sons in the throne (to preserve continuity and diminish the danger of assassination), in his founding and fortifying of new cities, his creation of a palatine office, modelled on the imperial consistory, his deliberate adoption of Byzantine pomp and ceremonial and his adaptation of Byzantine Court art and forms of coinage, created another, an alternative Byzantium in the West.[70] Internal reorganisation was accompanied by the crushing of external opposition and the removal of the old prohibition of marriage between Romans and Goths.[71]

Leovigild saw that religious unity was necessary. He alone, among Arian barbarian rulers, attempted a compromise solution by which conversion from Catholicism would be facilitated. This solution was a response to Hermenegild's aggressive Catholicism.[72] Leovigild's religious policy was at first very successful but its eventual failure led to the choice by his younger son, Recared, of the opposite answer to the problem, the adoption by the Arian king of the religion of the majority of the country.[73]

By his conversion to Catholicism Recared removed all reason or excuse for Byzantine intervention. He and his successors achieved in Spain a close harmony of Church and State, resembling that existing in Constantinople. But the situation, though satisfactory, might not last. The Third Council of Toledo in 589 celebrated a union of interests rather than of races, interests which might again divide. The Visigoths preserved their hegemony, the Hispano-Roman aristocracy its wealth and power, the Church was able to recover and apparently increase the privileged position it had enjoyed under the Christian Empire.

The fear of rebellion and the desire to avoid for the Church any appearance of complicity in a recent revolt, much more since this had been supported by the Byzantines, must have weighed heavily with John and Isidore. John of Biclar wrote during the reign of Recared.[74] He was bound to remember Re-

assassinating their kings. In fact four successive kings, from Amalaric to Agila, were assassinated (Isid., *Hist. Goth.*, xl, xliiif., xlvi).

[70] See Stroheker, *art. cit.* (n. 1), 265–67, and the references there given.

[71] Cf. Thompson, 33, for the gradual fusion of Romans and Goths.

[72] See below and n. 121.

[73] Gregory of Tours, vi, 18, believed that there were only "a few" Catholics left in Spain. Cf. Thompson, 20 and n. 81. For Leovigild's anti-Catholic measures cf. Thompson, 15–22, and my comments, "La Conversión," 31–33. For Recared's conversion cf. Gregory, ix, 15.

[74] The *Chronicon* contains references to events of 602 but these apparently derive from a revision of the work, probably due to a monk of Biclar (= Béjar in Lusitania). Cf. M. C. Díaz y Díaz, *Analecta sacra Tarraconensia*, xxxv (1962), 63–5. The work was probably finished in 590 because of John's elevation to the see of Gerona, which he already occupied in 592 (*PL*, lxxxiv, 318C).

cared's support of his father against Hermenegild and that Recared's succession and reign were possible because of Hermenegild's murder the year before Leovigild's death.[75] These considerations, together with his evident admiration for a great king of his own Gothic race, perhaps explain why John avoids, as far as possible, speaking any ill of Leovigild – or any good at all of Hermenegild.[76]

John of Biclar, followed by Isidore, sees in Hermenegild only the rebel.[77] The deliberate omission of Hermenegild's name in the anonymous *Lives of the Holy Fathers of Merida* is mainly interesting as representing the official version – perhaps one should say the official suppression – of history, as accepted by an uncritical provincial author several decades after the events had taken place.[78] It is interesting that, despite the successful imposition of the "official" view of Hermenegild as a mere rebel on most of our Spanish sources, he was seen as a martyr by one late seventh-century Spaniard, the strange hermit and poet, Valerius of Bierzo.[79] The same tradition was found in the (now lost) Ms. Aemilianensis of the *Epitome Ovetensis* of 881.[80]

By the conversion the Visigothic Crown gained the support of the Church and of the educated classes in general. Recognised by the papacy, the change was not immediately recognised by Byzantium. In 589 or 590 a Byzantine governor of Cartagena could still refer in an inscription to the Visigoths as "barbarian foes", but within a few decades his successor was appealing to King Sisebut as to a fellow Christian.[81] Whether the Spanish Church and Hispano-Roman culture were, in the end, to gain as much from the change as the Crown is another question and one that cannot be answered here. One can point,

[75] I do not wish to imply that Recared was responsible for Hermenegild's death – the responsibility was Leovigild's (cf. n. 44 above), but it must have been obvious that it was Recared who principally benefited from it. See "La Conversión," 26 n. 11.

[76] Cf. "La Conversión," 26 n. 12. For John's admiration of Leovigild cf. *s. a.* 569, 4 (Mommsen, 212; Campos, 80); cf. Isidore, *Hist. Goth.*, xlix.

[77] On Isidore's attitude cf. now H. Messmer, *Hispania-Idee und Gotenmythos* (Zürich, 1960), 132–7. M. C. Díaz y Díaz, "La leyenda 'A deo vita' de una moneda de Ermenegildo," *Analecta sacra Tarraconensia*, xxxi (1958), 267 n. 27, has recently pointed to an important variant in a Spanish MS. of Isidore, *Hist. Goth.* (MS. 'H' of Mommsen), which alludes clearly to the conversion of Hermenegild. For the dates of the *Chronicon* and the *Hist. Goth.* (624) cf. J. A. de Aldama, in *Miscellanea Isidoriana* (Rome, 1936), 63.

[78] *Vitas SS. Patrum Emeritensium*, v, 9, 4, ed. J. N. Garvin (Washington, 1946), 230, in describing Recared's conversion, quotes from Gregory, *Dialogi*, iii, 31 (see n. 44 above) but substitutes "Christum dominum" for Gregory's "fratrem martyrem," as Recared's model.

[79] Valerius, *De vana saeculi sapientia*, viii (*PL*, lxxxvii, 426D). Valerius does not appear to depend on Gregory the Great but he is not a very reliable source (cf. Duchesne, *L'Église au VIe siècle*, 573 f.).

[80] *MGH, AA*, XI, 288, *apparatus*.

[81] J. Vives, *Inscripciones cristianas de la España romana y visigoda* (Barcelona, 1942), 126 (no. 362); cp. the letter of the Patrician Caesarius to Sisebut (*MGH, Epist.*, iii, ed. Gundlach, 663 f.); cf. Stroheker, *art. cit.* (n. 1), 261.

certainly, to the Isidorian "renaissance," to the real accomplishments of Spanish art and letters in the seventh century.[82] On the other hand it is undeniable that, as, from 589 onwards, the Spanish Church became closely integrated with the State, it grew into a narrow isolationism, marked by increasing suspicion of the papacy. Toledo had become the Spanish Byzantium, almost the Spanish Rome.[83] It is difficult to say whether the State outdid the Church in the ugly zeal with which both Church and State pushed forward the anti-Jewish legislation that mars the Visigothic legal code and the Acts of the later Councils of Toledo.[84] The Church by this time had virtually become a department of the State. With a convenient servility it endorsed as the decree of heaven each successful "putsch" of the Visigothic nobility.[85] For this compliance, as for the legislation against the Jews, there were doubtless, as for most other things in Spain, Byzantine precedents.[86]

The 'artificial and ephemeral' Byzantinism of Leovigild and Recared was not deeply enough rooted, however, to endure. It is not enough, as M. Marrou has recently remarked, to wish to be Byzantine. The Visigoths lacked the solid armature of the empire. Their state, despite its Roman conception of "utilitas publica" and its recognition (unusual in barbarian kingdoms) of a division between the private possessions of the king and those of the Crown,

[82] See J. Fontaine, *Isidore de Séville et la culture classique dans l'Espagne wisigothique*, 2 vols. (Paris, 1959); H. Schlunk, "Arte Visigodo," *Ars Hispaniae*, ii (Madrid, 1947), 227–323.

[83] On the Spanish attitude towards Byzantium *saec.* VII cf. Fontaine, ii, 851. For Spanish relations with Rome see Lacarra, *art. cit.* (n. 11), 353–84, and the "Discussione," 407–412. He concludes (p. 384): "If the Visigothic Church did not separate itself in its dogmatic principles from the Universal Church and did not formally challenge the authority of the pope, in fact it lived enclosed in itself. It was not the object of special solicitude from Rome, nor did it receive with pleasure the observations it was occasionally sent." For a somewhat more favourable view cf. F. X. Murphy, *Mélanges J. de Ghellinck*, i (Gembloux, 1951), 361–73.

[84] See S. Katz, *The Jews in the Visigothic and Frankish Kingdoms of Spain and Gaul* (Cambridge, Mass., 1937), and the reflections of two Catholic historians, A. K. Ziegler, *Church and State in Visigothic Spain* (Washington, 1930), 197–99, and, more recently, A. Echánove, "Precisiones acerca de la legislación conciliar toledana sobre los judíos," *Hispania Sacra*, xiv (1961), 259–79. Cf. also B. Blumenkranz, *Juifs et chrétiens dans le monde occidental, 430–1096* (Paris, 1960), 105–34; E. A. Thompson, in *Nottingham Mediaeval Studies*, vii (1963), 29–32.

[85] Cf. Ziegler, 89–133, who considers, however, that the bishops had no other choice, and the remarks of C. Sánchez-Albornoz, *Cuadernos de historia de España*, v (1946), 86 n. 260.

[86] For a comparison between the role of the Archbishop of Toledo, as Primate of Spain, and that of the Patriarch of Constantinople cf. Lacarra, 375–78. The anti-Jewish measures of the Emperor Heraclius are sometimes supposed to have inspired those of Sisebut in 613 but Heraclius' measures appear to have come later, in 632 (Blumenkranz, 100 n. 143). However, Justinian had already legislated against the Jews and esp. the Samaritans (Ch. Diehl, *op. cit.* [n. 26 above], 328f.).

lacked a civil service which could resist the advance of feudalism.[87] Their strength sapped by the endless strife between great noble families, the Visigoths succombed to the first external threat of any importance.

The beginnings of the nationalism I have referred to are, I would suggest, visible in the Spanish chroniclers I have discussed. The defeat of Hermenegild made possible, for a time, a strengthening of the Visigothic kingdom. This led to the rise of a strong national self-consciousness, of which the most obvious propaganda manifesto is the *Laus Spaniae* of Isidore of Seville.[88] One would not wish to romanticize the figure of Hermenegild. He was one of a type of barbarian pretenders at the service of a would-be universal empire and an international, anti-Arian Church. It is impossible to separate in Hermenegild the religious and the political, the power grab and the pious conviction. It is ironical, however, that the knowledge of his undoubted Catholicism should have been suppressed in Spain by the Church for which he had claimed to be fighting and that that Church's greatest representative, Isidore of Seville, should have shared in the suppression of the truth, in the interest of the unity of the Kingdom.

II. Religious Formulas in the Coins of Leovigild and Hermenegild[89]

It may seem curious that no historian (as far as I know) has yet drawn adequate attention to the religious formulas in Leovigild's coins ("Cum Deo . . .") and connected them with Hermenegild's revolt and in particular with Herme-

[87] H-I. Marrou, in *Il Passaggio* (n. 53 above), 610; Stroheker, 270; C. Sánchez-Albornoz, e.g. in *I Problemi della civiltà carolingia = Settimane di Studio*, i (Spoleto, 1954), 109–126.

[88] Text in *MGH, AA*, XI, 267. The word "imperium" is here first applied to Spain. For the revival in Asturias and León of the "imperial" pretensions of the Visigoths – shown also by their use of the title "Flavius," etc. – cf. J. López Ortiz, in *Escorial*, vi, 15 (1942), 43–70, and R. Menéndez Pidal, *El imperio hispánico y los cinco reinos* (Madrid, 1950). The word "nationalist" can, of course, only be used in a qualified sense. Cf. the works cited in *Isidoriana* (León, 1961), 59 and n. 123. For continued interest in Byzantium, shown in 8th century Spanish chronicles, see C. E. Dubler, in *Al-Andalus*, xi (1946), 283–349, esp. 326–333.

[89] The interpretation and especially the dating of these coins involves particular technical problems that can obviously only be dealt with by a numismatist. In the discussion that follows I have been much helped by Mr. Philip Grierson, who worked independently over the material some years ago and who has very kindly allowed me to read and quote from the draft of a relevant chapter in a forthcoming book he is preparing on the pre-regal Visigothic coinage and the circumstances of the monetary reforms of Leovigild. It need hardly be said that I am alone responsible for any errors that may be found in this article. I shall refer throughout to the fundamental work on later Visigothic coinage, G. C. Miles, *The Coinage of the Visigoths of Spain Leovigild to Achila II = Hispanic Numismatic Series*, ii (New York, 1952), cited henceforth as Miles.

negild's celebrated coin, with the legend "Ermenegildi / regi a Deo vita." It is true that some scholars in the past have displayed an exaggerated tendency to make every Visigothic coin into a commemorative medal.[90] But though one must obviously proceed with caution, there can be no doubt that there are *some* Visigothic coins that were intended to be commemorative medals recording historical events. These Visigothic coins preserve some characteristics of the coinage of antiquity and particularly of the late Roman Empire. The ancient coin constituted, it has been said, "in a far higher degree than the modern, an expression of the State in its religious and symbolical aspect."[91] an instrument, in other words, of propaganda. The same thing is true of some coins of Leovigild and Hermenegild. One can cite the examples of Leovigild's coins recording the taking of Seville, Italica, Rosas and Cordoba.

The coins of Leovigild which I propose to study here, in relation to Hermenegild's coin "regi a Deo vita," are the four that bear religious formulas. Two of them were issued at Seville, one at nearby Italica and one at Rosas (Roda), in Catalonia. These coins of Leovigild and Hermenegild bear religious formulas which are not found in the rest of the Visigothic coinage. Leovigild issued two further commemorative coins in connection with his war against Hermenegild, "Cordoba bis optinuit" (584) and "Emerita Victoria" (582?), neither with legends religious in character.[92] As is well known many forgeries of Visigothic coins exist. There are few genuine coins of Hermenegild. Dr Miles recognised three with the religious legend as authentic but one of them he regarded as suspicious and Mr Philip Grierson, who has since been able to examine it, has no hesitation in regarding it as false.[93] There appears to be little doubt that three of the four religious legends of Leovigild are genuine, although two of these three – those of Italica and Roda – are each of them only represented by one coin known to survive.[94] Dr Miles believes that the other unique coin, "Cum Deo Spali adquisita," is genuine, but says "one must admit the possibility of its being a forgery."[95]

[90] See especially A. Fernández Guerra et al., *Historia de España desde la invasión de los pueblos germánicos hasta la ruina de la monarquía visigoda* (Madrid, 1891).

[91] H. Mattingly, *Cambridge Ancient History*, xii (Cambridge, 1939), 714.

[92] Miles, 190, 194f., and below, n. 123.

[93] Miles, 199f. P. Grierson, *Numismatic Chronicle*, 6th Series, xiii (1953), 80, rejects the John Hopkins coin (Miles, 200), while retaining as authentic the coins in the British Museum (Miles, Plate III, no. 14) and that listed by F. Mateu y Llopis, *Catálogo de las monedas previsigodas y visigodas del Gabinete Numismático del Museo Arqueológico Nacional* (Madrid, 1936), Plate VII, no. 73 and p. 228.

[94] See Miles, 192 and 185, Plates III, 1 and II, 6. The coin of Italica is in the collection of the Hispanic Society of America; that of Roda was formerly in the collection of Don Manuel Vidal Quadras y Ramón and is now in Paris (Miles, 18f.).

[95] Miles, 191 and Plate II, 17. The coin is apparently in the Museu Municipal at Lisbon. F. Mateu y Llopis, *Revista de Archivos, Bibliotecas y Museos*, lxi (1955), 314 n. 34, following Don Pio Beltrán, believes it to be a forgery.

The question of the *dates* of these coins is clearly of crucial importance. From the *external* evidence of contemporary history it seems clear that the coin of Italica, "Cum De(o) o(btinuit) Etalica," should be dated to 583, for the fortification of Italica preceded the taking of Seville and this, in its turn, preceded the capture of Hermenegild at Cordoba, an event Professor Thompson has shown should be dated February 584.[96] The first coin celebrating the fall of Seville, "Cum D(e)o optinuit Spali", is presumably of 583 or 584; it was succeeded by another type with the same legend but with a facing bust replacing the cross-on-steps. The coin "Cum Deo Spali adquisita" still has the cross-on-steps, so that, if genuine, it would also be of 584, the date of the fall of Cordoba, commemorated by what is generally taken to be the first issue of the new type with two facing busts.[97]

There remains the coin of Rosas. This coin, with the legend "Cum D(e)o i(ntravit) Roda," cannot be so easily dated. On the *internal* evidence of type evolution, which we shall turn to in a moment, Miles dates it to "between 578 and *ca*. 583, possibly 581, the year of Leovigild's campaign against the Basques."[98] We have no ground, however, for supposing the Basques inhabited Northern Catalonia, where Rosas is situated. John of Biclar, writing of 581, records, "Leovigild occupies a part of Vasconia and founded a city, called Victoria."[99] Leovigild's campaign in 581 was clearly confined to the *Western* end of the Pyrenees. Fernández Guerra supposes the Rosas coin commemorated the suppression of a rebellion in the Narbonense in 578. But no such rebellion as Fernández Guerra postulates is known to us from the contemporary sources.[100] Early in 585, on the other hand, there is contemporary evidence for a war with the Franks – the *only* such evidence in Leovigild's reign. The Narbonense was invaded by Franks and had to be "liberated" by Recared, acting for his father.[101] Rosas is on the Mediterranean coast, very near to the border of the Narbonense. Is it not probable that the coin refers to this campaign?[102] We shall see presently the importance of this point.

From the *external* evidence, then, the three or four religious coin-legends of Leovigild can most probably be dated to 583–85. It is more difficult to date from external evidence the coin "regi a Deo vita" of Hermenegild. On this

[96] Thompson, *art. cit.* (n. 1), 14, based on indications in Gregory of Tours. For a note on John of Biclar's dating cf. "La Conversión," 38 n. 38.

[97] So Miles, 45; cf. below, p. 505.

[98] Miles, 85. See below, n. 114.

[99] John, *s. a.* 581, 3 (Mommsen, 216; Campos, 90): "Liuuigildus rex partem Vasconiae occupat et civitatem, quae Victoriacum nuncupatur, condidit."

[100] Fernández Guerra, *op. cit.* (n. 90), i, 335 f. Cf. M. Torres, in Menéndez Pidal, *op. cit.* (n. 2), 101 f.

[101] John of Biclar, *s. a.* 585, 4 (Mommsen, 217; Campos, 93). See also Gregory of Tours, *Hist. Franc.*, viii, 30.

[102] The same view was already briefly indicated by F. Mateu y Llopis, *Analecta sacra Tarraconensia*, xix (1946), 13. The view of Fernández Guerra is still maintained by L. G. de Valdeavellano, *Historia de España*, i² (Madrid, 1955), 289.

coin we have recently had the important article of Professor M. C. Díaz y Díaz. Dr. Mateu y Llopis, in various publications, had seen in this coin an "allusion to the precarious state of the monarch [scil. Hermenegild] in Seville or in Córdoba, besieged by his father, i.e., about 583."[103] Díaz y Díaz, on the other hand, holds the coin "reproduces the religious acclamation, which, perhaps in the moment of his anointing and consecration as King, he received from the clergy." Díaz produces an interesting parallel between the acclamation on this coin, "a Deo vita," and those found in the Acts of the Third Council of Toledo in 589, directed to Hermenegild's younger brother, Recared.[104]. In order to maintain the parallel he returns to the traditional view that the "regi" of the coin is in the dative and that the formula should accordingly be translated "life to the King from God." In a reply to this article, Dr José Vives, on the other hand, maintains the view put forward before by him and adopted by Mateu y Llopis, that "regi" is a continuation of the "Ermenegildi" of the obverse and is, therefore, in the *genitive* and stands for "regis."[105] Dr Vives holds that his criticism of Díaz y Díaz's article does not affect the historical interpretation of the coin the latter has put forward.

Mr Grierson, independently of Díaz y Díaz, in his chapter on the coinage reforms of Leovigild, written in 1954, also saw the Hermenegild coin-legend as deriving from one of the acclamations of the coronation ritual. "The phrase *N* ... *regi vita*," to quote his own words, "is a regular feature of all medieval rituals, which go back to the formal acclamations of late Roman times. The idea of using such a phrase on the coinage came perhaps from North Africa, where 'vita' had appeared on the bronze of Carthage in the reign of Justin II, but the practice later spread to Constantinople itself, where "multos an(nos)," another of the ritual acclamations, was used on the gold of the late seventh and early eighth centuries."[106] "Vita" does not occur on coins earlier than the reign of Justin II (565–78), and a North African parallel so close in time to Hermenegild greatly reinforces Díaz y Díaz's case for the connection between Hermenegild's coin and his coronation, a connection which certainly seems to provide the best explanation as yet put forward for the coin-legend, unique in Visigothic Spain.[107] Díaz dates the coronation tentatively to 582 but this

[103] Mateu y Llopis, *Analecta sacra Tarraconensia*, xiv (1941), 83, also in *Catálogo* (n. 93 above), 228. [104] Díaz y Díaz, *art. cit.* (n. 77 above), 264, 267f.

[105] *Analecta sacra Tarraconensia*, xxxii (1959), 31–4.

[106] Cf. W. Wroth, *Catalogue of the Imperial Byzantine Coins in the British Museum*, i (London, 1908), 99–101; ii, 332, 335, 358f. For the "vita" acclamation see also E. Petersen, *Heis Theos, epigraphische, formgeschichtliche und religionsgeschichtliche Untersuchungen* (Göttingen, 1926), esp. 144 n. 2.

[107] The bronze coin of Byzantine Carthage, with the legend (Wroth, i, 99): "Dni Iustino et Sofi[e] Au[gustis]" (obverse), and, in the exergue, "Vita," also provides an example of a coin with the names of the rulers in the dative. However, it is difficult to see "Ermenegildi" as a barbarous dative. Cf. "La Conversión," 40 n. 49.

seems to me too late. It is clear that Hermenegild's conversion had taken place at least as early as 580. His coronation should probably be dated to the same year and with it the famous coin.[108]

After examining the external evidence we have, then, the following position with regard to the four or five types of coin with religious formulas. Hermenegild's is the earliest, most probably issued in 580, at latest in 581.[109] Leovigild's are later – they range between 583 and 585. Let us look now at the *internal* evidence for the dates of the coins deducible from a study of the evolution of types. It will be simplest to begin with Miles' discussion of this subject,[110] taking into account Mr Grierson's interpretation of the sequence of types. Four series of coins succeeded each other. We may tabulate them as follows:

1. The first type struck in Leovigild's reign, as by earlier kings, is that of the "pseudo-imperial coins with blundered imperial legends, profile bust and stylized Victory reverse."[111]

2. These were succeeded by Leovigild's second series, 'mintless' coins, with the same types as the pseudo-imperial coins but "with the king's name substituted for part or all of the imperial legend." Miles argues we should date these 'mintless' issues to the period 568–78.

3. The third type, with a reverse bearing a cross on four (or three) steps (and with mint names) cannot be earlier than 578 when this use of the cross was adopted by the Byzantine Emperor Tiberius II. Miles supposes that Leovigild was striking coins with this reverse at a number of mints in Northern and Southern Spain from 579–584 "at the latest."

4. The fourth type, with the facing busts, was "introduced at Cordoba in 584 ... and [almost] all mints issued coins with facing busts after abandoning the cross-on-steps type. Two years (584–586) is the minimum we can allow for the types with facing busts." Miles believes this type may have been introduced after the suppression of Hermenegild's rebellion in 584, in recognition of Recared's "now exclusive position as heir to the throne."[112]

[108] Díaz y Díaz, *art. cit.*, 269 n. 37. One cannot avoid the "eodem anno" of John of Biclar, referring to Hermenegild's marriage and rebellion (n. 39 above). Hermenegild's conversion certainly preceded his revolt (cf. n. 46 above). Cf. the inscription with the reference to the second year of Hermenegild (Vives, *op. cit.*, n. 81, 127, no. 364): "anno feliciter secundo regni domini nostri Erminigildi regis, quem persequitur genetor su(u)s dom(inus) Liuuigildus rex in cibitate Ispa(li) indi(c)tione" (following the correction of J. Mallon, *Memorias de los Museos Arqueológicos Provinciales*, ix-x [1948–49], 320-28). Mallon has shown that the inscription lacks the last two words after "indi(c)tione," and that these words would most probably have been "tercia decima," "quarta decima" or "quinta decima," i. e. 580, 581 or 582. This indicates that Hermenegild's reign was considered to begin *at latest* in 581. Mallon notes that the inscription is dated in the Byzantine manner, yet another sign of Byzantine influence in the Baetica of Hermenegild.

[109] See the preceding note. [110] Miles, 43–50.

[111] Here, and in the next sentence, I quote the unpublished work of Mr. Grierson.

[112] Miles, 45 f.

If we look at the five coin-legends that concern us here we can see that Hermenegild's religious legend, "regi a Deo vita" together(with his, probably later, "regi incliti") appears on the *second* type of coin listed, that with a profile bust on the obverse and a Victory on the reverse. Leovigild's first three – or four – "Cum Deo" issues, from Italica, Seville and Rosas, represent part of the *third* series. Leovigild's last (fourth) series includes a reissue of "Cum Deo optinuit Spali," with facing bust on obverse and reverse. Since the relative order of succession of these series is assured it is at once evident that our arguments from external evidence are confirmed and that Hermenegild's coin is *prior* to Leovigild's religious legends. Some of the limiting dates proposed by Miles for these series seem, however, less certain than their relative order and certain criticisms of these dates have been advanced. The beginnings of the last series seems easiest to date. Don Pio Beltrán, in a recent article, agrees that the type with two facing busts implies the association of Recared as king and was created in 584. But he also observes that one cannot tell whether all mints followed the same rhythm or began at one and the same time to mint the same type.[113] This being so, the change, e.g., at Rosas, from Leovigild's third to his fourth series might well take place later than at Seville, far nearer to Cordoba, the first place where we know facing busts were introduced. This would corroborate our suggested dating of the Rosas "Cum Deo" coin as late as 585.[114]

We have no means of dating exactly the beginning of either the second or the third series, with, respectively, a Victory and a cross-on-steps on the reverse. The latter cannot, as has been noted, be *earlier* than 578. We have argued above that Hermenegild's coin with its religious legend is associated with his coronation and should probably be dated 580. Beltrán believes Hermenegild was imitating Leovigild's second series of 'mintless' coins, already in circulation.[115] If this was so, he thinks it probable that Leovigild may have reacted, first with the coin bearing a bust on the obverse and a Victory on the reverse, as on the 'mintless' series, but this time with "Tole-to rex" on the reverse;[116] and secondly with the Byzantine cross-on-steps type which accompanies the religious formula "Cum Deo" at Italica, Seville and Rosas. The third of Leovigild's series, with the cross-on-steps, would begin, then, in 580 or 581 and continue until 584.[117] The fact is, however, that there is no proof that even Leovigild's second 'mintless' series, with his name and the Victory reverse is earlier than Hermenegild's revolt, and Mr. Grierson, in his unpub-

[113] P. Beltrán Villagrasa, *Numario hispánico*, ii (1953), 31, 36.

[114] Miles (p. 45) agreed it could be as late as 584. Mr. Grierson is also of the opinion that the coin is a little later in date than the rest of the group dated by Miles to 579–84.

[115] Beltrán, 33. Like Mateu y Llopis, *art. cit.* (n. 103), 83, and Miles, 24, Beltrán seems to think that Hermenegild's coin, "regi incliti," is earlier than his "regi a Deo vita." As I believe Díaz y Díaz is right in connecting the latter legend with Hermenegild's coronation, I assume it appeared on his first issue.

[116] Beltrán, *loc. cit.* This coin appears to be lost. Miles (p. 44 n. 4) is somewhat doubtful of its authenticity but Beltrán and Grierson think it genuine.

[117] Beltrán, *loc. cit.*

lished work cited above, argues strongly in favour of the thesis that it was Hermenegild, not Leovigild, who was responsible for initiating the regal coinage of the Visigoths. To summarize his arguments here would be to deform them. I can only say they seem to me convincing. It would appear that we have here a close parallel to Leovigild's religious policy. Mr. Grierson, speaking of "the earliest coinage of Leovigild" observes that it "bears every mark of diffidence, hesitation and lack of decision." These remarks would apply equally to Leovigild's policy towards the Catholic Church before 580, when, as far as we can tell from the scanty evidence available, his evident tolerance, extending at times to financial support for Catholic emigrés from North Africa, was interrupted by spasmodic bursts of persecution.[118] Hermenegild's conversion and revolt precipitated matters. Hermenegild's alliance with Byzantium, attested by Spanish and non-Spanish literary sources alike, is equally clearly reflected in his coinage.[119] His first coin-legend, "regi a Deo vita", seems inspired, as we have seen, by a contemporary coin of Byzantine Africa, but with the very significant addition of the words "a Deo," absent from the Byzantine bronze, stressing the orthodox character of the reign, a point, of course, unnecessary to stress in Byzantium. The danger to Leovigild of Hermenegild's revolt lay in the support Hermenegild might receive from Catholic Hispano-Romans (and Goths), as well as from foreign Catholic allies, especially the Byzantines.[120]

Leovigild was forced to reply to his son's challenge and he did so by his summons in 580 of an Arian Synod at Toledo, which opened a definite anti-Catholic campaign. He also, as would now appear, began to issue successive series of coins. The use of the cross-on-steps type, in particular, which both Beltrán and Grierson date to after 580, is, very probably, an affirmation of Leovigild's own orthodoxy. We can find an exact parallel to this in the text of Leovigild's address to the Arian Synod of 580, quoted by John of Biclar. This ran as follows: "Those coming from the Roman religion *to our Catholic Faith* need not be baptised, but only cleansed by the imposition of hands, the reception

[118] For a grant of land to the African Abbot Nanctus and his monks cf. *Vitas SS. PP. Emeritensium* (n. 78 above), iii, 2f. (esp. 8–10), pp. 154–8. Leovigild's banishment of John of Biclar seems to have taken place *ca.* 576 (Mommsen, 208; Campos, 18f.). This may be an isolated case of persecution, perhaps due to suspicion of a Gothic cleric who had spent no less than seventeen years in Byzantium (n. 21 above).

[119] P. Grierson, *loc. cit.* (n. 93), 84 n. 17, points out that Hermenegild – as contrasted with Leovigild – "apparently reverted to the full imperial standard" (of fineness of gold). Perhaps one should now say that Hermenegild *maintained* the imperial standard, from which Leovigild later diverged. F. Mateu y Llopis, *Archivo español de Arqueología*, xvi (1943), 172–93, and xviii (1945), 34–58, argues that almost all Visigothic coin types are copied from Byzantine originals. This view is criticized by W. Reinhard, *ibid.*, 220, and especially xx (1947), 125–9 (on p. 126 he points out that neither the profile bust on the obverse nor the Victory of the reverse of Hermenegild's coins derive from Byzantine models but from earlier Visigothic coins).

[120] See above, esp. n. 59.

of communion and the utterance of the formula 'Glory to the Father *by* the Son *in* the Holy Spirit'."[121] In this text Leovigild, in reply to the Catholic threat, affirms his own orthodoxy. *His* is the Catholic Faith.[122]

I have pointed out Leovigild's use of Byzantine models for his internal reorganisation of the Visigothic kingdom. In his coinage we have a clear example of his policy. In reply to Hermenegild's coins, with their religious acclamation borrowed in part from Byzantium, Leovigild will place the Byzantine cross-on-steps on his own coinage and will commemorate his victories over the Catholic usurper as God-given. Leovigild could indeed learn from his enemies and not least from his most formidable enemy, his son.

Leovigild's earliest "Cum Deo" legends commemorate the crucial episodes of the civil war, the fortification of Italica (583), the fall of Seville (583–584). The formula does not appear on the coin commemorating Leovigild's second capture of Cordoba ("Cordoba bis optinuit"), acquired from the Byzantines twice, first by war in 572, secondly by gold in 584, perhaps because this success was not strictly part of his war against his son.[123] That it does appear on the Rosas coin is intelligible if we are right in dating this coin in 585 and in connecting it with the war against the Franks, for Leovigild was fighting here against Guntram of Burgundy, who claimed to be intervening precisely because of the death of Hermenegild (and the exile of Hermenegild's Frankish wife, Ingundis, Guntram's niece).[124] In any case, two of the three instances – these that appear the earliest – when the "Cum Deo" formula is found on undoubtedly genuine issues of Leovigild (Italica and Seville) are indisputably connected with the king's war against his son. We may conclude, therefore, that we are justified in interpreting the formula, together with the earlier assumption of the cross-on-steps reverse, as a clear riposte to Hermenegild, propaganda to counter propaganda, scarcely less obvious than a written manifesto, and probably more effective in an age when books were only accessible to a limited few.

Harvard University
Cambridge, Mass.

[121] John. *s. a.* 580, 2 (Mommsen, 216; Campos, 90): "De Romana religione *ad nostram catholicam fidem* venientes non debere baptizari, sed tantummodo per manus impositionem et communionis preceptionem ablui et gloriam patri per filium in spiritu sancto dari." Mommsen corrected "a nostra catholica fide," but the MSS. have "ad nostram catholicam fidem," which must be correct since Leovigild is speaking ("Liuuigildus rex . . . dicens," as John says). I adopt the reading "preceptionem," which is that of J. B. Pérez's best MS., Segorbe, Bibl. Cap. 1. Readings of this (now lost) MS. are listed by M. C. Díaz y Díaz, *art. cit.* (n. 74 above), 74–76. A marginal note in another of Pérez's MSS., Escorial, &. IV. 23, has "ablui" (the other MSS. have "pollui" or "polui"). Flórez, *España Sagrada*, vi^3, 425, and Campos adopt "ablui."

[122] For the parallel case of the Vandal King Hunneric see above and n. 27.

[123] Nor does the "Cum Deo" formula appear on the Merida coin, sometimes dated (e.g. by Miles, 45) 582, to accord with Gregory of Tours, *Hist. Franc.*, vi, 18, which has the cross-on-steps reverse (Miles, 194 f.). But is it certain that this is a commemorative coin? Cf. Beltrán, *art. cit.* (n. 113 above), 34.

[124] Gregory of Tours, *ibid.*, viii, 28.

ADDITIONAL NOTE

The views put forward in this article have been criticised by several authors. Luís Vázquez de Parga, San Hermenegildo ante las fuentes históricas (Madrid, Real Academia de la Historia, 1973), re-examines the sources against the historical context; he aims to re-establish the credit of the Spanish chronicles and, to a certain extent, of Leovigild. E.A. Thompson, The Goths in Spain (Oxford, 1969), pp. 64-78, discusses the rebellion of Hermenegild at some length and offers different interpretations of some of its episodes. Roger Collins, "Mérida and Toledo: 550-585", in Visigothic Spain: new approaches, ed. E. James, (Oxford, 1980), pp. 189-219, in an important study which casts much light on the diversity and local life of Visigothic Spain, stresses the "cultural affinity" of Byzantium and Baetica, rather than the influence of the former on the latter. His view (pp. 215f) of Hermenegild's rebellion as essentially a Baetican reaction against Leovigild's strong rule, is attractive. I do not think, however, that one can escape the combined evidence of Gregory of Tours (whose testimony is undervalued by Mr Collins) and of the coinage described in my article. Taken together, these sources continue to suggest to me that what we have in the Spanish chronicles is a deliberate suppression of the religious side of the rebellion. I also cannot see why, as Mr Collins maintains (p. 217) "the official conversion of Hermenegild must have occurred either in the last stages of the rebellion, say 583, or in the period between its final extinction and the prince's death in 585." This is to ignore the connection between Hermenegild's coin, with its religious inscription, and his coronation (see my Study II, pp. 504f); the coronation clearly marked him as a rebel, and it should be dated to ca. 580.

Further light on this episode can be expected from the forthcoming article by J. Fontaine and P. Cazier, "Qui a chassé de Carthaginoise Sévérianus? Observations sur l'histoire familiale d'Isidore de Séville", to appear in the Memorial to Cl. Sánchez-Albornoz (Buenos Aires). This article helps to explain the differences between Leander of Seville's hostility towards the Goths - linked with his support of Hermenegild - and Isidore's pro-Gothic attitude.

III

HISTORIOGRAPHY IN VISIGOTHIC SPAIN

To interpret « Historiography in Visigothic Spain » in a strict sense would mean limiting this paper to the *Chronicle* of John of Biclar, the *Histories* and *Chronicle* (and perhaps the *De viris*) of Isidore of Seville, and the *Historia Wambae* of Julian of Toledo, five works in all. To understand the view (or views) of history existing in Spain under the Visigoths one has to take other writings into account as well. Since Biblical history is part of history (and for Christians the greater and most important part) one has to consider the way Biblical history was presented, not only in Isidore's *Chronicle*, but, in more popular shape, in sermons and tracts. And, since the history of the Church is, for Christians, the continuation of Biblical history, one has also to consider the *Passiones* of Martyrs and the lives of later saints produced in Spain as part of Spanish historiography [1].

(1) Abbreviations used: *MGH*, *AA* = *Monumenta Germaniae historica, Auctores antiquissimi* ; *SRM* = *ibid.*, *Scriptores rerum Merovingicarum* ; *PL* = *Patrologia latina*, ed. J-P. Migne; Campos = Julio Campos, *Juan de Biclaro, obispo de Gerona. Su vida y su obra*, Madrid 1960; Díaz = M. C. Díaz y Díaz, *Index scriptorum latinorum medii aevi hispanorum*, Madrid 1959 (cited by numbers, not pages). I cite the *Chronicon* of John of Biclar by the editions of Mommsen (*MGH*, *AA*, XI) and of Campos; Isidore, *Chronicon* and *Historiae* by Mommsen (*ibid.*); Isidore, *De viris illustribus*, by the new edition of C. Codoñer Merino, *El « De viris illustribus » de Isidoro de Sevilla* (Theses et Studia

Even when one includes these sources one is still far worse off for Spain than for France in the sixth and seventh centuries. There is nothing in Spain to compare to the historical and hagiographical writings of Gregory of Tours. The great series of legal texts incorporated in the *Leges Visigothorum* are only indirectly of assistance here, though Spanish Church Councils are of greater value [2].

Spanish historians create no new models in historical writing. They use models already available, the Chronicle – where they follow Jerome and his continuators –; the *De viris*, short collections of biographies, where they walk in the footsteps of Jerome and Gennadius; and lives of saints, where the model was established in the West by the translation of Athanasius' *Life of Anthony*, Sulpicius Severus' Martinian writings and (later) by Gregory the Great's *Dialogues*. Spanish writers compose *Passiones* of the martyrs on earlier (partly Spanish) models. The only historical works of Visigothic Spain without undisputed models behind them are Isidore's *Histories* and Julian of Toledo's *Historia Wambae*, though neither of these works was the first in its genre.

More interesting than the models used by Spanish historians, or than the precise sources drawn upon, – in

philologica Salmanticensia, XII), Salamanca 1964, and by *PL*, LXXXIII; Julian of Toledo, *Historia Wambae*, by Levison, *MGH*, *SRM*, V. General works on the subject are few in number. One may cite B. Sánchez Alonso, *Historia de la historiografía española*, I, Madrid 1941, 63-90; M. Ruffini, *Le origini letterarie in Spagna*, I, *L'epoca visigotica*, Turin 1951; W. Levison, *Deutschlands Geschichtsquellen im Mittelalter*, I, Weimar 1952, 81-91. In this study I have taken into account the *Chronicon* of Hydatius (*MGH*, *AA*, XI), although this was written before Spain became in any real sense Visigothic. I am grateful to Professor Herbert Bloch of Harvard University and to Dr. C. R. Ligota of the Warburg Institute for reading and commenting on this paper before its delivery.

(2) Cf. J. Fontaine, « Die westgotische lateinische Literatur, Probleme und Perspektiven », *Antike und Abendland*, XII (1966), 64-87, at 71f.

general well established for the major works[3] –, is the question of the *use* to which these models and sources were put. In other words, what were the *aims* pursued by our historians? To understand this one has to look more closely at their models and also at the history of the fifth and sixth centuries.

The tradition of *Christian* history, of history as recording the action of Providence, was established by Eusebius of Caesarea in the form in which it was known to later ages. Both Eusebius' *Chronicle*, in Jerome's translation, and his *Ecclesiastical History*, as translated by Rufinus, were known in Visigothic Spain[4], while Eusebius' interpretation of the history of Rome in Biblical terms, with Rome as the chosen instrument of God in place of Israel, is found in early fifth-century Spanish writers, in Orosius and in Prudentius' *Contra Symmachum*[5]. Eusebius' vision of Constantine as a Messianic figure, as a « new and greater Moses », was known to Spain through the *Ecclesiastical History*[6]. For Eusebius the fortunes of the

(3) By Mommsen for the works published in *MGH*, *AA*, XI, and by G. von Dzialowski, *Isidor und Ildefons als Literarhistoriker* (Kirchengeschichtliche Studien, IV. 2), Münster i.W., 1898, for Isidore, *De viris*. Campos has added many parallels (rather than direct sources) and Codoñer further details.

(4) Isidore, *Versus*, xi (Díaz, 123), ed. C. H. Beeson, *Isidor-Studien* (Quellen und Untersuchungen zur lateinischen Philologie des Mittelalters, IV. 2), Munich 1913, 162, cites Eusebius and Orosius as historians, without mentioning specific works. Eusebius' and Jerome's *Chronicle* is known to Hydatius, John of Biclar and Isidore, *Chronicon*; Eusebius' *Historia ecclesiastica* is used in the last named work.

(5) For Orosius see R. W. Hanning, *The Vision of History in Early Britain*, New York 1966, 37-42, with the references there given. Orosius was used by Isidore, *Historia Gothorum*, and by Julian, *Historia Wambae* (e.g., c. 7, p. 506). Isidore cites Prudentius in *Versus* (x, p. 161), as well as Orosius (preceding note). Cf. *Contra Symmachum*, I, 415-505 (the speech of Theodosius). See A. A. Castellán, « Roma y España en la visión de Prudencio », *Cuadernos de historia de España*, XVII (1952), 20-49, esp. 29-40.

(6) Eusebius, *Eccles. Hist.*, IX, 9; *Life of Constantine*, 1, 12, 20, 38. See F. E. Cranz, « Kingdom and Polity in Eusebius of Caesarea », *Harvard Theological Review*, XLV (1952), 47-66, at 56.

Church and the Roman Empire were inseparable, since Constantine's conversion. « The imperial government », in Baynes' words, was « a terrestrial copy of the rule of God in Heaven » [7]. Eusebius' views were repeated in Byzantium with certain variations to which I shall return, by fifth-century historians [8]. As Walter Kaegi has remarked, « it was far more difficult for *western* Romans to perceive any divine political and military rewards for imperial piety » [9]. In 400 Prudentius had seen Constantine and Theodosius achieving God's purposes. Later generations looked in vain for another Theodosius and the Eusebian model – the *identification* of Christianity and the Roman Empire – might seem doomed to break down in the general collapse of the Empire in the fifth-century West. Yet what *other* model was available, through which the world could become intelligible and the new order acceptable to Western Romans? St. Augustine's denial of the Eusebian assumptions, his *separation* of the heavenly City of God from the earthly city of man, was too radical to win general assent [10]. One possible course was open to Western Church historians and it was generally adopted. If you could not have the Basileus and Autokrator of Constantinople, the clear heir of Eusebius' Constantine, as your master, then you must find a Western Constantine to substitute for him. If you could not continue to maintain that you, as Romans, still dominated the world and could be plausibly identified with God's chosen race – since al-

(7) N. H. Baynes, *Byzantine Studies and other Essays*, London 1955, 168. See also Cranz's article and, now, F. Dvornik, *Early Christian and Byzantine Political Philosophy ; origins and background* (Dumbarton Oaks Studies, IX), Washington, D;C., 1966, II, ch. 10, esp. pp. 614-22; for Western echoes of Eusebius' views see pp. 626-30, 725.

(8) See below and n. 62.

(9) Walter E. Kaegi, Jr., *Byzantium and the Decline of Rome*, Princeton 1968, 204. (The italics are mine).

(10) See Cranz, p. 64; Hanning, *op. cit.*, 32-37; Dvornik, 726.

most all Western Romans were now ruled by barbarians – then you could identify the local dominant tribe, Franks or Visigoths, as God's instrument, and attribute to *its* ruler the aura of Constantine, a little dimmed perhaps but still visible [11].

This process of *transferring* the Providential mantle with which Eusebius had invested Rome and Constantine to lesser shoulders proved more painful and prolonged in Spain than in other countries. No clear substitute for the Empire appeared in Spain until the end of the sixth century, with Leovigild. Until then there had been no urgent necessity and reason – as there had been in Italy with Theodoric and in Gaul with Clovis – to reconcile Roman and barbarian traditions. The fifth and most of the sixth centuries constitute the obscurest age in the history of the Iberian Peninsula, but the few sources we have, coming from different parts of Spain, Hydatius in Galicia, Maximus in Saragossa, lives of saints from Cantabria and Mérida, agree in portraying a completely *fragmented* world, in which much of Spain was still ruled by « Romans », that is by the local aristocracy and bishops [12]. The most interesting local historian of this period, when the fate of Spain was still undecided, is Bishop Hydatius of Aquae Flaviae in Galicia (now Chavez in Portugal). His aspira-

(11) Cp. Gregory of Tours, *Historia Francorum*, II, 31, ed. B. Krusch and W. Levison, *MGH*, *SRM*, I², Hannover 1951, p. 77. 8f; Gregory the Great, *Registrum*, XI, 35, 37, ed. P. Ewald and L. M. Hartmann, *MGH*, *Epistulae*, II, Berlin 1899, pp. 304, 309; John of Biclar (cited below, n. 75). Cf. E. Ewig, « Das Bild Constantin des Grossen in den ersten Jahrhunderten des abendländischen Mittelalter », *Historisches Jahrbuch*, LXXV (1956), 1-46, esp. 26-29.

(12) Cf. Hydatius, e.g. 174, 186, 246 (*MGH*, *AA*, XI, pp. 29, 30, 35); Maximus, *Chronicorum reliquiae* (*ibid.*, 222f) (Díaz, 79); Braulio, *Vita S. Emiliani* (Díaz, 156), ed. L. Vázquez De Parga, Madrid 1943; *Vitas SS. Patrum Emeritensium* (Díaz, 214), ed. J. N. Garvin (Catholic University of America, Studies in Medieval and Renaissance Latin Language and Literature, XIX) Washington 1946. Cf. K. F. Stroheker, « Spanische Senatoren der spätrömischen und westgotischen Zeit », *Madrider Mitteilungen*, IV (1963), 107-32.

tions to continue Jerome's universal *Chronicle* are in sharp contrast with what he could achieve [13]. He is anxious to see Providence at work in the world but for him there is *no* clear vehicle of divine action. It has been well said that he « cannot trust either the Empire or the barbarians » [14]. A century after Hydatius' death about 469 the position had only grown more complex. The Visigoths had only begun to attempt to conquer the Peninsula in the 470s. They met with considerable opposition even in Northeast Spain in the early sixth century and hardly touched the South up to 552, when most of Baetica was taken over, apparently with little difficulty, by a Byzantine expeditionary force [15]. Between the orthodox Byzantines in the South, the (now Catholic) Sueves in the Northwest and the Catholic Franks across the Pyrenees the hold of the Arian Visigoths on Toledo and central Spain in the 560s seemed tenuous to a Catholic historian of Gothic blood, John of Biclar [16].

John of Biclar's *Chronicle* is short but repays careful study. Through it one may understand later Spanish historians. In John's pages one can follow the Byzantini-

(13) Cf. Hydatius, Praef. (pp. 13f.), also the useful article of C. Torres Rodriguez, « El Cronicon de Hidacio », *Compostellanum,* I (1956), 765-801.

(14) J. J. Carreras Ares, « La historia universal en la España visigoda », *Revista de la Universidad de Madrid,* VI (1957), 175-97, at p. 182.

(15) See R. D'Abadal y De Vinyals, *Del Reino de Tolosa al Reino de Toledo,* Madrid 1960, also my article, « Coins and Chronicles: Propaganda in sixth-century Spain and the Byzantine Background », *Historia,* XV (1966), 483-508, at 494-96.

(16) John of Biclar, *s. a.* 569 (Mommsen, 212; Campos, 80): « *Liuuigildus germanus Liuuani regis superstite fratre in regnum citerioris Hispaniae constituitur, Gosuintham relictam Athanagildi in coniugium accipit et prouinciam Gothorum, quae iam pro rebellione diversorum fuerat diminuta, mirabiliter ad pristinos revocat terminos* ». Isidore says the same thing in different words (*Historia Gothorum,* 49, p. 287. 16f.). Martin of Braga, *De trina mersione,* 3, ed. C. W. Barlow, 257, records the presence of Suevic legates in Constantinople, probably in the 570s. The Sueves were also in touch with Guntramn of Burgundy (*ib.,* 254 n. 9).

sation of the Visigothic realm stage by stage. John's *Chronicle* begins with Byzantium as the centre from which the world is seen [17]. This is hardly surprising since John spent seven (or, according to another manuscript reading, seventeen) years as a young man in Constantinople. According to his younger contemporary, Isidore, he was there « trained in Greek and Latin learning » and probably ordained priest [18]. He only returned to Spain in the late 570s. He evidently began to write his *Chronicle* in Constantinople and the entries from 567 to 577 are mainly concerned with the East and reveal direct knowledge of events in the Byzantine capital [19]. The *Chronicle* begins with a (somewhat optimistic) account of Justin II's return to Chalcedonian orthodoxy [20]. Soon we see Byzantium fighting the idolatrous Persians – in defense of the faith of the Armenians

(17) M. C. Díaz y Díaz, « La transmisión textual del Biclarense », *Analecta sacra Tarraconensia*, XXXV (1962), 57-76, shows that the « edition » of the *Chronicon* as we have it was made in 602, probably by a monk in John's monastery of Biclar, but the work itself was finished in 590. J. Fontaine, « Conversion et culture chez les Wisigoths d'Espagne », *La Conversione al Cristianesimo nell'Europa dell'Alto medioevo = Settimane di studio del Centro italiano di studi sull'alto medioevo*, XIV, Spoleto 1967, 87-147, at p. 109 n. 30, remarks: « Toute l'histoire des années 567 à 580 [a slip for 590] est mise en perspective par rapport à la dernière année et au Concile III de Tolède ». I would agree, provided one does not understand by this that, from the time John *began* the *Chronicon* it was designed to end in this way. In other words, the detailed knowledge of events in Constantinople and the whole focus of the *Chronicon* up to 577 seem to me to show that John was writing it year by year from the 560s, although he appears to have made some changes in the 580s, in the light of later events (see below and n. 26).

(18) Isidore, *De viris*, 31 (Codoñer, p. 151): « *Hic, cum esset adolescens, Constantinopolim perrexit, ibique graeca et latina eruditione nutritus, septimo demum anno in Hispanias reversus est* ». Arévalo's edition (*PL*, LXXXIII, 1105) reads « *post decem et septem annos* » ; Campos (p. 18) also prefers seventeen to seven, which I find difficult to accept (see n. 19). See Fontaine, « Conversion », 108-111.

(19) Cf., e. g.. John, *s. a.* 568,1, 573,4,6, 575,1, 576,2,5, 577,1 (Mommsen, 211, 213-15; Campos, 79, 83, 85-87). These entries seem to show that John was in Constantinople for at least nine years (see preceding note).

(20) John. *s. a.* 567,2 (Mommsen, 211; Campos, 78). See « Coins » (cited n. 15 above), 487f.

and Iberians of the Caucasus –; defeating the Moors in North Africa – where various tribes receive, *at the same time,* association with the Empire and the faith of Christ – in John, as in Eusebius, the two things are evidently inseparable; fighting pagan Avars in the Balkans, Lombards in Italy and Visigoths in Spain, both tribes, as John knew well, Arian heretics [21]. Among the concise entries of the *Chronicle* the news of a great Byzantine victory over the Persians in 575 stands out; there is no such extensive entry again until 589 [22]. This victory clearly impressed John, as it did the population of Constantinople [23]. In John's *Chronicle* Byzantium was still capable of converting to Christianity and of assimilating barbarians in North Africa, Saracens and Caucasian tribes [24]. It is to Byzantium that defeated Western barbarians flee with their treasures [25]. Byzantium is still incomparably the greatest of Christian powers. There would seem little doubt that the young John saw it as the Eusebian vehicle of God's action in this world [26]. To arrive at this view John did not have to go back to Eusebius, though he had probably read him. The Eusebian view of the Empire, restated in its essence by the church historians of fifth-century Byzantium, was again put forward by John's contemporary, Eva-

(21) *Ibid., s. a.* 567,3, 569,1,3, 576,5, 576,1, 570,2 (Mommsen, 211, 212, 214; Campos, 78, 79, 86, 80).

(22) Mommsen, 214; Campos, 85.

(23) See Campos, 122f.

(24) John, *s. a.* 569,1, 575,3, 576,2 (Mommsen, 212, 214; Campos, 79, 85f.). See Campos, 109f., 123f.

(25) *Ibid., s. a.* 572,1, 573,1 (Mommsen, 212f.; Campos, 81f.).

(26) Carreras Ares (cited n. 14), 185, may exaggerate slightly when he calls John's work « una historia imperial con un apéndice continuado de historia española », but this seems nearer the truth than to see John's interest in Spain as predominant in his work from its beginning. The lack of explicit formulation of Eusebian views with regard to Byzantium in the *Chronicon* may be due to John's later revision of the work by 590, after the conversion of Recared and the Goths. Cf. n. 17.

grius Scholasticus [27]. It seems extremely probable that this living tradition of Eusebian historiography was known to John, « trained », as he was, « in Greek [as well as] Latin learning », and that it influenced the presentation first of Byzantium and (more obviously) of the Visigoths in his *Chronicle* [28].

Gradually Spain assumes importance in the work. The entry for 569, which records how Leovigild became king and « marvellously restored the province of the Goths », must represent a later judgement, for this restoration took years to effect [29]. But, throughout the 570s, John records, with admiration and zeal, Leovigild's campaigns, by which the independent regions of the North and Northwest were conquered and the Byzantines in the South repeatedly defeated [30].

With Leovigild the *fragmentation* of the Iberian Peninsula, which had begun with the barbarian invasions of 409, was succeeded at last by *unification*, *political* unification in the 570s, *religious* unification in the 580s, attempted by Leovigild under the sign of Arianism and achieved, after grave crisis and civil war, by his younger son and successor Recared, under that of Catholicism [31]. The Arian

(27) See G. Downey, « The Perspective of the Early Church Historians », *Greek Roman and Byzantine Studies*, VI (1965), 57-70, esp. 60-63, 65f., 67, also Kaegi, *op. cit.* (n. 9), 190f., 219-21. See below and n. 61. John refers to Eusebius in his Praef. (Mommsen, 211; Campos, 77).

(28) This question is not discussed by Campos. He lists (pp. 207-11, see also 69-71) a number of « loca », to which he refers in his apparatus to the *Chronicon*, but it is not clear whether or not he thinks John *used* any specific Byzantine source. Even if one cannot show verbal quotations, the derivation of ideas is clear.

(29) See nn. 16-17 above.

(30) John, *s. a.* 570-577 (Mommsen, 212-15; Campos, 80-87).

(31) See Fontaine's article, cited above n. 17, also my « La Conversión de los Visigodos: notas críticas », *Analecta sacra Tarraconensia*, XXXIV (1961) 21-46; « Coins » (n. 15 above), and now K. Schäferdiek, *Die Kirche in den Reichen der Westgoten und Suewen bis zur Errichtung der westgotischen Katholischen Staatskirche* (Arbeiten zur Kirchengeschichte, XXXIX), Berlin 1967 137-233.

Leovigild and his two sons, the Catholic rebel Hermenegild and the successful convert Recared, all deliberately attempt to imitate Byzantium – an overpoweringly impressive model for sixth-century kings. Leovigild founds cities in the Roman manner, creates his sons co-rulers or Caesars, and sets up a Court at Toledo – until the 550s merely a provincial city; Toledo as a great capital is a creation of the Visigothic monarchy as Constantinople is of Constantine –; he creates his own independent coinage, which imitates that of Byzantium [32], and, again in contrast to his more tolerant predecessors, insists, in the Byzantine manner, on religious uniformity in his kingdom. His sons behave in the same way – if Hermenegild does not precede him by his coinage and emphasis on religion [33]. With Leovigild and his sons the Visigoths come of age politically in the only way possible in sixth-century Spain: they create an imitation Byzantium in the West.

It is surely significant that both the principal « manager » of the Third Council of Toledo, Bishop Leander of Seville, and John of Biclar, the historian of the double unification of Spain, political and religious, had spent long periods of time in Constantinople and were familiar with Byzantine culture [34]. These men set the standards

(32) Cf. « Coins », 501-508. *Later* Visigothic coinage is not as deeply and continuously indebted to Byzantine models as has been suggested. See W. Reinhart, in *Archivo español de Arqueologia*, XX (1947), 125-29. For Leovigild in general see K. F. Stroheker, « Leowigild », in his *Germanentum und Spätantike*, Zürich-Stuttgart 1965, 134-91. His article « Das spanische Westgotenreich und Byzanz », *Bonner Jahrbücher*, CLXIII (1963), 252-74, is reprinted in the same volume, pp. 207-45. On Toledo as a capital cf. E. Ewig, « Résidence et capitale pendant le haut Moyen Age », *Revue historique*, CCXXX (1963), 25-72, at 31-36.

(33) « Coins », 506f.

(34) For Leander's role at Toledo cf. John, *s. a.* 590 (Mommsen, 219. 9; Campos, 98): « summa tamen synodalis negotii penes sanctum Leandrum Hispalensis ecclesiae episcopum ». Leander spent several years (580-83 or 580-85) in Constantinople. Cf. Gregory the Great, *Registrum*, V, 53a (*MGH*,

to be followed. To understand Spanish historiography under the Visigoths – or simply the history of Spain in the sixth century – it is essential to realize that *all* our historians wrote *after* the 580s, *after* the two decisive decades of unification [35]. Spanish historians of the age marvel at and celebrate this unification, and seek to reinforce it whenever it is threatened [36].

I have shown in an earlier article how coins were used as royal (and religious) propaganda by both Leovigild and his hostile son, Hermenegild [37]. In Visigothic Spain, as in the ancient world and Byzantium, coins were declarations of royal policy and power and attempts to ensure its success. Otto von Simson has demonstrated how the Emperor Justinian's artistic programme at Ravenna was part of his creation of a « sacred fortress » of Byzantium on reconquered Italian soil [38]. Where Roman rulers used

Epistulae, I, 353f.); Isidore, *De viris*, 28 (Codoñer, 149f.; *PL*, LXXXIII, 1103B). For his closeness to Recared cf. *Reg.* IX, 227a, *ib.*, II, 221.19-22; I, 41 (I, 57. 9-11). That he could read Greek is shown by the dedication to him of a work « graeco eloquio » by John the Faster, Patriarch of Constantinople (Isidore, 26, Codoñer, 147f.; *PL*, 1102A). Leander was probably responsible for the introduction into Spain of the custom of reciting the Creed during Mass, « secundum formam orientalium ecclesiarum » (*PL*, LXXXIV, 351D; *Concilios visigóticos e hispano-romanos*, ed. J. Vives, Barcelona-Madrid 1963, 125).

(35) The study of J. Orlandis, « Algunas observaciones en torno a la ' tiranía ' de San Hermenegildo », in his *El Poder Real y la Sucesión al trono en la Monarquia - Visigoda* (Estudios Visigóticos, III), Rome-Madrid 1962, 3-12, is valuable for the term « tyrannus » but fails to take fully into account the circumstances under which John of Biclar and Isidore wrote. See also p. 309 below.

(36) One example of this tendency is Isidore's comment on the division of the kingdom between two kings, Liuva and Leovigild (*Historia Gothorum*, 48, p. 286f.): « *sicque regnum duos capuit, dum nulla potestas patiens consortis sit* ». This is not taken from John of Biclar, Isidore's source for this passage. Isidore probably had in mind Leovigild's disastrous step in making his sons « consortes regni » (John, *s. a.* 573,5, Mommsen, 213; Campos, 83), information not repeated by Isidore. On the term « consortes » cf. Orlandis, *op. cit.*, 4-6.

(37) « Coins and chronicles » (cited n. 15 above).

(38) Otto G. von Simson, *Sacred Fortress, Byzantine Art and Statecraft in Ravenna*, Chicago 1948. See also G. Mathew, *Byzantine Aesthetics*, London 1963.

new civic buildings as instruments of propaganda, Justinian used churches. Toledo was a Spanish reflexion of Ravenna, the sacred fortress of another religious monarchy [39]. Here, as in Constantinople, every aspect of Court life, from the time Leovigild, as Isidore says, was first raised in royal dress on a throne above his fellow Goths [40], was organized to display the magnificence and invincibility of the Crown. Sisebut's dedication of a church to St. Leocadia in Toledo in 618 was recorded as an event of great importance by Isidore and remembered by writers two centuries later. While promoting a flourishing cult of this previously unknown martyr, the foundation was, for royal policy, as important as a great military victory [41]. The dedication of chapels on the walls of Toledo by Wamba in the 670s was another attempt to combine religion and royalty, to provide the « royal city » of the West with the supernatural protection Constantinople had long enjoyed [42].

As in Byzantium the minor arts were at the monarchy's service. If Visigothic Toledo has virtually disappeared there still remain from Visigothic Spain the splendid votive crowns, without parallel except in Constantinople, decorated with Byzantine jewelry and dedicated by Kings. They are comparable to Byzantine « imperial art », with its ivories, royal portraits or purple codices, signs of piety

(39) See Ewig, article cited n. 32 above.

(40) Isidore, *Historia Gothorum*, 51 (p. 288.14f.).

(41) Isidore, *Chronica*, 416a (p. 480): « *Ecclesiam quoque sanctae Leocadiae Toleto mire fundavit* ». See Eulogius of Cordoba, *Liber apologeticus martyrum*, 16 (Díaz, 477), *PL*, CXV, 859C; C. García Rodriguez, *El Culto de los Santos en la España romana y visigoda* (Monografías de historia eclesiástica, I), Madrid 1966, 246-53.

(42) J. Vives, *Inscripciones cristianas de la España romana y visigoda*, Barcelona 1942, 125 (n. 361); Díaz, 240.

and proofs of power [43]. The surviving Spanish rural churches, also strongly Byzantine in style, give one some idea of what Toledo must have been [44].

Written history in Visigothic Spain should be seen in perspective, as occupying a place in the arsenal of royal propaganda – a *minor* place because only a few men could be reached by the written word in the seventh century, compared to the crowds which could be dazzled by the churches erected by kings in Toledo, their sanctuaries adorned by hanging votive crowns, providing the setting for the Church Councils, the Coronation service or the « Order when the king goes out to battle » in the *Liber Ordinum* [45].

Not all historical writing in Visigothic Spain can be classified as royal propaganda. I shall come later to popular presentations of Biblical history and to hagiography. But the major works which survive – the works of John of Biclar, Isidore, Julian of Toledo, the *Vitas Patrum Emeritensium*, were inspired (the last to a lesser extent) by the Court of Toledo. Recared's decision to bring the Goths into the Catholic Church – a decision which the Church could hardly afford to have reversed – necessarily made leading churchmen the close allies of the monarchy. One has, therefore, to consider the policies of Visigothic kings. They were concerned to control the Church – both

(43) On the votive crowns see H. SCHLUNK, « Arte visigodo », *Ars Hispaniae*, II, Madrid 1947, 311-320; J. FERRANDIS TORRES, « Artes decorativas visigodas », *Historia de España*, ed. R. MENÉNDEZ PIDAL, III, 2nd ed., Madrid 1963, 682-92, with the additions of M. LÓPEZ SERRANO, *ibid.*, 768-73. Cf. G. MATHEW, *op. cit.* (n. 38 above), 78-93, 95-98, and, for the use of imperial images, also DVORNIK, *op. cit.* (n. 7), II, 652-56, 686f., 694, 733f.

(44) See SCHLUNK, *op. cit.*, 270-306; LÓPEZ SERRANO, *op. cit.*, 738-51. See also SCHLUNK, « Relaciones entre la peninsula ibérica y Bizancio durante la época visigoda », *Archivo español de Arqueología*, XVIII (1945), 177-204.

(45) M. FÉROTIN, *Le Liber Ordinum* (Monumenta ecclesiae liturgica, V), Paris 1904, 498-505, 149-53.

as an instrument of power and because concern for the Church was the *right* occupation for the Vicar of God. Hence the « Tomes of the Most Holy Faith » or directives addressed by Kings, from Recared onwards, to Church Councils; royal correspondence with bishops (of which Sisebut's letters give us examples); the many laws issued on Christian morals; the support given to the bishops' attempts to educate the people of Spain in Christian principles as well as to suppress internal dissent by attacks on Jews and pagans [46].

During the seventh century Spain was often involved in civil war. The danger that the tiny dominant minority of the population, the Gothic aristocracy, would « destroy themselves » was present to all thinking minds [47]. Rebels were usually able to count on help from external enemies [48]. Hence the need to preserve strict internal unity and control the frontiers. The Seventh Council of Toledo, in 646, asks: « Who does not know how many crimes have been committed by the tyrants and deserters who pass to the enemy?... They have caused great harm to the fatherland and imposed a ceaseless strain on the army of the Goth » [49]. Many clergy were involved in these

(46) Cf. Recared to Toledo III (589); Chintila's decree for Toledo V (636); Receswinth to Toledo VIII (653); Ervigius to Toledo XII (681) and Toledo XIII (683); Egica to Toledo XV (688), XVI (693), and XVII (694), *PL*, LXXXIV, 342-45, 393f., 412-15, 468-70, 487-89, 511f., 528-31, 552-54; ed. Vives (cited n. 34), 108-16, 231f., 261-67, 380-84, 412-14, 449-52, 483-88, 523-27. See A. K. Ziegler, *Church and State in Visigothic Spain*, Washington, D.C., 1930. See the passages cited below, n. 82, and on Sisebut, pp. 284 f.

(47) See Isidore, *Historia Gothorum*, 46 (p. 286.7-10): « *videntes Gothi proprio se everti excidio et magis metuentes, ne Spaniam milites auxili occasione invaderent* ».

(48) E. g. Sisenand in 631 or Paul against Wamba in 672-73. Cf. Fredegarius, *Chronica*, IV, 73, ed. B. Krusch, *MGH*, *SRM*, II, 157, and below, p. 301 and n. 166.

(49) Toledo VII, c.1 (*PL*, LXXXIV, 403f.; Vives, 249f.): « *Quis enim nesciat quanta sint hactenus per tyrannos et refugas transferendo se in externas partes inlicite perpetrata, ...quae et patriae diminutionem afferent et exercitui Gothorum indesinentem laborem inponerent?* »

rebellions. The Council decreed they should be deprived of their rank and only receive communion, after penitence, at their death [50]. Long after the Byzantine danger was gone the Visigothic State would not allow an eminent ascetic to travel to the East, perhaps in part because he wanted to go through France [51]. Jungmann has remarked that church life in Spain is marked throughout the seventh century by a warlike atmosphere [52]. The touchiness of Spanish Councils and of leading bishops such as Braulio and Julian at the papacy's occasional interventions in Spain, the laws of Church and State against Jews, the existence of pagan practices as late as 693 and the violent attempts to suppress them, all these things are evidence supporting the view of Spanish unity as fragile [53].

Church historians played their part in ensuring unity. They celebrate victories over the main external enemies, Byzantines and Franks, and either castigate rebels or – more effectively – suppress evidence of internal disunity. I have discussed elsewhere the way in which John of Biclar, Isidore, and the author of the *Vitas Patrum Emeritensium* deliberately suppress the fact of the Catholicism of Hermenegild – the champion supported by at least part of the sixth-century Spanish church against the

(50) *Ibid.* (*PL.* 404f.; Vives, 250f.).

(51) See *Vita S. Fructuosi* (Díaz, 261), xvii, ed. F. C. Nock (Catholic University of America, Studies in Mediaeval History, N. S., VII), Washington, D.C., 1946, 123, with the variant version printed by M. C. Díaz y Díaz, « A propósito de la ' Vita Fructuosi ' », *Cuadernos de Estudios Gallegos*, VIII (1953), 149-178, at 178.

(52) J. A. Jungmann, in *Zeitschrift für katholische Theologie*, LXIX (1947), 53.

(53) See, e.g., J. Mª. De Lacarra, « La iglesia visigoda en el s. VII y sus relaciones con Roma », *Le Chiese nei regni dell'Europa occidentale e i loro rapporti con Roma sino all'800 = Settimane di studio*, VII.1, Spoleto 1960, 353-84; S. Katz, *The Jews in the Visigothic and Frankish Kingdoms of Spain and Gaul*, Cambridge, Mass., 1937; S. McKenna, *Paganism and pagan survivals in Spain up to the fall of the Visigothic Kingdom*, Washington, D;C., 1938.

Arian monarchy. This outstanding example of official suppression of history can, fortunately, be corrected by the use of non-Spanish literary sources and of coin evidence. Other probable examples of the same tendency to provide an excessively favourable picture of the past can be suggested, for instance the omission by Isidore of the religious issue when dealing with the reigns of Euric, Agila and Witiza [54]. Another sign of the adoption of royal directives by church chroniclers is the exaltation of the Goths and the increasingly systematic depreciation of Byzantines and Franks. John of Biclar is only at the beginning of this process. He celebrated the rise of the Visigothic kingdom as another Byzantium, but he never ceased to be interested in Byzantium itself [55]. Isidore's *Historia Gothorum* ends with the definite triumph within

(54) See n. 15 above. J. L. Romero, « San Isidoro de Sevilla, su pensamiento histórico-político y sus relaciones con la historia visigoda », *Cuadernos de historia de España*, VIII (1947), 5-71, at 58 n. 30, lists some of these instances of suppression of history by Isidore. Orlandis, *op. cit.* (n. 35), p. 12, holds that « prudencia política » explains the attitude to Hermenegild. But the contemporary sources not only do not name Hermenegild at the hour of Catholic triumph in 589. They deliberately suppress the religious element in his rebellion, his Catholicism, and this (in Isidore's case) when writing some thirty years later (the *Vitas* of Mérida are later still). The « objectivity » of John of Biclar and Isidore (stressed by Orlandis, pp. 10 and 35) therefore leaves a good deal to be desired. Nor can I see an absence of « juicio personal peyorativo » in Isidore's phrase in *Hist. Goth*, 49 (p. 287.14): « *Hermenegildum deinde filium imperiis suis tyrannizantem obsessum exsuperavit* » (this phrase sums up John's account but is Isidore's own and his *only* mention of Hermenegild in the *Hist.*). John of Biclar's record of the « mors turpissima » of Hermenegild's murderer, Sisbert (*s. a.* 587,4, Mommsen, 218; Campos, 95) is not (*pace* Orlandis, p. 12) comparable to the suppression of Hermenegild in the *Vitas*. It is simply a reference to the death inflicted (it is not said by whom) on Sisbert. For a theory explaining this entry see Fontaine, « Conversion » (cited n. 17), 145, n. 87. Cf. Schäferdiek, *op. cit.* (n. 31), 154, 204.

(55) Note how the triumphant account of the Third Council of Toledo is followed at once (590,2) by the (false) report that the « imperator Persarum Christi suscepit fidem et pacem cum Mauricio imperatore firmavit », an entry exactly comparable to that on the Garamantes in 569,1 (Mommsen, 212, 219; Campos, 79, 99). With John's attitude compare that of Avitus of Vienne, writing to Clovis c. 496 (cited, n. 92 below): « Gaudeat equidem Graecia principem legisse nostrum: sed non iam quae tanti muneris donum *sola* mereatur ».

the Iberian Peninsula of the Gothic monarchy [56]. Yet it is still against Byzantium that the Goths measure themselves, and the one defeat of the Goths by the « Romans » [Byzantines] recorded is ascribed to an unworthy (and unChristian) deception, when the Byzantines attack on a Sunday [57]. At the same time it can be shown that both John and Isidore greatly exaggerate Visigothic victories against the Franks [57 bis]. For Julian of Toledo the Roman Empire has ceased to exist; the enemy is the Franks and he employs against them his unbridled rhetorical talents [58]. Just as Byzantine church historians virtually

(56) *Hist. Goth.*, 62 (p. 292), also « Recapitulatio », p. 295 (cited below, n. 150).

(57) *Ibid.*, 42 (p. 284.21ff.). The (Arian) Visigoths « adveniente die dominico deposuerunt arma, ne diem sacrum proelio funestarent ».

(57bis) The letters of Bulgar, governor of Visigothic Gaul (Septimania) in 610-612 are instructive (ed. W. GUNDLACH, *MGH*, *Epist.*, III, Berlin 1892, 677-85). Bulgar is clearly afraid of an attack by Theodoric and Brunhild (see n. 99 below). He is involved in difficult negotiations with a bishop representing them (pp. 680f.). King Gundemar has to pay sums of money to another Frankish ruler, King Theudebert, to obtain peace (pp. 678f.). The Visigoths are evidently in an inferior position vis-à-vis the Franks. Note also Bulgar's remark (p. 681.18-22) that Recared had handed over two places in Septimania to Brunhild, « *pro stabilitate concordiae* ». This hardly sounds like the crushing Visigothic victories chronicled by John and Isidore (n. 68 below).

(58) Julian, *De comprobatione sextae aetatis* (DÍAZ, 268), I, 21 (*PL*, XCVI, 554A-B): « *Regnum autem quartum, quod perspicue pertinet ad Romanos, ferreum est, quod comminuit et domat omnia ; sed pedes eius et digiti ex parte ferrei, ex parte sunt fictiles ; quod hoc tempore manifestissime comprobatur. Sicut enim in principio nihil Romano imperio fortius et durius fuit, ita in fine rerum nihil imbecillius, quando et in bellis civilibus et adversus diversas nationes aliarum gentium barbarorumque videtur indigere auxilio* ». For some comments on this work and on the *Historia Wambae* see below, pp. 299-303. That Bishop Maximus of Saragossa wrote the same type of history is indicated by the fragments that survive (see n. 12 above), e.g. by his entry on the defeat of Attila (*MGH*, *AA*, XI, p. 222): « *His diebus Gotthi contra Hunnos dimicant in campis Catalaunicis, in quo proelio Theodoredus rex occubuit et Gotthi victores extiterunt* ». Here, as in the shorter version of Isidore's *Hist. Goth.*, 25 (p. 277.28f.), there is no mention of Roman participation in the battle or of Aetius. These passages were noted by H. MESSMER, *Hispania-Idee und Gotenmythos*, Zürich 1960, 95f.

expressed imperial propaganda so Spanish historians became royal propagandists [59].

It is hardly surprising that Spanish historians followed Byzantine examples. John of Biclar, as I said, was familiar with Byzantine erudition at first hand. If later historians in Spain could not read Byzantine historians in Greek they could read them in Latin, in the *Historia tripartita* commissioned by Cassiodorus and written by Epiphanius. It has long been known that this work was used by Isidore in his *Chronicle* and *De viris* but the implications of this fact for Spanish historiography have not been explored, perhaps because the *Historia tripartita* itself has received so little attention and its value has generally been underestimated [59 bis].

Cassiodorus' work is a careful selection from three fifth-century Byzantine church historians, Socrates, Sozomen and Theodoret [60]. Perusal of this work must have reinforced – while altering to some extent – the historical model constructed by Eusebius. Sozomen and, even more,

(59) For Byzantine historians see DOWNEY and KAEGI, cited n. 27 above. The case of Gregory of Tours is much less clear, despite MESSMER's remarks (pp. 64-72, 124-26); cf. FONTAINE (n. 17 above), 112-14.

(59bis) H. HERTZBERG, « Ueber die Chroniken des Isidorus von Sevilla », *Forschungen zur Deutschen Geschichte*, XV (1875), 289-360, at pp. 335-37, 359f., points to probable use of books III, VI-IX, XII of the *Hist. trip.* MOMMSEN, in his apparatus to the *Chron.* (pp. 466f.) agreed. The *Hist. trip.* is also probably used in Isidore, *De viris*, 6 (Codoñer, p. 137), although the editor is doubtful of this (p. 79 n. 25). It is probably used in the « African Appendix » to the *De viris* (which may in fact be Spanish in origin) and certainly in the Spanish additions first found in MS. León 22 (see nn. 128, 139 below).

(60) See the critical edition by W. JACOB and R. HANSLIK, *Cassiodori-Epiphanii Historia ecclesiastica tripartita* (Corpus scriptorum ecclesiasticorum latinorum, LXXI), Vienna 1952, and the useful article by M. L. W. LAISTNER, *Harvard Theological Review*, XLI (1948), 51-67, reprinted in LAISTNER, *The Intellectual Heritage of the Early Middle Ages*, Ithaca, N.Y., 1957, 22-39. C. E. DUBLER, « Sobre la crónica arábigo-bizantina de 741 y la influencia bizantina en la peninsula ibérica », *Al-Andalus*, XI (1946), 283-349, at pp. 295, 327, 333, holds that fragments of Byzantine historians were present in Spain and that Byzantine authors were used as « models » by Spanish writers but he does not prove this, at least for the Visigothic period.

Theodoret, emphasize, much more than Eusebius, the deference that the Christian prince owes to the priesthood and his « duty to assist the Church by imposing the priests' decisions in matters of faith on all Christians, even by force »[61]. The *Historia tripartita* contains, for instance, Theodoret's legendary version of the clash between St. Ambrose and Theodosius I, with the spectacular triumph of Ambrose[62]. But in general the *Historia* presents the Christian ruler as the ideal prince acting as « a channel of God's control over the course of history »[63]. One need only refer to the picture, mainly drawn from Socrates, of the very undistinguished Emperor Theodosius II, whose armies are portrayed as winning miraculous victories because of his virtues and prayers[64].

Both the exaltation of the « sacerdotium » in some parts of the *Historia tripartita* and the portrait of the ideal prince may help to explain some apparent contradictions between Isidore's theory of the just king in the *Sententiae* and his laudatory portraits of individual kings in the *Historiae*[65]. Even in the *Sententiae* Isidore is of his age in admitting

(61) Dvornik, *op. cit.* (n. 7), II, 789. The whole discussion of Sozomen and Theodoret (pp. 786-95) is most valuable.

(62) IX, 30 (pp. 540-46). Cf. also the account of the relations between Ambrose and Valentinian I (VII, 8, pp. 394-96), the dialogue between Pope Liberius and Constantius II (V, 17, pp. 237-41), on which cf. Dvornik, 730f., and the emphasis on Theodosius II's respect for the priesthood (X, 27, p. 620). All these passages are taken from Theodoret.

(63) Downey, cited above (n. 27), p. 63.

(64) XI, 17-18 (pp. 651-56); XII, 12 (680f.). Theodoret also contributed to this portrait (X, 27-28, pp. 619-22), while Sozomen's allocution to Theodosius II (I, 1, pp. 4-9) contains, as Dvornik says (p. 789) « the entire Hellenistic terminology derived from Eusebius on the ideal emperor », although he makes some significant additions of his own.

(65) See Laistner, pp. 58-60. On Isidore's theory see M. Reydellet, « La conception du souverain chez Isidore de Séville », *Isidoriana*, León 1961, 457-66. For the portraits see n. 85 below. See also E. Ewig, « Zum christlichen Königsgedanken im Frühmittelalter », *Das Königtum*, Lindau-Constance 1956, 30-6.

the Christian king's right to intervene in church affairs [66]. Here one may detect the influence not only of historical texts and of earlier Latin Fathers but of Acts of Councils and papal letters which were known in Spain. The *Collectio Hispana* contains, for instance, the Acts of Chalcedon, with Marcian's address to the assembled bishops and imperial decrees confirming the Council's decision; it also contains the deferential letter of Pope Anastasius II to Emperor Anastasius I, with its statement: « The heart of Your pious Clemency is the holy shrine of the public welfare, and, since God has appointed you to rule as His vicar over the world, it is by your instrumentality that the evangelical and apostolic statutes will find no opposition in stubborn pride » [67]. Such statements helped to form the minds of Spanish churchmen in a Byzantine pattern, which emerges most clearly in John of Biclar and Julian of Toledo.

Portrayal of Visigothic rulers as God's Vicars, new Constantines, is one of the most striking signs of the Eusebian and Byzantine patterns history assumed in Spain. The application of Biblical examples to the Visigoths appears in John of Biclar, when he compares the victory of Recared's Duke Claudius, « with scarcely three hundred men » over « some 60,000 Franks » to that of Gideon in

(66) See esp. *Sententiae* (Díaz, 111), III, 51, 4-6 (*PL*, LXXXIII, 723f.).

(67) *PL*, LXXXIV, 161f., 173-78, 807-12, esp. 809D : « *Pectus clementiae vestrae sacrarium est publicae felicitatis, ut per instantiam vestram, quam velut vicarium praesidere iussit in terris, evangelicis apostolicisque praeceptis non dura superbia resistatur* ». The translation (from Mansi) is that of Dvornik, p. 809. Some of Pope Leo the Great's letters to Byzantine emperors are also contained in the Hispana (e.g. 711ff., 715-24, 725-46). They are extremely deferential, although most of the instances where Leo speaks of the priestly character of the empire (see Dvornik, 772-76), do not seem to be included in the Collection. In ep. 59, col. 729C, Leo speaks of Marcian's « priestly feelings » (sacerdotalem affectum). On the other hand, the *Hispana* does not include Gelasius I's trenchant pronouncements (on which see Dvornik, 804-9).

the Book of Judges over the Midianites [68]. Julian of Toledo also repeatedly adduces Old Testament examples and parallels [69]. The Spanish Liturgy similarly compares the King to Moses and David, his enemies to Pharaoh and Amalech [70]. But actual examples are less prominent in Spain than what Peterson called « political theology », the application of Eusebius' idea of the ruler, which had become standard political ideology in Byzantium, to the West [71].

The idea that Constantine stands at the beginning of the present period of history, fundamental to Byzantine churchmen and church historians of the fifth and sixth centuries, is found in John of Biclar, where Recared *is* the new Constantine [72]. In John, in Isidore and – most crudely – in the *Vitas Patrum Emeritensium*, Recared is contrasted with Leovigild, the saint, the holy king, against the unjust heretical ruler [73]. For John and the *Vitas* God

(68) John, *s. a.* 589,2 (Mommsen, 218; Campos, 97). It is perhaps of interest that Isidore does not repeat this comparison, although he uses John here (*Hist. Goth.*, 54, p. 289).

(69) See below and n. 162.

(70) Cf. the hymn « In profectione exercitus » (Díaz, 358), ed. C. Blume, *Analecta hymnica medii aevi*, XXVII, Leipzig 1897, 270. See also the « Ordo quando rex cum exercitu ad prelium egreditur », in Férotin, *op. cit.* (n. 45), 149-53.

(71) E. Peterson, *Der Monotheismus als politisches Problem*, Leipzig 1935, 71f. See Cranz (cited above, n. 6), 53f.

(72) Ewig (cited above, n. 11), 9, notes that Tiberius was adopted and proclaimed Caesar by Justin II in 574 under the name Tiberius Constantinus. This occurred while John was in Constantinople (see above, n. 19) though he does not cite Tiberius' full name in his *Chronicon*. Isidore, *Origines* (Díaz, 122), V,1,7, sees a new era of legislation beginning with Constantine, and also of Church legislation and life (VI,16,2-6; this is less clear in the *Chronicon*, 329-334, pp. 465f.). Cf. the *Historia tripartita* (n. 60 above), which begins with the vision of Constantine (I, 4, 7, p. 17); Kaegi, *op. cit.* (n. 9), 220, 230.

(73) John, e.g. *s. a.* 580,2, contrasted with 587, 5 (Mommsen, 216, 218; Campos, 89f., 95). Isidore, *Hist. Goth.*, 52-56, esp. 52 (p. 289.1-3). *Vitas* (n. 12 above), V,ix,1-6 (pp. 228-30). Recared's restitution of goods confiscated by his father paralleled the action of Justin II in 567 (cf. L. Bréhier, *Vie et mort de Byzance*, Paris 1948, 35); perhaps this parallel influenced John's recording the fact (*s. a.* 587,7, Mommsen, 218; Campos, 96).

vindicates Recared's cause against the Franks even when he is not present himself, as – for a Byzantine historian – God vindicated Theodosius II's cause against the barbarians, although Theodosius never left his palace to lead his armies [74]. In John's account of the Third Council of Toledo, in 589, Recared « renews » the example of Constantine the Great and Marcian, « in *our* time », « rooting up » Arianism and completing the task Constantine began [75]. The Acts of the Third Council of Toledo (a Council « managed », as I said, by another churchman familiar with Byzantium, Leander of Seville) also present Recared as Constantine. He appears, like Constantine at Nicaea, « in the midst [of the bishops, and] having joined with the priests of God in prayer, full of divine inspiration », addresses the Council, like Marcian at Chalcedon, making it clear that his decision has been responsible for the conversion of the Goths, that *he* has called together the Council and that he expects the Bishops to carry out his wishes [76]. Eusebius' view of Constantine « as an idealized *type* rather than an individual – a glorious type in whom

(74) John, *s. a.* 589,2 (Mommsen, 218.28-30; Campos, 97): « *in hoc ergo certamine gratia divina et fides catholica, quam Reccaredus rex cum Gothis fideliter adeptus est, esse cognoscitur operata, quoniam non est difficile deo nostro, si in paucis, una in multis detur victoria* » ; *Vitas*, V,xii,5 (p. 246): « *Deus... precibus excellentissimi Reccaredi principis sanguinem innocuum ulciscens, rompheali iudicio protinus de inimicis mirificam fecit ultionem* ». Cp. the *Hist. tripartita* (cited, n. 64 above).

(75) John, *s. a.* 590,1 (Mommsen, 219.10-29; Campos, 98f.). Cf. nn. 11 above and 76 below. Gregory the Great, *Registrum*, IX, 228 (*MGH*, *Epistulae*, II, 221f.) virtually hails Recared as a new Constantine, saying: « *Audita quippe novi diebus nostris virtute miraculi quod per excellentiam tuam cuncta Gothorum gens ab errore Arrianae hereseos in fidei rectae soliditate translata est, exclamare cum propheta libet : ' Haec est immutatio dexterae excelsi '* [Ps. 76,12] ».

(76) *PL*, LXXXIV, 341-45; ed. Vives, 107-16. The phrases translated are: « *ecce in medio eorum adfuit serenissimus princeps, seque cum Dei sacerdotibus orationi communicans, divini deinceps flamine plenus* ». Cp. Marcian's address at Chalcedon and the decrees confirming the Council, in the Hispana (*PL*, LXXXIV, 161f., 173-78).

is revealed the triumph of the Church »[77], appears again in John of Biclar and the Acts of Toledo III. The « Laudes » the bishops of 589 sing, an example of Byzantine ruler-worship transferred to the West, and probably directly modelled on the « Laudes » addressed to Marcian at Chalcedon, hail Recared in Byzantine language as a truly « Apostolic » man[78]. This stylized form of royal appearance and address is repeated, together with the « Laudes », in later Councils of Toledo[79].

The idea of the ruler as « the Lord's Anointed », derived from the Old Testament, had been combined in Byzantium with Hellenistic philosophy to create the idea of one « legitimate ruler over the entire Christian world,... God's image and representative on earth, as God's viceroy charged with the maintenance of peace in the Christian world, with the Christian mission to the ' barbarians ', and with the preservation of law », himself « Lex animata »[80]. The emperor in Byzantium was assigned « an easily understood place in the divine plan of history »[81].

(77) Hanning, *op. cit.* (n. 5), 32.

(78) *PL*, LXXXIV, 345C; Vives, 117: « *Ipse novarum plebium in ecclesia catholica conquisitor. Ipse mereatur veraciter apostolicum meritum qui apostolicum implevit officium* ». The direct model for the « Laudes » of Toledo was probably the text of Chalcedon. The text in the *Hispana*, as we have it, has shortened the « Laudes » (*PL*, 162f.); the full text of the acclamations compared Marcian to Constantine, David, Paul, the apostles, and hailed him as priest-emperor (J. D. Mansi, *Sacrorum Conciliorum nova et amplissima collectio*, VII, Florence 1762, 169f., 177). Constantine is seen as an apostle in the *Vita Constantini*, IV, 60. (If this passage is an interpolation into Eusebius' text, as Dvornik, pp. 747-59, believes, this would not affect its later influence).

(79) E. g. Receswinth before Toledo VIII (653) or Ervigius before Toledo XII (681); *PL*, LXXXIV, 411, 467; Vives, 260f., 380. « Laudes » in Toledo IV (633), V (636), VI (638), etc. *PL*, 386C, 392A-B, 402B; Vives, 221, 230, 246. See Ewig, cited above (n. 65), 26-30.

(80) P. J. Alexander, in *Speculum*, XXXVII (1962), 348 (slightly changed). On the idea of the emperor as « incarnate law » cf. Dvornik, *op. cit.* (n. 7), II, chs. 10 and 11. For sixth-century Byzantine works cf. pp. 706-16, for Justinian pp. 716-23.

(81) Alexander, *loc. cit.*

In Visigothic Spain the king occupied essentially the same place. Certainly a king such as Sisebut or Receswinth had as little doubt as Justinian that it was to him that God had « given the rule of the faithful », and that bishops were to decide matters in a way, as Receswinth said, « pleasing to God and to My Faith » [82]. The Spanish Church enhanced the king's position by the rite of anointing at Coronations, for which there is no Christian precedent; it was adopted certainly from 672, very probably earlier [83]. The Church blessed the king about to go out to war as God's champion [84]. Its historians echoed this view. Isidore celebrated not only Recared but Suinthila as a saint [85]. Julian of Toledo saw Wamba, at war, as « protected by an escort of angels » [86].

(82) For Sisebut see below. Receswinth's « Tome », addressed to Toledo VIII (653), ends (*PL*, LXXXIV, 415B; Vives, 266), with the instruction that the bishops were to deal with the Jews, « *de his iubeatis ardenter et verissime Deo ac fidei meae placitam sententiam dare, ut sicut mihi divina pietas regimen fidelium dedit cum quibus se a me et glorificari cognoscit, ita quoque infidelium adsequi tribuat lucrum* ». The idea of the royal missionary or the « episkopos ton ektos », to quote the famous phrase of the *Vita Constantini*, IV, 24, appears here, as in Sisebut (below, p. 285).

(83) Anointing is attested for Wamba and later kings; see the *Laterculus regum Visigothorum* (Díaz, 241), *MGH*, *AA*, XIII, 468. This text becomes more detailed in its record of individual kings as time proceeds. The fact that earlier rulers are not stated to be anointed is therefore not conclusive. Julian of Toledo, *Historia Wambae*, 3 (p. 502) does not record the ceremony as a novelty in 672: he speaks of anointing in the « accustomed place » (locum sedis antiquae). Toledo IV, c. 75 (*PL*, LXXXIV, 384A; Vives, 217), with its stress on 1 Chronicles 16,22, « Do not touch my anointed », may indicate the ceremony existed in 633; perhaps it had been recently introduced, to bolster up the position of the usurper Sisenand. Cf. the *Liber Commicus* (Díaz, 640), ed. J. Pérez and A. González y Ruiz-Zorrilla (Monumenta Hispaniae Sacra, ser. Lit., II.2), Madrid 1955, 535-37, with very interesting readings « In ordinatione regis », from Wis. 9,1-12, Rom. 13,1-8 and (most strikingly) Luke 4,16-22. The use of the last passage shows that the king was « anointed to preach » and heal men's afflictions. We are not far from the « rois thaumaturges » of later centuries.

(84) See n. 70 above.

85) *Hist. Goth.*, 55-56, 64 (pp. 290, 293).

(86) *Historia Wambae*, 23 (p. 520.2-5): « angelorum excubiis ». Cf. the « Ordo » and hymn cited above (n. 70).

The only non-clerical historian of Visigothic Spain is King Sisebut. His reign, from 612 to 621, is one of the most important in the seventh century. His victories over the Byzantines probably decided their fate in Spain [87]. His decrees against the Jews were of signal importance for the future [88]. His religious foundations, his letters, his *Life of Desiderius* and his appeal to Isidore to write the *De natura rerum*, with its teaching against superstition, and the *Origines*, all reveal him as a Byzantine type of ruler, above all concerned with orthodoxy [89].

Sisebut's correspondence displays him at work as a Catholic King, reprimanding a bishop straying from his flock or one present at wild beast shows. The letters are filled with Biblical texts and phrases borrowed from Pope Gregory the Great [90]. His letter to his son Theudila, who had become a monk, is a sermon on the major vices and virtues [91]. The most ambitious surviving letter was addressed to the young Lombard King Adaloald and his mother Theodelinda. It is an anti-Arian sermon, denouncing Arianism as the source of wars, famine and plague; a contrast is drawn with the « Catholic peace » in which the

(87) See Isidore, *Hist. Goth.*, 61 (p. 291.22-26), and, more clearly, « Recapitulatio », 70 (295.1-4); also *Chron.*, 415 (p. 479). Fredegarius, *Chron.* IV, 33 (*MGH, SRM*, II, p. 133) saw Sisebut as triumphing completely over the Byzantines.

(88) See Katz, *op. cit.* (n. 53 above).

(89) J. Fontaine, *Isidore de Séville et la culture classique dans l'Espagne wisigothique*, II, Paris 1959, 868 n. 1, already suggested that Sisebut thought of himself as rivalling Justinian as a theologian. On Sisebut and the *De natura rerum* see *ibid.*, 454-57, and J. Fontaine (ed.), *Isidore de Séville, Traité de la Nature* (Bibliothèque de l'Ecole des Hautes Etudes Hispaniques, XXVIII), Bordeaux 1960, 4f., 151-59. See n. 100 below.

(90) Sisebut's *Epistulae* (Díaz, 87-92), ed. W. Gundlach, *MGH, Epist.* III, Berlin 1892, 662-75. The letter to Isidore (in verse) in Fontaine, *Isidore, Traité*, 329-35. The letters to Bishops Cecilius of Mentesa and Eusebius of Tarragona (pp. 662f., 668f.) illustrate Sisebut's views. He quotes from Gregory, *Reg.* I, 41 in the first letter and from *Reg.* IX, 230 in that to Theudila (p. 669).

(91) *Ibid.*, pp. 669-71.

« Gothic empire » now flourishes [92]. Citations from at least nine books of the Bible are combined with adroit flattery of Theodelinda. There are verbal parallels between the letter and Isidore's works [93]. However, the same style is used as in Sisebut's other prose writings so that it seems that, in logic, one must either conclude that *all* Sisebut's works were written by Isidore (or some other cleric) or, more probably, that Sisebut, when acting as a royal missionary, was writing the same language as his friend and correspondent [94].

Bruno Krusch, when editing Sisebut's *Life of Desiderius of Vienne*, complained that Sisebut did not attempt to describe « *mores hominum sine ira et studio* » [95]. Sisebut would have been surprised by such an idea. His work is an interesting combination of court history and hagiography. While seeking to edify the reader by the portrait of a miracle-working ascetic [96], Sisebut is also writing propaganda against the Franks. The portrait of Theodoric

(92) On this letter see FONTAINE, « Conversion » (cited, n. 17 above), 134-37 (cf. also 127f.), also O. BERTOLINI, in *La Conversione*, 350 and n. 60, JUNGMANN, cited above (n. 52), 65. See esp. p. 672.15-20. One wonders if Sisebut was drawing on letters like that of Avitus of Vienne to Clovis or Nicetius of Trier to Queen Clotsinda (really to Alboin); see *MGH*, *AA*, VI.2, 75f.; *MGH*, *Epist.*, III, 119-22.

(93) Cp. Sisebut, p. 675.14-16: « *Igitur ubi Deo Patri Deus Filius equalis ostenditur, de thesauris s a c r e l e g i s velut f l o r u m capita delecta collegimus et sub uno congesta exhaurientes eterni regis dona porreximus* », and Isidore, *Quaestiones in Vetus Testamentum*, In Genesim, Praef., 2 (*PL*, LXXXIII, 207B): « *In hoc opusculo exsequentes intexuimus, veterum ecclesiasticorum sententias congregantes, veluti ex diversis pratis f l o r e s lectos ad manum fecimus* ». Also Praef., 1 (*ib.*): « *Historia s a c r a e l e g i s non sine aliqua prenuntiatione futurorum gesta atque conscripta est* ».

(94) Cf. FONTAINE's suggestion, p. 135 n. 74, for the sources of the letter; on p. 136 he points out another parallel with Isidore. For Receswinth as royal missionary see n. 82 above.

(95) *MGH*, *SRM*, III, Hannover 1896, 623: « *patet auctorem motibus animi adeo deditum ad historiam conscribendam minus idoneum fuisse* ».

(96) Sisebut, *Vita vel passio S. Desiderii episcopi Viennensis* (DÍAZ, 86), *loc. cit.*, 1 (p. 630.4f.): « *pro imitatione praesentium, pro aedificatione hominum futurorum, pro sanctis exercendis studiis succedentium temporum* ».

and especially that of Brunhild as persecutors of Desiderius is modelled on *Passiones* of martyrs [97]. Theodoric's and Brunhild's actions are inspired by the Devil; they use magic arts against Desiderius [98]. Sisebut describes their deaths with loving care [99].

Is it to Sisebut that we owe, in addition to the *Origines* and *De natura rerum*, the composition of Isidore's historical works [100]? The first edition of Isidore's *Chronicle* should be dated in 615, the composition of the *De viris* in 615-618 and the first redaction of the *Histories* by 621 [101]. All these works were, therefore, written during Sisebut's reign. No dedication survives for the *Chronicle* or *De viris* and that of the *Histories* to King Sisenand may not be authentic; at most it merely implies Isidore sending Sisenand a copy of a work completed before his accession in 631 [102]. It is possible that earlier dedi-

(97) *Vita*, 15 (634.27f.): « *Nunc de* p a s s i o n i b u s *eius, qualiter sanctam animam omnipotenti Domino consignavit* ». Cf. 18 (636.11-16), the description of the cohort responsible for Desiderius' death, with the use of words such as « *funestis, teterrimus, ultroneus, rabiens* ». Desiderius is « *Martyr Christi* » (636.17).

(98) *Vita*, 8 (632.26f.); 16 (635.18-22), etc.

(99) *Ibid.*, 19-21 (636f.). Cp. the contemporary letters of Bulgar (*MGH*, *Epist.*, III, 677.21-25; 679.14-20), where Theodoric and Brunhild are said to be « *adsueta diffundentes venena* », and are seen as about to bring in the pagan Avars against other Franks (and Visigoths). Bulgar hopes for divine punishment of Brunhild as « author of strife » (« iurgiorum auctrix », p. 677.32). See also Fontaine, *Isidore de Séville* (n. 89 above), II, 841.

(100) See Isidore's letter to Sisebut (ep.vi), preceding the *Origines*, ed. Lindsay, and *Isidore, Traité*, ed. Fontaine, 167f.

(101) Cf. J. A. De Aldama, « Indicaciones sobre la cronología de las obras de S. Isidoro », *Miscellanea Isidoriana*, Rome 1936, 57-89, at 63, 65; Codoñer, 18-20. The date of the first redaction of the *Histories* is less certain. Mommsen, *AA*, XI, 254, refused to accept the view of H. Hertzberg, *Die Historien und die Chroniken des Isidorus von Sevilla*, Göttingen 1874, that the shorter version ended with Sisebut. Since it contains the notice of Sisebut's death it must have been finished later. But there seems a definite break with Sisebut's death and the account of Suinthila appears to be a postscript. L. Vázquez De Parga, « Notas sobre la obra histórica de San Isidoro », *Isidoriana*, León 1961, 99-105, at 104, does not solve this difficult question.

(102) Messmer, *op. cit.* (n. 58), 105f., attempts to support the authenticity of this dedication, which is doubted by Vázquez De Parga (*loc. cit.*). Cf. Díaz y Díaz, *cit. infra* (n. 106).

cations to Sisebut may have been suppressed after the overthrow of Sisebut's son, Recared II, by Suinthila in 621, when Isidore's second edition of the *Histories*, with its praise of Suinthila, was published in 624 [103]. The revision of this second edition was very sketchy; it did not change the *Recapitulatio* of the *Historia Gothorum*, with its concluding outburst of praise for Sisebut [104]. The first edition of the *Chronicle* also ended with high praise for Sisebut, not eliminated in the second edition of 626 [105]. There is no doubt Sisebut was the most cultivated king who reigned during Isidore's episcopate; Isidore's friendly relations with him and Sisebut's own historical work both suggest very strongly that Sisebut persuaded Isidore to undertake at least the *Chronicle* and *Histories* [106].

Can we discover, from *internal* evidence, why Isidore wrote these works [107] ? In general Isidore seems to have

(103) The accounts of Sisebut's death are contradictory in the two editions of Isidore's *Hist.* (61, pp. 291f.), one edition suggesting poison, and no cause is given for the rapid death of Recared II: it seems that Isidore is avoiding blaming Suinthila.

(104) *Hist. Goth.*, 70 (p. 295.1-4), cited n. 150 below.

(105) *Chron.*, 415-416 (pp. 479f.). Note that no censure of Sisebut is expressed here for having converted the Jews by force; cp. *Hist. Goth.*, 60, p. 291.14-17, but Isidore much attenuates the force of this censure by stating « *sive per occasionem sive per veritatem Christus adnuntietur* », a virtual acceptance of Sisebut's action, which was also confirmed by IV Toledo in 633, under Isidore's presidency (c. 57, *PL*, LXXXIV, 380A; Vives, 211). Later opinion in Spain certainly approved of Sisebut's action. Cf. the *Continuatio Isidori Hispana*, 15 (Díaz, 397), *MGH*, *AA*, *XI*, 339.29f.

(106) M. C. Díaz y Díaz, « Isidoro en la Edad Media hispana », *Isidoriana*, 346f., also inclines to accept Sisebut's agency here. On Sisebut see also the articles of W. Stach, cited in *Isidoriana*, 62 n. 135; Díaz y Díaz, « La cultura de la España visigótica del s. vii », *Caratteri del secolo VII* = *Settimane di studio*, V, Spoleto 1958, 829f.

(107) Isidore's historical works have been the object of relatively little attention. Only the *De viris* has been critically edited recently (n. 1 above). Mommsen's edition of 1894 is generally considered unimprovable. Vázquez de Parga (n. 101 above) disagrees and promises a new edition. Some articles on the historical works are reviewed in *Isidoriana*, 58f. I have found H. Messmer, *op. cit.* (n. 58), helpful over details, although inclined to carry theses too far. See A. Borst, « Das Bild der Geschichte in der Enzyklopädie Isidors von Sevilla », *Deutsches Archiv für Erforschung des Mittelalters*, XXII (1966), 1-62

had a very concrete purpose in view when he wrote. His shorter works, such as the *Allegoriae*, *Differentiae*, Book II, *De ortu et obitu patrum*, and *Prooemia*, are intended as manuals for the Spanish clergy. Book I of the *Differentiae* could have been used in a school [108]. The immediate usefulness of other works such as the *De ecclesiasticis officiis* and *Regula monachorum*, does not need demonstration. Let us turn to the *Chronicle* and *De viris*, for which Isidore had models at his disposal, the *Chronicle* of Eusebius-Jerome and Jerome's *De viris* [109]. Both these works had been written for a clearly discernible apologetic purpose. The *Chronicle* of Eusebius was to demonstrate the greater antiquity and superiority of Biblical to pagan history, while Jerome's *De viris* was to show the adversaries of Christianity that the Church too had « eloquent philosophers » and « doctors » [110].

In the West Jerome's translation and continuation of Eusebius was continued or imitated by – among others – Prosper and Hydatius in the fifth, Victor of Tunnuna and John of Biclar in the sixth century. Jerome's *De viris* was continued by Gennadius. These writers were all known to Isidore [111]. The immediate concern with anti-pagan apologetic disappears in the fifth century but it is largely replaced by a concern with *heresies*. This is common to all the writers I mention, although Hydatius,

(108) For the *Differentiae*, I, see FONTAINE, cited above (n. 2), 76f.

(109) For the *Chron.* see Isidore's Praef. (p. 424). The *De viris* is preserved with the earlier *De viris* of Jerome and Gennadius in most manuscripts and Isidore knew his predecessors' works. See CODOÑER, 17 n. 3, 62.

(110) Cf. A. D. MOMIGLIANO, « Pagan and Christian Historiography in the Fourth Century A. D », *The Conflict between Paganism and Christianity in the Fourth Century*, Oxford 1963, 83ff.; Jerome, *De viris*, Prol., ed. E. C. RICHARDSON (Texte und Untersuchungen, XIV), Leipzig 1896, 2.

(111) Prosper, Hydatius, Victor and John are used in Isidore's *Chron.* and in other works, Gennadius in *De viris*, 16 (Codoñer, 143; old numbering 29, *PL*, LXXXIII, 1098B).

for instance, living in Galicia and cut off by the invasions from the East, knows much less about developments in the Eastern Church than does Prosper, let alone Gennadius, in Gaul [112]. Victor of Tunnuna and John of Biclar, the two Western chroniclers closest to Isidore in time, are very much concerned with heresy. Victor, who is the only chronicler later than Jerome specifically cited by Isidore [113], covered the period 444-565. Apart from the Vandal persecution in his own North Africa, Victor scarcely refers to the West. For many years the only entries in his *Chronicle* deal with the ecclesiastical troubles and – to a lesser extent – with the civil wars of the Eastern Empire [114]. The picture he conveys is that of a ceaseless struggle for survival on the part of the defenders of the Council of Chalcedon. They are persecuted by the emperors of Byzantium from Leo I to Anastasius I, again by Theodora and, eventually, by Justinian. In the end Justinian appears as no better than the persecuting Arian Vandal Kings in North Africa [115]. John of Biclar, continuing Victor's *Chronicle* from 567 to 590, apparently accepts his point of view on Justinian but he is more concerned with Arianism in Spain than with the anti-Chalce-

(112) See n. 13 above. Hydatius' dependence on chance sources for information about the East is shown by his *Chron.*, 106 (*MGH*, *AA*, XI, 22); this entry displays great interest in heresy, combined with several mistakes about Nestorianism. For Gennadius cf. P. Courcelle, *Les Lettres grecques en Occident, de Macrobe à Cassiodore*, 2nd ed., Paris 1948, 221ff.

(113) Isidore, *Chron.*, 1 (p. 424.5): « *inter quos praecipue Victor Tonnonensis ecclesiae episcopus* ».

(114) From 473 to 538 there appears to be only one entry dealing with the West (outside North Africa), that of 497 (*MGH*, *AA*, XI, p. 192.32-34) on the schism in the papacy.

(115) The apparently final triumph of heresy in 553, due to Justinian, is significantly (« *his ita gestis* ») followed by an earthquake in Constantinople (p. 203.22). For Victor Justinian's views are « *nova superstitio* » (p. 205.25). Note one of the last entries (p. 206.3-5), where a defender of the « Three Chapters », in exile at Constantinople, is buried « *iuxta confessores, quibus Ugnericus Wandalorum rex linguas absciderat* ».

donian movement in the East, which seemed in abeyance [116].

Isidore is more ambitious in his scope than either Victor or John. His *Chronicle*, as he says, is a chronological summary (« temporum summa ») of history from Creation until his own time [117]. It is the first to introduce the scheme of the six ages of the world, found in Augustine, into a *Chronicle* [118]. In Isidore's account of history before Christ one can find traces of anti-pagan apologetic such as references to the beginning of the cult of the gods [119]. Isidore also notes the prior antiquity of Hebrew

(116) Since Justin II appeared to have returned to Chalcedonian orthodoxy (John, *s. a.* 567, 2, Mommsen, 211; Campos, 78). See above and n. 75.

(117) Isidore, *Chron.*, 2 (p. 425.1). Cf. *Origines*, I, 43, ed. Lindsay, « *et per historiam summa retro temporum annorumque supputatio conprehenditur* ». (On the discussion of history in the *Orig.* cf. FONTAINE, *Isidore de Séville*, I, 180-85).

(118) *Chron.*, 2-3 (p. 425), *Orig.*, V, 38, 5. AMOS FUNKENSTEIN, *Heilsplan und natürliche Entwicklung*, Munich 1965, p. 155 n. 202, holds that Isidore misunderstood Augustine's use of the « ages ». If so, this mistake was corrected by Julian of Toledo, *De comprobatione sextae aetatis*, III, 1 (*PL*, XCVI, 569f.). I must disagree with Funkenstein's theory that Augustine's view of the rest of time as « the old age of the world in which men could only await an end hidden from them » (I quote from the review of Funkenstein by B. S. SMITH, in *Speculum*, XLIII, 1968, 509-11) dominated historians until the eleventh century. It is true that Isidore concludes his *Chron.* (418, p. 481) by remarking (following *De civitate Dei*, XXII, 30): « *Residuum saeculi tempus humanae investigationis incertum est* », but this is to discourage millenarism. The tone of Isidore's works, particularly the *Hist. Goth.*, is generally agreed to be strongly optimistic, in contrast to the pessimism of Gregory the Great. Cf. FONTAINE, *Isidore de Séville*, II, 867f., and the articles of STEIDLE and ROMERO, cited in *Isidoriana*, 58f. Funkenstein's comments on Isidore are practically confined to the *Origines* and here he does not use Fontaine's work. It is also mistaken to cite Taio, *Sententiae* (DÍAZ, 209), III, 4 (*PL*, LXXX, 853-55) as independent evidence for Spanish thought on the « ages » when this passage (esp. 854D-855A) is derived verbatim from Gregory, *Hom. in Evangelia*, I, 19, 1 (*PL*, LXXVI, 1154).

(119) E. g. *Chron.*, 24 (p. 430): « *His temporibus primum templa constructa sunt et quidam principes gentium tamquam dii adorari coeperunt* ». This is not clearly derived from *De civ. Dei*, XVI, 2. Cf. also 22 (430.10f.), 38, 40 (433), 47, 50, 56 (434), the last entry recording the construction of the temple at Delphi *after* Moses received the Law. Jerome and Augustine are the sources for most of these notices but Isidore makes small changes (esp. in 38). In ge-

to Greek letters [120]. Many classical legends also appear, however, often culled from Augustine, not Jerome. They seem to serve only Isidore's « curiosity » [121]. Pagan authors are used as well as Christian, notably the fourth-century Eutropius' *Breviarium* and Rufius Festus [122]. No doubt these were sources sufficiently « neutral » in tone to be safely used [123]. Eutropius is the main source for Isidore's account of the Roman emperors – of whom we are told as much as of the rise of the Church [124].

The *fusion* of Christian and pagan sources in the *Chronicle* is typical of Isidore [125]. Would it, however, be true to say that Isidore has *no* definite purpose in the *Chronicle* ? Can one apply to this work a recent judgement on the *De viris*, that it was written « without any bias, without a concrete ideological purpose » [126] ? Can this judgement be maintained even of the *De viris* ?

neral, the theme is not stressed, as it is, e.g., by Martin of Braga (*op. cit.* infra, n. 176), 7, pp. 186ff., etc. Cf. CARRERAS ARES (cited above, n. 14), 190 and n. 50. See also Isidore, *Orig.*, III, 22,2.

(120) E. g. *Chron.*, 62 (435): « *Cadmus regnat Thebes, qui primus Graecas litteras adinvenit* ». (Only « Cadmus - Thebes » is from Jerome). In 55 (434) we are told that the Jews received the Law and letters together by Moses. The brief chronicle in *Orig.* V also includes these two notices.

(121) *Chron.*, 66-72, 75, 77-80, 84-85, 93 (pp. 435-38). Isidore adds some notices from other sources, e.g. 97 (438), the « discovery » of Latin letters by the nymph Carmentis (cf. *Orig.*, I, 4, 1, on which FONTAINE, I, 61).

(122) Cf. H. HERTZBERG, cited above (n. 59bis), pp. 340-43. Isidore also used the anonymous *Chronica urbis Romae* or *Chronica urbana* and *Liber de viris illustribus* (Mommsen, *AA*, *XI*, 395; Hertzberg, 339f., 307).

(123) Cf. MOMIGLIANO, cited above (n. 110), 88. Isidore could, e.g., use Eutropius for his notice on the institution of a census (156, p. 444).

(124) See *Chron.*, 235-328 (pp. 453-65). Out of about ninety entries some thirty-five are concerned with Christianity; the proportion increases greatly from the late second century. The only extensive entry is 247. Cp. the notices of Trajan (264-65) and Antoninus Pius (273), pp. 458f.

(125) Cf. *Isidoriana*, León 1961, 48, and FONTAINE, *Isidore de Séville*, *passim*, e.g. his comments (I, pp. 182f.) on the short list of historians in *Orig.*, I, 44.

(126) CODOÑER, pp. 17f.: « En su catálogo [the *De viris*] se reduce a dejar constancia de unos determinados escritores, con un sentido casi de índice, sin partidismo ninguno, y sin una finalidad ideológica concreta ». FUNKENSTEIN,

There are certain arguments in its favour. Isidore is no doubt a providentialist historian but this is less clear in the *Chronicle* and the *De viris* than in the *Histories* [127]. It is also now generally agreed that Isidore's genuine *De viris* does not include thirteen chapters largely devoted to North African authors and to defenders of the « Three Chapters », which were considered inextricably bound up with the cause of the Council of Chalcedon – against Justinian [128]. But an analysis of the thirty-three chapters of the *De viris* certainly by Isidore shows that sixteen of these entries, or almost half, are concerned with heresy. (The subject that interests Isidore next to this is asceticism, with which nine entries deal) [129]. Of the sixteen entries dealing with heresy, seven (perhaps eight) deal with Arianism or anti-Arian writers, four with anti-Chalcedonian movements in the East and their opponents [130]. When Isidore recorded his predecessors' writings he was clearly more concerned with the question of heresy than with anything else [131].

op. cit. (n. 118), pp. 70-72, considers that, from Isidore onwards, all historians were interested in was maintaining an unbroken record of the facts. This greatly oversimplifies the picture of early medieval historiography.

(127) Cf. *Hist. Goth.*, 28-29 (pp. 278.31-279.10), apparently an addition by Isidore to his sources' account of the Huns. References to the accomplishment of prophecies in Isidore are often taken verbatim from his sources (e.g. *Hist.*, 19, p. 275-19-21, is taken from Hydatius, 414, p. 18, with the characteristic Isidorian reservation of « *a quibusdam creditur* »).

(128) See the discussion in Codoñer, pp. 20-41. The author's view as to the date of these 13 chapters, often known as the « African Appendix », appears to vary between s. VII and VIII (pp. 34, 40) but she considers it was written or at least reached its definite form in Spain, where it is known by the ninth century (pp. 26, 34 n. 38). See n. 139 below.

(129) Chapters 1-3, 9-10, 12, 14, 18-20, 22, 25, 28-31 are concerned with heresy (29 is the only doubtful case but Licinian's work on Baptism [Codoñer, p. 150] was almost certainly directed against Arianism); chs. 6, 13, 15, 23, 26, 28, 30-32 with ascetic or monastic subjects. Chs. 4, 8, 13, 16, 25, 31 and 33 deal with historians or hagiographers.

(130) With Arianism: chs. 1, 14, 20, 22, 28-31; with anti-Chalcedonianism chs. 10, 18-19, 25.

(131) See also *Orig.* VIII, 3-5, and *De haeresibus* (Díaz, 110), ed. A. C. Vega, Escorial, 1940.

Isidore's attitude to the Three Chapters cannot be said to be impartial. His *Chronicle* has six entries dealing with « Acephalites », the name given to the radical Monophysites, opponents of the Council of Chalcedon [132]. While Isidore draws on Victor of Tunnuna he is not entirely dependent on him [133]. Isidore was himself confronted with the « Acephalite » heresy in 619, when called upon, at the Second Council of Seville, to confute a Syrian bishop [134]. It is worth noting that this event occurred during the years Isidore was writing and revising his historical works [135]. Isidore's entries in the *Chronicle* illustrate his remarks on Justinian and the defenders of the Three Chapters in the *De viris* [136]. Isidore records Justinian's triumphs but his general judgement on him is extremely unfavourable [137]. His heresy overshadows his victories. Justinian, Isidore writes, « accepted the heresy of the Acephalites and, proscribing the Council of Chalce-

(132) *Chron.* 385, 386a, 389a, 394a, 397a, 401a (pp. 473-76). 385 is found in both editions of the *Chron.* Cf. also *Orig.*, VIII, 5, 66.

(133) *Chron.*, 385 (p. 473) seems to be clearer in its judgement on the « Acephali » than Victor. The notice « *Acephalorum haeresis orta est* » appears in the short Chronicle in *Orig.*, V, 39, 39.

(134) See *PL*, LXXXIV, 598-608; Vives, 171-85. Cf. J. Madoz, « El Florilegio Patrístico del II Concilio de Sevilla (a.619) », *Miscellanea Isidoriana*, Rome 1936, 177-220. See also Braulio, *Renotatio librorum divi Isidori* (Díaz, 159), *PL*, LXXXII, 67D; *Continuatio Isidori Hispana*, 16, *MGH*, *AA*, XI, 339f.

(135) See above and n. 101.

(136) See n. 130 above. Codoñer, pp. 72, 74f., holds that Isidore shows no inclination in either direction on the Three Chapters. It is true that he it reluctant to go beyond the sources he employs (p. 77) but the *De viris* cannot be considered in isolation. In the *Chron.*, 397a (n. 138 below) Isidore is perfectly clear in defending the Three Chapters. Therefore, when he says (*De viris*, 18, p. 144) that Justinian « *tria capitula damnare contendit* » (the identical words used in the *Chron.*), or (25, p. 147) that Victor was exiled for defending them, his meaning is clear. This apart from the question of the additions to the work (n. 139 below).

(137) For the triumphs see *Chron.*, 398-399b (pp. 475f.), mainly based on Victor of Tunnuna. The entry on Belisarius' conquest of North Africa in *Hist. Vandalorum*, 83f. (pp. 299f.) is entirely based on Victor.

don, compelled all the bishops in his kingdom to condemn the Three Chapters »[138]. This hostile attitude to Justinian appears again in additions to the *De viris* in MS. León 22, which the work's recent editor considers may be due to Braulio or even to Isidore himself[139].

Isidore's *Historia Gothorum* (to which his other two *Histories* are merely appendages) is of particular interest because, unlike his *Chronicle* and *De viris*, it has no clear model. It has not been shown that Isidore knew Jordanes' *Getica*[140]; when the two authors are compared, Isidore is far less exaggerated in his praise of the Goths[141]. Isidore's additions to his sources are small though significant – for instance, adapting Orosius, he remarks that Valens, « who had consigned *such fine souls* [the Goths] to eternal fire [through converting them to Arianism] might deservedly be burned alive »[142]. (The description of the Goths' souls is Isidore's). Many other small changes are intended to « improve » the picture of the Goths presented by Isidore's sources, and amount to very skilful editing[143]. Isidore's general ideology of the Goths appears in the *Laus Spaniae*, which precedes, and the *Recapitulatio*, which follows, the *Historia*. The precedents and verbal sources for the *Laus Spaniae* have been carefully analysed

(138) *Chron.*, 397a (p. 475): « *Iste Acefalorum haeresim suscepit atque in proscriptionem synodi Calchedonensis omnes in regno suo episcopos tria capitula damnare contendit* ». See also n. 149 below.

(139) Codoñer prints these additions (p. 27). On p. 28 she suggests Braulio or (more hesitantly) Isidore as their author but on p. 33 she says they must be later than s. VII. Why?

(140) Messmer, *op. cit.* (n. 58), p. 86, points out that Isidore may at least have heard of Cassiodorus' original work. On the *Hist. Goth.* cf. Fontaine, « Conversion » (cited above, n. 17), 117f.

(141) Cp. Isidore, 5 (p. 269) and Jordanes, *De origine actibusque Getarum* 21 (*MGH*, *AA*, V.1, p. 87).

(142) *Hist. Goth.*, 9 (p. 271.22f). Isidore also probably invents the Catholic Goths (10, p. 271).

(143) Cf. Messmer, 91f., 93-95.

but no known precedent exists for the intimate association of Spain and the Goths in a historical work. Isidore completely *transforms* the meaning of his sources. This is particularly clear in his use of two works of St. Cyprian. Isidore transforms St. Cyprian's praise of virginity into praise of Spain and Cyprian's praise of « Ecclesiae gloriosae fecunditas » into that of « Geticae *gentis* gloriosa fecunditas ». He also changes a passage in Cyprian where he questioned the « security » of even the richest of this world. Isidore affirms that the « Gothorum florentissima gens » enjoys Spain and its great riches (« opes largas »), « imperii felicitate *secura* » [144]. Sources or close parallels to the *Recapitulatio* have not yet appeared. The view it conveys is extremely clear. « Rome herself, the conqueror of all peoples, submitted to the yoke of captivity and yielded to Gothic triumphs, and the mistress of *all* nations served the Goths as a handmaid » [145]. The *Historia* ends with the conquest by the Visigoths of the « Romans » (Byzantines) in Spain [146].

If Isidore's *Chronicle* and *De viris* have a direction it is against heresy. If Isidore's *Historia Gothorum* has a direction it is against Byzantium [147]. These works have the same purpose – they constitute a declaration of independence on the part of Visigothic Spain and an affirmation of its worth against the ancient mistress of the

(144) See J. Madoz, in *Razón y Fe*, CXVI (1939), 247-57, and *ibid.*, CXXII (1941), 229-31. The use of St. Cyprian is brought out in the second article. The passages used are *De habitu virginum*, 3, and *Ad Donatum*, 13. Cf. Isidore, p. 267.6, 23-25.

(145) *Hist. Goth.*, 67 (p. 294.9-11): « *Roma ipsa victrix omnium populorum subacta captivitatis iugo Geticis triumphis adcederet et domina cunctarum gentium illis ut famula deserviret* ». The translation follows closely that of G. Donini and G. B. Ford, Jr., *Isidore of Seville's History of the Kings of the Goths, Vandals, and Suevi*, Leiden 1966, p. 31.

(146) See below and n. 150.

(147) See above and n. 57, also Fontaine, *Isidore de Séville*, II, 868f.

Mediterranean world, still overshadowing politically in the early seventh century, when it continued to hold the North African coast, much of Italy, the islands of the Mediterranean and the command of the sea, and overshadowing culturally, in literature and art [148]. Isidore's verdict that Justinian, the greatest of Byzantine emperors, was a heretic was, in its day, a declaration of theological independence [149]. The *Historia Gothorum* proclaimed *political* independence. The *Recapitulatio* concludes on a triumphant note. « But after the prince Sisebut took up the sceptres of the kingdom, they [the Goths] have advanced to such a height of felicity that they proceed with their arms not only over land but over the *seas* themselves, and the Roman [Byzantine] soldier is the servant of those whom he sees that so many nations and

(148) See, e.g., P. Goubert, *Byzance avant l'Islam*, II.2, Paris 1965, 122-4, 219f.; A. H. M. Jones, *The Later Roman Empire, 284-602*, I, Oxford-Norman, Oklahoma 1964, 298-302, 315; A. R. Lewis, *Naval Power and Trade in the Mediterranean A.D. 500-1100*, Princeton 1951, 38-49. The different versions of Isidore, *Chron.* 414 (p. 479) show that the vicissitudes of Byzantium under Heraclius continued to interest Isidore. One version of 414 ends in 615, another in 626 and the last in 631. The first and second versions show Byzantium in great straits but the third remarks: « [*Eraclius*] *a re publica Romana multas in Oriente deficientes patrias et a Persis invasas dicioni priscae restaurat ac de Persis victoriose triumphat* ».

(149) J. Madoz, « El Concilio de Calcedonia en S. Isidoro de Sevilla », *Revista española de teología*, XII (1952), 189-204. Isidore, *Orig.*, VI, 16, 6-9, records only the first four General Councils as « synodi principales ». It is interesting to compare Damian of Pavia's letter of 680 (*PL*, LXXXVII, 1261-5, esp. 1264A), where Justinian's Council is added to the first four and Justinian is especially praised, with Isidore, and with John of Biclar's account of III Toledo, where Marcian at Chalcedon is the last emperor referred to as defending the faith (cf. above and n. 75). In 684 the XIV Council of Toledo, receiving the Acts of Constantinople III, ordered they should be placed immediately after those of Chalcedon (thus omitting Justinian's Council); c.7, *PL*, LXXXIV, 507D; Vives, 444f. If both the additions to Isidore, *De viris*, in MS. León 22 and the « African Appendix » to the work are Spanish (see above and nn. 139, 128) this reinforces the Spanish Church's refusal to accept Justinian's Council.

Spain itself serve [150]. The « freedom » of the Goths, one of the main themes of Isidore's *Historia*, which he shows them maintaining against all odds, now finally triumphs over the « Roman insolence » of the soldiers of the Basileus [151].

Isidore did not write a *History of Spain* but a *History of the Goths*, God's new chosen race. What one finds in him cannot be accurately termed nationalism. Unlike other scholars I am unable to find any « intuition of Spain » in his pages [152]. There was no « Hispano-Visigothic nation » in Isidore's time [153]. There was a Catholic Gothic monarchy maintaining a fragile hold over the provinces of Hispania and part of Gaul; to this Isidore gave his complete adherence; in the glorification of *this monarchy* a regional patriotism found its satisfaction, but this regional feeling, expressed in the *Laus Spaniae*, is not new – it had already appeared in Orosius and Prudentius

(150) *Hist. Goth.*, 70 (p. 295.1-4): « *Sed postquam Sisebutus princeps regni sumpsit sceptra, ad tantam felicitatis virtutem provecti sunt, ut non solum terras, sed et ipsa maria suis armis adeant subactusque serviat illis Romanus miles, quibus servire tot gentes et ipsam Spaniam videt* ». The translation is largely that of Donini and Ford, p. 33.

(151) « *Romanas insolentias* », *ibid.*, 54 (p. 290.1). Cf. MESSMER, 96-99; *Recap.*, p. 294.18-19: « *his tamen libertas magis de congressione quam de petita contigit pace* ».

(152) I refer particularly to the article by J. L. ROMERO, cited above (n. 54), p. 54. Despite Romero's repeated reservations one finds him again and again (pp. 20, 26, 57, etc.) referring to nationalism or to « national independence » when discussing Isidore, although these concepts are totally anachronistic when applied to the sixth century.

(153) ROMERO, 59. J. Mª. DE LACARRA, « Il tramonto della Romanità in Hispania », *Cuadernos de trabajos de la escuela española de historia y arqueología en Roma*, XI (1961), 19-32, at 29f., also seems to me to exaggerate somewhat when he speaks of « il nuovo ideale ispanico ». It is highly dubious that a « Gallo-Frankish » nation existed either in 600. Cf. E. SESTAN, *Stato e nazione nell'alto medioevo*, Naples 1952, 186-90. I entirely agree with L. VÁZQUEZ DE PARGA's remark (*Isidoriana*, León 1961, 106) that Isidore « no ha hecho historia nacional, sino dar una historia de pueblos no romanos, con independencia, y considerar en la *laus Hispaniae* a España unida al pueblo godo. Pero no hay propiamente concepto de nacionalidad ».

though in Isidore it is warmer and more glowing. But what *is* new in Isidore is the exaltation of the *Goths*, not that of Spain [154]. Isidore does not write national but royal history.

Professor Momigliano pointed out some years ago that, while Christians in the fourth century « invented ecclesiastical history and the biography of the saints », Byzantine military and political historians such as Procopius remained « basically pagan in outlook and technique » [155].

The nearest thing to a political and military historian in Visigothic Spain is Julian of Toledo, in his work entitled *History of the Most Excellent King Wamba, of the expedition and victory by which he overcame the province of Gaul rebelling against him in a famous triumph* [156]. This *Historia*, clearly written shortly after the event (673) is perhaps more classical in spirit than any other work from Visigothic Spain, certainly than any other historical work. There are reminiscences of Virgil and Pliny and a clear inspiration seems to stem from Sallust [157]. An explicit motive for the work – one with which Isidore would have sympathized – is to provoke the young to virtuous and warlike deeds [158]. The use of dialogue and imaginary speeches enlivens the story.

Much in this work denotes its ecclesiastical author, who was to become Archbishop of Toledo in 680. Long before 680 Toledo's position as the cultural and eccle-

(154) For a different view of the *Laus Spaniae* cf. J. A. MARAVALL, *El concepto de España en la Edad Media*, 2nd ed., Madrid 1964, 21f. See CASTELLÁN (cited above, n. 5).

(155) MOMIGLIANO, *loc. cit.* (n. 110), 88f.

(156) DÍAZ, 264. See n. 1 above.

(157) Cf. FONTAINE, cited above (n. 2), 84.

(158) *Hist. Wambae*, 1 (p. 501.8-10) : « *Solet virtutis esse praesidio triumphorum relata narratio animosque iuvenum ad virtutis adtollere signum, quidquid gloriae de praeteritis fuerit praedicatum* ». Cf. Isidore, *Orig.*, I, 43.

siastical centre of Spain was established, though its Archbishop was officially confirmed as the head of the Spanish Church only in 681, in the first Council presided over by Julian [159]. Julian had the opportunity to be in closer and more continuous contact with successive kings than either John of Biclar or Isidore. His *Historia* is clearly the voice of Court circles at Toledo. It is the only historical work surviving from these circles after Isidore's time, apart from a brief list of Visigothic kings [160]. Since Julian was a leading theologian and Biblical scholar he was able to use Biblical exegesis and providentialist history in the Court's service. Biblical parallels are stressed. Wamba, the holy champion of God, is singled out by a miracle at his anointing [161]. He is made to quote 1 Kings, when insisting his army should be pure, and the Psalms after his victory [162]. The rebel Paul « prophesies » his own destruction [163]. Julian considers that Paul is punished in part because he added sacrilege to tyrannicide, « madly » placing a crown given to a saint's shrine on his head [164]. The « hidden judgement of God » appears in his overthrow [165]. The attacks on « Gaul » (here meaning Septima-

(159) On Julian see my « El ' Prognosticum futuri saeculi ' de San Julián de Toledo », *Analecta sacra Tarraconensia*, XXX (1957), 5-61, esp. pp. 5-11, with bibliography (the articles by F. X. Murphy are particularly important).

(160) *Laterculus regum Visigothorum* (DÍAZ, 241), *MGH*, *AA*, XIII, 464-68. Cf. also DÍAZ y DÍAZ, article cited (n. 106), 350 and n. 23.

(161) *Hist. Wambae*, 4 (p. 504.2-6): « *signum salutis* ».

(162) *Ibid.*, 10 (p. 510.11ff.): « *Exemplum mihi praebere debet Eli sacerdos ille in divinis litteris agnitus*... » Also 25 (p. 520.25ff.): « *Quo viso, princeps, protensis cum lacrimis ad caelum manibus, ait : ' Te, Deus, conlaudo, regem omnium regum, qui humiliasti sicut vulneratum superbum et in virtute brachii tui conteruisti adversarios meos* ' » (Ps. 88,11). Cf. Wamba's speech in the *Iudicium in tyrannorum perfidia promulgatum* (DÍAZ, 239), p. 533.15-18, which also seems inspired by 1 Kings.

(163) *Hist. Wambae*, 11 (pp. 510f.), the interpretation of « *religiosus princeps* », Wamba. Cf. also 25 (p. 521.6-8): « *Impleta satis plene est in isto prophetialis illa sententia* » (Ps. 36,35f.).

(164) *Ibid.*, 26 (p. 522.3-11).

(165) *Ibid.*, 20 (p. 518.16): « *miro occultoque Dei iudicio* ».

nia, the province ruled by the Visigoths) in the *Historia* and especially in the *Insultatio in tyrannidem vilis Galliae*, also by Julian, are extraordinary in their violence, in their praise of the Goths and hatred of Gaul, which has called in « barbarians », including the Franks, against its anointed king[166]. Like Cassiodorus with the Ostrogoths, Julian is careful to apply the term ' barbarians ' only to peoples hostile to the race which rules his own land. His attack on « Gaul » is partly aimed at the Franks, who are depicted as terrified at Wamba's approach[167]. In his use in the *Insultatio* of personifications, by which « Spania » addresses and insults « Gallia », Julian seems to be drawing on a rhetorical model which I suspect may well be the anonymous fifth-century *Altercatio ecclesiae et synagogae*, possibly by a Spanish author and, in any case, probably known in Visigothic Spain[168]. The speeches of the Church against the Synagogue in this treatise seem made to be

(166) E.g. *ibid.*, 8 (p. 507.18f.): « *Fit tamen tota Gallia repente conventiculum perfidorum, perfidiae speleum, conciliabulum perditorum* ». Cf. the *Insultatio* (DÍAZ, 265), pp. 526-9.

(167) Cf. *Hist. Wambae*, 29 (p. 524.25-27): « *Tanta enim virtute animi atque constantia circumpositas b a r b a r o r u m gentes* [*Wamba*] *non solum non extimuit, sed contempsit* ». On the Franks cf. also 8 (p. 507.20f.); 9 (508.16-21); 13 (513.22f.); 24 (520.18ff.), and esp. 27 (523.2-14), where Wamba is said « *occasionem cum Francis proeliandi operiens, nec solum istius causae, sed et praeteritas gentis suae cupiens vindicare iniurias* », and the Franks avoid battle, « *Franciae munitissimae urbes iam ultimum sui, ut ferebatur, excidium deplorarent* ».

(168) See my edition of the *Altercatio*, *La « Altercatio » y la basilica paleocristiana de Son Bou de Menorca*, Palma de Mallorca 1955 (also in *Boletín de la Sociedad Arqueológica Luliana*, XXXI [1953-60], 69-132). The ascription to Bishop Severus of Minorca is disputed but not the fifth-century date. MS. Monte Cassino 247, which represents one of the two main branches of the tradition, contains « Spanish symptoms ». There is also a definite relationship between the *Altercatio* and the *Epistula* of Severus (ed. G. SEGUÍ, *La carta enciclica del obispo Severo*, Rome-Mallorca 1937). If both are not by Severus then the *Epistula* draws on the *Altercatio* (the reverse relationship is most improbable), in which case it may be considerably later. This is the view of B. BLUMENKRANZ, *Les auteurs chrétiens latins du moyen âge sur les juifs et le judaisme*, Paris 1963, 106-110, who places the work in Visigothic Spain. I hope to return to this question.

employed for Julian's purpose and there are a number of close verbal parallels [169].

Julian is also the author of the *De comprobatione sextae aetatis* of 686, perhaps the last of a series of apologetic works directed by Spanish bishops against the Jews in the seventh century [170]. Unlike the works of Isidore and Ildefonsus of Toledo on the same subject, Julian's work appeals throughout to history and chronology to prove that the « sixth age » – in which, according to the Jews with whom Julian was arguing, the Messiah should come –, had already arrived [171]. The fact that Julian's work

(169) One should also note that the use of an anti-Jewish polemical work by Julian in the *Insultatio* would fit in with his view of the rebellion as largely inspired by Jews. Cf. *Insultatio*, 2 (p. 526.23f.): « *sed super haec omnia Iudaeorum consortiis animaris* ». Cf. *Hist. Wambae*, 28 (p. 524.14-17). For Julian's own polemical anti-Jewish work see below. I note below the main parallels between the *Insultatio* and the *Altercatio*.

Ins. 1 (526.8f.): « *Ubi est illa libertas tua, in qua male libera de erecto tibi fastus supercilio adplaudebas ?* » Cp. *Alt.* (p. 38.114f.): « *Si adhuc regnas, liberam te esse cognosco* ». *Ins.* 2 (526.29-527.3): « *Agnosce, misera, agnosce quid feceris ! Sufficiat tibi inter febres amisisse memoriam. Nunc iam, depulsa febrium labe, nutricem te scandali recognosce, fomitem mali, matrem blasfemantium, novercam infidelium, negotiorum privignam, prostibulorum materiam, proditionis speleum, fontem perfidiae, animarum interemtricem* ». Cp. *Alt.* (p. 50. 357): « *Audi misera, audi infelicissima !* »; (p. 39. 139): « [Synagoga]: *Hic me miseram errasse cognosco*... (144f.) [Ecclesia]: *Certum habeo quod legisti, sed quae legisti retinere non potes, et ipsum agnosco redire* »; (p. 50.377): « *Crimen memoriam tollit* ». With the last words of the passage from *Ins.* cp. *Alt.* p. 56. 522-28, esp. 527-28: « *Gladius tuus per apicem mucronis madido adhuc cruore distillat, et revinci desideras ?* », which is closer to *Hist. Wambae*, 2 (p. 502.8f): « *Nisi consensurum te nobis modo promittas, gladii modo mucrone truncandum te scias* » (part of a probably imaginary speech by a noble to Wamba, persuading him to accept the throne).

(170) Cf. Blumenkranz, *op. cit.*, nos. 95, 96, 106, 110 (Julian's work). No. 96, which is probably not by Isidore, may be later than Julian.

(171) Cf. esp. *De comprobatione*, I, 23-27, and III (*PL*, XCVI, 555-559, 569-86). Eusebius, Jerome and Tertullian are cited to support Julian's arguments. In I, 19 (552D) he exhorts the Jews to verify his statements from their own historians (« *fideles vestras historias* »). Isidore and Ildefonsus naturally refer to Biblical prophecies and to the disappearance of the Jewish kingdom to support their case but one cannot compare these references, standard in anti-Jewish apologetic, to Julian's technique.

was directly commanded by King Ervigius, whose legislation attempted to enforce the mass conversion of Spanish Jews, makes it hard to see in the work a purely theological purpose [172]. It may be classed as apologetic history in the interest of the Visigothic monarchy, from which the Spanish Church was by now hardly separable.

Let us finally consider some other works produced in Visigothic Spain which are close enough to historical literature to deserve treatment here, first sermons and tracts with resumés of Biblical history and then hagiography, in its various forms. Unlike the works of John of Biclar, Isidore, Sisebut and Julian of Toledo, these works do not contain explicit royal propaganda but they are still part of a general attempt made by the Church under royal encouragement to educate the people of Spain [173]. This attempt included the presentation of « Christian history » in several forms.

Martin of Braga's *De castigatione rusticorum* (the correct title; *correctione* has no real manuscript authority) was written in the Suevic kingdom about 572, before the Sueves were conquered by the Visigoths. It was known to Isidore and was used by the eighth-century missionary to Germany, Pirminius, probably a Visigoth [174]. With Martin's work, one should compare Valerius of Bierzo's *De vana saeculi sapientia*, written about a hundred years

(172) See the dedication to Ervigius (*PL*, XCVI, 537-40, esp. 538f.): « *Contra hunc, inquam, detestabilem impietatis errorem et manifestissimam caecitatem respondere me augustum caput et mens serena tuae Celsitudinis praecipit* ». Cf. B. BLUMENKRANZ, *Juifs et chrétiens dans le monde occidental 430-1096*, Paris 1960, 120-31. My critical edition of Julian's works will appear shortly.

(173) Cf., in general, J. FERNÁNDEZ ALONSO, *La cura pastoral en la España romanovisigoda*, Rome 1955. Cf. the « Tomes » cited above, n. 46.

(174) DÍAZ, 26, 394. For the title cf. A. M. KURFESS, in *Aevum*, XXIX (1955), 181-86. An English translation of Martin's work using Kurfess' corrections to Barlow's edition, appears in my book, *The Conversion of Western Europe 350-750*, Englewood Cliffs, N. J., 1969.

later [175]. Martin of Braga traces the story of the world from Creation through the Fall of angels and men and the Flood to the rise of pagan gods. Valerius is much briefer, when dealing with strictly Biblical history, than Martin but adds an account of the Apostles' mission and dwells on the martyrs and the new type of martyrs, monks and hermits [176]. Both authors stress the contrasts of Hell and Heaven with which men's history ends [177].

Valerius' tract shows how Biblical history naturally ran on into that of the Church. The conscious promotion of the cult of Apostles and martyrs appears in c. 13 of the Fourth Council of Toledo (633), which decreed: « Let hymns, masses, prayers, orations, supplications... be composed; if none of these are used in church all ecclesiastical services will be unattended » [178]. The period after the conversion of Recared in 587 and particularly between 633 and the Arabic Invasion in 711 saw the composition of the greater part of the Liturgy misleadingly called Mozarabic. Between thirty and forty of the roughly one hundred hymns by Spanish authors in this Liturgy were probably composed in the seventh century [179]. Mas-

(175) Díaz, 290.

(176) Martin, *De castigatione*, 3-8, 13-14, ed. C. W. Barlow, *Martini episcopi Bracarensis opera omnia* (Papers and Monographs of the American Academy in Rome, XII), New Haven 1950, 184-89, 192-96; Valerius, *De vana saeculi sapientia*, 5-11 (*PL*, LXXXVII, 425-28). Cf. also his *De genere monachorum* (Díaz, 289), *ibid.*, 437. The long description of hermits in *De vana*, 10, is characteristic of Valerius and contrasts with Isidore's suspicion of hermits. Cf. J. Fernández, cited below (n. 198), 277f. Valerius is also exceptional in Spain in counting Hermenegild as a martyr (8, col. 426D).

(177) Martin, 14 (pp. 194f.); Valerius, 12-13 (cols. 428-30). As usual Valerius' pen runs away with him (in contrasting Josaphat and Jerusalem). He lacks Martin's sense of proportion.

(178) *PL*, LXXXIV, 371B; Vives, 197: « *Componuntur ergo hymni, sicut componuntur missae sive preces vel orationes sive conmendationes seu manus impositiones, ex quibus si nulla dicantur in ecclesia, vacant officia omnia ecclesiastica* ».

(179) J. Pérez de Urbel, « Origen de los Himnos Mozárabes », *Bulletin Hispanique*, XXVIII (1926), 5-21, 113-139, 209-45, 305-20. At p. 306 we are

ses, prayers and *Passiones* of martyrs were written, particularly in honour of local Spanish martyrs, in order to hold the attention of the local congregations. *Passiones* were written in Spain before 711, for saints of Saragossa, Toledo, Alcalá de Henares, Barcelona, Gerona, Seville, Avila and Mérida [180]. Other *Passiones* were imported, the East contributing more than Gaul, Italy and Africa combined [181].

Other more ambitious works were also composed in seventh-century Spain in honour of local saints who were confessors not martyrs [182]. The most important single hagiographical work is the *Vitas Patrum Emeritensium*, perhaps written at Mérida about 630. It is a curious blend of royal history, hagiography and anti-Arian propaganda [183]. The sketch of Leovigild draws heavily on

told that « about 40 » hymns were written before 711. DÍAZ, *Index*, 158, 336-67, lists 33. About six of these he is doubtful either as to their date or their origin. I cannot see why he omits the hymn « In ordinatione regis » (ed. C. BLUME, *Analecta hymnica*, XXVII, 269, or in J. P. GILSON, *The Mozarabic Psalter*, London 1905, 281), inc.: « Inclite rex magne regum, / consecrator », which is surely Spanish and seventh century.

(180) A. FÁBREGA GRAU, *Pasionario hispánico*, 2 vols. (Monumenta Hispaniae Sacra, Ser. lit., VI), Madrid-Barcelona 1953-55, edits and discusses these texts. He lists (I, pp. 262-4) the *Passiones* which he thinks were composed *saec.* VII. Eight are considered *saec.* VII by DÍAZ, 93, 95, 137, 215, 235, 310-11, 316. Fábrega Grau's theory of a *Passio de communi*, composed soon after 592, and serving as the basis for later *Passiones* of individual martyrs (pp. 67-78, 257f., etc.) is rejected by B. DE GAIFFIER, « Sub Daciano praeside », *Analecta Bollandiana*, LXXII (1954), 382-93. DÍAZ Y DÍAZ, in *Revista de Archivos, Bibliotecas y Museos*, LXIII (1957), 453-63, emends a number of texts published by Fábrega but provides good reason for thinking that the *Passio Leocadiae* (*Index*, n. 93) was *saec.* VII, not VIII, as de Gaiffier. Neither Díaz y Díaz nor C. GARCÍA RODRIGUEZ, *op. cit.* (n. 41), e. g. p. 311, accept Fábrega's theory of a *Passio de communi*.

(181) FÁBREGA GRAU, I, 255f., GARCÍA RODRIGUEZ, 393-417 (on Eastern influence esp. 414-417).

(182) GARCÍA RODRIGUEZ, pp. 335, 346, 354f., believes that only one confessor (St. Martin of Tours) received a general, as opposed to local, cult in Visigothic Spain.

(183) Ed. cit. (n. 12). Cf. FONTAINE, « Conversion » (cited, n. 17), 118-22. See above and nn. 73-74.

Sisebut's portraits of the royal persecutors in his *Life of Desiderius*, while the pictures of Bishop Masona and Recared use Gregory the Great's description of Hermenegild in the *Dialogues* (but the Mérida author suppresses all mention of Hermenegild)[184]. The account of Leovigild is a good example of what Professor Momigliano has called the mass invasion of historiography by devils[185]. Leovigild is practically possessed by the Devil. The scene between Leovigild and Bishop Masona is modelled on the *Passiones* of martyrs[186].

One should also refer to Braulio of Saragossa's *Life of St. Aemilian*, a hermit-monk who died in 573, and to the later *Life of St. Fructuosus*, which is apparently the work of two writers, one of whom may also be the author of the *Vitas* of Mérida[187]. Braulio's purpose in writing is clearly stated – the work is to be read on the Feast of St. Aemilian, during his mass. Braulio uses the *Lives* of Anthony and Martin of Tours and compares Aemilian to these heroes[188]. The Mérida *Vitas* are clearly written to the greater glory of the Church of Mérida. The author attempts to provide a local version of Gregory's *Dialogues*

(184) Cf. the use of the *Vita Desiderii* in *Vitas*, V, iv, 2, v,1,3 (pp. 198, 200), etc. Gregory, *Dial.*, III, 31 is used for Masona's resistance to Leovigild in V, iv,4 and for Recared in V,ix,4 (pp. 198, 230). Cp. also *Sermo in natale S. Vincentii M.* (Díaz, 320), *PL*, LIV, 503C, Vincent as « assertor veritatis », with *Vitas*, V,ix,5 (p. 230), « religionis divinae assertor ».

(185) Momigliano, cited (n. 110), 93.

(186) *Vitas*, V,vi,16-23 (pp. 212-6). Cf. also the attempt to kill Masona by mounting him on an untamed horse (*ib.*, 24-28, pp. 216-8).

(187) Braulio's work is cited above (n. 12), that of St. Fructuosus and Díaz y Díaz's article on it n. 51. Here (pp. 158-62) Díaz distinguishes two authors, the first of cc. 9-14 (ed. Nock, pp. 101-115) and the second of the rest. The first author may come from Mérida and is close to the *Vitas*. Nock (p. 38) already saw two authors at work.

(188) c. 12 (ed. Vázquez de Parga, pp. 18f): « *Isti divinitus superna concesserat gratia, vere ut coniceo caelicolis Antonio Martinoque vocatione, educatione per omnia similis* ». Cf. c. 27 (p. 28): « *O alterum Martinum qui in pauperem vestivit Christum !* ». For the purpose of the work cf. the prefatory letter to Fronimian, esp. pp. 5f.

and so to *confirm* the truth of Gregory's stories of visions and the future life [189]. This is combined with the propagandistic purpose to which I have alluded [190]. The *Vita Sancti Fructuosi* uses the same sources as the earlier works and seeks to exalt, in a fairly legendary manner, the great monk of Galicia [191]. Ildefonsus of Toledo's *De viris* is another example of local hagiography, much more than of literary history [192]. Paschasius' earlier *De vitis patrum*, partly translated from the Greek, is comparable to many *Passiones* in importing Eastern asceticism into Spain [193].

Valerius of Bierzo's hagiographical compilation has been analyzed by Professor Díaz y Díaz, who has shown

(189) See Praef. (p. 136) and cp. Gregory, *Dial.*, esp. IV, mainly devoted to visions of the future life, with *Vitas*, I. Gregory's *Dialogues* are also probably used in Braulio's *Vita S. Emiliani* (cf. I. M. Gomez, in *Dict. d'hist. et géo. ecclés.*, XV, Paris 1961, 410f.).

(190) See above and nn. 73-74.

(191) The *Vita* uses the *Vitas* of Mérida (see n. 187 above), the *Vita Martini* and *Dialogi* of Sulpicius Severus and Gregory, *Dial.* Cf. Díaz y Díaz, cited above (n. 51).

(192) Ildefonsus of Toledo, *De viris inlustribus* (Díaz, 220), *PL*, XCVI, 195-206, despite the references in the Praef. to Jerome's, Gennadius' and Isidore's works with the same title, is much more local hagiography of Toledo than literary history. On it cf. Sr. A. Braegelmann, *The Life and Writings of St. Ildefonsus of Toledo* (Catholic University of America, Studies in Medieval History, N. S., IV), Washington, D.C., 1942, 32-59; J. Madoz, in *Estudios eclesiásticos*, XXVI (1952), 476-80. The note is set from Praef. 2 (197B), where Toledo is called glorious « *ex hoc quod coram timentibus Dominum iniquis atque justis habetur locus terribilis, omnique veneratione sublimis* ». Ildefonsus sets out the wonders that attend the bishops of Toledo and the terrible punishments that visit their detractors among the local clergy (a well known hagiographical « topos »). Of the 14 chapters seven are devoted to bishops of Toledo and five to other Spanish bishops. There is a very strong monastic bias. Ildefonsus' world is one of monasteries and martyrs' shrines (cf., e. g., 2, 199B-C). For the schism in the Church of Toledo which he conceals cf. J. Rivera Recio, in *Hispania Sacra*, I (1948), 239-68. Julian of Toledo's *Elogium* of Ildefonsus (Díaz, 276) and Felix's *Vita* of Julian (*ib.*, 309) are both far richer in information than the whole of Ildefonsus' work, and are closer to Braulio's *Renotatio* (n. 134 above). Redemptus' *Obitus B. Isidori* (Díaz, 136), *PL*, LXXXI, 30-32, is a short piece comparable to Uranius' account of the death of Paulinus of Nola (*PL*, LIII, 859-66).

(193) Paschasius, *De vitis patrum*, VII (Díaz, 31), *PL*, LXXIII, 1025-62; cf. Barlow, *op. cit.* (n. 176), 294. See Ruffini, *op. cit.* (n. 1), 102f.

that it includes the *Lives* of Anthony, Hilarion, Germanus, probably that of Augustine, texts from Cassian, a series of chapters from Rufinus' *Historia monachorum*, and other Eastern and Western monastic texts [194]. The compilation also comprised some of Valerius' own writings, such as his account of Egeria's pilgrimage to the East [195]. Valerius' autobiographies are really a form of hagiography [196]. Their language often recalls that of Sisebut's *Life of Desiderius* [197]. Valerius' « persecutors », who include a bishop, clergy and monks, are modelled on the « tyrants » of the *Passiones*, while the Devil's direct attacks on him seem inspired by the *Lives* of Anthony and Martin [198].

To conclude. In Visigothic Spain historical models inherited from the Late Roman Christian Empire were applied by a series of historians close to the Court to the local scene. In John of Biclar one can see the transference of the focus of Eusebian history from the orthodox em-

(194) M. C. Díaz y Díaz, « Sobre la compilación hagiográfica de Valerio de Bierzo », *Hispania Sacra*, IV (1951), 3-25, esp. 10f., 22.

(195) Díaz, 285, ed. Z. García Villada, in *Analecta Bollandiana*, XXIX (1910), 377-99. Cf. C. M. Aherne, *Valerio of Bierzo* (Catholic University of America, Studies in Mediaeval History, N.S. XI), Washington, D.C., 1949, 48-51.

(196) Díaz, 292, 294, 295, but Aherne's edition, with translation (pp. 68-159) is preferable to that given by Díaz, as well as being much more accessible outside Spain. The poetical works of Valerius are edited by Díaz, *Anecdota wisigothica*, I (Acta Salmanticensia, XII,2), Salamanca 1958.

(197) Cp. *Vita Desiderii*, 18 (*MGH*, *SRM*, III, 636.11-16): « *homines funesti et vultu teterrimo, quorum erat frons torba, truces oculi...* », with Valerius, *Ordo querimoniae*, 2 (Aherne, 75.15-17): « [*Flainus*]... *cute teterrima, ... frons picea nigriore... truculentus velut saevissima bestia ; frendens...* ».

(198) The behaviour, e. g., of the priest Justus (*Ordo querimoniae*, 6, ed. Aherne, 91.44-47) is surely modelled on that of a pagan persecutor. The Devil attacks directly in cc. 7f. (pp. 97ff). Cp. Sulpicius Severus, *Vita Martini*, 24, 4,8, ed. J. Fontaine, *Sulpice Sévère, Vie de St. Martin*, I (Sources chrétiennes, CXXXIII), Paris 1967, 308. Cf. J. Fernández, « Sobre la autobiografía de San Valerio y su asceticismo », *Hispania Sacra*, II (1949), 259-84).

peror at Constantinople to the orthodox king at Toledo [199]. John, Isidore, and Julian of Toledo were doing essentially the same work as architects, sculptors, jewellers and designers of coins in Visigothic Spain. They were promoting the glory of the Visigothic Crown, using Byzantine models to assist in the creation of what was almost a rival Byzantium in the West. The failure to understand the essentially militant and propagandistic nature of our historians has led scholars to misunderstand the nature of sixth-century Spain. We are told, for instance, that when Byzantine forces reached Spain in 552 they were regarded as complete strangers to « the Spanish community ». What authority is given for this statement? Isidore of Seville's *Historia Gothorum*, written some sixty-five years later, in a world completely different from the fragmented Spain of 552, under the Catholic monarchy of Toledo, by a man closely associated with the Crown [200]. There is no reason to suppose that *any* « Spanish community » existed in 552. That anyone should think so today is a sign of the phenomenal success Isidore's royal history still enjoys after thirteen hundred years.

Beside this court history we have religious history, presented to the people in sermons, tracts, *Passiones* of martyrs, hymns and lives of confessors. The direct purpose of these works was the edification and instruction of

(199) See above, pp. 270f. B. Steidle, « Der heilige Isidor von Sevilla und die Westgoten », *Benediktinische Monatschrift*, XVIII (1936), 425-34, states that Isidore transfers the « Diadem » of Rome to the Visigoths. This is true, if one understands by « Rome » not merely classical Rome but the Roman Empire contemporary with Isidore, Byzantium.

(200) *Ibid.*, 47 (p. 286). Isidore does not, of course, use the phrase « Spanish community » but he does record the arrival of the Byzantines in a hostile spirit. His remarks here (p. 286.17-19) show that he is looking back from Sisebut's or Suinthila's reign: « *Adversus quos* [the Byzantines] *h u c u s q u e conflictum est : frequentibus antea proeliis caesi, n u n c v e r o multis casibus fracti atque finiti* ».

the people of Spain under the Church although the goal of unification under a Christian monarchy was also served. Eastern models influenced this literature and the Liturgy in general as they did the more ambitious royal histories [201].

Of the historians who survive from the Spain of these centuries John of Biclar had the advantage of possessing a wider training, acquired at Constantinople, than either Isidore or Julian [202]. He seems to have absorbed most thoroughly the Byzantine (fundamentally Eusebian) vision of history. With John we are living in the Constantinian era and Biblical typology is brought in to illuminate the figure of the final hero, the new Constantine, Recared [203]. In Isidore's *Chronicle* reiteration of the Eusebian apologetic motif is muted. By comparison with Prosper, Victor of Tunnuna, John of Biclar or even Hydatius, Isidore might appear (and has appeared to some scholars) as basically an « érudit », filing pieces of information in their appropriate slots without much interest in presenting a unified picture. I have tried to show why I think this an unfair view of him. Braulio of Saragossa, telling us that Isidore « made known the fatherland's past, the history of all time », sums up Isidore's *Histories* and *Chronicle* well [204]. His *Chronicle* is a useful manual for clergy as well as an example of his « curiosity » at work [205]. There is a definite, at times overriding, concern with heresy in

(201) Cf. J. Scudieri Ruggieri, « Correnti esotiche e impronte dimenticate nella cultura ispanica dell'alto medio evo », offprint from *Cultura Neolatina*, XIX (1959), 80 pp., at 26-8, with references there given.

(202) See above and n. 18. Isidore's knowledge of Greek was, at best, slight (cf. *Isidoriana*, 38) and that of Julian is disputed (*ibid.*, 354 n. 45).

(203) See above, p. 281.

(204) Braulio, *PL*, LXXXII, 67D.

(205) The *Chronicle* is used by Julian of Toledo, *De comprobatione sextae aetatis*, III (*PL*, XCVI. 581f.). For its use on a more modest scale by Eugenius of Toledo cf. Díaz, in *Isidoriana*, 350 and n. 24.

both *Chronicle* and *De viris*. The *Historia Gothorum* shows us conclusively that Isidore's historical, like his other works, had a very definite direction. As a work of art Julian of Toledo's *Historia Wambae* surpasses his predecessors' achievements. The ability to focus intensely on a year in time and a limited area in space is not found in Isidore, nor is a sacred halo focused so intensely on Isidore's kings as on Wamba by Julian.

The importance of Isidore's and Julian's works for the future is not my subject today. For many centuries they inspired the historians of medieval Spain and in the sixteenth century, when Spain was once more reunited under the control of its centre, the « Meseta » again dominating the peripheries, as in Visigothic Spain, the court historians of the Catholic Kings and of Philip II celebrate the Goths as ancestors of the Kings of Castille and (with somewhat greater reason) look back to Isidore as their own spiritual forebear [206].

(206) Cf. MARAVALL, *op. cit.* (n. 154), 19-27, 32, 303f., 318f., 321-37, esp. 326, and the general articles by M. C. DÍAZ Y DÍAZ and L. LÓPEZ SANTOS, in *Isidoriana*, e. g. 383f., 425-28. For a later period see, e. g., SAAVEDRA FAJARDO, *Corona gótica, castellana y austriaca* (1st ed., 1646), or *Historia de los Reyes Godos...*, by Julián de Castillo, Burgos 1582. Cf. the articles by R. LIDA, « Sobre Quevedo y su voluntad de leyenda », *Filología*, VIII (1962), 273-306, and « Quevedo y su España antigua », *Romance Philology*, XVII (1963), 253-71, esp. 267. PIERRE CHAUNU, in *Revue d'histoire économique et sociale*, XLI (1963), 176, suggests the comparison of the Visigothic period with the sixteenth century as possible because of the apparent dominance of the Meseta over the periphery of Spain in both periods.

IV

ST. JULIAN OF TOLEDO IN THE MIDDLE AGES

aint Julian of Toledo is the last of the great prelates of Visigothic Spain of whose life we know anything significant and whose works survive to y appreciable extent. His writings are in many ways as interesting as those any of his predecessors, even the greatest; while in erudition he is the equal Isidore of Seville, he surpasses him in originality.[1]

We have no exact date for Julian's birth but it seems reasonable to supse that he was born about 642, possibly some years earlier and certainly in ledo.[2] He was of Jewish descent, but his parents were already Christian ıen he was born.[3] We know he was the pupil of St. Eugenius (II) of Toledo dit 646-657), the poet and editor of Dracontius,[4] for he speaks of Eugenius the *Prognosticum* as "praeceptor noster."[5] Julian must also have studied der St. Ildefonsus (sedit 657-667), famous for his *De Virginitate perpetua ıtae Mariae*; he became a deacon in 667 after the death of Ildefonsus and a iest, no doubt at the then canonical age of 30, some five years later, out the time of King Wamba's accession and consecration at Toledo in 2; these last events and the civil war soon after, in the Pyrenees and Septiania, Julian described in what was probably his first work of importance, e *Historia de Wambae regis Gothorum Toletani expeditione*.[6] It was probably also

This article is based on part of my mbridge thesis for the Ph.D entitled "A itical Edition of the *Prognosticum futuri ıuli* of Saint Julian of Toledo." In the ening pages I have used my communican to the Second Congress of Patristic ıdies at Oxford in 1955, "Towards a Criti- Edition of the Works of St. Julian of ledo" (*Studia Patristica*, ed. K. Aland and L. Cross, I, Berlin, 1957, 37-43). I hope discuss the MS. tradition of the *Prognosticum* an article in *Sacris Erudiri*.

[1] Cf. J. Madoz, *Segundo Decenio de Estudios re Patristica española* (1941-50), Madrid, 51, 142. The older bibliography on Julian to be found in U. Chevalier, *Répertoire des rces historiques du Moyen Age, Bio-bibliographie*, Paris, 1907, 2687, and in an article by I.A.W." (Mrs. Humphrey Ward) in *Dicnary of Christian Biography*, ed. Smith and ace, III, London, 1882, 477-481. A more cent bibliography in T. Ayuso Marazuela, *Vetus Latina Hispana*, I, Madrid, 1953, 9 ff., or in E. Cuevas and U. Domínguez l Val, *Patrologia Española* (in appendix to e Spanish trans. of Dr. Altaner's *Patrologie*), adrid, 1956, 122*. Neither of these recent bliographies are complete. Cf. the biblioaphical note in my article "San Julián de ledo," *Analecta Sacra Tarraconensia*, XXX, 58, pp. 13-16, and the very full biblioaphical references in Dr. Murphy's two articles, cited below in note 13. For editions cf. note 6 below.

[2] Cf. M. Manitius, *Geschichte der Lateinischen Literatur im Mittelalter*, I, Munich, 1911, 129.

[3] The *Continuatio Isidoriana Hispana* of 754 (ed. Mommsen, Mon. Germ. Hist., *Cronica Minora*, II, 349) records Julian's Jewish descent. Because Felix, his all but immediate successor at Toledo, does not mention Julian's Jewish blood in his *Vita Iuliani* (*PL* 96, 445-452) the idea has been indignantly rejected by Florez and is still considered dubious by Cuevas and Domínguez del Val (*Patrologia Española*, 115*). The fact that Felix does not give *any* account of Julian's ancestry lends weight to the suggestion that the *Continuatio* is right.

[4] Eugenius' works are edited by Vollmer in Mon. Germ. Hist., *Auctores Antiquissimi*, XIV, 1905, together with Eugenius' editions of some of Dracontius' poems.

[5] E.g. *Prognosticum* III. 17 (*PL* 96, 504B).

[6] This was edited by Levison in Mon. Germ. Hist., *Scriptores Rerum Merovingicarum*, V, 1910, 500-535, the only one of Julian's major works to have received a critical edition in modern times. For the rest we have to depend on Cardinal de Lorenzana's edition of 1785 (*Sanctorum Patrum Toletanorum quotquot extant Opera*, II, Matritii, 1-384) reprinted in *PL* 96, 445-816. Cf. E. Dekkers, *Clavis Patrum Latinorum*, Steenbrugge, 1951, nos.

before he became a bishop that Julian formed his two collections of te: from Augustine, one "ex decade psalmorum beati Augustini"; the oth "excerpta de libris S. Augustini contra Iulianum haereticum collecta."[7] the *Historia* he had shown a mastery of rhetoric and a knowledge of the class remarkable for his age.[8] These two Augustinian anthologies foreshadowed later works of theological compilation, based on an arsenal of patristic lea ing. No doubt he had become well known to Wamba by means of the *Histor* which may possibly have been commissioned by the King and certainly be the stamp of official history. When Ildefonsus' undistinguished successor bishop of Toledo, Quiricus, died in 679, or early in 680, Julian was appoint by Wamba to succeed him. He was consecrated on the 29th of January, 68 he died ten years later, on the 6th of March, 690, and was buried in t church of St. Leocadia in Toledo.[9] During these ten years Julian presid over four of the national Councils of Toledo.[10] He became involved in theological controversy with Rome and could not fail to be concerned wi the violent political changes of his time. During the first year of his episcopa there occurred the deposition of Wamba from the throne. For his actions Primate of Spain Julian has been harshly criticized by Catholic historia such as Mariana and Baronius[11] as well as by German Protestant scholars the last century.[12] Some have seen in him an attitude towards the Holy S bordering on hostility if not on schism; others have detected in his politics overmastering desire to assert the primacy of Toledo and an unscrupulo readiness to aid in the deposition of Wamba, who, on this theory, is suppos to have offended the "clerical party" and Julian in particular. In rece years these accusations have been sifted and assessed critically, notably Dr. F. X. Murphy in two important articles.[13] This is not the place to ent again into these complicated questions. It is enough to say that the mo serious charges lack corroboration in the original sources. It is no long possible to think of Julian either as an incipient Gallican or as the evil influen behind the collapse of Visigothic Spain. He was certainly a scholar, for h time, of the first rank, a formidable theologian and a bishop not likely

1258-1266. A new edition is being prepared for the Corpus Christianorum, edited by Dom Dekkers.

[7] Cf. Felix, *Vita Iuliani*, 10 (*PL* 96, 450A).

[8] Scholars have detected reminiscences of Livy, Sallust and Virgil (cf. Levison, p. 492, notes 5 and 6; Manitius, *op. cit.*, 131).

[9] Felix, *Vita*, 12 (*PL* 96, 451 ff.).

[10] The XIVth Council (in 684) consisted of the bishops of the Province of Cartagena, together with representatives of the other five metropolitan Sees of Spain besides Toledo. The Acts of the XIIth to the XVth Councils are best edited by González (reprinted by Migne in *PL* 84, 467-526).

[11] Cf. Mariana, *Historiae de rebus Hispaniae*, Toledo, 1592, 278-280; Baronius, *Annales ecclesiastici*, Ad. An. 685, nn. 5, 6 and 7; Ad. An. 688, nn. 3-5, Mainz, 1601, VIII, cols. 735, 749. Cf. also P. B. Gams, *Die Kirchengeschichte von Spanien*, Regensbu 1874, II. 2, 237, etc.

[12] E.g. A. Helfferich, *Enstehung und Geschic des Westgothenrechts*, Berlin, 1858, 190-20 F. Dahn, *Die Könige der Germanen*, VI², Lei zig, 1885, 463-70; Paul à Wengen, *Julia Erzbischof von Toledo*, St.-Gall, 1891, *passi* F. Görres, "Der Primas Julian von Toledc *Zeitschrift für wissenschaftliche Theologie*, 4 1902-03, 524-553.

[13] "Julian of Toledo and the Condemn tion of Monothelitism in Spain," *Mélanges de Ghellinck*, Gembloux, 1951, 361-37 "Julian of Toledo and the Fall of the Vi gothic Kingdom in Spain," *Speculum*, 2 1952, 1-27. It may, perhaps, be suggest that at times Dr. Murphy attempts to pro too much. His picture of Julian as a passi bystander is not convincing, nor is his sugg tion that Erwig may have been innocent.

ɔw the position of the Church in Spain or that of his own See of Toledo be lightly challenged. Possibly in his defence of his prerogatives against ʼal power or of the purity of his faith against the unfounded suspicions of man theologians he went further, at times, than he should have done but ther in the one case nor in the other does he appear to have been actuated selfish considerations. The fact of his inclusion in the Mozarabic Calendars d the cultus given him, soon after his death, in Toledo and later throughout ain would indicate that he was long and happily remembered as a "Saint the people" as well as a defender of ecclesiastical liberty against royal rusion and as one of the greatest of the Doctors of the Visigothic Church.[14]

In spite of his many other responsibilities as Primate of Spain and his atively early death at about 48, Julian apparently always found time to ite. If it is probable that he took a large part in the compilation of the anish collection of Canon Law, the *Hispana*,[15] it is certain, from what his ɔgrapher, Felix, tells us, that he revised both the Visigothic *Liber Missarum* d the *Liber Orationum* or the local office of Toledo.[16] Dom Férotin, indeed, lieved the manuscript of the *Liber Sacramentorum* that he edited in 1912 ght well be a copy of Julian's revision of the Missal.[17] It has up to now ɔved impossible, however, to prove his authorship of any but a few isolated ısses, ascribed to him by Elipandus in the eighth and Samson of Cordova the ninth century.[18]

Felix records the existence of seventeen works by St. Julian.[19] Of these ly five are certainly known to survive. The poems, in which he may have celled his master, Eugenius, the letters, which must have proved as full of erest to us as those of Braulio of Saragossa,[20] the sermons, of which we ve so few to-day that come without doubt from Visigothic Spain, all these, gether with Julian's revised liturgies and seven more works of theology, are her lost or can not certainly be identified as his.[21] The five works known Julian's are the *Prognosticum futuri saeculi* (of 688-89), the *Apologeticum de*

⁴ Cf. Z. García Villada, *Historia eclesiastica España*, II, 1, Madrid, 1931, 278 ff. St. ian was accorded cultus in Toledo by 858 *Acta Sanctorum Iunii*, VI, Pars I, Antwerp, 15: "Mart. Usuardi Monachi," 140; B. de iffier, "Les Notices Hispaniques dans le rtyrologe d'Usuard," *Analecta Bollandiana*, 1937, 279). Later he is commemorated wo Mozarabic Calendars of Silos (Férotin, *Liber Mozarabicus Sacramentorum*, Paris, 2, 457) and in a Calendar (s. XII) of Oña de Gaiffier, in *Anal. Boll.* 69, 1951, 282-).

¹⁵ Cf. Fr. Maassen, *Geschichte der Quellen und Literatur des Canonischen Rechts*, I, Graz, 70, 820 f.; P. Séjourné, *Le dernier père de lise : Saint Isidore de Seville*, Paris, 1929, 323, f.

¹⁶ Felix, *Vita Iuliani*, 11 (*PL* 96, 450B).

¹⁷ L. Férotin, *Le Liber Mozarabicus Sacratorum*, xvi f.

¹⁸ Elipandus cites the Post Pridie of the Missa Generalis defunctorum as by Julian, in letters of 793/4 and 799 (*Concilia Aevi Karolini*, 2, 111-119; *PL* 96, 875). Cf. Férotin, *Le Liber Ordinum*, Paris, 1904, cols. 417-423. Samson of Cordova quotes (H. Florez, *España Sagrada*, XI², 432, 487) from a Mass, In VIII⁰ Dominico de Quotidiano (Férotin, *Le Liber Mozarabicus*, 623-626).

¹⁹ Felix, *Vita*, 7-11 (*PL* 96, 448-450).

²⁰ Most recently edited by J. Madoz, *Epistolario de San Braulio de Zaragoza*, Madrid, 1941. Cf. on Braulio the excellent monograph by C. H. Lynch, *Saint Braulio, Bishop of Saragossa (631-651), His Life and Writings*, Washington, D.C., 1938.

²¹ Some of the sermons might be among the homilies in British Museum, MS. Add. 30, 853. The lost works are listed by Ayuso Marazuela and Cuevas and Domínguez (see above, note 1). Cf. note 33 below. Prof. Bischoff is to publish some *Versus ad Modoenum* from MS. Paris. Lat. 8093 (s. VIII/IX).

tribus capitulis, the treatise *De sextae aetatis comprobatione* (both of 686), ' 'Αντικειμένων and the *Historia Wambae*. To these the late P. García Villada, S claimed to have added a fragment of the first *Apologeticum fidei* sent to Pc Benedict II in 684, while he agreed with Dom Morin in identifying the *Remediis Blasphemiae* mentioned by Felix with a work published by Cardi Mai as by an unknown author. Neither of these two attributions have gc unchallenged nor would the two discoveries add significantly, were tl generally accepted, to the corpus of Julian's writings.[22] A more serious cla is made for Julian's authorship of the *Ars Grammatica* published by Cardi de Lorenzana in Rome in 1797, but this too is not as yet accepted by critics. It is clear that the work comes from seventh-century Spain and knowledge of the classics therein displayed, though often acquired at seco hand, reminds one of the author of the *Historia Wambae*, but there are di culties in the way of proving his authorship.[23]

Outside Spain St. Julian was principally known to the Middle Ages the author of the *Prognosticum futuri saeculi*.[24] His other works are only rar recorded in the catalogues of mediaeval libraries and are found in f manuscripts. Many of them were, no doubt, irrecoverably lost at the ti of the Arabic invasion in 711, only some twenty years after his death, during the course of the immediately succeeding centuries, and copies ne left Spain. Of the books which are preserved, the treatise *De sextae aet comprobatione* was written for a particular controversy and it does not se to have interested the Middle Ages.[25] Only two manuscripts survive and

[22] Cf. J. Madoz, "San Julián de Toledo," *Estudios Eclesiasticos*, 26, 1952, 50, 62-65. The *Chronicle*, the *Commentarius in Nahum* and the other spuria printed in Migne, *PL* 96, are no longer claimed as Julian's except by some who find the reference in the *Commentarius* to the preaching of St. James the Apostle in Spain significant. On the other hand there has never been any doubt as to the authenticity of the *Elogium Ildefonsi*, although it is not mentioned by Felix; it has been recently edited by J. Madoz, *San Ildefonso de Toledo a través de la pluma del Arcipreste de Talavera*, Madrid, 1943, 13, from MS. León 22.

[23] On the *Ars* cf. C. H. Beeson, "The Ars Grammatica of Julian of Toledo," *Miscellanea Fr. Ehrle*, I, Rome, 1924, 50-70. W. M. Lindsay, *Julian of Toledo*, "*De Vitiis et Figuris*," Oxford University Press, 1922, 41, suggested that part of the work, at least, might be "nothing more than notes taken from Julian's lectures." The work is ascribed to Julian in the Catalogues of St. Riquier (831); Lorsch (s. IX) and Fulda (s. XVI). Cf. M. Manitius, *Handschriften Antiker Autoren in Mittelalterlichen Bibliothekskatalogen*, Leipzig, 1935, 335. It is preserved in seven MSS. (besides those listed by Lindsay add: Chartres 92 (47), s. IX, presumably destroyed in 1944, and Reg. I 1586, s. IX).

[24] It is the only work by Julian knowr Sigebert de Gembloux (*c.* 56) and the Ano mous Mellicensis (*c.* 52) (apud Fabric *Bibl. ecclesiastica*, Hamburg, 1788, 99, 1 It is also the only work by him known to Franciscan compilers of the *Registrum An* (s. XIII) or to their follower Boston of B (*c.* 1410).

[25] Julian had been asked by King Er (680-687) to reply to a Jewish claim that sixth age of mankind, in which, according the current interpretation of the "weeks" Daniel, the Christ was to be born, had not come. Julian held, on the contrary, that sixth age had begun with the birth of Chr He proved his case by extensive quotat from the Old and New Testaments and fr both Greek and Latin Fathers. It is a possible that he knew the discussions in Babylonian Talmud as to the ages of world (T. B. *Sanhedrin*, 97 a, b). Cf. A. Williams, *Adversus Judaeos*, Cambridge, 19 220 f.; S. Katz, *The Jews in the Visigothic Frankish Kingdoms of Spain and Gaul*, Ca bridge, Mass., 1937, 36 f.

ɔw that four more existed that appear now to be lost.[26] The *Apologeticum tribus capitulis* was, in part, embodied in the Acts of the XVth Council of ledo of 688. Its manuscript tradition is therefore that of the Collection spana, which appears not to have been formed before *c.* 700.[27] The manu-ipt tradition of the *Historia Wambae* is entirely Spanish.[28] The ᾽Αντικειμένων s somewhat better known than the *De sextae aetatis comprobatione.*[29] This lection of Patristic opinions on controversial or difficult passages of the Old New Testaments is yet another confirmation of the extent of Julian's rning and is held, without undue exaggeration, by one modern scholar to "not an unworthy forerunner" of Abailard's *Sic et Non.*[30] There are some een manuscripts containing all or part of the work known to me and it is ntioned in the catalogues of the Papal libraries at Avignon and Peniscola.[31] Both the ᾽Αντικειμένων and the *De sextae aetatis comprobatione* were well known the authors of Mozarabic Christianity. To them Julian was evidently a ısiderable theological authority. He is cited by the Bishops of Spain in 3-94 and by Elipandus of Toledo in 798 in their respective letters to the hops of Gaul and to Alcuin. He is cited, together with Eugenius II and efonsus of Toledo and Isidore of Seville, as the author of various liturgical mulas. He is one of the "holy and venerable Fathers of Toledo," "noster ianus."[32] This testimony does not stand alone. In the correspondence of ɔarus of Cordoba there is a letter from one (unnamed) bishop to another, itten *c.* 860, where two sentences of Julian—taken from a lost work—are oted and their author is spoken of with the greatest respect, in terms applied Julian in his own day to a Doctor of the Church such as Augustine.[33] In

[6] The existing MSS. are Paris, Bibl. Nat. :. 12139 (s. XIII) from Fleury and Madrid, l. Nac., 6687 (s. XIV). The lost MSS. are se of Eberbach (used for the *editio princeps* Hagenau, 1532); the "MS. très ancien" of Remi at Rheims (*Voyage Littéraire de deux igieux Bénédictins*, Amsterdam, 1730, II, ; that of St. Augustine's, Canterbury (*vide* Cat. of 1497 in M. R. James, *The Ancient raries of Canterbury and Dover*, Cambridge, 3, 237, No. 436) and that known to Ph. ɔbe, *Nova Bca. MSS. Librorum*, Paris, 1653, I hope to publish a critical edition of this rk, as of the *Prognosticum*, in the *Corpus istianorum.*

[7] Cf. E. Dekkers, *Clavis Patrum Latinorum*, 1790; C. W. Barlow, *Martini Episcopi carensis Opera Omnia*, New Haven, 1950, 99. The best existing edition of the *logeticum* is that of González (in *PL* 84, -520—preferable to that of De Lorenzana, 96, 525-36).

[8] As may be seen from Levison's edition, d above, note 6. Since 1910 one of the S. listed (Segorbe, Bibl. Capitular G est, . XVI) has been lost. Copies, however, st—Toledo, Bibl. Cap. 27-26 and Madrid, l. Nac. 1376.

[29] At one time the authenticity of the ᾽Αντικειμένων was attacked but it is now universally admitted (cf. Manitius, *Geschichte*, I, 132 f.).

[30] F. X. Murphy, in *Speculum*, 27, 1952, 7.

[31] A critical edition is being prepared by Padre Lorenzo Galmés O.P. of Valencia University. The oldest MSS. are Munich, Lat. 13581 and Monte Cassino 187, both s. IX. Cf. Ehrle, *Historia Bibliothecae Romanorum Pontificium*, I, Rome, 1890, 384,342; M. Fauçon, *La Libraire des Papes d'Avignon*, II, Paris, 1887, 107 f.

[32] Cf. *Epistola ad Alcuinum* (Mon. Germ. Hist., *Epistolae Karolini Aevi*, II, n. 182, p. 305.12, 30-34; p. 306.36 f.); *Epistola Episcoporum Hispaniae* (Mon. Germ. Hist., *Concilia Aevi Karolini*, I, p. 113.10-18; p. 117.25 f.).

[33] *Epist. Episcopi* (*Anonymi*) *ad alterum episcopum directa*, inter epistolas Albari Cordubensis, 10.3, ed. J. Madoz, *Epistolario de Alvaro de Cordoba*, Madrid, 1947, 194: "Numquid non iuxta beati Iuliani Toletani Metropolitani episcopi venerandum eloquium: 'insani capitis censetur esse, et vani, qui illic pedes erexerit, ubi capitis ratio non suaserit'." *Ibid.*, 4 (p. 198): "Et ideo iuxta beati Iuliani egregii doctoris sententiam; 'Non minoris est

the same way Tuseredus, in a letter to Bishop Ascaricus written shortly bef 800, speaks of "librum beati Iuliani, non Pomerii, sed Toletani, qui vocita Anticimena."[34] If Tuseredus knew and valued the 'Αντιχειμένων Abbot Sams of Cordoba, in his *Apologeticum* written in 864, knew this work, the *Prognostic* and the *De sextae aetatis*, and was able to identify some of Julian's liturgi compositions.[35] The *De sextae aetatis* was also used by Albarus of Cordo who derived from Julian some of his ammunition in his controversy with apostate Bodo Eleazar.[36]

In the Christian North, too, where there was slowly coming into bei the Spain of the Reconquista, Alfonso III and his historians looked back the vanished glories of Visigothic Toledo of which they could catch a glim in the pages of the *Historia Wambae*. Both the *Epitome Ovetensis* (also cal the *Chronicle of Albelda*) of 883 and the contemporary *Chronicle of Alfonso* draw heavily on the *Historia* in their account of Wamba's reign.[37] T authors of these works doubtless possessed the *Vita Iuliani* of Felix and h seen the high praise given to Julian by the *Continuatio Isidoriana* of 754.[38] Th were not slow themselves to praise and copy their illustrious predecess historian and primate of Spain.[39] The tradition of the *Historia Wambae*, is, we have said, exclusively Spanish. The work was known in Spain but bet known in the earlier than in the later Middle Ages. Later historians tend to copy not the *Historia* itself but Lucas of Tuy's version of it, made in thirteenth century.[40]

Outside Spain the *Prognosticum futuri saeculi* constituted Julian's main cla to fame but it does not seem to have been very widely read in his own count We know of one copy at Oviedo in 882.[41] It may indeed be suggested th this list represents either the original books acquired by Eulogius of Cordo

providentiae necessitati imminenti consulere, quam plenitudinis discretionis gubernaculum adhibere'."

[34] Tuseredus, in *PL* 99, 1238D.

[35] Samson cites Julian nine times in all. He cites the *De sextae aetatis* (*Apol.* II. Praef. 10: *España Sagrada*, XI[2], 386); the *Prognosticum* (II. 2 = *Apol.* II. 20: *ibid.*, 467 f.); the 'Αντιχειμένων several times (e.g. *Apol.* II. 27: *ibid.*, 512) and two passages from a Mass (cf. note 18 *supra*). Julian to him is "Beatus," "sanctus" or "venerabilis doctor."

[36] Cf. Albarus, *Epist.* 14.2-6 (ed. Madoz, 213-220) of *c.* 840, where passages from the *De sextae aetatis*, I. 6 (?), 10, 20, 21, 25-27 are used.

[37] Cf. the *Epitome* in Mon. Germ. Hist., *Cronica Minora*, II, 374 and the *Chronicle of Alfonsus III*, ed. Z. García Villada, Madrid, 1918, 54 f.

[38] The *Cont. Isidoriana*, 50 (*Cronica Minora*, II, 349) speaks of Julian as born of Jewish stock "ut flores rosarum deinter vepres spinarum, productus omnibus mundi partibus in doctrina Christi manet preclarus, qui etiam a parentibus Christianis progeni splendide in omni prudentia Toleto ma edoctus, ubi et postmodum in episco extitit decoratus." It also speaks of *Apologeticum* (*ibid.*, 350), recording, no do in an exaggerated form, Julian's triumph, uses the *De sextae aetatis*, III. 15 at the enc its Chronicle. The *Continuatio* was proba known to Alfonso III and his historians García Villada, *Crónica de Alfonso III*, 41

[39] Cf. the *Chronicle* (ed. García, 5 "beatum metropolitanum Iulianum leg qui historiam huius temporis liquidissi contexuit."

[40] The 12th-century *Chronicle of Silos* (c ed. Florez, *España Sagrada*, XVII[2], 264 uses the *Historia* as does Lucas, Bishop of T 1239-49, in his *Chronicon mundi*, III. version of the *Historia* is printed by Lorenzana together with the original (*PL* 761-808). D. Rodrigo Ximénez copies Lu (cf. Levison's edition of the *Historia*, 493

[41] G. Becker, *Catalogi Bibliothecarum Anti* Bonn, 1885, Cat. 26, No. 12, p. 60.

48, in his voyage to Navarre and especially to St. Zacarias in the Pyrenees more probably, copies of these works made in Spain.[42] And it is true that ies of the *De Civitate Dei*, of the *Aeneid*, of Juvenal's *Satires* and Prudentius' ems and of Aldhelm's *Aenigmata* are found in both lists.[43] There are, how-r, some thirty-five works in the Oviedo Catalogue not mentioned among logius' importations, nor indicated in his correspondence. Moreover, it be shown that almost all the books at Oviedo, classical or Christian, were own in Visigothic Spain and a good proportion of the Christian works idore, Eugenius of Toledo, Apringius of Beja) were by Spanish authors;[44] library included even the heretical Elipandus.[45]

The library at Oviedo was founded by Alfonso the Chaste, *c*. 800, when he e "et librorum bibliotheca"; but two at least of the books listed in 882—a le (No. 1) and the Codex Canonum (No. 26)—were ascribed by the nittedly somewhat uncertain authority of Morales, who saw them in 2, to the scriptorium of Toledo before the Arabic invasion.[46] It is, there-e, possible that the manuscript of the *Prognosticum* at Oviedo in 882 was a y made at Toledo, conceivably a copy very close to the original. Christians ng before the invasion may have taken northwards to the Asturias not y the relics but also the writings of the great Archbishops of Toledo, as, so are now told, the priests of Merida conveyed their relics, including those St. James the Apostle, to Galicia and founded there a shrine destined to ieve a fame equal to that of Rome and Jerusalem.[47] But this, alas, is mere culation, for we are not likely to discover to-day a manuscript no longer Oviedo in 1572.

Apart from this manuscript, we know of two codices in the Visigothic ipt from San Millan de la Cogolla, now at Madrid, of the tenth and venth centuries respectively;[48] of the fragment (s. XI) at Burgo de Osma

[42] Cf. Albarus, *Vita Eulogii*, III. 9 (*PL* 115, f.); J. Madoz, *Epistolario de Alvaro de Cor-*, 28 f.; C. M. Sage, *Paul Alvar of Cordoba: ies on his Life and Writings*, Washington, ., 1943, 15-18; Madoz, *Segundo Decenio de dios sobre Patristica española*, 183-85.

[43] Cf. Nos. 7, 39, 40, 41, 32 in the Cat. in ker, *op. cit*. To these we may add Nos. 34 38 (Dicta Catonis and Ovid (?)), which cited by Albarus (*Epist*. 20; 2.2, ed. doz, 280; 101).

[44] Cf. Nos. 13, 28, 8: copies of Gregory (?) Ezechiel (No. 3) and *Homilies* (No. 9), of *De Civitate Dei* (No. 7) and of Cassian, *lationes* (No. 10) were all no doubt at edo before the Arabic invasion since they used by Julian. Juvencus, Avitus and ulius (Nos. 30, 31 and 33) were to be nd at Seville s. VII (cf. *Versus Isidori*, X, C. H. Beeson, *Isidor-Studien*, Munich, 3, 161). Corippus (cf. No. 35) is cited by Julian in the *Ars Grammatica*.

[45] No. 22.

[46] Cf. J. Tailhan, "Appendice sur les Biblio-ques espagnoles du haut Moyen Age," in *Nouveaux Mélanges d'archéologie, d'histoire et de littérature sur le Moyen Age*, ed. Ch. Cahier, série 3, IV, Paris, 1877, 300-304. The *Viage* of Morales was only published (at Madrid) in 1765. Cf. pp. 93 f. In the view of late mediaeval historians such as Ximenez (s. XIII) the relics *and writings* of Ildefonsus and Julian were taken to the Asturias by Bishop Urbanus *c*. 720 (Ximenez, *Rerum in Hispania Gestarum*, IV. 3, ed. Schottus, p. 70). Florez (*España Sagrada*, V, 1750, 330-336) has shown the relics were translated by Cixila *c*. 777, not by Urbanus (cf. Risco, *ibid*., XXXVII, 1789, 282 f.).

[47] Here I follow the interesting and perhaps the first remotely plausible attempt at an explanation for the rise of Compostella put forward by Dom Justo Pérez de Urbel, in his "Orígines del Culto de Santiago en España," *Hispania Sacra*, 5, 1952, 1-31, and restated by him in the *Historia de España*, ed. by D. Ramón Menéndez Pidal, VI, Madrid, 1956, 57.

[48] MSS. Madrid, Archivo Historico Nacional, 1279 (s. X) and Madrid, Bibl. Real

(Cod. 98); and of the lost manuscripts of Ripoll (ascribed by Villanueva the eleventh century)[49] and of the Cistercian Monasterio del Espiña, n Valladolid, seen by Morales in 1572 and destroyed in a fire in 1731.[50] Th are five other surviving manuscripts in Madrid and Barcelona containing whole or part of the work, and there are five catalogues of books, other tl that of Oviedo, stretching from the ninth to the fifteenth century, wh mention it.[51] Perhaps it is possible to compare this relative neglect of Julian's work on the Last Things with the surprising absence of manuscri of Beatus from the monasteries of Castille.[52]

It is interesting to compare the Spanish attitude to Julian with t prevailing outside Spain. Elipandus and his supporters in the Adoptio controversy appeal to him as to the other Toledan Fathers in 793-94 but Council of Frankfort is not impressed. Alcuin, the probable author of *Epistula synodica*, sent in reply to the Spanish letter, remarks that it is strange that Spain, guided by such Doctors as those his opponents cite, sho have fallen into the hands of the infidels. No author has taught the here professed by the Spaniards unless it is their masters (Ildefonsus, Eugen Julian), whose names would be unknown to the universal Church unless tl were revealed by this schism.[53] On the other hand, Alcuin takes pains point out some years later, there is nothing unorthodox in the works of Spanish Fathers he has read. There is nothing heretical in the *Prognostic* which is a work "ex sanctorum floribus collecta Patrum."[54] Julian might be a Doctor of the Church, to be put on a level with Gregory the Grea but he had written at least one book that was to earn him the heart-felt, if always articulate, gratitude of the Middle Ages.

We have spoken of the relative neglect of the *Prognosticum* in Spain. I not think that will appear too strong a term to use when we consider extraordinary success enjoyed by this book everywhere else in Europe in Middle Ages. This can be seen from the number of manuscripts ex ing today. I have listed[56] 153 more or less complete codices and twe three others containing some part of the work. Of the 153 more or

Academia de la Historia, Aem. 53 (s. XI). The text of these MSS. is very corrupt.

[49] Villanueva, *Viage Literario a las Iglesias de España*, VIII, Valencia, 1821, 51.

[50] Cf. Morales, *Viage*, 190; De Lorenzana, *Admonitio* to his edition of 1785 (p. 2 = *PL* 96, 453). There was also a MS. at the Escorial, burnt in 1671 (cf. G. Antolin, *Cat. de los Códices Latinos de la Real Bibl. del Escorial*, V, Madrid, 1923, 414 f.).

[51] Cats. Nos. 98-102 in the list in the article cited in note 60 below.

[52] I owe this suggestion to my friend Dom Justo Pérez de Urbel, who, however, suggests in a recent letter to me that Beatus failed to interest "el espiritu fuerte y renovador de Castilla" because of the excessively Mozarabic context of his work and its insistence on the rapidly approaching end of the world. These objections clearly do not apply to *Prognosticum*.

[53] *Epistula synodica* (Mon. Germ. H *Concilia Aevi Karolini*, I, 145.22-30). Alcuin, *Adversus Felicem*, VII. 13 (*PL* 226 f.).

[54] Alcuin, *Adversus Elipandum*, II. 8 (*PL* 266B), written in 799.

[55] Cf. *Epist. synodica* (*ibid.*, 145.35-40). this episode cf. E. Amann, in *Histoir l'Eglise*, ed. A. Fliche et V. Martin, Paris, 1947, 143 f.; R. de Abadal y Vinyals, *La Batalla del Adopcionismo*, Ba lona, 1949, 106 f.

[56] In my article "San Julián de Tole *Analecta Sacra Tarraconensia*, XXX, 1958, 26-43; cf. also first unnumbered note to article.

nplete copies we have no less than thirteen of the ninth century,[57] ten of tenth[58] and twenty-six of the eleventh.[59] Other evidence of the popularity the *Prognosticum*, especially in the earlier Middle Ages, is its frequent ntion in mediaeval catalogues of books. I have listed[60] over 100 such alogues which include the work. It was to be found, often in two or three ies, in almost all libraries from the ninth to the twelfth centuries. And, we shall see, it was not allowed to remain unread on the shelves. It was d by a succession of writers from Alcuin to Peter the Lombard, and in the rteenth century it was translated into Anglo-Norman verse.

At first sight it may appear difficult to explain why the book was so popular, y it enjoyed, as the late Padre Madoz put it, "rápida y brillante fortuna" he Middle Ages.[61] No doubt the title, *Prognosticum futuri saeculi*, translated Idalius, Bishop of Barcelona, in his letter thanking Julian for the work, as raescientia futuri saeculi," a foreknowledge of the future life, was attractive, the work in itself, although at times, as at Reichenau,[62] placed with lections of visions, had nothing visionary about it. Why then, as Père de ellinck asks, was it preferred to such much more sensational works as the *phecies* of Pseudo-Methodius, which promised to reveal the secrets of the ure life?[63] The answer to the problem presented by the extraordinary pularity of the book appears to come from an examination of its form and ntent. Let us take its form first.

The *Prognosticum* is not in the least an original work. It is, as the author s in his Letter-preface to Idalius of Barcelona, a collection of the sayings the Doctors of the Church on the problems connected with Death, Judgement, Hell and Heaven.[64] But it is not a simple anthology. It is one of the t of a new type of treatise. Its chief merit, in the eyes of its first readers, s the fact that it contained much learning in a small space. Julian insists in Preface on the "brevity" (*brevitas*) of his book[65] and Idalius' reply is ical of the reaction of many later readers. He praises the book's "studiosa

[57] MSS. Angers 275; Cambridge, Corpus ; Chicago, Newberry Library, f. 2; sel, Theol. 4°.6; British Museum, Harl. o; Paris, Bibl. Nat., Lat. 2341; *ibid.* 2826; . 12269; *ibid.* 13400; Reims 414; Vatican, . Lat. 255; Vienna 890; Zurich, Car. C.

[58] MSS. Admont 3; Bamberg, Patr. 108; drid, Archivo Hist. Nac., 1279; Paris, . 2833A; *ibid.* 6649; *ibid.*, 17448; St.-Gall ; Turin, G. V. 3; Wolfenbuttel 4452; ich, C. 34.

[59] Nos. 5, 10, 16, 29, 31, 44, 47, 48, 53, 58, 68, 70, 73, 84, 87, 88, 94, 103, 104, 124, , 129, 130, 131, 142 in the list cited in e 56 above.

[60] In *Analecta Sacra Tarrac.*, XXX, pp. 48-

[61] Madoz in *Historia General de las Literaturas pánicas*, ed. G. Díaz-Plaja, I, Barcelona, 9, 131.

[62] Cf. Cats. 34-35 (842 and s. IX²) in my list cited in note 60. In the first Cat. the book is apparently bound with the 3rd and 4th Books of Gregory's *Dialogi*, "et liber Fursei de visione eius, et nonnullae visiones excerptae de libris gestorum Anglorum Bedae et de visione Barontii monachi et liber visionis Wettini, fratris nostri, quam Heito [Bishop of Basle 836] episcopus descripsit et Walafrid, frater noster, metricis versus subsequens illam decoravit" (P. Lehmann, *Mittelalterliche Bibliothekskataloge Deutschland und der Schweiz*, I, Munich, 1918, 259.6-10).

[63] J. de Ghellinck, "En Marge des Catalogues des Bibliothèques médiévales," *Miscellanea Fr. Ehrle*, V, Rome, 1924, 354.

[64] *Epistula ad Idalium* (*PL* 96, 455 f.). The book had grown out of a conversation between Julian and Idalius, who had come to Toledo for the XVth Council, on Good Friday, 688.

[65] *Ibid.*, 456A.

brevitas" and says: "Evidenter enim et dubia effugata et obscura in luc producta sunt, cum et antiquorum patrum decreta *et novae brevitatis ind* artificii vestrii fructuoso labore ad medium sunt deducta. Manet ergo illorum sententia veritas, ex vestro autem labore nova et verissima brevitas. The work contained much learning. Julian had an excellent library and knew how to use it.[67] Padre Madoz was able to show, in one of the articles he published, that St. Julian almost certainly possessed and co read Greek Fathers in the original; Epiphanius, for example, or St. J Chrysostom.[68] He possessed and had read almost all the Latins. The re was a new and more scientific type of theological manual, a system attempt to ascertain and state in compressed form the opinions of the Fat on a number of debatable points.

There had existed, of course, before this, anthologies of patristic teachi In the fifth century we have Prosper's *Sententiae ex operibus S. Augustini* anc the sixth the *Excerpta ex operibus S. Augustini* of Eugippius.[69] Julian him appears to have compiled one such work in the (lost) *Excerpta de libris Augustini contra Iulianum haereticum collecta.*[70] But in the *Prognosticum* Julian not merely compiling another anthology. He was writing a practical man principally intended, no doubt, for the instruction of his clergy. In *Sententiae* of Isidore he had a model he could follow, for in the *Sententiae* Isid had written the "first Latin compendium of faith and morals,"[71] and *Prognosticum* owes more to this work than to the compilations of Prosper Eugenius. The works of Isidore, Taio of Saragossa (in his *Sententiae*)[72] Julian constitute a great technical advance on these Augustinian collecti and in the progress they achieved were not to be surpassed by the author the Carolingian Renaissance. They were the first essays in a type from wh descended, in the course of time, the books of *Sentences* and the *Summae* of twelfth and thirteenth centuries. The Spanish bishops provided their reac with well-arranged collections of texts from the Fathers, "grouped un doctrinal headings, and containing brief, systematic and reasoned expositi of Christian teaching."[73] The writings of the earlier Fathers had gener been inspired by particular controversies. Their doctrinal teaching was usually arranged in a systematic order and it was not always easy to find w they thought on a particular point. Isidore, Taio and Julian enabled scholars of the earlier Middle Ages to discover, without great loss of time,

[66] *Ibid.*, 459A.

[67] I hope to publish a study of Julian's library. We know of the presence of some 55 works by 22 Christian authors in his collection.

[68] Cf. J. Madoz, "Fuentes teológico-literarias de San Julián de Toledo," *Gregorianum*, 33, 1952, 399-417. In this connection we should not forget the growing Byzantine influence on Visigothic law, art and court ceremonial in the late 7th century (cf. H. Schlunk, in *Ars Hispaniae*, II, Madrid, 1947, 247, 266, 306, and for Byzantine influence on the Spanish liturgy, A. Baumstark, "Orientalisches in altspanischer Liturgie," *Oriens Christianus*, 10, 1935, 1-37).

[69] *PL* 51, 427-496; *CSEL* 9.

[70] His *Liber Sententiarum, ex decade psalmc B. Augustini breviter summatimque colle* (Felix, *Vita*, 10) may have more clo resembled Taio's *Sententiae.*

[71] D. Stout, *A Study of the Sententiarum tres of Saint Isidore of Seville*, Catholic Uni sity of America, 1937 (available to m microfilm), p. 29.

[72] Edited by Risco, *España Sagrada*, XX 1776; reprinted in *PL* 80, 727-990.

[73] Stout, *op. cit.*, 5. Cf. J. de Ghellinck *Mouvement Théologique au XIIe siècle*, 2e Bruges, 1948, 116 f.

ching of the Church on a particular question or the solutions provided by Fathers to a scriptural problem. One can easily understand the usefulness such works as the *Prognosticum* in a monastery with only a small library. t it was not only the smaller houses that welcomed these new works. At ichenau in 822, for instance, we find three copies of Isidore's *Sententiae*.[74] find the abbot of St.-Riquier grateful for the gift of the *Sententiae* of Taio.[75] t Taio's work was never very widely known. It was primarily a compila- n of texts taken from Gregory the Great, and the existence of the work of erius[76] to a large extent made it unnecessary.[77] On the other hand the *gnosticum* responded to an interest and to a need satisfied by no other rk. This was the acute interest felt by the people of the Middle Ages in Last Things and their need to know more of all the problems connected h them.[78] The content of the *Prognosticum*, in other words, assured its cess even more than the form in which it was written, for it provided Middle Ages with its first and most influential treatise *De Novissimis*.

If Julian, in his *De sextae aetatis*, following Isidore in his *Chronica*,[79] refused provide his readers with calculations of the probable duration of time ore the end of the world and the Last Judgement, he was no less intent n other Visigothic writers on the Last Things. The text of Ecclesiasticus 40 came naturally to him as to Isidore.[80] A modern historian has com- nted with reason on the extent to which the Spanish bishops of this age re, one might almost say, obsessed by the thought of the rapidly approach- end of the world and of its transience and unimportance in the light of world to come.[81] In the *Prognosticum* Julian wrote of subjects which erested him passionately and which had the same interest for the succeed- generations of mediaeval Christendom. In Julian's work they could read inflamed rhetoric of Cyprian, the exegesis of Jerome, the etymologies of lore and some of the finest passages of Augustine, Gregory, Origen, Cassian l Chrysostom. They could find there curious analyses of the problems of Resurrection of the Body, and dramatic stories such as that of the con- sion of Gennadius by a series of dreams to belief in the Immortality of the ıl, or of the appearance of a father to a son desperate for lack of the

⁴ Lehmann, *Mittelalterliche Bibliothekskata-* , I, 249.16-18.

⁵ Cf. Becker, *Catalogi*, Cat. 6, No. 21, p. 14 3-833). There was also a copy at St. ndrille in 831 (*ibid.*, Cat. 7).

³ *Liber de expositione veteris ac novi testamenti iversis libris S. Gregorii M. concinnatus* (*PL* 683-916).

⁷ MSS. of Taio's work known to me in- le Barcelona, Archivo de la Corona de gon, Ripoll 49 (A.D. 911); Madrid, Acad. a Historia, Aem. 33 (s. VIII ex.), used by co; Berlin, Görres 37 (s. IX); Laon, 319 IX); Paris, Bibl. Nat., Nouv. Acq. Lat. 3 (s. IX); Oxford, Bodleian, Laud Misc. (s. IX); Stuttgart, Patres 37 (s. X).

³ Sigrid Undset, in *Kristin Lavransdatter*, n she describes the few books that composed Lavrans' library, shows her usual understanding of the minds of mediaeval people. Apart from the Sagas and the Gospels and Psalter in Latin, Lavrans' most valued book was one of discourses and visions concerned with the future life.

[79] Julian, *De Sextae aetatis*, III, 34 (*PL* 96, 584B); Isidore, *Chronica*, 418 (Mon. Germ. Hist., *Cronica Minora*, II, 481).

[80] Cf. Isidore, *ibid.*, 481.7-10; Julian, *Epist.*, *ad Idalium* (*PL* 96, 457B).

[81] Cf. Dom Justo Pérez de Urbel, *Los monjes españoles en la edad media*, I, Madrid, 1933, 341. Cf., e.g., Idalius, *Epist. ad Iulianum* (*PL* 96, 459C); Quiricus, *Epist. ad Ildefonsum* (*ibid.*, 193D). Cf. Gregory the Great, *Moralia*, *Praef.* (*PL* 75, 511); F. H. Dudden, *Gregory the Great*, London, 1905, II, 427-437.

knowledge his father had not given him before his death.[82] What is the nat
of the fire of Purgatory? What is the use of burying the dead in or n
churches? Why is Hell held to be under the earth? How can an incorpor
spirit suffer corporeal fires? Do the blessed pray for those in Hell? Can
dead recognize the souls of those they never knew in this world? Can
dead be moved by thought of the living who were dear to them? Shall
need food or clothes in the future life? How do those rise again who
eaten by wild beasts in this life? What will be the order of the Last Jud
ment? After the Last Judgement in what part of the world will be the f
to which the wicked are destined? What will happen to the Saints in
conflagration of the world? Shall we see God in the Beatific Vision with
eyes of our (risen) body?[83] These and many more questions Julian as
and, to the best of his ability, answered from the resources of the earlier tra
tion which he had so perfectly assimilated and made his own.

We have dwelt at some length on the form and content of the *Prognosti*
because they alone can furnish the full explanation for the phenome
success of the work. No doubt it owed this success in part, also, to the ti
and place where it was written. In the late seventh century Spain was s
the country "best equipped to furnish MSS. to the rest of Europe.
M. Courcelle has recently emphasized the influence of the teaching of Cas
dorus and of his manuscripts from Vivarium on Anglo-Saxon and Caroling
culture.[85] But Cassiodorus' influence was relatively slight compared to t
exercised by Isidore of Seville. Julian's works travelled in the wake of Isidor
It is not surprising to find that with the *Prognosticum*, as with the *Ars Gramma*
attributed to Julian and with Isidore's works, the greater part of the work
distribution was to fall to the Irish and the Anglo-Saxons. They "combine
as Dr. Beeson has remarked, "a zeal for discovering and copying MSS. w
facilities for distribution that were unsurpassed in the Middle Ages—a str
of monasteries extending from the Islands to Northern Italy—in unin
rupted communication with one another through the constant journeying
these restless islanders."[86] In the ninth century the *Prognosticum* was to
found in all the principal libraries influenced by the "Celts," at Reiche
and St.-Gall, as at Bobbio and Fulda. It either appears in the contempor
catalogues or else we know of manuscripts of that period proceeding fr
these centres.[87] This would argue early Celtic use of the work. When
find manuscripts in other libraries such as Lorsch (s. IX) or Cremona (98
it can be argued that these are copies made from the manuscripts at Fu
and Bobbio.[88]

In the ninth century, however, scriptoria in France seem to have pla
a more considerable rôle than any elsewhere in the copying of the w
Of the thirteen surviving ninth-century manuscripts, eight were proba

[82] Cf. *Prognosticum*, II. 33; 27 (*PL* 96, 494 f.; 489).

[83] Cf. *ibid.*, II. 19-20; I. 19; II. 7; II. 17; II. 25; 24; 27; III. 25-26; 29; 33; 43; 49; 54 (*PL* 96, 474-521 *passim*).

[84] C. H. Beeson, in *Miscellanea Fr. Ehrle*, I, 50.

[85] P. Courcelle, *Les Lettres Grecques en Occident, de Macrobe à Cassiodore*, 2e éd., P 1948, 313-388.

[86] Beeson, *loc. cit.*

[87] Cf. Cats. Nos. 33-36, 88 in the list c in note 60; MSS. St.-Gall 264; Turin, G. Kassel, Theol. 4°.6; Cambridge, Corpus

[88] So Edmund Bishop, *Liturgica Histo* Oxford, 1918, 170 n. 1.

itten in France, as against two certainly or probably written by scribes "Celtic" centres or who had been influenced by Celtic masters or dels.[89] In the tenth century we may assume the great monasteries were eady provided with copies of the work (often, as at St. Martin of Tours, irbach and Bobbio, they would have two or three copies), and we find a ponderance of manuscripts from German houses—Admont, Bamberg, issenburg.[90] In the eleventh century the manuscripts from the scriptoria Southern Germany are surpassed in number by the copies produced by the glish and Italian houses.[91] In the twelfth century, with the monastic orms and the foundation of new orders, the scriptoria of France and rmany were again active in making copies of the *Prognosticum*.[92]

The number of manuscripts of a patristic work that survives to-day is ally only a fraction of the total number that must have existed in the ddle Ages. The *Prognosticum*, moreover, was not a work to interest especially great collectors from the sixteenth to the nineteenth century, who are so gely responsible for having saved what has been saved from the débris of cessive Reformations and Revolutions. Only very rarely were manuscripts he *Prognosticum* provided with costly and interesting illuminations.[93] Only eptionally were they the product of well-known scribes. The manuscripts re meant to be read rather than looked at, and the subject-matter of the k was not now of great interest. Once it was known that it had been blished and was to be found in such standard collections as the *Bibliotheca rum* of Margarin de la Bigne[94] it ceased to be interesting.[95] So it is that the surviving manuscripts that contain the whole or part of the work can only nish a very relative indication of the number of copies in circulation in the

[89] MSS. probably written in France: gers 275; Chicago, Newberry Library, 2; Paris, Lat. 2341; *ibid.* 2826; *ibid.* 69; *ibid.* 13400; Reims 414; Reg. Lat. 255 a fragment (Munich, Georgianum, fol. 8°447). MSS. of "Celtic" character: pus 399; Kassel, Theol. 4°.6. Others: ish Museum, Harl. 3060 (German); nna 890; Zurich, Car. C. 132; B.M. Add. 16-21217 (fragments from a German (?) .).

[90] Admont 3; Bamberg, Patr. 108; Wolfen-tel 4452.

[91] 11th-century MSS. written in South many: Munich, Lat. 5127; *ibid.*, 18538b; ., 18948. Written in Italy: Florence, rentiana, Plut. XXIII. 23 (?); Monte sino 324; Padua, Seminario Vescovile, ; Vatican, Ottob. Lat. 452; *ibid.*, Vat. . 1201; *ibid.*, 5051. Written in England: mbridge, Clare 30; B.M., Cotton, Titus XX; *ibid.*, Royal, 12. C. XXIII; Bodleian, d. Misc., 546; University College, 104.

[92] Some 20 MSS. written in France and ut the same number in Germany, together h 9 English and 5 Italian copies. Here ermany" includes Austria and Holland; and "France" Belgium.

[93] MS. Madrid, Arch. Hist. Nac. 1279 (s. X, Visigothic script) has some curious illustrations. MS. Paris, Bibl. Nat., Lat. 12270 (s. XII, Corbie) has a picture of the donor, Herbert Dursens. This MS. was the only copy of the *Prognosticum* to be included in either of the recent French exhibitions of illustrated MSS., covering the whole of the Middle Ages, held in the Bibl. Nationale in 1954 and 1956. No MS. of the work was included in the similar Italian exhibition in Rome in 1954. One late MS. (Bibl. Nac. 4276, s. XIII/XIV) at Madrid has some interesting miniatures.

[94] Many (especially French) MSS. have a reference at the beginning of the *Prognosticum* to the appropriate volume of one or other of the editions of the *Bibl. Patrum.* Cf., e.g., the Angers MS. 275, fol. 64.

[95] This is not to say, of course, that one does not find the *Prognosticum* included in some great collections from De Thou (MS. Paris, Lat. 2837) to Phillipps, who had three MSS. (Brussels, II. 954; Chicago, Univ. Library, 147 and the lost MS. 13287).

Middle Ages. Through the catalogues we know of over 100 copies, of wh only some thirty can be identified with surviving manuscripts. To these manuscripts we must add the vanished Phillipps MS. 13287; the two cop till 1944 at Chartres (MSS. 193 and 249) and the manuscripts of Va Clericorum, of St. Ghislain, near Mons, and of Aulne-sur-Sambre, victims of an earlier *zeitgeist*.[96] More important for our purpose there are four first editions of the fifteenth and sixteenth centuries. In all we kn that some ninety manuscripts existed of which the whereabouts are not n known. It is generally calculated that for each surviving manuscript (o popular work such as the *Prognosticum*) ten copies existed in the Middle Ag On this basis, if we calculate the existence of 10,000 copies of the *Etymolo* of Isidore, it is perhaps not unreasonable to suppose that there were at time in being between 1,500 and 2,000 manuscripts of the *Prognosticum*.

The *Prognosticum* appears to have been more widely read in the earl than in the later Middle Ages. From the ninth to the twelfth century i found in almost all libraries.[97] The success it enjoyed during the Caroling Renaissance is matched by its popularity in the eleventh and twelfth centur It was copied in many Cistercian houses[98] and at Cîteaux itself it was incluc in the number of books reserved for reading in Chapter or for distribution

[96] To these lost MSS. of uncertain date we must add the MS. "très ancien" of Arnaud de Pontac (+ 1681), for which see *Catalogue Générale des MSS. des Bibl. Publiques des Départements*, 2e série, XXIII, Paris, 1894, p. xxxv (No. 14). Then there are the codices of Ripoll, La Espiña and the Escorial mentioned above (notes 49-50); the MS. of Wells (Leland, *Collectanea*, IV, p. 156) and the unidentified MSS. of Petavius and Cardinal Ottoboni. Of the three MSS. of the former (for which cf. Montfaucon, *Bibliotheca Bibliothecarum MS. Nova*, I, Paris, 1739, 67: 1249, 940, 95) one is presumably Reg. Lat. 452 and another Leyden B.P.L. 225. Neither Ott. Lat. 141 nor 452 seems to be the same as the MS. noted by Montfaucon (I, 189): "Juliani Episcopi Toletani ad Braulium Rothomagensem (!!): cod. vetus. Not. 12." There is also the lost MS. of St. Remi, Reims (*ibid.*, II, 1234: Cod. 51) and the two copies seen by Nicolas Antonio in the possession of Martin Vasquez Siruela (*Bibl. Hispana Vetus, apud PL* 96, 430C). The Phillipps MS. 13287 (s. XII ex.) was sold in 1913, lot 643, and again in the G. Dunn Sale, February 1914, No. 1280. It had been one of the MSS. of Sir W. Betham in 1854 (*Records of Ireland*, etc., No. 103). (I am indebted to Mr. A. N. L. Munby for answering various queries about the Phillipps MSS.) The Vallis Clericorum MS. is listed by Montfaucon, II, 1301. Haenel, *Catalogi*, 175 (in 1826) lists, as at Laon: "Isidori tr. de dubiis; Iuliani libri tres prognosticorum (cod. antiquiss.)." This d not appear at Laon in 1849 (*Cat. Gén. . Départements*, 1 série, I, 1849). The activi of the Conte Guglielmo Libri spring to m as a possible explanation of almost any appearance of a MS. during the period of visits to French provincial libraries, bu appears he purloined nothing from La For the St. Ghislain MS. cf. A. Sande *Bibl. Belgica MS.*, I, Insulis, 1641, p. 247 (vols. listed) and P. Faider, *Cat. des MSS Mons*, Paris-Ghent, 1931, xxiv ff.; P. Poncelet, in *Annales de . . . Mons*, 1897, 3 404, could only find about 40 survivors of 109 vols. still existing in 1794. For the Au (Cistercian) MS. cf. Sanderus, II, 1643, 2 decuria decima. Sanderus also lists a MS his Cat. (II, 28) of the Burgundian Collect at Brussels.

[97] Cf. E. Lesne, *Les Livres*, "*Scriptoria*" *Bibliothèques du Commencement du VIIIe à la du XIe Siècle*, Lille, 1938, 775: "Presque to les bibliothèques possèdent le livre de visi et prophéties dit 'Prognosticon Juliani'."

[98] In all we have 12 MSS. known to co from Cistercian houses, and fragments fr Himmerod, Alcobaça and Clairvaux. know of the lost MSS. of Aulne and Espiña and of Altzelle in Saxony, from wh the 1536 edition was taken. The *Prognosti* is also found in the Cats. of Clairva Cîteaux, Heilsbronn and Meaux in Yo shire: Cats. Nos. 30, 32, 55 and 81 in the in the article cited in note 60 above.

brethren.[99] At Cluny in a list of books for Lent we find it chosen by the nk Hugh, and it was again selected by Robert the infirmarian of Cluny in ;2.[100] Nor is the work's appearance in quotation in the books of "Flores" tuitous. We find it quoted in volumes from La Sauve, St. Germain, tines and Clairvaux in the twelfth century; in others of Arras, Himmerod l Marchiennes in the thirteenth and in the fourteenth century in manu- ipts from Norwich and Alcobaça.[101] The evidence for the statement that ook was *read* (and not merely copied) in the Middle Ages is always limited l difficult to assess, but it may be suggested that all these signs of the uence the book enjoyed, the unexpected places, as in the twelfth-century tiary from France now in the Vatican (Reg. Lat. 258), where we find it oted and known, are all proofs, distinct and curious, of its immense popu- ity. It is not surprising to find Père de Ghellinck including the *Prognosticum* "le tableau des principales sources auxquelles s'alimente la pensée de nos es."[102]

It may be useful to examine some specific instances where Julian's work be shown to have influenced later writers. It is often difficult to be sure ether it was Julian they were copying or whether they were making ect use of his sources. For instance, Alcuin, as we know, had read the *gnosticum*.[103] The work may have served as a source for his *De Fide S. nitatis*.[104] It seems more probable, however, that Alcuin was making ect use of Augustine. In the same way Sr. Veiga Valiña has produced allels between the *Prognosticum* and the *De Sacramentis* of Hugh of St. tor.[105] But it is possible Hugh was using Gregory's *Moralia*, XIV. 56. nore definite instance when it seems certain Julian was being used is to be nd in Haymo of Halberstadt, *De Varietate Librorum*, III, 7; 27-28 (*PL* 118, ; 946 = *Prog.*, II, 10; 18, III. 42). In III, 7 Haymo cites a passage of ianus Pomerius' lost work *De Animae Natura*, exactly as it is found in the *gnosticum*.

There are, however, more interesting proofs of Julian's influence than this. m Leclercq has recently pointed to the influence of the collection of texts m Augustine's *De Cura* and *De Civitate Dei* to be found in the *Prognosticum* the composition of some *Lectiones in vigilia defunctorum* in MS. Paris Lat. 33 A (s. X).[106] The influence of the *Prognosticum* can, indeed, still be seen

 "Libri legendi in conventu seu dividendi ribus ad legendum": Cat. 32 (No. 646).

)0 Cats. 8 and 10.

)1 MSS. Nos. 157, 170, 172, 175; 153, 156, ; 160, 163 in the list of MSS. in the article d in note 56 above.

)2 "En Marge des Cats. des Bibl. médié- s," *Misc. Ehrle*, V, 353.

)3 Cf. note 54 above.

)4 Cf. the *De Fide*, III. 20; 22 (*PL* 101, 54) with *Prog.*, III. 18, 32; 60, 62 (*PL* 96, , 513; 524).

)5 Cf. *De Sacramentis*, II. 17 (*PL* 176, f.) and *Prog.*, III. 27-29 (*PL* 96, 509 f.). A. Veiga Valiña, *La doctrina escatológica de San Julián de Toledo*, Lugo, 1940, 36. Burchard of Worms also uses the *Prog.* at least twice (III. 47; 49) in his *Decretorum l. xx*, XX. 109, 110 (*PL* 140, 1058). Cf. J. de Ghellinck, *Le Mouvement*, 430. He could have found the work at Lobbes where he received his educa- tion (cf. Cat. 40). Nine of 22 chapters in pars 18 of the *Summa* in MS. Vat. Lat. 1345 are taken from the *Prog.* (N. Wicki, *art. cit. infra*, note 120).

106 J. Leclercq, in *Revue bénédictine*, 54, 1942, 21 n. 2, 22 and n. 2, points to the probable use of *Prog.* III. 62; 20-22 (*PL* 96, 524; 505 f.) and II. 26-27 (*ibid.*, 487 f.) in the *Lectiones*. Cf. Leclercq, *ibid.*, 23.

in the selection of readings from the *De Cura* in the 2nd Nocturn of the Off in the Roman Breviary for November 2nd.[107]

In folios 1-34 of MS. Boulogne-sur-Mer 63 (s. XI[1]) (originally an in pendent volume) it would appear that we have a copy of a manuscript k by Aelfric for his personal use and in which he had entered Latin sermo etc., for translation. It is possible "that he owned this copy of his origi collection in which he had one or two extra items added. Whether it v Aelfric's personal property or not, it is believed to have been written by English scribe, probably in England."[108] What is certain is that the excer from the *Prognosticum* on folios 1-10 of this manuscript are the principal sou of an unpublished Old English homily by Aelfric probably intended for Octave of Pentecost.[109] Miss Raynes considers that it is "at least possible t Aelfric compiled the extracts himself. In one or two places in the Old Engl homily he seems to show a knowledge of parts of the *Prognosticum* not incluc in the extracts." The extracts are taken from all parts of the *Prognostic* They are often not in the order of the original and at times a passage "paraphrased instead of being quoted, but on the whole the source is follov closely."[110]

This instance of the influence of the *Prognosticum* on Anglo-Saxon literat would indicate that the work was present in some English libraries before Conquest. After the Danish invasions there was little left of the libra known to Aldhelm and Alcuin. But by the late tenth century new libra were being built up again, and in about 984 Bishop Aethelwold presen books to Peterborough "which are in all likelihood representative of Winchester library"[111] and which include a work probably to be identif with the *Prognosticum*.[112] Another centre of the monastic revival was Worces under Oswald which was in close touch with Fleury. We know of the existe of two copies of the work at Fleury[113] and so it is not surprising to find anot in the Cat. s. XI ex., probably of the Worcester library and a manuscr (Clare, Cambridge, 30) of the eleventh century from Worcester. The cc which Boston of Bury recorded at Ramsey might have come from Worces or from Fécamp (Cat. 5) at the time of Herbert of Losinga. The Canterb books were almost all burnt in 1067; one of the manuscripts at St. Augustin we know to have come there through Thomas of Gotesle, who arrived in eleventh century from St. Bertin (cf. Cat. No. 83). In the same way the s. ex. manuscript noted among the books of William of St. Carileph in 1c

[107] St. Odilo of Cluny (s. XI in.) appears to have been responsible for the celebration of All Souls' Day which still obtains (cf. H. Leclercq, "Mort," *Dict. d'Archéologie Chrétienne et Liturgie*, XII. 1, Paris, 1935, 34-38). In the Nocturn L. iv is taken from the *De Cura*, II and III (cf. *Prog.* I. 18: *PL* 96, 473); L. v from IV. 6 (cf. *Prog.* I. 19: *ibid.*, 474); L. vi from XVIII. 22 (cf. *Prog.* I. 18; 19: *ibid.*, 473; 474).

[108] E. M. Raynes, "MS. Boulogne-sur-Mer 63 and Aelfric," an article to appear in *Medium Aevum*. I have to thank Miss Raynes for her kindness in lending me her articl typescript and also photostats of folios 1-1 the MS.

[109] This is shortly to be edited by Profe Pope from eight MSS. at Cambridge Oxford.

[110] Raynes, *ibid.*

[111] Ramona Bressie, "Libraries of British Isles in the Anglo-Saxon Period," *The Medieval Library*, ed. J. W. Thomps Chicago, 1939, 123.

[112] Cf. Cat. 63.

[113] Cat. 4. Cf. Bressie, *art. cit.*, 122.

S. Laud Misc. 546; Cat. No. 66) was no doubt written after the Conquest, t was not imported from France as was probably the manuscript at Battle niversity Coll. MS. 104). It is curious to see the reverse process taking ce—manuscripts written in England going abroad at this time. We know *Prognosticum* was among the books given by Abbot Seaweald of St. Peter's, h, to St. Vaast d'Arras after he had had to leave England (Cat. 11). It robable that the Boulogne manuscript crossed to St. Bertin at this time as find it noted in the Cat. s. XII in. (No. 13).

The *Prognosticum*, as we have seen, had served as a source for an Old glish homily of Aelfric's. In the late thirteenth century it was to serve as original for a long poem in Anglo-Norman verse.[114] The Catalogue of erborough (dated by Gottlieb *c.* 1300) includes: G. XV. Eruditio Juliani discipulum ejus. Gallice.[115] To my mind there is no doubt that this is a rence to the poem recently edited by M. Bonjour from two manuscripts at ndon and Oxford and a fragment at Cambridge.[116] The poem, in the ndon manuscript, is entitled "Tractatus in Romanis de S. Juliano episcopo lerico suo." It is a free translation or rather adaptation of the *Prognosticum*. ıses most of the work, up to III. 38, but there are frequent changes in the ler. Other changes are in the order of ideas. The author of the poem, om M. Tanquerey[117] supposes, perhaps without sufficient reason, to be a yer, has added at the beginning some 400 verses on the problem of sin l evil of which the original is not to be found in the *Prognosticum*. Further-re he has made numerous omissions and has substituted his own for certain St. Julian's explanations, e.g. on the necessity of death. Where Julian uses gustine to insist that without death Faith would be too easy and would se to be Faith, our author relies rather on certain arguments more likely convince his audience, such as the danger of over-population of the rld.[118] He has a sense of the dramatic. The brief description in the *De a* of the father who dies without telling his son where he can find a receipt, lack of which he is later tormented by his father's creditor, reproduced in *Prognosticum* (II. 27) is expanded by the author of the poem into seventy-ee lines of drama. The idea of a dialogue, M. Bonjour suggests, the poet taken from the *Dialogi* of Gregory, translated into Anglo-Norman by re Angier early in the thirteenth century. Certainly the device has bled him to give his poem movement and drama. The bishop and his rk are real characters. M. Bonjour concludes that if, in the poem, the ideas l controversies of the original have lost some of their depth the translator been able to give them a human setting full of movement and life.

[114] Edited by M. Adrien Bonjour, *Dialogue Saint-Julien et son Disciple, Poème Anglo-mand du XIIIe siècle.* (Anglo-Norman ts—VIII), Oxford, 1949. It begins: "Ici mence un estoire, / De sein Julien la noire" and consists of 2,000 verses.

[115] S. Gunton, *The History of the Church of rburgh*, London, 1686, 221 (this reference ot noticed by M. Bonjour).

[116] The editor bases his text on MS. ndon, British Museum, Royal, 8. E. XVII, s. XIII/XIV. He gives the variants of Oxford, Bodleian, Rawlinson Poetry 241, s. XIV in. There is also a fragment in MS. Gonville and Caius College, Cambridge, 307, *c.* 1300.

[117] F. J. Tanquerey, in *Mélanges . . . Antoine Thomas*, Paris, 1927, 427-443 (cited by Bonjour, pp. xxi-xxvi).

[118] Cf. *Prog.*, I. 9 and *Dialogue*, 609 f. (p. 19). Cf., however, verses 575-992 (p. 18), where Augustine's reasons are given.

We have seen that in the earlier Middle Ages the *Prognosticum* was pres in almost every library, that it was known to and used by scholars such Aelfric and Haymo of Halberstadt. It is satisfactory to be able to show t it was used as a source by Peter the Lombard in his treatise "De Novissimi The late Père de Ghellinck pointed to some instances where he considered Lombard made use of the *Prognosticum.*[119] Recently it has been suggested t on some of these occasions a direct use of the sources seems more probable

The *Prognosticum*, we have remarked, appears to have been less wid appreciated in the later than in the earlier Middle Ages. The Preach Orders and the Colleges, of course, possessed copies[121] but they are very and far between in comparison with the great and lasting success of the w in monastic and Cathedral libraries. The gaps in the list of Catalogues be noted. They include most of the Courts of Renaissance Italy—the libra of the Pandolfini and the Medici, of such men as Giovanni Pico della Mir dola, of Santa Justina of Padua in 1453 (which numbered 1,337 manuscrip of Ferrara, of Urbino and the great library of the Aragonese Kings of Nap on which Professor T. de Marinis has recently given us, in *La Biblioteca dei d'Aragona* (Milan, 4 vols., 1947-52), a work "numquam satis laudandum." On the other hand the list includes almost all the great libraries of the earl pre-scholastic ages. Apart from its inclusion (two copies) in the Avignon a Peniscola Catalogues, in the Sorbonne List of 1338 (as a chained book in Great Library), in the first list of books given to Oxford University in 1439 Duke Humphrey and earlier in the successive Inventories of the Louvre, *Prognosticum*, the Catalogues tell us, was almost exclusively known to monasteries, Benedictine and Cistercian, and to the houses of the Augustin and Premonstratensian Canons.[123] It was not included, so far as I know, any of the Catalogues of the Friars' considerable libraries, such as, for instan that of the Austin Friars at York in 1372 or that of the Franciscans at Sie in 1481.[124] Nor do we find it in the Catalogues of Colleges at Oxford a Cambridge. Durham and Canterbury possessed copies but sent none

[119] *Le Mouvement Théologique*, 239 f. and cf. "En Marge," 354.

[120] N. Wicki, "Das Prognosticum . . . als Quellenwerk der Sentenzen des Petrus Lombardus," *Divus Thomas*, 31, 1953, 349-60. The Lombard refers to Julian (IV. Dist. XLIV, 7, ed. Collegii S. Bonaventurae, 2ª ed., Ad Claras Aquas, 1916, II, 1003) and quotes a passage, taken from Gregory by Julian, from *Prog.*, II, 17. The following passages, taken from Augustine and Cassian, are also in the *Prog.* (II. 9; 15; cf. p. 1004).

[121] E.g. MSS. Bruxelles 4485 (s. XIV); British Museum, Royal 6. E. III (s. XV); Paris, Lat. 2692 (s. XV).

[122] MS. 98 (Paris, B.N. Lat. 2338, s. XV) belonged to the Conte d'Ugento and passed from him to the Kings of Naples, but it was a late acquisition and is not included in any of the Inventories of their Library. In the same way the inclusion of a copy of the work in Sanderus' list (*op. cit.*, II, 1643, 28) of Burgundian Collection at Brussels is not su cient to prove its presence in this library the 15th century, since it is not found in of the Cats. from 1404 to 1487 printed Peignot and Barrois. Apart from Naples only Italian princely library that certai possessed a copy was that of Visconti-Sfo (MS. Paris, Lat. 6368, s. XIV).

[123] From the Cats. and the surviving M one can name at least 90 Benedictine and Cistercian houses and some 20 houses Canons which possessed the work.

[124] Cf. M. R. James, "The Catalogue the Library of the Austin Friars at Yor *Fasciculus Ioanni Willis Clark dicatus*, Ca bridge, 1909, 2-96; N. Papini, *L'Etr Franciscana*, I (unico), Siena, 1797, 118- The former library possessed 646 volun the latter about 1350.

ırham or Canterbury College.[125] The *Prognosticum* seems to have found as :le favour with the University-trained monk in fifteenth-century England as th the Italian prelates of an earlier age, whose collections, when they died, re shipped as "spolia" back to Avignon in the 1340's by Guillaume de zières, "nuntius et collector in regno Sicilie citra Farum,"[126] or with the andinavian book-collectors of the later Middle Ages.[127]

But if the *Prognosticum* suffered a comparative neglect during the later iddle Ages it became again of interest after the invention of printing. The *tio princeps* appears to have been published at Milan *c.* 1490,[128] but it was t until the sixteenth century that the work attained a new fame. Two itors, Cochlaeus in 1536 and Bugnaeus in 1554, realized the possibilities of : work as ammunition against the Protestants.[129] The milder Böetius Epo s more cautious. He was inclined to hold that the intemperate supporters the Church did her more harm than her open opponents.[130] After Böetius o's edition of 1564 there were no more separate editions but the *Prognosticum* s included in each reprint of the standard *Bibliotheca Patrum.*[131] As time ssed, the interest in the work awakened by the controversies of the sixteenth ıtury died away and it tended to be forgotten. Yet it had served the earlier ıturies of mediaeval Christendom well for it had provided those centuries th their standard work on the Last Things, the first treatise *De Novissimis.*

25 Cf. *Catalogi Veteres Librorum ecclesiae ıedralis Dunelm* (Surtees Society Publ. 7), ıdon, 1838, 39 and 39-40 and N. E. D. ckiston, "Some Durham College Rolls," *Collectanea*, 3rd Series, ed. M. Burrows xford Historical Society), Oxford, 1896, 38 (List of 1315); W. A. Pantin, *Canterbury lege, Oxford*, I (O.H.S., New Series, VI), ford, 1947 (for 1941), *passim.* Cf. also Sir M. Powicke, *The Medieval Books of Merton lege*, Oxford, 1931.

26 *Vide* M-H. Laurent, "Guillaume des zières et la bibl. pontificale à l'époque de ment VI," *Mélanges A. Pelzer*, Louvain, :7, 579-603.

27 Cf. C. H. Christensen, "Scandinavian raries in the Late Middle Ages," in *The dieval Library*, ed. J. W. Thompson, 477-. Only one copy of Augustine's *De Civitate* is to be found in all the records of Danish diaeval libraries (p. 483).

28 According to the British Museum horities, but L. Polain, *Catalogue des livres rimés au 15e siècle des bibliothèques de Belgique*, , Brussels, 1932, p. 532, ascribes it to the nter Thierry Martens of Alost and dates it 487. It is an 8° (18.3 × 11.2 cm.), 30 pp. lines), numbered Ai-Eiv. The title-page rely reads: "Incipiūt prenosticata Iulia/ni nerii urbis toletane epis/copi de futuro ılo." I know of the following copies: lleian, 4°.M.II. Th. Seld.; B.M. I. A. 36; I. A. 49037; Paris, Bibl. Nat., Rés. D. 11164 (Campbell, 1435); Brussels, Bibl. Royale, 3237.

129 Cf. Cochlaeus, Letter to the bishop of Merseburg; Bugnaeus, *Epist. Nuncupatoria* to Petrus à Danielo. Cf. J. de Ghellinck, in *Miscellanea J. Gessler*, I, Louvain, 1948, 530-547. It is interesting to note that Cochlaeus' edition has a note in the margin opposite I. 12 referring to the execution of More and Fisher in 1535 (the year before his edition appeared). The note (fol. C^v) reads: "Hoc consilium egregie nuper secuti fuerint Johan. Epūs Roffen, et Tho. Mor. in Anglia per martyrium. Anno. 1535." In the British Museum copy it has been almost inked out by some Protestant reader.

130 Cf. p. 3: "Atque dubitari quidem non immerito potest, utrumnam hactenus magis nocuerint Reipublicae Christianae, an ne Religionis invitae temerarii oppugnatores, an vero eiusdem intemperantes et maledici et virulentes et male sani propugnatores."

131 The edition of 1564 was used. Margarin de la Bigne included it in the third volume of his *Sacrae Bibliothecae SS. Patrum* (Paris, 1575) and it was reproduced in subsequent editions of this standard collection (Paris, IX, in 1589, 1624 and 1644; Cologne, VII, 1618 and in Vol. XII of the *Maxima Bibl. veterum Patrum*, published in Lyons, 1677, p. 590). The last edition served as the main source for De Lorenzana's editors in 1785.

Developed with all "the ultra-literal interpretation of the Bible and unlimit confidence in the method of deduction" which Julian had learnt from Grego the Great, the work had satisfied the curiosity of the faithful on "all sorts inaccessible problems."[132] It had helped to enable its readers to forget times the wretched enough circumstances of their lives and to enter ir consideration of the glories and terrors of the life to come.

[132] Cf. Pierre de Labriolle, *Histoire de la littérature latine chrétienne*, 3e éd., revue par Gustave Bardy, Paris, 1947, II, 805 f.

V

JULIAN OF TOLEDO IN THE *LIBER FLORIDUS*[1]

Some years ago, in an article in this *Journal*, I attempted to trace in outline the influence of the works of Julian, Archbishop of Toledo (680–90) during the Middle Ages.[2] Of these works by far the most influential was Julian's *Prognosticum futuri saeculi*. I have published elsewhere lists of 176 complete or fragmentary manuscripts of this work and of 102 mediaeval catalogues of books which mention it.[3] Both these lists could now be expanded[4] and some other instances of the use of the *Prognosticum* by mediaeval authors could be produced.[5] It is my aim here to show that Julian's work was drawn on by Lambert, canon of St.-Omer, in his *Li[ber] Floridus* (*c.* 1120), for a number of passage[s] which Delisle was unable to find the sourc[e] The text of the *Liber Floridus* used is ta[ken] from the original manuscript of Lamb[ert] Ghent, Bibliothèque de l'Université, 92.[7] [For] the text of the *Prognosticum* I have used [my] forthcoming critical edition, while giv[ing] references to Cardinal de Lorenzana's editi[on] as reproduced in Migne, *P. L.* XCVI, c[ols.] 453–524.

It would be interesting to discover [the] actual manuscript of the *Prognosticum* used [by] Lambert. We know he drew largely on [the] Benedictine library of St. Bertin.[8] A ma[nu]script from St. Bertin, now at Boulogne-s[ur-]Mer (63, saec. XI[1], fols. 1–10) contain[s a] series of important *excerpta* from the *Progn[os]ticum*.[9] Miss E. M. Raynes has shown t[hat] these *excerpta* were the principal source of

[1] This note arose out of a seminar on the *Liber Floridus* held at the Warburg Institute in June 1962 by Professor H. Bober and Professor H. Swarzenski and is offered as a slight contribution towards the definitive study of the miniatures and text of the *Liber* which is so badly needed.

[2] "St. Julian of Toledo in the Middle Ages", this *Journal*, XXI, 1958, pp. 7–26.

[3] "El 'Prognosticum futuri saeculi' de san Julián de Toledo", *Analecta sacra Tarraconensia*, XXX, 1957, pp. 5–61.

[4] I now have notes on ten more MSS., including one (Piacenza, Bibl. della Cattedrale 13), which, according to Professor B. Bischoff, is saec IX[1], from the region of Salzburg. I have also noted six more mediaeval catalogues which contain the work; the earliest is one of Caaveiro, in Galicia, dated 936 or 966. *Addenda* and *corrigenda* to my earlier lists will be included in an article on the MS. tradition of the *Prognosticum*, to appear in *Sacris erudiri*, as a companion to my critical edition, to appear in the *Corpus Christianorum*.

[5] E.g. the considerable use made of the work by Honorius "Augustodunensis", in his very popu[lar] *Elucidarium* (cf. V. Lefèvre, *L'Elucidarium et les lucida[ires]*, Paris, 1954, index, p. 536).

[6] See L. Delisle, "Notice sur les manuscrits du 'L[iber] Floridus' de Lambert, chanoine de Saint-Om[er]", *Notices et extraits des manuscrits de la Bibliothèque Natio[nale] et autres bibliothèques*, XXXVIII, Paris, 1906, pp. 5[77–]791. Delisle usually only gives the *incipit* and *exp[licit]* of each extract.

[7] Cf. Delisle, pp. 581–88. I am grateful to Profe[ssor] Bober for lending me photographs of the MS.

[8] Cf., e.g., Delisle, pp. 687, 689, 694.

[9] See, on this MS., the descriptions in *Catal[ogue] générale des manuscrits des bibliothèques publiques des dép[arte]ments*, 1st ser., IV, Paris, 1872, p. 613, and in B. Fe[hr], *Die Hirtenbriefe Aelfrics*: Bibliothek der angelsächsisc[hen] Prosa, IX, Hamburg, 1914, pp. x–xiv.

ɔublished Old English homily by Aelfric.[10] t possible that this manuscript was used by nbert? Although written by an English be, probably in England, it appears to 'e reached St. Bertin at an early date. The allel passages assembled below show that nbert's excerpts from the *Prognosticum* are :n very close to the text of MS. Boulogne [11] On the other hand there are a number :xcerpts in Lambert which are not to be nd in this manuscript.[12] If, as I think it is ually certain, Lambert used the Boulogne ;., he must have also had access to another and more complete copy of Julian's work. Such a manuscript is actually indicated in catalogue of the library of St. Bertin drawn up saec. XII *ineunte*, which registers "Iuliani pronostica".[13] This cannot correspond to the Boulogne MS., which does not contain Julian's name and is simply headed (fol. 1): "Hunc sermonem ex multis excerpsimus, de libro qui dicitur *Pronosticon.*" This second, presumably complete, copy of the *Prognosticum* at St. Bertin is apparently lost.[14]

[10] See E. M. Raynes, "MS. Boulogne-sur-Mer 63 Aelfric", *Medium Aevum*, XXVI, 1957, pp. 65–73, d in my earlier article in this *Journal*, p. 22. I have hank Miss Raynes (Mrs. Edwards) for lending me photostats of the MS. for the second time.

[11] The MS. was at St. Bertin by saec. XIII at st (cf. Fehr, p. x). Note especially passages nos. 6, , 9–12 below.

[12] Nos. 1, 3, 14, 15, 16 and 18. Other passages ıd in Lambert are incomplete in the Boulogne MS. s. 13 and 17).

[13] G. Becker, *Catalogi bibliothecarum antiqui*, Bonn, 1885, p. 183, No. 128; cf. *Analecta sacra Tarraconensia*, XXX, 1957, p. 49. I cannot find any entry corresponding to MS. Boulogne 63 in this catalogue, which is, however, extremely brief in its description of MSS. The MS. of the *Prognosticum* indicated by the catalogue is possibly the same that we find among the books written at St. Bertin by order of Abbot John (+ 1095): "librum Effrem vel Pronosticorum" (*Mon. Germ. Hist., Scriptores*, XIII, Hannover, 1881, p. 642).

[14] I use the following abbreviations: G = MS. Ghent 92; D = Delisle, *op. cit.*, n. 6 *supra*; B = MS. Boulogne 63. In the notes I have not indicated unimportant variants in B.

Lambert (G, fol. 6; D, p. 614, No. 11)

ıis noster Christus est perficiens nos, ipse t refectio et laudatio nostra in secula ulorum. Ibi erit vere maximum sabbatum ı habens vesperam.

Prognosticum, III. 62[15] (col. 524 B–C)

Finis noster Christus perficiens nos, ipse erit et refectio et laudatio nostra, quem in saecula saeculorum laudabimus, . . . Ibi erit . . . vere maximum sabbatum non habens vesperam.

G, *ibid.* (continues); D, *ibid.*

ıis igitur desideriorum nostrorum Christus ıc erit, qui sine fine videbitur, sine fastidio abitur, sine fatigatione laudabitur.

Ibid., 60 (col. 524 A);[16] B, fol. 9v

Finis igitur desideriorum nostrorum Christus tunc erit, qui sine fine videbitur, sine fastidio amabitur, sine fatigatione laudabitur.

G, *ibid.* (continues); D, *ibid.*

nc vere erit sabbatum nostrum cuius finis ı erit vespera, sed dominicus dies vel oc'us et eternus, qui Christi resurrectione ratus est. Ibi vacabimus et videbimus, ebimus et amabimus, amabimus et laudanus. Ecce quod erit in fine sine fine. Nam is alius noster est finis, nisi pervenire ad ;num, cuius nullus est finis? Amen.

Ibid., 62 (col. 524 C–D)[17]

Tunc vere erit sabbatum nostrum, cuius finis non erit vespera, sed dominicus dies vel octavus aeternus, qui Christi resurrectione sacratus est [paratus, *varii codd.*]. Ibi vacabimus et videbimus, videbimus et amabimus, amabimus et laudabimus. Ecce quod erit in fine sine fine. Nam quis alius noster est finis nisi pervenire ad regnum, cuius nullus est finis?

G, fol. 100; D, p. 663 (No. 154)

atus Augustinus dicit: Unus est paradisus, i primorum hominum vita extitit, alter 'o celestis ubi beatorum anime transferun- et expectant receptionem corporum ɔrum.

Ibid., II. 1 (col. 475 C);[18] B, fol. 3

Unus est terrenus paradisus, ubi primorum hominum corporaliter vita extitit; alter coelestis, ubi animae beatorum statim ut a corpore exeunt transferuntur, atque . . . expectant receptionem corporum suorum.

[15] From "Ibi erit" this is an (acknowledged) excerpt n Augustine, *De civitate Dei*, xxii. 30 (Corpus iptorum Ecclesiasticorum Latinorum, XL. 2, 568.19).

[16] From Augustine, *ibid.*, p. 666.4 f.

[17] Cf. *ibid.*, p. 670.9–16. One of the best MSS. of the *Prognosticum* has "Amen" after the *Explicit* of the work.

[18] Julian is using, without acknowledgement, Isidore, *Differentiae*, II.xii.32 (*P.L.* LXXXIII, col. 75 A–B), not Augustine.

5. G, *ibid.*; D, *ibid.* (No. 155)

Augustinus: Duo inferna, alter superior terra, alter inferior sub terra esse creditur.

Ibid., 4 (col. 477 A);[19] B, fol. 3r–v

duo esse inferna manifestius dicit [Augu nus], ut unus infernus superior terra, al vero infernus inferior sub terra esse accipiat

6, G, *ibid.*; [D, *ibid.*]

Anima vero que semel in infernum proiecta fuerit ibidem perpetuo manebit.

Ibid., 14 (col. 480 C); B, fol. 3v[20]

Quod hi qui semel fuerint in infern proiecti, ibidem erunt perpetim permans

7. G, *ibid.*; [D, *ibid.*;]=G, fol. 220; D, p. 702

Resurgent omnes homines tam magni corpore vel in statura in qua futuri erant si vixissent in mensuram etatis Christi ad quam pervenit in mundo cum resurrexit a mortuis annorum scilicet XXX[ta] trium.

Ibid., III. 20 (col. 505 C–D);[21] B, fol. 6

resurgant corpora mortuorum . . . in e aetate et robore, usque ad quam Christ hic pervenisse cognovimus (circa trigi quippe annos . . .) . . . in mensuram aet plenitudinis Christi. Resurgent ergo om tam magni corpore, quam vel erant vel fut erant aetate juvenali . . .

8. G, *ibid.*; D, *ibid.* (No. 156)=G, fol. 220; D, p. 702

Augustinus: Humanitatem Christi cum iudicabit orbem, iusti et iniusti visuri sunt; divinitatis vero eius dulcedinem non videbunt nisi soli iusti, sicut dicit apostolus, "Tollatur impius ne videat gloriam Dei".

Ibid., 8 (col. 501 B);[22] B, fol. 6v

Christus Dei Filius cum ad iudicium ven faciendum, omnes pariter humanitatem e et iusti et iniusti visuri sunt. Divinitat tamen eius iniusti non videbunt, quae iu tantum visura promittitur . . . testa Esaias, qui dicit: "Tollatur impius ne vid maiestatem Domini."

9. G, *ibid.*; D, *ibid.*=G, fol. 220; D, p. 702

Item Augustinus dicit: Electi non solum eos cognoscent quos in hoc mundo noverant, sed velut visos recognoscent bonos quos numquam viderunt sine iudice.

Ibid., II. 24 (col. 487 A);[23] B, fol. 4

Fit autem in electis quiddam mirabili quia non solum eos agnoscunt quos in h mundo noverunt, sed velut visos ac cogni recognoscunt bonos quos nunquam videra

10. G, *ibid.*; D, *ibid.*

Augustinus: Non impiorum sed sanctorum tantum anime norunt quid agitur a viventibus in mundo.

Ibid., 31 (col. 492 B); B, fol. 4v[24]

Quod non impiorum sed sanctorum tant animae noverint quid possit a viventibus a

11. G, *ibid.*; D, *ibid.* (No. 157)=G, fol. 220; D, p. 702

De monstris et de bimembris dicit Augustinus: Absit, inquit, ut bimembrem aut hominem duplicem resurrecturos credamus,

Ibid., III. 28 (col. 510 A);[25] B, fol. 7

Absit enim ut illum bimembrem, . . . ab inquam, ut unum hominem duplicem . resurrecturos existimemus.

---

[19] Julian alludes to Augustine, *Enarrationes in Psalmos*, 85.13, n. 17.36–38 (*Corpus Christianorum*, XXXIX, p. 1190), which he proceeds later to quote.

[20] The text is that of the chapter-heading. B's text is closer to that of G: "Anima denique que semel in infernum proiecta fuerit, ibidem erit perpetuo permansura".

[21] Julian is quoting, with acknowledgement, from Aug. *De civ. Dei*, xxii. 15–16 (pp. 623. 25–27; 624. 19–20). B's text is closer to that of G: "Resurgent . . . magni corpore et in illa statura, in qua erant viventes vel futuri erant si vixissent, in mensura vero etatis plentitudinis Christi, hoc est in illa etate et in illo robore ad quam Christus pervenit in mundo."

[22] Augustine is not here explicitly cited by Julian, and I have not found his source; it seems unlikely, however, that Lambert is using Augustine directly. is curious that Lambert should attribute a quotat from Isaiah (xxvi. 10) to St. Paul. The text of somewhat closer to that of G though not identic ". . . divinitatem vero eius non videbunt nisi soli iu sicut Isaias dicit: 'Tollatur impius ne videat mag tatem Domini'."

[23] The source of Julian here is actually Grego *Dialogi*, iv. 34, ed. Moricca, p. 280, ll. 12–14, ci with acknowledgement. B has "cognoscunt . noverant . . . viderunt", as G.

[24] The text is that of the chapter-heading. B rea "Non enim impiorum sed sanctorum tantum ani norunt quid possit a viventibus agi in seculo."

[25] Julian is quoting Augustine, *Enchiridion*, 87 (*P* XL, col. 273), with acknowledgement.

. G, *ibid.* (continues); [D, *ibid.*]

l cecos vel debiles, sed cum integro numero :mbrorum corporis sine deformitate sur- nt.

. G, fol. 230; D, p. 705 f. (No. 263)

ıgustinus, Hieronimus, Julianus Toletanus iscopus. Resurrectio communis omnibus t bonis et malis, immutatio autem solis ta est iustis, que utique glorificationem inuat vite eterne.

. G, *ibid.* (continues)

cit beatus Augustinus quod in tercio celo paradisus, in quo fuerat Paulus apostolus ɔtus, et ubi anime beatorum locantur exute rporibus.

. G, *ibid.* (continues)

eg.: Sunt quorundam iustorum anime que :elesti regno quibusdam adhuc mansionibus ferentur, quia de perfecta iustitia aliquid nus habuerunt.

. G, *ibid.* (continues)

lianus episcopus: Spiritus illi qui nec tam rfecte santitatis hinc exeunt ut ire in para- ιum post depositionem suorum corporum ssint nec tam criminose vixerint, ut cum ıbolo dampnari mereantur, ecclesia pro eis : efficaciter supplicante expiati, beata im- ortalitate ac regni celestis facti participes, eo sine ullo defectu permanebunt.

. G, *ibid.* (continues)

eg. [margin]: Credendum est quod ante :ributionem extremi iudicii, iniusti in quie quosdam iustos conspiciunt, ut eos lentes in gaudio non de suo solum sup- icio sed etiam de illorum bono crucientur; sti vero in tormentis intuentur impios, ut nc eorum gaudium crescat, quia malum nspiciunt quod misericorditer evaserunt, ntoque maiores ereptori suo gratias referunt, ıando vident in alios quid ipsi perpeti relicti tuerunt.

Ibid., 30 (col. 511 C); B, fol. 7[26]

Quod hi qui de hac vita debiles exierunt, cum suis integris membris in resurrectione futuri sint.

Ibid., 16 (col. 504 B);[27] B, f. 6

Nam iuxta quod beatus Augustinus, Hieronimus, Julianus Pomerius caeterique testantur, resurrectio communis omnibus erit bonis et malis, immutatio autem solis danda est iustis, quae utique glorificationem insinuat aeternae beatitudinis.

Ibid., II. 2 (col. 475 D–476 B)[28]

Legimus in beato Augustino, . . . quod in tertio coelo sit paradisus, in quo fuerit Apostolus raptus, et ubi animae beatorum locantur exutae corporibus.

Ibid., 8 (col. 478 C)[29]

Nam sunt quorundam iustorum animae, quae a celesti regno quibusdam adhuc mansionibus differuntur, . . . nisi quod de perfecta iustitia aliquid minus habuerunt.

Ibid., 10 (col. 479 B)[30]

Iulianus Pomerius dicit: Spiritus illi qui nec tam perfectae sanctitatis hinc exeunt, ut ire in paradisum statim post depositionem suorum corporum possint, nec tam criminose . . . vivunt, . . . ut cum diabolo . . . damnari mereantur, ecclesia pro eis hic efficaciter supplicante, ac poenis medicinalibus expiati, corpora sua cum beata immortalitate recipient, ac regni coelestis facti participes, in eo sine ullo defectu suae beatitudinis permanebunt.

Ibid., 32 (col. 493 B);[31] B, fols. 9, 4v

in homiliis papae Gregorii . . .: "Credendum est quod, ante retributionem extremi iudicii, iniusti in requie quosdam iustos conspiciant, ut eos videntes et conspicientes in gaudio, non solum de suo supplicio, sed etiam de illorum bono crucientur. Iusti vero in tormentis semper intuentur iniustos, ut hinc eorum gaudium crescat, quia malum conspiciunt quod misericorditer evaserunt, tantoque maiores ereptori suo gratias referunt, quanto vident in aliis quod ipsi perpeti, si essent relicti, potuerunt."

---

[26] The text is that of the chapter-heading. The text B is closer and follows almost immediately on the t passage used by G: "vel debiles ceci fuerunt, cum egro numero membrorum corporis sine deformitate urgent".

[27] The references here (and below, no. 16) to Julianus merius, whose (lost) work, *De natura animae vel quali- eius*, is often quoted by Julian of Toledo, were sunderstood by Lambert. B omits "Nam iuxta . . . tantur" but has "*data* est iustis", as G.

[28] Julian is referring to Aug. *De Genesi ad litteram* 12.34 (Corpus Script. Eccles. Lat., XXVIII. 1, p. 432), which he proceeds to quote.

[29] Julian is quoting, with acknowledgement, from Greg. *Dial.* iv. 26 (p. 263.15–18).

[30] See n. 27 above.

[31] Julian is quoting from Greg. *Hom. in Evangelia* II.40.8 (*P.L.* LXXVI, col. 1308 D–1309 A). B does

18. G, *ibid.* (continues); D, *ibid.* (p. 706)

Iudicii tempus vel diem incognitum nobis dominus voluit esse, Matheo et Marco testantibus non propheta nec angelus neque Filius nisi Pater solus diem novit ultimum consummationis seculi. Non arbitrandus est hoc ipse Filius ignorare cum per prophetam dicat, "Dies ultionis in corde meo", indicat se quidem scire, sed nolle hominibus indicare.

Ibid., III. 1 (col. 497 B)[32]

Iudicii tempus vel diem incognitum no Dominus voluit esse . . . legimus: "De autem illa et hora nemo scit, neque angeli coelo, neque Filius, nisi Pater solus." . . . n arbitrandus est hoc ipsum Filius ignorasse, Nam dum dicat idem Dominus per prop tam: "Dies ultionis in corde meo", indicat quidem scire, sed nolle omnibus indicare.

not contain the whole passage copied in G. It omits "Iusti vero . . . evaserunt". It reads, however, "conspiciunt, ut eos videntes in gaudio", as G.

[32] The end of this passage from Julian ("Nam dum dicat . . . omnibus indicare") is taken, without ackno ledgement, from Isidore, *Sententiae*, I.xxvii.1 (P LXXXIII, col. 595 A).

ADDITIONAL NOTE

The two articles reproduced here represent a selection of my work on Julian of Toledo. Apart from the articles referred to above in Study IV, p.7, I have discussed "Las fuentes de san Julián de Toledo", in Anales Toledanos 3 (Toledo, 1971), pp. 97-118, and a work wrongly attributed to Julian in "The Prognosticum futuri saeculi of St. Julian of Toledo and the Tractatus published by Mai", in Classica et Iberica, a Festschrift in honor of the Reverend Joseph M-F. Marique, S.J., ed. P.T. Brannan, S.J. (Worcester, Mass., 1975), pp. 339-344. My critical edition of the Prognosticum, the De comprobatione sextae aetatis, the Apologeticum de tribus capitulis, and of the two surviving letters of Idalius of Barcelona, was published, together with a reprint of older editions of Julian's Historia Wambae (by W. Levison) and of a letter in verse to a certain Modoenus (by B. Bischoff), in S. Iuliani Toletanae sedis episcopi Opera, pars 1 (Corpus christianorum, Series latina, CXV) (Brepols, Turnhout, 1976). The long introduction to this edition included a revised list of manuscripts of the Prognosticum, raising it to 186 complete or fragmentary copies (see Study IV above, p. 14). Further minor additions might be made.

My suggestion (in "Las fuentes", p. 101) that, in the Prognosticum, III, 5, Julian might be translating John Chrysostom directly from the Greek, has been corrected by Jean-Paul Bouhot, "Un pseudo-témoin du De natura animae de Pomère. Une homélie de Jean Chrysostom citée par Julien de Tolède", Revue des études augustiniennes 23 (1977), 113-23, who points out that Julian was using an earlier Latin version, printed as sermon 155 of Pseudo-Augustine. Aelfric's use of the Prognosticum (noted in Study IV, p. 22) has been fully explored by Milton McC. Gatch, Preaching and Theology in Anglo-Saxon England: Aelfric and Wulfstan (Toronto, 1977), pp. 129-146. Professor Gatch prints all the excerpts contained in MS. Boulogne-sur-Mer 63. One should also refer to the very thorough review of this book by John C. Pope, Speculum 54 (1979), pp. 129-36, which stresses the influence of Julian on Aelfric. We still await the edition of the Antikeimena of Julian, entrusted to other hands.

Roger Collins, "Julian of Toledo and the Royal Succession in Late Seventh-Century Spain", in Early Medieval Kingship, ed. by P.H. Sawyer and I.N. Wood (Leeds, 1977), pp. 30-49, in giving us a useful commentary on the Historia Wambae, questions (pp. 40f) my view of the Historia as official historiography, designed to glorify King Wamba (see Study III above, pp. 299f). While I think that Mr Collins greatly undervalues the influence of the Old Testament on "the theory and practice of Visigothic kingship" (see now Study I above, pp. 32f), I would agree that one should see the Historia as having a didactic purpose. I do not see this purpose as contradicting its panegyrical form and intention, A full study of the Historia is expected in Suzanne Teillet, Des Gots à la nation gotique. Les origines de l'idée de nation en Occident du IVe au VIIe siècle (Paris, 1984).

VI

The East, Visigothic Spain and the Irish

I propose in this paper to raise a question to which I am certainly not able to provide a definite although I shall suggest a possible answer for the consideration in particular of historians of early Irish art. As the solution I shall suggest involves the transmission of a number of late patristic works it may, I think, usefully be discussed here.[1] It has struck me for some time as curious that, while most recent scholarship is agreed in finding considerable and clear evidence of Eastern and especially of Coptic influence on Irish artists in the sixth, seventh and eighth centuries no specific study seems to have been attempted of how this Eastern influence reached Ireland.[2] Åberg produces a number of reasons against the likelihood that it came indirectly through Lombard Italy, Merovingian France, Germany or England. He

[1] I am indebted to Dr. Ludwig Bieler, Dom Eligius Dekkers O.S.B., Prof. J. Fontaine and Prof. Fr. Wormald for their kindness in reading this paper and giving me their criticisms of it.

[2] Cf. e. g. F. Henry, Irish Art, London 1940; Idem, Art Irlandais, Dublin 1954; Nils Åberg, The Occident and the Orient in the Art of the Seventh Century I, The British Isles, Stockholm 1943; M. and L. de Paor, Early Christian Ireland, London 1958. F. Masai, Essai sur les Origines de la Miniature dite irlandaise, Bruxelles-Anvers 1947, admits Eastern influence on Celtic art which he holds is English not Irish in inspiration. On his highly controversial work cf. the reviews of L. Bieler, in: Speculum 23, 1948, 495–502 and M. Schapiro, in: Gazette des Beaux-Arts 6e période, 37, 92e année, 1950, 134–38; the articles of F. Henry and S. P. O. Riordain, in: Studies 37, 1948, 267–82. The most important contributions to the discussion of the origins of Insular art since 1947 are those of C. Nordenfalk, Before the Book of Durrow, in: Acta Archaeologica 18, 1947, 141–174 and F. Henry, Les Débuts de la Miniature irlandaise, in: Gazette des Beaux-Arts, vol. cit., 1950, 5–24. The arguments advanced by these authors cannot be said to be met by M. Masai in his recent Il monachesimo Irlandese nei suoi Rapporti col Continente (Arte), in: Settimane d Studio del Centro Italiano di Studi sull'Alto Medioevo IV, Spoleto 1957 139–163. Cf. Nordenfalk, Early Medieval Painting, Lausanne 1957, 118.

does not, apparently, so much as consider the possibility of a transmission of Eastern art through Visigothic Spain.[1] This omission seems to me all the more surprising when we recall the fact that the remains of seventh century art in Spain are far more extensive than in France or Italy and that its connections with the East have been clearly demonstrated.[2]

Certain historians of art, notably Mlle Micheli and Dr. P. Meyer, have noted the remarkable similarities – not only in the use of interlace but in what may be called an anti-realist attitude, "a refusal of reality", to use a phrase of Mlle Henry's, in the portrayal of human beings – between Irish and Spanish art: these similarities may arise from a simultaneous or successive use of the same Eastern models.[3] Mlle Micheli, writing in 1939, held that this question was important for the very origins of Irish illumination.[4] Unfortunately no detailed study of the parallels between Spanish and Irish illumination has yet appeared. The overriding difficulty, of course, consists in our all but complete lack of Spanish illuminated MSS earlier than the early tenth century, even though the imagery of seventh century MSS may be reconstructed to some extent by the comparative study of Visigothic sculpture and of later Mozarabic illumination.[5] Art historians

[1] Cf. Åberg, op. cit., 31, 35, 40, 120, 128, etc. Mlle Henry (Irish Art, 45) suggests Eastern influence may have come through Rome (but cf. 56, 95). For a later period D. Talbot Rice, English Art 871–1100, Oxford 1952, suggests transmission from Syria "by way of South Italy and Spain to Ireland" (p. 100). Cf. G. Menéndez Pidal, Sobre Miniatura española en la Alta Edad Media, corrientes culturales que revela, Madrid 1958. He admits Irish influence on Spanish art of the Mozarabic period but (p. 37) can find no evidence for a connection between the monasticism of the British Isles and of Spain (on this cf. infra p. 454, n. 4).

[2] Cf. E. Camps Cazorla, El Arte Hispanovisigodo, in: Historia de España III, ed. R. Menéndez Pidal, Madrid 1940, 435–666; H. Schlunk, Arte Visigodo, in: Ars Hispaniae II, Madrid 1947, 227–323; Idem, Relaciones entre la Peninsula Ibérica y Bizancio, in: Archivo español de Archeologia 18, 1945, 177–204. For Eastern influences in Spain after the Arabic Invasion cf. G. Menéndez Pidal, op. cit.; A. Grabar, in: Arte del Primo Millennio: Atti del II° Convegno per lo Studio dell'Arte dell'Alto Medio Evo Pavia 1950, Torino, n. d., 312–319.

[3] Cf. G. L. Micheli, L'Enluminure du haut Moyen Age et les influences irlandaises, Bruxelles 1939, 169ff.; P. Meyer, Evangeliorum Quattuor Codex Cenannensis III, Bern 1951, 48. 50; F. Henry, Art Irlandais, 56ff.

[4] Micheli, op. cit., 169. Cf. F. Masai, Essai, 118 note 200.

[5] Cf. H. Schlunk, Observaciones en torno al problema de la Miniatura Visigoda, in: Archivo español de Arte 18, 1945, 241–65. Recently M. C. Díaz y Díaz, La cultura de la España visigotica del siglo VII, in: Settimane di

can, therefore, still dismiss apparent similarities with a shrug of their shoulders and a vague reference to the Celtic element common to Spain and to Ireland, to the same process of "stylisation", or to "la maladresse commune à tous les artisans barbares".[1]

I do not mean to deal directly here with the question of artistic relations between Spain and Ireland, though I shall mention at the end of this paper one parallel that seems illuminating. Instead I propose to indicate, necessarily in outline, some of the other evidence we possess for the very close relations between the two countries, particularly close, it is true, from the mid-seventh century onwards but also demonstrable as existing earlier, possibly before 600, a time when Eastern influences must, as Åberg notes, have been of great importance in Ireland in their contribution to the formative stages of Irish Christian art.[2] This evidence is drawn from the manuscript tradition of certain Latin authors, notably North African and Spanish: we find them copied and quoted by the Irish at such an early period that we are bound to assume they had travelled by ship direct to Ireland from Spain.

The assertion that such a journey was possible at this time may seem surprising but in fact we know that these voyages took place. The existence of trade between the Eastern Mediterranean and Spain in the sixth and seventh centuries is well attested.[3]

Studio V 2, Spoleto 1958, 823, has lamented our general lack of Spanish MSS of the seventh century. The Ashburnham Pentateuch cannot be used to fill the gap since its origin is still disputed, Lowe, Codices Latini Antiquiores (henceforth abbreviated as CLA) V, Oxford 1950, n. 693a, believing it comes from an "Eastern region, outside the main Latin stream", while C. Nordenfalk, Early Medieval Painting, Lausanne 1957, 101–4, following W. Neuß, Die Katalanische Bibelillustration, Bonn–Leipzig 1922, 61, holds it is probably Spanish.

[1] Cf. W. Neuß, Die Apokalypse des hl. Johannes in der altspanischen und altchristlichen Bibel-Illustration I, Münster i. W. 1931, 279; F. Masai, Essai ur la Miniatusre, 24 n. 25. C. Nordenfalk, Early Medieval Painting, 165, stresses the difference between Mozarabic and Irish illumination (though cf. ibid., 121. 163).

[2] Cf. Åberg, op. cit., pp. 15ff. 35, etc.; Henry, Les Débuts de la Miniature irlandaise (cited p. 442, n. 2).

[3] Trade revived after its, interruption by the Vandal fleet in the Fifth Century (against this view cf. N. H. Baynes, in; Journal of Roman Studies 19, 1929, 230–233). Cf. H. Pirenne, in: Mélanges Bidez II, Bruxelles 1934, 677–87; P. Lemerle, in: Settimane di Studio V 2, Spoleto 1958, 726; the sea route is more likely in the Seventh Century than the land route through the Balkans, by which books travelled earlier (cf. F. J. Babcock, in: Journal of Theological

From Carthage ships coming from Alexandria or Constantinople could gain the South of Spain, sail up the Guadalquivir to Seville or up the Guadiana to Mérida or continue round into the Atlantic to reach Braga and the North.[1] These ships brought with them travellers and artists from the East, with, in their luggage, books, Greek authors – mostly, though not always, in Latin translations; Eastern silks and jewels such as adorn the treasures of Visigothic kings.[2] In Spanish art of the sixth and seventh centuries historians now descry successive waves of Eastern influence, coming either indirectly via North Africa, Ravenna or Sicily or directly from Constantinople, Syria or Egypt.[3] Over Spanish monasticism Egypt exercised the same predominant influence as over the religious life of Ireland.[4]

Studies 33, 1931–32, 167–180). Fructuosus of Braga ca. 650 had apparently no difficulty in finding a ship from Spain to the East (cf. E. A. Thompson, in: Hermathena 90, 1957, 59–60).

[1] Cf. the Vitas Sanctorum Patrum Emeretensium, ed. J. N. Garvin, Washington 1946; Jacques Fontaine, Isidore de Seville et la culture classique dans l'Espagne Wisigothique II, Paris 1959, 831 ff. Martin of Braga seems to have reached Braga ca. 550, by ship direct from the East (cf. his Epitaph, ed. C. W. Barlow, Martini episcopi Bracarensis Opera Omnia, New Haven 1950, 283; Idem, in: Folia 6, 1952, 6), not, as Dom A. Mundó, in: Settimane di Studio IV, Spoleto 1957, 88, holds, via Gaul. H. Schlunk, Arte Visigodo (cf. p. 443 n. 2 above), 283, holds the existence of some of the sculptures of this period in Galicia is "inexplicable apart from direct relations by sea with the East".

[2] The presence of Eastern artists in Spain is evident to Schlunk, Relaciones (cited p. 443 n. 2 above). We know of Eastern clergy in Spain in the Sixth and Seventh Centuries (cf. Migne, PL 83,779; PL 84,820. 823. 611) as of Spaniards in the East (cf. Fontaine, op. cit., 846–848). There were Greek books at Braga and presumably at Biclar; (cf. Barlow, in: Folia 1, 1946, 109 ff.; Isidore, De viris 44 (PL 83,1105). Books were sent to the East (cf. PL 96,204) and appear to have influenced Latin scriptoria there (E. A. Lowe, in: Scriptorium 9, 1955, 194, but cf. J. Gribomont, in: Analecta Bollandiana 75, 1957, 105–134). The influence of Eastern silks on monuments near Lisbon is noted by Schlunk, Arte Visigodo, 268 ff. Some of the jewels in the Guarrazar treasure are Eastern (Idem, Relaciones, 202 ff.).

[3] Cf. Schlunk, Relaciones, passim; Arte Visigodo, 249 ff. 266. 306; P. Palol de Salellas, Esencia del Arte Hispánico de Época Visigoda: Romanismo y Germanismo, in: Settimane di Studio III, Spoleto 1956, 65–126.

[4] Cf. A. Mundó, Il monachesimo nella penisola iberica fino al secolo VII, in: Settimane di Studio IV, Spoleto 1957, 85 ff. For Egyptian influence on the Mozarabic liturgy cf. A. Baumstark, Orientalisches in Altspanischer Liturgie, in: Oriens Christianus, D. S. 10, 1935, 3–37; for the cult of Eastern Saints in Spain P. David, Études historiques sur la Galice et le Portugal du VIe au XIIe siècle, Lisbon–Paris 1947, 231 ff.; A. Fábrega Grau, Pasionario Hispánico (siglos VII–XI), Madrid–Barcelona 1953, 191–216. 222–224. 232–235.

There seems no doubt that some of the Eastern ships that had reached Northern Spain continued on their way to the British Isles. We know this not merely from the unhappy experiences of Arculf, wrecked somewhere in Britain on his way from Italy to France in the early 680's but from the contemporary Greek Life of St. John the Almoner of Alexandria, who died in 616.[1]

It would, I fear, be rash to maintain that all or even the majority of African or Spanish authors were transmitted to the rest of Europe via Ireland. Some Spanish writings, especially those of the late seventh century, never left Spain during the Middle Ages[2]; others, for instance the canonical *Collectio Hispana*, did so only after the Arabic Invasion of 711 and went first to France[3]; others again, for instance the *Orationale Visigothicum*, went to Italy.[4] Yet there is reason to believe that there was surprisingly little contact between Spain and France after the Battle of Vouillé in 507 and that Rome in the seventh century was almost entirely ignorant of developments in Spain.[5] On the other hand we can show that some Latin authors were certainly or probably transmitted from Spain to Ireland. What follows are only some

---

[1] On Arculf cf. D. Meehan (ed.), Adamnan's De Locis Sanctis, Dublin 1958, 6–11. Cf. Vita S. Johannis Ellemosynarii, auctore Leontio 10, ed. H. Gelzer, Freiburg–Leipzig 1893, 18ff. (trans. by E. Dawes and N. H. Baynes, Three Byzantine Saints, Oxford 1948, 216–218); R. S. Lopez, in: Byzantion 18, 1948, 141–47. On the Vita cf. G. R. Monks, in: Speculum 28, 1953, 349–62.

[2] E. g. the Historia Wambae of Julian of Toledo, ed. W. Levison, Monumenta Germaniae Historica, Scriptores Rerum Merovingicarum V, Hannover-Berlin 1910, 500–535.

[3] Cf. G. Le Bras, in: Settimane di Studio V, Spoleto 1958, 897ff. Another instance is Ildefonsus of Toledo's De Virginitate Perpetua S. Mariae (ed. V. Blanco, Madrid 1937), which only left Spain in the tenth century.

[4] Apart from the Orationale (ed. J. Vives, Barcelona 1946) other Spanish MSS reached Italy in the 8th century and were copied there (e. g. Verona LXI, for which see Lowe, CLA IV, 511).

[5] For the lack of contact between Spain and France cf. Le Bras, loc. cit. (n. 3 above); Fontaine, Isidore de Seville II, 835–41. Cf., however, the always useful warning of Dom Wilmart, in: Revue bénédictine 28, 1911, 354. The unsatisfactory relations between the Papacy and Spain in the 7th Century are well known (cf. e. g., F. X. Murphy, in: Mélanges J. de Ghellinck I, Gembloux 1951, 361–73). The Spanish Sacramentary used in the Schab-codex (Ambros. M. 12 sup.), edited by Dom Dold, in: Texte und Arbeiten 43, 1952, appears to come from the part of Visigothic Gaul lost in 507 and cannot, therefore, serve as a proof that relations existed between Spain and Gaul at a later date.

notes on the problem. They make few claims to originality, none to completeness.[1]

It is not improbable that certain Eastern writers such as Theodorus of Mopsuestia, translated into Latin in Africa in the sixth century, came to Ireland from Spain.[2] The case is better established when we come to the *Disticha Catonis* or to the *Libellus ad Gregoriam* of Arnobius Iunior.[3] It seems certain for a fragment from a lost work of Lactantius, found in an Irish MS at Milan.[4] It is provable beyond reasonable doubt when we come to Juvencus, to certain Priscillianist writings, to the early transmission of Isidore, to Eugenius and to Julian of Toledo.[5]

---

[1] The transmission of texts from Spain through Ireland to England is noted in passing by P. Lehmann, in: Settimane di Studio V, 864ff. A complete study is impossible until we possess a critical catalogue of all existing insular MSS and of MSS deriving from insular prototypes. B. B. Boyer, in: Classical Philology 42, 1947, 209ff., announced the preparation of such a catalogue and said it would comprise 550 MSS. This catalogue has unfortunately not yet appeared. Meantime we have only a few adequate studies of some major scriptoria, e. g. of Würzburg by B. Bischoff and J. Hofmann, Libri Sancti Kyliani, Würzburg 1952; of St.-Gall by A. Bruckner, Scriptoria Medii Aevi Helvetica II–III, Geneva 1937–38; J. Duft and P. Meyer, Irish Miniatures in the Abbey Library of St.-Gall, Berne 1954, and E. A. Lowe's Codices (cf. p. 443 n. 5 above), now nearing completion, for MSS before 800. For studies of Bobbio MSS cf. P. Collura, in: Aevum 30, 1956, 247–66 (full bibliography, with few omissions; one is Henry's article of 1950, cited p. 442 n. 2 above). For MSS of Spanish authors from A. D. 500 onwards we now possess an invaluable guide in M. C. Díaz y Díaz, Index Scriptorum Latinorum Medii Aevi Hispanorum, Salamanca 1958 (recte 1959). There is also great difficulty in assessing the sources of Irish works since many of these works still remain unpublished.

[2] Theodore is listed in Isidore, De viris 4 (PL 83,1085). Neander, followed by Harnack, Dogmengeschichte III, Tübingen 1905, 312 thought his works may have influenced the rise of Adoptionism. Against this link between Nestorianism and Adoptionism cf. E. Amann, in: Histoire de l'Eglise, ed. Fliche et Martin, VI, 2nd ed. Paris 1947, 132. 139. On his use by the Irish cf. M. L. W. Laistner, in: Harvard Theological Review 40, 1947, 19–31.

[3] Cf. Disticha Catonis, ed. M. Boas, Amsterdam 1952; Idem, in: Rheinisches Museum für Philologie 79, 1930, 183–196; Libellus ad Gregoriam, ed. G. Morin, Études, textes et découvertes, Maredsous 1913, 383–439. There is a fragment in Irish script in Clm 29051b, saec. VIII/IX and Clm 6434, saec. VIII ex., is copied from an Irish exemplar (cf. B. Bischoff, in: Sacris Erudiri 6, 1954, 210 n. 1).

[4] Ambrosianum F. 60 sup. (CLA III, 1938, 331; IV, 1947, p. XXIII), saec. VIII ex., written in Irish script at Bobbio, contains a fragment of Lactantius, De motibus animi in a collection of extracts: the latest author represented is Isidore (cf. Fontaine, Isidore de Seville, 761 and n. 2).

[5] For other Spanish authors, e. g. Taio of Saragossa, we must await critical editions now in preparation.

The editor of Juvencus for the Vienna Corpus believed that all his manuscripts descended from an archetype in insular script.[1] The oldest complete MS appears to be Corpus, Cambridge 304 (saec. VIII[1]) which Lowe believes probably written in Spain, but we possess a fragment written in Ireland or an Irish centre in Northumbria in the seventh century, while there are two copies among the *Libri scottice scripti* of St. Gall.[2] Furthermore the verses on the evangelists that preface Juvencus in some of the oldest MSS[3] also appear in three early Irish Gospels and seem to have influenced the distribution of symbols in the Book of Durrow.[4] Juvencus is as well known to Columban and Adamnan as to Isidore, Julian of Toledo and Eulogius of Cordoba.[5]

The manuscript at Würzburg containing the *Tractatus* by Priscillian (or Instantius) comes from Italy[6] but for other Priscillianist writings transmission via Ireland appears assured. We may instance the so-called *Fides S. Ambrosii*, whose oldest MS is Ambrosianum I. 101 sup., copied at Bobbio (saec. VIII), probably from an Irish exemplar.[7] The Priscillianist 'Monarchian' prologues are best preserved, as Dom Chapman pointed out long ago, in the Irish MSS[8]; they are cited in the Seventh Century by Cummean in his Commentary on Mark and in two later anony-

[1] Cf. Huemer, CSEL 24, 1891, p. XXXVII: *unum exemplar quod litteris anglosaxonicis saeculo ut videtur septimo scriptum.* This needs correction as a fragment has been discovered in Vat. Lat. 13501 (CLA I, 1934), saec. VI/VII, possibly Italian (cf. H. Thoma, in: Classical Review 64, 1950, 95ff.).

[2] Cf. CLA II, 1935, 127; VIII, 1959, 1172; P. Lehmann, Mittelalterliche Bibliothekskataloge Deutschlands und der Schweiz I, Munich 1918, 71.

[3] E. g. Corpus 304, Montpellier 362, Paris, Lat. 9347, Turin C. 68.

[4] The verses appear in the Rushworth Gospels (Bodl. Auct. D. 19, pre-820); in the MacDurnan Gospels at Lambeth (saec. IX) and in Fulda, Bonif. 3 (s. VIII). Cf. H. J. Lawlor, Chapters on the Book of Mulling, Edinburgh 1897, 23–28; P. McGurk, in: Sacris Erudiri 8, 1956, 253 n. 1.

[5] Cf. Columban, ed. G. S. M. Walker, Dublin 1957, 194. 184; Adamnan, De Locis Sanctis, ed. D. Meehan, Dublin 1958, 60. 92. For Isidore cf. Fontaine, Isidore, 833 n. 1, etc.

[6] Cf. B. Bischoff, Libri Sancti Kyliani, Würzburg 1952, 89. Schepss, CSEL 18, 1889, X, had thought the MS might have belonged to St. Kilian.

[7] Cf. CLA III, 1938, 352; K. Künstle, Antipriscilliana, Freiburg 1905, 58–60; A. D'Alès, Priscillien, Paris 1936, 121; Idem, in: Recherches de Science Religieuse 26, 1936, 606ff.

[8] Cf. J. Chapman, Notes on the Early History of the Vulgate Gospels, Oxford 1908, 278ff.; A. Dold, in: Zentralblatt für Bibliothekswesen 52, 1935, 125–35 (CLA VIII, 1959, 1195).

mous Irish commentaries on the Gospels[1]. Finally, from the last and most obscure partisans of the heresy the Irish received and transmitted the Apocrypha found in MS Augiensis 254 and the *De Pascha* attributed to Martin of Braga.[2] Given these facts it is perhaps not surprising that an Irish commentary of the seventh century in MS Augiensis 233 appears to be influenced by Priscillianism.[3] We may recall here the transmission of Bachiarius, accused of Priscillianism if never a Priscillianist; of the two surviving MSS of his *De fide* by far the oldest is a MS in Irish script of the late seventh century from Bobbio.[4] His *De lapso* is cited by an anonymous Irish commentator of the late eighth century.[5]

In his great work *Isidor-Studien* C. H. Beeson emphasised the role of the Irish in the transmission of Isidore of Seville. He listed thirty-nine MSS that he believed to derive from insular exemplars or to have been written or corrected by insular scribes.[6] He also noted twenty-seven MSS in insular script.[7] He does not, in general, distinguish between Irish and Anglo-Saxon hands. and the place of the Anglo-Saxons in the transmission of Isidore is undoubtedly considerable – some ten fragments of eighth century MSS written by them that were unknown to Beeson have ap-

[1] Cf. B. Bischoff, Wendepunkte in der Geschichte der lateinischen Exegese im Frühmittelalter, in: Sacris Erudiri 6, 1954, 258. 259. 262.

[2] Cf. D. De Bruyne, in: Revue bénédictine 24, 1907, 318–335 (the fifth fragment [p. 329. 80ff.] uses the Irish De XII abusivis saeculi). On the MS cf. CLA VIII, 1959, 1110. On the De Pascha (ed. C. W. Barlow, Martini episcopi Opera, 259–75, as a genuine work) cf. P. David, in: Bulletin des Études portugaises et de l'Institut français au Portugal 14, 1950, 283–99; Idem, Un traité priscillianiste du Comput Pascal, Coimbra 1951. A. Cordoliani, in: Revista de Archivos, Bibliotecas y Museos 62, 1956, 692–94, and Díaz y Díaz, Index Scriptorum, 13, follow David. On a recently discovered Priscillianist text in a Prague MS (pre-794) cf. O. Stegmüller, in: Zeitschrift für katholische Theologie 74, 1952, 450–63. The MS shows Irish-Northumbrian influence in its decoration (cf. Bischoff, apud A. Dold and L. Eizenhöfer, in: Texte und Arbeiten 38–42, 1949, 34ff.).

[3] Cf. M. Esposito, in: Journal of Theological Studies 21, 1919–20, 318.

[4] Ambrosianum O. 212 sup. (CLA III, 1938, 361). The other MS is Barcelona, Ripoll 151, saec. X–XI, for which cf. J. Madoz, in: Revista española de teologia 1, 1940–41, 457–88. A. R. Natale, Studi Paleografici, Milan, n. d. 1950, 63–74, thinks the Milan MS is saec. VIII.

[5] Cf. Bischoff (n. 1 above), 242–45.

[6] Isidor-Studien, Munich 1913, 122 and note 1. He took care to note the likelihood of many more such MSS being found (he was not able to see for himself many of the MSS he lists in his work).

[7] Ibid., passim. Cf. the works of Bischoff, Duft and Meyer and Collura cited in p. 447 n. 6 above.

peared in Lowe's *Codices* so far.[1] Nevertheless Isidore's writings came first, it would seem, to Ireland.[2] The number of seventh century MSS of Isidore is very small. Of the seven generally thought to be of that century two were probably written in Spain or Septimania; one in France, perhaps at Fleury; three at Bobbio and one, perhaps the earliest of all, the fragment of the *Origines* now numbered St. Gall 1399 a. 1, either in Ireland or at Bobbio.[3] This fragment is of great importance textually for it appears to be by far the earliest representative of a family of MSS deriving from the final edition of the work due to Braulio (post 633); this family, Porzig had held, only left Spain in the mid-ninth century.[4]

---

[1] Cf. also Weimar Fol. 414a, saec. VIII/IX, probably from Fulda (M. L. W. Laistner, in: Medievalia and Humanistica 2, 1944, 28–31).

[2] Cf., for another view, C. H. Beeson, Isidor-Studien, Munich 1913, 120ff. where he maintains France was the great centre for distribution of MSS, and Idem, in: Classical Philology 42, 1947, 73–87. Isidore was certainly known saec. VII in France and Italy. Cf. Anspach, art. cit. below p. 451 n. 1.

[3] In Spain or Southern France: St. Gall 226 (CLA VII, 1956, 929); Autun 27 + Paris, n. a. l. 1629 (CLA VI, 1953, 727a). In France, perhaps Fleury: Paris, Lat. 6400 G (CLA V, 1950, 564a; cf. CLA VI, p. XXI). At Bobbio: Ambros. S. 36 sup. (CLA III, 1938, **364); Vat. Lat. 5765 (CLA I, 1934, 43, corrected by IV, 1947, p. XXI); Ambros. C. 77 sup. (CLA III, 317: s. VIII; saec. VII according to Díaz y Díaz, Index Scriptorum, 34). The St. Gall MS is described by A. Dold, in: Texte und Arbeiten I 31, 1940, 5 n. 1; 77; 85–88; by J. Duft and P. Meyer, Irish Miniatures, 66. 81 and pl. XXXV; by Lowe, CLA VII, 1956, 995. Cf. E. Dekkers, in: Sacris Erudiri 9, 1957, 110–114. According to Duft it was written in Ireland in the middle of the 7th Century, according to Lowe it was "written in an Irish centre, presumably on the continent, possibly at Bobbio".

[4] Cf. W. Porzig, Die Rezensionen der Etymologiae des Isidorus von Sevlila, in: Hermes 72, 1937, 129–170, especially 166. As Dom Dold points out (Texte und Arbeiten 31, 1940, 88) the readings of the fragment most closely resemble Leyden, Voss. Lat. F. 74, MS 'C' in Lindsay's edition, one of Porzig's and family. Fontaine, Isidore de Seville, 405 n. 2, and Díaz y Díaz, Index Scriptorum, 40, though with some reserves, prefer Porzig's classification, incomplete as it is, to Lindsay's. M. Fontaine has observed to me personally that supposing the St. Gall fragments really derive from the final edition due to Braulio that would suggest to him transmission of their archetype from Saragossa through Southern France, possibly to Bobbio. I do not think, however, that this is any more likely than transmission from Saragossa via Braga to Ireland. (We have no idea of when the fragments reached St. Gall. If written in Ireland, as Duft holds, they might have come to the abbey with other Irish MSS in the 9th century.) It is perhaps worth noting that while we know Braulio was in correspondence with Fructuosus of Braga, to whom he sent books, we have no clear evidence of similar contacts between him and Cata-

Isidore is used by Irish writers from very early on. The anonymous *De duodecim abusivis saeculi*, written 630–650, uses the *Origines*[1]; Lathcen († 661) the *De ortu et obitu Patrum*[2], and the Pseudo-Isidorian *De ordine creaturarum* (saec. VII med.) the *Differentiae*.[3] In the early eighth century the *De ecclesiasticis officiis*, the *Sententiae*, the *Synonyma*, the *Chronica*, the *Historia Gothorum*, the *Epistula ad Massonam* (probably the first instance of its use outside Spain) and the *Origines* are used by the compilers of the *Collectio Hibernensis*.[4] In the eighth century Isidore is used by almost all the Irish writing in Latin. He is quoted by the *Paenitentiale Bigotianum* (700–25)[5]; in the grammatical works of Malsachanus and Cruindmelus[6]; in the sermons preserved at Cracow[7]; by Virgilius of Salzburg in his *Cosmographia*[8]; by the

onia or Septimania (cf. J. Madoz, Epistolario de San Braulio de Zaragoza, Madrid 1941, 186–206; cf. 48).

[1] In general, for the use of Isidore by writers of the 7th, 8th and 9th centuries cf. A. E. Anspach, Das Fortleben Isidors im VII. bis IX. Jahrhundert, in: Miscellanea Isidoriana, Rome 1936, 323–356. Cf. S. Hellmann, Texte und Untersuchungen, Ser. III, 4, Leipzig 1909, 2; E. Dekkers, Clavis Patrum Latinorum, Steenbrugis 1951, n. 1106.

[2] Anspach, art. cit., 337ff., attributed Lathcen's Ecloga to Isidore himself but Lathcen's authorship is now generally recognised (cf. Dekkers, Clavis, n. 1716; P. Grosjean, in: Sacris Erudiri 7, 1955, 94ff.).

[3] Cf. M. C. Díaz y Díaz, in: Sacris Erudiri 5, 1953, 147–166. The Origines are used in the anonymous Versus cuiusdam Scotti de alphabeto, saec. VII[1], according to M. Manitius, Geschichte der lateinischen Literatur im Mittelalter I, Munich 1911, 190–192.

[4] Cf. Anspach, art. cit., 327ff.; S. Hellmann, Sedulius Scottus, Munich 1906, 136–44; G. Le Bras, in: Revue des Sciences Religieuses 10, 1930, 248 nn. 2.3; P. Fournier and G. Le Bras, Histoire des Collections Canoniquesen Occident I, Paris 1931, 62. The Collectio appears to have been compiled between 700 and 725 in Ireland on the basis of an earlier collection containing extracts from Isidore. A critical edition is in preparation for the series Scriptores Latini Hiberniae.

[5] According to T. P. Oakley, in: Speculum 8, 1933, 490 n. 6, this work was composed on the continent. J. F. Kennedy, Sources for the Early History of Ireland I, New York 1929, 241, followed by J. T. McNeill and H. M. Gamer, Medieval Handbooks of Penance, New York 1938, 148, holds it is "an original Irish production". Isidore is used (cf. McNeill and Gamer, 153).

[6] Cf. Manitius, op. cit., 521–525.

[7] Cf. P. David, in: Revue bénédictine 49, 1937, 78; E. Dekkers, Clavis, n. 1122; Bischoff, in: Sacris Erudiri 6, 1954, 221 and n. 2 (MS Italian, written ca. 800, but the sermons are by an Irishman).

[8] The authorship of this work has been demonstrated by H. Löwe, in: Mainz, Akademie der Wissenschaften und der Literatur: Abhandlungen der geistes- und sozialwissenschaftlichen Klasse, 1951, no. 11.

Pseudo-Isidorian *Liber de numeris*[1] and in the *Liber monstrorum de diversis generibus*.[2] He is utilised in the anonymous Irish commentary on the whole Bible and in some ten other shorter commentaries among those listed by Professor Bischoff.[3] Already in the seventh century the *Origines* are used by Cennfaelad in his *Auraicept Na n-Éces* and by the lost "Old Irish Chronicle" from which all extant annals appear to descend.[4] Very early on, too, the Irish paid Isidore the compliment of ascribing the authorship of their works to him and more than one of their books traversed the Middle Ages and modern times "sous le pavillon isidorien".[5]

After Isidore works continued to be transmitted from Spain to Ireland. Eugenius of Toledo's edition of Dracontius seems to have travelled that way; perhaps the *Romulea* preceded it and came from Galicia where Martin of Braga seems to have read it ca. 580.[6] Julian of Toledo's *Ars Grammatica*, written before 690, within fifteen years at the most had been read by Aldhelm and Bede.[7] Further evidence of its Irish transmission has recently

[1] This work uses Isidore, Liber numerorum (Clavis, n. 1193; Díaz y Díaz, Index Scriptorum, n. 107), for which cf. C. Leonardi, in: Bullettino dell'Instituto Storico Italiano per il Medio Evo e Archivio Muratoriano, n. 68, 1956, 203–231. The L. de numeris was apparently written ca. 775. I have not seen R. E. McNally, Der irische Liber de numeris. Eine Quellenanalyse, Diss. Munich 1957.

[2] Dekkers, Clavis, n. 1124; Manitius, op. cit., 114–118. P. Lehmann, in: Settimane di Studio V, 868, believes it was written on the continent saec. VIII exeunte.

[3] Cf. Bischoff, art. cit. p. 449 n. 8 above, passim.

[4] Cf. Auraicept N an-Éces, the Scholar's Primer, ed. G. Calder, Edinburgh 1917, pp. XXXIII–XXXVII. For the date of Cennfaelad's death cf. pp. XXVIIff. See also N. K. Chadwick, in: Studies in early British History, Cambridge 1954, 247; P. Grosjean, in: Sacris Erudiri 7, 1955, 95 n. 2; 98. On the "Old Irish Chronicle" cf. J. Carney, Studies in Irish Literature and History, Dublin 1955, 349. He regards it as of Southern (Clonmacnoise) rather than Northern origin and believes the original copy of Isidore, to which British events were added, may have been dated 645 (pp. 363. 372ff.). The Irish saga Táin Bó Fráich, written ca. 700, uses the Origines (Ibid., 82ff.).

[5] E. g. the De XII abusivis saeculi (cf. above, p. 451 n. 1) in some MSS; the Pseudo-Isidorian De ordine creaturarum, De numeris (cf. p. 451 n. 3 and 1 above) and De veteri et novo testamento quaestiones (Dekkers, Clavis, n. 1194; Díaz y Díaz, Index Scriptorum, 44).

[6] Cf. Fr. Vollmer, Monumenta Germaniae Historica, Auctores Antiquissimi XIV, Berlin 1905, pp. XVIII XXXVI,; C. W. Barlow, Martini ... Bracarensis Opera, 276.

[7] Anspach, art. cit., 338ff. held that this was difficult to credit: he ascribes the Ars, clearly erroneously, to Isidore. Cf. C. H. Beeson, The Ars Grammatica of Julian of Toledo, in: Miscellanea Fr. Ehrle I, Rome 1924, 54–56.

come to light in a MS at Naples and in further investigations into MS Bern 207.[1]

I should need another paper to bring out the influence of the Mozarabic Liturgy on the Irish and English liturgical books. Since Edmund Bishop's famous chapter in *Liturgica Historica*, Abbot Capelle has demonstrated the probable transmission of the practice of singing the Creed at Mass from the East to Spain, from Spain to Ireland and thence to England.[2] Recently Dom Gamber has pointed to the possible derivation of the *Missa cottidiana Romensis* found in the *Missale Gothicum*, Bobbio and Stowe from the text sent by Pope Vigilius I (+ 555) to Profuturus of Braga.[3] C.W. Jones has shown how the African collection of tracts dealing with the date of Easter passed through Spain, where it was added to and revised, reaching Ireland before 633.[4]

---

[1] MS Naples IV A. 34, saec. IX, a codex showing Insular influence and having probably come to Naples from Bobbio where it may have been copied from a MS from Corbie, contains works of Julian, Bede, Aldhelm, Alcuin, Virgilius Maro, etc. Cf. C. H. Beeson, in: Classical Philology 42, 1947, 82. 86. For Bern 207 cf. R. Derolez, in: Scriptorium 5, 1951, 3–19 (especially p. 11); Idem, Runica Manuscripta, the English Tradition, Bruges 1954, 174ff.; CLA VII, 1956, 568 (p. 6), where the MS is dated 779–97. It should be said that Beeson, The Ars Grammatica (cited p. 452 n. 6 above), while holding the archetype of all our MSS of the Ars was probably copied from a MS in insular script and was probably itself insular, thinks it reached the British Isles via France, though he agrees that the reverse process may have taken place (pp. 67, 69). For another work of Julian, the Prognosticum, insular influence is again evident in the transmission (cf. J. N. Hillgarth, in: Journal of the Warburg and Courtauld Institutes 21, 1958, 7–26).

[2] Cf. E. Bishop, in: The Book of Cerne, ed. A. B. Kuypers, Cambridge 1902, 277–283 (it now appears Cerne was in part copied from an 8th Century Northumbrian collection; cf. W. Levison, England and the Continent in the Eighth Century, Oxford 1946, 295–302); Liturgica Historica, Oxford 1918, 161–63. 165–202; B. Capelle, in: Recherches de théologie ancienne et médiévale 6, 1934, 249–60. On "Spanish Symptoms" in general cf. L. Brou, in: Hispania Sacra 7, 1954, 467–85, with bibliography; Idem, in: Sacris Erudiri 9, 1957, 94–108 and the forthcoming article of J. Janini, Liturgia Trinitaria española en los Misales Gelasianos del siglo VIII, in: Anthologica Annua 7, 1959, 9–93.

[3] Cf. K. Gamber, Sakramentartypen (Texte und Arbeiten 49–50), Beuron 1958, 51. Dom Gamber has indicated to me personally, however, that a direct transmission of the same text from Rome to Galicia and Ireland independently cannot be considered unlikely. Cf. his article Ein römisches Eucharistiegebet aus dem 4./5. Jahrhundert, in: Ephemerides Liturgicae 74, 1960, 103–114.

[4] Cf. C. W. Jones, Bedae Opera de Temporibus, Cambridge, Mass. 1943, 75–77. 97. 105. 112ff. Cf. P. Grosjean, cited by K. Hughes, in: Irish Historical Studies 11, 1959, 232ff. Eastern influence in Spanish and Irish legislation on the amounts that should or could be left to the Church and the poor is descri-

From what part of Spain did these works reach Ireland? We should naturally be inclined to think of Galicia, the part of Spain nearest Ireland and connected with her by the Atlantic trade route since pre-historic times, as being most closely in touch with the British Isles.[1] Galicia, an independent kingdom under the Sueves from the fifth century until 585, still enjoyed considerable autonomy in the Seventh Century.[2] Galician monasticism, differing in many ways from that of Southern Spain, has interesting points of contact with Ireland.[3] The existence, moreover, of a centre of émigrés from Britanny at Britonia in North Galicia, with its Celtic bishops and important monastery, is attested from 561 until 675.[4] Eastern influence is very notable in Galicia from the fifth to the seventh century.[5] In the late sixth century, when the Pannonian Martin of Braga presided over the church of the Suevic kingdom, we find at Saamasas, in the same province of Lugo as Britonia, a relief that is a clear representative of the contemporary style of Ravenna.[6] A century later St. Fructuosus erected

---

bed in the important work of E. F. Bruck, Kirchenväter und Soziales Erbrecht: Wanderungen religiöser Ideen durch die Rechte der Östlichen und Westlichen Welt, Berlin-Göttingen-Heidelberg 1956, chaps. VI and VII.

[1] For the earlier period cf. J. Raftery, Prehistoric Ireland, London-New York 1951.

[2] Cf. R. Gibert, in: Settimane di Studio III, Spoleto 1956, 568; R. d'Abadal, ibid. V, 1958, 687 ff.

[3] Cf. C. J. Bishko, in: American Journal of Philology 59, 1948, 394; Idem, in: Speculum 23, 1948, 579. For Irish influence on Spanish penitentials cf. S. Gonzalez Rivas, La penitencia en la primitiva Iglesia española, Salamanca 1950, 133–139. It is interesting, too, to find St. Finnian of Clonard in a Spanish abridgement of ca. 800 of the Hieronymian Martyrology (cf. P. Grosjean, in: Analecta Bollandiana 72, 1954, 347–350).

[4] Today Santa Maria de Bretoña, Pastoriza, near Mondoñedo. The first bishop known is Mailoc, who attended the Second Council of Braga (572); David suggests he is the same as the Maliosus of Braga I (561). It is unlikely that he is identical with a North British prince brother of Gildas (cf. J. Fonssagrives, St. Gildas de Ruis, Paris 1908, 52–54; J. Pérez de Urbel, Los monjes españoles I, 2nd ed. Madrid 1945, 191 ff.). Apart from signatures to the acts of Spanish Councils Britonia appears in a 6th century document whose authenticity has been vindicated by P. David, Études historiques sur la Galice et le Portugal du VIe au XIIe siècle, Lisbon-Paris 1947, 44. 57 ff., and in a 7th Century list of sees that may have been drawn up by Julian of Toledo (cf. J. Leclercq, in: Hispania Sacra 2, 1949, 93). Cf. S. Ruíz, Britonia, in: Dict. d'histoire et géographie ecclésiastique 10, 1938, 767–69.

[5] Cf. M. Martins, Correntes da filosofia religiosa em Braga, séculos IV–VII, Porto 1950, 23–40.

[6] Cf. H. Schlunk, Arte Visigodo (cited p. 443 n. 2 above), 247 and fig. 255.

near Braga a church that has been described as the most Byzantine in the peninsula.[1] We have already seen the rapid transmission of Priscillianist works, probably written in Galicia, from Spain to Ireland. On the other hand the very early arrival of Isidore's works in Ireland may argue direct dispatch from the *scriptorium* at Seville into whose workings M. Fontaine has recently given us some interesting glimpses.[2] This possibility is confirmed by an argument from the history of art to which we shall come in a moment.

It is natural to assume that books from Spain would be most immediately welcomed in Southern Ireland, in the monasteries of Munster and Leinster that have given us most of the earlier theology of the Irish church, especially, perhaps, in the monastery of St. Carthach at Les Mór, associated with a group of authors whose existence has recently been revealed to us by P. Grosjean and that included Lathcen of Clonfertmulloe († 661), who certainly knew one of Isidore's works.[3] But Spanish influence penetrated further than Lismore in County Waterford. P. Grosjean has reminded us of the great significance of the Fahan Mura cross, with its Greek inscription of the late seventh century presenting a "litteral not to say servile" version of a doxology first appearing in the Fourth Council of Toledo in 633.[4] The presence in this remote cemetery in the extreme North of Ireland of a Spanish formula only promulgated half a century before is striking visual evidence of the influence of seventh century Spain on Ireland and it is none the less significant in that the cross should be covered by decoration of markedly Eastern origin.[5] Another curious instance of the simultaneous action of

---

[1] Cf. Ibid., 283.

[2] Cf. Fontaine, Isidore de Seville II, 782–84.

[3] Cf. P. Grosjean, Sur quelques exégètes irlandais du VIIe siècle, in: Sacris Erudiri 7, 1955, 67–98. See also R. Flower, The Irish Tradition, London 1947, 28. 40. 77 ff. Virgilius Maro, whose relations with Ireland and use of Isidore are known, is possibly connected with this same group of scholars (Grosjean, 82–84).

[4] Ibid., 97 ff. (cp. Masai, Essai sur la miniature, 86). Cf. R. A. S. MacAlister, in: Journal of the Royal Society of Antiquaries of Irеland 49, 1929, 89 ff.; idem, Corpus Inscriptionum Insularum Celticarum II, Dublin 1949, n. 951.

[5] On this decoration cf. F. Henry, Irish Art, 56; N. Åberg, op. cit. (p. 442 n. 2 above), 35 ff.; C. Nordenfalk, in: Acta Archaeologica 18, 1947, 168–171, who points out the resemblance to the interlace in MS Durham A. II. 10, while the Fahan inscription recalls the Greek text of the Pater Noster in the same MS.

Eastern and of Spanish influences on Irish or Northumbrian art has been recently pointed out to me in the Echternach Gospels by my friend O. K. Werckmeister of Berlin.[1] In the page representing the symbol of St. Matthew the attitude of the figure is based on a Coptic prototype. But this prototype does not explain the curious form in which the draperies are arranged, quite without parallel in Irish art. As this shows striking similarity with metalwork earlier in date than the Gospels and only to be found in the South of Spain, it may be concluded that the actual stylisation of the figure took place there and was transmitted to Northumbria by a Spanish illuminated MS.[2]

I end, then, as I said I would do, with a question. Is it not possible that we may have in Spain the link historians have been looking for, between the East and the Far West, between the arts and literature of late antiquity and the Irish and Anglo-Saxon artistic and literary renaissance?[3]

---

[1] Werckmeister informs me that a demonstration of this connection will appear in a study he has in preparation on the meaning of insular representations of enthroned figures. I am very grateful to him for allowing me to quote his conclusions here. I have written "Irish or Northumbrian art" since the origin of the Echternach Gospels appears to be still in dispute; most scholars, e. g. Lowe, CLA V, 1950, 578, Masai, Essai sur la miniature, 133, and, I should add, Werckmeister himself, regard it as Northumbrian and date it saec. VII–VIII or VIII[1], while Nordenfalk, Early Medieval Painting, 113, dates it "ca. 690, Ireland (?)". It seems to me that the depiction of a Roman tonsure in the page cited does not in any way exclude an origin in Southern Ireland, which had accepted this tonsure ca. 635. It would not be surprising to find Spanish artistic influence in a region where, as we have seen, Spanish authors were read at an early date.

[2] Another possible parallel between Spanish and Irish art is indicated by R. Crozet, in: Études Mérovingiennes, Paris 1953, 60ff., between a sculptured panel at Braga (saec. VI) and the Book of Kells, f. 1r. Cf. G. Gaillard, ibid., 135ff.

[3] As P. Joseph de Ghellinck, Littérature Latine au Moyen Age I, Paris 1939, 53ff., remarks, it is not surprising, when we recall the position of the Spanish Church saec. VII, enjoying, in its Councils above all, "une incontestable superiorité sur toute l'Europe chrétienne à ce moment", that its writings should have attained such success in the British Isles. (P. de Ghellinck believes, like Beeson (cf. p. 450 n. 2 above), that Spanish works reached the Isles via France; he does not mention the possibility of artistic connections.) Cf. now my sequel to this paper, Visigothic Spain and Early Christian Ireland, in: Proceedings Royal Irish Academy, Ser. C, 1962.

VII

VISIGOTHIC SPAIN AND EARLY CHRISTIAN IRELAND[1]

It may be as well to begin with a word of explanation for the double appearance of my friend Dr. Werckmeister and myself here to-day in response to the kind invitation with which you have honoured us. Some such explanation is, perhaps, needed to indicate how our two independent addresses are related, and as I have to speak first, it seems to fall to me to provide it.

This paper is, in a sense, a continuation of a communication read at the Third Patristic Congress, held at Oxford in September, 1959.[2] This communication ends with the question: " Is it not possible that we may have in Spain the link historians have been looking for between the East and the Far West, between the arts and literature of late antiquity and the Irish and Anglo-Saxon artistic and literary renaissance ? " This question was largely directed to art historians who, with great respect be it said, and with one or two honourable exceptions, seemed to me to have either completely ignored the possibility of artistic relations between Spain and Ireland or to have been content to dismiss them with an easy formula or with a shrug of contempt for—to quote M. Masai—" la maladresse commune à tous les artisans barbares."[3]

When I delivered my paper at Oxford I already hoped that Dr. Werckmeister, who had then begun to work on this problem, would eventually provide us with

---

[1] The revised and expanded form of an address given to the Royal Irish Academy on May 23rd, 1960. Dr. O. K. Werckmeister's address, which followed mine, will also appear in the *Proceedings*. I am very grateful to Mrs. N. K. Chadwick for reading and criticizing this paper in typescript and to Mr. Philip Grierson for enlightening me on several numismatic questions. I have to thank Dr. J. Duft (St-Gallen) and Dr. J. Raftery (Dublin) for providing photographs and for permission to reproduce them. My indebtedness to Professor B. Bischoff and to Professor J. Fontaine is indicated below. I should like to dedicate the paper to my friend Professor Ludwig Bieler in token of gratitude and admiration.

[2] " The East, Visigothic Spain and the Irish," to appear in *Studia Patristica*, IV, Berlin, 1961, 442-456. This paper contains full bibliographical notes to which, to save space and avoid repetition, I shall sometimes refer.

[3] Cf. F. Masai, *Essai sur les Origines de la Miniature dite irlandaise*, Bruxelles-Anvers, 1947, 24 n.25. For criticism of Masai cf. my earlier paper, n.2. M. P. Hornik, in *Arte del Primo Millennio: Atti del II° Convegno per lo Studio dell' Alto Medio Evo . . . Pavia . . . 1950*, Turin n.d., 322, observes: " It would be very tempting to look for the historical background in which these uninterrupted Oriental influences on Ireland around 600 would receive their proper setting." The most important recent work on early Hiberno-Saxon art is the volume of text by T. D. Kendrick, T. J. Brown, R. L. S. Bruce-Mitford *et al.*, *Evangeliorum Quattuor Codex Lindisfarnensis* . . ., II, Olten-Lausanne, 1960. Cf. also the recent article (which often takes a different view to that of the authors I have just cited) by G. Haseloff, " Fragments of a Hanging-Bowl from Bekesbourne, Kent, and Some Ornamental Problems " in *Medieval Archæology* 2 (1958) 72-103. Cf. below, n. 40, and, for further bibliography, O. K. Werckmeister (*art. cit. supra*, n.1).

an answer to the question I had raised. You will soon be listening to Dr. Werckmeister and his presence here releases me from outlining for you the artistic connections he appears to me to have established.

In my Oxford paper I was concerned to indicate some of the evidence, other than artistic, for the close relations between Spain and Ireland, particularly close, it is true, from the mid-seventh century onwards, but also demonstrable as existing earlier, possibly before 600, a time when they could, of course, have played an especially important part in contributing to the growth of Christian civilization in Ireland in the obscure period between the middle of the fifth and the end of the sixth century. I based myself principally, as I shall do to-day, on the manuscripts of certain Spanish authors; we find them copied and quoted by the Irish at such an early date that it is difficult not to assume that they had travelled by ship direct to Ireland from Spain. I spoke then especially of Juvencus,[4] of certain Priscillianist writings,[5] of Isidore and of some later Spanish authors. Given the short time at my disposal and in order not to repeat myself unnecessarily I propose to concentrate attention to-day mainly on the transmission of the greatest writer of Visigothic Spain, Isidore of Seville.[6]

Before we enter on a discussion of the possible routes that Spanish MSS. may have taken to reach Ireland it may be as well to glance for a moment at the political and intellectual map of Europe in the late sixth and seventh centuries. By 600 Justinian's attempt to restore the Roman Empire in the West was long over but although it had achieved nothing that was to endure it had effectively ruined, with its destruction of the Vandal and Ostrogothic kingdoms, the chances of a renaissance of Latin culture either in Italy or in North Africa. Nearly a century before its conquest by Islam, Christian Africa, for so long the leading church of the West, falls silent; Italy is absorbed in ceaseless conflict between Lombard and Byzantine; France sinks into decadence. The optimism of Isidore of Seville stands out in sharp relief against the pessimism of Gregory the Great and Gregory of Tours, who seem weighed down by the evils of the times, by the appalling collapse of civilization before barbarism. There is an obvious reason

---

[4] I should now wish to lay less emphasis on the transmission of Juvencus. N. Hansson, *Textkritisches zu Juvencus*, Lund. 1950, 27 ff. and 28 n.34, has shown that Huemer's belief that all the MSS. descend from an archetype in insular script of the seventh century is erroneous. Cf. also H. Thoma in *Classical Review* 64 (1950) 95 ff.

[5] According to A. Mundó, " Preparando la edición crítica de Baquiario," in *Bracara Augusta* 8 (1957), 88-97, at 89, the *De lapso* of Bachiarius, if not a Priscillianist certainly accused of Priscillianism, is cited by Gildas. (Dom Mundó informs me that his thesis on Bachiarius, when it appears, will contain a discussion of his " Fortleben.") On the other hand Dom Mundó establishes the probability that it was Gennadius who revised Bachiarius's *De fide*. In this case the exemplar of the saec. VII MS. in Irish script (Ambros. O. 212 sup. = E. A. Lowe, *Codices Latini Antiquiores* (henceforth abbreviated as *CLA*), III, Oxford 1938, 361), which contains the first recension of the work, together with the first recension of Gennadius, *De ecclesiasticis dogmatibus*, probably came to Bobbio from Southern France, not via Ireland, as was implied in my previous paper (p.449). For an early Irish commentary on Orosius cf. P. Lehmann, *Erforschung des Mittelalters*, II, Stuttgart, 1959, 31 ff. It makes much use of Isidore.

[6] For recent work on Isidore I may, perhaps, be allowed to refer to my paper, " The Position of Isidorian Studies, A Critical Review of the Literature since 1935," to appear shortly in *Isidoriana*, Léon, 1961, 11-74. Cf., in the same publication (317-44), the fundamental article of Professor B. Bischoff, " Die europaische Verbreitung der Isidorischen Werke." I have to thank Professor Bischoff for allowing me to read this in typescript.

for this optimism of Isidore. His country, one of the first Mediterranean lands of the Empire to suffer invasion by the barbarians, had been one of the first to recover its unity, or rather to find a new unity that could resist attack. It had been able, unlike Vandal Africa and Ostrogothic Italy, to repel the Byzantine " Reconquista."[7] In Spain the work of Leovigild had been completed and crowned by the conversion of his son.[8] In 587-89, led by King Recared, the dominant Visigothic race entered the Church and the unity of Spain as an independent kingdom was achieved for the first time, a unity that was to be made complete in Isidore of Seville's lifetime by the final expulsion of the Byzantines in 629. The *Laus Spaniae* of Isidore is a manifesto of Spain, powerful and united, flourishing happily under the rule of enlightened and Catholic monarchs.[9] Like all manifestos, the *Laus Spaniae* needs, no doubt, to be treated with caution as historical evidence. Behind the Byzantine ceremonial, the Byzantine type of coinage, the workshops producing Byzantine jewelry and textiles, there was no Byzantine tradition of Empire and, in contrast with the Imperial Civil Service, only factions of the Visigothic nobility, always ready to spring at each others' throats. The power of Toledo was much less real than it appeared. Nevertheless, in the early seventh century in the West, between the age of Justinian's " Reconquista " and that of the advance of Islam, Spain stands out politically as far stronger and more united than any other country, Toledo as the nearest reflection of Byzantium.[10] In addition to its political strength Spain enjoyed intellectual and spiritual resources that succeeded in creating a genuine national artistic style and a revival of Christian thought, both without comparison in contemporary Western Europe. The Visigothic churches, not by their size but in the beauty, precision and richness of their sculpture and

---

[7] " In 550 the question could have been asked—would the Mediterranean become a Byzantine lake ? Would Justinian add Spain to his trophies ? " (P. Goubert, " Influences Byzantines sur l'Espagne Wisigothique " in *Etudes Byzantines* 4 [1946] 111-133, at 131).

[8] Cf. the recent article by Professor E. A. Thompson, " The Conversion of the Visigoths to Catholicism " in *Nottingham Mediæval Studies* 4 (1960), 4-35, and my critique, " La Conversión de los Visigodos: Notas críticas " in *Analecta sacra Tarraconensia* 34 (1961) 21-46.

[9] The text of the *Laus Spaniae* is in *Mon. Germ. Hist., Auctores Antiquissimi*, XI, 267, or Migne, *PL* 83, 1057-58. Cf., for its authenticity—doubted by W. Stach—in *Historische Vierteljahrschrift* 30 (1935-36) 429 n. 22—and its sources, J. Madoz in *Razón ye Fé* 116 (1939) 247-57, and, *ibid.*, 122 (1941) 228-40.

[10] Cf. my previous paper (*cit. supra*, n.2), p.445, and, for the influence of Byzantine law in Spain at the time of Heraclius, R. S. Lopez in *Byzantion* 16 (1942-43), 445-61, esp. 449 ff. Spain is at one and the same time immensely influenced by Byzantium and in opposition to the Empire, an opposition that appears not only in the political situation but also in Isidore's writings. Cf., most recently, J. Fontaine, *Isidore de Séville et la culture classique dans l'Espagne wisigothique* (henceforth cited as Fontaine, *Culture*), II, Paris, 1959, 851. In the following remarks on Isidore I am much indebted to this great work. Isidore was almost entirely ignorant both of the Greek language (cf. Fontaine, *Culture*, II, 849 ff.) and of contemporary Byzantium, just as most of his Byzantine contemporaries were of events in the West (cf. G. Ostrogorsky in *Dumbarton Oaks Papers* 13 [1959] 12-14, 20). For possible Spanish suspicion of Byzantium *c.* 655 cf. the imprisonment of St. Fructuosus of Braga when he attempted to leave for the East (*Vita Fructuosi*, c.17, ed. F. C. Nock, Washington, 1946, 123, or in *PL* 87, 468), commented on by E. A. Thompson, in *Hermathena* 90 (1957) 58-63. It is not clear to me that Fructuosus wished to visit Byzantium itself, as Thompson supposes; the monastic centres of Egypt and Syria might well have interested him more. The *Vita* speaks merely of " partem occupans orientis." His imprisonment might have been due to suspicion of possible dealings, not with Byzantium, but with the Moslems, who occupied Egypt and Syria.

masonry, constitute a small counterpoise to the great churches of the East.[11] Their artistic achievement is excelled, in a different field, by the works of the Spanish Fathers who, in their writings and especially in the Creeds of the Councils of Toledo, accomplished a stride forward in the development of doctrine.[12]

The exceptional political conditions obtaining in Spain had enabled that country to succeed Africa as the guardian of the tradition of classical and Christian letters, a tradition impoverished but still alive. The Spanish church in the seventh century enjoyed " an incontestable superiority over all [Western] Europe."[13] Yet she seems curiously isolated from the rest of the Church and very far indeed from Ireland, her only possible spiritual rival. There is at first sight an enormous difference between even a Columban or an Adamnán and a Hispano-Roman bishop such as Isidore of Seville or Braulio of Saragossa, whose relations with the Court at Toledo and the " studiosa societas " of the great lay and spiritual princes of Spain recall at times to a modern historian the subtle preciosity of the fifth- and sixth-century bishops of Gaul and Italy, a Sidonius Apollinaris, an Ennodius of Pavia.[14] Yet in the Spain of Isidore's time there is an essential ambiguity. On the one hand Spain was still, in the seventh century, a land both visually and spiritually linked in a thousand ways to the world of late antiquity, a Mediterranean land turned towards Africa and the East from which she received so much of her artistic and intellectual inspiration.[15] On the other hand, while internally the texts yield us evidence of the growth of pre-feudal conditions on the great estates of the Visigothic nobility,[16] externally the North and West of Spain looked towards the Atlantic, towards Merovingian France and, through routes pursued since prehistoric times, towards Britain and Ireland.[17] In Isidore of Seville, too, there is ambiguity. On the one hand there is a genuine veneration for the classics and an attempt, often unavailing, to make his own their love of harmony and order, a dry objectivity, an effort to attain clarity at

---

[11] For the Spanish art of this period and its connections with the East cf. esp. E. Camps Cazorla, " El Arte Hispano-visigodo " in *Historia de España*, ed. R. Menéndez Pidal, III, Madrid, 1940, 435-666; H. Schlunk in *Ars Hispaniae*, II, Madrid, 1947, 227-323; Idem. in *Archivo espanol de Arqueologia* 18 (1945), 177-204; P. Palol de Salellas in *I Goti in Occidente = Settimane di Studio* III, Spoleto 1956, 65-126.

[12] Cf. the recent works on the Councils of Toledo, notably those of J. Madoz, esp. *Le Symbole du XIe Concile de Tolède*, Louvain, 1938, and *El Simbolo del Concilio XVI de Toledo*, Madrid, 1946.

[13] J. de Ghellinck, *Littérature latine au moyen âge*, I, Paris, 1939, 54.

[14] So Fontaine, *Culture*, II, 790.

[15] So far, it seems to be agreed, we must follow Pirenne in his characterization of the Germanic kingdoms of the Mediterranean world as " sub-spätantik." Cf. K. F. Stroheker in *Saeculum* 1 (1950), 462 ff. (on Spain, 456 ff.) and, in a similar sense, O. Halecki, *The Limits and Divisions of European History*, London-New York, 1950, 36 ff., M. Deanesly, *A History of Medieval Europe, 476 to 911*, London, 1956, 134, and L. G. de Valdeavellano in *Moneta e Scambi nell'alto Medioevo = Settimane di Studio* VIII, Spoleto, 1961, 204-206. Almost all the works—over a hundred—reviewed by A. Riising, " The Fate of Henri Pirenne's Theses on the Consequences of the Islamic Expansion " in *Classica et Mediaevalia* 13 (1952), 87-130, esp. 119-127 (on the cultural development), contrive to ignore the history of Spain, at least before 711. Cf. now *Problems in the European Civilisation. The Pirenne Thesis. Analysis, Criticism and Revision*, Boston, 1958.

[16] On this question cf. the works of C. Sánchez-Albornoz (listed by Fontaine, *Culture*, II, 808 n.3), e.g. in *I Problemi della civiltà carolingia = Settimane di Studio* I, Spoleto, 1954, 109-26.

[17] For these routes cf. e.g., J. Raftery, *Prehistoric Ireland*, London-New York, 1951, 85 ff., 112, 187, etc. Cf. below n. 145.

all costs, discernible in Spanish literature in subsequent ages.[18] The calming influence of Isidore's classical love of order, no less than the usefulness of his systematic repertory of erudition, help to explain his attraction for Irish writers subject to the influence of the very different æsthetic found in Virgilius Maro[19] and the *Hisperica Famina*.[20] But this classical side of Isidore is not the whole of him and perhaps not the side that mainly appealed to the Irish. His very respect for the pagan classics, as essentially " antiqui," authorities to be considered with the same attention accorded to the Christian Fathers, his remoteness from the traditional Christian hostility to the pagans, these things bring him closer to the Irish and the Anglo-Saxons than to Gregory the Great.[21] It is not for nothing, too, that he has been called a " Zauberkünstler," a word not to be understood here as meaning a mere conjuror but an artist in magic, who, in Vossler's words, takes possession of all things, even of history, by signs, formulas and sacred numbers.[22] This side of Isidore, his spirit of curiosity, his taste for the rare and the marvellous, for the glittering, the strange, the inaccessible, as conspicuous in some books of the *Origines* as in the Byzantine jewelry of Guarrazar, all this reveals a spiritual kinship with the Irish artists and writers of

---

[18] Cf. the remarks of Fontaine, *Culture*, II, 826, 871 n.2.

[19] Virgilius Maro was commonly used by the Irish. Cf. B. Bischoff, " Il Monachesimo irlandese nei suoi rapporti col Continente " in *Il Monachesimo nell'alto Medioevo e la formazione della civiltà occidentale = Settimane di Studio* IV, Spoleto, 1957, 127. It now appears to be generally agreed that he may have spent part of his life in Ireland; cf. N. K. Chadwick in *Studies in Early British History*, Cambridge, 1954, 244 ff.; P. Grosjean, *art. cit. infra* (n. 37), 82 ff.; B. Bischoff, *art. cit. infra* (n. 103), 20. Virgilius's use of Isidore is clear; cf. M. Manitius, in *Philologische Wochenschrift* 49 (1929) 1111. H. Zimmer's attempt to place him saec. V (*art. cit. infra*, n. 48, 1910, 1031-1098, 1118 ff.) is, therefore, hopeless, but his article contains proof of early Irish use of Virgilius.

[20] This influence was not, of course, universal, but it was very important in Ireland. On the *Hisperica Famina* cf. P. Grosjean, " Confusa Caligo " in *Celtica* 3 (1956), 35-85. He believes the *Hisp. Fam.* was a school text and, as such, was liable to various re-editions, of which four are (in part) preserved. Some of these " editions " were very probably Irish, at any rate it appears the work in some form was known in Ireland saec. VI (pp. 80 ff.). But he admits (p. 59 n. 1), like Roger, that it could be saec. VII and adds: " J'irais même jusqu'au VIIIe pour les textes qui nous sont parvenus." Version B was known to Aldhelm (p. 61 and cf. p. 64). Niedermann and Jenkinson may be right in holding that this version and A, at least, were written in Ireland (p. 63). R. A. S. Macalister, *The Secret Languages of Ireland*, Cambridge, 1937, 69, suggested that Isidore was among the sources of Hisperic Latin (his words are: " For general information they had the compilation of the dry-as-dust Isidore of Seville "). P. Grosjean (p. 57) is uncertain as to the use of Isidore. On p. 44 he notes that " arcator " in *HF* A 231 = scholar, i.e., bearer of a sack or container of books, " arca." For the use of " arca " as a container of books he can only find one early example in Jerome, *In Mt.* 23, 6 (*PL* 26, 175B) and another later one in Aldhelm, *Aen.* 89 (*MGH*, *AA* XV, 138). " Arca " as a container of books appears also, however, in Isidore, *Versus* xi, ed. C. H. Beeson, *Isidor-Studien*, München, 1913, 162: " Historias rerum et transacti tempora saecli Condita membranis haec simul *arca* gerit." (For " arca " in Bobbio so-called " ex-libris " cf. B. Bischoff *apud* T. D. Kendrick *et al.*, *op. cit. supra*, n. 3, p. 113, n. 7. An " arcam cum diversis codicibus membranis et chartis monastherii " also appears in the *Regula Magistri*, c. 17, ed. H. Vanderhoven, F. Masai *et al.*, Bruxelles, etc., 1953, 206. 20-21). For Isidore's *Versus* in Northumbria saec. VII-VIII cf. below, n. 110, and for stylistic comparisons between Spaniards and Irish, below, n.24.

[21] On Isidore cf. Fontaine, *Culture*, II, 785-806: " Culture païenne et culture chrétienne," and *idem*, in *Information littéraire* 9 (1957), 208-15. On the Irish cf. L. Bieler, *art. cit. infra*, n. 24, and H. Zimmer, *art. cit. infra*, n. 48, p. 576.

[22] Cf. K. Vossler, " Isidor von Sevilla " in *Hochland* 39 (1946-47), 420-28, at 423: " Beinahe möchte man ihn für einen Zauberkünstler halten, der mit Zeichen, Formeln und heiligen Zahlen nicht nur der natürlichen Dinge, sondern auch der Weltgeschichte habhaft zu werden sucht, so in seinem ' *De viris illustribus* ' und in seinen Chroniken. Und doch ist es kein Magier . . . kein Künstler." Vossler is cited by Fontaine, *Culture*, II, 813 n. 3.

his day.[23] Isidore's exuberant baroque style in the *Synonyma* is, too, strangely at variance with his theory as expressed in the *Origines*: its influence was not to be confined to Spain, where it began an age of baroque prose comparable to that of the seventeenth century, but spread to the British Isles and further still.[24]

These few general considerations are an attempt to suggest an explanation for something that, possibly, needs no explanation—since it constitutes an obvious fact—the incredibly rapid diffusion of Isidore's works over Western Europe within his own century. Together with these works, and before they had been written, Spain appears to have been transmitting manuscripts to the rest of Europe and notably to Ireland. No complete study of the works transmitted via Ireland is yet possible. All one can attempt at this stage are a few notes on some authors. Those most likely to prove worth investigating after the Spanish appear to be the Africans. Unfortunately we lack, as yet, satisfactory critical editions of most African Christian authors before or after Augustine, including Cyprian.[25] In view of the very close relations between North Africa and Spain from before the Barbarian Invasions one wonders if three important manuscripts of the fourth or fifth centuries—a copy of the Gospels and two manuscripts of Cyprian—in early, probably African, uncial, that almost certainly came from Ireland to Bobbio, had travelled previously to Ireland via Spain.[26] This line of descent—Africa-Spain-the British Isles—may be traced for the African grammarians Pompeius and Marius Victorinus, who are both cited in succession by Isidore, Julian of Toledo and Bede.[27]

But here we are at once confronted with various difficulties. " From Spain," as Saxl says in one of his lectures, " learning migrated to Wearmouth, Jarrow

---

[23] On Isidore cf. Fontaine, *Culture*, II, 883, who does not make the comparison with the Irish.

[24] On Isidore's style cf. now J. Fontaine, " Théorie et pratique du style chez Isidore de Séville " in *Vigiliae Christianae* 14 (1960), 65-101. Fontaine points out one should speak of contrast rather than contradiction between the *Synonyma* and the *Origines*. A comparison of the style or styles of the Spaniards and the Irish is yet to be made. Cf., meanwhile, the observations of Mrs. N. K. Chadwick in *Studies in Early British History*, 247: she is inclined to suspect the influence of newer rhymed strophic continental forms such as those already practised in Spain on Luccréth moccu Cérai (saec. VII). Fontaine, *art. cit.*, 77, n. 28, compares the Spanish " stilus rhetoricus " to the Latin of the *Hisperica Famina*; cf. already L. Bieler, " The Island of Scholars," in *Revue du moyen âge latin* 8 (1952), 225, cited by P. Grosjean in *Celtica* 3 (1956), 58, n. 1, and W. Meyer in *Nachrichten v. d. Koniglich Gesellchaft d. Wiss. zu Göttingen*, Philol.-hist. Klasse (1913), 110 ff.

[25] It should prove interesting to study the transmission of later African authors such as Fulgentius of Ruspe. Dom C. Lambot in *Revue bénédictine* 48 (1936), 225 and n. 2, points to a curious identity in the formulas for designating authorship to be found in MSS. of Fulgentius, of Isidore's *Origines*, and perhaps of Leander, not found elsewhere. He thinks, however, that this may well be fortuitous. Cf. also the remarks of Dom J. Leclercq on MS. Paris, Bibl. Nat., Latin 3794 (saec. XI-XII), which contains sermons of Fulgentius and excerpts from Isidore and may be Spanish in origin (*Rev. bénéd.* 56 [1945-46], 93 ff.)

[26] The MSS. are described by E. A. Lowe, *CLA*, IV, Oxford, 1947, nn. 458, 464, 465. The possible connection between Africa and Ireland consists in the fact that one of these MSS. (Turin, Bibl. Naz., G. VII. 15) is ruled " on the hair-side, several leaves at a time after folding, an Insular practice and otherwise unknown in MSS. of such antiquity " (*CLA*, n. 465). There is also a later Bobbio tradition that St. Columban brought the MS. with him. L. Bieler (*art. cit. infra*, n. 32), 272, also thinks the three MSS. came to Bobbio via Ireland.

[27] Cf. Fontaine, *Culture*, I, 193, 196 (the use of Marius Victorinus by Isidore is much less certain than that of Pompeius but he was certainly used by Julian of Toledo).

and York, from York to Tours, from Tours to Fulda."[28] So much is generally recognized. The stages between Spain and England remain, however, in dispute. In the past, one must admit, historians, in their picture of the transmission of culture in the early Middle Ages, tended to see the Irish everywhere, the Anglo-Saxons and the Italians nowhere. There came a very natural reaction and of late we have had the picture rather drastically reversed ![29] We must, therefore, be very cautious in our interpretation of the evidence and would do well, I think, to avoid *a priori* advocacy of any one of the likely routes for the transmission of manuscripts to the exclusion of the rest. The fact that Aldhelm, for instance, apparently possessed a work read a short time before by Julian of Toledo, or even a work of Julian himself,[30] does not *in itself* prove that these works came to Malmesbury or Sherborne either via Ireland or via France. Similarly, the presence of a Spanish work in a Bobbio manuscript may be explained either by its exemplar having come from Ireland or by its having come direct to Bobbio from Spain or through the South of France. All this is obvious enough. What I feel is dangerous is the view that we sometimes find to-day that it is, *a priori*, more likely a Spanish work travelled to Bobbio direct from Spain or to Malmesbury or Jarrow via Rome or Bobbio rather than that it arrived at Bobbio, Malmesbury or Jarrow by way of Ireland.[31]

This question may appear a mere " querelle de grammariens " but, on reflection, it will be seen that it involves a number of problems that concern early medieval culture and that are by no means unimportant. I may, therefore, at this point be allowed a slight digression. The view I have mentioned, that can be said to concentrate attention on Bobbio or on Northumbria rather than on Ireland, appears to spring from two causes, both negative and largely due to historical accident. The first is the lack of early insular codices that can certainly be held to have been written in Ireland itself, compared with the relatively large number surviving from Bobbio or, in Anglo-Saxon manuscripts from Northumbria. This lack of manuscripts from Ireland can only rationally be ascribed to the destruction wrought by Viking raiders and by later barbarians.[32] But it has led to the theory of Franz Steffens, who maintained that Bobbio was the home of the first inventors of insular abbreviations.[33] More reasonably, Lindsay, for instance, could hold that the oldest surviving MS. of the *Origines* of

---

[28] F. Saxl, *Lectures*, I, London, 1957, 241.

[29] Cf. e.g., P. Lehmann in *Downside Review* 71 (1953), 409; J. Duft and P. Meyer, *The Irish Miniatures in the Abbey Library of St. Gall*, Olten-Berne-Lausanne, 1954, 14, 16, 45, etc. The most extreme instance of this reaction is, of course, M. Masai's work cited above, n. 3.

[30] On Aldhelm's use of Julian cf. my Oxford paper (cited n. 2 above) 452 f.

[31] Reference to Map 40 in the *Atlas of the Early Christian World* by F. Van der Meer and C. Mohrmann, London, etc., 1958, 32, will assist understanding of the following pages.

[32] Most scholars would presumably not be prepared to discount, with M. Masai (*op. cit. supra*, n. 3, pp. 61-63) the probability of large-scale destruction of MSS. by the Vikings. For a discussion of the early insular MSS. that survive, and of work on the subject, cf. L. Bieler, " Insular Paleography, Present State and Problems," in *Scriptorium* 3 (1949), 267-94.

[33] On this theory and the insuperable difficulties it involves cf. Lowe, *CLA*, IV, p. xxiv. For the saec. VII MSS. certainly or probably written at Bobbio cf. ibid., xx-xxv.

Isidore was one written at Bobbio.[34] From this and similar apparently established facts obvious conclusions appeared to follow.[35] The second cause for the excessive emphasis placed on Bobbio and on Northumbria as against Ireland was the ignorance generally prevailing until recently of most of the early Irish literature in Latin. As long as much of this literature remained unpublished or, if published, was relegated to the appendices of the Fathers, Cyprian, Jerome, Augustine *et al.*, as long, in fact, as its date and origin were unknown, it was clearly impossible to use it to study Irish culture at home or abroad. Recent researches, notably those of Professor Bernhard Bischoff, have brought much light into these shadows.[36] We now have a number of not inconsiderable works, mainly Biblical commentaries and grammatical texts, that we can be reasonably certain were written in Ireland in the seventh century.[37] Some of these works make considerable use of Isidore (among other Spanish authors).[38] On the other hand, the number and importance of the works composed at Bobbio or in Northumbria in the seventh century are slight, to say the least.[39] This com-

---

[34] Cf. W. M. Lindsay's review of C. H. Beeson, *Isidor-Studien*, in *Deutsche Literaturzeitung* 34 (1913), col. 3167. He refers to MS. Vat. Lat. 5763. Lowe, *CLA*, I, Oxford, 1934, 39 and IV, p. xxv, dates the MS. saec. VIII med. and does not believe it was written at Bobbio. (Cf., however, A. R. Natale in *Miscellanea G. Galbiati*, II, Milan, 1951, 251 ff.) J. F. Kenney, *The Sources for the Early History of Ireland*, I, New York, 1929, 674, while acknowledging that ample evidence exists for the use of Isidore in Ireland, is doubtful whether *any* MS. of his works written there survives.

[35] Beeson, notably, stressed the role of Irish foundations on the Continent in the diffusion of Isidore (cf. *Isidor-Studien*, 120 ff.).

[36] Cf. especially B. Bischoff, " Wendepunkte in der Geschichte der lateinischen Exegese in Frühmittelalter " in *Sacris Erudiri* 6 (1954), 189-281; *idem*, " Il Monachesimo irlandese nei suoi rapporti col Continente " in *Il Monachesimo* (*op. cit. supra*, n. 19), 121-38. To say this is not to forget the work of earlier scholars, notably M. Esposito. Cf., however, the very small number of Irish works of saec. V to VII listed in J. H. Baxter *et al.*, *Index of British and Irish Latin Writers A.D. 400-1520*, Paris, 1932, 7 ff.

[37] e.g. the Commentary on St. Mark of Ps-Jerome, probably by Cummean (*c.* 633), in Migne, *PL* 30, 589-644 (cf. Bischoff, " Wendepunkte," 257-59); the *De mirabilibus sacrae scripturae* of Ps-Augustine, written in 655, for St. Carthach's monastery at Lismore, in *PL* 35, 2149-2200 (cf. P. Grosjean, " Sur quelques exègetes irlandais de VIIe siècle " in *Sacris Erudiri* 7, 1955, 67-98, esp. 71); the *De ordine creaturarum* of Ps-Isidore (*PL* 83, 913-954), on which cf. M. C. Díaz y Díaz in *Sacris Erudiri* 5 (1953), 147-66 (the work uses the *De Mirabilibus* and can be dated *paulo post* 650; cf. also *infra*, n. 74) and the anonymous *Ars ad Cuimnanum* (cf. *infra*, n. 103).

[38] The Commentary on Mark may use Isid., *Allegoriae*; cf. G. Wohlenberg in *Neue kirchliche Zeitschrift* 18 (1907), 465. The *De ordine creaturarum* certainly uses the *Differentiae* (Díaz, *art. cit.*, 157-59) and perhaps the *Origenes* (ib., 151 n. 2). For the anonymous *Ad Cuimnanum* cf. *infra*.

[39] On the culture of Bobbio at this time cf. the prudent reservations of P. Lehmann, " Panorama der literarischen Kultur des Abendlandes in 7 Jahrhundert " in *Caratteri del secolo VII in Occidente* = *Settimane di Studio* V. 2, Spoleto, 1958, 855-59. J. Fontaine, " Théorie et pratique " (*art. cit. supra*, n. 24), 77 n. 28, points to the use of Sisebut, *Vita Desiderii*, by Jonas at Bobbio in his *Vita Columbani* of 641. G. Haseloff (*art. cit. supra*, n. 3) suggests (p. 90) that Bobbio " may have played the essential part of a cultural clearing-house " in transmitting Copto-Syrian artistic influences to Ireland. He points in particular (p. 91) to " the fact that the first examples of new style-traits and motifs from the East " found in Ireland are later than the foundation of Bobbio. He acknowledges, however, the continuation of direct contact between the East and Ireland and remarks (p. 90): " But the necessary creative process . . . took place, there can be little doubt, on Celtic soil in Ireland itself." While mentioning the Greek inscription on the Fahan Mura slab as a means of dating the slab he does not remark that the formula is Spanish in origin or discuss possible relations between Spain and Ireland (cf. n. 140 below). For Northumbria cf. the following note.

parison is not very startling but it enables one to correct the one-sided and misleading picture presented by the surviving manuscripts if considered by themselves. The picture is, in fact, so complicated that any simple opposition of Irish to Northumbrian, or of Northumbrian to Southern English culture, would be merely a travesty of the truth. On the one hand Irish influence in Northumbria clearly did not come to a sudden end in 664 with the Synod of Whitby and, on the other hand, neither Irish nor continental influences were limited to Northumbria. Sir Frank Stenton has stated the position clearly: " The strands of Irish and continental influence were interwoven in every kingdom and at every stage of the process by which England became Christian." The rapid development of Northumbrian culture was due very largely to the great diversity of the sources on which it drew. But its artistic expansion came about more rapidly than the flowering of its literary culture. The first Northumbrian author of local origin, apart from the anonymous monk of Whitby, author of the first Life of St. Gregory the Great, was Bede himself, who did not begin to write until *c.* 702, and his dependence on Irish scholarship, at least for his early works, is very evident.[40] Meanwhile, apart from the rediscovery of Irish writings of the seventh century, the finding of the saec. VII fragments of Isidore at St. Gall has added another—and very significant—early manuscript to the few already known to proceed from Ireland.[41]

We can trace some of the possible routes by which books and works of art appear to have moved in the sixth and seventh centuries. We have, on the one hand, the routes taken by Eastern trade. There is a revival of Byzantine relations with the West in the sixth and seventh centuries, a revival that accepted and sought to sustain by diplomacy and the payment of tributes or bribes the

---

[40] Cf. F. M. Stenton, *Anglo-Saxon England,*[2] London, 1947, 125; C. E. Whiting in *Bede, His Life, Time and Writings,* ed. A. H. Thompson, Oxford, 1935, 1-38, and *infra.* A new edition of the Life of Gregory the Great (ed. F. A. Gasquet, Westminster, 1904) is badly needed. For its date cf. C. W. Jones, *Saints' Lives and Chronicles in Early England,* Ithaca N.Y., 1947, 64 ff. Before 716 Wearmouth-Jarrow possessed scribes capable of writing the Codex Amiatinus (cf. now E. A. Lowe, *English Uncial,* Oxford, 1960, 8-13). If T. J. Brown and R. L. S. Bruce-Mitford (*op. cit.*, n. 3 *supra*, p. xxiii, etc.) are right in dating the Book of Durrow *c.* 680 and the Echternach Gospels, Durham A. II. 17 and the Book of Lindisfarne all within the next twenty or thirty years, and in ascribing the three later manuscripts to the Lindisfarne scriptorium, the development there would be even more rapid and remarkable; on this point cf. Werckmeister (*art. cit.* n. 1 *supra*), n. 104. I feel that Mr. Bruce-Mitford (p. 117) exaggerates the importance of Northumbria from the point of view of " scholarship and poetry " (as opposed to art) in the late seventh century when he says: " England, and more particularly, as it seems to us, its Hiberno-Saxon North, led the Europe of its day." Here he forgets not only Ireland itself but also Visigothic Spain. J. Ryan, " Irish Learning in the Seventh Century " in *Journal of the Royal Society of Antiquaries of Ireland* 80 (1950), 164-171 (esp. 168-71), provides a necessary corrective to M. Masai's exaltation of Northumbria at the expense of Ireland. I would agree with Professor Haseloff (*art. cit. supra*, n. 3), 97, that " Ireland occupied a paramount position in the seventh century as a centre of education for the Anglo-Saxons and other nations." The main Irish monasteries have, of course, long been known to us from references in the Annals. Unfortunately the obits of scribes are seldom recorded in the Annals for the seventh century. K. Hughes, " The Distribution of Irish Scriptoria and Centres of Learning from 730 to 1111 " in *Studies in the Early British Church,* Cambridge, 1958, 243-73, notes (p. 249) that the eighth century evidence does not favour M. Masai's thesis of Irish dependence on Northumbria.

[41] Cf. *infra*, pp. 182-185.

military conquests of Justinian.[42] The direct sea route from the East to the Far West " continued to pass by way of Carthage as it had done from remote antiquity."[43] From North Africa one route would diverge to Southern France, to Marseilles, to Toulouse, where, in the fifth century, when it was the Visigothic capital, we find strong Byzantine influence, and to Narbonne, still, after 507, under Spanish control.[44] Another route from Africa continued on to Southern Spain. The existence of relations between the Eastern Mediterranean and Spain in these centuries is attested both by literary documents and, even more strikingly, by archæological finds and artistic influences, and they do not seem to have diminished after the final expulsion of the Byzantine troops *c.* 629.[45] From Carthage ships coming originally from Alexandria or Constantinople could gain the South of Spain, sail up the Guadalquivir to Seville or up the Guadiana to Mérida or continue round into the Atlantic to reach Braga and the North.[46]

[42] Mr. Philip Grierson, " Commerce and Trade in the Dark Ages, a Critique of the Evidence " in *Trans. of the Royal Hist. Society*, Fifth Series, 9 (1959), 123-40, points out (pp. 131 ff.) that the various " alternatives to trade," i.e., plunder and, more important in the present context, tributes of different kinds, notably those paid by Byzantium to the Franks and Lombards, " in their total bulk far overshadowing transfers of bullion for commercial purposes," were in all probability " more important than trade itself " (p. 140). The idea advanced by Dr. H. L. Adelson, *Light Weight Solidi and Byzantine Trade during the Sixth and Seventh Centuries*, New York, 1957, (cf. p. 136), and in *American Hist. Review* 65 (1960), 271-87, that the striking of these " solidi " was due to a " concerted effort at building up the trade of Byzantium with the West " and that they were minted specially by the Byzantine Government for merchants trading with the Germanic world, has to be rejected since merchants were forbidden by Byzantine legislation on pain of death to export gold from the Empire (cf. Grierson, *art. cit.*, 140, and his review of Adelson's book in *Hamburger Beiträge zur Numismatik* 14 [1960] 702 ff.; on this book cf. also J. P. C. Kent in *Numismatic Chronicle* 19 [1959] 237-40). It seems more probable that the light weight " solidi " were used for political payments.

[43] Fontaine, *Culture*, II, 846. Cf. my Oxford paper (*cit. supra*, n. 2), 444 n. 3. A. R. Lewis, *Naval Power and Trade in the Mediterranean A.D. 500-1100*, Princeton, 1951, 18-20, and W. H. C. Frend, " North Africa and Europe in the Early Middle Ages " in *Trans. Royal Hist. Society*, Fifth Series, 5 (1955), 61-80, esp. 69 ff., hold the attacks of the Vandal fleet in the fifth century had only a temporary effect in disrupting trade. Cf. also C. Courtois, *Les Vandales et l'Afrique*, Paris, 1955, 205-209. It used to be said that Irish monks reached Carthage in the seventh century (cf. P. W. Joyce, *A Social History of Ancient Ireland*, I,[2] London, 1920, 345, 466, following W. Reeves, in *P.R.I.A.* 7 (1857-61), 514-22, esp. 521, and in turn copied by later writers, e.g., N. Åberg, *The Occident and the Orient in the Art of the Seventh Century*, I, Stockholm, 1943, 10) but this idea is due to a misunderstanding of the dedication of the *De mirabilibus sacrae scripturae* (cf. *supra*, n. 37).

[44] Byzantine influence at Toulouse was especially notable in the important (destroyed) mosaics of La Daurade, on which cf. A. Grabar, *Martyrium*, I, Paris, 1946, 411 ff.; II, 124 ff., 171; R. Rey in *Annales du Midi* 61 (1949), 249-74; G. Boyer, ib., 68 (1956), 47-51; J. Hubert, *L'Architecture religieuse du Haut Moyen Age en France*, Paris, 1952, 80. For a later period cf. M. Durliat, " Un groupe de sculptures wisigothiques à Narbonne " in *Études Mérovingiennes*, Paris, 1953, 93-101, and A. Dupont, *Les cités de la Narbonnaise première depuis les invasions germaniques jusqu'a l'apparition du consulat*, Nîmes, 1942, 205-15.

[45] Cf. n. 10 *supra*; Schlunk (*op. cit. supra*, n. 11), 247, 266; Palol de Salellas (*cit. ibid.*), 86; Valdeavellano (*art. cit.*, n. 15 *supra*), 213-216. Another route between Italy and Eastern Spain in the seventh century is attested by the discovery of bronze jars in Majorca and Catalonia (none have been found in Southern France); cf. P. de Palol Salellas, *Bronces hispanovisigodos de origen mediterráneo. I. Jarritos y patenas liturgicos*, Barcelona, 1950 (cf. " Conclusiones," 167-74). In Southern Spain eastern influences were very strong saec. VI. J. de C. Serra y Ràfols in *Atti dello VIII Congresso Internazionale di Studi Bizantini*. 2 = *Studi Bizantini e Neoellenici* 8, Roma, 1953, 241-45, studies a mausoleum or martyrium at " La Cocosa," 12 km. south of Badajoz, which he dates saec. VI and considers even more Byzantine than S. Fructuoso de Montelios, in Galicia (saec. VII), which it closely resembles. For Coptic influence on the prototypes of the Beatus manuscripts cf. also J. Camón Aznar, in *Spanische Forschungen der Görresgesellschaft*, 1, 16, Münster Westf. 1960, 30.

[46] Cf. my Oxford paper, 445 n. 1. Eastern influence is notable in Galicia as early as saec. V; cf. C. Torres in *Cuadernos de Estudios Gallegos* 12 (1957), 53-64.

There seems no doubt that some of the Eastern ships that had reached Northern Spain continued on their way to the British Isles.

Our strongest archæological evidence for these voyages consists of the Eastern Mediterranean pottery, much of it evidently intended to provide for Celtic liturgical needs, recently found in the West of England, especially North Cornwall, South Wales and Southern Ireland—almost all the sites where it has been found are on the coast.[47] It is not found north of a line from Dublin to Anglesey and it has been suggested that this may indicate the distance to which Mediterranean traders were prepared to sail.[48] The continental dating of this pottery is not yet fixed but pottery very similar in type is dated *c.* 425-600.[49]

---

[47] Cf. C. A. Ralegh Radford, " Imported Pottery found at Tintagel, Cornwall " in *Dark-age Britain, Studies presented to E. T. Leeds*, ed. D. B. Harden, London, 1956, 59-70, esp. 68-70 (the site at Tintagel was occupied saec. V to IX by a large Celtic monastery); S. P. Ó Ríordáin in *P.R.I.A.* 47, Sect. C (1941-42), 127, 132 ff. (on very similar pottery found at Garranes, Co. Cork) and now the synthesis, collecting and correcting earlier work, by C. Thomas, " Imported Pottery in Dark-age Western Britain " in *Medieval Archæology* 3 (1959), 89-111, cited henceforth as Thomas. The numismatic evidence sometimes brought forward to support the idea of early contacts between the East or Spain and the British Isles is far from impressive. G. C. Boon, in *Med. Arch.* 3 (1959), 84, has recently pointed out that most of the evidence for finds of Byzantine coins in Britain is dubious. There is hardly any coin evidence of this period from Ireland. I know of only one Merovingian gold coin found near Trim; cf. J. Lindsay, *Notices of the remarkable Greek, Roman and Anglo-Saxon and other medieval coins in the cabinet of the author*, Cork, 1860, 12 (I owe this reference to Mr. R. H. M. Dolley of the British Museum). P. Le Gentilhomme, in *Revue numismatique*, 5ᵉ série, 8 (1945), 19 ff., states that Visigothic coins (of the post-Leovigild regal series) have been found in England but gives no references. He refers (p. 20) to a coin of Wittiza said to have been found at Skåne in Sweden, but this is now known to be a modern forgery (cf. G. C. Miles, *The Coinage of the Visigoths of Spain Leovigild to Achila II*, New York, 1952, 496). A. R. Lewis, *The Northern Seas, Shipping and Commerce in Northern Europe A.D. 300-1100*, Princeton, 1958, 120, states that Visigothic pieces were found at Sutton Hoo, but this is erroneous (cf. T. D. Kendrick *et al.*, " The Sutton Hoo Finds " in *British Museum Quarterly* 13 [1939] 126; C. H. V. Sutherland and P. Grierson, " Les trésors de Sutton Hoo et de Crondall [VIIᵉ siècle]," in *Exposition internationale de numismatique, Catalogue*, Paris, 1953, 49-53). For severe, but just, critiques of Lewis's book cf. R. H. M. Dolley in *Spink and Sons' Numismatic Circular* 66 (1958), 255, and P. Grierson in *English Hist. Review* 76 (1961), 311-15. Le Gentilhomme, *loc. cit.*, 7 (1943-44) 96, refers to Visigothic coins of the pre-regal series found in Kent and cites C. Roach-Smith, *Collectanea Antiqua*, I, London, 1848, 7, who describes a coin found near Faversham. P. Grierson, " The Canterbury (St. Martin's) Hoard of Frankish and Anglo-Saxon Coin-Ornaments " in *British Numismatic Journal* 27 (1953), 39-51, discusses some coins, etc., several of which come from Southern Gaul and some of which show " Visigothic " influence, but they may well have come from territory under Frankish control after 507. " The word ' Visigothic ' in this connexion must be used with some reserve " (p. 45, n. 3). There are, in fact, very few authenticated finds of genuine Visigothic coins in northern lands in seventh- or eighth-century hoards. I know only of the coin of Sisebut (struck at Seville) found at Wieuwerd (cf. P. C. J. A. Boeles, *Friesland tot de elfde eeuw*,[2] S'Gravenhage, 1951, 513), apparently not noticed by Miles, *op. cit.* (for the date—saec. VII[1]—cf. J. Lafaurie, " Les routes commerciales indiquées par les trésors et trouvailles monétaires mérovingiens " in *Moneta e Scambi* (*op. cit.* n. 15 *supra*), 231-78, at 239, 250). One or two coins of Suinthila from Tarragona were found in 1820 in the Mons hoard (saec. VIII,[1] or possibly VII; cf. Lafaurie, 254; Miles, 276 n. 4). For the Bordeaux hoard cf. *infra*, n. 65. Lewis refers (*art. cit. infra*, n. 55), 276, to a Visigothic coin of Seville (saec. VIII) found at Domburg in Frisia but this coin is not to be found in P. Le Gentilhomme, *Mélanges* (*op. cit. infra*, n. 65), 56-64, which Lewis cites as his authority.

[48] Thomas, 101. He notes, however (p. 100), that the lack of Eastern pottery north of this line may be explained by the importation of wine " in cask, or at any rate in small wooden containers to some Northern Irish and Western Scottish centres." We may remark that " Gallici nautae, de Galliarum provinciis adventantes," reached the neighbourhood of Iona in the period 563-97; cf. Adamnan, *Vita S. Columbae*, I, 28, ed. A. O. Anderson, London, 1961, and the commentary by H. Zimmer, " Uber direkte Handelsverbindungen Westgalliens mit Irland in Alterthum und frühen Mittelalter" in *Sitz. d. Kön. Preuss. Akad. d. Wiss.* (1909), 368.

[49] Thomas, 104.

This Eastern Mediterranean pottery is found in the British Isles, mainly on fifth- or sixth-century sites.[50] Its direct arrival by sea and not partly by land across France from Marseilles to Bordeaux is indicated by the absence of finds in Bordeaux or the Narbonne gap, though, significantly enough, it has been found at Barcelona.[51] It has been suggested that this pottery ceased to be imported at the time of the collapse of the Byzantine attempt to maintain Justinian's " Reconquista " in the West.[52] But one doubts if this collapse—a slow process; the Byzantine troops were only expelled from Spain *c.* 629 and after that they continued to hold the fortress of Ceuta across the Straits of Gibraltar until *c.* 711—would have affected trade with the British Isles, probably only carried out in any case by a few ships.[53] Moslem naval attacks do not seem to have been as effectual in the seventh century in hindering Mediterranean trade as was once thought.[54] We might more plausibly connect the diminution in the import of pottery with the waning of the " Celtic thalassocracy " which, according to some scholars, had linked Ireland, West Britain, Brittany and, perhaps, Spain, after the Anglo-Saxon conquest of the Severn valley and Chester at the beginning of the seventh century.[55] And we might also refer to the general shift, beginning *c.* 600, of the main trade route from the East, away from the old line leading to Marseilles to a new orientation from North Italy over the Alps and up the Rhine.[56] There seems no doubt, however, that ships from the Mediterranean, although probably in smaller numbers, continued to reach the British Isles in the seventh century. We know this from the contemporary Greek Life of St. John the Almoner of Alexandria, who died in 616 and, later, from the unhappy experiences of Arculf in the 680's.[57] There is also archæological evidence for

---

[50] Thomas, 104, says: " It is hard to show any clear case of importation in the seventh [century]." On p. 101, however, pottery of two of the sub-types discussed is shown to be present at Gwithian (Cornwall), a site dug by Thomas, in the period 525-800, although much less frequent than in the earlier period, 450-525.

[51] Thomas, 91 ff. Cp. n. 45 above (Palol de Salellas on finds of bronze jars).

[52] Thomas, 105, citing a view of Radford.

[53] As Thomas observes (*loc. cit.*), and cf. n. 54 below for the type of ship probably used.

[54] R. S. Lopez, " The Role of Trade in the Economic Readjustment of Byzantium in the Seventh Century " in *Dumbarton Oaks Papers* 13 (1959), 69-85, remarks (p. 71): " No one any longer believes that it [the coming of the Arabs] had catastrophic consequences for trade." It is hard to believe, however, that the Moslem advance into North Africa, already begun by 670 (though Carthage did not fall finally until 698) had no serious consequences for commercial and artistic relations. Spanish sources record two Moslem naval attacks on Spain in the late seventh century, the first under Wamba (672-80)—cf. *Crónica de Alfonso III* (a. 883), ed. M. Gómez-Moreno in *Boletín Real Acad. Historia* 100 (1932), 610 (later recension in *PL* 129, 1113C)—the second under Egica and Wittiza (*c.* 700); cf. *Continuatio Isidori Hispana* (754), c. 74, ed. Mommsen in *Mon. Germ. Hist., Auctores Antiquissimi* XI, 354·9 ff. It is curious that the *Vita S. Johannis Elemosynarii* (+ 616), auct. Leontio, cc. 10, 13, cited by Lopez, *art. cit.*, 71 and n. 7, should mention a new name for a ship (δόρκων = gazelle). Lopez thinks this was probably a swift vessel, possibly designed to escape pirates. This was the type of ship which the *Vita* (c.10) describes as reaching the British Isles (cf. n. 57 below).

[55] So A. R. Lewis, " Le commerce et la navigation sur les côtes atlantiques de la Gaule du Ve au VIIIe siècle " in *Le Moyen Age* 59 (1953), 262 and n. 49. St. Columban still travelled to France via Brittany *c.* 590; cf. Zimmer (*art. cit. supra*, n. 48), 395 ff. (*contra* G. S. M. Walker, *S. Columbani Opera = Script. lat. Hiberniae* II [Dublin, 1957] xix).

[56] This is stressed by Haseloff (*art. cit. supra*, n. 3), 90 and references in his n. 107.

[57] Cf. my Oxford paper (*cit. supra*, n. 2), 446. G. Mickwitz in *Wirtschaft und Kultur, Festschrift zum 70. Geburtstag von Alfons Dopsch*, Leipzig, 1938, 77, held the story of the

continued on page 179

continued contacts with the East, and especially Egypt, in the glass found in different parts of England and Scotland.[58]

In contrast to the routes taken by travellers and traders from the East we have those of Irish influence, travelling North to Iona and South from there to Lindisfarne with St. Aidan in 635; from Ireland itself in the same year to Burgh Castle (near Yarmouth) in East Anglia, with St. Fursey; about the same time to what was to be Malmesbury with Aldhelm's first master, Máel-dubh.[59] Other routes linked Ireland to Brittany and from Brittany there were lines branching out to St. Gall and Bobbio and a possible (though less well documented) line to Spain, to the Celtic See of Britonia in North Galicia, not far from the Eastern influence that, spreading inland from Braga, had reached the province of Lugo by the same date (the late sixth century) as the first mention of Britonia in the texts.[60]

Spanish works left Spain in the early Middle Ages in different directions. Although I am here concerned only with the relations between Spain and Ireland, it is necessary, in order to see these relations in perspective, to say a little first of Italy and France before speaking of the British Isles. Some manuscripts, then, went to Italy. But if we look at the evidence recorded in Professor Lowe's *Codices latini antiquiores* it is clear that most of these manuscripts, now at Verona, Vercelli, Lucca and elsewhere, left Spain after the Arabic Invasion, when a number of refugees escaped to Italy, taking with them such precious codices

[58] Cf. on this D. B. Harden, " Glass Vessels in Britain and Ireland, A.D. 400-1000 " in *Dark-age Britain* (*op. cit. supra*, n. 47), 149, 154-56. On the fifth-century glass from Egypt at Tintagel cf. *idem*, ib., 70. One should also refer to the decoration of Greek crosses in circles and marigolds found in Spain and Ireland, discussed by A. W. Clapham, " Notes on the Origins of Hiberno-Saxon Art " in *Antiquity* 8 (1934), 43-57, esp. 48-50.

[59] For St. Fursey and Burgh Castle and their possible connection with the Sutton Hoo finds cf. F. Henry, " Irish Enamels of the Dark Ages and their Relation to the Cloisonné Techniques," in *Dark-age Britain* (*op. cit. supra*, n. 47), 81-83, and Haseloff (*art. cit. supra*, n. 3), 93, 102. As Haseloff rightly points out (p. 94) archæological evidence shows that Irish influence was exercised in Southern England as well as in Northumbria. For Máel-dubh's pupil, Aldhelm, cf. *infra*, nn. 100-101.

[60] Cf. my previous paper (*cit. supra*, n. 2), 454, and *infra*, p. 189. Britonia is the modern Santa Maria de Bretoña, in the village of Pastoriza, near Mondoñedo, province of Lugo, Galicia.

continued from page 178

voyage to Britain in the *Vita* was " eine reine Legende " but few legends are without some basis in fact and the finds of pottery and glass (cf. n. 58 *infra*) have uncovered the basis for this account of Leontius. A. R. Lewis (*art. cit. supra*, n. 55), 284 and n. 151, and in *Northern Seas* (*op. cit. supra*, n. 47), 130 n. 113, thinks the *Vita* refers to a " Portus Britanniae " in the Asturias (= La Coruña [which is in Galicia !]). But the contemporary name for La Coruña was Brigantia, not Britannia (cf. Orosius, *Hist.*, I, 2, 71 and 81, ed. C. Zangemeister, Wien, 1882, 27.1, 29.7). There seems to be a confusion here between the See of *Britonia* (cf. n. 60 below), in Galicia, with dependencies in the Asturias, which was not on the sea, and the port of *Brigantia*, with its lighthouse, mentioned by Orosius [*loc. cit.*], which also possessed a mint (cf. Miles [*op. cit. supra*, n. 47], 127 ff.). They are clearly distinguished in a document of 572-582, *apud* P. David, *Etudes historiques sur la Galice et le Portugal du VIe au XIIe siècle*, Lisbon-Paris, 1947; cf. pp. 44, 32. I fail, furthermore, to see how one can translate the Greek phrase (*Vita S. Johannis Elemosynarii*, ed. H. Gelzer, 19. 15) "τὰς νήσοὺς τῆς βρεττανίας " except as " the islands of Britain " (it is so translated by E. Dawes and N. H. Baynes, *Three Byzantine Saints*, Oxford, 1948, 217). Lewis's argument from the lack of gold-mining in Cornwall and its continuation in Galicia in this period is not conclusive since (1) we lack reliable contemporary evidence for gold-mining saec. VII in either region, and (2) the payment was made in gold *coins* (cf. the " nomisma " of the text), not ingots, and there is no need to suppose these coins were struck locally or from the gold of local mines.

as the famous *Orationale* in Verona.[61] In the seventh century contacts between Spain and Italy were slight. They seem to have been more friendly and more frequent during the pontificate of Gregory the Great than they became later but the relationship seems then to have been orientated from Italy towards Spain and not vice versa.[62] Towards the end of the century the Papacy displays remarkable ignorance of contemporary events in Spain.[63] When we find seventh-century Spanish works, including Isidore, at Bobbio at an early date we have a right to hold that their derivation via Ireland is, *a priori*, quite as probable as their arrival direct from Spain.

The main routes by which Spanish manuscripts left Spain in the seventh century appear to have been via Southern France and via the British Isles. It is interesting to look at the surviving seventh-century manuscripts of Isidore. Of the nine that are generally thought to be of that century one was written in Spain, where it remains, two in Southern France or Spain, two in France—one in an unknown scriptorium, the other probably at Fleury, no less than three at Bobbio and one either in Ireland or at Bobbio.[64]

---

[61] Verona LXXXIX (84); cf. Lowe, *CLA*, IV, 515; J. Vives and J. Claveras, in J. Vives, *Oracional Visigótico* = *Mon. Hisp. Sacra*, Ser. liturg. 1, Barcelona, 1946, xiii-xv, xxxiv ff. J. Serra Vilaró, *San Prospero de Tarragona y sus discipulos refugiados en Italia en el año 711* = *Bibl. Histórica de la Bibl. Balmés*, Ser. II, 16, Barcelona, 1943, takes the legendary *Translatio* of the relics of the martyrs of Tarragona (*BHL*. 3206) too seriously (cf. B. de Gaiffier, in *Analecta Bollandiana* 66 [1948] 315 ff.) but we must suppose some such voyage of Spanish émigrés as he reconstructs in order to explain the journey of the *Orationale* from Spain to Verona via Sardinia. Some MSS. from Spain clearly reached Italy before the Invasion, e.g. the exemplar of Verona LXI (59), for which cf. Lowe, *CLA*, IV, 511. For the (very few) references to Isidore in Italy saec. VII cf. A. E. Anspach in *Miscellanea Isidoriana*, Roma, 1936, 344 (cf. also n. 93 *infra*). The earliest use of Isidore is to be found in the Continuator Prosperi Havnensis *c*. 625 (he uses the *Chronicon*). This was in Northern Italy. The *Chronicon* was also known in 624 to a Frankish author, the so-called Appendix to Marius of Avenches; cf. Mommsen, in *MGH*, *Auct. Ant.*, IX (1892) 267; XI (1894), 397, 489. For an Isidore MS. (of the *Sententiae*) copied at Verona saec. VIII from a Visigothic model cf. *CLA*, IV, 507; B. Bischoff, *art. cit. supra* (n. 6).

[62] Cf. Fontaine, *Culture*, II, 739-41, 842-46; Palol, *Bronces* (*op. cit. supra*, n. 45).

[63] Quiricus, Archbishop of Toledo, died in January, 680 but in September-December, 682 the Pope was still ignorant of any change in the Primatial See of Spain. Cf. R. Aigrain in *Histoire de l'Église*, ed. A. Fliche et V. Martin, V,[2] Paris, 1947, 256; for relations between Spain and the Papacy saec. VII the latest study is that by J. M^a. Lacarra, " La iglesia visigoda en el s. VII y sus relaciones con Roma," in *Le Chiese nei regni dell'Europa occidentale e i loro rapporti con Roma sino all'800* = *Settimane di Studio* VII. 1, Spoleto, 1960, 353-84.

[64] I. In Spain Escorial R. II. 18 (part of the text of the *De natura rerum*; cf. J. Fontaine, *Isidore de Séville, Traité de la nature* = *Bibl. École Hautes Études Hispaniques* 28, Bordeaux, 1960, 20 ff.). II. In Southern France or Spain: (1) St. Gall 226 + Zurich RP 5 + 6, containing fragments of the *Synonyma*, dated by Lowe, *CLA*, VII (1956) 929, saec. VII[2]; (2) Autun 27 + Paris, Bibl. Nat., n.a.l. 1629, the *Quaestiones in Vetus Testamentum* = *CLA*, VI (1953) 727a (saec. VII ex.); cf. also R. P. Robinson, *MSS. 28 and 107 . . . of Autun* = *Mem. Amer. Acad. in Rome* 16, Rome 1939, and Mundó, *art. cit. infra*, n. 68, p. 173, who holds it was probably written in Catalonia, perhaps at Urgell. III. In France, locality unknown: Münster, in Westphalen, Staatsarchiv Msc. VII 2a, *excerpta* from the *De ecclesiasticis officiis* = *CLA*, IX (1959), 1235 (saec. VII ex.); Lowe (ib. vi ff.) remarks of this previously unknown fragment that it is, " unless I err, the oldest Isidore MS. in existence." But its very close resemblance to Bern 219 (*CLA*, VII, 860), pointed out both by Lowe and by Professor Bischoff (*art. cit. supra*, n. 6), would date it saec. VII ex., as the Bern MS. was written shortly before 699-700. Bischoff thinks both MSS. were probably written in, or near, Reims. Lowe points to insular influence in the Bern MS. IV. In France, perhaps Fleury: Paris, Lat. 6400G, the *De natura rerum* = *CLA*, V (1950) 564a (saec. VII-VIII); cf. also *CLA*, VI, xxi; Fontaine, *op. cit.*, 25 ff. The *De officiis* in the same MS. (*CLA*, V, 564b) is only slightly later, according to Bischoff (*art. cit.*). V. At Bobbio: (1) Milan, Ambros. S. 36 sup., part of the *Quaest. in Vetus Test.* =

continued on page 181

A number of manuscripts from Spain no doubt reached French centres by way of Narbonne in Visigothic Septimania, although here again most of the movement of manuscripts in this direction seems to have taken place after the Arabic Invasion. It appears also that in the later part of the seventh century communications between North and South of France were relatively infrequent and that relations with Spain via the Rhône valley were less important than communications by sea from Southern Spain to the Garonne. We may note the presence of numerous Visigothic coins—some, struck at different mints: Tarragona, Mérida, Seville and Toledo, of recent date—in the Bordeaux hoard of *c.* 670.[65] In contrast, the contemporary hoards of La Baugisière (La Vendée) and Buis, in the Rhône valley (*c.* 650), are without Spanish coins and are essentially of local composition.[66] The Buis hoard consists only of Burgundian and Austrasian money, although this includes Merovingian coins from Marseilles and Uzès, near the political border of Septimania. The apparent falling off of communications between North and South is accompanied by a decline of the cities of the Rhône and Moselle valleys and of most of the cities of Septimania.[67] The importance of this region, so evident in the fifth and sixth centuries before the Visigothic capital settled at Toledo *c.* 570, was, therefore, markedly less pronounced in the seventh but valuable manuscripts were still transcribed there and others travelled through it towards the North.[68] The only existing seventh-century manuscript of Isidore's *Synonyma* and one of the two saec. VII manuscripts of his *Quaestiones in Vetus*

---

[65] Cf. P. Le Gentilhomme, *Mélanges de numismatique mérovingienne*, Paris, 1940, 5-51. Unfortunately the evidence of the Bordeaux hoard appears to be open to question in view of the three " Visigothic " forgeries which are supposed to have formed part of it and of the general unreliability of the early nineteenth-century list used by Le Gentilhomme. Cf. Miles (*op. cit. supra*, n. 47), 165; J. Lafaurie in *Revue numismatique*, Ser. 5, 14 (1952), 229-35. Here Lafaurie suggests a date *c.* 700 for the hoard (Le Gentilhomme put forward *c.* 675-77) but in his later *art. cit. supra*, n. 47, p. 255, he returns to *c.* 670. For the restraint with which coins found in hoards should be interpreted as evidence of trade cf. P. Grierson, *art. cit. supra*, n. 42, and in *Moneta e Scambi* (*op. cit.* n. 15 *supra*) 330. We shall await with interest the exhaustive repertory of hoards and isolated finds of Merovingian coins of saec. VI-VII the preparation of which is announced by Lafaurie, ib., 269 n. 68.

[66] Le Gentilhomme, ib., 95-130. Cf. esp. the maps showing the origin of the coins in the La Baugisière and Buis hoards (pp. 98, 101). For the few Visigothic coins of saec. VII[1] found at Wieuwerd and Mons cf. n. 47 *supra*; cf. also the *art.* by J. Lafaurie there cited, esp. 252, 255.

[67] Cf. E. Salin, *La civilisation mérovingienne*, I, Paris, 1949, 429 ff., and (on the increasingly regional character of the economy) 131 ff. For Septimania cf. also A. Dupont (*op. cit., supra*, n. 44), 203 ff., 214 ff., etc.

[68] Cf. A. Mundó, " El Commicus palimpsest Paris Lat. 2269. Amb notes sobre litúrgia i mss. visigòtics a Septimania i Catalunya " in *Liturgica* 1 = *Scripta et Documenta* 7, Montserrat, 1956, 151-275, and also MS. Toulouse 364 + Paris Lat. 8901 (*CLA*, VI, 836), dated *ante* 666-667, transcribed at Albi from what appears to have been a Visigothic exemplar.

---

continued from page 180

CLA, III (1938)**364 (saec. VII); for the identification of the fragment cf. E. Dekkers in *Sacris Erudiri* 9 (1957), 110-14. (2) Vat. Lat. 5765, index of chapters of the *De officiis*; cf. *CLA*, I, 43, corrected by IV, xxi. (3) Milan, Ambros. C. 77 sup., the *Sententiae*, dated in *CLA*, III, 317, saec. VIII, but saec. VII by Beeson, *Isidor-Studien*, 44, and by M. C. Díaz y Díaz, *Index Scriptorum Latinorum Medii Aevi Hispanorum*, Madrid, 1959, 34. VI. Ireland or Bobbio: St. Gall, 1399 a.l. (cf. *infra*, n. 75). For the possible presence of one of the *Versus Isidori* in Florence, Laur., Amiatino I (*CLA*, III, 299, saec. VII-VIII) cf. *infra*, n. 110, and for Paris, Lat. 10910 (*CLA*, V, 608) *infra*, n. 72.

Testamentum were among these codices.[69] Beeson's view was that the manuscripts of Isidore came first to France and, *from there*, were spread to the different parts of Christendom, above all by Irish monks.[70] Le Bras, however, has pointed out that Isidore was well known in the British Isles a century before his works effectively penetrated France. The same comparison can be drawn if we consider the diffusion of the Spanish canonical collections.[71] The main evidence for the knowledge of Isidore in Northern France comes from the *Liber scintillarum* of Defensor of Ligugé (near Poitiers), written *c.* 700.[72] Defensor cites the *Sententiae* many times, the *Differentiae* once, the *Synonyma* frequently and the *De officiis* eleven times.[73] It has only recently been noticed, however, that an unidentified quotation ascribed by Defensor to Jerome is really taken from Pseudo-Isidore, *De ordine creaturarum*, now known to be an Irish work.[74] In view of this contact with Irish learning we may wonder if Defensor did not derive his knowledge of Isidore's genuine works, at least in part, from the not far distant Breton centres in close touch with Ireland.

We have already alluded to a seventh-century manuscript of Isidore, written in Ireland or at Bobbio (cf. Plate XLV). This codex is only known to us from the fragments discovered recently by Dom Dold, Dr. Duft and Professor Bischoff,

---

[69] St. Gall 226 and Autun 27 (cf. *supra*, n. 64). The exemplars of the Münster fragment and of Paris, Lat. 6400G (Fleury) must also have passed through Southern France. Cf. Fontaine, *Isidore, Traité de la nature* (*op. cit. supra*, n. 64), 71 ff., and *idem*, *Culture*, II, 840-41, who, however, seems to me to present too simplified a picture of the evidence when he says (p. 71 n. 1): " C'est *sans doute* [my italics] cette voie qu'ont empruntée également les *Origines* pour se diffuser en Europe."

[70] Beeson, *Isidor-Studien*, 120 ff. In *Classical Philology* 42 (1947) 73, he observes that Spain " furnished Isidore MSS. to Italy and France and probably England, while the author was still living."

[71] Cf. G. Le Bras in *Revue des sciences religieuses* 10 (1930), 246, n. 4; *idem* in *Caratteri del secolo VII* (*op. cit. supra*, n. 39), 897 ff. R. Naz in *Dictionnaire droit Canon* 6 (1954), 69, points out Isidore's apparent ignorance of Gallican canonical collections.

[72] The other instances of use of Isidore in France collected by Anspach (*art. cit. supra*, n. 61), 335 ff., do not amount to much, apart from the use of the *Chronicon* by Ps-Fredegarius (cf. n. 61 *supra*). The most recent editor, J. M. Wallace-Hadrill, *Fredegarii Chronicorum lib. IV*, London, etc., 1960, assumes (p. xxii) that the first " compilator " of this work, a Burgundian, " finished his work in 613-14," but in this case he can hardly have incorporated part of Isidore's *Chronicon*, whose first redaction was only finished in 615 (cf. Mommsen in *Mon. Germ. Hist., Auct. Ant.*, XI, 407 ff.; J. A. de Aldama in *Miscellanea Isidoriana*, Roma 1936, 62 ff.). It seems one must return to Krusch's theory, as modified by W. Levison, in his revised edn. of W. Wattenbach, *Deutschlands Geschichtsquellen im Mittelalter*, Weimar, 1952, I, 109-113, and date the incorporation of Isidore to *c.* 658. It is certainly found in MS. Paris Lat. 10910 (cf. B. Krusch, in *MGH, Script. Rerum Merov.*, II, 9; Mommsen, *loc. cit.*, 398; *CLA*, V, 608), by far the oldest MS. of Fredegarius, written saec. VII-VIII, possibly in Metz (cf. Wallace-Hadrill, xlvii). For earlier use of Isidore's work in Gaul cf. *supra*, n. 61.

[73] Cf. *Defensoris Liber Scintillarum*, ed. H. M. Rochais = *Corpus Christianorum*, Ser. lat. 117, Turnhout, 1957, " Index scriptorum," 250-53. On Defensor cf. P. Lehmann, *art. cit. supra*, n. 39, pp. 863 ff.

[74] Cf. M. C. Díaz y Díaz in *Hispania sacra* 11 (1958), 483. The quotation is in c. lxxii, 19, ed. Rochais, 215. For the *De ordine creaturarum* cf. *supra*, n. 37. According to Díaz y Díaz (*loc. cit.*) the majority of the citations in Defensor not identified by Dom Rochais seem to come from the Latin version of St. John Chrysostom, *De reparatione lapsi* (mentioned by Isidore, *De viris* 19: *PL* 83, 1093). Díaz believes this work was either translated into Latin in Spain saec. VI ex., or entered Western Europe by way of Spain since the whole MS. tradition derives from Spanish texts. The work is present in MSS. that transmit the compilation of Valerius of Bierzo (saec. VII²).

and now collected under the "signatura" St. Gall, 1399 a.1.[75] They represent the only seventh-century manuscript of the *Origines* that survives and one of the earliest Irish manuscripts in existence. It has been much discussed in recent years. While Dr. Duft has ascribed it to Ireland Dr. Lowe has considered that it was "written in an Irish centre, presumably on the Continent, possibly at Bobbio." His two reasons for this judgment are "the script and type of membrane," which "seems parchment, not vellum."[76] He describes the script as "Irish cursive minuscule" and compares it to that of three other manuscripts, Dublin, Trinity College 55 (= Usserianus Primus, which he dates saec. VII in.), Milan, Ambros. C. 26 sup. (Basilius, saec. VII ex.) and Ambros. D. 23 sup. (Orosius, saec. VII).[77] Of these the manuscript whose script is closest to that of the St. Gall Isidore appears to be Usserianus I. Dr. Lowe believes that, like the two Milan manuscripts, it was probably written at Bobbio, one of his main grounds being the "Roman cursive influences in the script," also found in St. Gall 1399 a.1. Professor Bernhard Bischoff, in a personal letter he kindly allows me to quote, points out that, in the early period of Irish script, before it was fully formed, we can equally well suppose cursive or half-cursive models in Ireland as on the Continent and that vellum need not, in this period, have been the only writing material used in Ireland, to the exclusion of parchment. Statistics too, as he points out, show that the transmission of manuscripts from Ireland to the Continent was certainly far more frequent than transmission from Bobbio to St. Gall or to Ireland. Furthermore, there is a very close resemblance between the script of the St. Gall fragments and that of some wax-tablets now in the National Museum, Dublin. These tablets reveal the same "cursive" characteristics as Usserianus I and the Isidore fragments.[78]

---

[75] Cf. A. Dold and J. Duft, *Die älteste irische Handschriften-Reliquie der Stiftsbibliothek St. Gallen mit Texten aus Isidors Etymologien = Anhang von Heft 31 der Texte und Arbeiten nebst einer Erweiterung*, Beuron, 1955, 12 pp., 2 facs.; also L. Bieler, *art. cit. supra*, n. 24, pp. 271 ff.; Lowe, *CLA*, VII (1956), 995. B. Bischoff, *art. cit. infra*. n. 103, p. 17, n. 43, dates it "etwa in die Mitte des VII Jhs," as do Dold and Duft; Lowe dates it merely "saec. VII." (Cf. now Bischoff, *art. cit. supra*, n. 6). My plate reproduces details from the verso of the one surviving folio.

[76] Lowe, *loc. cit.*

[77] Cf. *CLA*, II, 271; III, 312, 328. Professor Bischoff, *apud* T. D. Kendrick *et al.*, *op. cit. supra*, n. 3, p. 113 n. 7, tentatively dates Ambros. D. 23 sup. saec. VII in. Cf. also, on these MSS., L. Bieler in *Speculum* 23 (1948), 501.

[78] There follows a quotation from Professor Bischoff's letter of 22nd February, 1960: "Es ist natürlich schwierig und eher vermessen, in der Frage des Ursprungs des St. Galler Isidor-Fragments eine bestimmte Meinung haben zu wollen. Wenn die Schrift desselben, und auch die Schrift des Cod. Usserianus I 'kursive' Elemente zeigen, so halte ich es für moglich, dass die Iren nicht nur in Bobbio mit Kursive bekannt wurden, sondern dass ein Teil der Schriftwerke, die zu ihnen nach Irland gelangten, in Kursiven oder Halbkursiven geschrieben war und diese Schriften auch wirkten, solange die irische Schrift noch nicht ihren späteren Kanon gefunden hatte. Und auch auf der materiellen Seite des irischen Buchwesens halte ich in der Frühzeit eine Entwicklung und gelegentliches Schwanken für möglich, so dass auch vellum nicht von Anfang an ausschliesslich gebraucht worden sein muss. Statistisch ist die übertragung von Hss. aus Irland auf des Festland gewiss unendlich viel häufiger gewesen als eine Ausstrahlung von Bobbio nach St. Gallen oder nach Irland. Bezüglich der Schrift kommt hinzu, dass auch die Schrift des in einem irischen Torfmoor gefundenen Wachstafelbuches im Ir. Nationalmuseum, Dublin, die gleichen 'kursiven' Züge zeigt, wie Usser I (und wie Isidor), und dass diese Wachstafeln von einem Bobbieser in das irische Moor versenkt worden seien, kann ich nicht glauben."

Professor Bischoff here alludes to the tablets found in a bog at Springmount, Co. Antrim (Plate XLV). They were briefly described by E. C. R. Armstrong and R. A. S. Macalister in 1920,[79] but their importance does not seem to have been generally realized, perhaps because Armstrong and Macalister made no attempt to date them.[80] They may have been thought to have been of roughly the same date as the tablets from Maghera, which seem to be fourteenth-century.[81] These latter tablets contain grammatical notes by some schoolmaster of the time, the Springmount tablets contain Psalms XXX-XXXI (Vulgate numbering) and are evidently monastic in origin. They were found near the site of a medieval monastery.[82] We may hope that Professor Bieler will one day give us a detailed description and publication of these tablets, whose importance is at once clear when they are dated (by Professor Bischoff) in the seventh century. Their existence shows that the cursive elements in the script of the Isidore fragments and of Usserianus I were present in Irish scriptoria at the time these manuscripts were written and earlier, for it certainly seems improbable, as Professor Bischoff observes, that a monk of Bobbio was responsible for sinking the tablets in an Irish moor![83] It seems more reasonable to suppose the Isidore manuscript was written in Ireland than at Bobbio and that it reached St. Gall from Ireland, probably in the ninth century, together with other Irish manuscripts.[84]

Dom Dold and Dr. Duft, in their discussion of the St. Gall fragments, have pointed out that textually the manuscript seems closer to Lindsay's MS. " C " (Leiden, Voss. lat. F.74), of saec. IX *med.*, than to other manuscripts.[85] It would be of great interest to be able to prove the relationship of the St. Gall Isidore to the Leiden MS., for the latter is one of a family of manuscripts which Porzig has shown to derive from the final, longer edition of the *Origines* due to Braulio (*post* 633); this family, Porzig held, only left Spain in the mid-ninth century, and

[79] " Wooden Book with Leaves Indented and Waxed, found near Springmount Bog, Co. Antrim " in *Journal Royal Society Antiquaries Ireland* 50 (1920), 160-166, with facs. Our Plate (II) reproduces the most legible of the tablets. For mentions of wax-tablets in Lives of Irish Saints cf. e.g., Lorcin, *art. cit. infra*, n. 119, 233, n. 82, 236, n. 97.

[80] Armstrong merely remarks (p. 161): " The excellent condition of the wooden leaves and the appearance of the leather straps do not suggest that the book belongs to an early date. It may, however, go back as far as the mediæval period." Macalister does not attempt to date the tablets.

[81] On these cf. J. H. Todd, " Remarks on some Fragments of an Ancient Waxed Table-book, found in a Bog at Maghera, County of Derry, and presented to the Royal Irish Academy by the Rev. J. Spencer Knox, A.M." in *Transactions of the R.I.A.* 21 (1848), Antiquities, 3-15 and Plates 1-3. (I am grateful to Professor Bieler for obtaining for me a microfilm of this paper.) These tablets are also now in the National Museum, Dublin, but they are, as Professor Bieler kindly confirms in a recent letter, so thoroughly darkened that no script is now discernible. On the basis of Todd's plates Professor Bischoff tells me he would agree with Todd's dating of the tablets saec. XIV.

[82] Macalister (*art. cit.*, 163-65) attempted a transcription of the tablets. The text has some *Vetus Latina* readings. For the site cf. ib., 160.

[83] Cf. *supra*, n. 78.

[84] Dr. Duft (*op. cit. supra*, n. 29), 27 ff., holds that most of the Irish manuscripts at St. Gall arrived at this time, or later.

[85] Dom Dold (*art. cit. supra*, n. 75), 6, notes " höchstens eine schwache Verwandtschaft " between the two manuscripts. Cf. Dr. Duft, ib., 9. The Leiden Ms. is divided into two halves (cf. W. M. Lindsay, *Isidori . . . Etymologiarum sive Originum libri XX*, Oxford, 1911, I, vii). The second half (ff. 107r col. II sq.), containing *lib.* XI, which concerns us here, was written, as Professor Bischoff kindly informs me in a letter of 6th January, 1961, by several hands in the style of Fulda, and therefore presumably *at* Fulda.

travelled via Italy.[86] Unfortunately the fragments that survive of the St. Gall manuscript are not sufficient for us to be able to reach a definite conclusion on this point. Since Porzig has queried the reliability of Lindsay's collation of the Leiden manuscript (which was communicated to him by Kuebler)[87] I have checked Lindsay's edition for the relevant passage (*Orig.* XI, i, 40-53) with a microfilm of the manuscript. Kuebler's collation seems, for this passage at least, fairly accurate, but there are some slips and, because of this, one or two cases not noticed by Dom Dold—who was relying on Lindsay—when " C " and St. Gall 1399 a.1. agree.[88]

The Anglo-Saxons played a very considerable part in the diffusion of Isidore's works but it seems they came first to Ireland. For the *Origines* we have not only the St. Gall fragments but also important Bobbio manuscripts of the eighth century that represent the earlier and shorter recension.[89] The *Differentiae*, Isidore's first work, soon reached Ireland. It, and the *De ortu et obitu patrum*, are quoted by Irish authors before 661 and it has been suggested that an important interpolation in *c.* 70 of the *De ortu* is due to an Irish editor.[90] The case of the *De natura rerum* is interesting; owing to the new critical edition by Professor Jacques Fontaine it is possible to discuss it at some length. The editor has given us in his introduction a very careful study of the diffusion of the work in pre-Carolingian Europe.[91] It reached Fleury in the seventh century and was soon copied there in a manuscript still preserved (Paris, Bibl. Nat., Lat. 6400G).[92] The first author to quote the work (or rather the *Epistula* of Sisebut attached to it) has, however, until recently been thought to be Aldhelm of Malmesbury, in his *Epistula ad Acircium*, which can be dated between 685 and 705.[93] Professor Fontaine has shown that the existing manuscripts should

---

[86] Cf. W. Porzig, " Die Rezensionen der Etymologiae des Isidorus von Sevilla " in *Hermes* 72 (1937), 129-170 (esp. 167).

[87] Ibid., 130; cf. Lindsay, *loc. cit.* (n. 85 *supra*).

[88] Cf. *Orig.* XI, i. 46 (Lindsay, vol. II, no pagination, line 11): " vocant graeci "; ib. 52 (line 15): " confringant " for " confrangant." Cf. Dold-Duft, *art. cit.*, 5.

[89] Cf. MS. Ambros. L. 99 sup (= *CLA*, III, 353, " written doubtless at Bobbio "); cf. also F. Bartoloni, " Note paleografiche " in *Bulletino dell'Istituto Storico Italiano per il Medio Evo e Archivio Muratoriano* 62 (1950), 141, 152 n. 1. For MS. Vat. Lat. 5765 cf. n. 34 *supra*, esp. the *art.* of Natale.

[90] I refer not to the later Irish work, *De ortu et obitu patrum*, an imitation of Isidore's *De ortu*, written in Germany saec. VIII^2 (cf. R. E. McNally, " Isidoriana " in *Theol. Studies* 20 (1959), 436, n. 28) but to the interpolation in c. 70 of the original work suggested by M. C. Díaz y Díaz, " Die spanische Jakobus-Legende bei Isidor von Sevilla " in *Historisches Jahrbuch* 77 (1958), 467-72, esp. 469 n. 18 (cf., however, the seemingly conclusive objections raised by Bischoff, *art. cit. supra*, n. 6). For early use of the *Differentiae* and *De ortu* in Ireland cf. n. 38 *supra*; P. Grosjean, *art. cit. supra*, n. 37, pp. 94 ff.

[91] Fontaine, *op. cit. supra*, n. 64, " La diffusion du ' De natura rerum ' en Europe de Sisebut à Charlemagne," 69-83, illustrated by a map.

[92] Cf. n. 64 *supra*.

[93] Fontaine dates it 685, citing (p. 74, n. 2) R. Ehwald, in his edition of Aldhelm, *MGH*, *Auct. Ant.* XV, Berlin, 1919, xviii. (The passage citing Sisebut is on p. 80.) Ehwald suggests *c.* 685, M. Manitius, *Geschichte der lateinischen Literatur im Mittelalter*, I, Munich, 1911, 136, *c.* 695. The only limiting dates in external history are the accession of King Aldfrith (= Acircius) of Northumbria in 685 and Aldhelm's becoming Bishop of Sherborne in 705. I do not myself think we can date the *Epistula* as early as 685 since it uses the *Ars Grammatica* ascribed (probably falsely) to Julian of Toledo (cf. n. 30 *supra*) and this was

continued on page 186

be divided into those containing the (original) short recension, the two of the " recension moyenne," with the addition of c.48, and the long recension, containing c.44 and the " mystic " passage in c.1.[94] Chapter 48 was probably added by Isidore himself but the long recension, with its two additions, appears to be the work of a cleric outside Spain but familiar with Isidore's style and methods. It is contained in the Anglo-Saxon and German group of manuscripts and Fontaine ascribes it to Northumbria.[95] The fact that the insular group of manuscripts of the long recension sometimes agrees with the Spanish MS. Escorial R. II. 18 (saec. VII) in presenting a reading preferable to that of the French manuscripts of the short recension makes Fontaine believe that England " a reçu originellement le traité dans une version plus proche de l'archétype, et peut-etre antérieure aux MSS. wisigothiques qui sont à l'origine des groupes français."[96] Fontaine considers four possible routes from Spain to England, two of which would take the work via Ireland, the direct route by sea to Ireland and the indirect way thither via France. Like Beeson he is more willing to consider a transmission via the Irish continental foundations than one direct to Ireland itself,[97] and he thinks Aldhelm's use of the work need not have been due to an Irish exemplar reaching Malmesbury.[98] It is true, of course, that by 685, the earliest possible date for Aldhelm's *Epist. ad Acircium*, English pilgrims were visiting France and Italy and returning laden with books. Aldhelm himself visited Rome in 692-93.[99] But long before he visited Rome and for some sixteen years before he went to Canterbury in 671 to study under Theodore and Hadrian, Aldhelm had been the pupil of the Irish Máel-dubh.[100] His whole style was formed on Irish models, he appears to have corresponded all his life with a number of Irish scholars or scholars trained in Ireland—one of whom, at least, reveals a knowledge of the *De natura rerum*, and recent investigations have disclosed to some extent the measure in which he was indebted to Irish scholar-

[94] Fontaine, *op. cit.*, 19-45.

[95] Ibid., 79 ff.

[96] Ib., 77. He continues: " Ce fait s'expliquerait bien par la transmission en Angleterre d'une ' édition irlandaise ' *sans doute* [my italics] continentale et antérieure à la diffusion du traité dans les *scriptoria* de la France septentrionale, attestée par nos témoins français." Cf., for another view, B. Bischoff, *art. cit.* (*supra*, n. 6): " Möchte ich die Anschauung vertreten, dass die direkte Verbindung von Spanien nach Irland keine geringe Rolle spielte." Cf. also J. M. Wallace-Hadrill, " Rome and the Early English Church: Some questions of Transmission " in *Le Chiese* (*op. cit. supra*, n. 63, VII, 2), 537 ff.

[97] Cf. nn. 69, 70, 96 *supra*. For Fontaine's discussion of the routes cf. *op. cit.*, 75-78 and his map. The other two routes he suggests as possible are that direct from Spain to England (for Sherborne read Malmesbury; Aldhelm clearly knew the *De natura rerum* before he began his brief episcopate in 705) and that through France and across the Channel.

[98] Ibid., 78.

[99] Cf. Duckett, *op. cit. infra*, n. 100, pp. 69-72.

[100] Cf. E. S. Duckett, " Aldhelm of Malmesbury " in her *Anglo-Saxon Saints and Scholars*, New York, 1947, 3-97.

continued from page 185

probably not written before 687 at the earliest. Aldhelm also cites other works of Isidore; cf. Ehwald, " Index locorum," 545, and J. D. A. Ogilvy, *Books known to Anglo-Latin Writers from Aldhelm to Alcuin (670-804)* = *Med. Acad. of America, Studies and Doc. 2*, Cambridge (Mass.), 1936, 48. Fontaine does not discuss the citation of the *De natura rerum*, c. 17. 1, *c.* 700 by the Anonymous *Cosmographia* of Ravenna, c. 5, ed. M. Pinder and G. Parthey, Berlin, 1860, 13.8 = ed. J. Schnetz, *Itineraria Romana*, II, Leipzig, 1940, 5.

ship.[101] It is of interest, therefore, to note that an anonymous Irish grammatical work, contemporary with Aldhelm and possibly earlier than the *Epistula ad Acircium*, used several works of Isidore, notably the *Differentiae*.[102] This grammatical work appears to represent the same teaching that Aldhelm would have received orally from Máel-dubh.[103] There can be no doubt that it makes direct use of the *De natura rerum*. A few parallel passages will suffice:

De natura rerum, III.1 (Fontaine, p. 183)	*Anonymus ad Cuimnanum* (MS. St. Paul in Kärnten 25.2.16, f.29r, col. 1)
Feria quasi a fando dicta quasi faria, eo quod in creatione mundi per singulos dies dixit Deus fiat; . . .	feriae a fando dictae quasi fari eo quod in creatione mundi per singulos dixit Deus quassi fando fiat . . .
Ibid., 3-4 (p. 185)	Ibid.
3. Quartum ab stella Mercurii quam quidam candidum circulum dicunt. Quintum ab stella Iovis quam Phaeton dicunt. Sextum a Veneris stella quam Luciferum asserunt, quae inter omnia sidera plus lucis habet. Septimum ab stella Saturni, quae sexto caelo locata triginta annis fertur explere cursum suum.	IIII. a stella Mercorii quam quidam candidum circulum dicunt. V. a stella Iovis quam Foeton dicunt. VI. a Veneris stella quam luciferum adserunt quae inter omnia sidera plus *lucem*[a] habet. VII. a stella Saturni.
4. Proinde autem gentiles ex his septem stellis nomina dierum dederunt, eo quod per eosdem aliquid sibi effici extimarent, dicentes habere ex aere ignem, ex sole spiritum, ex luna corpus, ex Mercurio linguam et sapientiam, ex Venere voluptatem, ex Marte fervorem, ex Iove temperantiam, ex Saturno tarditatem.	proinde autem ex his stellis gentiles nomina feriis debere eo quod per *easdem*[b]aliquid sibi effici *exaestimarent*[c] dicentes habere *ex aerae ignem*[d], ex sole spiritum, ex luna corpus, ex Mercorio linguam et sapientiam, ex Venere *voluntatem*[e], ex Marce fervorem, ex Iove temperantiam, ex Saturno tarditatem.

a. lucem *sicut* " ASB " *inter codd.* Isid. b. easdem *sicut* " B^2V " c. exestimarent " B^1," existim- *plures codd.* d. ex aere ignem *hab.* " E^2LASB," *om. cett.* e. voluntatem " VAS."

---

[101] The most important of his Irish correspondents was Cellanus of Péronne (cf. Ehwald's edn., *cit. supra*, n. 93, 498 ff.), of the English trained by the Irish, King Aldfrith of Northumbria (cf. n. 93 *supra*) and Eahfrith (Ehwald, 486-94). For the " Scottus " who used Isidore's work cf. *infra*, n. 109. P. Grosjean has recently demonstrated Aldhelm's use of the *Hisperica Famina*; cf. his *art. cit. supra*, n. 20, pp. 66 ff.

[102] Professor Bischoff (cf. n. 103 *infra*) dates this Irish grammatical work late seventh-century.

[103] Cf. on this work B. Bischoff, " Eine verschollene Einteilung der Wissenschaft," in *Archives d'histoire doctrinale et littéraire du moyen age* 25 (1958), 5-20, esp. 14-20. It is addressed to Cuimnanus and hence Professor Bischoff has called it " Anonymus ad Cuimnanum." The only complete MS. is St. Paul in Kärnten 25.2.16 (Anglo-Saxon, saec. VIII[1]). I am very grateful to Professor Bischoff for allowing me to use his transcript of this manuscript. His text will appear in the series *Scriptores latini Hiberniae*. I must also thank Professor Fontaine for lending me his edition of the *De natura rerum* in page-proof. Apart from the *De natura rerum* and the *Differentiae*, the *Anon. ad Cuimnanum* uses Isidore's *Origines* and *De officiis ecclesiasticis*.

We find from this comparison that in the seventh century the *De natura rerum* of Isidore had become a " manual of cosmography " not only, as Fontaine says, in Southern England but in Ireland.[104] Not long after, it was known to Bede and it seems more than probable that it came to him, too, via Ireland. C. W. Jones has pointed out the dependence of the Northumbrian schools, for the *Computus* in particular, on " Irish knowledge and methods." He observes that " Bede's works show that Northumbrian education owed comparatively little to Rome and the Augustinian mission. . . . Except for those works which Bede expressly assembled for the composition of his *History*, . . . I can find no indication of a stream of literature from the South which in any way equals the obvious stream from Ireland."[105] The Irish, in their turn, drew heavily on Isidore and their *Computus* serves to supplement his writings, especially *Orig*. V-VI, but also the *De natura rerum*, which is quoted at length in their manuscripts.[106] Whether Ireland originally received the work in one or other of the " editions " distinguished by Professor Fontaine remains uncertain for the present; the variants we have noted in the *Anonymus ad Cuimnanum* seem to correspond to the " long recension " (which includes MSS. " ASB " and contaminated " V " and " L ")[107] but they are not of sufficient importance to be decisive. Fontaine, while holding that the long recension comes from Northumbria, already suggested the possibility of its being the fruit of Irish erudition, perhaps by Adamnán of Iona.[108] We know that the continental Irish, at least, possessed the original short recension.[109] Aldhelm and Bede appear to have used the same edition or the " recension moyenne." Given the fact of Irish influence on both these authors and the presence, now established, of the treatise in Ireland saec. VII, we may reasonably conclude that Ireland received the work before England, no doubt in one of the two earlier editions, transmitted it unchanged to Malmesbury and Northumbria where, if not in Ireland itself, an Irish scholar or a scholar trained in Irish erudition produced the long recension which was taken by English missionaries from England to Germany in the eighth century.[110]

---

[104] Cf. Fontaine, *op. cit.*, 75. We may note the insertion of extracts from the *Sententiae* of Isidore, under the heading *De natura rerum*, in the *Collectio Hibernensis* (700-725); Anspach (*art. cit.* n. 61 *supra*, p. 328) and Bischoff (*art. cit.* n. 6 *supra*) think this might be due to the presence of both works in one MS. (as, e.g., Paris, Bibl. Nat., Lat. 6413).

[105] C. W. Jones, *Bedae Opera de temporibus* = *Med. Acad. America, Publ.* 41, Cambridge (Mass.), 1943, 111 ff.

[106] Cf. Jones, *op. cit.*, 130, and 394 ff. (from MS. Bern 417, saec. IX).

[107] Cf. Fontaine, *op. cit.*, the " stemma codicum," p. 70 bis.

[108] Ibid., 80.

[109] Cf. ib., 72 ff., 76, referring to MS. Clm 14300 (= *CLA*, IX [1959] 1294, saec. VIII-IX), which Fontaine associates with the circle of Virgil of Salzburg, and to MS. Ambros. H. 150 inf., from Bobbio, saec. IX in. A " Scottus " in correspondence with Aldhelm also used the work (*MGH*, *epist.* III, Berlin, 1892, 237.21, cited by Fontaine, 75 n. 3). The letter is dated between 688 and 705.

[110] One of the manuscripts of the long recension (Fontaine's " A " = Basel F. III. 15f. = *CLA*, VII [1956] 848, saec. VIII) was written in England in Anglo-Saxon minuscule and reached Fulda " at an early date." Three others (Fontaine's " FWZ ") were almost certainly written at Fulda saec. VIII. Isidore was, of course, well represented at Wearmouth-Jarrow (cf. Ogilvy, *op. cit. supra*, n. 93, pp. 47 ff.; M. L. W. Laistner, " The Library of the Venerable Bede " in *Bede, His Life* [*op. cit. supra*, n. 40], 237-66) but he does not seem to have been greatly prized there as an authority (cf. Laistner, 256; Jones, *op. cit. supra*, n. 105, p. 131, on which cf. Fontaine, *op. cit.*, 79 n. 1 and J. M. Wallace-Hadrill, *art. cit.* [n. 96 *supra*], 544 ff.). Bede used Isidore, *Versus* vii, in his *Epist.* 3, 12, ed. Jones, *op. cit.*, 312, and the same verse appears in Codex Amiatinus (= *CLA*, III, 299, saec. VII-VIII); cf. Beeson, *Isidor-Studien*, 144.

A discussion of the transmission of other works of Isidore will have to await the critical editions of his other writings, some of which are already in an advanced state of preparation.[111] In my previous paper at Oxford I enumerated certain early instances where he is used by the Irish. Professor H. Bober has recently drawn my attention to another instance where an Irish work of 689 appears to use him.[112] In fact it can be said that Isidore is omnipresent in the Irish writings of the late seventh, eighth and ninth centuries.[113]

From what part of Spain did the works I have mentioned reach Ireland? From what I have said it appears they often came direct, not via Bobbio or via England. Some may have come from Southern Spain but it seems likely more came via Galicia. I have already alluded to Britonia, a Celtic See in Galicia, probably founded from Brittany, whose existence is attested from the late sixth century onwards but which may have been founded in the fifth.[114] With its Celtic origin and important monastery it may have played the part of intermediary.[115] Its first bishop, who is known to us, has, however, the Brittonic, Welsh or, more probably, Breton (not very probably Irish) name of Mailoc, and the names of his successors that appear among the lists of episcopal signatures at Spanish Councils in the seventh century are not clearly Celtic.[116] The suggestion, tentatively advanced by S. Ruiz, that Mailoc is identical with a North British

---

[111] Cf. my paper *cit. supra*, n. 6, esp. Section II.

[112] This work is found in MS. Clm 14456 (saec. IX[1]), on which cf. C. W. Jones, *Bedae Pseudepigrapha: Scientific Writings falsely attributed to Bede*, New York-London, 1939, 48 ff., 125.

[113] Cf. e.g., the way Isidore is used in the " Reichenau school book," i.e., MS. St. Paul in Kärnten 25.2.31b, saec. IX, noted by B. Boyer, *apud* J. W. Thompson, *The Medieval Library*[2], New York, 1957, 692 ff. F.2v of this Irish MS. has an extract from *Orig.* II, xxviii. Place-names in the MS., as R. Flower, *The Irish Tradition*, London, 1947, 28, points out, indicate North Leinster as the district of its composition. Flower (p. 40) holds " our wandering Leinster scholar " belonged to the circle of Sedulius Scottus.

[114] The first bishop known to us is Mailoc, who signed the Acts of the Second Council of Braga in 572; P. David, *Études historiques* (*op. cit.* n. 57 *supra*), 60, suggests that he is identical with the Maliosus (see unknown) of Braga I (561). Cf. for these Councils, the critical edition by C. W. Barlow, *Martini Episcopi Bracarensis Opera Omnia = Amer. Acad. Rome, Papers and Monographs* 12, New Haven, 1950, 115.27, 123.21. Professor K. Jackson (cf. n. 116 *infra*) tells me, however, that the difference between the two names is too considerable for them both to indicate the same person. As no Councils were held (as far as we know) in the Suevic kingdom before 561 we have no means of knowing whether the See of Britonia existed in the fifth century.

[115] Cf. the references in my Oxford paper, 454, and J. Vives, *Inscripciones cristianas de la España romana y visigoda*, Barcelona, 1942, n. 359.

[116] I am very grateful to Mrs. N. K. Chadwick (Cambridge), Professor K. Jackson (Edinburgh) and Dr. Melville Richards (Liverpool) for answering questions as to the names of the Bishops of Britonia. Apart from Mailoc the only name which Dr. Richards thinks might be Celtic is Bela (who signed the Acts of Braga III in 675; cf. *PL* 84, 592). Dr. Richards connects Bela with the Welsh *rhy-fel* " war " and such names as *Belinos* (personal name) and *Belisama* (river-name). Mrs. Chadwick has pointed out to me that the name *Beli* occurs in various medieval Welsh texts, e.g., a pedigree (saec. X[1]) in the Harleian Genealogies (A. W. Wade-Evans, *Nennius's History of the Britons*, London, 1938, 101) and the entries in the Cambrian Annals, s.a. 613, 627, 722, 750 (*Beli* or *Belyn*); cf. Wade-Evans, 89, 92 ff. Mrs. Chadwick also refers to the heathen Celtic god *Belenus*, on whom cf. esp. M. Ihm, in Pauly-Wissowa, *Realencyclopädie*, III, 1, Stuttgart, 1897, 199-201. The name of the earlier priest of Britonia, Mactericus (653; cf. *PL* 84, 429D) also has elements that Mrs. Chadwick thinks might be paralleled in Celtic forms.

prince, the brother of Gildas, is quite unconvincing.[117] There is no need, however, to make our belief in the connection between Spain and the British Isles depend on the role possibly played by Britonia.[118] The more one studies late seventh-century Spain the more important Galicia appears. Its monasticism had interesting points of contact with that of Ireland. For the Galician, as for the Irish, ascetic, "se faire moine implique se mettre à l'étude des lettres."[119] The Galician Saints, Fructuosus of Braga, Valerius of Bierzo, seem at times Irish saints transplanted.[120] Many years ago Zimmer compared the type of episcopal life lived by St. Martin of Tours with that of Early Christian Ireland.[121] More recently Professor G. B. Ladner has observed that " Martin of Braga's position [saec. VI²] as ' monastic bishop ' and the subsequent development of monasticism in Galicia makes one wonder whether there may be at least parallelism between such Spanish phenomena and the abbot-bishops of fifth-, sixth-, and seventh-century Britain and Ireland. Could the monastic organization of the Irish Church," he goes on to ask, " still rather enigmatic as to its origins, be a peculiarly inverted adaptation to Celtic rural clan society of the western Mediterranean and Gallic,

---

[117] Cf. S. Ruiz in *Dict. hist. géo. ecclés.* X, Paris, 1938, 768, following the earlier suggestion of J. Pérez de Urbel, *Los monjes españoles*, I, Madrid, 1933, 191 ff. The *Vita Gildae* of Vitalis of Rhuys (saec. XI)—quite unreliable anyhow as a historical source—says of Mailoc that he founded a monastery, "Lyuhes, in pago Elmail " = Lowes, in Ewael, Radnorshire (cf. *MGH, Auct. Ant.*, XIII, 91.22); on the *Vita* cf. F. Lot, *Mélanges d'histoire bretonne* (*VIᵉ-XIᵉ siècle*), Paris, 1907, 207-66 and, on Gildas's family, ib., 262 ff.

[118] E. Bishop, in *The Book of Cerne*, ed. A. B. Kuypers, Cambridge, 1902, 280, already remarked ". . . . the ' Celtic ' See of Bretoña . . . suggests itself as a means of communication with the Irish Church." Dom L. Gougaud in *Dict. archéol. chrét. et liturgie*, II, 2, Paris, 1910, 2293, disagreed, observing " rien ne prouve que cette colonie celtique ait entretenu des relations avec l'Irlande ni même avec la Bretagne," and Bishop withdrew his suggestion (in *Liturgica Historica*, Oxford, 1918, 181). I would not now be inclined to place as much emphasis on Britonia as I did in my Oxford paper. H. Glunz, *Britannien und Bibeltext = Kölner Anglistische Arbeiten* 12, Leipzig, 1930, 77, n. 38, 88, speaks of direct Irish influence on Spanish Biblical texts, coming through Galicia. L. J. Hopkin-James, *The Celtic Gospels, their Story and their Text*, London, 1934, lxiii, is more cautious.

[119] The formula is that of A. Lorcin, " La vie scolaire dans les monastères d'Irlande aux Vᵉ-VIIᵉ siècles " in *Revue du moyen âge latin* 1 (1945), 221-36, at 229. Whence did the Irish monks derive their passion for knowledge ? It is hardly a universal accompaniment of the monastic vocation and was certainly not derived from Egypt, though it was from there that Irish forms of asceticism ultimately came (cf., on this crucial difference between the two countries, F. Henry, *Irish Art*, London, 1940, 34; Lorcin, *loc. cit.*). No doubt British monasticism, in its turn influenced by Lérins, was influential here (cf. J. Ryan, *Irish Monasticism, Origins and Early Development*, London, etc., 1931, 107-116; in *Le Chiese* [*op. cit.* n. 63 *supra*], p. 586, he states his belief that " the Irish Monastic system in fact derives directly from Lérins "). Zimmer (*art. cit.* n. 48 *supra*, and elsewhere) argued that Irish culture and scholarship derived from Gallic scholars of saec. V. I do not think we can exclude the possibility of Spanish influence arriving later than this. Dom Justo Pérez de Urbel (*op. cit.*, n. 117 *supra*, I, 377), speaking of the Spain of saec. VII, observes with reason: " Era tan grande la curiosidad de aquellos hombres del s. VII, que dondequiera que brillaba un espíritu superior, no tardaba en aparecer un montón de discipulos." The words could equally well be applied to Ireland in the same century.

[120] Pérez de Urbel, *op. cit.*, II, 17, already remarked that St. Fructuosus " tiene todas las predilecciones topográficas del monje celta." Even if the *Vita Fructuosi*, as M. C. Díaz y Díaz in *Rev. española de teología* 17 (1957), 36, points out, is an unreliable document, it is certainly saec. VII. It is interesting that Fructuosus is here described as being fond of founding monasteries in islands off the Galician coast and off Cadiz (cf. ed. Nock, *cit. supra*, n. 10, 97, 115); cp. the Irish habit of founding monasteries on all but inaccessible islands such as Skellig Michael. Fructuosus, like St. Brendan and other Irish saints, " had a great inclination for sailing on the sea " (" et dum multa illi intentio esset navigandi in mare," Nock, 97).

[121] H. Zimmer, *art. cit. supra*, n. 48 (1909), 558 ff.

originally urban, fusion of monasticism and clericate . . . ? "[122] If, however, as Professor Ladner seems to imply, Spanish monasticism may have exerted an influence on that of Ireland in the early period, later on Irish monasticism certainly influenced that of Galicia. Professor C. J. Bishko holds that the " Galician penitential system " is " probably Irish-inspired." According to him its " establishment in the province hardly antedates 650 "[123]; it may well have been associated with an attempt, in the generations immediately after the death of St. Fructuosus of Braga (*c.* 665), "to 'monasticize' the entire Church of Galicia under abbot-bishops and monastically living priests."[124] The Sancta Communis Regula, a monastic federation of houses round Braga, and stretching North-east to Bierzo, near Astorga, under the control of the abbot-bishop of Dumium and Metropolitan of Braga, resembles the Irish association of houses under the control of the successor of St. Colmkille, the Abbot (though never Bishop) of Iona, later of Kells.[125] If Irish art influenced the later art of Spain it may have been through Galicia, a region whose peculiar form of monasticism and collections of monastic rules had considerable influence on the later monasteries of Spain.[126]

But if Galicia was in contact with Ireland it was also in close touch with the East and with the great cultural centres of Spain.[127] The works of Isidore reached Braga almost, if not quite, as rapidly as they travelled to Saragossa and Toledo.[128] The relations between Braulio of Saragossa, appointed by Isidore " editor " of the *Origines*, and Fructuosus of Braga were close. We know of books sent from Saragossa to Braga.[129] A recent editor of Braulio's *Vita S. Emiliani* believes that it is possible that " all the manuscripts preserved go back to the one archetype copy sent by Braulio to Galicia at St. Fructuosus's request."[130]

---

[122] G. B. Ladner, *The Idea of Reform, its Impact on Christian Thought and Action in the Age of the Fathers*, Cambridge (Mass.), 1959, 396.

[123] C. J. Bishko in *Amer. Journal Philol.* 59 (1948), 394. The distinction between the " predominant Spanish or Visigothic monastic tradition " and Galician monasticism is stressed by Bishko in *Speculum* 23 (1948), 579.

[124] Ladner, *op. cit.*, 395 ff., citing, *inter alia*, Bishko's unpublished thesis, *Spanish Monasticism in the Visigothic Period*, Ph.D. Diss., Harvard, 1937. The *Regula communis* attributed to Fructuosus (*PL* 87, 1111-30) is not by him but by a later saec. VII author, according to Bishko, *art. cit. infra*, n. 125, 515; his view is accepted by M. C. Díaz y Díaz, *Index scriptorum* (*op. cit.*, n. 64 *supra*, n. 314).

[125] On the Galician federation cf. C. J. Bishko, " Gallegan pactual monasticism in the repopulation of Castile " in *Estudios dedicados a Menéndez Pidal*, 2, Madrid, 1951, 513-31.

[126] Cf. Bishko, *art. cit. supra*, n. 125 and in *Amer. Jour. Philol.* 59 (1948), 388. G. Fink, in *Hispania sacra* 5 (1952), 387 and n. 19, mentioned possible relations between Galicia and the British Isles and announced a forthcoming study of the subject (which has not, as far as I know, yet been published) to be based on Irish and Spanish manuscripts. J. Guilmain, " Zoomorphic Decoration and the Problem of the Sources of Mozarabic Illumination " in *Speculum* 35 (1960), 17-38, argues, not altogether convincingly, that much zoomorphic decoration in manuscripts from León and Castile comes from models, " for the most part, Franco-insular derivatives of Hiberno-Saxon archetypes." J. Camón Aznar (*art. cit.* n. 45 *supra*), 28 ff., believes in a " direct inspiration " of Mozarabic illumination by Irish models.

[127] For Eastern influence in Galicia cf. *supra*, n. 46; A. Mundó, " Il Monachesimo nella penisola fino al sec. VII. Questioni ideologiche e letterarie," in *Il Monachesimo* (*op. cit. supra*, n. 19), 86; J. Pérez de Urbel (*op. cit.*, *supra*, n. 117), I, 430,440.

[128] Cf. Anspach, *art. cit. supra*, n. 61, 326.

[129] Cf. J. Madoz, *Epistolario de San Braulio de Zaragoza*, Madrid, 1941, 48, 186-206.

[130] L. Vazquez de Parga, *S. Braulionis Vita S. Emiliani*, Madrid, 1943, xviii ff. The more recent edition by I. Cazzaniga in *Bolletino per la preparazione della edizione nazionale dei classici greci e latini*, N.S. 3 (1954), 22-40, was not available to me.

It seems probable that books travelling from Spain to Ireland would be most immediately welcomed in the South, in the monasteries of Munster and Leinster that have given us most of the earlier theology of the Irish Church, especially, perhaps, in the monastery of St. Carthach at Les Mór, associated with a group of scholars whose existence has recently been revealed to us by Père Grosjean and that included Lathcen of Clonfertmulloe (+ 661), who certainly used one of Isidore's works.[131] It is perhaps not accidental that Les Mór was one of the very few places in Ireland where what may be called a " double monastery " existed, that is, in this case, two houses, one of monks and one of nuns, side by side and under the same direction, though strictly separated.[132] Some, at least, of the Galician monasteries of the Sancta Communis Regula we have mentioned, for which the *Regula communis* (saec. VII[2]), wrongly attributed to St. Fructuosus, legislates, appear to have included monks and nuns in a much closer organization than that intended by Isidore or the Second Council of Seville (619).[133] They seem, however, to have had separate buildings.[134] It would not be surprising to find Spanish influence at work is Lismore in County Waterford. The monastery had been founded by St. Carthach in 636 when he was forced to abandon his earlier foundation of Rathan, further north, because of his adherence to the Roman method of calculating Easter.[135] Those who thought as he did were called by their opponents " Romani "[136] and, for spiritual as well as geographical reasons, they probably kept in closer touch with the Continent than the adherents of the Celtic Easter in Northern Ireland. It is significant that the letter of Calmanus (Colman ?) to Feradach, recently discussed by Professor Bischoff, should inform his " filius eruditissimus " of his acquisition " a Romanis " of a large number of manuscripts, containing, among other things, much improved texts of Sedulius and of Isidore's *De officiis ecclesiasticis*.[137] Professor Bischoff interprets the " Romani " of the text to mean Southern Irish in communion

---

[131] Cf. Grosjean (*art. cit. supra*, n. 37), and my Oxford paper (*cit. supra*, n. 2), 455 n. 3.

[132] Cf. *Vitas SS. Hiberniae*, ed. C. Plummer, Oxford, 1910, I, 197.

[133] Cf. the *Regula Communis* (*cit. supra*, n. 124), several of whose chapters apply to men and women. On the significance of this cf. I. Herwegen, *Das Pactum des hl. Fruktuosus von Braga* = Kirchenrechtliche Abhandl. 40, Stuttgart 1907, 59 (dom Herwegen later modified this view in *Revue bénédictine* 29 [1912] 97); S. Hilpisch, *Die Doppelklöster, Enstehung und Organisation* = Beiträge zur Geschichte des alten Mönchtums und des Benediktinerordens 15, Münster i. W. 1928, 52-55, and W. S. Porter, " Early Spanish Monasticism " in *Laudate* 10 (1932), 164.

[134] Cf. the two monasteries under the same direction and close together near Cadiz mentioned in the *Vita Fructuosi*, ed. Nock (*cit. supra*, n. 10), 115 ff. There is a good description of the different types of double monastery in Spain in J. Fernández Alonso, *La cura pastoral en la España romanovisigoda* = *Publicaciones del Instituto español de Estudios eclesiásticos, Monografías* 2, Roma, 1955, 492-97.

[135] Plummer (*cit. supra*, n. 132), xlv, n. 3 and Grosjean, *art. cit.*, n. 37 *supra*, 72. Cf., however, another explanation of St. Carthach's leaving Rathan in Ryan, *Irish Monasticism*, 327.

[136] Cf. J. F. Kenney, *Sources for the Early History of Ireland*, I, New York, 1929, 249.

[137] Cf. B. Bischoff, " Il Monachesimo " (*art. cit. supra*, n. 36), 128 ff.; *idem*, *art. cit. supra*, n. 6. There is a partial edition of the text, from MS. Bruxelles, Bibl. Royale 5665, by the Baron de Reiffenberg in *Bulletin de l'Acad. Royale des Sciences et Belles-Lettres de Bruxelles* 10 (1843), 368. The letter is not exactly dated but the cultural situation, as Professor Bischoff says, indicates an early period, at least saec. VIII. Fr. R. E. McNally, " *Dies Dominica*: Two Hiberno-Latin Texts " in *Mediæval Studies* 22 (1960), 355-61, has recently pointed to the use of the *De officiis ecclesiasticis* in two Celtic, probably Irish, documents of *c.* 800 or saec. IX[1], preserved in MSS. with Breton associations.

with Rome. If he is right we have here a clear instance of Southern Ireland transmitting manuscripts originating on the Continent to the North. It seems, too that it was from the South that some of the leading Irish missionaries set out to England, notably Máel-dubh to Malmesbury, St. Fursey to East Anglia, both about 635; their origin in the South, already, in 632, converted to the Roman Easter, would explain their easy relations with their diocesan bishops in England, in contrast to the difficulties St. Columban experienced in Gaul and the Irish from Iona in Northumbria.[138]

Spanish influence, however, also penetrated into the North of Ireland, and from there into Northumbria.[139] Père Grosjean has recently reminded us of the great significance of the Fahan Mura cross in Donegal, with its Greek inscription of the late seventh century presenting a " literal, not to say servile " version of a doxology first appearing in the Acts of the Fourth Council of Toledo in 633.[140] This doxology, which seems a typical piece of Irish scholarship in its showy display of a superficial knowledge of Greek, is, incidentally, the only ancient inscription in that language in the country.[141] The presence in this remote cemetery in the extreme North of Ireland of a Spanish formula only promulgated half a century before is striking visual evidence of the influence of seventh-century Spain on Ireland.

In this paper I have stressed the evidence drawn from the transmission of manuscripts, mainly because it happens to be the type of evidence with which I, personally, am most familiar. Plenty of other evidence exists. The influence of the Mozarabic Liturgy on Irish and English liturgical books was brought out,

---

[138] Cf. *supra*, nn. 59, 100.

[139] Cf. *supra* n. 110. W. Levison, *England and the Continent in the Eighth Century*, Oxford, 1946, 67, n. 3, 282, has observed that Isidore, *De officiis*, was used at Lindisfarne *c.* 700 to describe the qualities of St. Cuthbert.

[140] Grosjean, *art. cit.* (*supra*, n. 37), 97 ff. He remarks that the doxology " ne peut venir que d'Espagne " and is a link between Ireland and Spain saec. VII, on condition (1) that the inscription is not a later addition, and (2) that the slab is correctly dated s. VII. R. A. S. Macalister, " The Inscription on the Slab at Fahan Mura, Co. Donegal " in *Journal of the Royal Society of Antiquaries of Ireland* 59 (1929), 89-98, in fact dealt with the possibility that the inscription might be a modern forgery. If it is a forgery it is earlier than 1881 and it is extremely improbable that a forger who knew enough to use a correct script of saec. VII would have made the absurd mistake of writing " *τίμε* " instead of " *τίμη*," whereas this mistake is entirely conceivable in a monk of Fahan s. VII. P. Grosjean is no doubt right to wonder whether the date of the first appearance of the formula found in the inscription (633) may not have influenced art historians in their dating the slab saec. VII med. It is, however, possible to find a *terminus post quem* for the inscription by dating the decoration of the slab. Recently R. B. K. Stevenson, " The Chronology and Relationships of some Irish and Scottish Crosses " in *Jour. R. Soc. Antiquaries Ireland* 86 (1956), 84-96 (esp. 93-96), argued for a tenth-century date for the crosses of Carndonagh and Fahan Mura. I find his arguments unconvincing (he does not, for instance, consider the detailed parallels between the interlace of Fahan Mura and the Book of Durrow, brought out by Åberg, *op. cit. supra*, n. 43, or the arguments advanced by Nordenfalk in *Acta Archaeologica* 18 [1947] 141-74). His views have not been accepted by Haseloff (*art. cit. supra*, n. 3). The Book of Durrow is possibly to be dated *c.* 650 at latest it seems (as by T. D. Kendrick, T. J. Brown *et al.*, *op. cit. supra*, n. 3), *c.* 680. Fahan Mura must, accordingly, be assigned to the same period.

[141] Cf. R. E. McNally, " The *tres linguae sacrae* in Early Irish Bible Exegesis " in *Theological Studies* 19 (1958), 395-403; he remarks that Isidore's eulogy of Hebrew, Greek and Latin as *tres linguae sacrae* (*Orig.* 9, 1, 3) is often reflected in Irish reverence for the sacred character of the three languages. But repeated recourse to Hebrew, Greek and Latin in Biblical exegesis is peculiar to Hiberno-Latin commentaries. More often than not the Hebrew and Greek is pseudo, " mere pretensions of learnedness or inventions of Irish fantasy " (p. 396).

as long ago as 1907, by Edmund Bishop, and recent investigations have done much to confirm the views he sustained.[142] In the realm of paschal *computi*, too, Professor C. W. Jones has shown how the African collection of tracts dealing with the date of Easter passed through Spain, where it was added to and revised, to reach Ireland by 633.[143] Recently Dr. E. F. Bruck has pointed out Eastern influence in Spanish and Irish legislation on the amounts that should or could be left to the Church and the poor.[144] These different but converging lines of investigation seem to me to show that we are not confronted here with an ingenious hypothesis lacking real foundation but with something that may genuinely help to illumine the history of the Early Middle Ages. Perhaps we shall end by believing that after all the *Lebor Gabála* was not without some foundation in ascribing a Spanish origin to the Goidels and to Míl—Miles Hispaniae. "Does the later legend," we shall ask in the words of Kingsley Porter, " echo a historic fact ? "[145]

---

[142] Cf. my Oxford paper (*cit. supra*, n. 2), 453; B. Capelle, " L'introduction du symbole à la messe " in *Mélanges J. de Ghellinck*, II, Gembloux, 1951, 1003-27 (esp. 1009), however, now thinks Ireland received the custom of chanting the Creed at Mass from the East but not (as he maintained in 1934) through Spain. It does not seem to me that this new conclusion can be demonstrated and the chronological order remains clear—the East, Spain, Ireland, England. For " Mozarabic " formulas in Irish liturgical books cf. G. Manz, *Ausdrucksformen der lateinischen Liturgiesprache bis ins elfte Jahrhundert* = Texte und Arbeiten, Abt. 1, Beih. 1, Beuron, 1941. For other recent works on " Spanish symptoms," especially in the liturgy, cf. the references in Ladner (*op. cit. supra*, n. 122), 396, n. 46.

[143] Cf. C. W. Jones (*op. cit. supra*, n. 105), 75-77, 97, 105, 112 ff.

[144] E. F. Bruck, *Kirchenväter und Soziales Erbrecht. Wanderungen religiöser Ideen durch die Rechte der Ostlichen und Westlichen Welt*, Berlin-Göttingen-Heidelberg, 1956, chaps. VI and VII.

[145] A. Kingsley Porter, *The Crosses and Culture of Ireland*, New Haven, 1931, 4 (alluding to possible geological connections between Ireland and Spain in prehistoric times). For the legend cf. F. Lot, *Nennius et l'Historia Brittonum, étude critique*, Paris, 1934, 156; T. F. O'Rahilly, *Early Irish History and Mythology*, Dublin, 1946, 15, 195 and n. 1. Cf. also H. Zimmer in *Zeitschrift f. deutsche Alterthum u. deutsche Literatur*, N.F. 21 (1889), 285, n. 1.

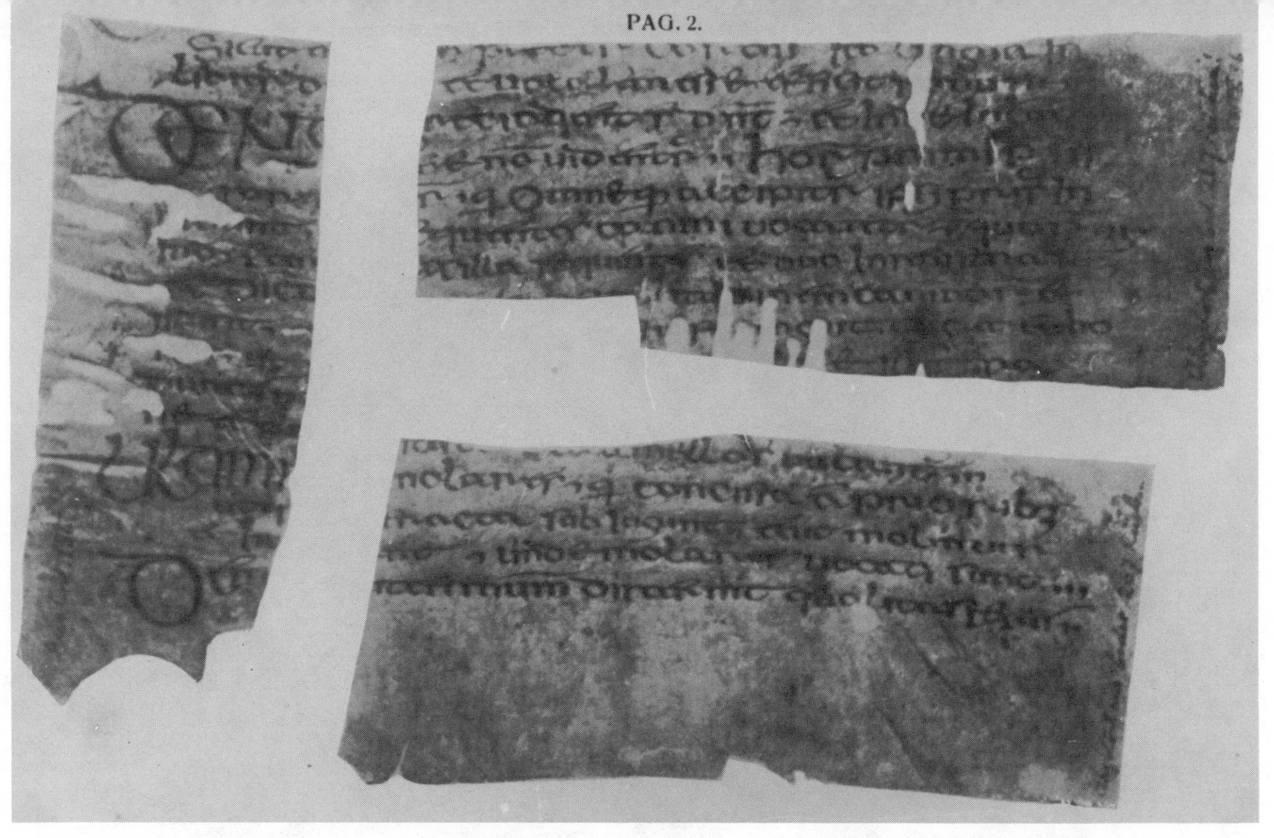

Fig. 1
Details of St. Gall Isidore saec. VII (cf. N. 75)

Fig. 2

Waxed tablet from Springmount, saec. VII (cf. N. 79)
Reproduced by courtesy of National Museum, Dublin

VIII

IRELAND AND SPAIN IN THE SEVENTH CENTURY

Some twenty years ago I published two studies on the relations between Ireland and Spain. In these articles I maintained that literary connections between the two countries are so strongly attested in the seventh century that it is most reasonable to suppose that they were direct. I held that Spanish works – especially, though not only, those by Isidore of Seville – came to Ireland before they reached England and at the same time that they reached France. From this connection I argued that certain important results followed.[1]

In general these views have proved acceptable to scholars writing on the period. In 1972, however, in his valuable discussion of the conversion of the Anglo-Saxons, Dr Mayr-Harting put forward some criticisms of the conclusions at which I had arrived and suggested that 'the Irish were not indispensable to introduce the Anglo-Saxons to Isidore's writings'. This view has been recently endorsed, without re-examination of the evidence, by Dr Edward James.[2] In the meantime a good deal of new evidence has emerged. It

[1] 'The East, Visigothic Spain and the Irish', *Studia Patristica* 4 (Berlin 1961) 442–56, and 'Visigothic Spain and early christian Ireland', *Proc Roy Ir Acad* (*C*) 62 (1962) 167–94. These articles were summarised in 'Old Ireland and Visigothic Spain', Robert McNally (ed), *Old Ireland* (Dublin 1965) 200–27.

[2] Henry Mayr-Harting, *The coming of christianity to Anglo-Saxon England* (London 1972) 127–8 (criticisms expressed with great courtesy). Edward James, 'Ireland and western Gaul in the Merovingian period', D. Whitelock, R. McKitterick and D. Dumville (ed), *Ireland in early mediaeval Europe: studies in memory of Kathleen Hughes* (Cambridge 1982) 362–86: 363. Dr James remarks that my theory was countered 'briefly but effectively' by Dr Mayr-Harting. Dr Vivien Law, *The Insular Latin Grammarians* (Woodbridge 1982) 24 n 61, refers to Mayr-Harting as criticising Professor Bischoff's 'thesis', which is much the same as mine (B. Bischoff, 'Die europäische Verbreitung der Werke Isidors von Sevilla', *Isidoriana* (León 1961) 317–44, reprinted in his *Mittelalterliche Studien* i (Stuttgart 1966) 171–94).

therefore seems useful to return to the subject. In this brief paper I shall at tempt to sketch the cultural context of seventh-century Western Europe an then to show some of the ways in which Spain contributed to the develop ment of early christian culture in Ireland. Finally I shall refer to the criti cisms expressed by the two scholars I have mentioned.

I begin by looking at the map of what one may for convenience call th literary production of the Latin-speaking church in the seventh century. B this time the more lasting effects of the barbarian invasions and of th counter-attack by Byzantium had become clear. In the world of Latin chris tianity North Africa had played from the beginning a leading role. In th fifth and sixth centuries the North African theologians still led the Lati church and North Africa also continued to produce grammarians, poets an historians. But after 600 one finds no successors to Fulgentius of Ruspe Priscian or Corippus. Long before Carthage fell to Islam in 697, internecin theological strife over the interpretation of Chalcedon appears to have ex hausted the energies of the Africans.

In Italy the Byzantine 'reconquest' had killed the Ostrogothic renaissance The long struggle between Byzantines and Lombards made any later reviva difficult. Italian works from the death of Gregory the Great to the middle o the eighth century (150 years) are covered in two pages of Dekkers's *Clavi* (France for the same period has four pages, Spain in contrast twenty-five) Except for Jonas of Bobbio, an Italian member of an Irish foundation virtually the only works listed are a few letters by three bishops and by som popes.[1] What culture survived in Italy was a provincial offshoot of Byzan tium.

The seventh century in France presents no figures comparable to Caesariu of Arles or Gregory of Tours. From the literary and codicological point o view France in this century has recently been described as a corridor be tween Italy and the British Isles. It was certainly not a centre radiating cul ture comparable either with Ostrogothic Italy in the early sixth century o with contemporary Visigothic Spain.[2] Pierre Riché, a scholar who has con tributed greatly to redress the earlier picture of unrelieved Merovingian 'de cadence', sees 'both religious education and monastic spirituality (as) at bes

[1] Eligius Dekkers, *Clavis patrum latinorum* (2nd ed., Steenbrugge 1961) 264–96. Thes pages do not include some special categories, such as hymns, grammarians, legal sources etc., but adding them to the respective 'national' totals would not greatly change the pro portions involved.

[2] J. Fontaine, addenda to his *Isidore de Séville et la culture classique dans l'Espagne wisi gothique* (which will appear as a third volume in the second edition). I have to thank Pro fessor Fontaine for allowing me to consult this material. Franz Brunhölzl, *Geschichte de lateinischen Literatur des Mittelalters* i (Munich 1975) 140–50.

mediocre (in seventh-century France). If any of the (bishops) wanted to study the Scriptures they went to Ireland'.[1]

In comparison to the silence of the African church in the seventh century and to the extreme poverty of Italy and – to a lesser extent – of France, Spain under the Visigoths presents a rich and varied picture, one in which Isidore of Seville, while outstanding, is not an isolated figure but has predecessors and successors distributed all over the peninsula from Braga to Barcelona and from Saragossa through Toledo to Merida. The 'moment of hope, of creation'[2] marked by the conversion of the Visigoths to Catholicism in 589 was to prolong its effects for a century. The same dissolution of the monarchy can be traced in Spain as in France but in Spain the process was more gradual. The civil wars and rebellions of the seventh century did not seriously affect the continuity of cultural centres such as Toledo. The survival of aristocratic episcopal families helped to maintain the cultural level. A relatively secure political climate made possible the transmission of texts to Spain from other parts of the christian West, notably from Italy and Africa, and their copying and use there. Thus anthologies of Latin poetry, biblical, patristic, grammatical and computistical texts could travel through Spain to France and the British Isles.[3]

The culture of these Spanish bishops (and of some exceptional lay aristocrats) was that of a small minority. The semi-literate authors of the inscriptions on slate found in cemeteries near the modern Portuguese frontier were no doubt more typical. It was, however, the 'high Latin' of Isidore and his colleagues which was conveyed to later readers outside Spain and this was vastly superior to that of the writers of Merovingian France. One does not find in the Spaniards what Brunhölzl describes in France: 'a gross disproportion between the pretensions one attempts to sustain and the capacities one possesses'.[4]

Fontaine, Díaz y Díaz and others have shown that Isidore's knowledge of

[1] P. Riché, 'Columbanus, his followers and the Merovingian church,' H. B. Clarke and Mary Brennan (ed), *Columbanus and Merovingian monasticism*, Br Archaeol Rep Int Ser 113 (Oxford 1981) 59–72, esp. 61, 63.

[2] J. Fontaine, in *Il passaggio dall'antichità al medioevo in occidente*, Settimane di Studio 9 (Spoleto 1962) 217.

[3] M. C. Díaz y Díaz, 'La trasmisión de los textos antiguos en la península ibérica en los siglos VII–XI', *La cultura antica nell'occidente latino dal VII all'XI secolo*, Settimane di Studio 22 (Spoleto 1975) 133–75: 174f, citing Traube on African texts. For Italy see J. Fontaine, *Isidore de Séville* ii (Paris 1959) 842–46. See, for example, the MS of Hilary written before 509/510 and restored in Spain (CLA I 1 a-c).

[4] Brunhölzl, *Geschichte*, 116. See J. Fontaine, 'De la pluralité à l'unité dans le "latin carolingien"?', *Nascita dell'Europa ed Europa Carolingia: un'equazione da verificare*, Settimane di Studio 27 (Spoleto 1981) 770–74.

the classics was far more limited than used to be thought. It is, for instance, doubtful if he had read much of Virgil other than secondhand, in excerpts. In Spanish libraries christian authors greatly outnumbered classical. But Isidore and later bishops possessed a range of encyclopaedic texts as well as grammatical works and they knew how to use both their patristic and their secular sources.[1]

Fontaine has brought out very clearly the extent to which Isidore was imbued with classical values. It is the more striking that his works should not have been merely consigned to 'winter storage' (as were many classical authors) in a few monasteries to await later rediscovery.[2] In contrast, Isidore's writings continued to act as a living force in cultural worlds completely remote from that in which they had been written. They were transmitted from a country where Latin had been spoken for over 700 years to one where it only existed as a cultural import. The clue here appears to consist in the very limitations of Spanish culture. In Spain, though classical *values* might persist, classical *models* had been reduced to their grammatical essentials and a new type of technical anthology, whether of grammar, ethics or theology, had emerged. The success of Isidore's *De natura rerum*, his *De officiis*, his *Sententiae*, of Julian of Toledo's *Prognosticum*, is bound up with the functional character of these works, with their (in general) sober style, and with the brevity so highly praised by their first readers.[3] The *Etymologies* of Isidore, while hardly brief, could be broken up and transmitted in separate books. Books I (on grammar) and IV (on medicine) were often so transmitted. The *Etymologies* as a whole had – to readers totally ignorant of the Roman world – the vast advantage of presenting an encyclopaedic approach to it through simple definitions. The book constituted a 'boiled-down' version of the whole of Hellenistic culture, of the arts, law, medicine, and a whole range of techniques. The work also provided a basic way to preserve Latin vocabulary and showed how to use it.[4] In this sense Isidore's works were calculated to assist the many readers of his time who, in the words of Gregory of Tours 'nomina discernere nesciunt'.[5] Braulio of Saragossa, Isidore's friend and the editor of the *Etymologies*, saw exactly what Isidore was trying to do though to describe it he was obliged to borrow with-

[1] Díaz y Díaz, 'La trasmisión,' 139, 146f. Compare André Vernet, 'La transmission des textes en France', *La cultura antica nell' occidente latino*, 89–123: 93.

[2] Fontaine, addenda to *Isidore de Séville* (cited above).

[3] See, for example, Braulio on Isidore in his *Renotatio* (ed. P. Galindo in C. H. Lynch, *San Braulio* (Madrid 1950) 358; PL 81, 16B) or Idalius on Julian of Toledo's *Prognosticum* (CCSL 115, 4.34, 5.68–73, 7.7).

[4] J. Fontaine, 'La naissance difficile d'une latinité médiévale (500–744): mutations, étapes et pistes', *Bull Assoc Guillaume Budé* 40 (1981) 360–68.

[5] Gregory of Tours, *In gloria confessorum*, prol. (MGH SRM 1.2.748.2).

ut acknowledgement (from Augustine) Cicero's praise of Varro. Isidore vas given to Spain by God, Braulio wrote, after so many disasters, 'lest we row old in rusticity' (ne usquequaque rusticitate veterascemus).[1]

Isidore was not only the author of the *Etymologies*. Brunhölzl says of him hat though most of what he wrote was compiled from earlier sources, 'the liversity of the domains he covers presupposes an astonishing breadth of piritual horizons'.[2] The extent of his appeal to readers outside Spain is pparent from a glance at the index to Lowe's *Codices Latini Antiquiores*. his shows that more manuscripts of Isidore are preserved from before 800 han of any other Latin author, apart from Augustine, and this despite the act that the distribution of Isidore's works only began about 615.[3] The uestion I am concerned with here is what works of Isidore appealed to vhich seventh-century readers. When one has established that one can perhaps suggest some reasons for this appeal.[4]

First of all, the gaps. One short work of Isidore, *De haeresibus*, appears never to have left Spain (and is only preserved there in one seventh-century nanuscript).[5] His *De fide catholica contra Iudaeos, Regula*, and *De viris illustribus* were not widely known until the eighth century, the last work not ven then.[6] I also cannot see much evidence for knowledge of the *Historiae*

Braulio, *Renotatio* (ed. Galindo, 358; PL 81, 17A). The translation by Claude W. Barow (*Iberian Fathers* ii (Washington DC 1969) 142) reads: 'lest we grow dull from boorish usticity'. See J. Fontaine, 'Cohérence et originalité de l'étymologie isidorienne', *Homeaje a E. Elorduy* (Deusto 1978) 113-44. [2] Brunhölzl, *Geschichte*, 90.

See the Index of Authors (by R. A. B. Mynors) in the *Supplement* to CLA (Oxford 971) 75. My count is 117 separate manuscripts containing works or fragments. For erome, including very small groups of letters, I find only 110.

The following remarks are particularly subject to correction because of the defective tate of Isidore's texts (not to mention those of many later authors). The long awaited ew critical edition of the *Etymologies* has only just begun to appear (Book XVII, ed. J. ndré, Paris 1981). In the last two decades we have new editions only of *De viris illusribus* (ed. C. Codoñer, Salamanca 1964) and of *Historiae* (ed. C. Rodríguez Alonso, eón 1975 (see below)). I do not here deal with the many mentions of Isidore in eighthentury authors. The recent reprint of Lindsay's edition of the *Etymologies*, with a panish translation (San Isidoro, *Etimologías*, ed. José Oroz Reta and Manuel-A. Marcos asquero (2 vols, Madrid: Bibl Autores Christianos 433-434, 1982-83)) is valuable for ts notes and especially for the long and detailed discussion of the political and cultural ackground to Isidore and of his whole literary production: Manuel C. Díaz y Díaz, 'Inroducción General', i 7-257. The following editions are here cited as about to appear: *ifferentiae* I (116 n 61), *De ortu et obitu patrum* (121 n 69) and *De officiis* (124 n 74). ee also the revised version of my paper in *Isidoriana* (1961), with bibliography for 936-75, to appear in *Studi Medievali* (1983).

M. C. Díaz y Díaz, *Index scriptorum latinorum medii aevi hispanorum* (Madrid 1959) o 110. The MS there dated saec. VIII is in fact saec. VII (CLA XI 1631).

The only two MSS of *De fide* registered in CLA are I 64 (saec. VIII^2, Italian) and V

outside Spain. Unfortunately the recent edition of this work does not dea satisfactorily with the manuscript tradition. It is customarily said that th *Historiae* is used (once) in the *Collectio canonum Hibernensis* of c. 700. I this were so it would be the only instance known to me of this work bein cited outside Spain in the century after it was written but in fact the *Histo riae* is not used in the *Collectio*.[1] These gaps appear to reflect a natural lacl of interest outside Spain in specifically Spanish concerns, namely the Jewisl problem and the desire to celebrate Spanish bishops (in the *De viris*) and th role of the Goths in history (in the *Historiae*).[2] One can point to the simila lack of interest in Ildefonsus and Julian of Toledo's later anti-Jewish apolc gias and in Julian's anti-Frankish *Historia Wambae* as compared to the grea popularity of his *Prognosticum* - his treatise on the last things - and to th early diffusion of his *Ars grammatica*.[3]

I have already pointed to the sparseness of the surviving works fror seventh-century Italy and France. It is necessary to bear this in mind whe considering the few mentions of Isidore one finds in Italian and Frankisl authors in this century. Even so, the instances when he is used are few in deed. In both Italy and France the *Chronica* was apparently the first, and for a long time, the *only* work to be known. It is cited within about a decad of the completion of its first version (that of 615) by one chronicler i France and another in North Italy.[4] Apart from this the main diffusion o

661 (VIII–IX, France ?). For the late saec. VIII translation into Old High German se my article, 'The position of Isidorian studies', *Isidoriana* (León, 1961) 65. For th MSS of *De viris* (none earlier than saec. IX) see C. Codoñer's edition (cited above), 87 103. For the *Regula* (known to Egbert of York saec. VIII) see M. C. Díaz y Díaz in *St dia Monastica* 5 (1963) 27–57.

[1] The quotation in H. Wasserschleben, *Die irische Kanonensammlung* (2nd ed., Leij zig 1885) XVII 15 (p 55) does not come from *Historia Gothorum* but from the *Chronic* 390, 396 (Mommsen, MGH AA 11, 470f).

[2] On *De viris* and *Historiae* see my article, 'Historiography in Visigothic Spain', *La stori grafia altomedievale*, Settimane di Studio 17 (Spoleto 1970) 261–311, and for *Historia* see Marc Reydellet, *La royauté dans la littérature latine de Sidoine Apollinaire à Isido de Séville*, Bibliothèque des écoles françaises d'Athènes et de Rome 243 (Rome 198 524–54.

[3] On the Spanish anti-Jewish apologiae see F. Parente, 'La controversia fra ebrei e cri tiani in Francia e in Spagna dal VI al IX secolo', *Gli Ebrei nell'alto medioevo*, Settimane Studio 26 (Spoleto 1980) 552–78; he points to the contemporary significance of thes works (which, of course, helped to 'date' them). For a comparison between the *fortun* of Julian of Toledo's different works see the prolegomena to the editions in CCSL 11 (1976); for the *Ars* see below, 11 n 5. Ildefonsus of Toledo's *De virginitate perpetu* first left Spain (by a sort of accident) saec. X; see Sr A. Braegelmann, *The life and writing of St Ildefonsus of Toledo* (Washington DC 1942) 129f.

[4] B. Bischoff, 'Die europäische Verbreitung der Werke Isidors', *Mittelalterliche Studie* i 171–94: 175. (For the different versions of Isidore's *Chronica* see my 'Historiography

ɜidore's works in Italy begins only *after* 700 and should probably be asso-iated with the arrival of exiles fleeing from Spain after the Islamic invasion f 711.[1] This is also true of France. There we have isolated references to the *'tymologies* by Theofrid, the first abbot of Corbie (a monk from Luxueil), /ho died after 683,[2] and to the *Sententiae* in the late seventh-century *Vita Vandregesili*. The ascetic collection made by Defensor of Ligugé, also bout 700, contains quotations from three or four works of Isidore.[3]

Let us turn to the British Isles. The first Anglo-Saxon writer of impor-ance, Aldhelm, only began to write in the 670s,[4] Bede about 702, at the ear-.est.[5] They are the first Anglo-Saxons to cite Isidore.[6] In contrast, apart rom St Columbanus, there is a long series of Irish Latin seventh-century uthors, many of whom cite Isidore. While Isidore's texts are principally rawn on by Irish exegetic, grammatical and computistic writers, they are lso used in more unusual works. A few details.

87 f). 'Fredegar' may also have known the *Chronica* but the date of the work is in dis-ute; see W. Goffart, 'The Fredegar problem reconsidered', *Speculum* 38 (1963) 206–41 he argues for c. 658).

De natura rerum is an exception, being known to the Ravenna cosmographer in the late eventh century; see Bischoff, 'Verbreitung', 175f.

Bischoff, 'Verbreitung', 176. David Ganz, 'The Merovingian library of Corbie', H. B. :larke and Mary Brennan (ed), *Columbanus and Merovingian monasticism* 153–72: 154.

See my 'Visigothic Spain and early christian Ireland', 182 and n 73, 74. The *Vita Wand-egesili* I 2 (MGH SRM 5, 13f) cited *Sent.* II xi 1, 6 (PL 83, 611f). Ian Wood, 'The *Vita Columbani* and Merovingian hagiography', *Peritia* 1 (1982) 63–80: 74, suggests that the *ent.* could have reached St Wandrille either from Ireland or via Bobbio or Luxueil. The date of Defensor is not established: it cannot be earlier than c. 700 since it uses the rish work *De ordine creaturarum* (see below) which, in its turn, uses the creed of a Span-sh council of 675; see below, 11 n 2. The seven MSS of Defensor in CLA are all dated aec. VIII^{2} or later.)

See the discussion in *Aldhelm: the prose works*, trans. Michael Lapidge and Michael Ierren (Woodbridge 1979) esp. 11–19, 136–51.

D. Whitelock, 'Bede and his teachers and friends', Gerald Bonner (ed), *Famulus Christi: ssays in commemoration of the thirteenth centenary of the birth of the Venerable Bede* London 1976) 19–39: 25; see Charles W. Jones, 'Bede's place in medieval schools', ibid. '61–85: 267.

Bischoff, 'Verbreitung', 183f. M. L. W. Laistner, 'The library of the Venerable Bede', ۸. H. Thomson (ed), in *Bede, his life, times, and writings* (Oxford 1935) 265, notes Bede's use of Isidore's *Chronica, De natura rerum, Etymologies* and (possibly) *Quaes-iones in vetus testamentum*. Many editions of Bede are incomplete in their indication of iis sources. Exceptions are mentioned by P. Meyvaert, 'Bede the scholar', *Famulus Christi*, 40–69: 63 n 19; see CCSL 118A (1967) and 121 (1983). One should now add the *Opera didascalica*, mainly edited by Charles W. Jones (CCSL 123A-C, 1975–80). Using hese editions one can increase the number of Isidore's works definitely used to include *Differentiae, Quaestiones, De ortu et obitu patrum*, and possibly also *Liber numerorum* ınd *Sententiae*.

The *Etymologies* is the work of Isidore most often used by the Irish. In the seventh century it is certainly used in Pseudo-Jerome's Exposition of the Gospels, in two commentaries on the Catholic Epistles,[1] in Laidcend's *Lori ca*,[2] in the *Hisperica Famina*,[3] in Virgilius Maro,[4] in the *De duodecim abusivi saeculi*,[5] in a newly discovered computus perhaps from the circle of Cum mian,[6] and, about 700, in the *Collectio canonum Hibernensis*.[7] It is also used in the vernacular *Auraicept na nÉces*.[8] In all it is used by at least ten separate authors, and this is a deliberately conservative estimate.[9]

Ten other works of Isidore can be shown to have been used by Irish au thors in the seventh century. They include all his important works other than the few which, as I said, do not appear to have left Spain at all in this early period.[10] What one should emphasise is the range of the Irish writers who use Isidore. Six works – the *Etymologies, De natura rerum, Differentiae De ortu et obitu patrum, Allegoriae,* and *Quaestiones in vetus testamentum* – are used in Irish exegetical writings.[11] Six works – the *Etymologies, De natura rerum, Differentiae, Chronica, Synonyma* and *De officiis* – are employed in the *Hisperica Famina* (which uses four works of Isidore), by Virgilius Maro

[1] B. Bischoff, 'Wendepunkte in der Geschichte der lateinischen Exegese im Frühmittela ter', *Mittelalterliche Studien* i 205–73 (no 11: p 240f). The two commentaries in que tion are edited by Robert E. McNally SJ in CCSL 108B (1973).

[2] Michael Herren, 'The authorship, date of composition and provenance of the so-calle *Lorica Gildae*', *Ériu* 24 (1973) 35–51.

[3] Michael Herren (ed), *The Hisperica Famina*: I, *The A-Text* (Toronto 1974) 20–22.

[4] Michael Herren, 'Some new light on the life of Virgilius Maro Grammaticus', *Proc Ro Ir Acad* (*C*) 79 (1979) 27–71: p 45–6.

[5] Siegmund Hellmann (ed), *Pseudo-Cyprianus: De XII abusivis saeculi*, Texte und Unte suchungen 34.1 (Leipzig 1909) 2.

[6] D. Ó Cróinín, 'A seventh-century Irish computus from the circle of Cummianus', *Pro Roy Ir Acad* (*C*) 82 (1982) 405–30: 413, 416.

[7] Wasserschleben, *Kanonensammlung* LXIV 7 (p 232).

[8] See A. Ahlqvist, *The early Irish linguist* (Helsinki 1983) 40–46; G. Calder, *Auraicep na nÉces* (Edinburgh 1917) xxxi–xl. See also F. J. Byrne, 'Seventh-century documents *Ir Ecclesiast Rec* 108 (1967) 164–82, esp. 166–7.

[9] I believe that *Et.* 15.34 is also used in Adomnán, *De locis Sanctis* II 30, 5 (ed. D. Mee han, Scriptores Latini Hiberniae 3 (Dublin 1958) 100 or CCSL 175, 222). For the use o Isidore in Ireland the most recent general study is that of Michael Herren, 'On the earlies Irish acquaintance with Isidore of Seville', Edward James (ed), *Visigothic Spain: new ap proaches* (Oxford 1980) 243–50. Some of the grammatical works assigned to Irelan saec. VII by Holtz (see below) also appear to use Isidore.

[10] That is, *De haeresibus, De fide catholica, Regula,* and *Historiae* (unless the last work i used by the *Collectio Hibernensis*: see above).

[11] *De natura rerum, Differentiae, Allegoriae* and *Quaestiones*, as well as the *Etymologies* are used in the commentaries cited above (n 1); *De ortu et obitu patrum* may be use there and is certainly employed by Laidcend in his *Egloga* (CCSL 145.3).

and in grammatical works such as the *Anonymus ad Cuimnanum* (which also uses four works), Malsachanus and (probably) the *Ars Ambrosiana.*[1] The *Etymologies* and the *De natura* are used in Irish computistical texts.[2] We also find two of the more 'original' Irish works of the seventh century citing Isidore. The ethical treatise *De duodecim abusivis saeculi*, in Laistner's view one of the most interesting works of the age, certainly uses the *Etymologies* and probably the *Sententiae* also.[3] The Irish author's approach links him to the *Collectio canonum Hibernensis,* which makes use of six of Isidore's works.[4] *De ordine creaturarum,* a biblical rather than 'scientific' approach to creation which still awaits a definitive study, uses *Differentiae* and *De officiis*.[5]

It is hardly necessary to point to the difference between the reception of Isidore in Ireland and elsewhere. Nowhere else, outside Isidore's own Spain, can one find anything approaching either the range of works used or the range of writers using them. Nor can one document the use of Isidore anywhere else outside Spain, except in the case of the *Chronica*, before the end

[1] V. Law, 'Notes on the dating and attribution of anonymous Latin grammars of the early middle ages', *Peritia* 1 (1982) 250-67: 260 remarks that 'no extant [grammatical] work (with the possible exception of the atypical Virgilius Maro) can as yet be attributed with certainty to an author working in the island of Ireland in this period'. L. Holtz, *Donat et la tradition de l'enseignement grammatical: étude sur l'Ars Donati et sa diffusion (IVe-IXe siècle) et édition critique* (Paris 1981) 264, 425-38, admits five such works, three of which - the *Anonymus ad Cuimnanum, Malsachanus* and *Ars Ambrosiana* - definitely or probably use Isidore, the *Anonymus* (which Law ascribes to 'an Irish milieu') using *De natura rerum, Differentiae, Chronica,* and *De officiis*. On this work see B. Bischoff, 'Eine verschollene Einteilung der Wissenschaften', *Mittelalterliche Studien* i 273-88. For Malsachanus see B. Löfstedt, *Der Hibernolateinische Grammatiker Malsachanus* (Uppsala 1965) 250.3f (*Differentiae*); for *Ars Ambrosiana*, Löfstedt's edition in CCSL 133 C (1982), 206f (possible use of *Etym.* and *Diff.*). For *Hisperica Famina* and Virgilius Maro Grammaticus see Michael Herren, *Hisperica Famina*, 20-22 and Michael Herren, 'New light on ... Virgilius', 45-6. For a critique of Löfstedt see V. Law, 'Malsachanus reconsidered: a fresh look at a Hiberno-Latin grammarian', *Cambridge Mediev Celt Stud* 1 (1981) 83-93.

[2] Ó Cróinín, 'A seventh-century Irish computus', 423-4.

[3] Hellmann, *Pseudo-Cyprianus: De XII abusivis saeculi.* The *Sententiae* appear to be used on p 34 but this is not a work often used by the Irish (it is however used in the *Collectio canonum Hibernensis*). See J. M. Wallace-Hadrill, *Early Germanic kingship in England and on the continent* (Oxford 1971) 56-7; M. L. W. Laistner, *Thought and letters in Western Europe* (2nd ed., London 1957) 144. On *Sententiae* see also Marc Reydellet, *La royauté dans la littérature latine*, 554-97.

[4] Wasserschleben, *Kanonensammlung. De officiis* and *Sententiae* are much used, *Quaestiones, Epistula ad Massonam* and *Chronica* less often, the *Etymologiae* once (LXIV 7 = p 232).

[5] *Liber de ordine creaturarum*, ed. Manuel C. Díaz y Díaz (Santiago de Compostela 1972) 35 f.

of the century. In Ireland, in contrast, we know that *De ortu* and the *Etymologies* were known to Laidcend by 661. Mr Ó Cróinín has shown recently that *De natura rerum* and the *Etymologies* were known to an Irish computist before 658. Virgilius Maro, who was also known to this computist, must therefore have made use of Isidore's *Etymologies* before that date.[1] The oldest existing manuscript of the work, it is now generally agreed, was written in Ireland before about 650.[2] Ireland had received a collection of tracts on Easter begun in North Africa and added to in Spain before c. 630.[3] It would seem that the group of Irish scholars who received these Spanish works—and which included computists, exegetes and grammarians—was mainly situated in south-east Ireland. These scholars appear to represent the 'Romani' referred to in contemporary texts; their location in the south enabled them to communicate with relative ease with continental centres of learning.[4] It is possible that there is a connection between this group and the lawyers responsible for the Old Irish classical tracts of the seventh and eighth centuries; it has been suggested that the fondness for etymology which these authors display owes something to Isidore's example.[5]

[1] Ó Cróinín, 'A seventh-century Irish computus', 424; and 'The Irish provenance of Bede's computus', *Peritia* 2 (1983) 229–47, which he kindly allowed me to consult before publication.

[2] St Gall, MS 1399 a.1 (CLA VII 995). See Bischoff, 'Verbreitung', 180. T. J. Brown, 'The Irish element in the Insular system of scripts to circa A.D. 850', H. Löwe (ed), *Die Iren und Europa im früheren Mittelalter* (2 vols, Stuttgart 1982) i 101–119: 104): 'I regard both the (Ussher) Gospels and the Isidore as native Irish products'. He dates the Gospels, the Isidore and the tablets from Springmount Bog (CLA Suppl. 1684) as approximately contemporary, i.e. to the first half or the middle of the seventh century. For the tablets (see my 'Visigothic Spain and early christian Ireland', 183f) see also Martin McNamara, 'Psalter-text and psalter study in the early Irish church (A.D. 600–1200)', *Proc Roy Ir Acad* (*C*) 73 (1973) 213f.

[3] Charles W. Jones, *Bedae opera de temporibus* (Cambridge, Mass. 1943) 74–7, 97, 105. For later bibliography see his introduction to Bede, *Opera didascalica* (CCSL. 123A (1975) xii-xv).

[4] For the 'Romani' see P. Grosjean, 'Sur quelques exégètes irlandais du VIIe siècle', *Sacris Erudiri* 7 (1955) 67–98 and, more recently, Michael Herren, 'The pseudonymous tradition in Hiberno-Latin: an introduction', John J. O'Meara and Bernd Naumann *Latin script and letters A.D. 400–900: Festschrift presented to Ludwig Bieler* (Leiden 1976) 121–31: 128–31). It now appears that Clonfert Mo-Lua, rather than Les Mór, may have been the main centre of these scholars (I follow Ó Cróinín in 'Irish provenance of Bede's computus', cited above).

[5] T. M. Charles-Edwards, 'The *Corpus Iuris Hibernici*', *Studia Hibernica* 20 (1980) 147, 160f. The curious view of Isidore as a convert from paganism which appears in Virgilius Maro (I follow the ingenious arguments of Michael Herren, 'Earliest Irish acquaintance with Isidore', 244, 249) combined with the idea held in seventh-century Ireland that the

There are signs that Spanish works later as well as earlier than Isidore were eceived in Ireland in the seventh century. An interesting example is the reed of the Eleventh Council of Toledo (675), which is used in the *De rdine creaturarum*.[1] Professor Holtz has traced the transmission of Pomeius Africanus's commentary on Donatus, which was known to Isidore and ulian of Toledo and then used by the Irish grammarians.[2] More significantly till, he sees Spain as providing (earlier on) the model for the 'mixed Irish verion' of the *Ars Donati*.[3] An anonymous Spanish commentary of the second alf of the seventh century on the qualities and defects of parts of speech vas preserved only by the Irish. It was known to Adomnán of Iona by 704.[4])ther Spanish works were probably mainly diffused via continental centres. 'his appears to be the case with Julian of Toledo, though his *Ars grammatica* vas very early on known to the Anglo-Saxons and a version of it to the Irish.[5]

Etymologies represented the *culmen* (or summa) of knowledge, shows that the Irish perceived something very important about Isidore, that (especially in this work) he deliberately tried to preserve profane culture as it was, not to integrate it into christian culture, ıs Augustine had wished to do. See also Díaz y Díaz, 'Introducción general', *Etimologías*, d. Oroz Reta and Marcos Casquero, i 196f.

Díaz y Díaz, *Liber de ordine creatur arum*, 36. For the transmission of Priscillianist exts see D. N. Dumville, 'Biblical apocrypha and the early Irish: a preliminary investigaion', *Proc Roy Ir Acad* (*C*) 73 (1973) 299–338: 322–30. For Juvencus see M. C. Díaz y)íaz, 'Al margen de los manuscritos patrísticos latinos', *Sacris Erudiri* 22.1 (1974–75) 1–74: 67f. Juvencus was well known in seventh-century Spain; a probably Spanish AS of saec. VIII[1] survives (CLA II 127). The next oldest MS (of saec VII *ex.*) comes from reland or Northumbria (from a centre under Irish influence) (CLA VIII 1172). A saec. VIII MS (CLA I 37) is probably from Bobbio. Díaz y Díaz's remarks on the transmission f Orosius (p 71f) are also interesting, but the Insular role here, though certain (see CLA I 328, saec. VII, (Irish, Bobbio?) and Suppl. 1687, Anglo-Saxon, saec. VIII[2], probably rom Northumbria), has yet to be clarified.

L. Holtz, 'Tradition et diffusion de l'œuvre grammaticale de Pompée, commentateur le Donat', *Rev Philol Hist Anc* 45 (1971) 48–83 esp. 64. Holtz sees one branch of the ransmission as coming from Spain via Ireland, the second from Toledo to Italy (p 78 n 1, 3).

3 Holtz, *Donat*, 305–7.

Ulrich Schindel, *Die lateinischen Figurenlehren des 5. bis 7. Jahrhundert und Donats Virgilkommentar*, Abh Akad Wiss Göttingen, Philol-hist Kl 3. F. 91 (1975); see esp. 65f. The work is only preserved in Basel, MS F. III. 15d., which was written in Ireland saec. VIII (CLA VII 847).

Its use by Aldhelm and Bede was argued by C. H. Beeson, 'The *Ars Grammatica* of Juian of Toledo'. *Miscellanea Fr. Ehrle* i, Studi e Testi 37 (Rome 1924) 50–70. On Bede see lso C. W. Jones's index to Bede, *Opera didascalica* (CCSL 123C (1980) 775f). Unfortuately he does not use the new edition by Maria A. H. Maestre Yenes, *Ars Iuliani Toletani Episcopi* (Toledo 1973) which, though not perfect, is fuller and superior to the unfindble edition of 1797. According to Maestre Yenes, the whole tradition descends from an nsular exemplar, p ciii. The three oldest MSS (CLA VII p 6 (568); VIII 1210; and Suppl 775) all have Irish or Anglo-Saxon connections. See Holtz, *Donat*, 460f.

The criticisms of the idea of direct links between Spain and Ireland to which I referred at the beginning of this paper appear to be based on several separate points. The lack of significance in this connection of the doxology at Fahan Mura, first emphasised by Dr Françoise Henry, must be accepted.[1] Dr Mayr-Harting is probably also correct in saying that we have no contemporary correspondence or accounts of travel between Spain and Ireland. But this does not mean that such a journey was impossible. Professor Charles Thomas's study of the archaeological evidence has shown that the finds of Eastern Mediterranean pottery (of the fifth to the early seventh centuries) in Cornwall, Wales, and (to a smaller extent) in southern Ireland and Scotland, provide evidence for 'direct, if casual and irregular trade' between the Mediterranean and the British Isles.[3] This trade clearly came through the Straits of Gibraltar.[4] These archaeological finds provide, in Thomas's phrase (applied to Gallo-Irish links), 'a raft for transmarine contact' which could involve 'ideas as well as trade goods'.[5]

I hope that the evidence I have already presented has shown how incorrect it is to say that Isidore 'quickly became known *everywhere* in the seventh century and no particular significance in the way of direct contact attaches to this being demonstrable in the case of Ireland'.[6] I am afraid that such a

[1] See F. Henry, *Irish art in the early christian period (to 800 A.D.)* (Ithaca, NY 1965) 127; taken up by Mayr-Harting (*Coming of christianity*, 128) and by James ('Ireland and western Gaul', 372–3). [2] Mayr-Harting, *Coming of christianity*, 127.

[3] Charles Thomas, *The early christian archaeology of North Britain* (Oxford 1971) 23.

[4] As is agreed, for instance, by Edward James, *The Merovingian archaeology of south-west Gaul*, Brit Archaeol Rep Suppl Ser 25 (Oxford 1977) 245, 258. See also J. W. Hayes, *A supplement to Late Roman pottery* (London 1980) esp. 525 (on finds in Portugal which 'provide the vital connecting link' between the Mediterranean and western Britain), and Charles Thomas, *A provisional list of imported pottery in post-Roman Western Britain and Ireland*, Inst Cornish Stud Spec Rep 7 (1981).

[5] Charles Thomas, 'Imported Late-Roman Mediterranean pottery in Ireland and Western Britain: chronologies and implications', *Proc Roy Ir Acad (C)* 76 (1976) 245–55, esp. 245, 247, 253. The origin in western Gaul of the pottery to which Thomas (and James, 382) refer is, as James acknowledges, not as yet proved. Mayr-Harting (85f), when speaking of the pottery in question, bases himself on older bibliography and appears not to know the earlier articles of Thomas, which maintained the same point of view as that expressed in 1971 and 1976. For the Mediterranean commerce of this age see A. R. Lewis, in *La navigazione mediterranea nell'alto medioevo*, Settimane di Studio 25 (Spoleto 1978) 481–501: 491, stressing the 'freedom of movement' of the sixth century and the early seventh.

[6] Mayr-Harting, *Coming of christianity*, 127 (the italics are his). The 'chances of survival' which Mayr-Harting mentions as favouring the evidence for early Irish knowledge of Isidore, as testified by extant manuscripts, might seem to others (when one thinks of the Viking raids on Ireland) to have worked against it! In a note to this passage (293 n 40)

statement betrays a lack of understanding of the meaning of the term 'transmission of texts'. When one speaks of a text being 'transmitted' one is not merely concerned with locating the places where the (generally few) extant copies were made. Important though that is, it is only a small part of the story. Texts are 'transmitted' essentially not from one place to another but from one person or group of persons to another. The main evidence for the transmission of ancient texts is the evidence of where and by whom they were used. This can consist in marginal notes and glosses; it can also - and this is more often the case - be found in the citations, explicit or (more generally) unacknowledged, by later authors. I have pointed out that, in the seventh century, it is only in Ireland that one finds a *group* of scholars able and willing to use Isidore. It would in fact have been surprising if his works had not arrived there, as the evidence shows they did, generations before they arrived (except in isolated instances) anywhere else outside Spain.

Dr Edward James, in endorsing Dr Mayr-Harting's conclusions, is mainly concerned to rebut an alternative to Zimmer's arguments for the importance of the Gallo-Irish connection. His article certainly strengthens Zimmer's case. I have no doubt that Latin learning, as well as wine, did reach Ireland from Gaul. But why stress one route to the exclusion of others? It is curious that Dr James should follow Mayr-Harting in arguing that Isidore was mainly transmitted via Gaul, for, in another work, he has shown the *lack* of communication between Spain and the Franks, at least via the most obvious route, Visigothic Septimania (Languedoc today), which he characterises as a frontier 'helping to isolate Spain from the rest of the western world'.[1] A recent study of the diffusion of Visigothic coinage seems to its author to indicate 'fairly important exchanges' in the seventh century between the Iberian Peninsula and Aquitaine (as earlier on up the Rhône valley). The evidence does not seem to me at all watertight.[2] But perhaps this question of routes is,

Mayr-Harting appears to suppose that the Isidore fragments at St Gall were written there; the accepted view is that they were written in Ireland (see 10 n 2 above).

[1] Edward James, 'Septimania and its frontier: an archaeological approach', Edward James (ed), *Visigothic Spain: new approaches* (Oxford 1980) 223-41: 241. See the criticism of this view by J. Fontaine in *Rev des études augustiniennes* 27 (1981) 444f. In his *Merovingian archaeology of south-west Gaul*, i 255, James finds 'only rare indications of contact with Visigothic Spain' in the tombs of Aquitaine.

[2] X. Barral i Altet, *La circulation des monnaies suèves et visigothiques: contribution à l'histoire économique du royaume visigot*, Beihefte der Francia 4 (Munich 1976) esp. 125-30. This statement is based mainly on the eighteen Visigothic coins probably found in the Bordeaux hoard: only three others (two at Mons and one at Wieuwerd) have been found in the rest of the Frankish kingdom (p 94f, 183). Barral does not appear to have considered the difficulties of using this type of evidence to prove 'exchanges'. See Philip Grierson, 'Commerce and trade in the Dark Ages, a critique of the evidence,' *Trans Roy Hist Soc ser 5* 9 (1959) 123-40. The dates given for the Bordeaux hoard (c. 695-702) are

in the end, secondary. Does it matter a great deal whether one travels from Toronto to London via New York or direct? The question is where one comes from and where one arrives. More crucial than the question of routes is that of reception. The crucial question here is where Spanish works first arrived in any important number and when they did so, and the answer to this question is Ireland, in the first half of the seventh century.

I suspect that the reason why what is really a secondary question has been blown up out of proportion is due to an anachronistic perception of the seventh century. A reading of Bede and of earlier writers does not, I submit, tend to show that Irish and Anglo-Saxons were unconnected or that they were engaged in constant rivalry but rather that they were interested in the same things: biblical exegesis, grammar, and the Easter question. If this is so, is it not more likely than not that one group would have borrowed from the other? In the past Irish influence on Anglo-Saxon culture may have been exaggerated. If so, this has been followed by an exaggeration in the opposite direction, the tendency to deny the evident priority of Hiberno-Latin over Anglo-Latin developments. I suggest that one should beware of drawing excessively sharp contrasts between the achievements of Irish and Anglo-Saxons, seeing the latter, for instance, as dedicated to the practical work of converting the pagans in Germany while the Irish are relegated to the role of pilgrims in search of 'holy solitude', who only became missionaries by a sort of happy accident.[1] In another sphere, is one justified in seeing the Irish as predominantly ascetics and exegetes, not fundamentally interested in secular, grammatical education? Exaggerated conclusions can be drawn from the 'synod' of Whitby and the arrival of Theodore and Hadrian at Canterbury in 669.[2] Did these events have such sudden and dramatic results? To quote Dr Law, 'Very little of Theodore's own writings survives and nothing of Hadrian's... We lack any information as to what books they brought with

very close to the Islamic invasion and the hoard could be the result of one Spanish exile's flight to France. See also James, *Merovingian archaeology of south-west Gaul*, i 229.

[1] So Vivien Law, *The Insular Latin grammarians*, Studies in Celtic History 3 (Woodbridge 1982) 98; many other examples of this view could be quoted. I do not think that the *Vita Columbani* bears it out. See T. M. Charles-Edwards, 'The social background to Irish *peregrinatio*', *Celtica* 11 (1976) 43–59 and Ian Wood, 'A prelude to Columbanus: the monastic achievement in the Burgundian territories', H. B. Clarke and Mary Brennan (ed), *Columbanus and Merovingian monasticism*, 3–32: 19: 'The Irish seem to have been inspired both by asceticism and by a desire to evangelize, and they passed this on to their continental foundations'. See also Riché, ibid., 65f.

[2] Law, *Insular Latin grammarians*, 7. Claudio Leonardi, 'Il venerabile Beda e la cultura del secolo VIII', *I problemi dell'occidente nel secolo VIII*, Settimane di Studio 20 (Spoleto 1973) 603–58: 648f points out that Boniface, the greatest of 'practical' Anglo-Saxon missionaries, wrote specifically for Bede's biblical commentaries when on his mission.

them from Rome'.[1] The contrast with what we *know* was available in Ireland in 669 – Isidore's works, for one – is so obvious as to be embarrassing. One wonders if it is possible to maintain that 'Irish influence was *eclipsed* by the arrival of the new teachers'.[2] Perhaps it is safer to say, with Professor Bullough, that 'books, the old Easter Tables excepted, were not put on an index in 664 or 710 or any other date'.[3] The continuance, rather than the abrupt cessation, of Irish influence in England seems nearer the truth.[4]

To sum up. The debt of seventh-century Ireland to Spain consists, it seems to me, in four main things. First, a computistical collection, received from Spain by about 630. This made it possible to work out the Easter question in a new and more scientific way. Secondly, Ireland received from Spain (as I think Professor Holtz has demonstrated) a synthesis of Donatus's grammatical teaching. Thirdly, it received the works of Isidore, including the *Etymologies*, Book I of which was, as Dr Law says, 'the shortest summary of Latin grammar available'.[5] A concentration on grammar – which the age had identified with science itself[6] – provided the 'starting point of the cultural movement of the seventh century (in Ireland)'.[7] Fourthly, Isidore's *Synonyma* gave Irish writers a new style, quite different from the sobriety of

[1] Law, *Insular Latin grammarians*, 8. See Lapidge and Herren, *Aldhelm: the prose works*, 8. In 'Notes on the dating and attribution of anonymous Latin grammars', Dr Law (258) stresses the 'frequent cultural contact' (from 597 onwards), which she sees as existing between the Anglo-Saxons and the Mediterranean world, in contrast with Ireland's 'far less regular' links with this world. Compare T. J. Brown: 'Until 669 Anglo-Saxon England was a cultural province of Ireland and a province in which Latin learning flourished much less vigorously than in Ireland itself' ('An historical introduction to the use of Classical Latin authors in the British Isles from the fifth to the eleventh century', *La cultura antica nell' occidente latino dal VII all'XI secolo*, Settimane di Studio 22 (Spoleto 1975) 237–93: 253–4).

[2] Law, *Insular Latin grammarians*, 8.

[3] Donald A. Bullough, 'The missions to the English and Picts and their heritage (to c. 800),' *Die Iren und Europa*, i 80–98: 94f (and references there cited).

[4] See T. J. Brown, 'The Irish element in the Insular system of scripts', *Die Iren und Europa*, i 106; Gerald Bonner, 'Ireland and Rome: the double inheritance of christian Northumbria', Margot H. King and Wesley M. Stevens (ed), *Saints, scholars and heroes: studies in medieval culture in honour of Charles W. Jones* (2 vols, Collegeville, Minn. 1979) i 101–116 (this article is mainly on Durham, MS A. II. 17, on which see now D. Ó Cróinín, *Peritia* 1 (1982) 352–62); Archibald A. M. Duncan, 'Bede, Iona and the Picts', R. H. C. Davis and J. M. Wallace-Hadrill (ed), *The writing of history in the middle ages: essays presented to Richard William Southern* (Oxford 1981) 1–42 (Bede's use of Irish annals). Clare Stancliffe, 'Early "Irish" biblical exegesis', *Studia Patristica* 12 (1975) 361–70: 367, correctly sees 'Ireland and England as an integral part of Western Europe, a geographical area for which the christian church with its concomitant Latin culture provided a unifying force'.

[5] Law, *Insular Latin grammarians*, 23.

[6] Holtz, 'Tradition et diffusion ... de Pompée', 48.

[7] Holtz, 'Irish grammarians and the continent in the seventh century', H. B. Clarke and Mary Brennan (ed), *Columbanus and Merovingian monasticism*, 135–52: 145.

Isidore's other works. This synonymic style was to be put to good use by the authors of the *Hisperica Famina*.[1]

The essentially practical aims of Irish scholars - which made them later palimpsest classical manuscripts at Bobbio to use them for patristic or grammatical texts - made them Isidore's natural readers and the natural disseminators of his works. Both Isidore, in his ruthless attitude to ancient (even patristic) authors - he can ransack Ovid and St Augustine with equal glee to find the grammatical example he wants - and the Irish were, in a sense, 'spoiling the Egyptians', taking from the ruins of antiquity what was useful for the age in which they lived. They were able, by their very ruthlessness, to transform the sources they received. Out of the sources he had Isidore created something new, a new synthesis of knowledge.[2] Out of the sources they received - from Spain, in large measure - the Irish created works to which no parallel existed in Spain. Building on Isidore they achieved greater sophistication than he possessed.[3] In another sphere, by 700 Adomnán could write the life of a saint which far surpasses any seventh-century Spanish *vita*. But even the greatest Irish writers of the ninth century would have been impossible without the rudiments received from Spain two centuries before.

A number of the Spanish contributions to Irish culture were passed on to England. This is undeniable in the case of Bede's use of computistical works and it is becoming increasingly clear also in the case of grammatical works.[4] In the first three quarters of the seventh century the Anglo-Saxons were more dependent on Ireland than on the continent. Further research will be needed to determine the exact channels of transmission. One that has been undervalued in the past must have been through the Anglo-Saxons who visited Ireland in search of learning.[5] Another channel, it is reasonable to suppose, connected the 'Romani' of southern Ireland to south-west England and so to Northumbria.[6] But it is enough to have shown that much learning reached Ireland from Spain generations before it was available elsewhere.

[1] Herren, *Hisperica Famina*.

[2] As is shown by J. Fontaine, in his great work *Isidore de Séville et la culture classique dans l'Espagne wisigothique*; for the approach he uses see 'Problèmes de méthode dans l'étude des sources isidoriennes', *Isidoriana* (León 1961) 115-30.

[3] As Holtz (*Donat*, 298) points out, speaking of Malsachanus.

[4] Bede's use of Irish works included the *De ordine creaturarum*, the computists and Virgilius Maro. See C. W. Jones's index to Bede, *Opera didascalica* (CCSL 123 C (1980) 735, 774f, 803) and his 'Bede's place in medieval schools', 281 n 45. On the use of Irish grammatical treatises by Boniface and Tatwin see Holtz, *Donat*, 319, 497f.

[5] See Charles-Edwards, 'The *Corpus Juris Hibernici*', 159-60; see also T. J. Brown, 'Historical introduction to the use of classical Latin authors in the British Isles', 292.

[6] This is suggested by Ó Cróinín 'The Irish provenance of Bede's computus' *Peritia* 2 (1983) 229-47: 244-5.

IX

The Position of Isidorian Studies: A Critical Review of the Literature 1936-1975

List of abbreviations; Preface; Bibliographies.

I. General Works. II. Authentic Works. III. Works of disputed authenticity. IV. The Sources of Isidore. V. Isidore and the Culture of his Age. VI. Church History, theology, history of dogma. a. Lives of Isidore. b. Canon Law and Moral Theology. c. Isidore and the Bible. d. Isidore in the history of dogma. e. Isidore in the history of the Liturgy. VII. The Influence of Isidore in the Middle Ages. Conclusions.

List of abbreviations

Opera Isidoriana

alleg. – allegoriae
chron. – chronica
diff. – differentiae
ep. – epistolae
fid. – de fide catholica contra Iudaeos
Goth. – historia Gothorum
nat. – de natura rerum
num. – liber numerorum
off. – de officiis ecclesiasticis
orig. – etymologiae seu origines
ort. – de ortu et obitu patrum
proem. – proemia
quaest. – questiones de Vetere Testamento seu mysticae expositiones sacramentorum
reg. – regula monachorum
sent. – sententiae
syn. – synonyma seu lamentatio animae peccatricis
vir. – de viris illustribus

General

ALTANER, in *Misc. Isid.* = B. ALTANER, *Der Stand der Isidorforschung. Ein kritischer Bericht über die seit 1910 erschienene Literatur*, in *Misc. Isid.*, pp. 1-32.

ALTANER, *Patrologie* = IDEM, *Patrologie. Leben, Schriften und Lehre der Kirchenväter*, Freiburg, 1966.

AST = *Analecta sacra Tarraconensia* (Barcelona).

AYUSO = T. AYUSO MARAZUELA, *La Vetus Latina Hispana*, I, *Prologómenos*, Madrid, 1953.

BALCL = *Bulletin d'ancienne littérature chrétienne latine* (Maredsous).

BTAM = *Bulletin de théologie ancienne et médiévale* (*Louvain*).

CD = *La Ciudad de Dios* (El Escorial).

CHE = *Cuadernos de historia de España* (Buenos Aires).

CLA = E. A. LOWE, *Codices Latinae Antiquiores*, I-XII, Oxford, 1943-71.

CPh = *Classical Philology* (Chicago).

CPL = E. DEKKERS and A. GAAR, *Clavis Patrum Latinorum*, Steenbrugis, 1961 - *SEJG* 3.

CUA, SMH = Catholic University of America, Studies in Medieval History.

CUA, SMRLLL = Ibid., Studies in Medieval and Renaissance Latin Language and Literature.

CUA, SST = Ibid., Studies in Sacred Theology.

DIAZ, Index = M. C. DIAZ Y DIAZ, *Index scriptorum latinorum medii aevi hispanorum*, 2 vols. Salamanca, 1958-59, (Acta Salmanticensia iussu Senatus Universitatis edita, Filosofía y Letras, XIII, 1-2).
[Another edition, identical in content, 1 vol., Madrid, Consejo Superior de Investigaciones Científicas, Patronato Menéndez Pelayo, 1959].

EE = *Estudios ecclesiásticos* (Madrid).

FONTAINE = J. FONTAINE, *Isidore de Séville et la culture classique dans l'Espagne wisigothique*, 2 vols Paris, *Études Augustiniennes, 1959*.

FONTAINE *Isidore, Traité de la nature* = J. FONTAINE, *Isidore de Séville, Traité de la nature, suivi de l'Epître en vers du roi Sisebut à Isidore*, éd. critique et traduction, Bordeaux, 1960 (Bibl. Hautes Études Hispaniques, 28).

HS	= *Hispania Sacra* (Madrid).
Isidoriana	= *Isidoriana. Estudios sobre San Isidoro de Sevilla en el XIV centenario de su nacimiento* León, 1961.
JTS	= *Journal of Theological Studies* (Oxford).
MA	= *Le Moyen Age* (Bruxelles).
MADOZ, *San Isidoro*	= J. MADOZ, *San Isidoro de Sevilla, Semblanza de su Personalidad Literaria,* ed. C. G. GOLDÁRAZ, León, 1960.
MADOZ, *Segundo decenio*	= IDEM, *Segundo decenio de estudios sobre patristica española (1941-50)*, Madrid, 1951 (Est. Onienses, I, 5).
MCNALLY	R. E. MCNALLY, *Isidoriana,* in *Theological Studies,* 20 (1959), pp. 432-42.
Misc. Isid.	= *Miscellanea Isidoriana,* Rome, 1936.
ML	= MIGNE, *Patrologia Latina.*
RABM	= *Revista de archivos, bibliotecas y museos* (Madrid).
RB	= *Revue bénédictine* (Maredsous).
REA	= *Revue des études anciennes* (Bordeaux).
REL	= *Revue des études latines* (Paris).
RET	= *Revista española de teología* (Madrid).
RHE	= *Revue d'histoire ecclésiastique* (Louvain).
RhMus	= *Rheinisches Museum für Philologie* (Frankfurt).
RMAL	= *Revue du Moyen Age latin* (Lyon-Strasbourg)
SEJG	= *Sacris Erudiri, Jaarboek voor Godsdienstwetenschappen* (Steenbrugge).
VChr	= *Vigiliae Christianae* (Amsterdam).

Preface

When, in 1936, there appeared in Rome a publication entitled *Miscellanea Isidoriana* it contained as its first article a lengthy bibliographical report by Dr. Berthold Altaner, *Der Stand der Isidorforschung. Ein kritischer Bericht über die seit 1910 erschienene Literatur*, that has proved invaluable to all later writers on Isidore. This article follows that of Dr. Altaner not only in its title but in its general plan. Its author is well aware of his debt to his predecessor.

Dr. Altaner in his *Bericht* mentioned some 120 publications dated from 1910 to 1935. This article attempts to cover the succeeding forty years although some publications of 1970-75, if not of earlier years, have probably escaped me. As it is, however, I find this article contains references to some 660 publications. At times, while struggling with this considerable mass of material, I must confess I have felt that too much has been written on St. Isidore. But if, like that other great Spanish Saint and Doctor, the Blessed Ramon Lull, Isidore continues to furnish an all too ready theme for the sentimental discourse or the profuse panegyric, he has also, as I hope to show, been the subject of a number of works of real value that geatly enhance our understanding of him and of his age. The advance these works have effected in Isidorian investigation also prepared and made possible the work of the Reunión Internacional of Léon in 1960.

Much of the material discussed here is difficult of access, especially outside Spain. I have to acknowledge my debt to previous bibliographers of Isidore. When Dr. Altaner wrote in 1936 the modern renewal of interest in the Spanish Fathers was only beginning. Today it can be said to have greatly progressed. My debt to the bibliographical publications registered below, especially to those of the late P. José Madoz, S. J., of P. Ursicino Domínguez del Val, O.S.A., of Dom Eligius Dekkers, O. S. B., of the late Mgr Teófilo Ayuso Marazuela, of Professor M. C. Díaz y Díaz and especially to the admirable bibliography of Professor Jacques Fontaine, will be evident to every scholar. At the same time I have to thank librarians inside and outside Spain for their assistance. I should like to mention especially here the late Rvdmo. Dr. José Vives, of the Biblioteca Balmesiana in Barcelona, and my friends Professor J. B. Trapp and Dr. C. R. Ligota of the Warburg Institute, London. It is due to the unfailing kindness and helpfulness of these and other librarians that I have been able to see all but a few of the works enumerated here*.

* This article includes my contribution to *Isidoriana* (León, 1961), pp. 11-74, with corrections and additions for 1960-1975. I am grateful to the Centro de Estudios Isidorianos León, for permission to reproduce my earlier article.

I am extremely grateful to my friends and colleagues Professor M. C. Díaz y Díaz and Professor J. Fontaine, who read and commented on the greater part of this article. Their criticism has saved me from many blunders. For those that may remain I am alone, of course, responsible. I am also grateful to Fr. B. de Gaiffier S. J., of the Société des Bollandistes, and to the late Fr. R. E. McNally S. J., who were kind enough to read and criticise Sections VI[a] and III respectively in their 1961 version.

Bibliographies

For bibliographies on Isidore before 1910 cf. Altaner, in *Misc. Isid.*, pp. 2 sqq., and for publications 1910-35, ibid., passim (1). This article is very complete. I have indicated a few omissions. General bibliographical periodicals that I have found especially useful are *L'Année Philologique* (Paris), *AST* (bibliographies to 1952), *Indice Histórico Español* (Barcelona, 1953-), *BALCL*, *BTAM*, *RHE*, and, for the publications of 1956- the new *Bibliographia Patristica*, ed. W. Schneemelcher (Berlin). Special bibliographies published since 1936 dealing with Spanish Patristics and Isidore, in chronological order (cf. also Section I below, General Works):

J. Madoz, *Un decenio de estudios patrísticos en España (1931-40)*, in *RET*, 1 (1940-41), pp. 919-62, especially 949-56.

R. B. Brown, *The Printed Works of Isidore of Seville, a trial check List*, Lexington, 1949 (University of Kentucky Libraries, Occasional Contributions, 5), i + 32 pp. This work is a secondhand compilation in which the author has made no attempt to distinguish between genuine and spurious works.

J. Madoz, *Segundo decenio*, pp. 115-122. Valuable as are all P. Madoz's publications (2).

E. Dekkers and A. Gaar, *CPL*, pp. 204-211. A new edition is in preparation.

W. Wattenbach and W. Levison, *Deutschlands Geschichtsquellen im Mittelalter*, I, Weimar, 1952, pp. 86-88.

Ayuso, pp. 506-508.

U. Domínguez Del Val, *Cuatro años de bibliografía sobre Patrística española (1951-54)*, in *RET*, 15 (1955), pp. 399-444, esp. pp. 429-34. Adds some works omitted by Madoz, *Segundo decenio*.

E. Cuevas and U. Domínguez del Val, *Patrología española* (appendix to the Spanish trans. of B. Altaner, *Patrologie*), Madrid, 1956, pp. 92*-99*, esp. pp. 98* sq. A certain lack of order.

B. Altaner, *Patrologie*, 1966, pp. 494-97.

Fontaine, pp. 889-926. This is far the best bibliography yet published but it does not aim to include everything on Isidore and omits some valuable articles, principally on his theology.

Diaz, *Index*, pp. 28-47. Cf. infra, Section II.

(1) For a review of Altaner's article cf. P. Heseler, in *Philologische Wochenschrift*, 58 (1938), pp. 303-306, who also indicates a few omissions.

(2) Cf. also J. Madoz, *El renacer de la investigación patristica en España, (1930-1951)*, in *SEJG*, 4 (1952), pp. 355-71; on Isidore 370 sqq.

MADOZ, *San Isidoro*, pp. 157-188. More useful for Spanish than for other works. Contains some recent publications, added by the editor of this posthumous work. Not always exact.

A. SEGOVIA, *Informe sobre Bibliografía isidoriana (1936-60)*, in *EE*, 36 (1961) pp. 73-126. Often second-hand. Does not distinguish between the important and the trivial. Occasionally useful, with regard to the MS. tradition and the influence of Isidore.

U. DOMÍNGUEZ DEL VAL, *Herencia literaria de padres y escritores españoles de Osio de Córdoba a Julián de Toledo*, in *Repertorio de historia de las ciencias eclesiásticas en España*, 1, Salamanca, 1967, pp. 1-85, esp. pp. 55-65. Contains the bibliography (with some omissions) to 1966.

J. FONTAINE, *Chronique de littérature wisigothique*, in *Revue des études augustiniennes*, 19 (1973), pp. 163-76, studies the years 1970-72; in a sequel, *Chronique d'histoire et de littérature hispaniques (paléochretiennes et visigotiques)*, ibid., 22 (1976), pp. 402-35, the years 1972-76.

I. GENERAL WORKS DEALING WITH ISIDORE, IN CHRONOLOGICAL ORDER

This is a selective list. It would be useless to list all recent histories of Spain, of medieval philosophy, etc., that dedicate a few pages to Isidore. In general I have omitted reprints of books first published before 1935, if the new edition adds nothing substantial to the old.

R. AIGRAIN, in *Histoire de l'Église*, ed. A. FLICHE et V. MARTIN, V, Paris, 1938, pp. 242-44.

J. DE GHELLINCK, *Littérature latine au moyen âge*, I, Paris, 1939, pp. 24-29.

R. MENÉNDEZ PIDAL, *Historia de España*, III, Madrid, 1940, pp. XXXIII-XLI.

J. PÉREZ DE URBEL, *Las letras en la época visigoda*, ibid., pp. 397-415.

P. DE LABRIOLLE, *Histoire de la littérature latine chrétienne*, 3e éd. revue par G. BARDY, II, Paris, 1947, pp. 818-23. Inadequate.

E. R. CURTIUS, *Europäische Literatur und lateinisches Mittelalter*, Bern, 1948, passim. 2nd ed. 1954. Cf. Section V below, and note 81. A work of great importance for Isidorian studies. Cf. also note 133 below.

A. CASTRO, *El enfoque histórico y la no hispanidad de los Visigodos*, in *Nueva revista de filologia hispánica*, 3 (1949), pp. 217-63, esp. pp. 252-58 (almost exactly reproduced in IDEM, *La realidad histórica de España*, México, 1954), Castro argues that Isidore and his contemporaries were not yet Spaniards in any real sense of the term. Cf. the reply (to the article) by C. SÁNCHEZ-ALBORNOZ, *España, un enigma histórico*, I, Buenos Aires, 1956, pp. 132-34, 242-47, a work that contains other valuable ' aperçus ' on Isidore (e. g., II, pp. 601 sq.).

J. Madoz, *Escritores de la España visigótica*, in *Historia general de las literaturas hispánicas*, ed. G. Diaz Plaja, I, Barcelona, 1949, pp. 119-24, 137 sq. Excellent general orientation.

Idem, in *Enciclopedia Cattolica*, VII, Città del Vaticano, 1951, pp. 254-58. Largely reproduces his study of 1949.

M. Ruffini, *Le origini letterarie in Spagna*. I. *L'epoca visigotica*, Torino, 1951, c. VII, pp. 115-148. A careful study.

A. Bernareggi, *Enciclopedia ecclesiastica*, V, Milano, 1953, pp. 122-25. Abundant if not very select bibliography.

A. M. Bozzone, in *Dizionario ecclesiastico*, ed. A. Mergati and A. Pelzer, II, Torino, 1955, p. 480.

L. García de Valdeavellano, *Historia de España*, I[2], Madrid, 1955, pp. 298-301. Not very critical.

E. Cuevas and U. Domínguez Del Val, *Patrologia española*[4], Madrid, 1956, pp. 92*-99*. Cf. the criticisms of M. C. Díaz y Díaz, *De patrística española*, in *RET*, 17 (1957), pp. 37-44.

M. L. W. Laistner, *Thought and Letters in Western Europe A. D. 500 to 900*[2], London, 1957, pp. 119-25.

F. L. Cross (ed.), *The Oxford Dictionary of the Christian Church*, London, 1957, pp. 705 sq.

E. Ewig, in *Die Religion in Geschichte und Gegenwart*, III[3], Tübingen, 1959, p. 906.

P. Riché, *Education et culture dans l'Occident barbare* (*VI*e-*VIII*e *siècles*), Paris, 1962 (2nd ed. 1967), esp. pp. 339-50.

J. Fontaine, in *Catholicisme*, VI, Paris, 1963, pp. 154-66. Idem, *Die westgotische lateinische Literatur. Probleme und Perspektiven*, in *Antike und Abendland*, 12, 1 (1966), pp. 64-87, esp. pp. 75-81.

A. Humbert, in *The New Catholic Encyclopaedia*, VII, New York, 1967, pp. 674-76.

U. Domínguez Del Val, in *Diccionario de historia eclesiástica de España*, II, Madrid, 1972, pp. 1211-14.

II. Authentic Works: editions, translations and manuscripts

Valuable lists of those works generally admitted as authentic are to be found in B. Fischer, *Vetus Latina, die Reste der altlateinischen Bibel*..., I, Freiburg, 1949, pp. 87-88; *CPL*, pp. 267-73; Ayuso, p. 505; Díaz, *Index*, I, pp. 28-44. The last named is the most reliable and also lists a very considerable number of MSS. of the different works. (He is content to omit those later than 1200). In this the author follows Beeson's classic work but greatly adds to the number of MSS. listed. A future edition could profit from the most recent volumes of Professor Lowc's *CLA*; cf. my review in *JTS*, N.S., 11 (1960), pp. 196 sq. The pages in the *Index* devoted to Isidore condense the results of recent research, much of it the author's own; apart from the works of Fontaine they constitute perhaps the most important contribution to general Isidorian scholarship in the period under review. J. MADOZ, *San Isidoro*, c. II, « Obra literaria », pp. 23-78, discusses the works of Isidore he considers authentic. He lists a number of MSS. His lists are based on Beeson's, with some Spanish additions, mostly taken from Antolin's catalogue of the Escorial Library. For Madoz's book cf. also below, Section I. B. BISCHOFF, *Die europaïsche Verbreitung der Werke Isidors von Sevilla, Isidoriana*, León, 1961, pp. 317 44, by his discussion of the early MSS. has greatly added to our understanding of the transmission of Isidore's works.

J. A. DE ALDAMA, *Indicaciones sobre la cronología de las obras de S. Isidoro*, in *Misc. Isid.*, pp. 57-89, has given us a reliable chronological scheme for Isidore's writings, based on a number of converging patterns taken from the dedications, precise references to historical events, the correspondence with Braulio, the use of the works of St. Gregory the Great and the *renotatio librorum divi Isidori* of Braulio. This scheme has been generally accepted; it has helped to secure the rejection by scholars as spurious of at least one work recently ascribed to Isidore (3).

M. DE POBLADURA, *Vicisitudes de una proyectada versión castellana de las obras completas de San Isidoro de Sevilla* (1772), *Salmanticensis*, 8 (1961), pp. 135-57, discusses a bilingual, annotated edition of Isidore proposed by the Capuchins of the Convento of San Antonio de Prado, in Madrid. The Consejo de Castilla did not grant permission because of the unfavourable opinion of the Real Academia de la Lengua, both as to the idea of translating Isidore and as to reprinting the edition of Madrid, 1599. Don Manuel Lardizával y Uribe considered a critical edition necessary. However, Bartolomé Ulloa produced an edition in 1778 (of the Latin text), which is simply a reprint of the 1599 edition, without even correcting its errors. This edition was used for the translation of the *Synonyma* published in 1944 (see below, n. 29), but it was soon eclipsed by Arévalo's edition. On this edition, the last published of Isidore's *opera omnia*, see C. EGUÍA RUIZ, *Un insigne editor de S. Isidoro, el P. Faustino Arévalo, S. I.*, in *Misc. Isid.*, pp. 364-84. In 1936 Professor A. E. Anspach was still engaged, as he had been for many years, on a new edition of Isidore for the *Corpus scriptorum ecclesiasticorum latinorum* of Vienna. Unfortunately, at the time of his death, this edition had not appeared. Dr. Anspach, however, published several works that he ascribed to Isidore, but whose authenticity remains in doubt. We shall come to them later (cf. infra, Section III). We now have J. M. FERNÁNDEZ CATON, *Catálogo de los materiales codicológicos y bibliográficos del legado científico del Prof. Dr. August Eduard Anspach*, in *Archivos Leoneses*, 19 (1965), pp. 29-120 (pp. 38-66 are concerned with Isi-

(3) Cf. infra. Section III, for the *Commonitiuncula ad sororem*, ed. ANSPACH.

dore), which reveals the extent of Prof. Anspach's labours. (See below, p. 13).

Before we turn to discuss studies of Isidore's individual works we should notice the publication from the important MS. 22 of Léon Cathedral (saec. IX) of fragments from the *origines* and the *laus Spaniae*, by R. R(ODRÍGUEZ) and A. Á(LVAREZ), *Los fragmentos isidorianos del códice samuélico de la Catedral de León*, in *Archivos Leoneses*, I (1947), 2, pp. 125-67 (4). In a different field L. GARCÍA RIBES, *Estudio de las traducciones castellanas de obras de San Isidoro*, in *RABM*, 56 (1950), pp. 279-320, has given us a useful account of Spanish translations of Isidore, medieval and modern (5). Fray JUSTO PÉREZ DE URBEL and Fray TIMOTEO ORTEGA published an excellent anthology of Isidorian texts in translation, *San Isidoro (Antologia)*, in the series *Breviarios de Pensamiento español*, Barcelona, 1940, 279 pp. (6).

In discussing the separate works of Isidore I follow the order of the *CPL*. One of the few works of Isidore critically edited since Arévalo's time has been the *Origines* or *Etymologiae* (7). (For the name cf. R. SCHMIDT, *Origines oder Etymologiae ? Die Bezeichnung der Enzyklopädie des Isidor von Sevilla in den Handschriften des Mittelalters*, in *Festschrift A. Hofmeister*, Halle, 1955, pp. 223-32, and FONTAINE, I, 11 n. 1). Lindsay's edition of 1911, although an advance on Arévalo's, has long been recognised as inadequate, using, as its does, insufficient MSS., and suffering greatly from its neglect of the actual as distinct from the ostensible sources used by Isidore. Arévalo's edition is still indispensable and has, on occasion, been proved to be right as against Lindsay's (8). FONTAINE's recent work on the sources of the Orig. has greatly facilitated the task of the future editor. (Cf. infra, Section IV). Meanwhile we have an attempt by W. PORZIG to improve on Lindsay's classification of MSS. which two leading authorities appear prepared to accept, at least as a working hypothesis (9). In an article (*Die Rezensionen der Etymologiae des Isidorus von Sevilla*, in *Hermes*, 72, 1937, pp. 129-70) based principally on MSS. in Swiss libraries, Porzig not only pointed out errors in Lindsay's collation of various MSS. but maintained the latter's division of his material into three families was mistaken and that in fact the real division lies between those MSS. containing a longer or a shorter recension, the longer deriving from Braulio's edition. Porzig's conclusions need to be verified, as he himself said, through a study of other MSS., notably of those in Paris, before they can be consi-

(4) Some of these fragments had already been published by F. FITA, in *CD*, 6 (1871).

(5) Cf. also J. MADOZ, in *RET*, 11 (1951), pp. 461 sqq.

(6) I. QUILES, *San Isidoro* (op. cit. infra, Section VIa), pp. 101-49, translates into Spanish passages from the *origines*, *differentiae* and *sententiae* that bear on philosophical problems.

(7) Henceforth abbreviated as well as the other Isidorian works.

(8) Cf. FONTAINE, I, p. 112 n. 1. Lindsay saw, of course, the importance of using Isidore's sources (cf. his edition, I, xiii), and in *Classical Quarterly*, 5, 1911, p. 42 sq.) but felt obliged to omit references to them so as not to swell the *apparatus* further. It is also fair – and necessary – to say that he did not intend his edition to be considered as in any way definitive.

(9) Cf. FONTAINE, I, p. 405, n. 2; DÍAZ, *Index*, p. 40 n. 61.

dered definitive but they seem more firmly based than the theories of Anspach ([10]).

Although no new edition of the Orig. has appeared in the last sixty years to replace Lindsay's we can record a number of emendations to the text of varying value ([11]), and also the discovery and publication of the only Seventh Century MS. (only surviving in fragments) that appears to exist, written in Irish minuscule, probably in Ireland, now St-Gall 1399 a.l ([12]). We can also record the appearance of the first complete translation

(10) For which cf. A. E. ANSPACH, *Taionis et Isidori nova fragmenta et opera*, Madrid, 1930, pp. 36-56. (Cf. ALTANER, in *Misc. Isid.*, p. 7). If we recognise (as we must) with G. MENÉNDEZ PIDAL (art. cit. infra, note 134) the importance of the Spanish tradition of the orig., we must not forget the equal or even greater importance of the non-Spanish tradition, all the more evident today after the discovery of the only 7th Century (fragmentary) MS. of the wark, which was written *outside* Spain (cf. infra, note 12). It cannot reriously be maintained that « esencialmente el resto de la tradición europea *sólo* (my italics) a través de este eslabón (the Mozarabic MSS.) queda encadenada a San Isidoro » (art. cit. p. 166). Sr. Menéndez Pidal does not refer to BEESON's *Isidor-Studien* or to PORZIG's article. He has, however, pp. 169-72, 177 sq. 180-87, 192, some interesting notes on various early Spanish MSS. of the Orig., and indicates some relations between them, especially between Escorial P. I. 8 (saec. IX) and Esc. & 1. 3 (a. 1047).

(11) Cf. J. H. OLIVER, in *RhMus*, 100 (1957), pp. 242-44, on Orig. 1, 24, 2: *ineptiam* for *inperitiam* (dubious: more convincingly J. H. GILLIAM, in *Hommages à León Herrmann*, Bruxelles-Berchem, 1960 (Coll. Latomus 44), pp. 413 sq., emends *inpuritiam*, the reading of two of Lindsay's MSS. and of Arévalo); W. T. AVERY, in *CPh*, 49 (1954), p. 189, on orig. 2, 18, 1 (useless); ID., ibid., 104, on orig. 3, 71, 9 (cf. FONTAINE, II, p. 528 n. 2); M. VAN DEN HOUT, in *VChr*, 2 (1948), p. 56, on orig. 3, 12, 1: *geometrae* for *geometriae* (accepted by FONTAINE, I, p. 400, n. 1); W. D. SHARPE, in *Traditio*, 14 (1958), pp. 377 sq., on orig. 4, 8, 9; *pityriasis* for *satiriasis* (possibly correct). A. ROTA, in *Atti*... (art. cit. infra, note 65) on orig. 6, 16, 12, holds the phrase in *Decret. Grat.* I, dist. XV. 1: *unde qui sibimet dissentiunt, non agunt concilium*; *quia non consentiunt in unum*, which is substantially maintained by the Correctores romani of Gratian but is omitted by Arévalo and Lindsay, is *genuine* Isidore; it lacks any serious support from MSS. H. SILVESTRE, in *MA*, 55 (1949), pp. 247-49, emends orig. 11, 2, 33: *Caesariensis* (i. e. Priscian of Caesarea) for *Caesar* (ingenious but unsupported by the MS. tradition); C. HÜNEMORDER, in *RhMus*, 110 (1967), pp. 371-84 on orig. 14, 4, 4: *aves Hercynias* (not *Hyrcanias*); W. T. AVERY, in *CPh*, 51 (1956), pp. 172-73, on orig. 15, 13, 1: *choragros* (as Arévalo) instead af *coragros*; J. VALLEJO, in *Emerita*, 16 (1948), pp. 227 sq., on orig. 15, 16, 2: *mille alium* for *mille adium*; Ibid., 268 sq., three other possibilities; *mille ad eum, milliadium* and *miliadium*; A. S. PEASE, in *American Journal of Philology*, 61 (1940), p. 80, on orig. 17, 1, 3: *fimavit* for *firmavit* (following Arévalo); L. SPITZER, ibid., pp. 357 sq., confirms the reading; J. ROUGÉ, in *Latomus*, 18 (1959), p. 650, on orig. 19, 19, 12: *rostrum* for *rastrum* (no MS. authority). A. MAZZARINO, in *Helikon*, 6 (19 66), pp. 232-36, on orig. 19, 22, 20, proposes to read (in the quotation from Naevius): *paleraque ex auro* (for *pulchra quae*). No MS. evidence is adduced. Variant readings in MSS. for *aphratum* (orig. 20, 2, 29) are noted by K. MRAS, in *Wiener Studien*, 61-62 (1943-47) p. 106 n. 22. Etymological and other commentaries an the *Orig.* infra, Section V.

(12) Cf. A. DOLD and J. DUFT, *Die älteste irische Handschriften-Reliquie der Stiftsbibliothek St. Gallen mit Texten aus Isidors Etymologien*, Beuron, 1955, 12 pp. + facs.; LOWE, *CLA*, VII (1956), n. 995. The question of the origin of the fragments is disputed between Ireland and an Irish continental foundation. (? Bobbio). DÍAZ, *Index*, p. 39 n. 60, indicates G. GOLDSCHMIDT, in *Gesnerus*, 2 (1945), pp. 151, 156-62, as publishing readings from a saec. VII papyrus of the orig. at Zurich. In fact, however, the papyrus at Zurich contains fragments of the *synonyma*, not the *orig.* (as such is is duly noted by DÍAZ, *Index*, 31 and n. 33; cf. *CLA*, VII, n. 929). GOLDSCHMIDT (loc. cit.) notes two MSS. of the *Orig.*, Zurich C. 150 (saec. XV) and C. 128 (s. XI-XII). For other MSS. (apart from DÍAZ, *Index*, 40 sqq.; *CPL*, n. 1186) cf. C. BALÍC, in *Studia mediaevalia in honorem R. J. Martin*, Bruges, 1948, p. 472 (Zagreb Cathedral 182, s. XII); C. J. HERINGTON, in *RhMus*, 101 (1958), pp. 353 sq.

of the work into Spanish, by L. CORTÉS Y GONGORA, *San Isidoro de Sevilla, Etimologías,* introd. general de S. MONTERO DÍAZ, Madrid, 1951 (Biblioteca de Autores Cristianos, 67), xx – 87* + 563 pp. Other fragmentary translations have appeared, not only into Spanish but into Russian (13). A problem that should be mentioned here was discussed by F. SAXL, in *Illuminated Mediaeval Encyclopaedias,* I, *The Classical Heritage* (14). Saxl produced arguments to show that there existed an illustrated « édition de luxe » of the Orig. which was used as a source by the Carolingian artist or artists who illuminated Rabanus Maurus' *de universo* and that the archetype of this illustrated edition was illuminated, probably in Spain, not long after the work was sent by Isidore to Braulio.

J. M.ª. FERNÁNDEZ CATÓN, *Las Etimologías en la tradición manuscrita medieval estudiada por el Prof. Dr. Anspach,* León, 1966 (also in *Archivos Leoneses,* 21, 1965, pp. 121-384), publishes a list of 967 MSS. of the orig. studied by Dr. Anspach. For the practical purpose of a new edition this list is of less use than BISCHOFF's discussion of the early MSS. (*Isidoriana,* pp. 339-41). Meanwhile a new edition has been set in train by Prof. J. FONTAINE of Paris and his collaborators. « *Comptes rendus* » of the « *Colloques isidoriens* » held at the Institut d'Etudes Latines of the University of Paris have been circulated to those interested. (The second « colloque » appears in *Revue d'histoire des textes,* 2 (1972), pp. 282-87).

What is proposed is an edition established by a different specialist for each separate book of the work, accompanied by translation into the particular editor's language, by full notes, and by a complete *index verborum* at the end (volume 21). All twenty books have now been assigned to different scholars. All non-Spanish MSS. earlier than 1000 and Spanish MSS. later than that date will be collated. The complete collation of MSS. will be preserved at the Institut de Recherche et d'Histoire des textes in

(Exeter Cathedral 3549 [B], s. XIII); H. SILVESTRE, in *SEJG,* 5 (1953), pp. 180 sq. (Bruxelles 5413-22, s. IX, excerpta); H. WEISWEILER, in *RHE,* 34 (1938), p. 248, 254 (Munich Lat. 16085, s. XII, excerpta); A. M. NEGRI, in *Riv. di filol. e di istruzione classica,* N. S., 37 (1959), pp. 260-77 (describes Bologna 797, French, s. XI, *ineunte,* containing an incomplete copy of Orig. 1). G. MARTÍNEZ DÍEZ, in *Anuario de Estudios Medievales,* 2 (1965), pp. 431 sq., studies the text of orig. 8, 5, in MS. Paris, Bibl. Nat., lat. 1460 (s. XIV). J. JIMÉNEZ DELGADO, *El ' de ortographia ' isidoriano del Códice Misceláneo de León,* in *Isidoriana,* pp. 475-93, publishes the text of orig. 1, 27 from MS. León 22. K. FORSTNER, in *Scriptorium,* 14 (1960), pp. 235-56, discusses MSS. fragments (Salzburg, St. Peter, of saec. VIII-IX containing orig. 9, 2 sq. and 5, 38 sq. He lists variant readings. Cf. also supra, note 10 and infra, note 96.

(13) ISIDORUS HISPALENSIS, *Ethimologiarum liber IIII De Medicina,* Masnou-Barcelona, 1945, 92 pp. + facs., containing a trans. of L. IV by D. BERMÚDEZ CAMACHO and C. E. ARQUÉS, is not mentioned by L. GARCÍA RIBES, art. cit. supra. The bibliography of *RHE,* 42 (1947), p. 540, mentions a publication entitled ISIDORUS HISPALENSIS, *Ethymologiarum de Musica,* Barcelona, 1946, but, from the description given, this seems to be a confusion with the work just cited. I have certainly never been able to find a copy of the *De Musica* of 1946 in any library inside or outside Spain. For the Russian trans. of selections from the *Orig.* cf. infra, Section V, n. 96.

(14) A lecture originally delivered in 1939 but published in his posthumous *Lectures,* London, 1957, I, pp. 228-41, and II, plates 55-64. The main difficulty with SAXL's theory is the absence af existing early illuminated MSS. of the *Orig.*.

Paris. The aim is to edit the long recension traditionally ascribed to Braulio, while making clear the passages omitted in other versions.

MARC REYDELLET, *La diffusion des Origines d'Isidore de Séville au Haut Moyen Age*, in *Mélanges d'Archéologie et d'Histoire de l'Ecole Française de Rome*, 78 (1966), pp. 383-437, has presented conclusions which modify earlier views. While the four families of MSS. distinguished by LINDSAY and PORZIG « subsist », the Spanish and French families now appear far less homogeneous than had been thought. It seems possible that Books 1-10 and 11-20 were often transmitted separately. In 1970 (in one of the « comptes rendus » already cited) M. REYDELLET proposed the collation of two Italian, five Spanish, eight French and two unclassified MSS. (apart from fragmentary evidence).

M. C. DÍAZ Y DÍAZ, *Los Capitulos sobre los metales de las Etimologías de Isidoro de Sevilla*, León, 1970 (La Mineria Hispana e Ibero-Americana, 7), 99 pp., edits orig. 16, 17-24, with a translation, notes and a valuable introduction. Díaz emphasizes the complexity of the textual tradition. He collates 32 MSS. He finds it hard to isolate the Spanish « family » or to see the French family as unitary. He does not find the supposed connection between a French family and the edition addressed to Sisebut or between a Spanish family and the later edition of Braulio convincing. DÍAZ sees Sisebut as receiving only Books 1-10 (this edition would correspond to MS. Milan, Ambrosiana, L. 99 sup., s. VIII), while the edition of Braulio is best represented by MS. Escorial T. II. 24 (s. IX *ex.*). Conclusions drawn from such a short portion of the orig. cannot be definitive but it is interesting to note how much further they go than those of REYDELLET, based particularly on his work on Book 9.

M. C. DÍAZ Y DÍAZ, *Problemas de algunos manuscritos hispánicos de las Etimologías de Isidoro de Sevilla*, in *Festschrift Bernhard Bischoff*, Stuttgart, 1971, pp. 70-80, discusses the following MSS: Madrid, Bibl. Nac. 10008 (saec. XII *ex.*); Paris, Bibl. Nat., nouv. acq. lat. 2169 (dated 1072); Escorial & I.3. (of 1047); Madrid, Bibl. Acad. Historia 76 (954), and 25 (946); Escorial & I.14 (*CLA* no. 1635); T. II. 24 (the *U* of Lindsay); P. I.8 and P. I. 7 (both saec. IX), P.I. 6 (saec. X) and Madrid, Bibl. Nac., Vitr. 14.3 (the *T* of Lindsay). His notes are of particular interest in revealing the excessive importance given by Beer and Lindsay to *T*; in displaying the relations between different Isidorian MSS. written in the Rioja, and in his discussion of the paleography of Mozarabic MSS. centered on Escorial & I.14. MIGUEL RODRÍGUEZ-PANTOJA, *Notas de ortografía isidoriana*, in *Habis*, 5 (1974), pp. 65-91, using the Hispanic MSS. of the orig., Book 19, which he is editing, studies changes in vocalism, e/i, i/y, o/u, ae/e, oe/i, the use of h, t/d, c/qu, and the assimilation of prefixes.

WILLIAM D. SHARPE has given us an English translation of orig. 11, 1-4(« De homine et portentis ») and of Book 4 (« De medicina »), ISIDORE OF SEVILLE, *The Medical Writings* (*Transactions of the American Philosophical Society*, N. S., 54, 2, 1964, 75 pp.). The translation is careful and is accompanied by a valuable introduction and full notes on classical and

Christian sources. See reviews by P. KIBRE, *Speculum*, 40 (1965), pp. 754-56; W. STONEMAN, *Manuscripta*, 9 (1965), pp. 176 sq.

Isidore's earliest surviving work, the *differentiarum libri ii* has been studied by G. BRUGNOLI, *Studi sulle Differentiae verborum*, Rome, 1955, pp. 133-50, and in *Il Liber de differentiis rerum di Isidoro di Siviglia, Vetera Christianorum*, 1 (1964), pp. 65-82. In his second study Brugnoli notes that Book 2 of the *differentiae* is Isidore's first attempt at a succinct statement of doctrine, a prelude to the *sententiae*. He believes that this Book was originally transmitted separately from Book 1, which is concerned with grammar. He questions the authenticity of Book 1. An edition in preparation by Prof. C. CODOÑER MERINO of Salamanca should clarity these points (15).

Some years ago M. L. W. LAISTNER, in *Medievalia et Humanistica*, 2 (1944), pp. 28-31 facs., published the text of the *de natura rerum* contained in the surviving fragment of an Anglo-Saxon MS. (Weimar Fol. 414a, saec. VIII-IX = *CLA* IX, n. 1369). He took this occasion to point out the inadequacy of Becker's edition in 1857 and to stress the necessity of a new edition based on a wider selection of MSS. This new edition was produced by M. JACQUES FONTAINE, *Isidore de Séville, Traité de la nature, suivi de l'Epître en vers du roi Sisebut à Isidore*, ed. critique et traduction, Bordeaux, 1960 (Bibl. Hautes Études Hispaniques, 28), XIV + 466 pp. (Both the treatise and the *epistula* of Sisebut were accompanied by French translations; the translation of the nat. was the first into any modern language). This was the first critical edition of an undoubtedly genuine major work of Isidore to appear since Lindsay's edition of the orig. in 1911. The text is preceded by a long introduction, divided into three main parts. We have, firstly, a study of the date (612-613) and origin of the work, its predecessors and plan, then of the MSS. employed and their relations, with the history of the diffusion of the text in Europe from Sisebut to Charlemagne, and, finally, of the language of the treatise. The editor bases his text on 17 MSS. (three of them fragments) which include all the known pre-Carolingian witnesses. He is able to show they represent three « editions », a short recension in 46 chapters, contained in six MSS., the « recension moyenne », with the addition of c. 48 (contained in the Ovetensis-Escorial R. II. 18, s. VII-and in Cambrai 937, s. VIII) and, lastly, the long recension in 48 chapters, containing c. 44 and the « mystic » passage in c. 1. This is found in seven English, German and Italian MSS (16). An examination of the internal evidence indicates the second recension is probably due to a subsequent addition of c. 48 by Isidore himself but the long recension, with its two additions, appears to be the work of a later cleric, perhaps in Northumbria, familiar with Isidore's style and methods. The construction of a *stemma codicum* confirms us in the view that the essen-

(15) The work is contained in the Exeter MS. described by HERINGTON (art. cit. supra, note 12). One might also add to DÍAZ's list of MSS. (*Index* n. 101) Paris Lat. 4841 (s. IX, frag.) and St. Paul in Kärnten 25, 2, 35 (s. IX-X).

(16) It is impossible to determine to which « edition » two incomplete MSS. belong. (Chapters are numbered here as in FONTAINE's edition). Cf. also infra, note 94.

tial difference lies between the French family of MSS., closely related to the one ancient Spanish MS., the Ovetensis, and the Anglo-Saxon and German group which contains the long recension. In a most interesting chapter, whose understanding is much assisted by a map which serves to supplement the *stemma codicum*, the editor discusses the diffusion of the work in pre-Carolingian Europe. Its first dated mention is by Aldhelm c. 685 (at Malmesbury in Southern England). Fontaine suggests four possible routes from Spain to Malmesbury, two of which would take the book via Ireland, but he himself inclines to suppose it reached England from France. It was copied there, probably at Fleury, before the Seventh Century was over (Paris lat. 6400G). The long recension, as paleographical evidence has already suggested and as a study of the historical background confirms, seems to have originated in Northumbria and to have travelled thence to Germany and Italy. The whole of this discussion, rigorously scientific in method as it is, succeeds in bringing to life in a new way the problems of transmission of classical and Christian learning in the Seventh and Eighth Centuries.

The third part of the introduction is the first critical study to appear of the language of Isidore of Seville (for Sofer's work, as Fontaine observes, is lexicographical). Fontaine studies successively the orthography and phonetics, the morphology, the syntax and the style of the *de natura rerum*. It is unnecessary to point out the immense usefulness of this study to future editors of other works of Isidore and of the other Spanish Fathers. The edition is accompanied by a detailed *apparatus* of sources, *testimonia* and parallels and by two further *apparatus*, one *critical*, limited to important variants, the other *general*, with all other variants, including orthographical. In the construction of the text Fontaine, using the results of his study of Isidorian orthography, manages to avoid both the excessive respect for scribal mistakes that characterises some other modern editions and the undiscerning « classicism » of Nineteenth Century scholarship. One of the few « lacunae » one might point to in this otherwise definitive edition is the absence of a discussion of the curious human figures that appear in some early MSS. notably in Paris lat. 6400G and 6413. Two studies of these illustrations, too recent to be of use to Fontaine, will fill this minor gap [17].

Since Fontaine's edition we have some valuable notes on MS. Escorial R. II. 18 by Prof. Díaz y Díaz, *La circulation des manuscrits dans la Péninsule Ibérique du VIII*e *au XI*e *siècle*, in *Cahiers de civilisation médiévale*, 12 (1969), pp. 226 f. Fontaine himself has published two additional

(17) Cf. B. Teyssedre, *Un exemple de survie de la figure humaine dans les MSS. précarolingiens : Les Illustrations du « De natura rerum » d'Isidore*, in *Gazette des Beaux-Arts*, 6e période, 56 (1960), pp. 19-34, who reproduces the miniatures with human figures in Paris Lat. 6400G and 6413, and O. K. Werckmeister, *Three problems of tradition in pre-Carolingian Figure Style : from Visigothic to Insular Illumination*, *Proceedings of the Royal Irish Academy*, 63, Series C (1963). Cf. also my article, ibid., cit. infra, note 146, for a suggestion that the long recension comes in fact from Ireland and not from Northumbria. On the *schemata* in the nat. and the orig. cf. H. Bober's article in *Essays... E. Panofsky*, New York, 1961.

studies on the MS. transmission of the *de natura rerum*. In *La diffusion de l'oeuvre d'Isidore de Séville dans les scriptoria helvétiques du Haut Moyen Age, Revue Suisse d'Histoire*, 12 (1962), pp. 305-27, he discusses the transmission of the work from 800 (where his edition left off) to 1000, on the basis of the MSS. still preserved in Swiss libraries. Studying those at Basle and Bern he is able to show the survival of the short recension (46 chapters) in the early ninth century in both France and Bavaria, and at the same time, its contamination by MSS. of the long recension. An examination follows of the MSS. of the treatise preserved at Saint-Gall, Einsiedeln and Zofingen (all acquired by or written at Saint-Gall or copied from its MSS). Copies of the work reached Saint-Gall from Verona, Chelles and Germany. Other copies were made there. The result was an attempt to produce a « critical » text, as copyists became editors.

In *La diffusion carolingienne du De natura rerum d'Isidore de Séville d'après des manuscrits conservés en Italie, Studi Medievali*, 7 (1967), pp. 108-27, FONTAINE carries a similar enquiry to Italy. Three Reginenses Latini (255, 310, 1260) and MS. Milan, Ambros. H. 150 inf. belong to or descend from the short recension; two Palatini Latini (834, 1448) represent the long recension. MS. Modena Est. 988 descends from a contaminated Italian sub-group of the eighth century, already isolated in Fontaine's edition.

If we turn to the exegetical works of Isidore, on the *allegoriae* there is nothing to record apart from L. MOLINERO's Spanish translation [18]. The question of St. James' presence in Spain has continued to attract attention to the *de ortu et obitu patrum*. M. C. DÍAZ Y DÍAZ, *Die spanische Jakobus-Legende bei Isidor von Sevilla*, in *Historisches Jahrbuch*, 77 (1958), pp. 467-72, edits c. 70 which concerns St. James, collating 38 MSS [19]. The passage refering to St. James preaching in Spain appears to be contained in the whole MS. tradition. Professor Díaz maintained, however, on the ground of its divergence from the source used by Isidore for the whole work and from Julian of Toledo's known views (*de comprobatione sextae aetatis*, II, 13), and also because of the incorrectness of its style that it was an interpolation. In a later article, *La literatura jacobea anterior al códice calixtino*, in *Compostellanum*, 10 (1965), pp. 638-661, esp. pp. 643-6, DÍAZ Y DÍAZ, influenced by observations of BISCHOFF (*Isidoriana*, pp. 334 f.) accepts the view that this passage is probably by Isidore (see also, below, Section IV, n. 78). C. Chaparro has a critical edition of the *de ortu* in preparation [20].

(18) *Algunas Alegorias de la Sagrada Escritura*, Buenos Aires, 1936, 39 pp.

(19) DÍAZ, *Index*, n. 103 lists several more early MSS. not used in his edition. We can add St Paul in Kärnten 25, 1, 35 (XXV a 9), saec. VIII-IX, also containing the *prooemia*.

(20) Cf. the use of the *de ortu* by Lathcen (+ 661) in Ireland; for the Irish *de ortu* cf. infra, Section III. On the phrase « sepultus in acha marmarica » (DÍAZ, art. cit., 472) cf. E. HONIGMANN, *Patristic Studies*, Città del Vaticano, 1953 (Studi e testi 173), pp. 79-81 (not cited by Díaz). Honigmann holds Achaia « seems the genuine name of the city in Marmarica » (it is the reading of a good number of DÍAZ's MSS.). Cf. also DÍAZ, *El lugar de enterramiento de Santiago el Mayor en Isidoro de Sevilla*, in *Compostellanum*, 1 (1956), pp. 881-85, and C. TORRES RODRÍGUEZ, *Arca marmorea*, ibid., 2 (1957), pp. 323-39. The latter holds

The authenticity of the *liber numerorum* first published by Arévalo from a copy of the only MS. known to him (Turin J. II. 7, saec. XI) has been recently questioned by certain critics (21). It is used, however, as authentic both by Fontaine and by C. LEONARDI, *Intorno al « Liber de numeris » di Isidoro di Siviglia*, in *Bullettino dell'Istituto Storico Italiano per il Medio Evo e Archivio Muratoriano*, n. 68 (1956), pp. 203-31. In this important article Leonardi corrects many readings of Arévalo's edition from the original MS. at Turin and also by comparison with Isidore's main pagan source, Martianus Capella. He also suggests emendations drawn from Isidore to the text of Martianus and points, in passing, to the different ends pursued by the two authors (22).

With regard to the other *opera exegetica* we can only register two new publications. Dom E. DEKKERS, *Fragmenta Patristica*, in *SEJG*, 9 (1957), pp. 110-14 has discovered a fragment (ML 83, 277-83) of the *mysticorum expositiones sacramentorum seu questiones in vetus Testamentum* in MS Ambros. S. 36. sup., saec. VII, probably written at Bobbio (= *CLA* III, n. **364, not identified by LOWE). He uses it, together with Isidore's sources, to correct readings in Arévalo (23). Dom G. MORIN, *La part de S. Isidore dans la constitution du texte du psautier Mozarabe*, in *Misc. Isid.*, pp. 151-63, edits critically a *praefatio in psalterium* he attributes to Isidore (24).

Among the dogmatic works, while the text of the *de fide catholica* has received little attention, the *sententiarum libri iii* has been the subject of a thesis by D. STOUT, *A Study of the Sententiarum libri tres of Isidore of Seville*, Washington, *CUA*, 1937. It is of interest but suffers from a failure to re-examine the sources of the work (25). We have two recent translations into Spanish by J. OTEO URUÑUELA, *Sentencias en tres libros*, Madrid,

the text is corrupt and should read *arca marmorea*, a phrase current at the time but later misunderstood outside Spain and « corrected » to agree with the Byzantine catalogues of sees. In MSS. later than the 12th Century the Spanish tradition was responsible for a return to the original reading.

(21) Cf. MCNALLY (p. 436 n. 26) and DÍAZ, *Index*, n. 107. The latter remarks « de libro genuino nil dicere licet: non me fugit magnam movere difficultatem quod sine scriptoris nomine in codd. traditur ». He adds two MSS. to those mentioned by Leonardi, but omits München Lat. 14334 (s. XV), probably copied from a Spanish exemplar according to B. BISCHOFF, *Eine verschollene Einteilung der Wissenschaften*, in *Archives d'hist. doctrinale et litt. du moyen âge*, 25 (1958), p. 9, n. 19; Bischoff (ibid., 9 sq., 18) also doubts the work's authenticity and holds (against Ehwald) that it was probably not used by Aldhelm. For the other *liber de numeris*, published in an appendix by Arévalo, cf. infra, Section III.

(22) LEONARDI (p. 23) thinks Isidore's knowledge of Martianus Capella was not only limited but probably secondhand. FONTAINE (I, pp. 380 sq., 442) apparently thinks it was direct and fairly close.

(23) Cf. also R. P. ROBINSON, *Manuscripts 27 (S. 29) and 107 (S. 129) of the Municipal Library of Autun*, New York, 1939 (Memoirs Amer. Acad. in Rome, 16), pp. 3-10 (on Autun 27, saec. VII and VIII). Cf., as well as DÍAZ, *Index*, n. 121, the MSS. listed by G. MEYER and M. BURCKHARDT, *Die mittelalterlichen Handschriften der Universitätsbibliothek Basel*, Obteil. B., I, Basel, 1960, p. 862.

(24) The attribution seems generally accepted; cf. *CPL*, n. 1197; DÍAZ, *Index*, n. 133. On the Isidorian editing of the Bible cf. infra, Section VIc, and, for the *liber de variis quaestionibus* infra, Section III.

(25) Cf. FONTAINE, II, p. 692 n. 3. On the *de fide catholica* cf. infra, Sections VId and VII and note 154.

1937, 2 vols., and by ISMAEL ROCA MELIA, Madrid, 1971 (Santos Padres Españoles, 2), pp. 215-525. This second translation, accompanied by a short introduction and notes, is based, unlike OTEO's version, on Arévalo's text, which is printed below it.

A new critical edition is in preparation by LAUREANO ROBLES. He has published *Isidoro de Sevilla y la cultura eclesiástica de la España visigoda, Notas para un estudio del Libro de las ' Sententias '*, in *Archivos Leoneses*, 24 (1970), pp. 13-185. He holds that the *Sententiae* should be dated between 618-633, and sees them as intended as a manual for the theological formation of the clergy. The introduction studies the meanings of *sententia* in classical and Christian thought. Isidore's work represents a great advance in systematization on the *Sententiae* of Prosper of Aquitaine. Robles studies the tradition of the work as shown by references in library catalogues and publishes a preliminary (unnumbered) list of over 440 MSS. (many descriptions are necessarily slight). He asks for corrections and additions. There is no attempt, as yet, to single out the older or more valuable MSS. with a view to an edition. Meanwhile, Prof. Fontaine informs me, P. CAZIER of Lille University is preparing an edition of *sententiae*, book I. (See now CAZIER, *Le Livre des règles de Tyconius. Sa transmission du De doctrina christiana aux Sentences d'Isidore de Séville, Revue des études augustiniennes*, 19, 1973, pp. 241-61). M. MURJANOFF has published *Eine patristische Mischandschrift mit dem ersten Reklamantenbeleg*, in *SEJG*, 16 (1965), pp. 465-69. He prints two pages from sent. I, 10, 2-12 from Leningrad Lat. F. v. I. 149 (saec. IX ex., North Italian (26).

In 1936 that veteran patristic scholar P. A. C. VEGA edited for the first time from the only MS. known (Escorial R. II. 18, saec. VII and VIII) a work he identified with the *de haeresibus* listed by Braulio: *S. Isidori Hispalensis Episcopi De Haeresibus liber*, Escorial, 1936 (Script. eccles. Hispano-latini veteris et medii aevi, 5) (27). M. C. DÍAZ Y DÍAZ, *De patristica española*, in *RET*, 17 (1957), pp. 37-39, suggested some doubts as to the work's authenticity but his arguments appear to have been answered by P. VEGA, *El « Liber de haeresibus » de San Isidoro de Sevilla y el Códice Ovetense*, in *CD*, 171 (1958), pp. 241-55 (28). There is, in any case, no dispute that the work is of the Isidorian age. Meanwhile, V. BEJARANO, *Algunas notas gramaticales al « De Haeresibus Liber » isidoriano*, in *Emerita*,

(26) For MSS. of the work, apart from DÍAZ, *Index*, n. 111, cf. a longer (no doubt incomplete) list in G. MEYER and M. BURCKHARDT, op. cit. supra, note 23, pp. 341 sq. (no dates given): HERINGTON, art. cit. supra, note 12; G. OUY, in *MA*, 64 (1958), pp. 115-31, on Paris lat. 2827 (s. XI) and E. M. BUYTAERT, in *Franciscan Studies*, N. S., 13. 2-3 (1953) p. 45, on Assisi 98 (s. XIII). We may add Bristol, City Reference Library 3 (s. XIII[1]) and Leningrad O. v. I, 17 and F. v. I. 14 (both s. XII).

(27) Also in *CD*, 152 (1936), 32 pp. I use the second edition of 1940 (38 pp.). ANSPACH, in *Misc. Isid.*, p. 356, points to use of the work as Isidorian in the *Liber glossarum* (s. VIII). A. MILLARES CARLO, *Los códices visigóticos de la catedral toledana*, Madrid, 1935, p. 67, holds the Escorial MS. comes from Córdoba; cf. also C. SÁNCHEZ-ALBORNOZ, in *Settimane di studio*, VI, Spoleto, 1959, pp. 643 sq.: G. MENÉNDEZ PIDAL (art. cit. infra, note 134) pp. 156-58, 163 sq.

(28) DÍAZ, *Index*, n. 110, now includes the work among the *opera genuina* but still with a certain reserve.

26 (1958), pp. 65-76, has provided us with a valuable list of emendations to P. Vega's edition. They consist essentially in a return to the readings of the Escorial MS. which are shown to be consistent with the grammar and style of the period.

The *synonyma* has been again translated into Spanish while its style has received attention from FONTAINE and from CASAS HOMS [29]. The article by J. FONTAINE, *Isidore de Séville auteur 'ascétique': les énigmes des Synonyma*, in *Studi Medievali*, 6 (1965), pp. 163-95, is the first extensive treatment this work has received; earlier authors seem unable to decide whether it is grammatical, ascetic, mystical or dogmatic in nature. The first Book is, Fontaine shows, an examination of conscience, the second proposes a rule of Christian life. Fontaine sees the work as a « manuel d'introduction générale à la spiritualité chrétienne », perhaps intended for the pupils of the episcopal school of Seville and probably among Isidore's *first* works, a prelude to the *sententiae*. Sr. Juan Antonio Peris is preparing a new critical edition. He has published *Algunas observaciones sintácticas al texto de los Synonyma de Isidoro de Sevilla, Durius*, 1 (1973), pp. 77-96. Here he argues that Arévalo modified the text of the work by attempting to make it conform to the rules of classical Latin. In *Particularidades estilísticas de los Synonyma de Isidoro de Sevilla. Contribución al establecimiento del texto*, ibid., pp. 309-21, he studies the style of the work, showing how this is related to its syntax (I have had to rely for my knowledge of these articles on the notices in *L'Année Philologique*). One should also refer to P. PETITMENGIN, *Notes sur des manuscrits patristiques latins*, I: *Fragments patristiques dans le MS. Strasbourg* 3762, *Revue des études augustiniennes*, 17 (1971), pp. 3-12 (esp. 8 sq.). Fols. 22-23 of this MS. contain fragments of syn. 1, 34-78 in Beneventan minuscule of saec. X-XI.

The historical works of Isidore have been described by B. SÁNCHEZ ALONSO, *Historia de la historiografia española*, I, Madrid, 1941, pp. 70 sq., 76-80, 82 sq., by F. R. PERMUY, *San Isidoro, historiador nacional*, in *Ilustración del Clero*, 35 (1942), pp. 293-300, 336-42, 376-80, who concentrates on the Goth., and by J. N. HILLGARTH, *Historiography in Visigothic Spain, La Storiografia Altomedievale*, Spoleto, 1970, (Settimane di Studio, XVII), 1, pp. 261-311, esp. pp. 287-99 (see also, below, Section VId) [30]. J. L. ROMERO has translated the *historiae vandalorum et sueborum* in *CHE*, 1-2 (1944), pp. 289-97. An English translation has appeared by G. DONINI and G. B. FORD, Jr., *Isidore of Seville, History of the Kings of the Goths, Vandals and Suevi*, Leiden, 1966, VIII + 46 pp. (2nd ed., 1970, XI + 45 pp.). The first edition is full of faults, most of which re-

(29) Cf. infra, Section V and note 85. The trans. is entitled *San Isidoro de Sevilla, De los Sinonimos*, trad. por M. ANDRÉU VALDÉS SOLIS, Madrid, 1944, 108 pp. It is based not on Arévalo's edition but on the earlier and inferior edition of Madrid, 1778. A. VIÑAYO GONÁLEZ, *Angustia y ansiedad del hombre pecador. Fenomenografia de la angustia existencial en los 'Soliloquios' de San Isidoro*, in *Studium Legionense*, 1 (1960), pp. 137-56, discusses the work in the light of modern philosophy and psychology.

(30) Cf., especially on the need for revising Mommsen's edition, L. VÁZQUEZ DE PARGA, *Aspectos criticos de las obras históricas de Isidoro*, in *Isidoriana*, pp. 99-105.

main in the second. The translators appear ignorant of Isidorian bibliography. They take no account of the shorter version of the *historiae*. No sources are indicated, so that one has no idea what is Isidore's own work, what is borrowed. There are no notes. See, also, the review by J. FONTAINE, *Latomus*, 26 (1967), pp. 205 sq.

CRISTÓBAL RODRÍGUEZ ALONSO's Oviedo University thesis of 1971, *Las Historias de los Godos, Vandalos y Suevos de San Isidoro de Sevilla, estudio, edición crítica y traducción*, has been published as No. 13 of « Fuentes y estudios de historia leonesa », León, 1975, 352 pp. (See the review by P. CAZIER, *Revue des études augustiniennes*, 22, 1976, pp. 427-29). After a short introductory section, which describes the hist., rather unconvincingly, as « national » history, the editor shows that the original title of the work, in its longer redaction, was *de origine getarum* (unfortunately this discovery is not clearly registered either in the apparatus or the title of the book). Returning to the view put forward by Hertzberg in 1874 the editor maintains convincingly that both versions of the hist. – the shorter, finished in about 619, and the longer, which reaches 624 – are authentic, and do not, as Mommsen suggested, both descend from a lost and defective archetype. The longer version has a distinctly panegyrical and apologetic character. While Isidore celebrates the triumphs of the king reigning in 624, Suinthila, he also expands greatly his references to religious themes. The *laus Spaniae* (for which see below) was probably composed at the same time. On the other hand the dedication to Sisenand, only present in a saec. XIII MS., should be considered apocryphal. (This conclusion was also reached, independently, by L. VÁZQUEZ DE PARGA, *Algunas notas sobre el Pseudo Metodio y España*, *Habis*, 2, (1971), pp. 143-64, esp. 153 sq.)

RODRÍGUEZ's study of Isidore's sources, in the hist. and the *laus Spaniae*, includes and completes the work of earlier scholars but his table of parallel passages (pp. 75-102) would be much more useful if it had been used in the apparatus to his edition. This represents an advance on Mommsen, who based his text, for the longer recension, mainly on Berlin MS. 1885. The present editor uses the MSS. known to Mommsen and two Spanish MSS., either unknown or only imperfectly known to him (Madrid, Bibl. Nac. 1513, saec. XIII, and Madrid, Real Academia de la Historia 78, saec. X-XI). Unlike Mommsen, he does not use the MSS. of one version to supply defects in the other but maintains the two apparatus separate. The main differences between Mommsen's edition and Rodríguez's are to be found in the text of the shorter version. The description of the MSS. and the *stemma* and *conspectus siglorum* have faults, pointed out by Cazier (see above). The translation and the *index verborum* (the latter due to J. M. DÍAZ DE BUSTAMANTE) will be useful. The absence of an *index nominum* is surprising. There is no attempt to trace the diffusion of the text (as Fontaine did for the nat.).

The authenticity of the *laus Spaniae* was questioned, on what seem inadequate grounds, by W. STACH, in *Historische Vierteljahrschrift*, 30 (1935-36), p. 429 n. 22; in fact it is contained in a number of early MSS.

and its use of sources is consistent with Isidorian authorship [31]. I. RODRÍGUEZ, *Cántico de San Isidoro a España, Helmantica*, 12 (1961), pp. 177-226, is a general article on the *laus*, discussing its classical antecedents, its probable sources (nothing seems to be added here to MADOZ's studies, cited below, Section IV), and its rhymed prose. He also translates it. J. JIMÉNEZ DELGADO, *El Laus Hispaniae en dos importantes códices españoles*, ibid., pp. 227-59, discusses MSS. León, Bibl. Capitular 22 and Madrid, Real Academia de la Historia 78. He publishes the text contained in the León MS. (not directly collated by Mommsen) and argues that three of its variants should be accepted, as against Mommsen's text (DÍAZ, *Index*, n. 116), *montibus frondea* (not *frondua*), *tibi cedat* (not *cedet*), and *nec... invideris* (not *invidebis*). These variants are not accepted in the new edition by RODRÍGUEZ ALONSO of the hist., which includes the *laus* (pp. 168-70; see his introduction, pp. 57-64).

An important article by H. KOEPPLER, *De viris illustribus and Isidore of Seville*, in *JTS*, 37 (1936), pp. 16-34, refuted Schütte's theories on the *de viris* and maintained the Isidorian authorship of the last 33 chapters in older editions, the first 13 being the work of an unknown African author of the Sixth Century. A new edition of the vir. by Professor C. CODOÑER of Salamanca University has appeared, *El ' De viris illustribus ' de Isidoro de Sevilla*, Salamanca, 1964 (Theses et Studia philologica Salmanticensia, 12), 167 pp. (See the reviews by J. FONTAINE, in REL, 42, 1964, pp. 556-59; A. M. [MUNDÓ], *Indice histórico español*, 10, 1964, p. 229). The edition is preceded by a long introduction on the work, its double redaction, its sources and textual tradition. The edition is based on 34 MSS., which the editor divides into two main families, a small « Braulian » group of Spanish MSS., which also contains further *Lives* by Braulio, Ildefonsus, etc., and a « pre-Braulian » family, without these additions, which appears to have travelled via Ireland or England. One can criticize the technique of the edition. The *apparatus* is very unwieldy. The use of a few *sigla* for hyparchetypes and the adoption of a different order for the *sigla* representing individual MSS., so as to bring out the differences between families, would have made the edition more intelligible.

More serious questions arise with regard to the question of the work's double redaction and the interpolations. It is unfortunate that the editor has not carried her investigations further. She is certainly right to distinguish two questions: (1) whether Isidore's work consisted of 33 or 46 chapters + preface, and (2) the question of the authorship of the interpolations found in the 46-chapter recension in the chapters common to both versions. One may accept her arguments (pp. 29 ff.) against the Isidorian authorship of the chapters not present in the short recension. What I do not find consistent is her attitude to the interpolations (published p. 27). On p. 28 she states that they are by Braulio, or possibly by Isidore himself (they are found in the important MS. Léon 22). But, on p. 33, she considers them later than saec. VII. The only reason for this view is appa-

(31) Cf. J. MADOZ, in *Razón y Fe*, 116 (1939), pp. 247-57; DÍAZ, *Index*, n. 116. There is a German trans. by B. STEIDLE, in *Benediktinische Monatschrift*, 18 (1936), p. 424.

rently the hostile attitude to Justinian and his supporters, evident especially in the addition to ch. 18. Prof. Codoñer considers Isidore neutral in the question of the Three Chapters (p. 72). She forgets that in the *Chronica* (397a) he clearly takes sides against Justinian. There is no reason here to reject the interpolations in MS. León 22 as non-Isidorian. As to the chapters not present in the short (33-chapter) recension, the inclusion of the obscure Peter of Lérida certainly indicates (as CODOÑER, p. 32) a Spanish author. I cannot see any reason for dating these chapters after 700. Another question connected with the *de viris* is unresolved. What is the origin of the interpolations contained in MS. Florence, Laurentiana, S. Crucis Plut. 22, 12 (saec. XIII), published pp. 37 f. ? To MUNDÓ (see above) they seem saec. VII and Spanish. Mr. C. M. LAWSON has pointed out to me the interest of the remarks on Justus of Urgel, who is « named as the author of the Spanish Psalter collects. Dom Wilmart and Dom Brou did not mention *his* name when attempting to decide who wrote them » (a reference to their joint edition, see *CPL*, no. 2015).

An editor has also been found for the *de ecclesiasticis officiis* ; not long ago Professer LOWE published a facsimile of a previously unknown Seventh Century fragment of *excerpta* of this treatise (*CLA*, IX, 1959, n. 1235: Münster i. W., Staatsarchiv Msc. VII 2a) which he believed was written in France and was the oldest Isidorian MS. in existence. K. FORSTNER (cited above, note 12) printed variant readings of a fragment at Salzburg (saec. IX), containing 2, 18 sq. Mr. C. M. LAWSON, *Notes on the de ecclesiasticis officiis*, in *Isidoriana*, León, 1961, pp. 299-303, showed that the rule, « codices antiquiores meliores, recentiores deteriores », did not apply to this work. In the introduction to his edition, an Oxford thesis for the degree of B. Litt, 1961, revised 1970 for publication, he greatly expands this picture.

Mr. Lawson shows that the original title was *de origine officiorum*. The division into books and chapters is not due to Isidore but had been made by the time of Braulio's *renotatio* [*ca.* 637]. The editor gives much weight to the sources of the work; he allows them to be decisive in reconstructing the text on occasion but can decide against the true text of a source, especially when a MS. of the source agrees with the reading of Isidore's MSS. Mr. Lawson has collated 31 MSS. and examined 103. He reduces the MSS. to three hyparchetypes, He has changed Arévalo's text (basically that of Grial, 1599) in 890 instances. He lists and examines a large number of MSS. containing *extracts* from the work and examines its use by the Irishman Colman (saec. VII?), the anonymous *Vita S. Cuthberti* (698-705), Ps-Germanus of Paris (*ca.* 700 ?), Ildefonsus of Toledo, the *Regula communis*, Valerius of Bierzo, Pirminius (d. 753), and many later authors. The textual tradition is examined in great detail. It is possible to follow the diffusion of the work via Toledo and Saragossa to Italy (*ca.* 640), from Italy to the British Isles. This whole discussion is as fascinating as is FONTAINE's in his edition of the *de natura rerum* (32).

(32) I am grateful to Mr. LAWSON for allowing me to see his edition in typescript. Unfortunately it is unlikely that it will be published as one volume. For the sources see also infra, Section IV. MSS: add to DÍAZ, *Index*, n. 104: Vat. lat. 5765 (s. VIII); St. Paul in Kärnten 25.2.35 (XXVa5), s. IX-X; Wien 751 (s. IX, frag.).

Prof. Díaz's edition of the *regula monachorum* has been ready for publication for some time. Díaz has discussed the MS. tradition in two studies, *Aspectos de la tradición de la Regula Isidori*, in *Studia Monastica*, 5 (1963), pp. 27-57, and *El manuscrito de Lérins de la Regula Isidori*, ibid., 7 (1965), pp. 369-82. He considers that the *regula* was addressed (between 615 and 624) to the monks of the unlocalized *coenobium Honoriacense*. Its MS. tradition is small, compared to that of other Isidorian works. It consists, on the one hand, of some Spanish *codices regularum* (Escorial a. I. 13, London, British Library, Add. 30055, Paris Bibl. Nat., lat. 10876 and a fragment in 13090), apparently descending from a model formed by Fructuosus of Braga in the late seventh century, and, on the other, of an interpolated recension, preserved in MSS. Valenciennes 288, CLM 28118 and Durham B. III.8. The interpolations tend to make the rule stricter. This indicates that they are later than Braulio's *renotatio*, for Braulio remarks on the *regula*'s mildness. They are *earlier* than Egbert of York, who cites one of them *ca.* 750. They are apparently Spanish and probably also proceed from Galicia. Isidore's *regula* was used in Spain, in conjunction with other *Rules*, until 1100 or later.

In his second article Díaz discussed further evidence for the text of the *regula*, existing in a partial copy of a lost MS. of Lérins. This lost MS. was apparently in Visigothic script and belonged to the uninterpolated family.

The new edition, with the first Spanish translation, of the *regula*, by J. Campos Ruiz, Madrid, 1971 (Santos Padres Españoles, 2), pp. 79-125, contains a brief introduction, which discusses the date (before 619 but this is not clearly established), the dedication (the *coenobium Honoriacense* may only have received the archetype of the interpolated family), and the sources (the notes on sources are based on Susín Alcubierre, see Section IV, below). The editor appears not to know Díaz's second article. He claims to have collated all the MSS. (except, apparently, the copy of the Lérins MS.) and the main editions. The *apparatus* does not bear this out. The Escorial MS. is cited four times, CLM 28118 once, the other MSS. seem to be cited via Díaz's first article. Only the first three interpolated passages are recorded in the *apparatus* (cf. Díaz, *Studia Monastica*, 5, 1963, pp. 32 ff.). Campos has also written a useful study of the deliberately simple vocabulary and style of the *regula*, *La Regula monachorum de San Isidoro y su lengua*, in *Helmantica*, 12 (1961), pp. 61-101. See K. S. Frank, cited, below, Section IV. The authenticity of the *prologus in libro canticorum*, edited by Anspach in 1930, has been accepted by specialists such as A. W. S. Porter, in *Ephemerides liturgicae*, 49 (1935), p. 127, and W. M. Whitehill, in *Jahrbuch für Liturgiewissenschaft*, 14 (1938), p. 108.

Of Isidore's *epistulae* only two, apart from the correspondence with Braulio, edited by J. Madoz, *Epistolario de San Braulio de Zaragoza*, Madrid, 1941 (Est. Onienses, I, 2), pp. 71-89, from MS. León 22 are regarded as genuine by Díaz, *Index*, nn. 124-25, those to Massona and to Elladius (33). The *Versus* edited by Beeson are also generally (and, I believe, rightly) considered authentic although P. VEGA, for one, stated his belief that they are apocryphal (in *CD*, 171, 1958, p. 257 (34).

III. WORKS OF DISPUTED AUTHENTICITY (35)

The best recent discussion of the many works that habitually travel « sous le pavillon isidorien » is that of Fr. R. E. McNALLY, *Isidoriana*, in *Theological Studies*, 20 (1959), pp. 432-42. This careful and scholarly disquisition dispenses me from going into the question of every work at one time or another ascribed to Isidore (36). It is, however, necessary to discuss in some detail the more important works recently so ascribed.

Among the works generally attributed to Isidore until recent years the *de ordine creaturarum* occupies an important place. Its authenticity was, indeed, questioned almost as soon as its first publication by D'ACHERY but it was admitted by Arévalo into his canon and only a few scholars, among them the great DUHEM, ventured to query his verdict (37). In a recent article, however, Prof. M. C. DÍAZ Y DÍAZ, *Isidoriana*, I: *Sobre el*

(33) Cf. also J. FERNÁNDEZ ALONSO (cit. infra, note 111). To MSS. of the *epist. ad Massonam* listed by DÍAZ, *Index*, n. 124, add Wien 751 (s. IX), indicated by W. LEVISON, *England and the Continent in the Eighth Century*, Oxford, 1946 p. 282. The *epist. ad Eugenium* is regarded as authentic by J. MADOZ, in *RET*, 2 (1942), p. 240; *CPL*, n. 1210 and McNALLY, MADOZ, *San Isidoro*, pp. 65 sq., also continued to regard the *epist. ad Leudefredum* as genuine. Cf. DÍAZ, *Index*, n. 453 (it is Spanish, s. VIII-IX). *The Letters of St. Isidore of Seville*, translated by G. B. FORD, Jr., Catania, 1966 (reviewed by J. FONTAINE, *Latomus*, 27, 1968, pp. 453 sq.); 2nd revised edition, Amsterdam, 1970. The 2nd edition (unlike the first) contains the admission that *Letters* 1, 6, 7 and 8 « are considered to be spurious ». Two of the *Letters* are from Braulio to Isidore. The 2nd edition also contains the Latin text, taken from *ML* 83, except for Letter 14 (from Lindsay's edition of the *Origines*).

(34) Cf. DÍAZ, in *RET*, 17 (1957), pp. 43 sq.; FONTAINE, II, p. 738 n. 2; MADOZ, *San Isidoro*, pp. 75-78; ID., in *EE*, 21 (1947), pp. 217-23. A Spanish trans. of *versus* in J. VIVES, *San Isidoro nuestro maestro y su biblioteca*, Barcelona, 1956, 35 pp. A. ORTEGA, *Los Versus Isidori*, in *Helmantica*, 12 (1961), pp. 261-99, reprints the critical edition of BEESON, with its *apparatus* (inaccurately reproduced) and some additional notes on sources, mainly furnished by MADOZ and FONTAINE.

(35) Under Section II supra I have mentioned objections against the authenticity of the *liber numerorum*, *de haeresibus*, *laus Spaniae*, part of the *de viris* and the *versus*. I again follow the order of the *CPL*, discussing, first the works it admits among the *opera genuina* but which are now considered dubious, then the *dubia* and lastly the *spuria* (*CPL*, pp. 274-77). The *liber de variis quaestionibus* is placed by the *CPL* among the last, whether rightly or wrongly is another question. Cf. infra.

(36) As will appear later I am not always in agreement with Fr. McNALLY. Cf., also, for lists of pseudo-Isidoriana, P. GLORIEUX, *Pour revaloriser Migne, tables rectificatives*, Lille, 1952, pp. 48-49; AYUSO, pp. 477-480, 505 sq.; DÍAZ, in *SEJG*, 5 (1953), pp. 149-51; ID., *Index*, pp. 44-47 (mentions many ascriptions in MSS. of works to Isidore). Cf. also MADOZ, *San Isidoro*, pp. 81-87. Cf. R. E. McNALLY, *Isidore pseudepigrapha in the Early Middle Ages*, in *Isidoriana*, pp. 305-316. L. ROBLES, *Prolegómenos a un ' Corpus Isidorianum '. Obras apócrifas, dudosas o espurias*, offprint from *Anales de la Universidad de Valencia*, (1971) 19 pp., lists 24 works or groups of works of questionable authenticity. The author informs me that this publication is merely a preliminary statement of his thesis, Valencia, 1971, which will be published by the Centro Superior de Investigaciones Científicas.

(37) P. DUHEM, *Le système du monde*, III, Paris, 1915, pp. 14 sq.

« *Liber de ordine creaturarum* », in *SEJG*, 5 (1953), pp. 147-66, put forward very serious objections to the work's retention as Isidorian. He pointed to its omission from Braulio's *renotatio*, a fact in itself difficult to account for, to the lack of support in the MS. tradition for the ascription to Isidore, and then proceeded to advance new and significant arguments based on the language of the treatise. While it contained words and constructions very different from those found in Isidore's undoubtedly authentic works it proved to be dependent on the *de mirabilibus sacrae scripturae* of Augustinus Hibernicus. The insular origin of the early MSS., together with the work's dependence on an Irish writer who, as P. GROSJEAN has since demonstrated, lived in the South of Ireland *ca.* 650, clearly combine to prove it is not Isidorian [38]. DÍAZ has now published a critical edition of the work, *Liber de ordine creaturarum, un anónimo irlandés del siglo VII*, Santiago de Compostela, 1972, 240 pp. Here, reinforcing earlier arguments, he shows that the work cannot be by Isidore, and that the MS. tradition originates in Ireland. He dates the work between 680 and 700. He uses 25 MSS. together with D'Achery's edition (from a lost MS.) for his edition, and traces the diffusion from Ireland to Bohemia, saec. VII-XV. The critical text is accompanied by a Spanish translation and by full notes and indices.

Two treatises entitled *de numeris* have been ascribed to Isidore. That published by Arévalo in an appendix (ML, 83, 1293-1302) has, at times, been considered possibly genuine (cf. *CPL*, n. 1193). It has recently been critically edited, with a very thorough study of sources and parallels, by Fr. R. E. MCNALLY, *Der irische Liber de numeris. Eine Quellenanalyse des pseudoisidorischen Liber de numeris*, Diss., München, 1957, XV-210 pp. [39]. He has shown that the work in its original form is Irish and was written between 750 and 775 in the circle of St. Virgilius of Salzburg; it was subsequently added to by another Irish scholar.

Two other works admitted as probably genuine by the *CPL* now appear to be inauthentic. Neither of them figure in Braulio's *renotatio*. On

(38) Cf. P. GROSJEAN, *Sur quelques exégètes irlandais du VIIe siècle*, in *SEJG*, 7 (1955), pp. 67-98. DÍAZ's arguments are accepted by MCNALLY and by FONTAINE, I, p. 14 n. 2. For MADOZ cf. infra, Section V.

(39) A new edition of this text by Fr. MCNALLY is to appear in the series *Scriptores latini Hiberniae* (Dublin). MCNALLY, *Christus in the Pseudo-Isidorian Liber de ortu et obitu patriarcharum*, in *Traditio*, 21 (1965), pp. 167-83, discusses the work, which is probably by the same author as the *Liber de numeris*. He transcribes an additional section on Christ from MS. Colmar 39 (from Murbach, s. VIII-IX), the oldest MS. R. E. REYNOLDS, in *Mediaeval Studies*, 34 (1972), pp. 113-51, discusses a number of MSS. of two pseudo-Isidorian works, the *epistula ad Leudefredum* (*CPL*, 1223) and the *de officiis vii graduum* (*CPL*, 1222). More recently Reynolds has returned to the theme in *The ' Isidorian ' Epistula ad Leudefredum: its Origins, Early Manuscript Tradition, and Editions*, a paper presented to the Visigothic Colloquy in Dublin (May, 1975), in *Visigothic Spain : new approaches*, Oxford, 1980, pp. 251-71 (with an edition of the work from MS. Escorial d. I. 1). A fuller treatment of the subject appears in *Mediaeval Studies*, 41 (1979), pp. 252-330. Reynolds considers the *epistula* Spanish though not by Isidore. It should be noted that DÍAZ, *Index*, pp. 32 sqq., has pointed to the presence in MS. León 22 (s. IX) of fragments that seem to resemble closely parts of the work edited by MCNALLY but which appear under the name of Isidore. For the other *de numeris* or *liber numerorum* cf. supra, Section II.

the *quaestiones de veteri et novo Testamento* (*CPL*, 1194), edited from what seems the only MS. (Pal. lat. 277) by Arévalo, see McNally, *The Pseudo-Isidorian De Vetere et novo Testamento quaestiones*, in *Traditio*, 19 (1963), pp. 37-50. McNally discusses this work in detail and re-edits it from the MS. He holds that it dates from about 750. Parallels to Irish Biblical works written in Southern Germany suggest that the author, if not himself Irish, drew his learning from Irish centres in that region. Isidore's *origines, de officiis, de fide catholica* and *differentiae* are used (40). Z. Garcia Villada edited a fragment *de Trinitate* (*CPL*, 1200) that he found in the Códice de Roda and ascribed to Isidore but it seems to consist merely of excerpts from his genuine works (41).

The *institutionum disciplinae* figures among the *dubia* after the list of works by Isidore in the *CPL* (n. 1216). It seems to be of some importance to reach a decision on the authorship of this work as it is frequently cited as a source for the cultural history of Visigothic Spain, for instance by J. Scudieri Ruggieri, *Alle fonti della cultura ispano visigotica*, in *Studi Medievali*, N. S., 16 (1943-50), pp. 1-47, especially 7, 31 sq., and by R. Menéndez Pidal, *Los Godos y el origen de la epopeya española*, in *I Goti in Occidente*, Spoleto, 1956 (*Settimane di Studio*, III), pp. 296-99 (42). Some eminent Isidorian scholars, among them Beeson, have thought the work authentic. It was first edited by Anspach in 1912 and again recently by P. Pascal, in *Traditio*, 13 (1957), pp. 425-31. Pascal employs not only Paris Lat. 2994A (s. ix), used by Anspach, which has an ascription to Isidore, but also Munich Lat. 6384 (s. x), first indicated by Cardinal Mercati, which has an ascription to Augustine. Pascal, like Anspach, favours Isidorian authorship. He points to the fact that several passages in this short work are found almost verbatim in undoubted Isidorian writings. One is bound, however, to agree with Fontaine (I, p. 14 n. 2) that the style is not the same and that the use of Pliny the Younger (not found elsewhere in Isidore) is highly significant. The Paris MS. appears, however, to contain paleographical evidence of a Spanish connection that is reinforced by the evident use of a number of Isidore's works (43).

(40) McNally, art. cit. supra, note 36 (in *Isidoriana*). Díaz, *Index*, p. 44, Madoz, *San Isidoro*, p. 81, and Bischoff, art. cit. (supra, note 21), p. 9 n. 18, agree the work is inauthentic.

(41) McNally apparently considers it authentic. Cf., however, Altaner, in *Misc. Isid.*, p. 10; Madoz in *RET*, 1 (1940-41), p. 953 sq.; Díaz, *Index*, p. 45. For the *epist. ad Eugenium* (*CPL*, 1210) cf. supra, Section II, note 33.

(42) Cf. also the discussion of *Settimane di Studio*, V, Spoleto, 1958, pp. 679 sq.; J. Fernández Alonso, *La cura pastoral* (op. cit. infra, n. 111), pp. 96 sq.; Madoz, *San Isidoro*, p. 82.

(43) Díaz, *Index*, p. 44, rejects the work with the phrase « stilus ac sermo Is. alienus ». It is perhaps worth noting that the Paris MS. contains Isidore's *differentiae*, fragments of the *orig.*, *sententiae* and *de officiis*, i. e. three of the four works in which parallels or verbal connections with the work have been found (it does not contain the *regula*); our work comes at the end after *opera genuina*. We may notice here the *Benedictio cerei* and *lucernae* (*CPL*, 1217-1217a); cf. Díaz, *Index*, nn. 150-51, who admits the latter is possibly Isidorian. On other fragments edited by Anspach cf. Díaz, *Index*, pp. 45 sq. On the *Hymnus SS. Iustae et Rufinae* (*CPL*, 1218) cf. ib., n. 340; infra, Section VI°.

The latest discussion of the work is by J. FONTAINE, *Quelques observations sur les Institutionum disciplinae pseudo-Isidoriennes*, in *CD*, 181 (1968), pp. 617-55. He stresses the small *extent* of the borrowings from Isidore and concludes that only the *origines* and *de officiis* are used. The ideas of the work and of Isidore, on the ages of man and on education in general, differ sharply. The work is far less religious in tone than Isidore, and far more detached from reality. Not only are its most striking sources classical (Sallust, Cicero, Pliny) not Christian, but there seems little evidence of any awareness of living in a Germanic kingdom. The famous reference to *carmina maiorum* seems to be connected not to Germanic customs but to the Roman practice of singing the praise of ancestors at banquets. Of the two MSS. cited the Paris MS. (partly in Visigothic script) was possibly written in the Pyrenees or Southern France, that of Munich in France. Fontaine does not venture to decide where this brief aesthetic exercise was composed; he does not reject my conjecture that it may be connected with the circle of the Visigothic exile Theodulf of Orléans. The nearest certain dating is between 620 and 850.

In 1935 A. E. ANSPACH edited under the title *S. Isidori Hispalensis Commonitiuncula ad sororem*, Escorial, 1935 (Script. eccles. Hispano-Latini veteris et medii aevi, 4), 100 pp., a short treatise previously ascribed to a bishop Adalger (ML, 134, 915-38) (44). Thirteen years later an article by A. VACCARI, *Un trattato ascetico attribuito a S. Girolamo*, in *Mélanges F. Cavallera*, Toulouse, 1948, pp. 147-62, re-examined the question. Anspach had used MSS., two of which attribute the work to Isidore. VACCARI pointed out that in other MSS. it was attributed to Augustine, Ambrose, Jerome and Caesarius of Arles. It is certainly not by any of these Fathers but the variety of attribution in the MSS., the lack of mention by Braulio or Ildefonsus, the non-Isidorian manner of using sources, including Isidore's own *sententiae*, and, finally, the difficulty of supposing a work if by Isidore, presumably directed to his only known sister, Florentina, would not even cite in passing the similar work Isidore's elder brother, St. Leander, had addressed to her (cf. *CPL*, 1183), these difficulties in combination are sufficient to remove the possibility of Isidorian authorship. The fact that the work uses Isidore but not Bede and is cited by Alcuin incline Vaccari to place it in the late Seventh Century; traces of Visigothic influence found by Anspach in the now destroyed MS. Chartres 69 suggest, if no more, a possible Spanish origin (45).

(44) Cf. the reserve shown by ALDAMA, in *Misc. Isid.*, p. 83 n. 100; C. LAMBOT, in *BALCL* 3 (1939-50), n. 64, and ALTANER, in *Theol. Revue*, 36 (1937), p. 58, with regard to this work.

(45) The MSS. of this work are also listed by H. ROCHAIS, in *RB*, 63 (1953), p. 251 n. 1. VACCARI's art. appears again, with some slight additions, as *Un trattato ascetico sballottato fra quattro dottori*, in his *Scritti di erudizione e di filologia*, Roma, 1958, (Storia e letteratura, 67) II, pp. 283-300. His arguments are accepted by MADOZ, *Segundo Decenio*, p. 119 [= *San Isidoro*, p. 85]; MCNALLY; DÍAZ, *Index*, p. 44; cf. *CPL*, 1219. A. C. VEGA, *El commentario al Cantar de los Cantares atribuido a Casiodoro, es español?*, in *CD*, 154 (1942), pp. 143-55, suggested that a commentary of Ps-Cassiodorus (*ML*, 70, 1055-1106) *might* be by Isidore. This attribution was not accepted by *CPL*, nn. 910, 1220; MADOZ, *Segundo Decenio*, pp. 117 sq.; DÍAZ, *Index*, p. 45; SEGOVIA, *EE*, 36 (1961), p. 87.

L. WALLACH, *Alcuin and Charlemagne*, Ithaca, N.Y., 1959, pp. 251 f, has argued against Alcuin's use of the work. G. BRUGNOLI, *Un opusculo pseudo-geronimiano in un codice farfense*, in *Benedictina*, 9 (1955), pp. 169-73, discussed the text in MS. Rome, Bibl. Naz. 174 Farf. 19 (saec. XIV). L. ROBLES, *Anotaciones a la obra del Pseudo-Isidoro Commonitiuncula ad sororem*, in *AST*, 44 (1971), pp. 5-32, lists more MSS. than ever before (66 in Latin, 10 in Italian and three in Catalan). He argues that the correct title is *Admonitio de laude caritatis*. The attributions in the MSS. are of no help in detecting the authorship. The sources are principally the *Vitae Patrum*, secondarily Cassiodorus and Isidore.

Arévalo edited a *liber de proprietate sermonum* (ML, 83, 1319-1332) which some MSS. contain together with genuine Isidorian works (*CPL*, 1226). In 1909 C. Pascal showed it was not by Isidore. In her excellent new edition M. L. UHLFELDER agrees with Pascal. The book seems to come from the Fourth or Fifth Centuries A.D. and bears no sign of Christian authorship (46).

We now come to the *Liber de variis quaestionibus*, by far the most important of the works recently ascribed to Isidore and that over which the most prolonged and (at times) acrimonious controversy has raged. Nor can it be said by any means that the end has yet been reached. The work was first published by Dom Martène and Dom Durand in 1717 from a MS at Angers (now Angers 285, s. x); they attributed it, certainly on rather flimsy grounds, to Rabanus Maurus. In 1940 P. A. C. VEGA reedited the work, using MS. Escorial S. I. 17 (s. VIII-IX), a fragment in Reg. lat. 281 (s. IX[1]) already printed by Arévalo in an appendix (ML, 83, 1243-48) and the 1717 edition: *S. Isidori Hispalensis Episcopi Liber de Variis Quaestionibus*, Escorial, 1940 (Script. eccles. Hispano-Latini veteris et medii aevi, 6-9), LXXXIV-287 pp. (47). In their separate introductions to the new edition, P. VEGA and Dr. ANSPACH produced a number of powerful arguments for the work's authenticity. It was, in fact, generally accepted as Isidorian until the appearance of J. MADOZ, *Una obra de Félix de Urgel falsamente adjudicada a San Isidoro de Sevilla*, in *EE*, 23 (1949), pp. 147-68 (48). P. VEGA's reply, *El « Liber de variis quaestionibus » no es de Félix de Urgel*, in *CD*, 161 (1949), pp. 217-68, elicited P. MADOZ's second article, *Contrastes y discrepancias entre el « Liber de variis Questionibus » y San Isidoro de Sevilla*, in *EE*, 24 (1950), pp. 435-58 (49). As a result of P. Madoz's articles a number of patristic scholars accepted his view that the *liber de variis quaestionibus* was not by Isidore but by the Adoptionist Fe-

(46) M. L. UHLFELDER, *De proprietate sermonum vel rerum, a Study and Critical Edition*, Rome, 1954 (Papers and Monographs of the Amer. Acad. in Rome, 15), 116 pp. A. C. VEGA, *De patrologia española. La Lamentatio Originis y el Lamentum paenitentiae del Ps. Isidoro, Boletin de la Real Acad. de la Historia*, 168 (1971), pp. 23-39, considers the *lamentum* a Carolingian work, probably from the circle of Alcuin (pp. 30 sq.). See DÍAZ, *Index*, n. 304.

(47) Part of the introduction first appeared in *CD*, 152 (1936).

(48) It is registered as Isidorian, e. g., by B. FISCHER, op. cit. supra, Section II, in 1949: Madoz's articles evidently produced a change of mind; cf. AYUSO, p. 480. Cf. (A. C. VEGA), in *CD*, 154 (1942), pp. 159-72 (a collection of reviews, etc.).

(49) For a brief summary of the arguments cf. H. BASCOUR, in BTAM, 8 (1959), nn. 980-82. MADOZ, *Segundo Decenio*, pp. 164 sq. (and *San Isidoro*, pp. 86 sq.) merely restates his position.

lix of Urgel and therefore of the late Eighth Century (50). Other specialists, including Dr. ALTANER, have apparently refrained from deciding between the arguments advanced by P. Madoz and P. Vega (51). Professor DÍAZ Y DÍAZ has maintained the work is neither by Isidore nor by Felix but is certainly Spanish and written either at the beginning or in the middle of the Eighth Century (52). The questions involved are very complex and cannot be gone into here. I think, however, that one thing at least has certainly been established by the controversy and that is that the *liber* is not by Felix of Urgel (53). His use of it does not, obviously, prove him the author. On the other hand I think one must agree that the work bears evidence of a doctrinal development that supposes the Monothelite controversy well advanced and also displays a doctrinal insecurity that contrasts with Isidore's undoubtedly genuine works (54). Here one should note that P. MADOZ's principal philological argument, the use of the verb *liniare* in the sense of represent or prefigure, both in the *liber* and in Felix of Urgel, is not as conclusive as Madoz believed. Since he wrote both P. Vega and Prof. Díaz have pointed to its use in the same sense in Gregory of Elvira (55). It has yet, however, to be found in Isidore's undoubtedly genuine works. Certain other of P. Madoz's arguments seem to me not to prove as much as he would wish, for instance his stress on the phrase *egregius doctor* in the *liber* or on the use of long and detailed chapter headings. Both these things are found in the Toledan school of the late Seventh Century as well as in the Adoptionists; they are notable especially in St. Julian of Toledo (56). This does not mean that I am about to suggest yet another author for the *liber* (57). No, but I think it is in the direction of the late Seventh Century and towards Toledo or Saragossa that one should look for an answer to this important question (58).

(50) E. g. *CPL*, 1228; McNALLY; AYUSO, p. 480.

(51) Cf. ALTANER, *Patrologie*[5], p. 460. Cf. note 122 infra.

(52) DÍAZ appears to vacillate slightly. In *De patristica española*, in *RET*, 17 (1957), p. 40, he speaks of the first quarter of the Eighth Century; in *Index*, n. 401, of the middle of the Century.

(53) P. VEGA (pp. 42-52 of the offprint of his art.) points out (1) that there is no evidence for the Jewish-Christian « ambiente » so clearly referred to in the *liber* in the region of Urgel in the late Eighth Century; in Moslem Spain few conversions from Judaism were likely (this important point is not, I think, fully appreciated by Prof. DÍAZ, art. cit. [note 52 supra] pp. 41 sq.); (2) the book cites no author later than Isidore; (3) it is never cited by any of Felix of Urgel's numerous friends or enemies as his, and (4) there is no MS. evidence for the attribution to Felix (the fragment in Reg. Lat. 281 goes under the name of Isidore; in the other two MSS. the work lacks its first folios).

(54) Cf. MADOZ, (1949), pp. 150-61; (1950), pp. 437-45; 450-58; VEGA, pp 13-32 of the offprint; DÍAZ, art. cit., pp. 40 sq.

(55) Cf. A. C. VEGA, in *España Sagrada*, LV, Madrid, 1957, pp. 137 sq.; DÍAZ, art. cit. p. 41 n. 141.

(56) Cf. Julian of Toledo, *prognosticum*, I, 9; II, 16; 19; 23 for the phrase *egregius doctor* (all passages checked with my edition). Isidore is himself described as *doctor egregius* by *Conc. Tol.* VIII (653); *ML* 84, 421C.

(57) A careful examination of the Biblical and patristic sources of the *Liber* and of Julian would tend to show independent use of the same authorities.

(58) ANSPACH, in his preface to the *Liber*, pp. lxxi sq., argues Burchard of Worms, *Decretum* XX, 109-110 (*ML*, 140, 1058), who here cites Isidore, was using the *Liber* c. 86 + some lost work of Isidore also copied by Julian of Toledo. It is much more likely that Bur-

L. Castán Lacoma, *Un opúsculo apologético de San Isidoro, inédito*, in *RET*, 20 (1960), pp. 319-60, publishes, for the first time, from MS. Madrid, Real Academia de la Historia. Emil. 3 (saec. xiii), a work entitled in the MS., *Isaiae testimonia de Christo domino*, with no ascription to Isidore, which Anspach (*Taionis et Isidori nova fragmenta et opera*, p. 69) had already identified, with considerable probability, with one of those listed in the *abbreviatio*. The work « coincides completely, not only in its ideas but often in its text, with the *de fide catholica*, lib. i ». The author admits the possibility that it is an extract from the *de fide* but argues it is an authentic work of Isidore, earlier in date than the *fid*. This must remain doubtful: it is highly probable that a later author mingled his own errors with a « remaniement » of the *fid*. The work is not mentioned by Braulio, and the *abbreviatio*'s authority is slight. Castán Lacoma's views are summed up in *Isidoriana*, pp. 445-56.

IV. The Sources of Isidore

During the forty years covered by this review the investigation of Isidore's sources has continued. We may note, however, a certain change of direction and, possibly, also a more moderate degree of expectation as to the results that this research might attain than has at times existed in the past. In the Nineteenth Century in particular an excessive importance appears to have been attached to « Quellenforschung », as if, as H.-I. Marrou observed, the essence of an historical phenomenon could be reduced to knowledge of its origins, of the contacts or external influences it may have undergone (59). Here I cannot do better than cite Professor Fontaine. He remarks as follows: « On ne peut accéder à la véritable originalité d'Isidore de Séville que par une triple démarche. D'abord, un bilan aussi complet et detaillé que possible de ses sources directes et indirectes. Ensuite, une observation minutieuse des coupures, additions et modifications auxquelles Isidore soumet le texte qu'il emprunte. Enfin, la réfé-

chard was using Julian, *prognosticum*, III, 47, 49 (ML, 96, 518 sq.) and this is also indicated by the use of the *Liber*, though he does mention Ivo of Chartres. The most hopeful line of advance with regard to the *Liber* would appear to lie in a thorough examination of the sources of the work. (I now understand from Prof. Díaz that a recent thesis on the *Liber* by his disciple, A. Palacios, has succeeded in clarifying the date and origin of the work by way of the sources.) Cf. on the *Commentarii in libros genesim et regum* (*ML*, 50, 893-1208), in MS. Autun 27 (s. vii-viii), attributed to Isidore by F. Fita in 1910, P. Bellet, *Claudio de Turin, autor de los comentarios « In genesim et regum » del Pseudo-Euquerio*, in *Estudios Biblicos*, N. S., 9 (1950), pp. 209-23, who shows they are by Claudius of Turin (cf. already, against Fita, Altaner, in *Misc. Isid.*, p. 12). Madoz, *San Isidoro*, pp. 84 sq., accepts Bellet's reasoning. J. Madoz, in *RHE*, 34 (1938), pp. 5-20, demonstrated the authenticity of the Creed of Toledo IV (633) and its Isidorian authorship as against Künstle's idea of a derivation from Toledo I (400). M. C. Díaz y Díaz, *Un poema pseudoisidoriano sobre la creación*, *Studi Medievali*, S. 3e, 11 (1970), pp. 397-402, publishes a poem *de fabrica mundi* attributed to Isidore in two Spanish MSS. (Madrid, Bibl. Acad. Historia, 78, and Bibl. Nac. 8831) but probably saec. ix in date.

(59) H-I. Marrou, in *RMAL*, 3 (1947), p. 380, n. 6.

rence à la realité contemporaine sous tous ses aspects. Ainsi seulement peut-on espérer se replacer dans le mouvement original de la création isidorienne et restituer le lecteur, l'écrivain, l'évêque, trop souvent isolés, dans l'unité d'une seule personne vivant en un temps et un lieu bien caractérisés: la Bétique du début du VIIe siècle » (60).

The aim he has so concisely expressed FONTAINE has himself admirably achieved in his great work, *Isidore de Séville et la culture classique dans l'Espagne wisigothique*. This book contains by far the most important study of Isidore's sources yet published. It contains much more than this and we shall come to it again when we discuss recent works on Isidore and the cultural history of his time (cf. Section V below) but it is necessary to say something here of the new results of Fontaine's research into sources. Apart from his work little that is new has been discovered as to Isidore's use of the pagan classics (61). The old theory that Isidore was using the lost *Prata* of Suetonius as a main source continues to find expression, for instance in A. ROSTAGNI, *Il proemio di Svetonio « De poetis » presso Isidoro, alla luce dell'antica precettistica*, in *Mélanges J. Marouzeau*, Paris, 1948, pp. 509-23. Rostagni tries to show the chapter *de poetis* (orig. 8, 7) derives entirely from Suetonius, *de poetis*. Curtius and Fontaine, on the other hand, hold it is drawn, according to Isidore's custom, from a variety of later sources (62). A direct use of Verrius Flaccus in orig. 1,27, sustained by L. STRZELECKI, *Studia isidorea*, in *Eos*, 40 (1939), pp. 28-40, seems equally improbable (63). V.-J. HERRERO LLORENTE, *Lucano en la literatura hispanolatina*, in *Emerita*, 27 (1959), pp. 45-52, argues that Isidore employs quotations from Lucan (1) to display Isidore's classical erudition and (2) that Isidore quoted Lucan from memory. Herrero Llorente does not, however, even consider the possibility that Isidore was using intermediary sources, including *scholia* on Lucan. On this cf. FONTAINE, II, pp. 575, 742-44 and *indices*, 967, 995. It is, in fact, clear that even Isidore's apparently most direct quotations from the classics are taken at second or third hand. Following in the steps of earlier critics, expanding the field of their study and improving on the methods they employed, Fontaine

(60) J. FONTAINE, in *REL*, 31 (1953), p. 300 n. 1.

(61) Cf. J. MADOZ's general work, *La literatura patristica española continuadora de la estética de los clásicos*, Zaragoza, 1950, which I know in the Eng. trans. in *Folia*, 7 (1953), pp. 67-85; 8 (1954), pp. 23-37. An invaluable general discussion by J. FONTAINE, *Problèmes de l'étude des sources isidoriennes*, in *Isidoriana*, pp. 115-130.

(62) Cf. FONTAINE, II, p. 749 n. 2. Orig. 8, 7 is also discussed by SALMON (cited below, note 133). Other scholars who favour to a greater or lesser extent the « Suetonian thesis » are G. R. WATSON, in *Journal of Roman Studies*, 42 (1952), pp. 56-62, on orig. 1, 24, 1 (cf. FONTAINE, I, p. 83 n. 1; the source is more likely Rufinus); J. VALLEJO, in *Emerita*, 17 (1949), pp. 263 sq., on orig. 19, 23, 1 (supposes direct or indirect use of Suet.) and S. F. BONNER, in *Hermes*, 88 (1960), p. 354 sq., on orig. 1, 21, who still follows the view of Reifferscheid that Isidore here derives from Suetonius's lost *de notis*. He does not know of FONTAINE's discussion (I, pp. 74 sq.) of the relations between Isidore and the Anonymous *de notis* in MS. Paris Lat. 7530. A. MENTZ, *Die tironischen Noten*, in *Archiv für Urkundenforschung*, 16 (1939), pp. 306-11 and K. CHRIST, in *Zentralblatt für Bibliothekswesen*, 61 (1947), p. 154, 158, are also faithful to the old thesis. On the older literature on the subject cf. ALTANER, in *Misc. Isid.*, pp. 13-15.

(63) Cf. FONTAINE, I, p. 93 n. 1.

has confirmed their finding that Isidore's sources are not to be found in the *versus in bibliotheca* or in the list of « loci citati » in Lindsay's edition of the *origines*. « Direct and massive » borrowings from the lost works of Suetonius, Varro or Celsus are shown to be highly improbable. Of the great pagan poets Isidore may possibly have made direct use of Ovid, more probably of Virgil, Martial and Lucretius.

Since Fontaine wrote G. GASPAROTTO has given us a series of articles on the sources used by Isidore in the *de natura rerum* (cc. 29-32 and 39) and in orig. 13, *Isidoro e Lucrezio, Memorie della Accademia Patavina di Scienze, Lettere e Arti*, Classe di Scienze Morali, 77 (1964-65), pp. 285-330; 78 (1965-66), pp. 73-130, 207-38; 79 (1966-67), pp. 39-58, 101-30, and *Le citazioni poetiche nel libro XIII delle 'Etymologiae' d'Isidoro di Siviglia, CD*, 181 (1968), pp. 668-81. In the articles in the *Memorie* Gasparotto shows how Isidore, in his treatment of natural phenomena (thunder, lightning, the rainbow, etc.) combines Christian and pagan sources but Lucretius is the main model used, particularly in the orig. where Christian sources scarcely appear. In the *de natura* Lucretius is sometimes used directly by Isidore, sometimes by way of St. Ambrose and Seneca. In the orig. Isidore uses Seneca and Servius but mainly Lucretius. Gasparotto maintains that Isidore also uses Varro, Apuleius, *de mundo*, Cicero's *Tusculan Questions*, Ovid, *Metamorphoses*, Lucan, and Virgil, *Georgics*. In the article in *CD* he shows how Isidore often cites verses from pagan poets to confirm the validity of his theories by their *auctoritas* and to emphasize the connection between etymology and poetry. Gasparotto analyses 19 quotations from pagan poets in orig. 13, eleven from Virgil, five from Lucretius, and one each from Pacuvius, Ovid and Martial. Many of these are probably not taken directly from the source. In a later article, in *Memorie*, 83 (1970-71), pp. 67-92, Gasparotto discusses Isidore's use of sources in orig. 13, 18, 5-6 and 14,6, 34. Isidore here used Sallust, Virgil, Florus, and Servius.

FONTAINE admitted the possibility that Isidore had direct access to parts of Cicero and of Sallust and that it was certain that he used Quintilian (64). Apart from these authors, and even normally then, Isidore's

(64) On Ovid cf. J. MADOZ, *Ovidio en los Santos Padres españoles*, in *EE*, 23 (1949), pp. 233-38 (on Isidore p. 236; dubious if direct use). A. MONTEVERDI, *Orazio nel medio evo*, in *Studi medievali*, 9 (1936), p. 162, supposes direct use of Horace in Isidore; FONTAINE (I, p. 168 n. 4), with reason, thinks this unlikely. H. L. W. NELSON (op. cit. infra, note 81), p. 16, points out that a historical « howler » in orig. 16, 20, 4 derives ultimately from Petronius, *Sat.* 50, 5-6; no doubt it reached Isidore indirectly. W. C. MCDERMOTT, *Isidore and Petronius*, in *Classica et Mediaevalia*, 23 (1962), pp. 143-7, produces another textual parallel between orig. 16, 16, 6 and Petronius, 50, 7-51. He believes that Isidore used Petronius and Pliny directly here. Sisebut, and presumably Isidore also, appear to have known Lucretius, according to J. MADOZ, in *Principe de Viana*, 7 (1947), pp. 3-12, which I know in Eng. trans. in *Folia*, 6 (1952), pp. 40-52; cf. also FONTAINE, *Isidore de Séville, Traité de la nature*, pp. 11, etc. J. MADOZ, *Nuevas fuentes de los 'Versus Isidori'*, in *EE*, 21 (1947), pp. 217-23, shows Isidore used Martial even more often than Beeson supposed. J. COUSIN, *Etudes sur Quintilien*, 2 vols, Paris, 1936, mentions various relations between Quintilian and Isidore. He follows Woehrer and Schaeffer, however, in holding that Isidore made exten-

use of pagan classics is indirect. The sources he actually employed were almost always late, of the Fourth or Fifth Centuries A. D. or even later, – Martianus Capella, Cassiodorus, late grammarians such as Servius, anonymous manuals or school textbooks, many of them now lost. A rearguard action has been waged by scholars of the Pontifical University of Salamanca against Fontaine's scepticism as to Isidore's classical learning (see A. ORTEGA, cited above, note 34, p. 267) but no one has been able to disprove Fontaine's negative conclusions, nor can this be done by repeating negative conclusions, nor can this be done by reapeating outworn generalizations, though Fontaine's views may be modified in detail by studies such as those of Gasparotto. The conclusions of Fontaine are confirmed by the results of other independent investigations on a smaller scale. A. TABERA, *La definición de furtum en las « Etimologias » de S. Isidoro* (orig. 5, 26, 19-20), in *Studia et documenta historiae et iuris*, 8 (1942), pp. 23-47, agrees with KÜBLER (*Isidorus Studien*, in *Hermes*, 25, 1890) in holding the immediate source of Isidore here is a juridical manual, now lost, composed in Spain before the Codification of Justinian; this manual drew on the *codex Theodosianus* for the passage used in c. 20; Varro is the ultimate source for c. 19 but he, also, reached Isidore through the manual (65) H. L. LEVY, in *Speculum*, 22 (1947), pp. 81 sq., has pointed to the *Breviarium Alaricianum* IX, 13, 1-2, possibly with additional matter omitted from our present MSS., as the source for orig. 8, 9, 9. G. BOYER, in *Droits de l'Antiquité et Sociologie Juridique, Mélanges H. Lévy-Bruhl*, Paris, 1959, (Publ. de l'Institut de Droit romain de l'Université de Paris, 17), pp. 46-62, discusses the definitions of arra in orig. 5, 25, 20-21 and 9, 7, 4-6. In the first passage the terms are the same as in Augustine, esp. Serm. 23, 8-9 (ML, 38, 158 sq.) and M. MASSEI, in *Bollettino dell'Istituto di Diritto Romano*, 1941, p. 284, had repeated the view already expressed that Isidore was using him. Boyer believes both authors used a juridical collection of *differentiae*, probably dating from the Fourth Century, although the institution of « arra » survived in Isidore's day. In orig. 9, 7, 4-6 the contra-

sive use of Celsus. M. STAROWIEYSKI *Isidore de Séville et la littérature classique, I: Littérature grecque, Meander*, 29 (1972), pp. 357-67, has an alphabetical list of the Greek authors mentioned by Isidore in the orig. and chron. In *II: Littérature latine*, ibid., 30 (1975), pp. 19-35, he has a similar list of Latin authors. He does not think Isidore knew most Latin (or any Greek) authors directly among those he mentions. Both articles are in Polish, with resumés in Latin.

(65) A. GUARINO, *Isidoro di Siviglia e l'origine dei codicilli*, in *Studia et documenta hist. et iuris*, 10 (1944), pp. 317-32, esp. pp. 317-21, discusses *codicillum* in orig. 5, 24, 14. He believes the source is probably close to, if not identical with, Justinian, *Inst.* 2, 25, pr. TABERA (art. cit., p. 24 n. 1) and BOYER (art. cit. infra, 62) think Isidore was ignorant of Justinian's codification. J. DE CHURRUCA, *Las fuentes de la definición de codicilo en san Isidoro de Sevilla, Anuario de historia del derecho español*, 34 (1964), pp. 5-30, holds that Isidore was not here drawing on the *Institutes* but on juridical or grammatical manuals. A. ROTA, *Lo Stato e il diritto nella concezione di Irnerio*, Milano, 1954, pp. 37, 41, thinks Isidore knew Just., *Inst.* and *Digest.* In *La definizione isidoriana di ' concilium ' e le sue radici romanistiche*, in *Atti del Congresso internaz. di diritto romano e di storia del diritto* (Verona, 1948), IV, Milano, 1953, pp. 213-25, ROTA holds orig. 6, 16, 12 derives from the Digest (I, 3 D. 2, 14). But this parallel depends partly on a phrase that seems to be an interpolation in Isidore, although Rota maintains it is genuine (cf. note 11 supra). Cf. also A. D'ORS, art. cit. infra, Section VIb.

diction with the earlier passage is explained by the use of a different source, probably a lexicographer interested in old Roman customs. The later definition corresponds exactly to the Semitic conception of « arra », the earlier and more precise passage, on the other hand, to the use of the term in the Greek and Hellenistic world. Both conceptions came to Isidore, however, through the late Roman legal traditions, of a popular and learned nature respectively. P. VALLETTE, *Isidore de Séville et la fondation de Milan*, in *Mélanges Ch. Gilliard*, Lausanne, 1944, pp. 93-102, has shown that the source for orig. 15, 1, 57, with its independent testimony to the legend of the foundation of Milan, is an anonymous poem meant to teach geography. Vallette's study supplements Philipp's researches on the sources of this passage. Often enough, as with Braulio so with Isidore, the real sources of a passage are not the pagan classics ostensibly cited but one of the earlier Fathers (66).

Discussing orig. 16, 17-24, DÍAZ Y DÍAZ (cited above, Section II, p. 14) pp. 32 sq., remarks that the way Isidore writes bears little relation to reality. His presentation of information taken from Pliny is not due to technical changes between Pliny's time and his own but (possibly) to a desire to simplify his written source. In his edition of these chapters Díaz notes Isidore's direct use of St. Jerome and of Servius. His use of Lucretius, Pliny and other sources is generally at second or third hand. In a later article, *La transmisión de los textos antiguos en la península ibérica en los siglos VII-XI*, in *La Cultura antica nell'occidente latino dal VII all'XI secolo*, Spoleto, 1975 (*Settimane di studio*, XXII), pp. 133-75, Diaz considers (pp. 136-42) that Isidore used Lucretius, Martial (perhaps through an anthology), and Virgil (though he may have been known through Servius). Ovid, Lucan, and Juvenal are almost certainly cited only at second hand. Of classical prose writers Díaz believes that Isidore used Pliny the Elder and the other encyclopaedic authors, Solinus, Placidus, and Martianus Capella, directly; he is less likely to have possessed Quintilian. Díaz follows JUAN DE CHURRUCA, *Presupuestos para el estudio de las fuentes jurídicas de Isidoro de Sevilla*, *Anuario de historia del derecho español*, 43 (1973), pp. 429-43, and in his book, *Instituciones de Gayo en san Isidoro de Sevilla*, León, 1975 (which I have not seen), in holding that Isidore only knew Gaius through elementary summaries of his work, although he cites him by name in his *versus*.

The case of the *laus Spaniae* is particularly interesting. J. MADOZ, *De laude Spanie. Estudio sobre las fuentes del prólogo isidoriano*, *Razón y Fe*, 116 (1939), pp. 247-57, pointed out various possible pagan sources. Later, in *Ecos del saber antiguo en las letras de la España visigoda*, ibid., 122

(66) Cf. FONTAINE, passim, e. g. II, p. 791. ROTA, *Lo Stato* (op. cit., supra, note 65), pp. 20-28, notes that Isidore's definition of *populus* (orig. 9, 4, 5) is not taken from CICERO, *De re publica*, I, 25 but from AUGUSTINE, *De civitate Dei*, XIX, 29, 2. L. ROBLES (cited above, Section II, p. 19), pp. 163-71, discusses the sources for orig. 2, 29, and particularly the statement on man as a microcosm. It seems unnecessary to conclude that Isidore is using any source except CASSIODORUS, *Inst.* 2, 3, 14, as was already noted by Mynors (p. 120). A more extensive use af Mynors' edition of Cassiodorus would have saved Robles (pp. 174-85) considerable trouble. See also FONTAINE, e. g. I, p. 248; II, pp. 939 sq.

(1941), pp. 228-40, he drew attention to the even clearer use of Cyprian, *de habitu virginum* 3 and *epist. ad Donatum* 13 in the same preface. More recently, DÍAZ Y DÍAZ, *Prudencio en la Hispania visigótica. Unas breves notas,* in *Corona gratiarum. Miscellanea patristica, historica et liturgica E. Dekkers,* II, Bruges, 1975, pp. 61-70, has noted reminiscences of Prudentius in the same work (p. 62). The sources of the *de viris* and the *historiae* have been carefully studied in the new editions by Codoñer and Rodríguez, respectively; see Section II, above.

In 1936 ALTANER could declare that Isidore's theological works, from the point of view of the investigation of sources, were « fast eine terra incognita » (67). Although very much remains to be done this is less true today. Two investigations of the theological works remain outstanding. J. MADOZ's *El Florilegio Patrístico del II Concilio de Sevilla (a.* 619), in *Misc. Isid.,* pp. 177-220, and Dr. A. C. LAWSON, *The Sources of the De Ecclesiasticis Officiis of St. Isidore of Seville,* Oxford thesis for the D. D. (Bodl. MS. Eng. Theol. C. 56), 1937 (68). Lawson's was the « first concerted attempt to trace the whole of the sources for one of S. Isidore's works » (69). The *Florilegium* of 619 contains 25 quotations from ten Fathers, arranged in chronological order and well selected to support the argument against the Syrian Acephalite bishop Gregory. Quotations from SS. Gregory Nazianzen, Gregory of Nyssa, Cyril of Alexandria and Pseudo-Basil (Didymus ?) are taken, with one exception, at second hand from Justinian, *Confessio rectae fidei adversus tria capitula* (ML, 69, 234-40); the exception may be from an earlier Latin translation. In the *Florilegium* Isidore, P. Madoz notes, follows, in his selection, not only a chronological order of authors but also the original order of the fragments selected in the works he employed. In the *de officiis,* on the other hand, he pursues the same minute process of adaptation and combination visible in his secular works. Far from being a servile copyist of his predecessors he composes a mosaic of texts, adapting them with slight but significant touches to the ends he proposes. Very few chapters of the *de officiis* are left without their sources being accounted for.

Isidore's respect for Origen is notable in various of his works (70). The influence of Origen's homilies on Isidore has recently been brought

(67) ALTANER, in *Misc. Isid.,* p. 30 (and cf. 12).

(68) LAWSON published a summary in RB, 50 (1938), pp. 26-36. In RB, 57 (1947), pp. 187-95 he indicated a new source for the *off.* and for the *fid.* in the *Consultationes Zacchaei Christiani et Apollonii Philosophi.* B. BOTTE, in *RTAM,* 11 (1939), p. 240, points out the *Statuta ecclesiae antiqua* is the source of off. 2, 13, 3. G. MORIN, in *RHE,* 34 (1938), p. 237, notes Isidore uses PS-JEROME, *De septem ordinibus ecclesiae..* Lawson had already noticed the use of both sources. Cf. now the general discussion of U. DOMÍNGUEZ DEL VAL, *La utilización de los Padres por San Isidoro,* in *Isidoriana,* pp. 211-221.

(69) LAWSON, in *RB,* 50 (1938), p. 30; cf. MADOZ in RET, 1 (1940-41), pp. 954 sq. Lawson's views on Isidore's use of his sources were confirmed in an independent investigation of his sacramental theology by J. HAVET (art. cit. infra, Section VId), esp. p. 92. A. C. LAWSON s thesis (as far as c. 31) has appeared in translation, as *Las fuentes del 'De ecclesiasticis officiis',* *Archivos Leoneses,* 17 (1963), 1, pp. 129-76; 2, pp. 109-37.

(70) FONTAINE, II, pp. 756 sq.

out by J. Châtillon (71). Optatus of Milevis was used by Isidore as were many earlier and later North African writers (72). Augustine is, of course, to Isidore the greatest of all his predecessors; he is constantly employed, sometimes in very unexpected ways (73). M. Pellegrino, *Le ' confessioni ' di S. Agostino nell'opera di S. Isidoro di Siviglia, Isidoriana,* pp. 223-70, prints 62 textual parallels between the *Confessions* and Isidore's works (41 passages are from the *sententiae,* 14 from the *quaestiones in Genesim*). He believes that Isidore drew on the work for the doctrine he needed without regard to the spirit of the original. P. Courcelle, *Reflexions d'Isidore de Séville sur la vie du jeune Augustin, Latomus,* 21 (1962), pp. 520-41 (= his *Les Confessions de St. Augustin dans la tradition littéraire, Antécédents et Posterité,* Paris, 1963, pp. 235-54), adds to the number of passages used by Isidore and holds that he was deeply affected by the *Confessions.* Although Isidore sometimes « schématise et durcit la pensée d'Augustin » and ignores many of the intimate aspects of the work, Augustine's psychological analyses contribute to Isidore's spiritual and ascetic teaching, for instance on friendship and conversion. Several centuries would pass before anyone studied the *Confessions* as closely as Isidore had done. L. Robles, *La presencia de san Agustín en las ' Sentencias ' de Isidoro de Sevilla, Estudios de Metafísica* (Univ. de Valencia, Catedra de Metafísica, Curso 1970-1971), pp. 109-22, emphasizes Isidore's skill in summing up Augustine's ideas (in the *Confessions*) in a more theoretical scholastic form, and often with additions of his own. Robles also lists instances of the uses of other works of Augustine by Isidore, especially in sent. 1. See Robles' doctoral thesis, *L'Anthropologie religieuse chez Isidore de Séville, étude historique des sources: I Sent., cc.* 11-13 (Montréal, 1960-61). In *El origen y la espiritualidad del alma, San Isidoro de Sevilla, San Agustín y la cuestión priscilianista, Escritos del Vedat,* 1 (1971), pp. 407-88, Robles discusses the possible use by Isidore of Augustine, Gregory of Elvira, Claudianus Mamertus, and Fulgentius of Ruspe. In a brief article I. Opelt, *Materialen zur Nachwirkung von Augustins' Schrift De doctrina christiana, Jahrbuch für Antike und Christentum,* 17 (1974), pp. 64-73 (esp. 67 f.), touches on Isidore.

(71) *Isidore et Origène, Recherches sur les sources et l'influence des ' Quaestiones in Vetus Testamentum d'Isidore de Séville,* in *Mélanges bibliques A. Robert,* Paris, 1957 (Travaux de l'Institut cath. de Paris, 4), pp. 537-47.

(72) Cf. Y. M.-J. Congar, *Cephas-Céphalè-Caput,* in *RMAL,* 8 (1952), pp. 5-42 and J. Madoz, in *EE,* 17 (1943), pp. 285-87. (Optatus the source af orig. 7, 9, 3: Augustine, *Sermo* 76, 1 of ibid., 2). On Isidore and North Africa cf. Fontaine, II, pp. 857-59. J. Havet (art. cit. infra, Section VId) esp. pp. 92 sq., stresses the importance of Tertullian and Cyprian among Isidore's sources. On Isidore's knowledge of Dracontius cf. D. Romano, *Studi Draconziani,* Palermo, 1959, pp. 90 sq.

(73) Cf. E. Nebreda, *Las grandes lineas de la teologia isidoriana y el influjo del obispo de Hipona, San Agustin, en el metropolitano Hispalense, San Isidoro,* in *Ilustración del Clero,* 31 (1938), pp. 41-51, 164-68, 249-54 (discusses Isidore's views on the Existence, Essence and Attributes of God, on the Trinity and on Creation and Angelology); R. Schmidt, in *Zeitschrift für Kirchengeschichte,* 67 (1955-56), pp. 288-317 (Augustine's division of history into six ages is taken up by Isidore and Bede); M. van den Hout, in *VChr,* 2 (1948), p. 56 (the source of orig. 3, 12, 1 is Aug., *De ordine,* 1, 2, 3). Cf. Rota, cit. supra, note 66.

A. LINAGE CONDE, *Isidoro de Sevilla, De monachis, Studia Patristica,* XIII, Berlin, 1975, pp. 479-86, commented on the classification of monks in orig. 7, 13, 3-4. Isidore here used Augustine, *de opere monachorum*, and Cassian, *conlationes* 18. Among later Christian writers the influence of Cassiodorus is well known (74). It has been debated whether or not Isidore knew the Rule of St. Benedict (75). Dom Pérez de Urbel's list of parallels was reinforced by a note by J. JANINI in *AST,* 31 (1958), pp. 259 sq. (Isid. reg. 9, 8-9 depends on Benedict, *reg.* 39,1). On the other hand hand R. SUSÍN ALCUBIERRE, *Sobre las fuentes de la regula Isidori, Salmanticensis,* 14 (1967), pp. 371-94, argued that Isidore did not use Benedict. He showed that the main inspiration of the reg. was drawn from Augustine, *disciplina monasterii* and *regula ad servos Dei,* and considered the parallels between the reg. and other Isidorian works (off., sent.) and the *regula* of Pachomius. Among the considerable bibliography on the *regula* of Augustine, the article of M. VERHEIJEN, in *Augustiniana,* 4 (1954), pp. 258-68, may be cited as upholding the use by Leander and Isidore of the *disciplina monasterii* and the *epist.* 211, 5-16, in its feminine form (the *regula puellarum*), while U. DOMÍNGUEZ DEL VAL, in *RET,* 17 (1957), pp. 481-529 (esp. 493 sq., 523) believes that both authors cite the masculine and primitive version (the *regula ad servos Dei*); he also maintains Isidore's use of the *disciplina.* A. LINAGE CONDE, *La difusión de la regula benedictina en la península ibérica, Regulae Benedicti Studia, Annuarium internationale,* 1 (1972), pp. 297-325, at 302, believes the Rule of Benedict has « left abundant traces in the *regula Isidori* » (he cites a number of parallels). See also idem, *Los orígenes del monacato benedictino en la península ibérica,* I, León, 1973, 244 sq. LINAGE CONDE, *La única cita hispana conocida de la Regula Magistri,* in *Translatio studii. Manuscript and library studies honoring O. L. Kapsner, O.S.B.,* ed. J. G. PLANTE, Collegeville, Minn., 1973, pp. 202-23, rejects both the thesis of the Spanish origin of the *regula magistri* and the idea that it influenced Isidore (pp. 211-15); the latter idea had been advanced by G. PENCO, *Sulla diffusione della Regula Magistri, Benedictina,* 10 (1956), p. 194. Meanwhile A. DE VOGÜÉ, *La Règle d'Eugippe retrouvée, Revue d'ascétique et de mystique,* 47 (1971), pp. 233-66, identifies the *regula* of Eugippius cited by Isidore, vir. 13 (CODOÑER, p. 141) with a work in MS. Paris, Lat. 12634. K. S. FRANK, *Isidor von Sevilla, Das 'Mönchskapitel'* (*De eccles. off. II,* 16) *und seine Quellen, Römische Quartalschrift für christliche Altertumskunde und Kirchengeschichte,* 67 (1972), pp. 29-48, shows that here Isidore used Jerome, *epist.*, Cassian, and Augustine. In *Isidor von Sevilla, Regula Monachorum und ihre Quellen, Studia Patristica,* XIII, Berlin, 1975, 461-70, Frank argued that Isidore's sources in the reg.

(74) Cf. the general remarks of P. COURCELLE, in REA, 44 (1942), p. 86. R. A. B. MYNORS ' edition of the *Institutiones*, Oxford, 1937, reveals the use made by Isidore of Cassiodorus (cf. the list p. 193).

(75) Cf. J. PÉREZ DE URBEL, *Los monjes españoles en la Edad Media,* I, Madrid, 1933, pp. 496-508, and, against the doubts of Sr. P. J. MULLINS, (op. cit. infra, Section VId) pp. 69 sq., MADOZ, *Segundo Decenio*, p. 120, A. MUNDÒ, in *Il monachesimo nell'alto Medioevo*, Spoleto, 1957 (Settimane di Studio, IV), p. 102 n. 101, also supports Isidore's use of Benedict.

included Augustine, *disciplina monasterii*, the female form of the *regula*, other Augustinian works, Gregory the Great, *Moralia*, and earlier monastic sources. He showed that Isidore displayed independence in his choice and use of the materials available to him. Isidore was familiar with the works of St. Martin of Braga and made almost as much use of those of St. Gregory the Great as he did of St. Augustine (76).

Did Isidore make a direct use of Greek sources ? We know he could read Origen and some later Fathers, together with some late Greek manuals, but in translation (77). Lawson has suggested he may have read St. Cyril of Jerusalem in the original (78). Others are prepared to be more positive. But it is dangerous to rely on the late medieval *Vita* with its « latinis, graecis, et hebraecis litteris instructus » (79). If one cannot agree with FONTAINE (II, p. 849) that it is certain Isidore could not read Greek, it remains probable that his knowledge was very limited (80).

(76) Cf. A. FONTÁN, *La tradición de las obras morales de Martin de Braga*, in *Boletin de la Universidad de Granada*, 23 (1951), pp. 73-86 (believes Isidore knew the three minor treatises and the *de ira* and cites them as *volumen epistolarum* in vir. 35 [ML, 83, 1100]). On Gregory cf. R. WASSELYNCK, *L'influence des « Moralia in Job » de S. Grégoire le Grand sur la théologie morale entre le VIIe et le XIIe siècle*, Thèse, Lille. Fac. de théologie 1956, 3 vols. in 4°. (dactylographiée). I owe my knowledge of this work to O. LOTTIN, in *BTAM*, 8 (1958), n. 91. Isidore is studied. (WASSELYNCK later published *L'influence de l'exégèse de St. Grégoire le Grand sur les commentaires bibliques médiévaux*, in *RTAM*, 32, 1965, pp. 157-204; on Isidore pp. 158-60. In another article, *Les 'Moralia in Job' dans les ouvrages de morale du haut moyen âge latin*, ibid., 31 (1964), pp. 5-31, he discusses Isidore on pp. 6-11). FONTAINE, *Isidore, auteur ascétique* (cited above, Section II) studies the sources of the *synonyma*. The main sources are the Bible (esp. the Old Testament) and Gregory, *Moralia*. Gregory's spirituality is presented in such a way that the Old Testament and Stoic influences predominate over a message inspired by love for God and men. A similar change wrought by Isidore in Gregory's thought also appears in the *sententiae*. See FONTAINE, *La vocation monastique selon St. Isidore de Séville, Théologie de la Vie Monastique*, Paris, 1961, pp. 353-69, esp. 360-9. Isidore substitutes moralizing for Gregory's mystical perspectives in his discussion of monastic life.

(77) Cf. FONTAINE, II, pp. 756-59. M. SCHMAUS, in *Vitae et veritati, Festgabe für K. Adam*, Düsseldorf, 1956, p. 49 sq., notes Isidore s theology of the Trinity is more influenced by Greek than by Latin Fathers.

(78) LAWSON, in *RB*, 50 (1938), p. 35. Cf. A. VACCARI, *Una fonte del ' De ortu et obitu patrum ' di S. Isidoro*, in *Misc. Isid.*, pp. 165-75 (the source is the Greek *Vitae prophetarum*, saec. IV-V, of which the purest existing form is in MS. Marchal, now in the Vatican, no. 2125, saec. VII²; Vaccari thinks Isidore most probably used it in translation). His art. is reprinted in his *Scritti* (op. cit., note 45 supra, II, pp. 271-81). On the *Breviarum apostolorum* and the *de ortu* see B. DE GAIFFIER, *Le Breviarium Apostolorum, Analecta Bollandiana*, 81 (1963), pp. 104-16; he concludes that both works derive from an older compilation.

(79) As does J. M. JIMÉNEZ DELGADO, *Formación clásica de S. Isidoro*, in *AST*, 14 (1941), pp. 59-74; cf. the remarks of MADOZ, *Segundo Decenio*, p. 121; FONTAINE, I, p. 7 n. 1. R. RODRÍGUEZ SEIJAS, *San Isidoro, en la Pedagogia*, in *Revista española de Pedagogia*, 6 (1948), pp. 453-83, is still more fantastic; Isidore apparently knew Hebrew, Greek, Syriac, Egyptian (!) and Gothic. He also used Varro and Suetonius directly. S. CIRAC ESTOPAÑÁN, *Estudio de la Bizantinistica en España*, in *Universidad*, 16 (1939), p. 136, remarks, in passing, that Isidore's culture was not exclusively Latin but also Byzantine; he makes no attempt to prove this.

(80) I do not agree with Fontaine that the statement in vir. 39 (*ML*, 83, 1102) that John the Faster of Constantinople wrote a work in Greek that he addressed to Isidore's brother should *in itself* mean *Graecum est, non legi*. Cf. the reserves on this point of B. DE GAIFIER and P. COURCELLE, in their reviews of Fontaine (cit. infra, note 98). U. DOMÍNGUEZ

V. Isidore and the Culture of his age

A certain number of articles attempt to sketch briefly the significance of Isidore and especially of the orig. in the history of culture (81). Of greater importance are the appreciations, inside Spain, of Z. García Villada, *La obra de S. Isidoro de Sevilla. Valoración y sugerencias*, in *Misc. Isid.*, pp. 33-38, and of M. C. Díaz y Díaz, *La cultura de la España visigotica del siglo VII*, in *Caratteri del secolo VII in Occidente*, Spoleto, 1958 (*Settimane di Studio*, V. 2), pp. 813-44, esp. 820-29 and the discussion, ib., 889-97,

Del Val, *El helenismo de los escritores cristianos españoles en los siete primeros siglos*, *CD*, 181 (1968), pp. 479-82, also believes that Isidore had enough Greek « para poder defenderse en casos dificiles ». The general consensus of opinion, however, is that Isidore's Greek was very limited; cf. Madoz (cit. note 79 supra); Díaz, in Settimane di Studio, V. 2, Spoleto, 1958, pp. 841 sq.; B. Bischoff, in *Byzantinische Zeitschrift*, 44 (1951), pp. 29, 50, E. Delaruelle, in *Mélanges de la Société toulousaine d'études classiques*, I (1946), p. 213; Fontaine, II, pp. 849-51. Cf. also Mullins, op. cit. infra, Section VId, pp. 75-78.

(81) We may cite, « pour mémoire », A. de la Fuente González, in *Revista eclesiástica*, 10 (1936), pp. 473-85 (a note on the importance and encyclopaedic character of Isidore's works); A. Van de Vyver, in *Archeion*, 19 (1937), pp. 13 sq. (Isidore's position between Cassiodorus and Bede); E. M. Sanford, in *Classical Journal* 44 (1948-49), pp. 462-67 (brief notes on the Orig.); A. J. I. Van de Velde, *Le compendium du VIIe siècle oeuvre de Isidorus Hispalensis*, in *Actes du VIIe Congrès international d'Hist. des Sciences*, Paris, 1954 (Coll. des travaux de l'Acad. inter. d'Hist. des Sc., 8), pp. 615-19 (of very slight value); cf. Fontaine, I, p. 23, n. 2); more useful is H.L.W. Nelson, *Etymologiae van Isidorus van Sevilla. Een Boek op de grens van de antike en de middeleeuwse wereld*, Leiden, 1954, 39 pp. Cf. also Section IV supra and note 79. The celebration in 1960 of the XIV Centenary of Isidore's birth called forth a series of popular presentations of his life and thought. The *Crónica general de los actos celebrados en León (1 de mayo-31 octubre 1960) en conmemoración del XIV Centenario del Nacimiento de San Isidoro (560-1960)*, León, 1961, contains: L. Almarcha Hernández (bishop of León), *San Isidoro de Sevilla, semblanza de su personalidad literaria*, pp. 204-10; J. Rubio y García-Mina, *Lección magistral sobre San Isidoro*, pp. 165-8; J. Ibánez Martin, *Sabiduria, patriotismo y santidad*, pp. 219-35; R. Menéndez Pidal, *San Isidoro y la cultura de Occidente*, pp. 188-203. All these discourses were also published in *Archivos Leoneses*, 14 (1960). I have not seen L. López Santos, *San Isidoro de Sevilla*, in *Cátedra 1960-61. Prontuario del profesor*, ed. J. Rubio García-Mina, Madrid, 1960, pp. 363-74; A. Hernández Parrales, *El XIV Centenario del Nacimiento de san Isidoro, arzobispo de Sevilla*, in *Boletín del Instituto de Estudios Giennenses*, 7 (1960), pp. 9-31, nor I. Gutiérrez Zuluaga, *Los Origines de Isidoro de Sevilla y su trascendencia didáctica*, in *Revista española de Pedagogía*, 111 (1970), pp. 219-36; 112 (1970), pp. 311-28. The *Homenaje a San Isidoro de Sevilla* (Curso Académico 1960-61), Publicaciones del Instituto Nacional de Ensenanza Media « Cervantes » 2, Madrid, 1961, contains: F. Sánchez Faba, *La Astronomia en el ' Liber de natura rerum ' de San Isidoro*, pp. 9-32; E. Alvarez Lopez, *Breve aproximación a las ' Etimologias y algo sobre Botánica isidoriana*, pp. 33-73; Juan Durantez, *San Isidoro, educador de la Edad Media*, pp. 75-81; R. Ezquerra, *San Isidoro y la España visigótica*, pp. 83-94. See also L. Brunelle, *La pensée scientifique d'Isidore de Séville*, in *Scientia paedagogica*, 58 (1964), pp. 33-6, and J. Zaragueta, *San Isidoro de Sevilla, en su tiempo y en el nuestro*, in *Anales de la Universidad Hispalense*, 23 (1962) pp. 85-101. M. Starowieyski, *Isidore of Seville*, in *Meander*, 22 (1967), pp. 452-66 is the first account of Isidore in Polish (I am indebted to Dr. Ligota for my knowledge of it). It is an excellent *status quaestionis*, summing up Isidore's life, works and influence. F. Sánchez Faba, *San Isidro* [sic], *cientifico*, Cartagena, 1970, 76 pp., a general introduction to the scientific aspects of orig. and nat., is known to me from *IHE*, No. 79904. U. Pizzani, *Il filone enciclopedico nella patristica, da S. Agostino a S. Isidoro di Siviglia*, *Augustinianum*, 14 (1974), pp. 667-96, discusses encyclopedists from Varro to Isidore and (pp. 692-95) Isidore's attempt to restore ancient culture, which he sees as a complete failure.

and, outside, by K. Vossler and E. R. Curtius (82). Several books on Isidore have appeared. From inside Spain, apart from the general work of J. Fernández Alonso, *La cura pastoral en la España romanovisigoda*, Roma, 1955, which, necessarily, draws continually on Isidore and devotes considerable space to a discussion of Spanish culture et this time, we have the posthumously published work of J. Madoz (+ 1953), *San Isidoro de Sevilla, Semblanza de su personalidad literaria*, edited by C. G. Goldáraz, León, 1960, XX + 199 pp. This is really four articles, put together by the editor. If P. Madoz had published the book himself he would doubtless have avoided a certain amount of repetition and he might have changed certain things, e.g. the use of the *de ordine creaturarum* as authentic. The editor has left the text as P. Madoz wrote it and confined his additions to notes and bibliography. The last chapter (c. 4), pp. 119-56, was written in 1952 (cf. *RET*, 12, 1952, p. 622). It contains a general picture of Isidore, his sources, his view of the Bible, his theology, his philosophy of law, his view of the seven arts, the diffusion of his work and, finally, stresses his patriotism. Elsewhere in this study we have mentioned other chapters of this book (cf. supra, Bibliographies and Section II, infra, Sections VI a and b). We may mention here an article by J. Ruiz Goyo, in *Boletín de la Biblioteca Menéndez y Pelayo*, 18 (1938), pp. 249-59, which collects the teaching of Menéndez Pelayo on Isidore; I have not seen the article by Menéndez Pelayo in *Menéndez-Pelayismo*, I (1944), pp. 3-192, which may reprint some of his work on Isidore.

Fontaine's *Isidore* will be briefly described at the end of this Section. Some twenty-five years ago there appeared G. Mancini's *Osservazioni critiche sull'opera di Sant'Isidoro di Siviglia*, Pisa, 1955 (Studi di Letteratura Spagnuola, 5), 102 pp. (83). The author suffers from an apparent lack of access to much of the recent literature on the subject and from a tendency to limit his investigation, especially of Isidore's style, to the classical side of his subject. The title of his work promises, perhaps, more than the work provides. On the other hand M. Donati, *Il pensiero estetico in Isidoro di Siviglia e negli enciclopedisti medioevali*, in *Rendiconti della Accademia Nazionale dei Lincei*, S. 8, Classe di scienze morali, storiche e filol., 3 (1948), pp. 370-80, accentuates overmuch to my mind the « medieval »

(82) K. Vossler, *San Isidoro*, in *Arbor*, 2 (1944), pp. 17-25, reproduced in a special volume of *Arbor*, entitled *Historia de España*, Madrid, 1953, also in *Hochland*, 39 (1946-47), pp. 420-28 (= *Aus der romanischen Welt*, Karlsruhe, 1948, pp. 551-62). E. R. Curtius sums up Isidore's view of literary history and poetics in *Zur Literarästhetik des Mittelalters*, in *Zeitschrift für roman. Philol.*, 58 (1938), pp. 465-73 (= *European Literature and the Latin Middle Ages*, New York, 1953, pp. 450-57). Fontaine, I, p. 158 n. 2, criticises Curtius's deliberate neglect of sources; cf., however, ibid., p. 4 n. 3. For other aspects of Isidore cf. Curtius, *European Literature*, pp. 42-44, 75, 157 sq., 496 sq.

(83) The Spanish version, *San Isidoro de Sevilla. Aspectos Literarios*, Bogotá, 1955 (Publ. del Instituto Caro y Cuervo. Ser. minor, 4), 134 pp. seems less complete than the Italian.

(84) P. Pascal, in *Classical Journal*, 51 (1955-56), pp. 113, 115, similarly overemphasises « the great hostility of Isidore to secular learning », which, he admits, is « something of a paradox ». On this question cf. J. Madoz, in *Folia*, 8 (1954), cf. note 61 supra – pp. 33 sq., and the longer discussion by Fontaine, II, *Culture paienne et culture chrétienne*, pp., 785-806, also Id., *Le problème de la culture dans la latinité chrétienne du IIIe au VIIe siècle*, in *Information littéraire*, 9 (1957), pp. 208-15.

side of Isidore and his passive acceptance of the materials available to him. Did Isidore, we may ask, really have an absorbing desire to avoid all contact with classical culture ? (84). E. DE BRUYNE, *Études d'esthétique médiévale*, I, Brugge, 1946 (Rijksuniversiteit te Gent. Werken de Fac. van de Wijsbegeerte en Letteren, 97), pp. 74-107, has given us a longer study than Donati's of Isidorian aesthetic ideas. It suffers from a certain failure to see Isidore against the background of his age. Cf. FONTAINE, in *VChr*, 14 (1960), p. 98, n. 68, 99 n. 70. Recently FONTAINE has given us a valuable article, *Isidore de Séville et la mutation de l'encyclopédisme antique*, *Cahiers de l'histoire mondiale*, 9 (1966), pp. 519-38. Here he shows that Isidore's encyclopedism had roots going back for centuries, to the retreat of science into the compilation of extracts from earlier authors already found in Suetonius and Pliny. The orig. continues the Classical tradition while expanding it to include subjects such as Christian doctrine, Judaism and heresies. The practical aim of the work is stressed here, as in FONTAINE's major work (see below).

P. M. BASSETT, *The Concept of Christian Society and Culture in the Writings of Isidore of Seville: his suggestions concerning philosophical, historical and legal foundations for Visigothic Spain* [Dissertation, Duke University' 262 pp.,] I know through *Dissertation Abstracts* 28 A, 9 (1968), p. 3753. The thesis is concerned with the aims of Isidore, as deduced from his writings. In order to help create a stable society in Spain Isidore elaborated a philosophy of history and a new conception of authority, *officium*, not *imperium*, which uses but transcends Roman and Visigothic legal traditions. (This work can be obtained in microfilm or xerox from University Microfilms, Ann Arbor, Michigan 48106, U.S.A.).

Uncertainty over Isidore's sources has until recently prevented any serious study of his language or style. We have already noted (supra, Section II) Fontaine's analysis of the language of the *de natura rerum*. In an article the same author studies the *Théorie et pratique du style chez Isidore de Séville*, in *VChr*, 14 (1960), pp. 65-101. At first sight there appears to exist a flagrant contradiction between the sober classical theory of rhetoric in the *origines* and the *stilus isidorianus* so beloved of the Middle Ages and found especially in the *synonyma* (85). This contradiction, as is often the case with Isidore, is more apparent than real. The « grand style » found in other works besides the *synonyma*, e.g. in the *laus Spaniae*, is classical in comparison to that of Isidore's friend and correspondent, King Sisebut. It has been greatly influenced by Isidore's favourite Christian sources, the homilies of Cyprian, Ambrose, Augustine and Gregory the Great, and probably also by the contemporary Spanish Liturgy. On the other hand Isidore's theory is less austere than appears at first sight for it concedes great importance to *suavitas* and *dulcedo*, to *ornamenta verborum*. One should speak of contrast rather than of contradiction. If

(85) On the *synonyma cf.* J. M. CASAS HOMS, *interpretación filológica de los ' Synonyma ' de San Isidoro*, in *Actas del I Congreso español de Estudios Clásicos*, Madrid, 1958 (Publ. Soc. esp. de Est. Clásicos, 2), pp. 518-23, who points out the grammatical, rhetorical and philological interest of the work.

Isidore often appears dull and impersonal it is largely because of his didactic and pastoral purpose-that of a grammarian but also of a bishop-that inspires even the « methodical flourishes » we find in his works. The *regula monachorum* is the one work where Isidore is natural; he expressly says here he is using *sermo plebeius vel rusticus*. The same natural prose is found in his *epistulae* to Braulio. M. RABANA ÁLVAREZ, *La lengua hablada en tiempos de San Isidoro*, *Archivos Leoneses*, 24 (1970), pp. 187-201, uses the orig. but also the recently discovered *pizarras* (cited, without question, from the edition by M. GÓMEZ MORENO, Madrid, 1964), and other sources already used by R. MENÉNDEZ PIDAL, *Origenes del español*, Madrid, 1956; that is, he argues back from Mozarabic dialectic forms to the Visigothic period.

Scholars have commented on different philological and other points in the origines. I follow the order of the texts discussed. M. HUBERT, in *REL*, 49 (1971), pp. 290-313, argues that in orig. 1, 18-19, Isidore attempted a summary description of the liturgical recitation of Biblical and other texts, and that here he is followed by, and does not copy, the grammarian Audax. Several critics have endeavoured to elucidate the meaning of orig. 1, 24, « *De notis militaribus* », and especially the significance of the three Greek letters used. The source is in part Rufinus (cf. FONTAINE, I, p. 83, n.1). G. R. WATSON, in *Journal of Roman Studies*, 42 (1952), pp. 56-62, held that Rufinus and Isidore are dealing with *notae* used in a Roman casualty list. *Superstites* here would mean not only surviving soldiers but ' wounded and alive '. *Labda* would stand for ' wanting ' or perhaps ' deserter '. J. H. OLIVER, in *RhMus*, 100 (1957), pp. 242-44, while agreeing that a casualty list is intended, believes *superstites* means ' soldiers wounded but still *apti militiae* '. J. H. GILLIAM (art. cit. supra, note 11, pp. 408-15) argues convincingly that we do not have to assume a casualty list but rather a simple roll of names. *Superstes* means merely ' surviving '. *Labda* is not a « nota militaris » but denotes *impuritas*, Isidore here digressing from his subject. G. R. WATSON returns to the question in *Historia*, 11 (1962), pp. 379-83. He maintains that the context excludes Gilliam's interpretation. *Labda* denotes *inperitus*, a soldier who « failed » tests in basic training. J. ENGELS, *La portée de l'étymologie isidorienne*, in *Studi medievali*, ser. 3e, 3 (1962), pp. 99-128, studies orig. 1, 29. He traces its sources (notably Boethius, *On the Topics*) and proposes several corrections to the text. For Isidore most names have an *origo* which is also *veriloquium*, « that is they have been imposed *secundum naturam* ». J. JOLIVET, *Quelques cas de ' platonisme grammatical ' du VIIe au XIIe siècle*, in *Mélanges R. Crozet*, I, Poitiers, 1966, pp. 93-95, discusses the same passage. He considers Isidore « un Platon réduit à la grammaire ». G. DE POERCK, *Etymologia et origo à travers la tradition latine*, in *Gedenkboek E. A. Leemans*, Bruges, 1970, pp. 191-228, reflects on the nature of these two words from Cicero and Varro to Cassiodorus and Isidore. He studies Isidore (pp. 212-19), especially orig. 1, 29, 2, 30, and book 10. He disagrees with Engels as to the use of Boethius (the source is Quintilian, with some traces of Varro) and as to the corrections proposed for 1, 29, 1. On orig. 1, 32, 1 cf. M. NIEDERMANN, *Précis de phonétique historique du latin*,[3] Paris, 1953,

p. 16. On orig. 1, 32, 5 cf. Id., in *Rev. de philol. et litt. et d'hist. ancienne,* 22 (1948), p. 14. R. Muth, in *Wiener Studien,* 67 (1954), pp. 42 sq., holds orig. 1, 39, 18 reveals only a vague idea of the origins of epithalamia. J. L. Vidal, *Observaciones sobre centones virgilianos de tema cristiano. La creación de una poesia cristiana culta, Boletín del Instituto de Estudios Helénicos* 7, 2 (1973), pp. 53-64, studies the *versus ad gratiam domini* attributed to quidam Pomponius in orig. 1, 39, 26. L. Herrmann, *Tertulliana, I: Tertullien et S. Pomponius, Latomus,* 30 (1971), p. 151, maintains that the same passage makes it possible to be more precise as to the activity of Tertullian as the author of juridical works because of his relationship with Sextus Pomponius, the great jurist, whom Isidore shows was a Christian. R. Till, *Ein Bekenntnis des Scipio Aemilianus, Festschrift für K. J. Merentitis,* Athens, 1972, pp. 415-22, studies the maxim of Scipio, cited in orig. 2, 21, 4, describing the political rise of the ideal Roman noble. E. Orth, *Lekton = dicibile, Helmantica,* 10 (1959), pp. 221-26, discusses the different meanings of *lekton* and cites, among other authors, orig. 2, 22, 2. B. Loeschorn, *Die Bedeutungsentwicklung von lat. organum bis Isidor von Sevilla, Museum Helveticum,* 28 (1971), pp. 193-226, shows that the word eventually means both the human voice and the psalter but its most important meaning will be that of a musical instrument; see orig. 3, 19, 1, 21, 1. E. Pólay, *Iura,* 16 (1965), pp. 27-51, discusses the plan of Julius Caesar to codify Roman law. Orig. 5, 1, 5 is one of our two sources for this plan. C. O. Brink, *Limaturae, RhMus,* 115 (1972), pp. 41 sq., comments on the use of Servius on Aen. VI, 160, in orig. 6, 8, 3. R. R. Johnson, *Bicolor membrana, Classical Quarterly,* 23 (1973), pp. 339-42, notes that texts from Persius, orig. 6, 11, 4, and Jewish practice suggest that early classical parchment rolls were only inscribed on the recto, which was dyed yellow. A. Rota, *La definizione* (cited supra, note 65), comments on *concilium* and *coetus* in orig. 6, 16, 12-13. F. J. Dölger, *Antike und Christentum,* 6 (1950), pp. 82-85, cites orig. 6, 19, 4 for *missa,* which Isidore interprets as a dismissal (of catechumens). D. Wieluch, in *Vetus Testamentum,* 7 (1957), p. 418, registers the information contained in orig. 8, 4, 5 on the Essenes and points out its source is Ps-Jerome, in *Corpus haeresologicum,* I, ed. Fr. Oehler, Berlin, 1856. R. Lorenz, *Circumcelliones-cotopitae- cutzupitani, Zeitschrift für Kirchengeschichte,* 82 (1971), pp. 54-9, notes that to explain Isidore's (probably mistaken) interpretation of circumcellions as monks, in off. 2, 16, 7, S. Calderone, *Circumcelliones, La Parola del Passato,* 22 (1967), pp. 94-109, cited his assimilation of the word to *cotopitae* in orig. 8, 5, 53. But (Lorenz argues) the word *cotopita* should be explained by reference to Semitic languages, not to Coptic. It means an olive-harvester (and this is what a circumcellion was). J. G. Fernández, *Emerita,* 30 (1962), pp. 136 sq., notes that the contemptuous description of the Epicureans in orig. 8, 6, 15, stems from Lactantius. S. McKenna, *Paganism and Pagan Survivals in Spain up to the Fall of the Visigothic Kingdom,* Washington, 1938, (*CUA, SMH,* N. S. 1), p. 140, thinks orig. 8, 9, 3 refers to actual magical practices in Spain contemporary with Isidore. V. Pisani, *Helikon,* 5 (1965), pp. 146 sq., holds that *ola* in orig, 11, 1, 62, is a vulgar derivation from *ulna.*

G. CAMBIER, in *Latomus,* 19 (1960), pp. 59-64, finds that the *equiferos* of orig. 12, 1, 54, helps to explain *equus ferus* in Horace, *Sat.* I, V, vv. 50-51. A. SÁNCHEZ, in *Homenaje a San Isidoro* (cited note 81, above), pp. 95-110, discusses *catum a captura* (orig. 12, 2, 38). F. TIETZE, in *Glotta,* 28 (1939-40), p. 279, suggests *mus* (orig. 12, 3, 1 and 20, 3, 4) is an Iberian word. J. FRIEDRICH, ibid., 29 (1941-42), p. 61, believes it comes from the Greek. R. BALTAR [VELOSO], *Ostrea / Ostreum, Durius* 1 (1973), pp. 271-76, notes that orig. 12, 6, 52 is an example of confusion in the language of the period (I know this article only from *L'Année Philologique*). L. GAMBERALE, *L'acredula di Cicerone. Una variante d'autore ?, Studi italiani di filologia classica,* 43 (1971), pp. 246-57, argues that Isidore probably used the original edition of Cicero's lost *Prognostica* (fr. IV 4 sq.) rather than *de div.* 1, 14 in orig. 12, 7, 37.

P. D'HEROUVILLE, in *Les Etudes Classiques,* 10 (1941), pp. 321-28, compares orig. 13, 11 to descriptions of winds in Virgil and other classical authors. (On this subject see the bibliography in ISIDORE, *Traité de la nature,* p. 295). J. ROUGÉ, in *Cahiers d'histoire publiés par les Universités de Clermont-Lyon-Grenoble,* 8 (1963), pp. 253-68, discusses references to the island of Carpathos, *inter alia* orig. 14, 6, 24 and 19, 1, 11. A. M. SCHNEIDER, in *Nachrichten der Acad. der Wiss. in Göttingen,* 1952, Philol.-Hist. Klasse, 7, Göttingen, 1952, p. 160, holds the description of *basilica* as a king's hall in orig. 15, 4, 11 is « reine Lexikographenweisheit », unrelated to life in the Fourth (or, presumably, in the Seventh) Century. I. CAZZANIGA, *Alcune glosse latine, Studi classici e orientali,* 24 (1975), p. 174, comments on orig. 15, 12, 3. Following Varro he suggests inserting *dei* before *tuguria.* J. ANDRÉ, in *REL,* 28 (1950), p. 111, discovers the traditional meaning of *trames* in orig. 15, 16, 10. W. KASPERS, in *Zeitschr. für vergleichende Sprachforschung auf dem Gebiete der Indogerm. Sprachen,* 67 (1942), pp. 218 sq., comments on *cateia* in orig. 18, 7, 7. M. RODRÍGUEZ-PANTOJA, *En torno al vocabolario marino en latín : los catálogos de naves, Habis,* 6 (1975) pp. 135-52, compares the text of orig. 19, which lists 42 names for 31 ships and boats, with a North African mosaic of *ca.* 200, and with lists in Aulus Gellius and Nonius Marcellus. F. CAPPONI, in *Latomus,* 23 (1964), pp. 63-74, holds that Isidore's interpretation of *transenna* in orig. 19, 1, 24, as *funis extentus* was probably the original meaning. Isidore agrees here with Servius. G. P. SHIPP, in *Glotta,* 39 (1960-61), p. 153, holds that *agea* (quoted from Ennius) in orig. 19, 2, 4, originally comes from Doric Greek. E. SALIN and J. CHOUX, in *Bull. archéol. du Comité des travaux hist. et scient.,* 1946-49, pp. 815-20, show that a way of marking boundaries mentioned in orig. 19, 6, 7 (a passage inspired by Augustine, *De civ. Dei* XXI, 4, 3) still survived in Lorraine saec. VI-VII. Various authors have commented on Isidore's interpretation of *ascia* in orig. 19, 19, 12. Cf. P.-M. DUVAL, in *Mémoires de la Soc. Nat. des Antiquaires de France, Ser.,* 9, 3 (1954), pp. 74 sq., followed by J. CARCOPINO, *Le mystère d'un symbole chrétien : l'ascia,* Paris, 1955, p. 16. J. ROUGÉ, in *Latomus,* 18 (1959), pp. 649-53, maintained that *ascia* was never an agricultural implement but only a wooden tool used by coopers, wheelwrights and carpenters.

The source for Isidore here was probably Palladius, *De re rustica*, I, 43 [already suggested by Arévalo]. E. F. Leon, in *Transactions and Proceedings of the American Philological Association*, 84 (1953), pp. 176-80, believes that Isidore's definition of *molochinia* in orig. 19, 22, 12 is a misunderstanding of his source, Nonius Marcellus. J. Van den Bosch, *Capa, Basilica, Monasterium et le culte de Saint Martin de Tours*, Nymegen, 1959, pp. 12-15, shows that Isidore, orig. 19, 31, 3, has the same explanation as Gregory of Tours of *cappa* as a cape covering the head. P. Ruffel, in *Annales publiés par la Fac. des Lettres de Toulouse*, 2 (1953), *Pallas, Etudes sur l'Antiquité I*, pp. 124-39, comments on *caltula* in a series of texts that includes orig. 19, 33, 4. V. Pisani, in *RhMus*, 97 (1954), p. 288, compares *mozicia* in orig. 20,9, 4 with the Sardinian « moittsu ». P. Ortmayr, in *Wiener Jahreshefte*, 32 (1940), Beibl., pp. 39-40, comments on *falcastrum* in orig. 20, 14, 5 and J. Rougé, in *REA*, 59 (1957), p. 326, on *ciconia* in orig. 20, 15, 3.

A. Borst, *Der Turmbau von Babel, Geschichte der Meinungen über Ursprung und Vielfalt der Sprachen und Völker*, II, Ausbau, I, Stuttgart, 1958, pp. 446-55, comments on the remarks in the orig. on the origins of speech, on the stages of Latin from *prisca* to *mixta*, on the names of peoples. The diversity of languages for Isidore was a natural historical fact, ordained by God. No other author exercised so durable an influence on medieval ideas on this diversity and on the genealogies of peoples (p. 455).

N. Benavides, *La etnografía en San Isidoro, Archivos Leoneses*, 14 (1960), pp. 357-75 (and in *Crónica general en conmemoración del XIV Centenario del nacimiento de San Isidoro*, Léon, 1961, pp. 169-87), has a very general gloss on ethnography in orig. 9.

G. Kahlo, *Vermischte Randbemerkungen, Ziva Antika*, 22 (1972), pp. 186-88, lists a number of notices in the orig. which he claims have not yet been appreciated at their true value. Unfortunately he uses a saec. xvi edition and ignores the problem of sources. N. C. Conomis, *Greek in Isidore's Origines, Glotta*, 51 (1973), pp. 101-112, comments on and attempts to improve a number of the Greek terms in the text. A. García Gallo, *Consideración crítica de los estudios sobre la legislación y la costumbre visigodas, Anuario de historia del derecho español*, 44 (1974), pp. 343-464, briefly discusses the testimony of Isidore, goth. 35, 51 (pp. 364-68).

J. Zeiller, *Isidore de Séville et les origines chrétiennes des Goths et des Suèves*, in *Misc. Isid.*, pp. 287-92, discusses the valuable evidence in the *historiae Gothorum et Sueborum*, unavailable elsewhere, for the early evangelisation of these peoples [86]. H. M. Klinkenberg, *Der Verfall des Quadriviums in frühen Mittelalter*, in *Artes Liberales. Von der antiken Bildung zur Wissen-*

(86) W. H. C. Frend, in *JTS*, N. S., 3 (1952), pp. 87-89, holds *circumcelliones* in off. 2, 16 (*ML*, 83, 796) means wandering ascetics or pseudo-monks, which is evidently the cor-, rect interpretation. F. Bolgiani, *La conversione di S. Agostino*, Torino, 1956, pp. 111-119 held there was no other example of the phrase *Tolle, lege* in Latin literature than Aug., *Conf.* VIII, 12, 29. P. Courcelle, in *REA*, 59 (1957), p. 379, points to its existence in Isidore, *versus* (ed. Beeson, p. 157).

schaft des Mittelalters, Leiden-Köln, 1959 (Studien und Texte zur Geistesgeschichte des Mittelalters, ed. J. KOCH, 5), pp. 1-32, esp. 13-22, has compared Isidore's ideas of the four arts that were later to form the *quadrivium* with those of Cassiodorus and Gregory the Great. He maintains, on the basis of certain textual changes in the transmission of ancient musical theory by Cassiodorus and Isidore, that they were already sceptical of Boethius' confidence in the power of man through the arts *agnoscere Deum*; the authority of Scripture is set against that of secular knowledge. In the two later authors' evaluation of numbers Scriptural symbolism becomes dominant over Pythagorean musical theory. Neither Cassiodorus nor Isidore, however, are as ready to abandon the culture of the past as is Gregory the Great (87). A. B. DURÁN, *Valor catequético de la obra « De Natura Rerum » de San Isidoro de Sevilla*, in *Atenas*, 9 [78] (1938), pp. 41-51, has stressed the catechetical intention of the nat., distinct from that of the *origines* (88). (We may recall, however, the fact that they were both originally addressed to the same person, Sisebut). E. ELORDUY, *San Isidoro, Unidad orgánica de su educación reflejada en sus escritos*, in *Misc. Isid.*, pp. 293-322, is correct in emphasising the preponderant role of grammar as a « ciencia totalitaria » in Isidore (89). A. MENTZ, who had already discussed the suject of stenography in Isidore (orig. I, 22) in earlier works, returns to it in *Archiv für Urkundenforschung*, 16 (1939), pp. 304-11 (90).

Three articles have discussed music in Isidore. Two of them are by F. J. LÉON TELLO, who contrasts the entirely theoretical notices of the orig., which only propose to explain the principal musical terms, with the more practical concern in the *de ecclesiasticis officiis* with the forms of liturgical chant (91). W. GURLITT, *Zur Bedeutungsgeschichte von « musicus » und « cantor » bei Isidor von Sevilla*, Mainz, 1950 (Akad. der Wissenschaften und der Literatur in Mainz, Abhandl. der geistes-und sozialwissenschaftlichen Klasse, 1950, 7), pp. 543-58, also believes in a complete separation between the theory in the orig. on the *musicus* (orig. 3) and the practical

(87) It is possible that Klinkenberg exaggerates the opposition of Scriptural and Pythagorean theory. Cf. FONTAINE I, 3e partie, « Déclin général des sciences exactes », esp. pp. 341-50, 441-50. It is possible to speak of Isidore's « Christian Pythagoreanism ». Klinkenberg does not mention the *liber numerorum*, discussed at length by Fontaine. (Cf. supra, Section II and note 21).

(88) Cf. also J. PÉREZ DE URBEL, *Pedagogia isidoriana*, in *Educación*, 1 (1941), pp. 7-14 (not available to me); R. RODRÍGUEZ SEIJAS (art. cit. supra, note 79); A. ALAEJOS, *Cómo enseñaba S. Isidoro de Sevilla*, in *Verdad y Vida*, 1 (1943), pp. 208-20, a fervent eulogy of little scientific value. Both the last two authors base themselves largely on the apocryphal *institutionum disciplinae* (cf. Section III supra).

(89) He exaggerates, however, the extent of Stoic influence on Isidore. Cf. FONTAINE, I, p. 150 n. 2. The importance of Isidore's emphasis on grammar, as determining the true historical or literal interpretation or interpretations of Scripture, is brought out by A. NEMETZ, *Literalness and the Sensus Litteralis*, in *Speculum*, 34 (1959), pp. 76-89, esp. 82-84.

(90) Cf. also J. G. FÉVRIER, *Histoire de l'écriture*, Paris, 1948, p. 489.

(91) F. J. LEON TELLO, *La teoria de la Mùsica en las « Etimologias » de San Isidoro*, in *Saitabi*, 8 (1950-51), pp. 48-58. His other article, *La teoria de la música en las obras de San Isidoro*, in *Música*, 1, 2 (1952), pp. 11-28, adds little that is new. He fails to discuss Isidore's sources.

emphasis on the *cantor* and on the liturgy (orig. 6, 19; 7, 12). This contrast seems somewhat forced. FONTAINE's study of sources reveals a certain influence of Isidore's experience on his theory (92).

L.-I. RINGBOM, in his works on the earthly paradise in medieval European and in Persian mythology, discusses the picture of *medium mundi* found in some MSS. as illustrating orig. 3, 52, and shows that a Persian myth presupposes the same cosmogram. Unfortunately Ringbom does not discuss the sources of the cosmogram in Isidore (93). The fundamental study of Isidore's astronomy is contained in FONTAINE, II, pp. 453-589. In an earlier article, *Isidore de Séville et l'astrologie*, in *REL*, 31 (1953), pp. 271-300, FONTAINE points out that Isidore's attitude to astrology is not entirely (as has been believed) dictated by his sources but is also influenced by the need to combat Priscillianism and contemporary astral superstitions. Isidore distinguishes clearly between these superstitions and natural astrology. Nevertheless his respect, in some cases undeserved, for the authors he used, explains his indulgence towards certain aspects of astrology. His intellectual curiousity, together with Jewish and Byzantine influences, combine to account for his tolerant attitude, very different from that of Augustine, and also, in its scientific approach, from the views of Gregory the Great and Gregory of Tours.

An important article on Isidore's geographical ideas is that of R. UHDEN, *Die Weltkarte des Isidorus von Sevilla*, in *Mnemosyne*, S. III, 3 (1935-36), pp. 1-28. The author describes the map in MS. Vat. lat. 6018 (saec. IX) of the orig. which, he holds, is the earliest detailed world map of the Middle Ages and is a copy of a « Darstellung » made by Isidore on the basis of a late antique map. According to G. MENÉNDEZ PIDAL (art. cit. infra, note 134) p. 189, the artists of the Beatus MSS. and the author of Vat. Lat. 6018-certainly made outside Spain-used similar models. The relation between Isidore and these models is not, however, clear. Two other articles are more general in nature and of less specific value (94). On

(92) Cf. FONTAINE, I, pp. 413-40, esp. 435-40. On early Church music cf. S. CORBIN, *L'Eglise à la conquête de sa musique*, Paris, 1960, cited by FONTAINE, in *VChr*, 14 (1960), p. 84 n. 42. On Isidore cf. CORBIN, pp. 180-82, 196-99.

(93) Nor does FONTAINE, although he indicates the sources of the chapter (II, pp. 494 sq.). RINGBOM first cited Isidore in this context in *Graltempel und Paradies, Beziehungen zwischen Iran und Europa im Mittelalter*, Stockholm, 1951) (Kungl. Vittelhets Historie och Antikvitets Akademiens Handlingar, 73), pp. 283-85, using an illustration derived (indirectly) from MS. St-Gallen 237 p. 63. Basically the same theory in *Paradisus terrestris, Myt, Bild och Verklighet*, Helsingfors, 1958 (Acta Societatis Scientiarum Fennicae, N. S. C. 1, 1), pp. 290 sq. (with the same illustration). This illustration does not seem to appear in most MSS. of the *orig.*

(94) Cf. S. MONTERO DÍAZ, *Ensayo sobre las ideas geográficas de San Isidoro de Sevilla*, in *Rev. Univ. Madrid*, 1 (1940), pp. 122-42; A. MELÓN, *La etapa isidoriana en la geografia medieval*, in *Arbor*, 28 (1954), pp. 456-67 (cites various studies but not Philipp's). G. MENÉNDEZ PIDAL (art. cit. infra, note 134) does not cite Philipp either. He is mainly concerned with the Beatus maps but notes the influence of a primitive representation of the three parts of the world (Asia, Europe, Africa) found in MS. Esc. R.II. 18 f. 24v (s. VII), at the end of Isidore *de natura rerum*. The possibility (for one cannot rate it higher) that this *rota* is part of the original text is reinforced by its presence – not observed by Menéndez Pidal – in two ancient non-Spanish MSS., Basel F. III. 15a (s. VIII ex.) from Fulda, and

Isidore's own geographical ideas, their nature and sources, as distinct from his influence on later geographers, Philipp's work remains the one essential study. P. CHARANIS, *Graecia in Isidore of Seville*, in *Byzantinische Zeitschrift*, 64 (1971), pp. 22-25, argues that when Isidore, in chron. 414, mentions the Slavs conquering Greece (ca. 615), he probably means Illyricum.

C. SANZ EGAÑA has given us a brief examination of the views on agriculture in the orig. (95). More unusual is a translation by O. DOBIASH-ROZHDESTVENSKAYA and V. A. BAKHTIN into Russian of selected passages from the orig., accompanied by copious notes on technical agricultural terms (96). I have not been able to see the work of I. ARIAS TOVAR and A. RUIZ MORENO, *La medicina en la obra de San Isidoro*, Buenos Aires, 1950, 205 pp., but it apparently consists mainly of extracts from the orig., nat. and the diff. SHARPE (cited Section II, above), in the introduction to his translation of Isidore's medical writings, has a useful discussion of the cosmological, medical and anatomical tradition behind Isidore and the use he made of it. He remarks (pp. 27 sq.) that orig. 11 is « strongly teleological » and « sometimes amounts to nothing more than a list of anatomical examples to document the beneficence of God [but] there are passages of genuine value to the historian of science ». Isidore's discussion of monsters « is rational and more than a little sceptical » (p. 31). His « medicine is derived entirely from books »; hence the slight treatment accorded surgery and the omission of midwifery, both crafts « learned by apprenticeship ». Orig. 4 was probably intended as a collection of definitions of medical terms, not as a practical manual. Isidore is remarkable in consistently ascribing natural causes even to epilepsy and lunacy, often seen as due to demonic possession (p. 33). His restatement of the rational tradition of classical medicine was of great value to later physicians (97).

Besançon 184 (s. IX in.) from Murbach. (Cf. FONTAINE, *Isidore, Traité de la nature*, pp. 31-34).

(95) *Los clásicos de la agricultura, la agricultura en las Etimologias de San Isidoro de Sevilla*, in *Boletin de la Biblioteca Agricola*, 37 (1956), pp. 165-72, known to me only from the bibliography in the *Indice histórico español*. I. GONZÁLEZ GALLEGO, *Apuntes para un estudio económico de la España visigoda (Las Etimologias y el Fuero Juzgo fuentes de historia ecónomica)*, in *Archivos Leoneses*, 21 (1967), pp. 89-107, is an outline, with little attempt to investigate the sources, of Isidore's remarks on agriculture, mining, industry, trade. Most of the information Isidore provides is certainly taken from pre-Visigothic sources.

(96) Cf. Akademia Nauk SSSR (USSR), Seria V. Trudi Instituta istorii nauki i techniki, Istoria Agrikultury, *Agrikultura v pamjatnikach zapadnogo sredneivekovja* (= Agriculture in the Monuments of the Western Middle Ages), Moscow-Leningrad, 1936, pp. 1-40 (= Veka vi-viii. *Agro-i zootechniczeskie fragmenti u Isidora Sevil'skogo, v Varvarskich Pravdach i Grigoria Turskogo*). The authors print trans. of passages from orig. 15, 13; 17, 2-4; 20, 14 and 12, 1, 2, 7 and 8. These trans. are said to be based on collations of Anglo-Saxon MSS. of saec. VIII-IX in Leningrad, (none such are mentioned in STAERK, *Les MSS. Latins de St. Petersbourg*, 1910, or in DÍAZ, *Index*, n. 122); in fact the variants from Lindsay's edition do not seem important. Some are due to misprints. (I should like to thank my friend Dr. C. R. Ligota for his assistance with this article).

(97) Slighter publications on the same subject, also unavailable to me. are those of E. SALGADO BENAVIDES, *S. Isidoro Hispalense. La Medicina y los médicos*, Madrid, 1949, 30 pp.; T. OLIARO, *La medicina nelle opere di Isidorus Hispalensis e nel Codice « Isidorus et alii de Medicina »*, Torino, 1935, on which cf. G. VERITÀ, in *Riv. di storia delle scienze mediche e na-*

J. Sola, *San Isidoro y la Ciencia Diplómatica*, in *Helmantica*, 12 (1961), pp. 301-42 (summary in *Isidoriana*, pp. 505 sq.) studies the remarks of Isidore on writing materials (orig. 1 and 6). It is very difficult to know how far these remarks are based on contemporary reality. They appear to be drawn from earlier writers, largely, probably indirectly, from Pliny.

We now come to what is in all probability the most important book on Isidore published not only since 1935 but, in my view, since the edition of Arévalo, M. Jacques Fontaine's *Isidore de Séville et la culture classique dans l'Espagne wisigothique*, 2 vols., Paris, 1959, xx + 1014 pp. The unanimous welcome the work has received from critics inside and outside Spain makes it superfluous to dwell here on its merits (98). Something must, however, be said. We have already seen the importance of the new results Fontaine has attained in his research on Isidore's sources (supra, Section IV). But Fontaine is, as we have also seen, in no danger of supposing that the pursuit of sources can provide us with all or perhaps with the most interesting of the answers we seek in reading Isidore. He never forgets that behind the question of sources is that of their personal use.

Fontaine concentrates his attention on orig. 1-3, the books that deal with the seven *artes*. Here the position of Isidore as mediator between classical antiquity and the early Middle Ages is perhaps more important and certainly easier to grasp than elsewhere. Fontaine begins with a study of grammar and rhetoric in Isidore (pp. 27-207, 211-337)-he underlines the dominance of grammar in Isidorian thought-, and continues with his treatment of the exact sciences, arithmetic, geometry, music (pp. 341-450). The fourth part is devoted to astronomy (pp. 453-589) and the fifth to philosophy (pp. 593-732). The sixth (pp. 735-888) is a synthesis which deals with the culture of Isidore. In this last part, the culmination and crown of the whole work, the results of the minute enquiries carried out in the rest of the book are put to admirable use in an examination of the

turali, 18 (1936), p. 210 (Oliaro transcribes part of a MS. in the Bibl. Angelica attributed to Isidore that appears to differ from the text of orig. lib. 4); A. Meyrelles de Souto, *Santo Isidoro Hispalense e a psico-somática*, in *Itinerarium*, 6 (1960), pp. 304-15 (a digression on orig. 4); Juan R. Zaragoza Rubira, *La Urologia en la España goda, Actas del II Congreso Español de Historia de la Medicina*, 1, Salamanca, 1965, pp. 75-84, and E. Prieto Escanciano, *Ensayo sobre las ideas psicológicas de San Isidoro*, in *Studium Legionense*, 2 (1961), pp. 161-210, and Zaragoza Rubira, *La psiquiatria en la España goda, Cuadernos de historia de la Medicina Española*, 10 (1971), pp. 109-17 (see *IHE*, No. 90840).

(98) We may mention here the following reviews: P. TH. Camelot, in *Rev. des Sciences philos. et théol.*, 44 (1960), pp. 577-79; J. Casas Homs, in *AST*, 31 (1958), pp. 387-91; P. Courcelle, *Isidore de Séville, auteur antique et médiéval*, in *REA*, 61 (1959), pp. 419-23; J. Daniélou, in *Recherches de Science Religieuse*, 47 (1959), pp. 610-612; M. C. Díaz y Díaz, in *JTS*, N. S., 11 (1960), pp. 194 sq.; B. De Gaiffier, in *Analecta Bollandiana*, 78 (1960), pp. 193-96; C. Mohrmann, in *VChr*, 13 (1959), pp. 243-47; I. Opelt, in *Gnomon*, 32 (1960) pp. 437-42; M. Pellegrino, in *Atene e Roma*, 4 (1959), pp. 171-78 (not seen); J. Perret, in *REL*, 37 (1959), pp. 312-14; A. C. Vega, in *CD*, 173 (1960), pp. 319-26; J. P. Massaut, *MA*, 67 (1961), pp. 567-72; J. Monfrin, in *Romania*, 83 (1962), pp. 120-23; G. M. Colombás, *RHE*, 56 (1961), pp. 101-07. J. Luis Cassani, *El método de Isidoro de Sevilla a través de un reciente trabajo de Jacques Fontaine*, in *CHE*, 33-34 (1961), pp. 300-13; Y.M. J. Congar, *St. Isidore et la culture antique, Revue des sciences religieuses*, 35 (1961), pp. 49-54;

profane authors in the library of Seville, of the methods of work pursued by Isidore, of Isidore in relation to pagan and Christian, to ancient and medieval culture, of Isidorian culture in the contemporary West and of the Isidorian Renaissance, its nature and limitations. The book ends with five detailed indexes. From this analysis it is evident that over half of it (pp. 27-589) consists mainly in an examination of orig. 1-3. The author, however, refers throughout to other parts of the orig. that deal with subjects related to those he is discussing and to other works of Isidore, including his religious treatises.

It is impossible to point out here the many ways in which Fontaine makes us aware of unsuspected aspects of Isidore and of his age. He is able to reveal the complex process of adaptation of pagan sources, the addition of new examples chosen from the Bible or Christian authors, the slow welding of the diverse elements into a whole. In considering the debated question of the « originality » of Isidore, Fontaine maintains that, apart from the fact that one cannot exclude the hypothesis of an entirely personal contribution to the orig. based on the teaching in turn received and given in the episcopal school of Seville, e.g. on the text of Virgil, Isidore's real originality consists in his choice of such diverse materials, in the range of his curiosity and in his taste for speculation. Fontaine, unlike most critics of Isidore, insists in seeing him clearly in the precise context of his age. As a result his « authentic interest in science, independent of theology », noticed by Sarton, stands out all the more and his respect for pagan sources, especially in his discussion of philosophy, appears all the more original. Fontaine rejects as incredible the picture with which we are sometimes presented of Isidore as two men, one the scholar wholly concerned with the past, the other the bishop and statesman concerned with the religious and political issues of his day. He sees Isidore's intellectual activity as an attempt to respond to the particular demands of his contemporaries, whether for theological or for profane instruction. Isidore's attempt to adapt pagan learning to Christianity was genuine if hesitating but it would be a mistake to judge the orig. by their success or failure to reflect contemporary reality. The work was not intended as a practical manual but rather as a dictionary to be consulted by scholars. The ideal of Isidorian teaching was certainly not fully realised but the rise in the standard of scholarship in Seventh as compared to Sixth Century Spain and the great profit derived from the Seventh Century onwards outside Spain from Isidore's works show they were suited and necessary to their time.

Since Fontaine's book, and apart from the « coloquio » on « la originalidad de Isidoro » held at León in 1960 (*Isidoriana*, pp. 509-23), we may mention the following studies as of particular importance. M. C. Díaz y Díaz, *Les arts libéraux d'après les écrivains espagnols et insulaires aux VII*e

and M. Cruz Hernández, *San Isidoro y el problema de la ' Cultura ' hispano-visigoda*, *Anuario de Estudios Medievales*, 3 (1966), pp. 413-23, also comment on the work, the article of Congar being the most valuable. Shorter notices by O. Lottin, in *BTAM*, 8 (1960), pp. 598 sq.; L. Van-Hove, in *Etudes Classiques*, 27 (1959), p. 460. A short article announced the work in preparation in *REL*, 23 (1945), pp. 77-79; cf. Madoz, *Segundo Decenio*, p. 121.

et VIIIe siècles, in *Arts Libéraux et Philosophie au Moyen Age*, Montréal-Paris, 1969 (Actes du IVème Congrès International de Philosophie Médiévale, Montréal, 1967), pp. 37-46, discusses the different classifications of the arts given in diff. and orig., especially the curious division of *physica* into seven disciplines, which include *astrologia* and *mechanica* (diff. 2, 39). The « vacillations » of Isidore when confronted with the need to classify the sciences reveal a lack of consistency in his use of earlier lists. M. González Pola, *La dialéctica arte liberal en San Isidoro,* ibid., pp. 873-86, is a discussion of orig. 2, 22-31, which adds very little to Fontaine.

A. Borst has given us two articles on the role of history in the orig., *Storia e lingua nell'enciclopedia di Isidoro di Siviglia,* in *Bullettino dell'Istituto Storico Italiano per il Medio Evo e Archivio Muratoriano*, no. 77 (1965), pp. 1-20, expanded in *Das Bild der Geschichte in der Enzklopädie Isidors von Sevilla,* in *Deutsches Archiv,* 22 (1966), pp. 1-62. These articles investigate Isidore's etymological approach to history (e. g. in orig. 7, 6, 23: « Heber transitus. Etymologia eius mystica est, quod ab eius stirpe transiret Deus, nec perseveraret in eis, tralata in gentibus gratia »), and of Isidore's general providentialist approach, in which Christ is the centre of history and the Christianisation of the world is already largely accomplished (see also below, Section VId). Borst points out Isidore's attempt to combine Christian and pagan sources so as to give his contemporaries the answer to their historical situation as Roman Christians living under Gothic rule. Commenting on H-I. Marrou's view, in *Isidore de Séville et les origines de la culture médiévale, Revue historique,* 235 (1966), pp. 39-46, that Isidore is not the last Roman encyclopedist but a founder of the Middle Ages, Borst rightly asserts that Isidore should not be subjected to our modern classifications but be seen as a man of his own time. The same view is taken by H. J. Diesner in his recent publications. His *Isidor von Sevilla und seine Zeit,* Berlin, 1973, 83 pp., attempts to portay Isidore *in* his time. Insufficient attention is here paid to Isidore's sources; see J. Fontaine, *REL*, 51 (1973), pp. 493-96. Diesner, *Zeitgeschichte und Gegenwartsbezug bei Isidor von Sevilla, Philologus,* 119 (1975), pp. 92-7, comments especially on orig. 18, 6, 9, while emphasising Isidore's interest in contemporary problems. One may also cite two other short articles, *Auf der Weg zum Feudalismus. Puer, homo, satelles bei Isidor von Sevilla, Wissenschaftliche Zeitschrift der Martin Luther Universität,* 22 (1973), 5, pp. 75-78, and *Amicitia bei Isidor von Sevilla,* in *Forma futuri. Studi in onore del Cardinale Michele Pellegrino,* Turin, 1975, pp. 229-31, commenting on Isidore's texts on friendship. The chronological limitations of this review preclude my discussing Diesner's major work, *Isidor von Sevilla und das westgotische Spanien,* Berlin, 1977 (Abhandlungen der sächsischen Akademie der Wiss. zu Leipzig, Philol.-hist. Klasse, 67.3), 128 pp.

Riché (cited, Section I), whose work has contributed greatly to our understanding of the context of Isidore's work, has some valuable pages on the goals he and other Spanish bishops pursued and on the limited nature of their attainments. Less valuable is the panegyric, centered on Isidore, by Sr. C. M. Aherne, *Late Visigothic Bishops, their Schools and the transmission of culture, Traditio,* 22 (1966), pp. 435-44. L. Robles, *La cultura religiosa de la España visigótica, Escritos del Vedat,* 5 (1975), pp. 9-54, provides a useful discussion of the background for Isidore's work. F. Martín Hernández, *Escuelas de formación del clero en la España visigoda,* in *La Patrología toledano-visigoda,* Madrid, 1970 (XXVII Semana Española de Teología), pp. 65-98, while often citing Isidore, contains little not already to be found in the work of Fernández Alonso (supra, p. 41). R. Gibert, *Antiguëdad clásica en la Hispania visigótica,* in *La Cultura antica nell'Occidente latino,* Spoleto, 1975 (*Settimane di studio* XXII), pp. 603-52, is less general than the title suggests, being almost entirely devoted to Isidore and especially to the orig. Most of the article registers Isidore's remarks on antiquity and follows Fontaine closely. On orig. 5, 1-27, devoted to law, Gibert's detailed comments (pp. 631-46) are particularly valuable. They illustrate Isidore's use of his sources in discussing many legal institutions no longer in existence in his day.

The article by J. Fontaine, *Fins et moyens de l'enseignement ecclésiastique dans l'Espagne wisigothique,* in *La Scuola nell'Occidente latino dell'alto Medioevo,* Spoleto, 1972 (*Settimane di studio* XIX), pp. 145-202, situates Isidore's contribution to education, in the most general sense, in the context of his sources and predecessors. Drawing particularly on off., and reg. but also on orig., sent., and other works, Fontaine shows that one should not consider monastic and episcopal education as totally distinct in Seville or elsewhere in Visigothic Spain. In both types of school what was aimed at was the study of the Scriptures and, for those considered sufficiently advanced to embrace them, of the authors of the great patristic age.

Commenting on a point raised in this last article, M. Banniard, *Le lecteur en Espagne wisigothique d'après Isidore de Séville: de ses fonctions à l'état de la langue, Revue des études augustiniennes,* 21 (1975), pp. 112-44, disagrees with Fontaine's interpretation of orig. 7, 12, 24 and argues that *miseranter pronuntient* describes not a ludicrous but a moving performance. Commenting particularly on off. 2, 11, Banniard maintains convincingly that Isidore's remarks reveal that a break between the written and spoken language had not yet taken place.

L. Boehm, *Der wissenschaftstheoretische Ort der historia im frühen Mittelalter,* in *Speculum historiale,* Freiburg i. Br.-Munich, 1965, pp. 663-93 (esp. 678-82), discusses the references to *historia* in the orig., especially 1, 41 (the sources used are Gellius and Servius) and the place of history as a division of grammar (orig. 1, 5, 4). A. Ferrari, *Octavio Augusto, según San Isidoro, Boletín de la Real Academia de la Historia,* 164 (1969), pp. 159-87, points out that Augustus is cited more often than any other Roman figure in Isidore (25 times). Ferrari ascribes a numerological significance to this fact; he forgets that Isidore attributes much less importance to Augustus than do most other Christian writers, who follow the tradition of Eusebius and Orosius.

VI. Church History, *theology, the history of dogma:*

a. Church History: Lives of Isidore

In the 1930s and 1940s we had a proliferation of popular, generally undocumented, Spanish biographies of Isidore. We may briefly enumerate those of F. Vera, *San Isidoro de Sevilla, siglo VII*, Madrid, 1936, 266 + ii pp.; A. Muñoz Torrado, *San Isidoro de Sevilla*, Sevilla, 1936, xvi + 320 pp.; M. Ballesteros Gaibrois, *San Isidoro de Sevilla*, Madrid, 1936, 121 pp. (not seen), and L. Araujo Costa, *San Isidoro, arzobispo de Sevilla*, Madrid, 1942, 192 pp. The best modern biography known to me is that of Dom J. Pérez de Urbel, *San Isidoro de Sevilla, su vida, su obra y su tiempo*, Barcelona, 1945, 284 pp., on which the more recent and less reliable (though almost equally readable) work of I. Quiles, *San Isidoro de Sevilla, biografia, escritos, doctrina*, Buenos Aires, 1945, 149 pp., largely depends. Isidore has also, as in the past, been the subject of a number of panegyrics or eulogies (99).

A. Beltrán, *Algunas cuestiones acerca del lugar del nacimiento de San Isidoro*, in *Anales de la Univ. de Murcia*, 1947-48, pp. 605-608, establishes the probability that if Isidore was born before c. 567 then he was born not in Seville but in the Carthaginense and very likely in Carthagena itself (100). Was he a monk ? J. Pérez Llamazares, *San Isidoro de Sevilla, monje ?*, in *Misc. Isid.*, pp. 39-55, argues from the silence of Braulio and the other early biographers and of Isidore's own works that he was not; he then attempts, less convincingly, to prove he was instead what was

(99) Cf. A. C. Vega, *Hacia la glorificación nacional de San Isidoro de Sevilla*, in *CD*, 153 (1941), pp. 209-25; J. Ibáñez Martín, *San Isidoro y la Cultura*, in *Revista de Educación*, 3, 5 (1943), pp. 7-16; P. Font y Puig, *San Isidoro de Sevilla como patrono de las Facultades españolas de Filosofia y Letras*, Barcelona, 1945 – not seen –; O. Díaz Caneja, *San Isidoro, gloria nacional*, in *Atenas*, n. 190 (1949), pp. 75-77; S. Montero Díaz, *Semblanza de San Isidoro*, Madrid, 1953, 18 pp. and J. Pérez Llamazares, *Grande de España, forjador de la unidad española: San Isidoro*, in *Hidalguia*, 5 (1957), pp. 225-40; Id., *Centenario glorioso*, ibid., 11 (1963), pp. 753-68; Id., *San Isidoro, seminarista*, ibid., 13 (1965), pp. 113-32; *San Isidoro, doctor egregio*, ibid., 14 (1966), pp. 729-46. A German translation of Pérez de Urbel's biography has appeared, *Isidor von Sevilla. Sein Leben, sein Werk und seine Zeit*, Cologne, 1962; it was severely reviewed by H. Grotz, in *Zeitschrift für katholische Theologie*, 86 (1964), p. 120. For a psychological study see A. Adnes, *Remarques psychobiologiques sur saint Isidore de Séville*, in *Isidoriana*, pp. 467-74. We may add the brief biographical and literary notices by C. Moro, in *Revista eclesiástica*, 10 (1936), pp. 373-79; N. Prandoni, in *Ambrosius*, 12 (1936), pp. 222-25; 13 (1937), pp. 21-27; 82-85 (not seen); and P. F. Mahoney, in *Catholic World*, 148 (1939), pp. 485 sq. (not seen).

(100) Beltrán cites A. Puig Campillo, *San Isidoro de Cartagena, Arzobispo de Sevilla*, Cartagena, 1948, 43 pp., which I have not seen. Apparently this author cites a hymn supposedly by St. Ildefonsus which says of Isidore *natus de Carthagine*. Beltrán believes this hymn is certainly not earlier than saec. xiii. Is it identical with the *hymnus s. Isidori* that Díaz, *Index*, n. 1109, thinks s. xii.

later known as a Canon Regular (101). J. MADOZ, *San Isidoro*, c. I, « Vida », pp. 3-21, in a general treatment of Isidore's life, draws special attention to the *liber de transitu S. Isidori* of Redemptus. Against the doubts of C. H. LYNCH, *St. Braulio, bishop of Saragossa* (631-651). *His Life and Writings*, Washington, 1938 (CUA, SMH, N. S. 2) pp. 51 and 206, he argues it is authentic. It is contained in a series of ancient MSS. (cf. DÍAZ, *Index*, n. 136) and its description of Isidore's reception of penance is in accord with contemporary sources, including Isidore's own works, as is the text of his confession.

M. ALIJA RAMOS, *Un poco de crítica sobre las antiguas biografias isidorianas*, in *Revista eclesiástica*, 10 (1936), pp. 587-601, attempted to show that the *abbreviatio*, forming c. 11 of the *vita Isidori* attributed to Lucas of Tuy (s. XIII), was in fact saec. VIII (102). But in fact the *abbreviatio* is only, as FONTAINE (I, p. 7 n. 1) has remarked, an interpolated version of the *renotatio librorum Isidori* of Braulio, which has been recently edited by P. GALINDO from MSS. León 22 and the interpolated Paris Lat. 2277 in his translation of C. H. LYNCH, *San Braulio*, Madrid, 1950, pp. 356-61. On the *renotatio*, the *abbreviatio*, Ildefonsus, *de viris*, and Redemptus cf. A. C. VEGA, *Cuestiones críticas de las Biografias Isidorianas*, in *Isidoriana*, pp. 76-87. J. VIVES, in *AST*, 21 (1948), pp. 157-74, has pointed out the unreliable character as historical evidence of one of Isidore's medieval biographers, Rodrigo de Cerrato. Another medieval biography of Isidore, by the Arcipreste de Talavera, has recently been published for the first time by P. MADOZ (103). J. LOPEZ ORTIZ, *San Isidoro de Sevilla y el Islam*, in *Cruz y Raya*, 36 (1936), pp. 7-63, has an interesting discussion of the legendary connections between Isidore and Mahomet and his followers; it would be more useful to scholars if it were not deliberately published « limpia de erudición y referencias bibliográficas ». Cf. the review by R. RICARD, in *Hespéris*, 22 (1936), pp. 194-95.

B. DE GAIFFIER, *Le culte de Saint Isidore de Séville, Esquisse d'un travail*, in *Isidoriana*, pp. 271-83 (reprinted in his *Études critiques d'hagiographie et d'iconologie*, Brussels, 1967, pp. 115-29) shows how hagiographical literature on Isidore increases from the saec. XII onwards. Erroneous statements in earlier authors are traced and corrected. Isidore was not canonised in 1598 nor was he declared Doctor of the Church until 1722. His relics were preserved at St. Riquier (saec. IX), at San Millán de la Cogolla (saec. XIII) and (some thought) at Bologna. He is seldom represented in art and few churches are consecrated to him.

A. VIÑAYO GONZÁLEZ, *Cuestiones histórico-críticas en torno a la traslación del cuerpo de San Isidoro*, in *Isidoriana*, pp. 285-97, discusses the jour-

(101) Other scholars disagree (e. g. PÉREZ DE URBEL, *San Isidoro*, pp. 32 sq.). Cf. J. FERNÁNDEZ ALONSO, *La cura pastoral en la España romanovisigoda*, Roma, 1955, p. 81. The epitaphs of Isidore, Leander and Florentina were edited by J. VIVES, *Inscripciones cristianas de la España romana y visigoda*, Barcelona, 1942, n. 272.

(102) Anspach (*Taionis et Isidori nova fragmenta et opera*, pp. 57-64) had already attemted to demonstrate this. Cf. the criticisms of ALTANER, in *Misc. Isid.*, p. 8; LYNCH, *St. Braulio* (op. cit. infra, note 136), pp. 214 sq.; DÍAZ, *Index*, n. 846; MADOZ, *San Isidoro*, pp. 78 sq.

ney of the relics of the saint from Seville to León in 1063. (See ID., *La Legada de S. Isidoro a León*, in *Archivos Leoneses*, 17, 1963, pp. 65-112; 18, 1964, pp. 303-43). F. SÁNCHEZ FABA, *Una imagen de S. Isidoro, obra de D. Francisco Salzillo*, ibid., pp. 499-504, discusses a wooden statue of 1755 in Cartagena. See also H. HOCHENEGG, *S. Isidor und seine Verehrung in Tirol*, in *Spanische Forschungen der Görresgesellschaft*, I, 20 (1962), pp. 214-24.

b. Canon Law and Moral Theology

In the last twenty-five years we have had no such detailed study as Dom P. SÉJOURNÉ's work on Isidore and his role in the history of canon law (Paris, 1929). A. ARIÑO ALAFONT, *Colección canónica hispana, estudio de su formación y contenido*, Avila, 1941, 144 pp., esp. pp. 103-114, while rebutting Tarré's view that the *Hispana* comes from Arles, and maintaining its Spanish origin, holds it is not proved that Isidore is the author. The work may be collective; it does not appear (in the Seventh Century) to have possessed an officia character [104]. J. RUIZ GOYO, *San Isidoro de Sevilla y la antigua colección canónica « Hispana »*, in *EE*, 15 (1936), pp. 119-36, holds it is probable that Isidore or someone under his orders is responsible for the collection. A recent treatment of the subject is that of J. MADOZ, *San Isidoro*, c. III, « La colección canónica ' Hispana ' », pp. 89-117, esp. pp. 98-111. He believes that various proofs converge to establish Isidore's authorship. The style of the prologue to the *Hispana* seems to mark it as Isidorian. Part of it is found again in the orig. (6, 16) but it appears that here Isidore is copying his own prologue. Furthermore, the prologue uses the *Decretum Gelasianum*, first certainly used by Isidore, vir. 18 (ML, 83, 1093). In vir. 16 (ib. 1092) Isidore similarly cites a letter of Pope Siricius found in the *Hispana* with an almost identical title. Because of these and other arguments Madoz is favourable to Isidore's authorship of the *Hispana* but he admits it is not definitely proved. The silence of Braulio and Ildefonsus is difficult to explain. Do they omit the work as a mere collection of documents from their lists of the *opera* of Isidore ? [105].

M. C. DÍAZ Y DÍAZ, *Pequeñas aportaciones para el estudio de la ' Hispana '*, in *Revista española de derecho canónico*, 17 (1962), pp. 373-90, esp. 386-90, questions the Isidorian authorship of the prologue and suggests

(103) *Vidas de S. Ildefonso y San Isidoro*, Madrid, 1952, (Clásicos Castellanos, 134). Study of Isidore, pp. lxv-ciii; text of life, 67-161. It is a trans. (dated 1444) partly based on the *Vita Isidori* attributed to Lucas of Tuy (DÍAZ, *Index*, n. 1082). but probably using other sources as well. The text is based on two MSS., Escorial b. III.1 (s. XV and XVI) and Madrid, Bibl. Nac. 1178 (a. 1578).

(104) ARIÑO ALAFONT is fóllowing, in his treatment of the question, Séjourné and Anspach (op. cit., note 102 supra, pp. 108-117).

(105) Cf. also R. NAZ, *Hispana*, in *Dict. droit canon*, 5, Paris, 1953, pp. 1159-62 and ID., *Isidore de Séville*, ibid., 6 (1957), pp. 66-74. He holds that all one can admit as certain is that the collection was composed under Isidore's influence.

that Leander of Seville may be its author. He also notes that the series of Decretals in the *Hispana* ends in 597, in Leander's episcopate. G. MARTÍNEZ DÍEZ, *La colección canónica hispana*, 1, Madrid, 1966, the editor preparing the new *editio maior*, considers, pp. 306-27, that Isidore edited the greater part of the collection, though it was added to later, and a « second edition » is due probably to Julian of Toledo (d. 690). CH. MUNIER, in his review of Martínez Díez, *Saint Isidore de Séville, est-il l'auteur de l'Hispana chronologique* ?, in *SEJG*, 17 (1966), pp. 230-41, remains doubtful of the Isidorian authorship, in view of a contradiction between chron. 108 and the *Hispana*.

The juridical ideas of Isidore are discussed by H. YABEN, *Las ideas jurídicas de San Isidoro*, in *Revista eclesiástica*, 10 (1936), pp. 561-74 and 11 (1937), pp. 3-18 (he also mentions their influence on the scholastics) and by M. GARCÍA-PELAYO ALONSO, *Los conceptos jurídicos fundamentales en San Isidoro de Sevilla*, in *Revista de ciencias jurídicas y sociales*, 17 (1934) pp. 375-97, who points out the sources of Isidore in Roman Law and the influence of his ideas on Natural and Civil Law and the Law of nations [106]. M. FORNASARI, *De consuetudine eiusque functione iuridica apud Patres*, in *Apollinaris*, 35 (1962), pp. 116-36, especially 118 sq., discusses orig. 2, 10 and diff. 1, 122. Isidore draws on the Digest and on Tertullian, *de corona*. Fornasari points out that Isidore is the first Father to distinguish between *consuetudo*, *lex and mos*.

F. FLÜCKIGER, *Geschichte des Naturrechts*, I, Zollikon-Zürich, 1954, pp. 396-401, also comments on orig. 5. Isidore, drawing on Tertullian, derives law from reason. Here again his later influence is considerable. His definition of Natural Law (orig. 5, 4) is inspired by Stoic and Roman legal ideas but also by the Fathers. Isidore's inclusion of *communis omnium possessio* among the characteristics of the Law of Nature is not to be understood (as by E. REIBSTEIN, *Die Anfänge des neueren Natur- und Völkerrechts*, Bern, 1949, p. 51) as advocacy of communism. The Law of Nature is contrasted with Positive Law, the Law of the State if it is derived from reason. S. RAMÍREZ, *El derecho de gentes*, Madrid, 1955, (Scientia 14), pp. 29-33, and A. D'ORS, *En torno a la definición isidoriana del ius gentium*, in *Derecho de Gentes y organización internacional*, I, Santiago, 1956, pp. 9-40, discuss Isidore on the *ius gentium*. D'Ors points out that the definition of *ius gentium* in Isidore is related to Justinian's *Instituta* and to Hermo-

(106) This last art. was omitted by ALTANER from his bibliography in *Misc. Isid.*, as were those of P. LÉON, *Doctrines sociales et politiques du moyen âge, Des origines au IXe siècles*, in *Arch. de Philos. du Droit et de Sociologie Juridique*, 2 (1932), pp. 247-67, who points (258-62) to the influence of Augustine and the Roman jurists in Isidore, and O. SCHILLING, *Der Kollektivismus der Kirchenväter*, in *Theol. Quartalschrift*, 114 (1933), pp. 481-92, who, like Flückiger (cit. infra) stresses (486 sq.) the contrast in Isidore between Natural Law that includes property being common to all and the *ius gentium*. I have not seen A. BECERRA BAZAL, in *Revista de la Escuela de Estudios Penitenciarios*, num. 103 (1953), pp. 27-30. According to U. DOMÍNGUEZ DEL VAL, in *RET*, 15 (1955), p. 433, it is of slight value and merely translates excerpts from orig., lib. 5. F. HIPOLA, *La técnica jurídica de San Isidoro de Sevilla*, in *Anales del Seminario de Valencia*, 1 (1961), pp. 159-262, toils throgh the works of Isidore but without any result worth the labour.

genian, *Epitomae iuris*. But certain differences indicate an advance towards the idea of international law as distinct from Roman *ius gentium* (cf., in the same sense, RAMÍREZ, p. 32) and, on the other hand, the influence of ecclesiastical legislation (107).

E. CHAMPEAUX, *La parenté fraternelle et la « prima stemma » d'Isidore*, in *Revue historique du droit français et étranger*, S. 4, 16 (1937), pp. 1-19, discusses the first of the three « stemmas » in orig. 9, 6, 28. He shows there was an attempt to « baptise » the primitive « stemma », i.e. to make the maternal relationship prevail over the fraternal. He does not discuss the question of whether the authentic text of Isidore has been interpolated.

R. BIDAGOR, *Sobre la naturaleza del matrimonio en S. Isidoro de Sevilla*, in *Misc. Isid.*, pp. 253-85, demonstrates clearly how Isidore (primarily in orig. 9, 7) used and adapted his pagan sources – mainly Roman legal texts and Servius on Virgil – and, by introducing ideas derived especially from Augustine, succeeded in stating the Christian doctrine that was accepted by the Middle Ages (108).

An. article of more general importance for Isidore's moral theology is that of PH. DELHAYE, *Les idées morales de saint Isidore de Séville*, in *RTAM*, 26 (1959), pp. 17-49. Delhaye points out the great similarity in doctrine between Isidore and Gregory, together with their totally different points of view. Gregory's morality is doctrinal and affirmative in tendency, Isidore's is practical and negative. We find in Isidore a concentration on the idea of sin, on precise and particular precepts in which there is notable a constant care for moderation. The difference between Gregory and Isidore is perhaps one of mentality, certainly it is largely due to their differing audience. Isidore stresses the importance of purity of heart, of intention. He distinguishes between « peccata leviora » and « graviora »: his lists of the latter are based on Cassian and Gregory; he enumerates sometimes eight, sometimes seven. The virtues are seen essentially as remedies against sin. Far the most important are the three theological virtues, especially Charity, given by the Holy Spirit. Sin is combatted by penance. Isidore's morality is linked with canon law and penitential practice, which, in the Seventh Century, was in a state of transition. He speaks of compunction but also of public penance and of a more common penance, more or less public. Compunction is not the same as contrition; it is a constant regret for being a sinful man. Delhaye shows Isidore, both in his *regula monachorum* and still more in his attempt to provide a rule of life for the clergy, insisting always on intellectual formation. Isidore also gave particular advice to married people, to slaves, to rulers, to

(107) A. GARCÍA GALLO, *San Isidoro Jurista*, in *Isidoriana*, pp. 133-141, emphasizes that Isidore « defines concepts and institutions but does not expound how they are regulated ». García Gallo's examples of the « originality » of Isidore (e. g. in his definitions of law and custom, orig. 5, 3) are not wholly convincing. See also below, Section VId.

(108) P. COLLI, *La pericope paolina Ad Ephesios V. 32 nella interpretazione dei SS. Padri e del Concilio di Trento*, Diss. Pont. Univ. Gregoriana, Parma, 1951, pp. 103-05, has some comments on quaest. in V Test., in Genesim, of slight importance.

kings. The theology he transmitted to the Middle Ages was a compendium of that of his predecessors (109).

S. GONZÁLEZ, *Tres maneras de penitencia*, in *RET*, 1 (1940-41), pp. 985-1019, discusses the three types of penance obtaining in the Spanish Church from saec. V to VIII: public penance (imposed by the Church); public penance, undertaken voluntarily from devotion, and private penance. Isidore is used throughout this study (110). Another article devoted especially to public penance in Spain is that of J. FERNÁNDEZ ALONSO, *La disciplina penitencial en la España romano-visigoda desde el punto de vista pastoral*, in *HS*, 4 (1951), pp. 243-311; he also examines the Isidorian texts (111).

J. FONTAINE, *Isidore de Séville (saint)*, in *Dictionnaire de Spiritualité*, VII, 2, Paris, 1971, cols. 2104-16, notes the difficulty inherent in studying Isidore's spirituality, and the danger of treating it separately from his « secular » works. Fontaine uses all Isidore's works to try to reveal his ideas on penance, on conversion, on the duties of different states of life, on the contemplative life (based on study and meditation of the Bible). Isidore's Stoic ethic contributed to the dryness and impersonality of his works, full of proscriptions and prohibitions, but it served his pastoral intentions well, as it had those of Martin of Braga.

FONTAINE, *La vocation monastique* (cited above, note 76), shows how Isidore, in the *de officiis*, the *origines* and the *sententiae*, seeks to go back to the oldest Latin sources, Jerome, *epist.* 22, Cassian and Augustine. Isidore sees monks as hierarchically above the laity, though below the lowest orders of clergy. But, in the *spiritual* order, monks come before the rest since they are entirely devoted to attaining holiness. The bishop must free any cleric wishing to become a monk. Isidore is suspicious, however, of the monastic « fringe », the semi-monks already denounced by Augustine. His *regula* is also mainly concerned with *discipline*. See M. C. DÍAZ Y DÍAZ, *La vie monastique d'après les écrivains wisigothiques (VIIe siècle)*, *Théologie de la vie monastique*, Paris, 1961, pp. 376 sq. G. G. SUÁREZ, *La vida religiosa en San Isidoro y San Fructuoso*, *Estudios*, 27.93 (1971) pp. 275-84, compares the rules of the two saints. On the role of reading

(109) Cf. also, on Isidore's moral legislation for his times, his insistence on intellectual formation, etc., J. FERNÁNDEZ ALONSO, *La cura pastoral* (op. cit. note 101 supra), pp. 81-95.

(110) Cf. also GONZÁLEZ, *El Sacramento de la Penitencia en la Iglesia española romano-visigoda*, in *EE*, 17 (1943), pp. 213-226; ID., *La penitencia en la primitiva iglesia española*, Salamanca, 1950 – a collected reprint of earlier articles –, pp. 125-27; brief notes that add little to the studies of POSCHMANN (cf. ALTANER, in *Misc. Isid.*, pp. 26 sq.) and MULLINS, (op. cit., infra, Section VId).

(111) On pp. 288-94 he discusses the texts of the *epistulae ad Elladium* and *ad Massonam*. This art. is largely reprinted in ID., *La cura pastoral en la España romano-visigoda*, Roma, 1955, pp. 511-73. Cf. also P. RÉGAMEY, *La componction de coeur*, in *La Vie spirituelle*, 44 (1935), Suppl., esp. pp. [65]-[83]: Gregory the Great's doctrine is taken up in the classical definition of Isidore, sent. 2, 12 (*ML*, 83, 613 sq.); B. WELTE, *Die postbaptismale Salbung*, ... Freiburg, 1939 (Freib. Theol. Studien, 51), pp. 72 sq. See G. MARTÍNEZ DÍEZ, *Algunos aspectos de la penitencia en la iglesia visigodo-mozárabe*, in *Miscelánea Comillas*, 49 (1968) pp. 5-19, who corrects González's views on important points.

in Isidore, reg. see J. ORLANDIS, *La lectio divina en el monacato visigodo, Ius Canonicum*, 7.1 (1967), reprinted in his *Estudios sobre instituciones monásticas medievales*, Pamplona, 1971, pp. 85-93.

c. Isidore and the Bible

The whole question of an Isidorian « edition » of the Bible has been revived by Mgr. T. AYUSO MARAZUELA, in various articles published in *Estudios Bíblicos* under the general title of « Contribución al estudio de la Vulgata en España ». He maintains that some of the extra-biblical elements in Spanish MSS. of the Vulgate belong to the original Isidorian revision and claims to have restored to Isidore the summaries preceding the Heptateuch, Kings, Chronicles, Esdras, Wisdom, Ecclesiasticus, the Prologue to the Minor Prophets and that to Hosea, the *incipit* and *explicit* to Kings and Chronicles, notes on the Hagiographa, and the arrangement of the Song of Songs (112).

Both S. M. ZARB, *S. Isidori cultus erga Sacras Litteras*, in *Misc. Isid.*, pp. 91-134, and A. TAPIA BASULTO, *El canon escriturístico en San Isidoro de Sevilla*, in *Ciencia Tomista*, 58 (1939), pp. 364-88, show that Isidore's canon was essentially that later defined by Trent. Deutero-canonical books he treated as inspired. Zarb also speaks of the exegetical works of Isidore, of the different « senses » of Scripture and of the rules for its interpretation (113). F. OGARA, *Tipología bíblica, según S. Isidoro*, in *Misc. Isid.*, pp. 135-150, deals with the mystical and allegorical interpretations of the Bible in Isidore at greater length, with special reference to the *allegoriae* and the *quaestiones in Vetus Testamentum*.

Various authors refer to Isidore while discussing the different patristic interpretations of Gen. 3, 15. T. DE ORBISO, *La Mujer del Protoevangelio*, in *Estudios Bíblicos*, N. S., 1 (1941-42), pp. 279-82, holds Isidore, in quaest. Gen. 5, 5-7 (ML, 83, 221), follows to some extent the Spanish tradition (especially evident in the anonymous *epistula ad amicum aegrotum de viro perfecto*) that Mary is to be identified with *ipsa*, but in reality he adopts the different view that *ipsa* is Eve, as symbol of the human race in its war with the devil. J. MADOZ, *Hacia los orígenes de la interpretación mariológica del Protoevangelio*, in *EE*, 23 (1949), pp. 299-305, maintains that Isidore's source here is not the anonymous *epistula* but Irenaeus, *adversus haereses*, III, 23, 7, and that *ipsa* for him is Mary (114).

(112) Cf. AYUSO, p. 505, and references, p. 507, and ID., *Algunos problemas del texto Bíblico de Isidoro*, in *Isidoriana*, pp. 143-191. On Isidore's revision of the Psalter cf. ZARB, art. cit. infra, pp. 115 sq., and G. MORIN, art. cit. supra (Section II and note 24).

(113) On the role of grammar in Isidore's exegesis cf. A. NEMETZ, art. cit. supra, note 89. A. TAPIA, *Las ciencias bíblicas en las obras de San Isidoro de Sevilla*, in *Estudios Bíblicos*, 8 (1936), pp. 49-79, underlines the profound knowledge of the Bible in Isidore. A. GARCÍA DE LA FUENTE, *San Isidoro de Sevilla, intérprete de la Biblia*, *CD*, 173 (1960), pp. 536-59, adds little to the earlier articles of ZARB and BASULTO. See also H. DE LUBAC, *Exégèse médiévale, les quatre sens de l'Ecriture*, 4 vols., Paris, 1959-64 (see the indices).

(114) Cf. also A. VACCARI, in *Colligere fragmenta, Festschrift A. Dold*, Beuron, 1952, pp. 34-39, esp. 36; J. MICHL, in *Biblica*, 33 (1952), pp. 476-505, esp. 495, 504 sq., and R.

F. Asensio, *Tradición sobre un pecado sexual en el Paraíso ?*, in *Gregorianum*, 31 (1950), pp. 163-69, discusses the text of quaest. Genesim, together with a text attributed to Isidore which appears to be a summary of his views. Against J. Coppens, in *Ephem. theol. Lovanienses*, 24 (1948), p. 408, Asensio holds that Isidore, following in his exegesis his model Augustine, was concerned primarily to establish the comparison between the process of the first Temptation and that of all subsequent temptation and sin. He will not, therefore, serve as a witness to Coppens's « lost tradition » of an expulsion from Paradise due to sexual sin.

d. *Isidore in the history of dogma and of philosophy*

Sr. P. J. Mullins, *The Spiritual Life according to Saint Isidore of Seville*, Washington, 1940 (Diss. = *CUA, SMRLLL* 13), xii + 212 pp., understanding « spirituality » as including almost all the theology of Isidore, has given us, in this carefully documented study, the most complete modern treatise we possess on the subject (115). The first two introductory chapters describe the Life and Character of Isidore and the Sources of his Doctrine (here Sr. Mullins follows Lawson, op. cit. supra, Section IV). There follow discussions of « The Foundation of the Spiritual Life » (penance and compunction); « The Way of Perfection » (the life of grace) and « The Ideal of Perfection » (in the clergy, the laity, in the religious state and in the life of contemplation) (116).

J. Madoz, *El Concilio de Calcedonia en S. Isidoro de Sevilla*, in *RET*, 12 (1952), pp. 189-204, demonstrates that Isidore, in his refusal to admit the Acts of the Second Council of Constantinople (553) as authentic, was inspired by African sources of the Sixth Century hostile to Justinian. But his anti-Nestorianism is perfectly clear (117). Two articles discuss the place of the Holy Spirit in Isidorian theology. S. González, *La inhabitación del Espíritu Santo según S. Isidoro de Sevilla*, in *Revista de Espiritualidad*, 1 (1941-42), pp. 10-33, shows that for Isidore the Third Person of the Trinity is the substantial and personal Love of Gold, *Sanctitas* or *Donum* of Father and Son. He inhabits the souls of the saints of the Old Testament and those of all the just of the New. J. Havet, *Les sacrements et le rôle*

Laurentin, in *Bulletin soc. franc. d'Etudes Mariales*, 12 (1954), pp. 101 sq. T. Gallus, *Interpretatio mariologica Protoevangelii (Gen. 3, 15) tempore postpatristico usque ad Concilium Tridentinum*, Roma, 1949, p. 23, also believes that Isidore adheres to the Mariological interpretation. This is denied by S. Stys, in his review of Gallus, in *Collectanea theologica*, 23 (1952), pp. 366-80, which I know from *BTAM*, 8 (1960), n. 2374. Laurentin takes the same view as Stys.

(115) Cf. M. Cappuyns, in *BTAM*, 5 (1946-49), n. 1159; Madoz, *Segundo Decenio*, pp. 119 sq.

(116) I have not seen J. Ruiz Goyo, *San Isidoro de Sevilla, maestro de la vida ascética*, in *Sal Terrae*, 25 (1936), pp. 343-51, cited by Madoz, in *RET*, 1 (1940-41), p. 951.

(117) Also related to Isidore's Christology are Madoz, *Le symbole du IVe Concile de Tolède*, in *RHE*, 34 (1938), pp.. 5-20; Id., art. cit. supra, Section IV, in *Misc. Isid.*, pp. 177-220, and J. Rivière, *Le dogme de la Rédemption après saint Augustin*, in *Rev. sciences religieuses*, 9 (1929), esp. pp. 319, 340, 502 sq.

de l'Esprit Saint d'après Isidore de Séville, in *Ephem. theol. Lovanienses,* 16 (1939), pp. 32-93, in an important article expounds the role of the Holy Spirit first in Baptism and Confirmation and then in the Eucharist. (1) According to Isidore all grace is already a participation in the Holy Spirit but it is at the Imposition of Hands that the special, personal Gift of the Spirit descends into the souls of the baptised. The ceremonies of ablution and chrismation destroy sin, original and actual, and through them the baptised enter into a new life. Imposition of Hands is not a sacrament but conveys the personal *donum Spiritus Sancti.* It is not clear whether Isidore is here merely repeating the common theology of the Spanish Church but it is certain that outside Spain in the Seventh Century this view of the Imposition of Hands was no longer held. More stress was laid on the postbaptismal chrismation. (2) The Holy Spirit is active in *all* Sacraments. Invoked, He descends on the waters of Baptism. This idea was drawn from Tertullian. Isidore's thesis on the efficacity of the Sacraments was derived from Cyprian; it was not a specifically Spanish theory but was held throughout the Church. (3) The Holy Spirit acts in the Eucharist. The Body and Blood of Christ, although present on the altar through the Words of Invocation, need to be sanctified by the Holy Spirit to become *sanctifying* to the faithful communicant. This complex operation is accomplished in the *oratio sexta* or *prex mystica* of the Spanish *Missa fidelium,* as Havet shows by a comparison of the Isidorian texts and those of the Spanish Liturgy. The Holy Spirit is invoked in the *Post pridie.* The same theory is found in the African Fathers, probably as early as Cyprian, also in Gaul and in the East. The influence of African theology is visible throughout Isidore's sacramental theology. The probable reason for the conservatism of his theory on the Imposition of Hands was his attachment to African writers, especially Tertullian and Cyprian. Tertullian influenced his Baptismal theology, Cyprian his Eucharistic. In contrast, Isidore at times is notably independent of Augustine, for instance over the Imposition of Hands, which Augustine does not stress. The texts on the Eucharist are collected and translated by J. Solano, *Textos eucarísticos primitivos,* II, Madrid, 1954, pp. 695-708 ([118]).

R. Schulte, *Die Messe als Opfer der Kirche. Die Lehre frühmittelalterlicher Autoren über das eucharistische Opfer,* Münster, 1959 (Liturgiewis-

(118) Angel Antón Gómez, *Die Typologie der Taufe bei Sankt Isidor von Sevilla,* Diss., Munich, 1959 (text in Spanish), 250 + 89 pp., studies Isidores typology of Baptism, the « figures » of Baptism in the Old Testament (the Spirit of God over the waters, the Ark, etc.) and of the New Testament and Baptism as entry into the church. Unfortunately the author is not aware of Lawson's thes:s on the sources of the *de officiis* (see Section IV above). I have not seen J. Guillén, *La Eucaristia en los Padres y escritores españoles,* in *España eucaristica,* Salamanca, 1952, pp. 23-39; according to U. Domínguez del Val, in *RET,* 15 (1955), p. 408, it is not always exact. On other aspects of Isidorian theology cf. H. Huber, *Geist und Buchstabe der Sonntagsruhe,* Salzburg, 1958 (Studia theol. moralis et pastoralis, 4), pp. 126-28, and J. M. Alonso, in *Estudios, Rev. de la Orden de la Merced,* 7 (1951), pp. 417 sq., who mentions Isidore's doctrine of the Beatific Vision but unfortunately concentrates attention on the *de ordine creaturarum* (cf. Section III supra) although hesitant as to its authenticity. For penitential theology cf. Section VIb supra.

senschaftliche Quellen und Forschungen 35), studies the Church as *ecclesia offerens* of each mass, or of the mass in general. The first part of the work (pp. 12-54) is dedicated to Isidore. It uses all his authentic writings. Isidore's treatment of Christian initiation is discussed by J. D. C. FISHER, *Christian Initiation. Baptism in the Medieval West, a study in the disintegration of the primitive rite of initiation*, London, 1965 (Alcuin Club Collections 47), pp. 88-93. Far less reliable is T. C. AKELEY, *Christian Initiation in Spain, c.* 300-1100, London, 1967, on which see my review in *Speculum*, 44 (1969), pp. 264-66.

Isidore's anthropology figures in two general surveys of the subject. According to G. MATHON, *L'Anthropologie chrétienne en Occident de St. Augustin à Jean Scot Érigène*, Thesis, Lille, Faculté de Théologie, 1964 (known to me from *BTAM* 9, no. 1396) Isidore restates the views of Augustine as the basis for moral and spiritual life. P. DAUBERCIES, *La théologie de la condition charnelle chez les Maîtres du haut moyen âge*, in *RTAM*, 30 (1963), pp. 5-54, only refers to Isidore occasionally but shows that he is in agreement with Gregory the Great and the general tradition in his low view of man's body. More « positive » expressions can also be found in Isidore as in other authors (though Isidore is not, p. 21, the author of the *de ecclesiasticis dogmatibus*) but they hardly detract from his fundamentally otherworldly attitude.

J. F. SAGÜES, *La doctrina del Cuerpo Místico en San Isidoro de Sevilla*, in *EE*, 17 (1943), pp. 227-57, 329-60, 517-46, has given us an exposition of the whole ecclesiology of Isidore while discussing the different symbols he uses for the Church. The Holy Spirit is not expressly called the Soul of the Church but is seen as such (119). Two studies describe the Isidorian doctrine of the Primacy of the Apostolic See. Both treat the *epistula ad Eugenium* as authentic (120). Even if it is not by Isidore, however, the essential theoretical orthodoxy of the Spanish Church is evident in *de ecclesiasticis officiis*, 2, 5 (ML, 83, 781 sq.) In practice there is visible a certain reserve in the Spanish attitude towards Rome, although this has at times been exaggerated. J. LÉCUYER, *Aux origines de la théologie thomiste de l'episcopat*, in *Gregorianum*, 35 (1954), pp. 56-89, discusses (pp. 72-74) the texts of off. 2, 5 and 7, orig. 7, 12 and the Second Council of Seville. For Isidore bishops and *presbyteri* share in the same priesthood; the episcopate is set apart with certain special powers but this is purely a matter of discipline and does not imply a distinct sacramental character. L. ROBLES, *Teologia del episcopado en San Isidoro, problemas que*

(119) Cf. MADOZ, *Segundo Decenio*, p. 122. Sagües uses the *liber de variis quaestionibus* (cf. supra, Section III) as authentic. On Isidore's doctrine of the Mystical Body cf. also GARCÍA-RODRÍGUEZ, art. cit., infra.

(120) Cf. A. C. VEGA, in *CD*, 154 (1942), pp. 23-56, 237-84, 501-24; 155 (1943), pp. 69-103 (esp. 154, 1942, pp. 501-510) (= *El Pontificado y la Iglesia española en los siete primeros siglos*, El Escorial 1942); J. MADOZ, *El Primado Romano en España en el ciclo Isidoriano*, *RET*, 2 (1942) pp. 229-55. See also J. M. LACARRA, *La Iglesia visigoda en el siglo VII y sus relaciones con Roma*, in *La Chiesa in Occidente*, Spoleto, 1960 (*Settimane di Studio*, VII), pp. 361 sq. On the *epist. ad Eugenium* cf. supra Section II, note 33.

plantea, in *Teología espiritual*, 7 (1963), pp. 131-67, sees Isidore as beginning to distinguish between bishops and priests but not yet clear if the distinction is one of sacramental powers or simply juridical. Isidore is concerned, as are all the bishops of the time, to exercise pastoral care over the whole of society, lay, clerical and monastic. « An excessive centralisation of powers » in the bishop is only slightly mitigated by the existence of metropolitans and church councils.

Two articles use Isidore as a source, one for the doctrine of the sacrament of ordination, the other for the rite of episcopal ordination itself. The first is that of MATIAS AUGÉ, C.M.F., *El sacramento del orden según los concilios españoles de los siglos IV-VII, Claretianum*, 5 (1965), pp. 73-93, the second by J. A. ABAD IBÁÑEZ, *El sacerdocio ministerial en la liturgia hispana », Teología del sacerdocio*, 5 (1973), pp. 353-97. F. MIAN, *Maiestatis communio, Augustinianum*, 13 (1973), pp. 205-14, compares the formula « unum propter maiestatis communionem » of orig. 7, 4, 1, and the Sunday preface for mass in the Roman rite.

J. MADOZ, *La muerte de María en la tradición patrística española*, in *EE*, 25 (1951), pp. 361-74, discusses some texts of Isidore and other authors. The peaceful death of the Virgin was admitted in Spain. Isidore is using Ambrose, Paulinus of Nola and Augustine. He is later cited by Tuseredus (s. VIII) (121).

The only known polemical work of Isidore (apart from his collection of texts against the Acephalite bishop Gregory; cf. Section IV, supra) is his *de fide catholica contra Judaeos*. A. L. WILLIAMS, *Adversus Judaeos, a bird's eye view of Christian « Apologiae » until the Renaissance*, Cambridge, 1935, who gives us (pp. 282-92) a detailed analysis of the work, maintains (p. 217) that Isidore had « no knowledge of traditional Judaism and can hardly have come into close contact with Jews ». This is not the view of B. BLUMENKRANZ, *Les auteurs chrétiens latins du Moyen Age sur les juifs et le judaïsme*, in *Revue des études juives*, N.S., 11 (1951-52), pp. 8-13. Blumenkranz sees in Isidore's attitude to the Jews a contradiction between his attempt to employ persuasion in the *de fide* and his sanction of pressure in the Fourth Council of Toledo. FONTAINE, in *REL*, 31 (1953), p. 294, n. 4, has suggested it is more accurate to see here a development due to external circumstances (122).

(121) The art. of M. GORDILLO, *La Asunción de Maria en la Iglesia española*, in *Razón y Fe*, 144 (1951), pp. 25-38, is superficial. Gordillo holds (p. 28) that the first indication of a Feast of the Assumption in Spain is in Isidore (ort. 67; ML, 83, 148 sq.). In fact this is not so; Isidore says that *nothing* is known of the death of the Virgin and that her tomb is said to be in the valley of Josaphat (cf., in the same sense, MADOZ, *San Isidoro*, pp. 37 sq.; M. JUGIE, *La mort et l'assomption de la Sainte Vierge*, Città del Vaticano, 1944, Studi e testi, 114, p. 270). J. R. GEISELMANN, in *Geist und Leben*, 24 (1951), pp. 361 sq., says Isidore and Bede merely hold Our Lady's bodily incorruption, not her Assumption. On this cf. B. CAPELLE, in *Ephem. liturgicae*, 66 (1952), pp. 243 sq. H. FRÉVIN, *Le Mariage de la sainte Vierge dans l'histoire de la théologie*, Thesis, Lille, Facultés Catholiques, 1951 (see *BTAM*, 8, 1960, no. 2175) sees Isidore, like most of the tradition, following Augustine in affirming that the Virgin was married because marriage is founded on mutual consent not on *copula*.

(122) BLUMENKRANZ considers the *liber de variis quaestionibus* authentic and discusses it (ibid., pp. 13-17). Cf. also ID, in *Theol. Zeitschrift*, 4 (1948), pp. 129 sq.; and his *Juifs et*

Several articles have been devoted to the philosophy of Isidore and in particular to his political ideas. (On his philosophy in general cf. FONTAINE, II, pp. 593-732). B. STEIDLE, *Der heilige Isidor von Sevilla und die Westgoten*, in *Benediktinische Monatschrift*, 18 (1936), pp. 425-34, discusses the *historia Gothorum*. He stresses Isidore's freedom – in contrast to earlier Fathers – from Roman or National pride, his optimism and his belief in the possibilities of Spain under the Visigoths. J. J. CARRERAS ARES, *La historia universal en la España visigoda*, in *Revista de la Universidad de Madrid*, 6 (1957), pp. 175-97 (esp. 177 sq., 189-97), commenting on the *chronica*, points out how the work is based on the Augustinian scheme of six ages (cf. supra, Section IV, note 73) and contains a chronological synthesis that was to serve as the basis of universal histories throughout almost all the Spanish Middle Ages. J. L. ROMERO, *San Isidoro de Sevilla, su pensamiento histórico-político y sus relaciones con la historia visigoda*, in *CHE*, 8 (1947), pp. 5-71, also notes the influence of Isidore's predecessors on his historical works. Isidore's political thought is governed by his belief in Providence, but, when he writes of the Roman Empire, he is also influenced by the circumstances of his own age, especially by his enmity towards Byzantium. Like Steidle, Romero emphasises Isidore's optimism; he notes his deliberate ignoring of Germanic culture; for him all order and civilisation are Roman in origin (123). B. GARCÍA-RODRÍGUEZ, *La Patria en S. Isidoro de Sevilla*, in *Ilustración del Clero*, 45 (1952), pp. 418-26, derives Isidore's idea of his country from his belief that different peoples are members of the Mystical Body of Christ (sent. 3, 49: *ML*, 83, 721).

FRANCISCO ELÍAS DE TEJADA, *Ideas políticas y juridicas de San Isidoro de Sevilla*, in *Revista general de legislación y jurisprudencia*, 108 (1960), pp. 225-58 (and, more briefly, with the same title, in *Anuario de Derecho*, 5, 1961-62, pp. 17-28), sketches the principal themes he sees in Isidore. (Unfortunately his bibliography is largely out-of-date; he considers several questionable works authentic and the *abbreviatio* as by Braulio; see above, Section VIa). Tejada stresses the influence of Augustine on Isidore's ideas, on the monarchy as the instrument of the church, on law, tyranny, and history. He notes the absence of nationalism in Isidore, the classicism of his *laus Spaniae*. More limited in scope but perhaps more useful is M. REYDELLET, *La conception du souverain chez Isidore de Séville*, in *Isidoriana*,

chrétiens dans le monde occidental 430-1096, Paris, 1960 (Études Juives, 2), pp. 46, 62, 82, 108 sq., 229-31, etc. Cf. also S. KATZ, *The Jews in the Visigothic and Frankish Kingdoms of Spain and Gaul*, Cambridge Mass. 1937 (Med. Acad. of America, Monographs 12), p. 35.

(123) Cf. also J. A. MARAVALL, *El Concepto de España en la Edad Media*, Madrid, 1954, pp. 11-18, (on the *laus Spaniae*, its character and influence); ID., in *Cahiers d'histoire mondiale*, 4 (1957-58), pp. 832 sq. On ROMERO's art. cf. FONTAINE, II, p. 817 n. 3. R. PRIETO BANCES, *San Isidoro y la justicia cristiana*, in *Archivos Leoneses*, 18 (1964), pp. 131-43, has some very general considerations on the subject. J. PÉREZ LLAMAZARES, *Las dos potestades*, in *Hidalguia*, 8 (1960), pp. 689-704, is an outline af Isidore s position on Church and State based on the Second Council of Seville and the Fourth of Toledo. P. M. ARCARI, *Idee e sentimenti politici dell'alto medioevo*, Milano, 1968 (Univ. di Cagliari, Pubbl. della Facoltà di Giurisprudenza, S. II, 1), xi + 1023 pp., has a good many references to Isidore but is very confused about him. See the review by [illegible] DUQ. ADAMS, in *Speculum*, 46 (1971), pp. 122-26, esp. 125.

pp. 457-66, a gloss on sent. 3, 47-51, and other texts. See also F. J. Fernández Conde, *El ' Agustinismo político ' y su importancia en la evolución historica del medioevo, Burgense*, 13. 2 (1972), pp. 457-88, at 468-70. H. J. Diesner, *Papsttum und Zeitgeschichte bei Isidor von Sevilla, Theologische Literaturzeitung*, 96 (1971), pp. 81-90, discusses Isidore's ideas on church and state in Spain and on relations with the papacy.

J. Y. du Quesnay Adams, *The Political Grammar of Isidore of Seville*, in *Arts Libéraux et Philosophie au Moyen Age* (Actes du IVème Congrès International de Philosophie Médiévale, Montréal, 1967), Montréal-Paris, 1969, pp. 763-75, is a careful investigation of key terms in Isidore's political thought which shows that variations in their use can reveal changes in his mind. *Populus*, one of these terms, can be interpreted by Isidore in traditional Roman terms as meaning civil society in its general legal aspect. It so appears in diff., orig., hist., and sent., though it is also applied to ecclesiastical groups. But *populus* is *also* often used by Isidore merely as a synonym for *gens* or *natio*, though in the hist. *gens* is generally used for the Visigoths. The connection with the use of *gens* in Jordanes and in the Visigothic Law Codes is suggestive.

R. Buchner, in *Historische Zeitschrift*, 207 (1968), pp. 568 sq., compares Isidore to Venantius Fortunatus and Gregory of Tours. Venantius sees a unity between Gallo-Romans and Italians (both are *romani*). Gregory belongs to the *regnum Francorum*; Italy is separate from his land. Isidore, also, sees *Itali* as distinct from *Hispani*. H. H. Anton, *Fürstenspiegel und Herrscherethos in der Karolingerzeit*, Bonn, 1968, (Bonner historische Forschungen 32), pp. 55-60, 388 sq., has a useful discussion of Isidore's ideas on kingship and tyranny and of his sources. He also shows how Isidore's thought influences that of later writers.

Hans Messmer, *Hispania-Idee und Gotenmythos. Zu den Voraussetzungen des traditionellen vaterländischen Geschichtsbildes im spanischen Mittelalter*, Zurich, 1960, 141 pp., esp. ch. 2, pp. 85-137. This section of the work is less questionable than ch. 1, devoted to Frankish historians. Glossing the hist., Messmer rightly stresses the devotion of Isidore to the Goths though, as Fontaine has noted (*Conversion*, cited below, p. 117 n. 46) this does not exclude Isidore's dependence on Roman tradition. Howver, the fact of Isidore's hostility to the Catholic prince and pretender Hermenegild needs explanation. In two articles, *La Conversión de los Visigodos : notas críticas*, in *AST*, 34 (1961), pp. 21-46, and *Coins and Chronicles : Propaganda in sixth-century Spain and the Byzantine Background*, in *Historia*, 15 (1966), pp. 483-508, I have suggested that the purely political interpretation of this question found in Messmer and E. A. Thompson *The Conversion of the Visigoths to Catholicism*, in *Nottingham Medieval Studies*, 4 (1960), pp. 4-35, was anachronistic. (More recently Thompson, *The Goths in Spain*, Oxford, 1969, pp. 76 sq., and elsewhere, has modified his position). The evidence of coins shows that religious motives were at least « affichés » by *both* the Arian King Leovigild and his son Hermenegild. Isidore can hardly be acquitted of assisting at the birth of the official version (or rather the official suppression) of history, which is consummated in the *Vitas Patrum Emeritensium*. For a broad approach to the difficult question of the conversion of the Visigoths to Catholicism in the 580s see J. FONTAINE, *Conversion et culture chez les Wisigoths d'Espagne*, in *La Conversione al Cristianesimo nell'Europa dell'Alto Medioevo*, Spoleto, 1967 (*Settimane di studio* 14), pp. 87-147; on Isidore's attitude pp. 117 sq. For a different view of Hermenegild as a « tyrant » in Isidore and elsewhere see also J. ORLANDIS, *El Poder Real y la Sucesión al Trono en la Monarquia Visigoda*, Rome-Madrid, 1962 (Estudios Visigóticos 3), pp. 3-12, 34 sq.

M. REYDELLET, *Les intentions idéologiques et politiques dans la Chronique d'Isidore de Séville*, in *Mélanges d'Archéologie et d'Histoire de l'Ecole Française de Rome*, 82 (1970), pp. 363-400, is the first detailed examination of the *chronica* for many years. Reydellet shows that Isidore, though he may have known Sallust, makes no real use of the great pagan Latin historians. Apart from Orosius (whose influence on him is less pronounced than one might expect) he only knew history as chronicle or epitome. For Isidore the chronicle is the ideal form of history, since his aim is « to embrace the whole evolution of man ». Hence the need for *brevitas*, which Isidore repeatedly stressed.

Isidore's adoption of the Augustinian division of history into six ages was deliberate. Isidore changed Augustine's scheme and began with the world's creation, not with Adam, because he wished to stress that history begins at God's behest. Isidore's emphasis on certain kingdoms and events is also deliberate. Many events referred to in the *origines* are omitted in the *chronica*, as irrelevant to the history of salvation through Israel. In the Sixth Age, beginning with the Birth of Christ, Isidore is even more selective. There are traces of anti-Jewish and anti-heretical propaganda, a complete absence of any mystical conception of the Roman Empire, before or after Constantine, and, at the end, a clear exaltation of the Visigothic kingdom, now officially Catholic, where the Jews had been « converted » and the Byzantines expelled, as against the Empire in the East. God's plan seemed very largely realized.

In *Historiography in Visigothic Spain*, in *La Storiografia Altomedievale*, Spoleto, 1970 ((*Settimane di Studio*, 17), pp. 261-311, esp. 287-99, I have tried to set Isidore's historical works in the context of the Visigothic kingdom, with its court art and court historians, imitating while seeking to be independent of Byzantium [124].

(124) On the historical works of Isidore cf. also supra, Section II. A. BARBERO DE AGUILERA, *El pensamiento politico visigodo y las primeras unciones regias en la Europa Medieval*, in *Hispania*, 30 (1970), pp. 245-326 (esp. pp. 264-77), in an article which ignores much recent work on the subject, comments on Isidore's political views on monarchy and tyranny and on IV Toledo c. 75. He sees this canon as contradicting Isidore's political theory on the Divine Right of Kings and as proof of the « economic identification » of the church's interests with those of the nobility (p. 277). A simpler explanation would be to see the church as sanctioning the seizure of power by Sisenand, as it sanctioned earlier and later « coups d'état »; though certain leading bishops (including Isidore, it seems) preferred a hereditary succession they had to go with the tide. The importance of c. 75 can be exaggerated; it hardly ever affected later royal successions.

e. *Isidore in the history of the Liturgy*

P. SÉJOURNÉ, *Saint Isidore de Séville et la liturgie wisigothique*, in *Misc. Isid.*, pp. 221-51, examines the evidence that can be found in the *de ecclesiasticis officiis* for the liturgy of the time. The assertion of Dom B. BOTTE, in *RTAM*, 11 (1939), p. 229 n. 26, that in the *de officiis* Isidore collects all he can find in the authorities available to him without worrying as to its practical significance for Spain, would seem dubious in the light of Dom Séjourné's article – to which, incidentally, Dom Botte does not refer [125]. A. C. LAWSON (op. cit. supra, Section IV and note 68) has confirmed the finding of Dom Wilmart that Isidore does not depend on Pseudo-Germanus of Paris but the latter on Isidore [126]. R. E. MESSENGER, in *Traditio*, 4 (1946), pp. 163 sq., following Dom J. Pérez de Urbel's earlier work in *Bulletin hispanique*, 28 (1926), believes that Isidore wrote a number of hymns. But for this there exists no proof; in his contribution to *Isidoriana*, *Los himnos isidorianos*, Dom PÉREZ DE URBEL only claims one hymn as probably Isidorian, that of SS. Iusta et Rufina (p. 111). Mgr. J. ENCISO, in *RET*, 3 (1943), pp. 485-92, shows Anspach's idea (*Taionis et Isidori nova fragmenta et opera*, pp. 86 sq.) that Isidore was the author of the prologue to the Mozarabic hymns was mistaken. The author is a later writer who is copying the Fourth Council of Toledo, cc. 13-14 [127].

(125) Cf. also the important art. of J. HAVET, cit. supra, Section VId, esp. pp. 61-72 (on the *oratio sexta* of the *Missa fidelium*). He suggests (p. 64) that Isidore might be the author of certain formulas of the Mozarabic Liturgy very close to off. I, 15, 2-3 (*ML*, 83, 752). A. GARCÍA DE LA FUENTE, in *CD*, 152 (1936), pp. 275-79, has some general observations of slight importance on the *de officiis*. Cf., for the Spanish or Mozarabic Liturgy in general, F. CABROL, *Mozarabe (la liturgie)*, in *DictArchChrLit.*, 12, 1. Paris, 1935, pp. 390-491, and the more recent arts. of L. BROU, in *HS*, 2 (1949), pp. 459-484; and J. PINELL, ibid., 9 (1956), pp. 405-27; 10 (1957), pp. 385-427; *Estudios sobre la liturgia mozárabe*, ed. J. F. RIVERA RECIO, Toledo, 1965; A. ROCHE NAVARRO, in *Archivos Leoneses*, 25 (1971), pp. 323-69 (the fullest bibliography so far published though without commentary).

(126) W. H. FRERE, *The Anaphora or Great Eucharistic Prayer*, London, 1938, p. 107, holds Pseudo-Germanus does not necessarily depend on Isidore. J. QUASTEN, *Oriental Influence in the Gallican Liturgy*, in *Traditio*, 1 (1943), pp. 55-78 and A. CHAVASSE, in *RMAL*, 1 (1945), pp. 117 sq., take the same view as Wilmart and LAWSON. A. VAN DER MENSBRUGGHE, *L'Expositio missae Gallicanae est elle de Saint Germain de Paris (+ 576)?*, in *Messager de l'exarchat du patriarche russe en Europe Occidentale*, 32 (1959), pp. 217-49 (esp. 220-26); defends the dependence of Isidore on the *expositio*, which he holds is by St Germanus; he has not seen the work of LAWSON. He is mistaken, moreover, – following Wilmart and Leclercq – in supposing that Isidore, *de officiis*, was hardly known in Frankish Gaul before saec. IX. We now know of a saec. VII MS. of *excerpta* from the work that comes from Gaul (cf. supra, Section II and n. 32). P. van der Mensbrugghe's article is not improved by the raillery, worthy of Henri Leclercq, he addresses to scholars such as Edmund Bishop and André Wilmart who are no longer able to defend themselves. Another study by the same author, *Pseudo-Germanus Reconsidered, Studia Patristica*, 5 (1962), pp. 172-84, is equally unconvincing. Two new editions of « Germanus » have recently appeared. K. GAMBER, *Ordo antiquus gallicanus* Regensburg, 1965 (Textus patristici et liturgici 3), who reprints Quasten's edition, with some notes, follows van der Mensbrugghe. The posthumously published edition of E. C. RATCLIFF, *Expositio antiquae liturgiae gallicanae*, London, 1971 (Henry Bradshaw Society 98), is directly based on MS. Autun 184 (saec. IX). The editor, who disbelieved in the attribution to Germanus, did not leave his arguments behind him.

(127) On music in Isidore cf. supra, Section V and notes 91-92.

Dom L. Brou, *Problèmes liturgiques chez Saint Isidore*, in *Isidoriana*, pp. 193-209, discusses the Isidorian authorship of the *benedictio lucernae* of Holy Saturday, established by MS. evidence and the citation by Elipandus in 799. Brou argues that Isidore was also the author of a melody for the *benedictiones* for the mass of the Ascension. On the other hand, there is no proof that the « Mozarabic » Missal and Breviary printed in 1500-02 (despite their attribution to Isidore) were drawn up by or have any close connection with him. See also Brou, « Etudes sur le Missel et le Bréviaire 'Mozarabes' imprimés», *HS*, 11 (1958), pp. 349-98.

VIII. The Influence of Isidore in the Middle Ages

A great historian has held that « the complete enumeration of later medieval works based on Isidore would have neither utility nor end » (128). Yet, in view of the fact that we possess as yet no attempt at a complete study of Isidore in the Middle Ages, it may be useful to collect some notes on recently published works that bear on the subject (129).

For many medieval historians the influence of Isidore was immense. E. R. Curtius has described the *origines* as the « Grundbuch des ganzen Mittelalters... Es hat nicht nur den Wissensbestand für acht Jahrhunderte gültig festgelegt, sondern auch deren Denkform geprägt » (130). Père Y. M.-J. Congar, in *RMAL*, 8 (1952), pp. 27 sq., has pointed out that Isidore for the Middle Ages, even more than Augustine, Jerome, Gregory or Aristotle, was « un maître en discours logique et en définitions, un premier instituteur qui lui a enseigné l'usage raisonné de sa langue », for he provided medieval men with « un instrument d'ordre et, avec ses limites, de précision dans la pensée ». For Congar (p. 37) the Lutheran Revolution and the Dispute of Leipzig (1519), in particular, mark the end of a world formed in the school of Isidore.

Are these claims exaggerated ? Only a complete investigation of Isidore's influence in the Middle Ages can fully answer this question (131). But in the meantime – the probably considerable meantime – we may look at a little of the evidence. One indication is the extent to which Isi-

(128) Mommsen, in *Mon. Germ. Hist., Auct. Ant.*, XI, Berlin, 1894, (Chronica Minora 11), p. 407.

(129) Cf. also supra, Section II; Section V; Section VIb. I am well aware that the notes that follow are incomplete. They are meant as an *indication* of the evidence available. See, also, Segovia, cited, above p. 8.

(130) Curtius, in *Zeitschr. für roman. Philol.*, 62 (1942), p. 475 (= *European Literature in the Latin Middle Ages*, p. 496) (cf. note 82 supra).

(131) As Fontaine (II, p. 888 n. 1) has already noted, no such work at present exists. L. Allevi, *L'influenza dell'ultimo dei padri, S. Isidoro di Siviglia (+ 636)*, in *La Scuola Cattolica*, 64 (1936), pp. 448-61, is a general commemorative art. and A. E. Anspach, *Das Fortleben Isidors im VII. bis IX. Jahrhundert*, in *Misc. Isid.*, pp. 323-56, only goes as far as the Ninth Century and has to be treated with reserve (he attributes several works to Isidore which are not by him, e.g. the *Ecloga* of Lathcen and the *Ars Grammatica* attributed to Julian of Toledo; cf. pp. 337 sq., 338 sq.).

dore's name and fame were exploited in the Middle Ages by the authors of commentaries on the Bible. In Fr. STEGMÜLLER's *Repertorium biblicum Medii Aevi*, III, Madrid, 1951, he occupies 30 pages (even Jerome has only 35), pp. 471-500. He is drawn on as a patristic source by writers on Canon Law, although it has been shown that he was more used by the *Hibernensis* (c. 710) than by later collections (132). From Isidore more than from any other author the Middle Ages drew – to choose almost at random – among many other things, their view of pagan religions, their classification of the ages of life – *iuventus, gravitas, senectus* –, their theory of tyrants as opposed to legitimate kings, their discussion of the Names of Christ and their Origenist conception of the relations between the Old and New Testaments based on the typological interpretation of Scripture (133). The Middle Ages may not, as Saxl believed, have received from Isidore in the *origines* a pictorial representation as well as a logical explanation of antiquity (cf. supra, Section II and note 14). But, on the one hand, the application of Isidorian texts, that began with the rudimentary representation of the three continents found in MS. Escorial R. II. 18 (saec. VII) – a representation copied and enlarged on throughout the Middle Ages – resulted in the increasingly complex maps in later Isidorian MSS. and especially in the Beatus commentaries, and, on the other, the *rotae* illustrations in the *de natura rerum* played a considerable rôle in transmitting to later centuries the idea of circular figures, which was to flower forth so amazingly in the rose windows of the medieval cathedrals (134).

(132) Cf. CH. MUNIER, *Les sources patristiques du droit de l'Église du VIIIe au XIIIe siècle*, Thèse, Univ. de Strasbourg, Mulhouse, 1957, p. 28.

(133) Cf. P. ALPHANDÉRY, *L'evhemérisme et les débuts de l'histoire des religions au moyen âge*, in *Rev. hist. religions*, 109 (1934), pp. 5-27, esp. 16-25 (on orig. 8, 11); J. DE GHELLINCK. *Iuventus, gravitas, senectus*, in *Studia mediaevalia in honorem R. J. Martin*, Bruges, 1948, pp, 39-59, esp. p. 40, 44-47 (on orig. 11,2 and diff. 1, 531, 2, 19-20, *ML*, 83, 63C, 81); F. FLÜCKIGER, op. cit. supra, Section VIb, p. 396 (on sent. 3, 48, 7: *ML*, 83, 719; cf. also W. PARSONS, in *Rev. of Politics*, 4, 1942, pp. 131 sq.); for influence of Isidore's ideal of the just king (sent. 3, 50; *ML*, 83, 721 sq.) as early as Jonas of Orléans, *de institutione regia*, 6 and the Council of Paris of 829 cf. E. EICHMANN, *Zur Symbolik der Herrscherkrone im Mittelalter*, in *Notter Antal Emlékkönyv*, Budapest, 1941, pp. 180-207, and H.-X. ARQUILLIÈRE, op. infra cit., pp. 149-51. E. R. CURTIUS, *Nomina Christi*, in *Mélanges J. de Ghellinck*, II, Gembloux, 1951, pp. 1029-32, discusses orig. 7,2; Isidore's source is the *Decretum Gelasianum*. (This art. is reprinted in CURTIUS, *Gesammelte Aufsätze zur romanischen Philologie*, Bern-München. 1960, pp. 373-75, a collection of arts, that contains numerous other references to Isidore). J. CHÂTILLON, art. cit. supra, note 71, p. 546, points to Isidore's transmission of Origenist views. P. B. SALMON, *The 'three voices' of poetry in medieval literary theory*, in *Medium Aevum*, 30 (1961), pp. 1-18, comments, *inter alia*, on the influence of orig. 8,7. W. J. BRANDT, *The Shape of Medieval History*, New Haven, 1966, pp. 1-11, claims that Isidore's physical theories underlie even late medieval views of nature.

(134) Cf. G. MENÉNDEZ PIDAL, *Mozárabes y asturianos en la cultura de Alta Edad Media, en relación con la Historia de los conocimientos geográficos*, in *Boletín de la Real Academia de la Historia*, 134 (1954), pp. 137-291 (cf. note 94 supra). On the *rotae* in the early MSS. of Isidore, *de natura rerum*, cf. FONTAINE, *Isidore, Traité de la nature*, pp. 15-18, 20-34, and, on their possible later influence M. TH. D'ALVERNY, *Le cosmos symbolique du XIIe siècle*, in *Archives d'hist. doctrinale et litt. du moyen âge*, 20 (1953), pp. 31-81, esp. p. 75 n. 3, 78; E. J. BEER, *Die Rose der Kathedrale von Lausanne und der kosmologische Bilderkreis des Mittelalters*, Bern, 1952 (Berner Schriften zur Kunst. 6), pp. 39 sq. (for Isidorian influence cf. also, ib., pp. 61 sq. etc.). For possible influence of the illustration of Isidore's idea of the griffin

Isidore's influence on the culture of his own age and land is evident. W. STACH and FONTAINE have described his relations with his contemporary, king Sisebut (135). LYNCH has commented on the correspondence between Isidore and his favourite disciple and, in a sense, « literary executor », Braulio (136). Isidore's second bibliographer, Ildefonsus, it appears, was not, as was once thought, his direct disciple, but Ildefonsus's use of Isidore is clear enough. From him he took, for instance, almost all the Biblical citations for his *de virginitate* (137). Julian of Toledo, too, uses Isidore, like Ildefonsus generally without acknowledgment (138). Isidore serves as a source for the Creeds of successive Councils of Toledo (139). After the Arabic Invasion he continues to be used by the few Christian chroni-

(orig. 12, 2, 17) in twelfth Century bestiaries on Suger of St. Denis cf. O. VON SIMSON, *The Gothic Cathedral*, New York, 1956, p. 113 n. 70. L. PRESSOUYRE, *Le cosmos platonicien de la cathédrale d'Anagni*, in *Mélanges d'archéologie et d'histoire* (École française de Rome), 78 (1966), pp. 551-93, comments (pp. 556-60) on the Isidorian *schemata.*

(135) Cf. W. STACH, *Bemerkungen zu den Gedichten des Westgotenkönigs Sisebut (Anth. Lat. Nr. 483)*, in *Corona quernea, Festgabe K. Strecker*, Leipzig, 1941 (Schriften des Reichsinstituts für ältere deutsche Geschichtskunde, Mon. Germ. hist. 6), pp. 75-96, esp. pp. 89 sq.; ID., *König Sisebut, ein Mäzen des isidorianischen Zeitalters*, in *Die Antike*, 19 (1943), pp. 63-76. See FONTAINE, *Isidore, Traité de la nature*, pp. 151-59, which uses and supersedes his earlier study in *Actes du Congrès de l'Association G. Budé*, Paris, 1949, pp. 156-58. L. J. VAN DER LOF, *Der Mäzen König Sisebutus und sein De eclipsi lunae*, *Revue des études augustiniennes*, 18 (1972), pp. 145-51, considers (*inter alia*) the relations of Sisebut with Isidore (esp. over the nat.), and whether his concern with literature differed from Isidore's. On Isidore in Spain see the articles of M. C. DÍAZ Y DÍAZ, *Isidoro en la Edad Media española* (in Latin literature), and L. LÓPEZ SANTOS, *San Isidoro en la Literatura medioeval castellana*, in *Isidoriana*, pp. 345-87 and 401-43. On Sisebut's *Carmen* see also V. RECCHIA, *Sisebuto di Toledo : il « Carmen de luna »*, Bari, 1971 (Quaderni di « Vetera christianorum », 3) on which see J. FONTAINE, *REL*, 49 (1971), pp. 514-16; B. DE GAIFFIER, *Analecta Bollandiana*, 91 (1973), pp. 147 sq.

(136) Cf. C. H. LYNCH, *St. Braulio, bishop of Saragossa (631-651), his Life and Writings*, Washington, 1938 (CUA, SMH, N. S. 2), pp. 33-54 (the Spanish trans. by P. GALINDO, *San Braulio...*, Madrid, 1950, adds little of importance to the original except a new edition of the *renotatio* for which cf. supra, Section VIa). The correspondence is edited from MS. Léon 22 by J. MADOZ, *Epistolario de San Braulio de Zaragoza*, Madrid, 1941, pp. 71-89.

(137) Cf. J. M. CASCANTE DÁVILA, *Doctrina mariana de San Ildefonso de Toledo*, Barcelona, 1958) (Colectanea San Paciano, Serie teológica 5), pp. 317 sq., 322 sq. For the use of the *de officiis* in Ildefonsus, *De cognitione baptismi* cf. A. BRAEGELMANN, *The Life and Writings of St. Ildefonsus of Toledo*, Washington, 1942 (CUA, SMH, N. S. 4), p. 64. Cf. also J. MADOZ, in *EE*, 26 (1952), pp. 467-505.

(138) Cf. A. VEIGA VALIÑA, *La doctrina escatológica de San Julián de Toledo*, Lugo, 1940, p. 150; J. MADOZ, in *Gregorianum*, 33 (1952), pp. 401, 403, 412 sq.; J. N. HILLGARTH, *Las fuentes de San Julián de Toledo*, in *Anales Toledanos*, 3 (1971), p. 116; also A. ROBLES, *Fuentes literarias del Antikeimenon de Julián de Toledo*, in *Escritos del Vedat*, 1 (1971), p. 134. For Taio of Saragossa's use of Isidore's sent. in his own *sententiae* see L. ROBLES, *Tajón de Zaragoza, continuador de Isidoro*, in *Saitabi*, 21 (1971), pp. 19-25. Taio makes less effort to summarize his sources than did Isidore and he depends more on Gregory the Great.

(139) For Toledo IV (633) cf. J. MADOZ, in *RHE*, 34 (1938), pp. 5-20; for Toledo VI (638) ID., in *Gregorianum*, 19 (1938), pp. 161-93; for Toledo XI (675), ID., *Le symbole du XIe Concile de Tolède*, Louvain, 1938, (Spicilegium Sacrum Lovaniense, 19), esp. pp. 112, sq.; for Toledo XVI (693) ID., *El simbolo del Concilio XVI de Toledo*, Madrid, 1946 (Est. Onienses, i, 3), p. 120. Cf. also J. DE J. PÉREZ, *La Cristologia en los simbolos toledanos IV, VI y XI*, Roma, 1939, esp. pp. 10-15, 17, 19, 28, 37 sq., 45, 47 sq., 50; C. RIERA, *Doctrina de los simbolos toledanos sobre el Espiritu Santo*, Vich, 1955, 182 pp.

clers of the Eighth Century, by the Chronicle of 741 and the *Continuatio Hispana* of 754 (140). In the Ninth Century, in Moslem Spain, he is a favourite source of Paulus Albarus of Córdoba (141). In the Tenth Century at Córdoba he is still evidently well known for it seems that the Moslem Ahmad al Razi then had access to a lost Mozarabic compilation dependent on Isidore (142). In 1012 the *sententiae* were well known in Catalonia, at Barcelona (143). In the Twelfth Century Isidore is one of the principal influences on the sermons and Biblical commentaries of St. Martin of León (144). In the Thirteenth the *laus Spaniae* inspires the glosses of bishop Vincent of Idanha-Guarda (+ 1248) (145). An article by M. MARTINS, *S. Isidoro na Idade Média Portuguesa* (560-1960), in *Broteria*, 70 (1960), pp. 275-83, notes the presence of MSS. of Isidore in donations of books from 959 onwards and discusses several Isidorian MSS. of Alcobaça, the Portuguese translation of the apocryphal *Collectum S. Isidori*, and some mentions of Isidore in medieval Portuguese literature.

The influence of Isidore was felt in the Seventh Century outside the Iberian Peninsula, notably among the Irish and Anglo Saxons (146). His influence is visible in *An Illustrated Medieval School-Book of Bede's « De natura rerum »*, described by H. BOBER, in *Journal Walters Art Gallery*,

(140) Cf. C. E. DUBLER, *Sobre la Chrónica arábigo-bizantina de 741 y la influencia bizantina en la Peninsula ibérica*, in *Al-Andalus*, 11 (1946), pp. 283-349, esp. pp. 298-303, 326. On the influence of Isidore, *de ortu*, on Beatus, *In Apocalipsin*, see M. C. DÍAZ Y DÍAZ, *Estudios sobre la antigua literatura relacionada con Santiago el Mayor*, *Compostellanum*, 11 (1966) pp. 639 sq.

(141) Cf. C. M. SAGE, *Paul Albar of Cordoba : Studies on his Life and Writings*, Diss., Washington 1943 (CUA, SMH, N. S., 5), esp. pp. 54 sq., 80, etc.; J. MADOZ, *Epistolario de Alvaro de Córdoba*, ed. crítica, Madrid, 1947 (Mon. Hisp. Sacra, ser. patrística 1), cf. *indices*, p. 288. G. MENÉNDEZ PIDAL, *Le rayonnement de la culture isidorienne. Les Mozarabes*, in *Cahiers d'histoire mondiale*, 6 (1961), pp. 714-31, has a good general discussion of the influence of Isidore's works.

(142) C. SÁNCHEZ-ALBORNOZ, *San Isidoro, ' Rasis ' y la Pseudo Isidoriana*, in *CHE*, 4 (1946), pp. 73-113, held the Arabic original of « Rasis » was used by the Pseudo-Isidorian *Chronica Gothorum*, which he dates saec. XI ex. R. MENÉNDEZ PIDAL, *Sobre la Crónica Pseudo Isidoriana*, in *CHE*, 21-22 (1954), pp. 5-15, dates the *Chronica* saec. X (that is, its lost Arabic original) and believes it derives independently from the same compilation, partly Isidore, also used by « Rasis ». DÍAZ, *Index*, n. 753, places the *Chronica* in saec. XI. A. BENITO VIDAL (ed.), *Cronica seudo isidoriana*, Valencia, 1961 (Textos Medievales 5), uses MS. Paris, Bibl. Nat., lat 6113, though in general he follows Mommsen's edition. See ID., *La fecha de la Crónica seudo isidoriana*, in *Saitabi*, 11 (1961), pp. 247-52; he thinks that the existing MS. was copied from a Visigothic original, written in Andalusia 1095-1144.

(143) Cf. F. VALLS-TABERNER, *Obras selectas*, II, Madrid-Barcelona, 1954, pp. 238-40. A. MUNDÓ, *Códices isidorianos de Ripoll*, in *Isidoriana*, pp. 389-400, discusses 25 MSS. which at one time belonged to Ripoll and contained works of Isidore.

(144) Cf. A. VIÑAYO GONZÁLEZ, *San Martin de León y su Apologética antijudia*, Madrid-Barcelona, 1948, esp. pp. 202-206, 211.

(145) Cf. G. POST, in *Speculum*, 29 (1954), pp. 198-209.

(146) Cf. B. BISCHOFF, art. cit. supra, note 21, and now his *Die europäische Verbreitung der Werke Isidors von S.*, in *Isidoriana*, pp. 317-344 (reprinted in his *Mittelalterliche Studien*, I, Stuttgart, 1966, pp. 171-94). Cf. also O. K. WERCKMEISTER, art. cit. supra, note 17, and his art., *The Meaning of the Chi Initial Page of the Book of Kells*, in *Friends of the Library of Trinity College, Dublin, Annual Bulletin* (1959-60); J. N. HILLGARTH, *The East, Visigothic Spain and the Irish*, *Studia Patristica*, 4 (1961), pp. 442-56; ID., *Visigothic Spain and Early Christian Ireland*, *Proceedings of the Royal Irish Academy*, 62, Series C (1962), pp. 167-94.

19-20 (1956-57), pp. 65-97. Clement Scottus is one of a series of Irish grammarians who use Isidore (147).

One should cite here MICHAEL W. HERREN, *The Hisperica Famina* : I. *The A-Text, a new critical edition with English translation and philological commentary*, Toronto, 1974. Herren sees the work as written in Ireland, probably saec. VII; he discusses Isidore's influence, pp. 20-22 (esp. that of orig. 9, 3, and, less certainly, of nat. and diff.). In his paper for the Visigothic Colloquy in Dublin (1975), to appear in *Visigothic Spain: new approaches* (Oxford, 1980), Herren developed these influences and also spoke of Isidore's influence on Virgilius Maro, a theme expanded in *Some New Light on the Life of Virgilius Maro Grammaticus, Proceedings of the Royal Irish Academy*, 79, Series C (1979), pp. 45 sq. I. N. SALUM, *A semana e o quotidiano, Lingua e Literatura*, 2 (1973), pp. 93-122, discusses the *divisiones temporis* in Isidore and Bede (I only know a reference to this article in *L'Année Philologique*).

There is no doubt of the incredibly rapid spread of Isidore's works on the continent in the eighth century. It seems that there are more manuscripts of his works listed in *CLA* than those of any other author, though this repertory ends in 800. In France perhaps the first author to make much use of Isidore was Defensor of Ligugé, who probably wrote *ca.* 700. See the critical edition by H-M. ROCHAIS, in *Corpus Christianorum, Series Latina*, 117, Turnhout, 1957, pp. 250-53, and his later Defensor de Ligugé, *Livre d'étincelles*, Paris, 1961-62, (Sources chrétiennes 77 and 86) 2 vols. Isidore's sent., syn., off. and (once) diff. are used. The sent. supplied a third of Defensor's extracts. The (probably saec. VII) *Aratus Latinus*, a badly translated version of the Greek of Aratos and his commentators, used the orig. and nat. The place and exact date of *Aratus* are still obscure. See H. LE BOURDELLÈS, *Naissance d'un serpent. Essai de datation de l'Aratus Latinus mérovingien*, in *Hommages à M. Renard*, Brussels, 1969 (Collection Latomus 101), pp. 506-14.

The influence of the *de ecclesiasticis officiis* is very notable among Carolingian theologians in their interpretation if not in the text of the Canon of the Mass (148). Claudius of Turin seems the first of a series of theolo-

(147) See J. M. SOLÁ-SOLÉ, in *Bibliotheca Orientalis*, 14 (1957), pp. 66-68. But it seems rash to assume that this text attributed to Isidore by Clemens but not found in his extant works was really drawn by him from « des sources beaucoup plus anciennes, voire même originales » or that Isidore « nous parle semble-t-il du point de vue des grammairiens phéniciens » (p. 67). Cf. G. BOYER (cited supra, Section V), p. 50 n. 1.

(148) See J. A. JUNGMANN, in *Zeitschr. für katholische Theologie*, 62 (1938), pp. 390-400; ID., *Missarum Sollemnia*, I, Freiburg, 1952, pp. 108 sq., also the list of liturgists in C. VOGEL, *Introduction aux sources de l'histoire du culte chrétien au Moyen Âge*, reedited, Spoleto, 1975, pp. 11 sq. For Spanish influence on Carolingian writers in general see L. WALLACH in *Didascaliae, Studies in honor of A. M. Albareda*, New York, 1961, pp. 508 sq.; he also (pp. 478 sq.) notes how Isidore's simplified formulation of the *Filioque* (orig. 7, 4, 4) was preferred to Augustine, *de Trinitate*, XV, 26, 47 by the authors of the *Libri carolini*. A. GRILLMEIER, in *Das Konzil von Chalkedon*, ed. GRILLMEIER and H. BACHT, 3 vols, Würzburg, 1951-54, II, pp. 814 sq., notes how Isidore transmitted African Chalcedonianism to the Middle. Ages On the influence of the sent. on attempts to systematize theology, from Carolingian times onwards, see L. ROBLES (cited above, Section II), pp. 37-42. L. OTT.,

gians of the early Middle Ages who use the *quaestiones in Vetus Testamentum* (149). Alcuin uses Isidore for his speculations on the seven arts (150). A. LENTINI, in *Aevum*, 27 (1953), p. 244, has noted the use of orig. 1, 3, 5 by the Ninth Century grammarian Hilderic. The Glossary of Karlsruhe (MS. Aug. CCXLVIII, saec. IX med.), probably from Corbie, uses the orig. and perhaps the *differentiae* (151). Remigius of Auxerre (+ 908) uses orig. 1, 3, 7; cf. H. SILVESTRE, in *MA*, 63 (1957), pp. 55 sq. Isidore is among the sources of the anonymous *De bestiis et aliis rebus*, a collection of chapters from the Latin *Physiologus* with various additions (152).

G. EHRISMANN has said of the translation into Old High German of the *de fide catholica* that it is a « notable and unique phenomenon in Old German literature » (153). On this translation cf. W. BRUCKNER, in *Festschrift G. Binz*, Basel, 1935, pp. 69-83, who believes the translation was made not at Murbach but near the French Court by an author equally familiar with Latin, German and French; and R. KIENAST, in *Festschrift für W. Stammler*, Berlin, 1953, pp. 11-24, who returns to the view that Murbach was the home of the translation which he dates 782-792. Bruckner's view seems, however, the more convincing of the two (154).

in *Das Konzil*, II, pp. 874-78, has some useful notes on Isidore and the early scholastic historians and canonists, as regards Chalcedon.

(149) Cf. CHÂTILLON, art. cit. supra, note 71, pp. 542-46.

(150) Cf. M.-TH. D'ALVERNY, in *Mélanges F. Grat*, I, Paris, 1946, pp. 249 sq. (citing orig. 1,1 and 2,24). L. STRZELECKI, in *Eos*, 40 (1939), pp. 40-48, shows ALCUIN, *Orthographia*, ed. KEIL, used orig. 1,27, as well as Cassiodorus.

(151) Cf. A. LABHARDT, *Contributions à la critique et a l'explication des gloses de Reichenau*, Thèse, Neuchâtel, 1936, ix + 107 pp., known to me only from the review by M. CAPPUYNS, in *BTAM*, 3 (1937-40), n. 548; also A. LABHARDT, *Glossarum biblicum codicis Augiensis*, CCXLVIII, Neuchâtel-Paris, 1948, pp. xiii sq.

(152) Cf. F. J. CARMODY, in *Speculum*, 13 (1938), pp. 153-59; H. SILVESTRE, in *MA*, 55 (1949), pp. 247-51. H. M. ROCHAIS, in *RB*, 67 (1957), pp. 141-50, describes the sources of the Carolingian *florilegium* in MS. Reims 443 (saec. IX), containing texts from Isidore, sent. and off. (cf. also an earlier description by A. WILMART, in *RB*, 34 (1922), pp. 235 sq.).

(153) cf. EHRISMANN, cit. VOSSLER, in *Arbor*, 2 (1944), p. 22.

(154) The *Répertoire des médiévistes européens*, Poitiers, 1960, p. 175 (n. 1138) misleadingly stated that Mr. K. Ostberg of London University had in preparation a new edition of Isidore, *de fide catholica*. Mr. Ostberg informed me that in fact he was working on the Old High German translation and, to that end, collating early MSS. of the Latin original, but he was not preparing a new edition of the Latin text. See the 3rd. edn. of the *Répertoire* (1971), no. 3202. For recent literature on the O.H.G. Isidore see W. HAUBRICHS, *Zum Stand der Isidorforschung, Zeitschrift für deutsche Philologie*, 94 (1975), pp. 1-15; see also e.g., apart from the works cited in the text, H. BRAUER, in *Die Deutsche Literatur des Mittelalters, Verfasser-Lexikon*, II, Berlin-Leipzig, 1936, pp. 558-60; J. FOURQUET, *L'ordre des éléments de la phrase en germanique ancien*, Paris, 1938, pp. 124-56; G. BAESECKE, in *Beiträge zur Geschichte der deutschen Sprache und Literatur*, 69 (1947), pp. 367-372; H. DE BOOR, *Geschichte der deutschen Literatur*, I, München, 1949, pp. 29-33, 39; T. A. ROMPELMAN, *Langobardisch en Duits*, Groningen, 1950 (Handel. 21 Nederlands philol. Congres), p. 34; G. NORDMEYER, *Syntax Analysis of the Old High German « Isidor »*, in *Wächter und Hüter, Festschrift für H. J. Weigand*, New Haven, 1957, pp. 29-38, and many other writers on Old German, e.g. D. RUPRECHT, *Tristitia, Wortschatz und Vorstellung in den althoch-deutschen Sprachdenkmälern*, Göttingen, 1959 (Palaestra 227), who also cites Isidore's teaching contained in the *differentiae*. See the bibliography by F. DELBONO, in *Studi Medievali*, S. 3ª, 9 (1968), pp. 277-319. E. ULRICH, *Die althochdeutschen Glossen zu Isidors Büchern über die Pflichten*, Diss. Halle, 1938, vi + 40 pp., discusses O.H.G. Glosses on the *de eccles. officiis*, con-

C. SILVA-TAROUCA, *Un codice di Pseudo-Isidoro coevo del falso ?*, in *Misc. Isid.*, pp. 357-63, discusses MS. Ottob. Lat. 93, which he dates c. 850, and connects with Tours; he sees it as the oldest MS. of Pseudo-Isidore. S. WILLIAMS, *The Pseudo-Isidorian Problem Today, Speculum,* 29 (1954), pp. 702-707, points to this article of Silva-Tarouca as having advanced the problem a decisive stage. He believes that Ps-Isidore originated 845-55 in a scriptorium of the diocese of Reims. Essentially the same view of the date and origin of the False Decretals (in the circle of the opponents of Archbishop Hincmar of Reims) is taken in the fundamental recent study of HORST FUHRMANN, *Einfluss und Verbreitung der pseudoisidorischen Fälschungen von ihrem Auftauchen bis in die neuere Zeit,* Stuttgart, 1972-74 (Schriften der Monumenta Germaniae Historica. Deutsches Institut für Erforschung des Mittelalters, 24). 3 vols. This work, which collects Fuhrmann's many earlier articles and expands them, complements the study of manuscripts by S. WILLIAMS, *Codices Pseudo-Isidoriani: a Palaeographical-Historical Study,* New York, 1971 (Monumenta Iuris Canonici, Ser. C: Subsidia 3). The bulk of Fuhrmann's work is an exhaustive study of the influence of Pseudo-Isidore to the time of Gratian. Another very important book, which often touches on Isidorian texts, though mainly concerned with canon law sources prior to the Pseudo-Isidorian forgeries, is that of HUBERT MORDEK, *Kirchenrecht und Reform im Frankenreich: Die Collectio Vetus Gallica, die älteste systematische Kanonessammlung des fränkischen Gallien. Studien und Edition,* Berlin-New York, 1975 (Beiträge zur Geschichte und Quellenkunde des Mittelalters, 1); see especially p. 375 (MSS. of the quaest.) and 511 (for the off.) (155).

R. T. MEYER, in *Traditio,* 12 (1956), pp. 398-405, points to three batches of « glossae collectae » from the orig. in Aelfric's *Vocabulary.* They may be interpolations due to a scribe and not to Aelfric himself. S. GONZÁLEZ, in *EE,* 18 (1944), pp. 367 sq., points to the use of Isidore in Burchard of Worms, *Decretum* (156). A. OLIVAR, in *HS,* 11 (1958), pp. 185 sq., notes the citation of a passage by Guitmund of Aversa (d. c. 1095) *in quodam missali hispano, quod dicunt sanctum dictasse Isidorum.* See *Isidoriana,* p. 195 n. 3. In MS. Munich, Lat. 19414 Isidore's orig. and off. are combined to form « a brief etymological description of the ecclesiastical offices ».

tained in three saec. IX MSS., all in Munich, Clm 6325, 19410 and 14461. The Latin text used seems closer to the older editions of Isidore, including that of Cochlaeus in 1534, than to Arévalo's. A grammatical study shows that behind the Bavarian MSS. we possess there was a (lost) original of saec. IX in., possibly coming from Fulda.

(155) Cf. also J. HALLER, *Nikolaus I und Pseudo-Isidor,* Stuttgart, 1936, esp. c. 9, pp. 155-72. R. GRAND, *Nouvelles remarques sur l'origine du Pseudo-Isidore, source du Décret de Gratien,* in *Studia Gratiana,* III, Bologna, 1955, pp. 3-16, maintains the theory that Ps-Isidore originated at Mans and is the work mainly of clerics from Western France. For later influence of Ps-Isidore cf., e.g., A. MICHEL, in *Studi Gregoriani,* 3, Roma, 1948, pp. 149-61 (= *Zeitschr. der Savigny-Stiftung für Rechtsgeschichte* 66, Kan. Abt., 1948, pp. 329-39) (in the Investiture Controversy); H. FUHRMANN, in *Zeitschr. für bayerische Landesgeschichte,* 20 (1957), pp. 136-51 (in the Synod of Hohenaltheim).

(156) González does not discuss the question of whether Isidore or Julian of Toledo are used in *Decr.* XX, 109-110 (cf. supra, note 58).

The *florilegium*, which uses other sources as well, was probably compiled in ninth-century Bavaria. See ROGER E. REYNOLDS, *A Florilegium on the ecclesiastical grades in CLM 19414: testimony to ninth-century clerical instruction*, in *Harvard Theological Review*, 63 (1970), pp. 235-59, who edits the text. Reynolds has pointed out elsewhere that no late patristic texts on clerical officers, their origins and duties were more important than Isidore's. They were transmitted and remodelled in many different forms, notably in the saec. IX *Institutio canonicorum*. In *Isidore's texts on the clerical grades in an early medieval Roman manuscript, Classical Folia*, 29 (1975), pp. 95-101, Reynolds studies MS. Rome, Bibl. Naz. Vitt. Em. 583 (saec. X-XI), which contains an unusual combination of passages on the grades, including orig. 7, 12, and passages from off. In *Excerpta from the Collectio Hibernensis in three Vatican Manuscripts, Bulletin of Medieval Canon Law*, N. S., 5 (1975), Reynolds identifies excerpts from off. and orig. 7, 12 in MSS. Vat. Ottobon. lat. 6 (saec. X-XI) and Archivio San Pietro H 58 (saec. XI?). J. TURVILLE-PETRE, *Translations of a lost penitential homily, Traditio*, 19 (1963), pp. 51-78, reconstructs a (probably saec. IX) Latin homily from translations into Old English and Old Icelandic. Isidore, off. and sent., are among the sources used. The *Summarium Heinrici*, I, ed. (lib. I-X) by R. HILDEBRANDT, Berlin, 1974, is almost all drawn from Priscian, Cassiodorus, Bede, and (especially) Isidore, orig. The work appears to be by a monk of Lorsch and is dated by the editor *ca.* 1020. In *Zur Ecbasis cuiusdam captivi v. 19, Mittellalteinisches Jahrbuch*, 9 (1973), p. 121, B. K. BRASWELL suggests that the source of v. 19 in this probably saec. XI text is not the Younger Pliny, as had been thought, but orig. 1, 21, 3.

A. BECCARIA, *I codici di medicina del periodo presalernitano (secoli IX, X e XI)*, Rome, 1956 (Storia e Letteratura 53), shows how the section on medicine in orig. 4 circulated widely and often anonymously in early medieval MSS. Y. VIOLE O'NEILL, *An 'Exordium membrorum' written in the tenth century*, in *Sudhoffs Archiv für Geschichte der Medizin und der Naturwissenschaften*, 51 (1967), pp. 363-67, discusses a treatise (in Montpellier, Faculté de Médicine, MS. 211) which seeks to sort out the contradictions between the physiological theories of diff. 2, 17 and orig., book 11. In religious literature R. BULTOT, in *RB*, 78 (1968), pp. 333-39, shows that the syn. was the main source of Pseudo-Anselm, *Exhortatio ad contemptum temporalium*, a work of unknown date (pre-1300) addressed to monks.

H. KOLB, *Isidors 'Etymologien' in deutscher Literatur des Mittelalters*, in *Archiv für das Studium der neueren Sprachen und Literaturen*, 205 (1968-69), pp. 431-53, studies the considerable use of the orig. by Otfrid of Weissenburg, *Evangelienbuch* (saec. IX), and by Conrad of Megenberg, *Buch der Natur* (*ca.* 1350). Examples of the use of Isidore in twelfth-century grammatical writings are given by R. W. HUNT, in *Mediaeval and Renaissance Studies*, 2 (1950), pp. 7, 31, and in 4 (1958), pp. 270-73.

Isidore's influence in the fields of political thought and of Canon Law, as we have already seen, was considerable. H.-X. ARQUILLIÈRE, *L'Augustinisme Politique, essai sur la formation des théories politiques du Moyen-*

Age[2], Paris, 1955, pp. 41 sq., points to the frequent use of sent. 3, 51 (ML, 83, 723 sq.) by the contemporaries of Gregory VII, Cardinal Deusdedit and Anselm of Lucca among others, and to its general success in the canonical collections. Isidore's attraction for these reformers was no doubt due to his having stated clearly the view that the function of the secular power in the Church was no mere obligation but its principal « raison d'être ». A. ROTA, *Lo Stato e il diritto nella concezione di Irnerio,* Milano, 1954, pp. 20-42 shows Irnerius used Isidore (157). Gratian's use of him is apparent from the studies of L. R. SOTILLO, *Las fuentes ibéricas del Decreto de Graciano,* in *Studia Gratiana,* II, Bologna, 1954, pp. 15-48 (esp. 39-42) and G. HUBRECHT, *La « juste guerre » dans le Décret de Gratien,* ibid., III, Bologna, 1955, pp. 161-177 (esp. 169 sq.) (158). Isidore is also a source of St. Bernard (cf. F. DE P. SOLA, in *EE,* 23, 1949, p. 217) and of the Victorines. Isidore, as FONTAINE (I, p. 14, n. 1) notes, is the main source of the *Didascalicon* of Hugo of St Victor, ed. C. H. BUTTIMER, Washington, 1939; cf. p. 138. H. WEISWEILER, in *Scholastik,* 20-24 (1945-49), pp. 59-87, 232-67, points to the influence of Isidore and especially of the *de ecclesiasticis officiis* in Hugo's *de sacramentis* (159). Richard of St. Victor also made much direct use of Isidore; cf. his *Liber exceptionum,* ed. J. CHÂTILLON, Paris, 1958 (Textes philos. du Moyen Age, 5), pp. 69 sq., 542 sq.

The influence of Isidore on St. Thomas Aquinas' philosophy of law has been described by P. M. VAN OVERBEKE, in *Rev. thomiste,* 55 (1955) pp. 519-64, esp. 539 sq., 554 sq., 557-64 (160). D. A. CALLUS, in *Studia mediaevalia in honorem R. J. Martin,* Bruges, 1948, pp. 268 sq., has noted his influence on Robert Kilwardby O. P. He was also much used by the compilers of more popular literature in the vernacular or in Latin. F. J. CARMODY, in *Speculum,* 11 (1936), pp. 359-70, shows how Brunetto La-

(157) ROTA suffers from the confusion found in U. CHEVALIER, *Répertoire, Biobibliographie,* I, Paris, 1905, n. 2285, when he divides Isidore into two, *Senior* (author of the orig.) and *Junior,* author of the *differentiae verborum.*

(158) According to CH. MUNIER (op. cit. supra, note 132), p. 160, Gratian probably used an abridgement of the orig.

(159) Cf. also L. OTT, in *Divus Thomas,* Ser. III, 27 (1949), pp. 180-200, 293-332 and L. CALONGHI, *La scienza e la classificazione delle scienze in Ugo di San Vittore,* Torino, 1956, (Pont. Athen. Sales, Fac. philos., Theses ad lauream 41)), neither of which were available to me. John of Salisbury was another assiduous reader of the orig. (G. THÉRY, cit. FONTAINE, I, p. 14 n. 1). For the influence of Isidore in the Twelfth Century one will naturally consult J. DE GHELLINCK, *L'essor de la littérature latine au XII*e *siècle,* 2 vols. Bruxelles-Paris, 1946 (Museum Lessianum, Sect. hist. 4-5, and ID., *Le mouvement théologique du XII*e *siècle. Études, recherches et documents* [2] Bruges-Bruxelles-Paris, 1948 (Ibid., ib., 10). PH. DELHAYE, in *RB,* 60 (1960), pp. 180-207 (esp. pp. 203 sq.) points out use of Isidore in a saec. XII *Florilegium* in MS. Bodley 633.

(160) Cf. also A. H. CHROUST, *The Philosophy of Law from St. Augustine to St. Thomas Aquinas,* in *New Scholasticism,* 20 (1946), pp. 26-71 (mentions Isidore pp. 31 sq.). F. SCHULZ, *Bracton on Kingship,* in *L'Europa e il Diritto Romano* (= *Studi in memoria di P. Koschaker*), I, Milano, 1954, pp. 23-70, is a revised version of an article which appeared in *English Historical Review,* 60 (1945), pp. 136-76. He has some brief notes (pp. 41 sq.) on the influence of Isidore, *orig.* 1, 29,3 and 9,3,4 and *sent.* 3, 48,7 (ML, 83, 719A). Bracton (+ 1268) used the Isidorian maxim: *Rex eris, si recte facias...* His immediate source was probably the anonymous saec. XIII compilation of *Leges Anglorum.*

tini's *Trésor* (1268) uses the *origines, sententiae, prooemia* and *de ortu et obitu patrum.* Cf. also CARMODY's critical edition, *Li livres dou Tresor de Brunetto Latini,* Berkeley-Los Angeles, 1948 (Univ. of California Publ. in Modern Philology, 22). The *origines* also constituted an important source of Guido delle Colonne's *Historia trojana* (1287); cf. R. CHIÀNTERA, *Guido delle Colonne...*, Napoli, 1956, pp. 241 sq. H. D. AUSTIN, in *Medievalia et humanistica,* 4 (1946), pp. 104-106, mentions the fact that Isidore is the second most important direct source of Uguccione da Pisa, *Magnae derivationes,* a dictionary used by Dante. P. RENUCCI, *Dante disciple et juge du monde gréco-latin,* Clermont-Ferrand, 1954, p. 167, thinks it no more than probable that Dante knew the Orig. themselves (cf., however, ibid., p. 192). J. A. MAZZEO, *Dante and Epicurus,* in *Comparative Literature,* 10 (1958), pp. 106-20, has pointed out that one of the two concepts of Epicurus in Dante, that found in *Inf.* X, is based especially on Isidore, orig. 8, 6. A. VALLONE, in *Studi danteschi,* 35 (1958), pp. 259-62, compares orig. 14, 6, 8 and *Purg.* XXVIII, 139-144; the comparison indicates, if it dos not conclusively prove, Dante's use of the passage in question (161).

In the later Middle Ages Isidore continued to be used as a source. H. HUESCHEN, *Der Einfluss Isidors von Sevilla auf die Musikanschauung des Mittelalters,* in *Miscelánea en homenaje a Mgr. H. Anglés,* Barcelona, 1, 1961, pp. 397-406, shows how Isidore's observations on music in orig. 3 and in off. 2, 12 and 1,5 were used by later medieval writers. Spanish theologians drew on Isidore when discussing the Jewish question. The *de fide* is used by Bernat Oliver (d. 1348) in his influential work, *Contra caecitatem Iudaeorum,* ed. F. CANTERA BURGOS, Madrid-Barcelona, 1965. A century later (in 1449) Alonso de Cartagena, in his *Defensorium unitatis christianae,* ed. M. ALONSO, Madrid, 1943, discusses at length the canons of IV Toledo (drafted by Isidore) and texts from orig., as well as Isidore's remarks on Sisebut's conversion of the Jews (see hist., 60). An anonymous *Compendium philosophiae* described by M. DE BOÜARD, in *Rev. thomiste,* 37 (1932), pp. 118-43, 301-330 (the oldest dated MS. is of 1320) makes much unacknowledged use of him. For Robert Mannyng (+ c. 1340) cf. D. W. ROBERTSON, in *Modern Language Notes,* 61 (1946), p. 511 (orig. 9, 7, 9 may be used). R. A. PRATT, *Chaucer and Isidore on Why Men Marry,* in *Modern Lang. Notes,* 74 (1959), pp. 293-94, believes Chaucer, in *Canterbury Tales* III (D) 257-262, was using orig. 9, 7, 29, either directly or, more probably, indirectly. The « English Chaucerian » Thomas Hoccleve (d. *ca.* 1450) drew on Isidore, *synonyma,* to reinforce his acceptance of the divine will. See A. G. RIGG, *Hoccleve's Complaint and Isidore of Seville,* in *Speculum,* 45 (1970), pp. 564-74. Christine de Pisan, in her poem, *Livre de la Mutacion de Fortune,* written 1400-1403, ed. S. SOLENTE, 2 vols., Paris, 1959, in the fourth part (vv. 7173-8070) uses two principal texts, Brunetto Latini and Isidore. She cites Isidore twice by name and uses *origines* libb. 1-3, following the original quite closely (cf. ed. cit., I, 1 sqq.,

(161) A. VALLONE also points out (p. 259) that many passages in DANTE, *De vulgari eloquentia,* ed. A. MARIGO, Firenze, 1957, may have drawn for their ideas on the orig.

lv-lix) (162). Nor did Isidore's influence end with the Middle Ages. The Spanish school of scholastic theologians and jurists, from Vitoria to Suárez, in their treatment of the Law of Nations (*ius gentium*), follow Isidore more closely than they do St. Thomas Aquinas, and, in another field, the *de fide catholica* continued to influence Christian *apologiae* against the Jews until well into the Nineteenth Century (163).

CONCLUSIONS

We may, perhaps, begin on a note of satisfaction. The old prejudices against Isidore seem to be losing some of their former force. There are still some historians content to repeat H. Leclercq's contemptuous phrase on the *origines*, « un grenier où se trouve remisée toute la défroque de l'antiquité (164) but, on the whole, a more enlightened attitude now prevails (165) The old view that Isidore was a mere compiler or a humble executant of the desires expressed by Augustine in the *de doctrina christiana* must also be abandoned (166).

In 1936, in *Misc. Isid.*, pp. 37 sq., P. Z. GARCÍA VILLADA put forward a programme for Isidorian studies that may have seemed at the time too optimistic but a surprising number of his suggestions have been or should shortly be realised (167). If we look, however, at what has been achieved we have no cause for self-congratulation for it is clear that much more remains to be done.

(162) Martinus de Leibitz, Fifteenth Century abbot of the Monasterium scottorum at Vienna, makes much use of Isidore in his *Trialogi ascetici aliaque opuscula*, ed. C. J. JELLOUSCHEK, Bresseo-Padova, 1932 (Scripta monastica, 13); I know this work only from the review by H. BASCOUR, in *BTAM*, 2 (1933-36), n. 726.

(163) Cf. S. RAMÍREZ, op. cit., supra, Section VIb, pp. 136-185; BLUMENKRANZ, *Les auteurs chrétiens latins*, cit. supra, Section VId; A. L. WILLIAMS, cit. ibid. E. ELORDUY, *San Isidoro interpretado por Suárez*, in *Archivos Leoneses*, 20 (1966), pp. 7-75, admits that Suárez's citations of Isidore are few in number compared with those of Augustine (85 compared with 475) but Isidore influenced Suárez's legal ideas.

(164) H. LECLERCQ, *L'Espagne chrétienne*, Paris, 1906, p. 309, cited by F. LOT. *La Fin du Monde antique et le début du Moyen Age*, éd. revue, Paris, 1951, p. 330.

(165) With some exceptions. F. S. LEAR, *St. Isidore and Mediaeval Science*, in *Rice Institute Pamphtets*, 23 (1936), pp. 75-105, collects (pp. 76 sq.) examples of facile condemnation of Isidore from medievalists of standing such as Haskins, Taylor, Lynn Thorndike, et al. We could add more recent examples of what FONTAINE (I, p. 19 n. 1) calls an « exécution hargneuse et facile » of Isidore, e.g. H. Aubin, in *Antike und Abendland*, 3 (1948),p. 107 (= *Vom Altertum zum Mittelalter*, München, 1949, pp. 94 sq.) (cf. FONTAINE, loc. cit.) or F. B. ARTZ, *The Mind of the Middle Ages : A.D. 200-1500, an Historical Survey*, New York, 1953, p. 193 (who cites LECLERCQ, loc. cit. supra, note 164).

(166) Cf. even E. GILSON, *Introduction à l'étude de Saint Augustin*, Paris, 1949, p. 161 n. 2; ID., *La Philosophie au Moyen Age, des origines patristiques à la fin du XIVe siècle*, Paris, 1947, p. 152: Isidore's « ne sont pas les sources d'une pensée, ce sont celles d'un dictionnaire ».

(167) E.g. the study of Isidore's Biblical text through the reconstruction of the *Vetus Latina Hispana*, and the Spanish MSS. of the Vulgate (cf. Section VIc supra). Some of P. García Villada's suggestions were perhaps too optimistic (cf. FONTAINE, I, p. 20).

To begin with the state of Isidore's works. The hopes expressed by Dr ALTANER, in *Misc. Isid.*, p. 30, and in *Der Stand der patrologischen Wissenschaft*, in *Miscellanea G. Mercati*, Città del Vaticano, 1946 (Studi e testi 121), I. p. 509, that more works of Isidore, hitherto unknown, would be published, have not been realised and it is doubtful, in my view, if they ever will be. I believe we now possess in print almost all the works known to Braulio, unfortunately in an edition (that of Arévalo) outstanding for its time but insufficient for ours. It has yet to be replaced by a modern critical edition of Isidore. This is the first and most obvious necessity of Isidorian studies. Without it the investigation of Isidore's sources, of his methods of work, of his language and style, of his influence, are all fatally handicapped. The promised *opera omnia* of Isidore in preparation by the late Dr. Anspach have not appeared. The investigation of Isidore's Biblical text has, however, been greatly advanced by the work of Mgr. T. AYUSO MARAZUELA (168). Professor DÍAZ Y DÍAZ, in his *Index Scriptorum*, has given us lists of MSS. of the *opera Isidoriana* which can, no doubt, be perfected, but which will serve as a point of departure for the new critical edition. The chronology and canon of Isidorian writings is much more clearly established, thanks to the labours, *inter alios*, of Prof. DÍAZ, FR. MCNALLY, and P. VACCARI, than it was in 1935 (169). A start, moreover, has been made on the edition itself. Apart from FONTAINE's edition of the *de natura rerum*, which we may surely call definitive, if that word bears any meaning, new editions are in preparation of the *differentiae*, the *de ortu et obitu patrum*, the *synonyma*, the *regula*, the *de ecclesiasticis officiis*, and the *sententiae*. Those of the *historiae* and the *de viris* are already completed. (170).

But this is clearly only a beginning. The great, almost insuperable, task of preparing a new and adequate edition of the *origines*, enormously facilitated by the work of Fontaine on its sources, still demands a renewed study of the vast MS. tradition that has called for a team of specialists. Without a text solidly based on an adequate MS. tradition, the *origines* will remain the privileged playground of scholars endowed with a zeal for ingenious or arbitrary emendation (cf. note 11 supra). Many of the theological works of Isidore – most of his *opera exegetica* and *dogmatica* – are still conspicuously neglected. They need a fresh study of their sources as well as of their MSS. This has only been begun by the work of P. JOSÉ MADOZ in *Misc. Isid* and of Dr. A. C. LAWSON (cf. Section IV supra).

The two fundamental necessities for Isidorian studies, then, are a new critical edition and a new and intensive study of sources. Until they are concluded all « conclusions » based on the present state of the evidence are bound to be provisional and liable to drastic revision. Yet, in the meantime, certain other « lacunae » should be indicated. There is a need for a study of Isidore's style and language; it can take as a point of departure

(168) Cf. Section VIc supra.
(169) Cf. Sections II and III supra.
(170) Cf. Section II supra.

FONTAINE's article in *VChr* and his edition of the *de natura rerum* (171). Linked closely with the study of style and language is the question of whether or not Isidore possessed an aesthetic theory distinct from that of his predecessors and successors. Is it possible to determine more precisely than Fontaine has done Isidore's place between the ancient and the medieval world, in relation, for instance, to Boethius, on the one hand, to Alcuin, on the other ? (172). There is an evident necessity, too, for a new critical biography of Isidore that will take into account the results of Fontaine's great enquiry and press into service the disciplines of archaeology, of economic and art history, for in the words of MARC BLOCH, « a historical phenomenon can never be understood apart from its moment in time » (173).

More notable than any of the « lacunae » we have indicated is the lack of recent work on the theology of Isidore. We still, as in 1936, lack « eine wissenschaftlich abschliessende Darstellung über die Bedeutung Isidors für die Kultur, Kirche *und Theologie* seiner Zeit » (174). This crucial gap in recent study is perhaps inevitable at present. It can be ascribed to two main causes. One is the disastrous absence we have already stressed of modern critical editions of Isidore's theological works and of investigations of their sources. The other cause appears to be the prevalence of the old view of Isidore as a compiler (and not even an intelligent compiler) that, one suspects – but would like to be proved wrong –, lingers on in the theological faculties of Europe and the U.S.A. even after it has disappeared from more secular circles. Again and again, in the course of this study, it has been remarked how inadequate this view on closer inspection proves to be. It explains neither Isidore's stylistic nor his astrological ideas (175). But the existence of this theory would account very well for the indifference of students or masters interested in Augustine or Thomas Aquinas but content to dismiss Isidore as, at best, an « agent of transmission » (176). It is, of course, perfectly legitimate to consider certain periods as more important than others for the development of Catholic doctrine and theological speculation. But if it is today generally accepted – as it appears to be – that it is not possible to understand either of these subjects without some understanding of the Middle Ages, it must be considered doubtful if one can understand the Middle Ages without knowing something, *at first hand*, of one of their greatest teachers. That, in fact, the study of Isidore's theological works can yield results as interesting in their way as that of his « secular » writings, is proved by the existence de-

(171) Cf. Sections V and II supra.

(172) Cf. FONTAINE, II, *Culture antique ou culture médiévale*, pp. 807-830.

(173) M. BLOCH, *The Historian's Craft*, Manchester, 1954, p. 35 (Eng. trans. of *Apologie pour l'Histoire, ou Métier d'Historien*).

(174) ALTANER, in *Misc. Isid.*, p. 30.

(175) Cf. the articles of FONTAINE in *VChr*, 14 (1960), and in *REL*, 31 (1953), cited supra, Section V.

(176) Cf. e.g., F. CAYRÉ, *Patrologie et histoire de la théologie*, II, Paris, 1947, pp. 254-63, esp. 259; J. TIXERONT, *Histoire des dogmes dans l'Antiquité Chrétienne*, Paris, 1912, p. 323, etc.

spite all existing obstacles, of the articles we have cited, both written over forty years ago, of Bidagor and Havet [177]. There appears to be no reason why the methods Fontaine has applied to the investigation of Isidore's technique of work should not be transferred to his *opera theologica*.

The study of Isidore's influence in the Middle Ages has hardly begun. It needs many a preliminary investigation before it can be built on secure and lasting foundations. It is possible that it can best be dealt with by nations – Isidore in France, in Italy, etc.

(177) Cf. supra, Sections VIb and VId.

INDICES

MODERN AUTHORS

REFERENCES TO GENUINE WORKS BY ISIDORE OR TO WORKS ATTRIBUTED TO HIM

ANCIENT AND MEDIEVAL AUTHORS AND WORKS

INDEX

General Note: The indexing of modern authors is selective. The last article included (IX) is not indexed here since it contains its own indexes. K = king, of the Visigoths, unless otherwise specified.